ITALY IN THE AGE OF THE RENAISSANCE
1380–1530

LONGMAN HISTORY OF ITALY

Italy in the Age of the Renaissance 1380–1530

DENYS HAY
AND
JOHN LAW

LONGMAN
London and New York

Addison Wesley Longman Limited,
Edinburgh Gate,
Harlow, Essex CM20 2JE, England
and Associated Companies throughout the world.

*Published in the United States of America
by Addison Wesley Longman Inc., New York*

First published 1989
Fifth impression 1996
Sixth impression 1998

British Library Cataloguing in Publication Data

Hay, Denys
Italy in the age of the Renaissance 1380–1530–
–(Longman history of Italy).
1. Italy, 1300–1494
I. Title II. Law, John E.
945'.05
ISBN 0–582–48358–1 CSD
ISBN 0–582–48359–X PPR

Library of Congress Cataloging-in-Publication Data

Hays, Denys.
Italy in the age of Renaissance, 1380–1530/Denys Hay and John Law.
p.   cm. – (Longman history of Italy)
Includes index.
ISBN 0-582-48358-1.   ISBN 0-582-48359-X (pbk.)
1. Italy – History – 1268–1492.   2. Italy – History – 1492–1559.   3. Renaissance –
Italy.   I. Law, John E (John Easton)   II. Title.   III. Series: Longman hisotry of
Italy (Unnumbered)
DG533.H392   1989   88-8829
945'.05 – dc19   CIP

Set in Lontron 202 11/12 pt Garamond
Printed in Malaysia (VVP)

Contents

CONTENTS

CONTENTS

List of genealogical tables and maps

Abbreviations used in the text

Art B.	Art Bulletin
A. S. I.	Archivio Storico Italiano
A. S. L.	Archivio Storico Lombardo
A. S. P. N.	Archivio Storico per le Provincie Napoletane
A. S. R. S. P.	Archivio della Società Romana di Storia Patria
A. V. (N. A. V.)	Archivio Veneto (Nuovo Archivio Veneto)
Boll. Stor.-Bib. Sub.	Bolletino Storico Bibliografico Subalpino
B. M.	Burlington Magazine
E. H. R.	English Historical Review
J. W. C. I.	Journal of the Warburg and Courtauld Institutes
Ren. Q.	Renaissance Quarterly
R. S. I.	Rivista Storica Italiana
S. V.	Studi Veneziani
T. R. H. S.	Transactions of the Royal Historical Society

Preface

The authors of this book have shared in its planning and take joint responsibility for its contents — although we would not subscribe to all that the other has written. We have scrutinised each other's chapters, and it may well be that a number of readers will be able to guess who was responsible for the first drafts. In any case it seems fair (since the emphasis of the work fell unevenly) to say that Hay originally drafted chapters 1, 2, 7, 8 and 12 and Law the remainder.

Both authors have found it hard work since the subject, which for convenience we may call the Renaissance in Italy, has been much studied and the extensive recent literature continues to produce work of originality and importance. Neither of us would claim that we have been able to absorb or evaluate all of the new work which, as may be seen from Chapter One, undergoes fairly rapid changes of emphasis. It is indeed a matter of astonishment that Italy and its problems, even in new guises, still attract so much interest. As the balance of research activity has shifted from the traditional concern with 'humanist' writings, it has continued to find in the great libraries and archives of Italy almost inexhaustible material for the current concern with social history. It is nevertheless a matter of regret that much research, especially by foreign historians, continues to concentrate on a few centres, making the task of doing justice to the history of Italy as a whole more difficult.

Finally, we might stress our belief that there is still a place of importance to be reserved for the study of politics, ideologies and humanism, as well as for the history of Italian cultural patronage — a subject which is being enriched as music catches up with the arts and literature as a subject of historical inquiry. Nevertheless, we have tended to tilt the balance of our expositions to an examination of public affairs. This presents a side of Italy more accessible to the 'barbarians' north of the Alps, as the political life on the southern slopes of the Alps, in the *Regno* and on the islands displays some striking resemblances to the 'feudal' north.

Denys Hay, Edinburgh
John Law, Swansea

Acknowledgements

Soon after the Preface was drafted our plans were set back by my having an illness which concluded by my being told not to work for some time. It was a typical act of kindness that John Law agreed to stitch together the *disjecta membra* and, while everything was more or less completed by then, it has fallen to him to undertake the final editorial co-ordination.

Denys Hay
October 1985

In preparing my contributions to this volume I have owed a great deal to the libraries of the Vatican, the British School at Rome, the Warburg Institute, the British Library and University College Swansea. For work on Venetian and Veneto material I would like to thank the Gladys Krieble Delmas Foundation; more generally, I would like to acknowledge the support of the British Academy. Mrs Glennis Jones has combined both patience and care in the face of many drafts and revisions. Thanks are also due to Martin and Alison Hicks for compiling the maps. Lastly, I would like to thank Denys Hay for his generous guidance and support — and not only in respect of this collaborative project.

John Law
December 1987

PART ONE

Introduction

CHAPTER ONE

Historiography

The period covered by this volume is bounded by dates chosen for more than convenience to distinguish an important stage in the tangled history of an Italy which was to be united, at least in principle, only in the third quarter of the nineteenth century. In 1376 Gregory XI returned from Avignon to Rome and although the institution and standing of the papacy were seriously affected by the Great Schism (1378–1417), the restoration of Rome as the papal capital had a complicating and growing impact on Italian affairs. In Florence the failure of the popular revolt of the *Ciompi* (1378) led to the entrenchment of a narrower oligarchic regime, run in the interests of the wealthier citizens and broadly typical of urban government throughout the Peninsula. Further north, in 1385 Giangaleazzo Visconti acquired the whole Visconti inheritance based on Milan, and went on to amass so much territory as to have a profound impact on the balance of power and the concept of lordship in Italy. In the kingdom of Naples, the deposition of Giovanna I in 1381 ushered in a period of intense rivalry between the two branches of the house of Anjou and the Aragonese crown which was to alter the distribution of power in the south and the islands.

Nor is the year 1378 far removed from critical events in the cultural history of the Peninsula. In 1374 Petrarch died, followed in 1375 by Boccaccio; but also in 1375 Petrarch's disciple Coluccio Salutati became chancellor of Florence. These years also saw the birth of three artists who were to have a considerable impact not only on the fine arts themselves but on the standing of the artist in society: the sculptors Ghiberti (1378) and Donatello (1386) and the architect Brunelleschi (1377). In the history of culture the period thus inaugurated has been called, for convenience, the Early Renaissance, and although many of its leading figures were Florentine, its characteristics can be traced through the Peninsula. The Sack of Rome in 1527 marks the end of the period, signalling as it does a fundamental shift in the balance of power in Italy. Cultural changes cannot be so pinpointed, but in literature the great verse masterpieces in the vernacular began to appear, while in the fine arts Mannerism replaced the High Renaissance style. Moreover in 1550, by using the term 'Rinascita', the artist and historian of the arts Giorgio Vasari

3

produced the word which in the French form, 'Renaissance', has been used to characterise the culture of fifteenth-century Italy and then that of all Western European civilisations in the sixteenth and seventeenth centuries.

There is something paradoxical in attempting to explain the history of a divided land when one's own assumptions are of a unitary state broadly equivalent to the area where English or French were spoken, albeit containing islands of linguistic separation and dialect. France and England had been governed – often misgoverned – by dynastic rulers for centuries before the time when the story of Italy is taken up in the following pages. Hence it seemed sensible to begin by attempting an account of what non-Italians thought of the land beyond the Alps. It is nevertheless deceptive to imagine any non-Italians – or Italians, for that matter – having a clear general picture of the Peninsula, divided by geography and, largely because of geography, by political organisation. Why, one is compelled to ask, did Italy not follow the line of development evolved in transalpine lands? One is driven to this question since Rome had been an imperial city and, however much this ancient imperalism may have concealed effective local autonomies, Rome itself remained one of the abiding ideals of the Italians. Even if it had declined into a merely emotive catch-phrase, 'civis Romanus sum' could from time to time rally a party or excuse a programme in the Middle Ages and the Renaissance.

The explanation is not far to seek. With the establishment of the centre of Roman government in Constantinople in the fourth century, the city of Rome came under papal management, and subsequently the popes had one policy which they pursued with intermittent effect, but fairly consistently: to prevent any lay ruler achieving sovereignty in Italy. Two areas invited the establishment of such rivals: the south and Sicily – the latter linked since the thirteenth century with Aragon, the most powerful force in the western Mediterranean – and the north of Italy, whose German 'emperors' offered a serious challenge, only finally destroyed (along with any hope of early unification in Germany), in the mid-thirteenth century, when the Hohenstaufen were eliminated effectively in the north at the same time as their rule in the kingdom of Sicily was ended. To achieve this involved the papacy inviting in French clients, the Capetian counts of Anjou, who in their turn cast envious eyes on Rome and the precariously held States of the Church which straddled central Italy. But overall the Angevins failed: they never succeeded in uniting the northern and southern parts of Italy. This had been the threat of the German emperors in the twelfth and thirteenth centuries, which the papacy had successfully foiled.

The popes were thus in large measure responsible for the failure of strong government to emerge in Italy; not only did they prevent it from developing under German and French princes, they proved incapable of providing it themselves – all the more so when circumstances in the fourteenth century compelled them to make Avignon their capital. However, far from signalling a resumption of power in Italy, the popes who took up residence in Rome in 1378 were frequently powerless, and the fifteenth century in peninsular history is one where attempts at pacification from the 1450s were the product of lay initiatives, and were to collapse with the Sack of Rome in 1530 with which this volume closes.

So tangled a tale discouraged the type of national history which we find, for example, in the *Grandes Chroniques* in France. With some remarkable exceptions, the history which was written in Italy in these centuries was parochial. What is astounding is its quantity and variety;[1] but if most of these histories are restricted to a narrow geographical perspective, the town within whose dominions the writer was at work could have wide economic and political interests. This was markedly the case with Florence; thus historians there from Giovanni Villani (d. 1348) were obliged to take a broader view, since their government was involved not only with other Italian states, not only with the papacy, but with the wider world of European trade and diplomacy. Hence Leonardo Bruni of Arezzo's *Historia Florentini Populi Libri XII* (from 1415) and its sequel, *Rerum Suo Tempore Gestarum Commentarium* (1440–41), offer more than a mere history of Florence, important though that is. Bruni, of course, caught the eye of scholars as a 'humanist', and his *History*, translated into Italian at the direction of the *Signoria* of Florence, was thus able to spread his approach to later scholars like Machiavelli.

There was, however, one Italian, from Forlì in the Papal States, who did try to survey the Peninsula as a whole. Though hampered by the little help he received to cover the kingdom of Naples, Flavio Biondo issued his *Italia Illustrata* over a period in the 1440s; he is to be regarded as the first and by no means the least influential of the chorographers – writers of those surveys which related antiquity to the present, which were to be extremely influential in all parts of Italy and, in time, in Europe at large; Camden's *Britannia* is an outstanding English example. Biondo was not writing history, and he pointed towards those descriptive pictures of his land, like Leandro Alberti's *Descrittione di tutta Italia* of 1550, which in turn formed the basis of the guide-book as it developed from 1800. But if Biondo was not writing as a historian in this work, he certainly was in his *Decades* (1437–42), virtually a history of Italy from the fall of Rome to his own day. As abridged by Pius II, the narrative of events became even more pronounced and gave a framework to Italy and to Italian history which long proved influential.[2]

From what has been said, one might well have expected a general survey of Italian politics to emerge in the *Liber de Vita Christi ac Omnium Pontificum* of Bartolomeo Platina (1474), like Biondo a papal official (see below, p. 126). In fact Platina's *History of the Popes*, popular with Protestants after the Reformation as well as with Roman Catholics, is not the history of Italy, or even of the Papal States, or even (one might add) of the popes – save perhaps to use them occasionally as examples of moral decrepitude. Above all it is not really a history of the papacy as an institution, some understanding of which is essential to the Italian story. The long-term influence of Platina was in the development after the Council of Trent of a series of important church histories.

However, two other Florentines followed in Bruni's steps and wrote histories of their town which, because of their wide-ranging and competent

5

political analyses, approach the point of being histories of Italy. The first of these is Niccolò Machiavelli, who wrote his history of Florence in 1520–24, after his much-celebrated *Principe* (1513) and *Discorsi* (1516–19) and after he had lost his official government positions on the return of the Medici. Guicciardini wrote, but did not publish, two partial histories of Florence in 1508–09 and 1527–30, but produced, again after he had left public service (in his case with the papacy), a monumental – and monumentally influential – *History of Italy*. This last was expressly aiming at a history of the Peninsula, and thus in an important sense is the first of the series of such works, but it was impossible for an official and diplomat of an important Italian town to look at Italian history as such. For example, in the dedication of the *History of Florence* to the Medici pope Clement VII Machiavelli mentions how the death of Lorenzo completely altered the Italian political scene: 'I have come to these times which, through the death of the Magnificent Lorenzo de' Medici, changed Italy's condition.' Machiavelli takes a wider view, but it is from a Florentine perspective.

For Guicciardini the turning point was really the French invasion of 1494: 'I have decided to write an account of what happened in Italy in our time, from the point when French armies, summoned by our own [i.e. Italian] princes themselves, began with great activity to disturb the land' and so led to decades of 'le calamità'.[3] Of course in a sense Guicciardini also goes back to Lorenzo de' Medici, for he paints the picture of Lorenzo's epoch as one of peace and prosperity and exaggerates the Florentine influence on events. But his great survey was not to be superseded for years, and then in ways which were determined by the needs of travellers on the one hand and antiquaries on the other. The travellers wanted descriptive works concentrating on current affairs, on the curiosities of the land; and they needed helpful advice on roads, inns, holidays and so forth. Such works began to appear from 1600 with the *Itinerary* of Francis Schott; before that, travellers had to depend on guides following the descriptive work of Leandro Alberti mentioned above. Schott's book was designed for the Italian part of what came to be known as the Grand Tour.[4]

Antiquarian studies were mainly localised and were largely concentrated on Roman monuments, pivoting on Rome itself. The literature on this was often significant and had lasting value,[5] especially since ancient buildings were treated as quarries by the builders of the Renaissance and Enlightenment. But from the time of Schott the antiquities of medieval Italy also began to inspire some remarkable scholarship. One great man deserves particular mention: Ludovico Antonio Muratori, for he not only published a vast amount of original source material – not least in his *Rerum Italicarum Scriptores*, to which medievalists must still turn – but he also compiled a general review in his *Annali d'Italia* (12 volumes: 1744–49). Muratori (1672–1750) did not really accomplish a proper history of Italy in his vernacular *Annali*; indeed, he demonstrated the difficulties of writing such a work. What was the historian of Italy as a whole to do? He had, first, to wait for a general awareness in the literary public of the existence of an Italy with a history to be written. Such a conviction gradually developed, not least in works like Ughelli's *Italia Sacra*[6] and in Girolamo Tiraboschi's *Storia della Letteratura Italiana* (13 volumes, 1772–82). Like the work of Ughelli and Muratori, Tiraboschi's contribution was to remain an indispensable work of reference virtually until our own day, when it is now being replaced by a number of collaborative works. Vasari on artists and architects (see below, pp. 8 and 306 ff) falls into a similar category, although his status as a 'primary source' means that he cannot be replaced by any number of subsequent authorities.

One significant pointer to the dilemmas of the Italian historian is the absence of national bibliographical aids such as are to be found in most other European countries. There are titles, but their contents are often vacuous. A signal example is Pietro Egidi's *La Storia Medioevale* (Rome, 1922) in the series 'Guide Bibliografiche'. Egidi himself is contemptuous of many of the general works which he discusses in his introduction, save only the *Storia della Storiografia Italiana* of Benedetto Croce, which is in fact mainly and explicitly limited to the nineteenth century. However, as the awareness of the unity of Italy deepened in the *Risorgimento*, the need developed to write 'Italian' history rather than the often localised studies which dominate the series of volumes listed, for example, by Egidi. The result, which continues to this day, was the emergence of histories of varying value, but all aiming at the story of the Peninsula as a whole. A notable feature of these works was that they were composed of separate volumes, each dealing with a separate period. The collaborative history is not, of course, confined to Italy – similar studies are found in France and England – but Italian history has of necessity had to accommodate itself to vigorous local studies. There was (despite, or rather because of, the papacy) no central political or administrative unity round which a general survey could be gathered, and the intense historical activity of the *Risorgimento* continued to express itself in local rather than on national terms.

This can be seen clearly in the periodical literature and the societies devoted to local history founded in the nineteenth and early twentieth centuries; for example, the publication of Italian journals devoted to the Trentino and the Alto Adige long anticipated the incorporation of these regions in the Italian state – thus anticipating history rather more successfully than the programme for the study of Albania, launched in Venice in 1939! The wealth of Italian local history can also be appreciated from the way the '*deputazioni di storia patria*', designed to publish source material as well as articles and monographs, have an overwhelmingly regional character. Despite this, a number of scholars embarked on the task of a 'national history' under the initial encouragement of the Milan publisher Vallardi. So far as the period covered by this book is concerned, the treatment of it by Luigi Simeoni in *Le Signorie* (Milan, 1950) is unquestionably useful – but mainly because it abandons a unitary narrative and instead combines two surveys under his title. Under broad period divisions Simeoni is content to tell regional history and then, but distinctly as far as possible, what we must (surely by 1988!) call national history.

The attentive reader of the following pages, however, will notice that the 'older' approach to Italian history is still being vigorously pursued. The only historical periodical explicitly linked to the name of Luigi Simeoni is devoted to the history of his native town, Verona;[7] the bibliographies attached to the chapters below not only draw on such local periodical literature but are also indebted to a new type of regional – and even parochial – history, generously sponsored, beautifully produced and admirably illustrated, but devoted to the history and culture of a circumscribed area. The pioneer work in this development was the *Storia di Milano* (from 1953) supervised by the Fondazione Treccani degli Alfieri. Others have followed on Naples, Mantua, Verona. Meanwhile collaborative histories of Italy are continuing, much influenced by the splendour of such local productions. An example relevant to the ensuing pages is N. Valeri's *L'Italia nell'Età dei Principati dal 1343 al 1516* (Milan, 1949). A thematic rather than a regional or chronological approach is more in evidence with two recent contributions to the 'storia d'Italia' genre, both published in Turin, by Einaudi and the Unione Tipografico-Editrice Torinese (U.T.E.T.).

However, in one area, cultural history, it has been possible to trace a more coherent 'Italian' development. For example, while regional studies of art and architecture are plentiful, they tend to exist within a framework defined by such issues as: the enhanced status of the arts, and even of the artist; the growing influence of the antique; the creation of the illusion of depth and space in painting. That the discussion of the various Italian 'schools' is related to the central concept of 'Renaissance' is in large measure due to the *Lives of the Most Excellent Painters, Sculptors and Architects* of Giorgio Vasari (1511–74). His Tuscan bias and his enthusiasm for the patronage of the Medici reveal a typically regional outlook and have skewed the later study and teaching of art history; but the breadth of his survey – especially in the second edition of his work – and his emphasis on central 'Renaissance' themes have proved inspirational and influential and have shaped later studies, both general and local (see below, p. 306 ff).[8] Moreover, the idea of the 'Renaissance' develops and changes as it comes to absorb vernacular literature by the seventeenth century and – albeit not until the nineteenth century – political change as well. In this way the Renaissance begins to assume the character of a turning point in European history – the 'birth of modern times'. Unquestionably the most influential scholar in this evolution was the Swiss historian Burckhardt, whose *Civilisation of the Renaissance in Italy* came out in German in 1860; it soon acquired the status of a historical classic, and when one sees it in modern illustrated editions it is hard to remember that it is over a hundred years old.

Burckhardt's study is in six parts. Perhaps the most remarkable is the first, which has the odd title 'The State as a Work of Art', but which is really an 'overview' – as it is now fashionable to adopt the German term 'Uberblick' – of Italian political development from the thirteenth century to the sixteenth. Burckhardt does not use the term 'Renaissance state', which has become so popular in the last forty years, but although many recent historians find his approach somewhat irrelevant and superficial, it did in fact anticipate their own much more detailed concerns with fiscal, demographic and social history. His second part is entitled 'The Development of the Individual' and links itself to the previous section by contrasting the effects on personality of despotisms and republics. It is also here that we find the discussion of the 'universal man', the idea of fame and vernacular literature. The third part, 'The Revival of Antiquity', covers the humanists, their patrons and the pervasive Latin which was to dominate education in all European countries until the 1800s. Part IV, 'The Discovery of the World and of Man', brings in natural science, the description of man and cities and 'life in movement', with its concluding discussion on the 'dignity of man', another Burckhardtian phrase destined to be much in the minds of recent scholars. 'Society and Festivals' is the fifth part, and while it contains matters which would seem peripheral to some modern historians, it deals with two themes of absorbing recent concern: women and 'festivals'. Finally Burckhardt turns to 'Morality and Religion'. In essence, this final section links the Renaissance and the Reformation. One must remember that the lonely professor at Basel was a Protestant. In brief, his judgement is that if the Italians did inaugurate the modern world, they paid a heavy price for it in scepticism and immorality.

Burckhardt transformed the Renaissance into a period of time. In the course of earlier centuries its purely cultural aspects – artistic and literary, and above all educational – had penetrated virtually every part of Europe, and one may doubt if there had been such generally accepted standards and styles since the thirteenth century or before the twentieth; then, although the norms of physical science were applied in theory to all intellectural disciplines, in many countries the dominance of humanist values was continued in, for example, the British 'public schools', the *lycées*, and above all in the *écoles normales* or *scuole normali* distributed throughout Napoleonic and post-Napoleonic Europe. The tenacity of such humanist concerns is vividly displayed in the contents of publications such as the Italian journal *Rinascimento* and the American *Renaissance Quarterly*.

Such studies are often essentially philological and thus, it would appear, drift apart from the Renaissance period as it is currently written about, and taught, where it increasingly conforms to the essentially sociological interests of many modern historians. Indeed, with the rapid decline in the mastery of the history, literature and above all the language of classical antiquity, much of the periodical *Rinascimento* must be unintelligible nowadays; it was not so when every boy (and a few girls) was drilled in little else by school or tutor, and when abler pupils could read Virgil in the original. This is certainly the picture of education and scholarship which applied in Europe, in the north and south of America and, to a lesser degree, in other areas where European influence predominated. Yet the mention of Europe can trip one up. In effect the Renaissance as sketched above was for long restricted to Western Europe. Beyond the Elbe, the tempo of cultural as of political change was different, although by the end of the last century Russians and other East Europeans were heavily influenced by the scholarship and literary ideas of Germany,

France and Britain. They were much occupied in writing about the Renaissance in their own countries in their own languages which sadly, but all too often, means they are not well known in Western Europe.

But the historians of Eastern Europe have not focused exclusively on their own renaissances; later medieval and Renaissance Italy have also attracted considerable attention. In part this manifests itself in the study of diplomatic history, as well as of ecclesiastical, cultural and economic points of contact. However, as is made clear by the recent work of the Russian Victor Rutenburg on popular unrest in fourteenth- and fifteenth-century Italy, historians of Eastern as well as of Western Europe and the English-speaking world have been drawn to the study of the social history of the period.[9] In large measure this has been encouraged and sustained by the wealth of Italian archives and libraries, not only in 'state papers' and official histories and the semi-public records of guilds, confraternities, the Church and notarial archives, but also in material of a more private nature: correspondence, diaries and family chronicles. Where Burckhardt saw individualism, ambition and an appetite for fame as leading characteristics of the age, and paid comparatively little attention to 'domestic life' or the community, modern historians are trying to explore and stress the bonds of society.

NOTES AND REFERENCES

1. Most recently, Eric Cochrane, *Historians and Historiography in the Italian Renaissance* (Chicago and London, 1981).
2. D. Hay, 'The Decades of Flavio Biondo', *Proc. of the British Academy*, vol. xlv (1959).
3. Prologue to the first book of the *History of Italy*.
4. The *Itinerarii Italiae Rerumque Romanorum* was published at Antwerp. Many Italian editions followed the first of 1615: E. S. de Beer, *Francois Schott's Itinerario d'Italia* (London, 1942); J. R. Hale, *England and the Italian Renaissance* (London, 1954), p. 123; J. W. Stoye, *English Travellers Abroad* (London, 1952). p. 199.
5. R. Weiss, *The Renaissance Discovery of Classical Antiquity* (Oxford, 1969).
6. D. Hay, *The Church in Italy in the Fifteenth Century* (Cambridge, 1977), pp. 2–3.
7. *Studi Storici Luigi Simeoni*, published by the Istituto per gli Studi Storici Veronesi.
8. Vasari's *Vite* were published in 1550 and, after extensive revisions, in 1568. An interesting insight into the influence of the work and the development of art history to the end of the nineteenth century is provided by the abridged and annotated edition by E. H. and E. W. Blashfield and A. A. Hopkins (London, 1898).
9. See the introduction by R. Manselli to Rutenburg's *Popolo e Movimenti Popolari nell'Italia del '300 e '400* (Bologna, 1971).

CHAPTER TWO

The structure of Italy: the Italian view and the outsider's picture

THE OUTSIDER'S PICTURE

By the late sixteenth and the early seventeenth century, adroit publishers were catering for an increasing number of men who were travelling more or less for the sake of it. The arrival of the guidebook, in something like its present form (routes, distances, sights to see, charges to pay, hostelries at which to stay and which to avoid) was the herald of the Grand Tour.[1] Before that time, one undertook journeys with a purpose. This was often diplomatic, military, above all religious (including pilgrimages) and commercial. Even Montaigne, one of the first northerners to inspect the Peninsula with a critical and sympathetic eye in his *Journal* of his travels in 1580 and 1581, was preoccupied with his health and the baths where he might improve it. As for the diplomats, from whom much might have been hoped, they seldom behaved or were required to behave as the Venetian emissaries did in their famous reports of the countries to which they were sent. Even as shrewd an observer as Commynes, whose mission of 1478 at the time of the Pazzi conspiracy gave him a rapid view of Florence just after the attempted murder of the Medici princes (*Mémoires*, Book vi, Chapter 4) and a longer chance to get to know the Peninsula as a companion of Charles VIII in his invasion (Book vii), was normally intent on his diplomatic and political tasks; the main exception, apart from a few asides, is his celebrated analysis of the Venetian state (Book viii, Chapter 180). This insertion, explicitly described as such, is so like a miniature version of a Venetian *relazione* that one wonders if it was provoked not only by the length of Commynes' visit – some eight months – but perhaps by a desire to emulate Venetian diplomatic practice.

But the vast majority of foreigners who crossed the Alps were either scholars making for Bologna or other celebrated universities in search of degrees in civil law, or pilgrims, the latter including a number of clergy who had (after the popes were established in Rome) business at the Curia. Of the former we have in some cases fairly complete lists of names, since matriculation registers were maintained and, as in Germany, matriculation was only for a year at a time; it was also organised by 'national' groups and these have been much studied. Unfortunately, although these ambitious clerks can be numbered,[2] we can find few traces of their views of Italy and Italians; no such nominal rolls exist for the much larger numbers of pilgrims, save accidentally in the records of a particular national hostelry or college. And the multitudes seeking graces of all sorts from the offices of the pope are a jungle of often indecipherable names, where only a diocese can lead one to the place of origin of the supplicant, recorded in often ill-kept registers.

Nor did the pilgrims and busy clergy seeking help from the departments of the Curia keep diaries. However, there is one interesting by-product of the pilgrimages, whether to Rome or through Rome to the Holy Land. A considerable number of works were prepared, often by former pilgrims, to aid the uninitiated voyager, and it is interesting to see in the *Pilgerbuch*, many of which have been published (and indeed, with the advent of printing, many of which were available in print by the end of the fifteenth century), the steady absorption of material of what might – roughly – be called, cultural items among the religious itineraries. The 'marvels of Rome' (*mirabilia Urbis*) were a separate genus of itineraries for those who had long wished to add the Pantheon, Trajan's Column, the Coliseum and other splendid antique gestures to their spiritual benefits while visiting *ad limina apostolorum*,[3] whether or not during a period of jubilee or on an individual pilgrimage, or more material gains from curial ordination (with virtually no questions asked about the canonical requirement being fulfilled) or a scrap of paper to help secure preferment to some distant living.

It was through this steadily growing interest in classical antiquities that a new view of the ancient world was gradually to evolve during the fifteenth and sixteenth centuries. It was mainly fixed on Rome. The Englishman who had seen the Roman Wall in Northumberland, the French who had grown up beside the Pont du Gard in Provence, even perhaps the Italian of such visibly Romanised centres as Lucca, Verona or Vicenza, did not treat the marvels of the city with less reverence and, as such reverence gradually buttressed itself on literature, they could become disciples and distributors of what a later age would call the values of the Renaissance.

For a foreigner there was no doubt that Italy was a land where the town was the essential political unit. This, indeed, ignored the mountains that dominated all of the Peninsula save the valley of the Po. But it was, as will appear, how the Italians saw the scene themselves and continued to do so for centuries, perhaps in effect until today. Judging from the attitudes of pilgrims and travellers, there can be no doubt which town took precedence. Milan, in size and industrial significance, was 'the greatest in Italy and might-ily inhabited and rich'.[4] Rome might have the greatest relics of the greatest saints; Milan could equip an army and its busy 'armament firms' produced perpetually the din of metalworking in the fourteenth and fifteenth centuries, a period of unending war. Rome, even after the popes were more or less securely established there from the 1440s, was negligible commercially (though a mighty borrower of money) and owed its tenacious attraction to ths extraordinary merits the visitor could acquire through indulgences, or those favours which needed the particular payments for membership of the various 'colleges' in the Curia, which in effect (as noted below, pp. 104 and 126) were a way of buying an annuity. It was the indulgences that were especially recorded in the *Pilgerbücherei*. Here (for example) are a few lines from the notes kept by the German Arnold von Harff, who came from the area near Cologne in the 1490s. Among many other graces one could begin, when entering the city from the north, at S. Maria del Popolo, with its daily indulgence of 3,000 years; and so to S. Maria Rotonda (the Pantheon) with daily a forty years' indulgence with 'as many quarantines' (a penance of forty days). And so on, until the German gives up: 'there are many other churches, with many relics, great pardons and indulgences, which would take too long for me to describe at present . . . I will therefore describe certain worldly matters which are to be found there.'[5]

If some of the foreigners regrettably omitted to record their views of Italy, we will observe later (p. 21 ff) that a few Italians looked at their land with curiosity in the later Middle Ages. But how can one describe it objectively? Its limits were fairly clear: the Alps to the north, the Adriatic and Tyrrhenian seas form evident barriers. But what of the islands? For many non-sailing Italians the islands were, it would appear, hardly to be counted; in any event, the biggest (Trinacria or Sicily) was under non-Italian rule, and Corsica was battled over between Catalans and Genoese; Malta had a language strange even by strange Italian linguistic traditions, and the Genoese and Venetians were in a sense pushing the boundaries of Italy south-east along the Mediterranean.

Nevertheless we must accept the territorial Italy more or less of our own day and attempt to describe it as it might have appeared to the few then curious enough to look over their city walls.

LATE MEDIEVAL AND RENAISSANCE ITALY: SOME FACTS AND FIGURES

When one tries to describe what any European peoples thought about their own countries' dimensions and the character of their peoples, the first two things to remember are that (until the mid-sixteenth century) there were few adequate maps save those made for sailors, and that few people were interested in them. It is true that some very beautiful examples have survived of the mariner's *portolan*, which were clearly intended for the use of landsmen for reference or picturesque armchair travels. It must be supposed that Dante referred to such a map. But such men were only a handful, even among the tiny minority of the learned, which is the second point to stress. The vast majority were limited by the horizons they could see, and it was the cartographical pioneers like Mercator (1512–94) who began to solve the problem of depicting a spherical object on a flat plane. Italy may well take some credit in these developments because of the elaborate drainage and canal construction in the country, especially in Lombardy; but increasingly exact estate measurement is found everywhere in fifteenth- and sixteenth-century Europe.

The measurement of a town or property did not, however, carry with it any automatic consciousness of the larger entity of which it formed a part. In Italy we are concerned with an area both very large by Western European standards and divided into a multiplicity of smaller political units. Yet even here we may be sure that the few men who might refer to themselves as Tuscans, Genoese or Sicilians were very unrepresentative of the mass. Even in Tuscany, when taxation reached out from Florence to burden *contadini* in the whole *dominio*, there were pockets in the hills where the tax collectors could hardly reach; as for the high Apennines and, in the north, the Alps, had they ever been under the total hegemony of any 'state', big or small, in antiquity or later? To some extent this is true all over the continent until the nineteenth century, but it is obviously more so with rugged Italy than with the douce champagne lands which were found to any extent only in the valley of the Po.

Who were the Italian, and how many of them were there in the period covered by this book?[6] To the first half of this question, some vague answer may be attempted if we go back to the conquest (how complete was it?) of the Peninsula by the Latini. It has been estimated that the Italian population rose from 7,300,000 in 1150 to 11,000,000 in 1300 and then declined, reaching a low of 8,000,000 in 1400, after which it slowly climbed to 11,600,000 by 1550, by which time estimates are firmer, owing to the research of K.J. Beloch and others and the more plentiful tax figures of the sixteenth century. This trend is, so far as one can judge, parallel to similar movements in Europe at large and the sharp decline in the fourteenth century begins, in Italy as everywhere else, before the Black Death of 1348. Equally interesting are the distribution figures which seem plausible for 1550; northern Italy (including Lombardy and adjacent areas) 4,746,000; the rest of mainland Italy 5,592,000; the islands (including, besides Sicily and Sardinia, Corsica, Malta and the Lipari group) 1,253,000. In considering these figures one must remember that they represent political boundaries at the time and not after the many adjustments, especially in the north, in later decades.[7]

One is not, of course, entirely reliant on taxation and similar figures, collected for purposes quite different from the needs of the modern statistical demographer. We have the whole pattern of deserted villages to mark the contraction of the fourteenth century. Again the Peninsula shared this experience with the rest of the continent. The phenomenon was not new. In an age which had available for all practical purposes only animal manure, the yield of all but the best land was quickly exhausted and a small community rapidly broke up, looking for fresh territory to exploit. Other long-term influences had the effect of attrition of the population, notably in Italy those areas subject to malaria, like the Tuscan or Roman *Maremma*, where the malady may not have been as dramatic as the first onset of the plague, but was equally devastating over a prolonged period. Likewise as towns expanded they attracted rural labour, and as fortified centres were created by aggressive lords, they too took their toll. Yet the size of towns tells its own story. The walls of Florence, finally enlarged in the decades around 1300, were not to be filled until the nineteenth century.

These processes were greatly intensified in the fourteenth-century atmosphere of regression. The clerical surveys of parts of the Papal States – and, even more general, the lists of the revenues due from parish churches which had vanished – bear witness to what an authoritative survey by Dr Christiane Klapisch-Zuber describes in an account on which these paragraphs rely heavily.[8] She points out that the decline and disappearance of villages, especially marked in the hill territory of north Italy and Tuscany (and of course intensified by epidemics from time to time) was accompanied by the rapid development of *mezzadria* or sharecropping, which incidentally greatly facilitated bourgeois exploitation of lands reasonably near towns. The Church, too, sometimes benefited from the agricultural decline. These trends were intensified in the area around Rome and southwards in the *Regno* and Sicily, where perpetual and brutal warfare benefited only a few rapacious families who took over the lordship of the destroyed settlements. This reintroduction of a sort of 'fiscal feudalism' was indeed common to the whole Peninsula at the end of the Middle Ages.[9]

These dwindling millions were, then, the 'Italians', most of whom did not so describe themselves. Why should they have done? Even the prominent and the literate would talk of being 'Venetian' or 'Florentine' only on occasions of formal diplomatic protocol – ambassadorial exchanges by harangue or letter – or the propaganda of humanist historians.

Nevertheless, to the outside world (as well as to a few Italians) the Peninsula was Italy; and there were reasons even for some of the inhabitants to become intermingled and confused about what a much later age would describe as nationality.

ITALIAN INTEGRATION

There was, it need hardly be stressed, a continuing tradition of *Romanitas*. The city conquered Italy before conquering the world of the Mediterranean, indeed beyond that the territory south of the Roman Wall in Britain and the *limes* of the Rhine–Danube on the Continent. The aura of the grandeur that had been Rome survived its shabbiness and lack of economic significance. If grass now grew in the Roman streets and Rome was, as has been said, a 'city of villages', it was still the resting place of Peter and Paul and (after 1462) Andrew, and so one of the great centres of pilgrimage of the Christian world, full also of other wonders of pagan antiquity. The city was a somewhat equivocal symbol of unity. Did one's allegiance (we speak of the learned and the politicians) lean towards republican Rome or imperial Rome? At any rate, there were good authorities for regarding the Alps as a bulwark against the barbarians and for Italy itself, mostly harsh and mountainous and in general terms most un-garden like, as the 'garden' of the Empire.

This potentially divisive Roman inheritance, republican and Caesarean, reminds one of the similar contrasting loyalties in nineteenth-century France. In the event, it was not to be as damaging. There were many important people who crossed the land from end to end, and if the 'courtly' Italian language Dante had advocated in the *De vulgare eloquentia* (see below, p. 22) did not emerge at once, or indeed for centuries, the seeds were sown in literature and art, and among the elites who governed the states large and small.

Not only, indeed, in literature and art, or among the elites. We should remember that, faced with economic disaster, the wretched could and did turn to migration to other parts of the Peninsula including the towns, where they might be able to settle down, so that vanishing villages could replace depleted urban centres. Below these relatively lucky migrants there were vagabonds pure and simple, ranging the land for the spoils they could find. Some vagabonds became mercenary soldiers and, in bands constantly changing in composition, moved up and down the land. Scholars were often on the move, as were clergy – looking for titles and promotion, often far from their home area. This floating population had to come to terms with a dozen major and many minor dialects. This was the real background of the *volgare* of later centuries.

It is very important to remember that the great and not so great families, counts, marquises, dukes, and simple lords sought alliances for themselves and their children, legitimate and illegitimate, in ways designed to enlarge their own influence and wealth. This is more readily displayed in genealogical tables, for which a famous – if not always reliable – series exists in the extensive work begun by Pompeo Litta.[10] But every study of the Visconti, or the Sforza, or the Este or the Gonzaga is predictably full of matrimonial diplomacy, often further complicated (as in the case of Francesco Sforza, Duke of Milan from 1450 to 1466) by large numbers of illegitimate children, and often revealing how connections could be made with distant houses. As in the case of the Visconti rulers of Milan, marriage alliances could be established with foreign (in the modern sense) noble or even royal dynasties, although the relative rarity of such alliances suggests that the ruling class looked first for marriage within the Peninsula. In the period few Italian princelings had foreign ambitions in a political or territorial sense, although marriage with foreign dynasties could bring both prestige and security. The point to remember is that a prince or princess joining a new spouse took with him or her a horde of personal servants, partly out of a desire to have beside him or her traditional 'familiars', partly in order to have access to trustworthy persons. This last is especially noteworthy in the case of high prelates, especially cardinals, who moved to the court of Rome (which was more truly at Rome after 1450 than it had been for centuries) with literally hundreds of their relations and dependants. The most extreme case of this was the positive invasion of Catalans under Calixtus III (d. 1458) and Alexander VI (1492–1503). They were, as natives of a state based on the west Mediterranean, perhaps more excusable, since they were more isolated and loathed in Italy; but one has only to look at other non-'Roman' popes to see the same phenomenon. After all, the chief attraction for many ambitious clerics of the Chair of St Peter was the opportunity it afforded for doing good turns to one's kith and kin. One may interpolate that the nobility and higher clergy were (and this frequently applied also to the daughters of noble families) educated in Latin grammar and increasingly familiar with the classics of antiquity. The Renaissance in literature thus helped to pave the road that was slowly to lead to a kind of Italian language, more or less common to the entire land. One must not exaggerate this. There were and still are pockets of German speakers and French speakers in the north; there are isolated areas in the south where the Byzantine legacy is reflected in the remnants of a Greek patois. Albanian is preserved in communities on the Adriatic coast. The Italians themselves are fond of saying that they have two languages – Italian and their own local patois – although it is to be doubted if this is truer of Italy than, say, of Somerset or Durham, let alone other parts of Europe.

Political expansion could also reduce the Peninsula's internal barriers. The Venetians, for centuries willingly confined to the lagoons and regarded as rather a race apart, in the course of the period acquired a large part of north-eastern Italy; they had – or so their propagandists could argue – only 'come into their own', in the sense that they had reunited the ancient Roman province of *Venetia*. Less tendentious and more direct and influential was the steady increase in Venetian investment on the Italian *terraferma*; the Palladian villas on the Brenta and elsewhere are later monuments to the extension of Venetian culture as well as property. The dominance of the wealthy over the areas surrounding the larger towns of Italy spread urban culture over a wider area, however irregularly. Further influences tending to a degree of integration were clergy moving about from one living to another, and lawyers employed as administrators.

As far as the clergy are concerned as instruments of integration, one of the striking features of attempts to reform religious orders in the later Middle Ages was the grouping together of reformed houses in 'Congregations' (see below, p. 131). Such groupings naturally tended to have a fair degree of geographical contiguity, and Italian Congregations seldom if ever crossed the Alps. The most active of the latter-day religious were the Franciscans, and both the Conventuals and the newer Observants (*c.* 1360) had separate organisations for the Peninsula and for northern Europe. These Congregations were, in fact, a source of continuous strife, especially among the Franciscans, split anyway by a schism which in the event no pope could heal, so that by the sixteenth century there were to be three distinct Franciscan Orders: Observants, Conventuals and Capuchins (1528); there were really four if we add in the separate order of Minims, founded by S. Francesco di Paolo (d. 1506), which did also have one or two convents outside Italy, owing to the patronage of King Louis XI of France.

These friars were frequently moved from one house to another within the Peninsula and were often intimately connected with policy as (rarely) advisers to princes and (more commonly) confidential emissaries. Indeed, Lorenzo de' Medici refused to allow S. Marco in Florence to belong to the Lombard Order of reformed Dominicans. The convent had been refurbished by the Medici, and Lorenzo insisted that it should form the centre of another Congregation, but the convent and the order illustrate the penetration by many clergy in parts of Italy in which they were strongest. Savonarola, later to be the prior of S. Marco, was a Ferrarese Dominican, famed as a preacher, who had earlier delivered courses of Lenten sermons in Florence. Indeed, the great preachers of Italy were great travellers too. S. Bernardino of Siena died in 1444 and is buried magnificently in L'Aquila in the Abruzzi, part of the kingdom of Naples. The Lenten sermons and the call by communities distracted by violence for the preaching of peace were found all over the country, although Savonarola is virtually unique in achieving the political domination of Florence for a time (see below, Chapter Seven, for further discussion of the clergy).

The political tensions of the Italian commune, whether under republican or princely government, also paradoxically led to influences making for a degree of unification. One of the commonest punishments inflicted on unsuccessful political opponents (short of execution) was exile. Hardly a sizeable town existed without its nucleus of exiles from other cities, frequently conspiring towards their return, attempting to steer their (often unwilling) hosts to lend their political support. The Peace of Lodi (see below, pp. 157–8) was partly intended to prevent this kind of internal disruption, as well as to unite the Italian states against invasion from over the Alps. That invasion, when it came in 1494, owed much to Milanese and other Italian exiles at the court of France.

The diaspora of preachers, even more than the scattering of politicians, suggests that there was a certain basic language shared by Italians, including many of the uneducated and illiterate. For example, on the Palazzo Pubblico of Siena, as throughout Italy, one can still see the light-radiating letters IHS, standing for the sacred name of Jesus, which the Franciscan S. Bernardino (1380–1444) and his followers propagated to stimulate devotion and the observance of the Christian message. A recent essay on popular melodies[11] – more recent, of course, than the period covered by this book, if the antiquity of many is impossible to date – suggests a linguistic division into three broad areas: a Mediterranean region – covering much of southern Italy and Sicily – a central area and a northern area, with Sardinia a separate unit. Admittedly this is based on 'specifically musical elements',[12] but it probably reflects the languages of the people as well as their music. The late medieval sermon was, of course, a highly dramatic performance and the preacher communicated by gesture and symbols, such as Bernardino's use of the sacred name IHS. But we have so many vernacular sermons preserved that we can be sure that they were not written down save to be spoken: Bernardino of Siena, Bernardino of Feltre, Savonarola are signal examples of sermon-writers who took immense pains to communicate to large audiences through the vernacular, even if they sometimes slipped a word or two of Latin into their texts; this odd, macaronic effect, perhaps normally confined to written texts and not reflected in the spoken word, reminds us that behind the varieties of the *volgare* lay the ancient literary language of the scholars of antiquity.

Also behind the *volgare*, need it be said, lay the literary language of the scholars, whether old-fashioned teachers of law and medicine – with an old-fashioned vocabulary which was nevertheless perfectly grammatical – or the *'umanisti'*, as the students were calling the teachers of that portion of the old *trivium*, rhetoric or style, on the basis of improved, sometimes rediscovered (for example Quintilian) Latin texts. This is a subject pursued further below (Chapter Twelve), but in the present context it is worth remembering that by the early fifteenth century no government could do without its secretaries and counsellors instructed in the new manner. From Coluccio Salutati, Chancellor of Florence 1375–1406, to the courtiers and servants of the popes after Calixtus III, a ruler of any stature had to have his letters and discourses prepared or delivered by an expert in the humanities.

Some of these humanists were as 'wandering' as medieval scholars. In general the tools of their trade were linguistic, a revived classical Latin as practised by a few schoolmasters in the fourteenth century and by nearly all schoolmasters and university teachers of rhetoric and 'poetry' by the end of the fifteenth. To the extent that the ordinary literate man was incapable of ready understanding of this mandarin language, the wandering literati, despite their frequent appeals and references to *Italia*, did little to cement together the varied bricks in the divided Italian house; after all, their predecessors, the wandering scholars of the twelfth and thirteenth centuries, had done little to crystallise the concept of Christendom. But Bruni and Poggio, returning to Florence after years in the papal Curia, or Filelfo, pestering every prince for patronage and wandering from city to city in search of wealth and admiration, these and others like them contributed to a growing cultural unity among the court elites. The papal Curia was especially prone to attract non-Romans in large quantities, as will be seen later (pp. 205–7).

Many humanists had only a notarial education. This was true of both Salutati and Bruni, and it says a good deal for the quality of the grammatical instruction they received that they were to become leaders in the cultural changes we label Renaissance; but notaries and lawyers with university degrees were agents of the humanities in other ways. For centuries it had been the practice of Italian city governments to hire for a fixed period, usually a year, a non-native as *podestà* or other chief magistrate, the idea being that he would be neutral in the squabbles of the town. Such a man was normally an LL.D., trained in the schools of Bologna, Padua or Pavia, and he arrived at the post to which he had been invited accompanied by a retinue (or *curia*) of notaries and clerks, knights and soldiers. His term of office was followed by a period when his exercise of his functions was subject to scrutiny (the *sindicato*).

For many men this form of public office became a career, and one which took them far afield. A signal example of such a career magistrate, so to speak, was the Roman Stefano Porcari. His great (and wretched) moment was to come (see below, pp. 205–6) when he tried to rouse the Roman mob in

1452–53 and miserably failed, ending his life on the scaffold. Before that he had exercised the office of *podestà* at a number of places. In 1427 and 1428 he was captain of the people at Florence (a supreme criminal jurisdiction, with headquarters in the Bargello); in 1432 he was *podestà* in Bologna, in papal territory; in 1434 *podestà* at Siena and in 1435 in Orvieto, again in the States of the Church. His career could be multiplied in many other examples and lends a characteristic uniformity to the legal system of the Mediterranean lands, and especially Italy itself. Several other magistracies were also often filled by lawyers and notaries drawn from territories outside that of the state which employed them temporarily.

One tends to think of Italy as unified by commerce, and indeed the bigger banking and merchant houses had their *filiali*, their agencies and branches, in the larger towns. But equally unifying were less happy peninsular phenomena – war, banditry and poverty. Certainly most of the troops and their captains who ravaged the land in the period were Italian; for example, the wars fought in the early fifteenth century to secure the kingdom of Naples were largely fought by Italian mercenary troops hired by each side. Indeed, from that conflict the historian Flavio Biondo (1392–1463) fathered the tradition of the Peninsula being dominated by two Italian schools of warfare: the rapid tactics adopted by Braccio da Montone (1368–1424) as against the cannier, more Fabian methods of Muzio Attendolo Sforza (1369–1424) and his disciples, notably his son Francesco, later Duke of Milan (1450) (see below, p. 84 ff).[13] Many princelings were in the service of the larger powers, and made an honest florin out of the almost perpetual wars of Italy: the Montefeltro of Urbino are one conspicuous example; the Malatesta of Rimini are another. But it is an illusion to suppose, as some older books would have it, that successful *condottieri* were rewarded with massive land grants, which enabled them to climb the social ladder. The only important example of this was Francesco Sforza, who in any case was married to the (admittedly illegitimate) sole heiress of the Visconti, Bianca Maria. Most of the other *condottieri*, even if they arrived at hereditary principalities, failed to get them or keep them: one thinks of Facino Cane, Piccinino, Gattamelata. Others, we must remember, were by inheritance 'feudal' lords of their lands, like the Montefeltro, the various branches of the Malatesta, and the unruly Colonna and Orsini in the region of Rome.

In practice a kind of hierarchy of mercenary captains developed. A prince or republic hired a captain general who in turn subcontracted with other lesser captains for the total he wanted, in a balanced force – infantry, artillery and so on. We should remember that there is nothing particularly Italian in these developments, which are equally to be found in the kingdoms of northern Europe. But we introduce the phenomenon in the Italian context to show yet another way in which men were moving round the country, begetting children, mingling dialects, indifferent to any sentiment which one could call patriotism and frequently going over into robbery and violence, not on behalf of their cynical paymasters but on their own account – as the pay-masters did not pay and the mercenary joined the hordes of the poor. To quote Fernand

Braudel, 'vagrants and bandits were brothers in hardship and might change places'.[14] Since marauders all over Europe hugged borderlands between so-called sovereign states (since in this way the bandits could often defy authority with impunity) the multiplicity of governmental authorities in Italy encouraged the robber bands to choose areas where they might readily slip out of one jurisdiction into another. The harshest poverty and the cruellest banditry (on sea as well as on land) seems to have come in the decades round 1600, but Italy had been blisteringly damaged by the French invasions, horrors like the Sack of Rome (see below, p. 222),[15] and almost perpetual invasions, 'legitimate' and illegitimate, down to the mid-sixteenth century, when disorder becomes, one might say, merely endemic in the Peninsula.

'The poor are always with us.' In Italy they were, or felt themselves to be, nearer help from begging to and at the great pilgrim centres where hospitals and confraternities, as well as devout well-to-do visitors from afar, might alleviate their hardship. Succouring the poor is one of the corporal acts of mercy enjoined on Christians and (along with more ruthless measures, such as forcibly expelling the out-of-work from a given community) was taken seriously in our period. So also was the doctrine which, for the simple who were innocent of theological niceties, was the hope of curtailing uncomfortable aeons in purgatory by indulgences. These could of course be purchased from pardoners who often omitted to qualify the efficacy of Grace; but they would also be obtained by the pious act of pilgrimage. This had always been notionally associated with poverty. For the poor shuffling down the roads to a holy place there was thus hope of alms on the way and at the end of the tramp, and beatitude after (for Rome was the pilgrimage centre most accessible to Italians) visiting the five great basilicas, especially in the comfortingly frequent years of Jubilee.

ITALIAN PICTURES OF ITALY

Such a subtitle conjures up the steady infiltration of 'landscape into art', to use Sir Kenneth Clark's title (1949). And it is true that in the last centuries of the Middle Ages – the Italian's Renaissance – it does become possible to gather contemporaneous images of the Peninsula, although most often such landscapes or townscapes form only the background to a religious painting, or less commonly to a secular subject or portrait. The initiative to this particular artistic development was, for once, not Florentine:

It is in Sienese painting that we must look for the sense of natural beauty which we have discovered in the poets of the early fourteenth century; and we find it in the work of Simone Martini and the Lorenzetti . . . [Simone] was at one with the finest Gothic art of France.[16]

Some Italian painters and writers were indeed beginning to 'view' Italy, if not to distinguish it consciously from other parts of Europe.

It was to Petrarch's Avignon that Simone went, and it is no accident that

Sir Kenneth Clark's discussion of the gradual detachment of landscape from its role as mere background begins, tellingly, with Dante's Dark Wood in the early lines of the *Divine Comedy* before going on to Petrarch and the garden delights of Boccaccio's *Decameron*. Not that Clark would have argued for landscape as s subject worthy of attention in its own right as an Italian invention or monopoly. Indeed, it is rather a product of northern Europe. Nevertheless it was absorbed and developed by the Bellini, Uccello, Piero della Francesca and others, so that it is possible for E. Sereni, in his history of the Italian agrarian landscape (see below, p. 72), to illustrate the world of the Peninsula from paintings of the time. Needless to say, the urban world is even better depicted visually. The grandees or town councils who commissioned paintings (and buildings) naturally expected them to reflect this background.

The preceding pages have doubtless suggested an Italy in which many men were on the move, so that the vernaculars could mingle with a fair degree of facility. It may be doubted if this satisfied the purists, and there were some fastidious or ambitious lovers of Italian as it might become, not as it was messily emerging. Such an advocate of a stylish and 'correct' Italian was Dante in his remarkable book on *Vernacular Literature* (*De vulgari eloquentia*). This work is introduced here, however, not because it was to be over the centuries a forlorn cry for 'courtly' Italian, destined never to be attended to, but because it is the first of three important books written by Italians at about this time and dealing with their own land; 'at about this time' since only one of the authors lived within the period. The work by Dante was written in approximately 1305; the next writer is Flavio Biondo, historian and papal servant, whose short account of Italy was written between 1448 and 1453 and was first printed in 1474; finally, in 1550 a Dominican friar called Leandro Alberti composed and published at Bologna his *Descrittione di tutta Italia*.

Dante's plea for a common and elevated style for the whole of Italy does not really concern us here, save to reinforce the feeling of a multiplicity of tongues, somehow not impeding contact, which has emerged in the previous pages. Here he is a witness to the notion intellectuals had of their land. To start with, his view – and those of many later writers – assumes a land running from north-east to south-west, with the northern boundary imposed by the Alps. If Dante had looked at *portolans*, as seems certain, these were crudely accommodated to a 'T and O' map of an earlier date so that Jerusalem remained at the centre of the world; thus, in viewing his Apennine divisions he writes of the right and the left of the Peninsula in a way contrary to modern practice. He compares the mountain divide to the sloping ridge of a roof. He then makes broad subdivisions: 'to the right . . . most of Apulia, Rome, the duchy of Spoleto, Tuscany, the March of Genoa; . . . to the left, part of Apulia, the March of Ancona, Romagna, Lombardy, the March of Treviso with Venice, Friuli and Istria . . . .'.[17] To reiterate, Dante's purpose was not to depict Italy but, having established the main divisions (all, we may note, of historical and political origin) to regard them as a linguistic problem. 'In this small corner of the world', he concludes, 'the number of linguistic varieties would reach not merely a thousand but even more'.[18]

Dante's aim had been to give Italy a true literary language and beyond that, we may suppose, to encourage a genuine Italian political unity. This was far from being the purpose of Flavio Biondo of Forli, and it would have been surprising in a man who was a papal servant naturally inclined to sympathise with the age-old desire of popes to divide and rule. Biondo is, of course, best known for his *Decades*, the first survey of medieval Christendom which, as the work progressed, became a history of Italy. This history, which ran from the fall of Rome to his own day, was mercilessly plundered by other historians and therefore had a brief but profound influence on historiography. Here we must note his insistence on the fall of Rome coinciding with the collapse of the towns; it is to their revival that he looks for the rebirth of a new and more vigorous Italy. But his *Italia Illustrata* is a shorter and much more unusual book – one, perhaps, which was more influential than the *Decades* since it promoted a movement of chorography which by the mid-sixteenth century penetrated nearly every European land. 'Chorography', says the dictionary, 'is a description of districts, more limited than geography, less than topography.' In practice, for Italy it was tracing the Roman origins of areas, especially towns; as it was in later work regarding areas where centurions had once held sway, like Camden's *Britannia*. In his *Italia Illustrata* Biondo followed this path, and gave ancient authorities for surviving places; to these he added information on famous men, both of antiquity and of more recent times, so that his small book became a kind of view of the regions in both 'chorographical' and historical terms. His aim – only partly fulfilled, since much depended on the help he solicited from local scholars – was to list the boundaries of his provinces, of which he identifies eighteen (derived ultimately from Pliny) and thus

proceeds to deal seriatim with towns, castles, rivers. In all this he follows wherever possible the ancient authorities, and never forgets that his aim is to relate ancient names with modern. But he regularly intersperses brief indications of scenery and notes the occasions when small places have momentarily had historic importance. When he discusses larger towns a succinct account is given of origins, of subsequent history, of the current situation, including the names of celebrated writers, and of families who have produced popes.

Since Biondo depended on local help, his work is markedly defective where such help is lacking, as in the *Regno*; the islands, including Sicily, he completely omits. It is perhaps explicable that the region which he treats most fully is his own, the Romagna;

as long as the sections on Tuscany or Rome and twice as long as the section on the Veneto. . . . It was the home of the revival of letters and the birthplace of the Italian general Alberigo da Barbiano, from whose indigenous militarism a happier political future for Italy seemed to Biondo to point. [19]

In its different way, Biondo's little book was as original as Dante's survey of the Romance languages; it certainly had more immediate effect, more diffused and general emulators. None the less, in the very nature of things, it was soon to be overtaken by other works – fuller, more up to date and, it must be noted, more useful to visitors to Italy. Leandro Alberti's *Descrittione di tutta Italia*, which came out ten times between 1550 and 1631 and also appeared twice in Latin in the late sixteenth century, came closer to being a *vade mecum* for travellers than the scholarly work of Biondo. Montaigne took it with him; a century later an alumnus of Edinburgh left a copy to Edinburgh University Library, significantly describing it as 'the best Classical Description of Italy' (1778). But by then, as noted earlier, we are well into the world of guidebooks.

Alberti's big book is, like the smaller work of Biondo, very uneven. He too depended on helpers, although as a Dominican provincial he travelled widely. He too omitted the islands, although promising their later inclusion, as they were to be omitted in much later works involving Italy, such as F. Ughelli's *Italia Sacra* (see below, p. 145).[20] His picture of the land was based on its resemblance to a human leg, from thigh to foot. Basing himself on Biondo's *Italia Illustrata*, he too sought to relate the ancient nomenclature of places to their modern equivalents. He had, of course, much more secondary material to fall back on. The larger scale of Alberti's work encouraged elaborate excursions into current affairs, economic and social, but (another Romagnol, like Biondo) he too gives his own province the lion's share of men and memories.

Yet neither Biondo nor Alberti does more than give incidental views about the Italians and the Italy of their own day. They are harking back (Biondo by command of Alfonso of Aragon) to the effort of relating antiquity to the present, not of analysing what made Italy different from other adjacent lands.

NOTES AND REFERENCES

This chapter may help to explain why it is so difficult to attempt a general bibliography for this, or indeed for many other periods of Italian history. Nevertheless there are a number of works which are useful for consultation: J. R. Hale (ed.). *A Concise Encyclopaedia of the Italian Renaissance* (London, 1981), containing a valuable article on 'National feeling'; *Encyclopaedia Italiana* (Rome, 1929–39); and Einaudi, *La Storia d'Italia* (Turin, 1972–76), one of the most useful of the recent Italian surveys of peninsular history. E. Cochrane gives an exhaustive survey of contemporary narratives in *Historians and Historiography in the Italian Renaissance* (Chicago, 1981). F. Braudel, *La Méditerranée et le Monde Méditerranéen*, first appeared in Paris in 1949. There have been several revisions since, and an English version (1971–73). This is a difficult book to use, but it has stimulating sections on all countries in the region.

1. The first Italian guidebook as such was by Francis Schott in 1600. On this see E. S. de Beer, *The Library*, ser. 4, XXIII (1942).
2. Cf. G. B. Parks, *The English Traveller to Italy*, i (all published). (Rome, 1954).
3. F. M. Nichols, *Marvels of Rome* (London, 1889). Cf. bibliography in Letts, *Von Harff*; below, n. 5.
4. Roger Barlow's paraphrase of the Spaniard Enciso's *Sumar de Geografia* (1518). ed. E. G. R. Taylor (Hakluyt Society, London, 1932). p. 54.

5. *The Pilgrimage of Arnold von Harff*, ed. M. Letts (Hakluyt Society, London, 1946), pp. 34–9; for the *Mirabilia* see Letts, note on p. 16, and his bibliography.

6. Einaudi, *Storia d'Italia*, vols V* and V** (Turin, 1974).

7. A. Bellettini in Einaudi, *Storia*, vol. V*, p. 487, and bibliography on pp. 5312, which omits to note the revised 1965 edition of vol. ii of K. J. Beloch's *Bevölkerungsgeschichte Italiens* (Berlin, 1937–61).

8. Einaudi, *Storia*, vol. V*; and below, pp. 35–44 on the family, and on the *Rationes Decimarum*. Dr Klapisch-Zuber has made a number of valuable contributions to the study of Italian social and demographic history.

9. Cf. P. J. Jones in vol. i (revised edn) of the *Cambridge Economic History of Europe* (Cambridge, 1966).

10. Pompeo Litta *et al.*, *Famiglie Celebri Italiani*, 10 vols (Milan, 1819–83; second series published in Naples, 1901–23). There is an index to this work in the British Library.

11. 'La Canzone Popolare', Roberto Leydi in Einaudi, *Storia*, vol. V**, pp. 1183–1279. esp. p. 1203.

12. The northern area of popular song has links with styles of north European character, the Mediterranean areas with styles basically common to northern Africa and southern Europe.

13. Flavio Biondo, *Italia Illustrata*.

14. Braudel, op.cit., vol. ii, p. 741; the whole section on poverty and banditry, pp. 734–56, is highly relevant.

15. See Eric Cochrane's volume in this series: *Italy 1530–1630*.

16. Clark, *Landscape into Art* (London, 1949), p. 6.

17. Ed. A. Marigo (Bari, 1938). pp. 80–86; cf. Hay, 'The Italian view of Renaissance Italy', in *Florilegium Historiale, Essays presented to W. K. Ferguson*, (ed. J. G. Rowe and W. H. Stockdale; Toronto, 1971). 'T and O' maps were so called because they were circular in design, with the Mediterranean effecting a tripartite division of the continents.

18. Marigo, op.cit., p. 88.

19. Hay, loc. cit., pp. 8–9.

20. The promised additional section on the islands appeared in 1561, and in the edition of 1568 each island was accompanied by a map; see the full study by C. R. Austin, *The Sources and Influence of the Descrittione di tutta Italia of Fra Leandro Alberti* (Unpublished Ph.D. thesis, University of Edinburgh, 1974).

PART TWO

Society, the state and the Church

CHAPTER THREE

Urban society

As mentioned in Chapter One, the archives and libraries of Italy contain a wealth of material for the study of the social history of the Renaissance, and in a few centres research has made rapid progress in recent years. Modern historians, sometimes equipped with methodologies (and even conclusions) borrowed from the social sciences and anthropology, have eclipsed the older certainties suggested by Marx or Burckhardt: that the Renaissance saw the triumph of the bourgeoisie, or the emergence of the individual. But the plethora of detailed local studies, often based on new approaches and new source material, makes it more difficult to arrive at an equally confident picture of Renaissance society as a whole. The relationship between city and *contado* will be discussed in the following chapter; this chapter will focus on two related issues: the position of the ruling elite in urban society and the nature and role of the family.

URBAN ELITES

The prevailing view of Italian urban society in the Renaissance is that it became more hierarchical, and that this development can be traced in both manners and institutions. It was behind the increasingly ostentatious palace-building of the period. It can also be detected in the appetite for titles and coats of arms bestowed by the princely and royal houses of Europe; as is discussed in Chapters Ten and Eleven, a craving for such honours was a feature of the signorial dynasties of northern and central Italy, but it permeated society more widely – as is shown, for example, by the imperial registers.[1] The emperor Sigismund's arrival in Italy in 1412 was prefaced and accompanied by the large-scale granting, or sale, of favours; he made the Miari family of Belluno counts, allowing them to incorporate the imperial eagle in their arms. In 1433 Corrado Trinci was among the prominent citizens of Foligno to be made count palatine and admitted to the imperial Dragon Order as the same emperor returned northwards from his imperial coronation in Rome. These fashions were far from absent in republican Florence. In 1401, Bonaccorso Pitti composed a sonnet to celebrate the privilege granted his family by Rupert of Bavaria: to incorporate his arms in theirs. Giovanni Rucellai appears to have been allowed by the Este of Ferrara to adopt one of their *imprese*; the device of a wind-filled sail was placed on the facade of his palace in the 1450s. Despite this Giovanni probably continued to regard himself as a citizen of Florence, but earlier Bonaccorso had been proud of the letters patent issued by Rupert proclaiming the nobility of the Pitti. The nature of nobility in general was a matter for active debate by humanists and jurists in the period.[2]

As will be further discussed in the following chapter, the hierarchical nature of society is also revealed in contemporary attitudes; some Venetian examples can illustrate the point from an urban context. In 1425 the doge argued that Durazzo was so plague-ridden that it would be improper to send nobles to govern it; its offices were better suited to Venetian citizens. When the noble merchant Andrea Barbarigo made his will in 1486, the charitable provisions made for poor nobles were double the value of those made for commoners. And contempt or condescension could be reciprocated. In his will of 1361 the wealthy citizen Antonio Arian stipulated that none of his children should marry into a noble family.[3] The heavy defeats suffered by Venice in the early years of the War of the League of Cambrai prompted fears of a popular revolt, provoked by the apparent failure of noble rule.

If evidence of this nature is rather impressionistic, institutional changes do suggest much more clearly that urban society was becoming more hierarchical in the period. Distinctions became increasingly marked between guilds associated with 'honourable' professions and occupations – law, medicine, large-scale commerce – and those of a more manual nature linked to the 'mechanical arts'. Concurrently, the place of the lesser trade and craft guilds in the government of both such large centres as Genoa, Florence and Naples and of the smaller communes of the Marches and Umbria, had either ended or was in decline. The lawyers, notaries, bankers and merchants who retained a role in communal government now did so less because of their guild status and more because of their wealth, their family background and their professional expertise. The conditions of citizenship became more restrictively defined, and the status itself no longer formed the basis for a prominent role in public affairs. Communal government came increasingly into the hands of a minority of the citizenry, variously labelled by historians as a nobility, a patriciate, an elite or a ruling group – of these terms, only the first had wide currency.

Some specific examples illustrate the general tendency. In 1380 the government of the city of Naples became largely the prerogative of five noble parties – which divided up the city geographically between them – which met and organised in their own lodges and which are called *sedie* or *seggi*, from the seats they controlled on the governing council. Admission to a *seggio* became more closely defined and controlled, and the ascendancy the nobility enjoyed is demonstrated by the fact that they swore homage to Alfonso I on

4 June 1443, a day before the 'people' of Naples performed the same cere-mony.[4] The last modification to the ranks of the hereditary Venetian nobility took place in 1382 with the inclusion of thirty new families. In Verona, the large Council of Five Hundred was officially abolished in 1405 to be replaced by a Council of Fifty, and in 1438 the city's College of Notaries formally excluded its members from abroad or the *contado* from its own government and the public offices at its disposal, reserving the lion's share of such positions for citizen members untainted by the 'mechanical arts'.[5]

If it is relatively easy to assemble the evidence pointing towards a more hierarchical society in which power was increasingly concentrated in fewer and more explicitly privileged hands, it is harder to explain the development itself. Particular, local, circumstances have to be taken into account. When the membership of the ruling council of Belluno was defined in 1424 – with the exclusion of those associated with the 'mechanical arts' – the reason was in part to reduce the grounds for faction among the leading families and their supporters. When the Medici returned to Florence in 1434, they exiled a large number of families who had previously been members of the *reggimento* (see below, Chapter Eleven, p. 253 ff).[6] More generally, the explanation possibly lies in large measure in the anxiety of already established families lest they be driven from power. This was a fear which may have been particu-larly acute in a period of grave economic and social upheaval following outbreaks of plague. In cities such as Florence, established families were fearful of economic and political decline in respect of 'new men' and immi-grants trying to profit from the opportunities and redistribution of wealth produced by a period of dislocation. Moreover, in Florence and Siena the extreme social unrest of the late fourteenth century possibly created a more defensive and elitist attitude on the part of the leading families, as the contempt shown by men like Filippo Villani, Giovanni Cavalcanti and Bonaccorso Pitti for the *'gente nuova'* and the *Ciompi* shows.

Furthermore, the same period was one of political change with the creation of more centralised territorial states; the leading citizens of communes newly subject to Venice or the Visconti were probably apprehensive lest changes of regime affect their position: their terms of surrender are characterised by an anxiety to defend the *status quo*. To such economic, social and political press-ures there should probably be added a basic tendency towards 'aristocratisa-tion'. The urban elites of Italy were far from detached from a more 'traditional', 'feudal' world. Naples, for example, was the seat of the Angevin and then the Aragonese royal courts, and the members of the city's noble *seggi* sought a sounder nobility through the acquisition of titles, fiefs and marriages to the baronial houses of the kingdom. The dividing line between urban and feudal nobilities was even more blurred in the case of Genoa where the leaders of the great clans, or *alberghi*, could combine without any sense of contra-diction, commerce, public office and property-ownership in the city with fiefs, lordships and castles in the hinterland. As mentioned above (and as demonstrated by Trexler), even the more strictly republican Florentines could not escape the allure of monarchy and nobility, while the passage of aristocratic pilgrims like Henry Bolingbroke, Duke of Lancaster (1392–93) aroused the attention of the chroniclers of Venice and the Veneto.[7]

In fact, as we shall see in Chapter Four (pp. 64–69), the influence of feudal society and attitudes on the urban elites of Italy does not appear so surprising if the political geography of the country is considered and once older, largely anachronistic, ideas are abandoned: of a 'modern', 'bourgeois' Italy distinct from a 'medieval', 'feudal' Europe. Nor should it come as a surprise that the social and political history of the period so often reveals a hierarchical view of society. The civic humanism of Florence, with its emphasis on a citizen's duty to participate in public life, was largely the rhetoric of an elite. The *Della Vita Civile* (1438–39) of Matteo Palmieri, one of its number, represents society as more oppressively hierarchical than John of Salisbury's vision of the body politic in the twelfth century, with 'the working masses and the humblest sector of the middle class' struggling 'for the good of the Republic'.[8] In Venice, noble humanists like Francesco Barbaro (1390–1454) and Lauro Quirini (*c.* 1420–*c.* 1479), as well as non-nobles like Giovanni Caldiera (*c.* 1400–*c.* 1474) and Francesco Negri (1452–*c.* 1523), did not question the right of the nobility to rule. Probably much more typical than the hostile and alienated Antonio Arian mentioned above was the citizen banker Angelo Condulmer, who made provision in his will of 1394 so that his daughters could all take noble husbands.[9]

But if Italian society in the Renaissance was closer to a European norm than was once supposed, it might suggest that the changes detectable in the period – towards a more differentiated hierarchy – should not be exaggerated. In the first place, the process met with little determined resistance. On matters ranging from the distribution of offices to the allocation of the tax burden, the Venetian republic could respond to and exploit 'popular' resentment against the self-created urban elites in its Italian and Dalmatian dominions without overturning or modifying the social and political structure. When the popular *seggio* of Naples protested in 1455 at the destruction of its *loggia* to make room for a tournament ground, Alfonso defused the crisis by admitting its leading families to one of the noble *seggi*. As that incident suggests, the urban elites or nobilities of Italy often lacked clear definition, beyond a longer enjoyment of the status itself, to distinguish them from the wealthier members of the *popolo*. Indeed in Naples, in periods of crisis and *interregna*, the popular *seggio* was granted a seat in city government, and definitively so after 1495. In Genoa, the 'closing' of the commune's constitution in 1528 saw the inclusion of a number of popular *alberghi*.

Elsewhere the ruling elite could be even less structured. In Florence, both contemporaries and historians agree that wealth, a distinguished lineage, advantageous marriage alliances and a record of uncontentious office-holding were prominent ingredients in the formula for political and social eminence. But the combination of such assets was neither essential nor an invariable guarantee of success; although historians have detected a narrowing of the republic's *reggimento* in political terms in the later fifteenth century, the patronage of the Medici contributed to maintain an element of social mobility, and to outsiders it could appear bizarrely open and ill-defined. In the 1430s the Spaniard Pero Tafur was amazed that a government that might include shoemakers could function so well; later in the century a Venetian ambassador sneered at a constitution that afforded a role to practitioners of the 'mechanical arts'.[10]

There is a considerable irony in that comment because the Venetian nobility, although one of the longest established and more closely defined of the urban elites of the Peninsula, had like the rest been self-created, while the unashamed involvement of its members in trade and finance failed to impress some critics. Against them Lauro Quirini argued in his *De Nobilitate* (*c.* 1449) that commerce was so useful to the republic that it was not an ignoble profession. Quirini also tried to answer the Florentine Poggio Bracciolini, whose own *De Nobilitate* of 1440 attacked heredity as the basis of nobility in Venice, as elsewhere. The Venetian response was that nobility derived from nature, but the unresolved character of this ongoing debate, and the fact that a powerful case could still be made for a nobility of personal virtue and excellence rather than of blood, further illustrates the confusion and imprecision surrounding the noble status claimed by many of the urban elites of the period.

This confusion stems in large measure from the fact that Italy lacked a single sovereign from whom all honours and status depended, and it is further reflected in the attitude to heraldry and knighthood in the Renaissance. For the most part, coats of arms appeared to have been the product of the inventiveness and opportunism of their owners. They were certainly not the preserve of feudal dynasties alone but were adopted by prominent urban families, as well as by cities and even rural communities. Nor does Italian Renaissance heraldry necessarily follow any laws; for example the history of the Medici arms − and in particular the choice of the number of gold balls, or *palle* − appears eccentric. The *Tractatus de Insigniis et Armis* written by the famous jurist Bartolus of Sassoferrato around 1355 launched no systematic study of the subject, and the only collections of Renaissance heraldry appear to be local. Similarly knighthood was generously conferred by recognised authorities like the popes and emperors, as well as by communal and signorial regimes. In one day in 1378 the rebellious *Ciompi* of Florence created sixty-seven knights.[11]

With imprecision surrounding the definition, composition and appearance of the urban nobilities of Renaissance Italy, it is perhaps hardly surprising that it would be inappropriate to describe them in terms of caste, as if they were aloof from the rest of society. In Venice, where the situation was probably more closely defined than elsewhere, the nobility embraced such a wide spectrum of wealth, political prominence and family size that it could almost be described more as a microcosm of society as a whole than an elite. As will be discussed below, its relations with the rest of the population were close, and the scrutiny of notarial material reveals how inextricably associated were the lives of nobles and commoners in matters ranging from the election of parish priests and the membership of confraternities to commercial and property dealings. More generally, the 'aristocratisation' of the urban elite should not be exaggerated. Goldthwaite has argued that their members did not flaunt their wealth and distinction through large numbers of servants and continued to regard the city, rather than their rural properties, as the centre of social and political activity.[12] Moreover, neither the town plans of Italian cities, nor the design of their public buildings, nor the evidence left by their diarists and chroniclers suggest that the conduct of the ordinary business of government was normally carried out in conditions of secrecy. This is not surprising. When the size of surviving consultative councils is considered in contemporary terms, they appear to have retained a representative character. The Greater Council of Venice in around 1500 was made up of about 2,000 members; in the context of a total population of about 100,000 and of a period when it would have been unthinkable to accord *contadini*, women, immigrants, the poor, the young or the clergy any place in government, that represents a considerable level of involvement. The same point can be made from smaller centres such as Belluno, where in the mid-fifteenth century around thirty families were represented in a greater council, out of a total population of about 2,000.

Finally, historians are becoming increasingly aware of institutions and modes of conduct that might have provided some compensation for those excluded from the elite, or might have prevented the emergence of a too-rigidly hierarchical society. If guilds were almost everywhere excluded from government, they did retain an important role in organising the economic, social and devotional lives of their members.[13] As we shall see in Chapter Seven (p. 136 ff), confraternities are being increasingly recognised as having a central position in the social and spiritual life of the community, embracing both 'nobles' and 'commoners'. There is growing evidence that neighbourhood organisations retained administrative as well as social, devotional and ceremonial functions. From his sympathetic scrutiny of the *gonfalone*, or district, of the Red Lion in Florence, F. W. Kent has shown how tightly knit such neighbourhood communities could remain, and how supportive they could be of greater families – like the Rucellai – while retaining the involvement of the less wealthy and prominent.[14] Probably studies of similar organisations – like the *ottine* of Naples – would reveal that vertical relationships were far more active and important than the impersonal concept of 'aristocratisation' would suggest.

This is certainly the conclusion suggested by recent research on the practice of patronage – beyond the more familiar context of the arts. Reciprocal ties of interest, obligation and friendship can be shown to have run through society. From the 'well-equipped laboratory' of Florentine social history it is possible to show how the greater families could draw on retinues from their estates, while in turn such dependants looked to their patrons for protection and favours. The interest and the generosity of the Medici towards the church of San Lorenzo allowed them to favour allies and dependants, while promoting their own cause in this world and the next. Giovanni Rucellai's own account of the wedding of 1466 between his son Bernardo and Nannina, granddaughter of Cosimo de' Medici, reveals him revelling in his new and powerful connections, as well as presiding over his own pyramid of clients, neighbours, poorer relatives and estate workers, who were his dependants but who reciprocated his friendship and were necessary to his sense of status. In Genoa patronage in the political and social sense was virtually institutionalised in the *alberghi*, where ties of dependence and obligation were expressed in clan membership.[15]

THE FAMILY

Although the basis of the Genoese *albergo* was the clan rather than the kin, it represented a formal association of families which had adopted or accepted a common name and which behaved – politically, economically, devotionally and socially – like an extended family. However, both Heers and other historians have shown that '*le clan familial*' can be found elsewhere and that the family, however precisely constituted, had a key role in all aspects of Renaissance society. This was very much appreciated at the time. Herlihy and others have suggested that the severe losses caused by repeated visitations of the plague encouraged a heightened interest in family life and concern for the rearing of children, and certainly the period sees a remarkable number of treatises, sermons and government decrees, as well as collective and individual charity, aimed at the family and the welfare of children.[16]

Perhaps the best-known treatise was written by Leon Battista Alberti (1404–72); identified by Burckhardt as an outstanding example of Renaissance individualism, Alberti in his *Della Famiglia* of the 1430s purported to follow conversations between members of his family held in Padua in 1421. He explored such central issues as family loyalty, relations with the state, sources of wealth, the management of the household, marriage and the upbringing of children. Understandably – in view of Leon Battista's resentment at being discriminated against for his illegitimate birth and the Alberti's exile from their native city of Florence – the *Della Famiglia* argues for mutual support within the family and self-reliance in its relations with the rest of society. By contrast, the Venetians Francesco Barbaro in his *De Re Uxoria* (1415–16) and Giovanni Caldiera in his *De Veneta Iconomia* (1463–64) stressed the contribution the family should make to the greater good of the republic.[17]

Less confidence is displayed by the Roman aristocrat Marcantonio Altieri who, in his *Li Nuptiali* of 1521, lamented the decline of the Roman nobility as revealed by the collapse of the pomp and ritual once attending its marriage ceremonies.[18] The family was also a matter of concern for governments with the commune of Florence, for example, legislating on matters ranging from homosexuality to the treatment of wet-nurses, while dowry payments and the care of abandoned children appear to have been popular areas of charitable activity. At various times in the fifteenth century, the commune of Siena appointed marriage brokers. Finally, as Italian governments became more narrowly oligarchic and aristocratic in character, an impetus was given to the collection of genealogical information; the Venetian diarist and historian Marino Sanudo (1466–1536) was obsessed by the family history of fellow-members of the nobility.[19]

The important role identified by contemporaries for the family can also be seen in the compilation of family diaries and chronicles, intended as private rather than as public records. The best-known of such *ricordi* are those of prominent Florentine families; for example the cloth merchant Giovanni Morelli was the author of *ricordi* covering the years 1393 to 1411 and combining family history with observations on such topics as paternal authority, marriage and relations with the state. But if *ricordi* are rarely as well written or as informative as those of Morelli, the practice of keeping family records was widespread both down the social scale and in other cities. According to Cohn, even Florentine artisans and labourers kept family account books and *ricordanze*; but certainly among the greater families of Venice and Pisa records were kept of births, marriages and deaths, offices held and property owned, transferred or claimed.[20]

If such material was intended for domestic consumption, families were also prepared to proclaim their achievements and status more publicly. Scholars could be commissioned to write the 'official' history of ruling families: Giovanni Simonetta's *Rebus Gestis Francisci Sfortiae* was designed to exalt the achievements of the new duke of Milan. Architects, artists and craftsmen could be employed on such projects as the family palace, *loggia* (meeting-place) and burial chapel. Alberti argued that a family's honour was expressed through the building of a palace and a *loggia*; he himself contributed to the design of Giovanni Rucellai's palace in Florence in the 1450s; in his will of 1491 Filippo Strozzi committed his heirs to finishing his palace, begun in 1489. Indeed, the palace and the burial chapel were the items of property a family was most anxious to retain. Both were likely to display the family's coat of arms, and this introduces the point that there were ways of celebrating a family's existence which were more within reach of a wider section of society than major undertakings in stone. The della Robbia firm in Florence produced affordable coats of arms in glazed terracotta. Other workshops turned out *cassoni*, painted chests to contain a bride's trousseau and designed to commemorate her marriage and the union of two families. Similar celebrations of what are now fashionably termed 'the rites of passage' were *deschi da parto*, decorated dishes or salvers, presented to a mother after childbirth. These, like family portraits and death masks, could be the work of highly accomplished artists. The *cassoni* workshop of the Florentine Apollonio di Giovanni – active between 1446 and 1463 – was not only highly productive but earned its master the title of 'the Tuscan Apelles'. The fact that Savonarola attacked the pagan nature of the scenes depicted on *cassoni* panels suggests that the market for such items was wide.[21]

The keeping up of appearances was related to the role the family could have in the pursuit and maintenance of power and influence. Rather notorious in this regard is the practice of most of the popes of the period to advance their relations and their clients to offices in Church and state, a practice that was vigorously pursued by Martin V (1417–31), anxious to rebuild papal authority after the Schism, and by the Spanish Borgia popes Calixtus III (1455–58) and Alexander VI (1492–1503), determined that their foreign origins should not prove a handicap. The Renaissance popes also tried to use their kin to secure, through marriage, alliances with other Italian families. For example in 1488 Innocent VIII agreed to the marriage of his illegitimate son Franceschetto Cibo to Maddalena de' Medici, daughter of Lorenzo and Clarissa, who was herself from the powerful Roman Orsini family. One consequence of this was the bestowal of a cardinal's hat on Lorenzo's son Giovanni on 9 March 1489. Since Giovanni was only fourteen it is not surprising that his elevation was kept secret, but dynasticism was normally less discreet. The marriage of Bernardo Rucellai to Nannina de' Medici in 1466 was remarkable for its pomp and ceremony and succeeded in 'rehabilitating' the Rucellai, previously compromised by marital links with the exiled Strozzi, with the regime.[22] As the case history of the Rucellai shows, marriage ties were not always a formula for success, but they continued to be seen as a possible way of reconciling enemies and making friends. In 1389 a Dominican friar suggested that intermarriage between Spanish and native families would reduce faction on Sicily, while the rivalry between the Oddi and the Baglioni of Perugia was punctuated by efforts at reconciliation through marriage.[23]

Families also sought to promote their interests through office-holding in Church and state. From 1466 all the bishops of Mantua were members of the ruling Gonzaga house, and the elevation of Francesco Gonzaga to the cardinalate in 1461 was understood to bring prestige and influence as well as worry and expense to the dynasty. Leading Florentine families sought ecclesiastical offices of importance in the city and its dominions to enhance their status, while the Venetian government felt the need to guard against the influence of noble families with members in the Church by excluding them from sensitive debates. In Venice, too, steps were taken to prevent the doge from favouring his family, while Savonarola observed that if the Florentines copied Venetian practice and created a doge, they should choose a man with no sons. In February 1464 the Sforza ambassador to Genoa reported that the doge and archbishop of the city, Paolo di Campofregoso, had no intention of accepting the lordship of the duke of Milan because he had an obligation to favour his friends, partisans and relatives.[24] In general communal governments legislated to limit the number of offices or seats on the communal councils a family could enjoy; but as such governments became more narrowly oligarchic and aristocratic in character, so the need to secure a right to participation increased. In sixteenth-century Lucca ancient but decaying families struggled to maintain their membership of the communal council, but where families proved too aggressive in the pursuit of their interests they could suffer reprisals. Papal dynasties and their clients fell abruptly from favour on the death of their principal patron, while the Alberti clan faced collective exile on the failure of a number of conspiracies against the Florentine regime.

But modern research is making clearer the importance of family ties outside the better-charted world of higher politics. The family was probably the means by which Florentines gained entry to confraternities.[25] It was the means by which leading families conferred favours and status on potential clients, for example by providing them with dowries or inviting them to stand as godparents to their children. In Genoa, belonging to an *albergo* afforded its lesser members protection. In general, the family could provide succour to less fortunate relatives, orphans and widows, while the foreigner without family or friends ran the dangers of the social outcast. The family could also determine its members' means of livelihood. At all levels, soldiering was an activity often passed from father to son. The same was true for civilian life and appears to have applied as much to the 'arts' as to the 'crafts'. The Bellini of Venice were remarkable for their talents, but less so for operating as a 'family firm'. Again in Venice the Alberghetti were a dynasty of cannon-founders, as the Antegnati of Brescia were leading makers of musical instruments in the sixteenth century. For the majority of the population, working on the land, the value of the family as a source of labour meant that the average household was larger and more likely to extend beyond the conjugal family than was generally the case with urban society. In San Gimignano poor peasant families abandoned their infant children to the hospital of S. Maria della Scala, but 'redeemed' them when they reached working age.[26]

The importance of the family in all levels of society has encouraged historians to try to describe its size, structure and behaviour, but for all its considerable achievements modern research remains at a reconnaissance stage.[27] The greatest progress has been made with the Florentine and Tuscan evidence, and while the material for other cities and regions remains relatively unexplored it is difficult to arrive at conclusions for Italy as a whole. Even for Tuscany the picture remains tentative. A major insight has been afforded from the study of the Florentine *catasto*, or tax assessment, of 1427, but for all its massive detail it has limitations for the demographer and the social historian. It was not a census, and some elements of the population remained excluded or under-represented: the very poor, foreigners, the clergy, Jews, women and young children. Moreover, as an undertaking it was overambitious. For example, the efforts of its assessors to secure accurate reporting of age were thwarted by a mixture of caginess and confusion, and the *catasto* of 1427 was not the first of a series, making it more difficult for historians to check and observe its information over a period of time. Not that there is a dearth of evidence to set against it, but where such evidence exists it tends to throw its light on a minority of the population: the better-off, more literate and record-conscious inhabitants of Florence itself.

Such imbalances may be considered almost inevitable; they probably also affect such areas of inquiry related to family history as the status and role of women. Although this subject has received a good deal of welcome attention in recent years, it was anticipated by Burckhardt, and not least in the rather inconclusive quality of the evidence and arguments offered. Burckhardt claimed to see a greater equality between the sexes in Renaissance society, but his examples are provided by a few stars from court and salon. Not only are these unlikely to be typical, but elsewhere, on the basis of Alberti's *Della Famiglia*, Burckhardt shows that wives were expected to be instructed by their husbands even in matters of household management. Modern research has enlarged on the number of identifiable cultured and characterful women. For example, the letters of the Florentine Alessandra Strozzi for the period 1447 to 1470 show her to have been thoroughly involved in trying to rescue the fortunes of a family suffering political disgrace and exile.[28] The Veronese humanist Isotta Nogarola (1418–66) impressed – and disturbed – her contemporaries with the extent of her self-acquired learning.[29]

On the other hand, the role of the majority can be shown to have been not nearly as positive, while the status of women can appear to have been inferior and even precarious; even Isotta Nogarola was mocked and criticised for deserting her proper calling in the home. Conventional wisdom continued to insist that women were the 'weaker vessels', subject by the natural order to the necessary guidance of men. More generally, in tax records women were under-represented, and heads of households appear to have been often more uncertain of the names, ages and even existence of their daughters than they were with their sons. Infanticide and abandonment are likely to have taken a greater toll of the lives of female children. Women were rarely left or granted the lands and properties most closely associated with their families. The search for a husband could inflate dowry payments, and mean that daughters had to marry beneath themselves in social and economic terms. Lower down the social scale, young girls whose families were unable to provide dowries were often placed in domestic service, brothels or badly run nunneries to join the 'scum and vomit of the world', as S. Bernardino charitably put it; girls 'adopted' as domestic servants were often subjected to sexual harassment. In Sardinian law less credence was given to female than to male witnesses, and the Florentine evidence suggests that in the period lower-class women found it increasingly difficult to defend their interests in the courts; women who had entered marriage with a dowry often found it hard to reclaim it on their husbands' death. Lastly, the evidence from women 'out at work' in the textile industries, the fields or the Venetian dockyards can be treated anachronistically if it is used to suggest 'equality of opportunity', just as the women tax returns reveal as living alone should not be seen as 'independent'.[30]

But if it is difficult to accept Burckhardt's picture of an enlightened equality between the sexes, it would probably be wrong to conclude that in practice the status of women was always inferior, passive and precarious – even if arguing from records largely compiled by and for men is only slightly less hazardous than arguing from silence. In view of the importance of the family to all levels of society, the role allowed by contemporaries to women in the home should not be undervalued by the modern historian, if only because the home should not be understood in narrow terms. Women like Margherita, the wife of the 'merchant of Prato' Francesco Datini, could become business managers; lower down the social and economic scale women worked in domestic industries and in agriculture. In patrician circles, the fact that there was normally an age difference between husband and wife might have underlined the authority of the former over his young bride, but it does not mean that the relationship remained unchanged; in fact the authority of the wife and mother in the household probably increased.

The property rights of women in Sardinia were far more extensive than on the mainland, but recent studies of the Venetian patriciate suggest that dowries should not be seen exclusively as burdens facing a woman and her kin, but also as assets which could gain for wives considerable influence and independence of action in the affairs of their families by birth and marriage.[31] The need felt by husbands to honour their new wives with gifts does not suggest that they always entered their new households as the pawns of marital strategy.[32] One woman who did appear to do so was Caterina Fieschi of Genoa (1447–1507). Despite a devout childhood that suggested a nun's vocation, political necessity placed her in an unhappy marriage with Giuliano Adorno. The conflict between her piety and his dissolution was apparently resolved in her favour and the couple embarked on a life devoted to humility and the care of the sick, in which Catterina appeared to combine sympathy and spirituality with formidable powers of organisation and physical stamina, qualities which led to her eventual canonisation.[33]

Taken together, such evidence as the career and cult of Catterina of Genoa, the popular cults associated with the Holy Family and the female saints and the intensified concern for the procreation and upbringing of children detectable in the period would make it reasonable to suggest that in practice women were more highly appreciated, and a more forceful presence in society, than the formal record would often indicate – if few husbands were as generous as Duke Lodovico of Savoy who, himself, increased his wife's dowry in 1456 as a tribute to her fecundity! This conclusion is supported by the enthusiasm for conjugal love which Herlihy and Klapisch-Zuber have found rehearsed by many of the civic humanists of the fifteenth century, while Goldthwaite claims that in the period literary invectives against women declined in fashion. Finally – if paradoxically – the power and influence which women could exercise over men are revealed in contemporary sermons, *ricordi* and *novelle* with their tales of scolds, the infidelity of young wives, the demands of widows and the dangers of female gossips.[34]

But the family life that could produce such stereotypes was not experienced by all. Though attracted to the towns in search of work, marriage and security, the poor found urban life extremely dangerous, with violence, disease, famine and plague taking a heavy toll within and without the family group. Studies on the urban poor in Verona and Tuscany reveal small families and a large number of single people.[35] Men appear to have postponed marriage until they had acquired the means to support a household and this, together with the social ills associated with rootless and impoverished young men, probably contributed to checking population growth. Men also appear to have delayed marriage in better-off households, partly for the same reasons but probably also because their fathers were reluctant to accept an early division of the family resources. But in the case of the better-off, enjoying superior living conditions and diet, delayed marriage appears to have produced larger and more stable households than was the case with the urban poor. Wealthier families also appear to have been less parochial than the poor in their search for marriage partners; but for historians the nature of family ties beyond the household has become a matter of debate.

Most agree that in some of the cities of Italy the *consorteria*, or clan, was no longer the force it had been in the thirteenth century; for example in sixteenth-century Venice the *casa* of the Contarini was made up of around two hundred male members, but it did not survive as a cohesive unit with shared political and economic objectives. Rather it had subdivided into branches, scattered throughout the city, each taking its name and identity from its own parish or palace.[36] However, this was not the case everywhere and the clan survived in political and economic terms on the islands, in the south, in the Papal States and – as the *albergo* – in Genoa.[37] In the north it survived in the smaller centres that less often come under the social historian's scrutiny. The early-fifteenth-century chronicle of Clemente Miari, a member of one of the leading families of Belluno, is largely devoted to the successes and reverses experienced by his kin and relatives by marriage.[38] The decline of the *consorteria* has been attributed, as in Florence, to the growing power of the state armed with anti-magnate legislation; in Venice it has been linked to a greater political stability and the unchallenged ascendancy of the nobility. Less clear is the nature of the familial groups left in its wake. One view, based largely but not exclusively on Florentine evidence, is that by this time the *consorteria* had been replaced by the conjugal household based on one set of parents and their children. It could establish economic and political links with other members of the father's kin, but it was just as likely to seek such associations among neighbours and other families unrelated by blood or marriage.

Supporting this view is the fact that historians working from contemporary or near-contemporary genealogies can develop an exaggerated sense of family unity by confusing survival or continuity between generations with solidarity within one generation; the simple but effective image of the family tree can suggest a greater unity of purpose between its branches than in fact existed. Evidence from as far apart as Florence and Trani emphasises the obvious point that common ownership of property and rights could be a source of discord and litigation rather than a guarantee and expression of family unity.[39] More-over, the elements of nostalgia or idealisation found in such works as Alberti's *Della Famiglia* can be overlooked, and the significance of the family home can be misread. The boom in palace construction in fifteenth-century Florence was certainly stimulated by family pride, but the buildings created most often housed the conjugal family rather than the clan, with younger sons and more distant relatives seeking their own residences.[40] Even where such property did remain in common ownership, its identity as a family residence could become diluted. In his will of 1415 the Florentine wool merchant Alberto Rinieri tried to insist that his new palace, built around 1400, should remain within the family. But he had no male heirs, and by 1469 those with rights in the building were anxious to get it off their hands. The realities of succession and the division of property had worked decisively against Alberto's sense of family.[41]

Lastly – and most importantly – Goldthwaite has concluded, from a detailed examination of the papers of four Florentine families covering the fourteenth to sixteenth centuries, that business was not normally conducted in the context of the wider family. The *fraterna* contract that could link the economic activity of close relatives in Venice, and could turn a *palazzo* into a warehouse and the base of operations for the family firm, points to a way of doing business largely absent from Florence. Of all the biographies studied by Goldthwaite, only Niccolò Capponi (1473–1529) and his brother Giuliano (1476–1565) had a close business partnership, and even that quickly fell apart on Niccolò's death. In general the accumulation, division and loss of family fortunes, the direction of business activity and investment and the degree of involvement in public life depended crucially on the abilities, priorities and health of individuals.

It would, however, be a mistake to see society exclusively in terms of rather isolated and self-reliant conjugal families. This would ignore the legislation designed to prevent the over-representation of individual families in government. It would ignore the concern the Medici, like other princes, showed for the marital strategies of other leading families. It would ignore the collective punishment meted out on the Pazzi after they had tried to overthrow the Medici in 1478; or to the Poggi of Lucca, whose ascendancy over a quarter of the city and influence in communal government came to an end in 1527 when they failed to overthrow the constitution: those members allowed to stay in Lucca changed their name.[42] More positively, it would ignore the interest and pride shown by contemporaries in the family in a wider sense. The gift of rings by the married women of a family to a new bride entering their ranks suggests how binding even ramified relationships by marriage were intended to be.[43] The Kents have also studied the records of a number of Florentine families and conclude that their sense of kin was more powerful and had a greater reality than Goldthwaite would allow. The Peruzzi, for example, had a strong sense of identity, probably enhanced by their rivalry with the Medici. Their palaces were densely situated round the church of S. Croce, where their tombs were located. They had a family *loggia* where policy was discussed, in a manner very reminiscent of the Genoese *albergo*. As revealed in his *Zibaldone*, or commonplace book, Giovanni Rucellai was thinking of his kin when he built a family *loggia* in the 1460s; in his will of 1465 Giovanni asked that none of his personal emblems be displayed at his funeral, only those of his lineage. And in the eyes of the Kents the Strozzi appear much more clannish than they do in Goldthwaite's account, with the palace-building of Filippo being eagerly followed by homesick exiled relatives in Ferrara and Padua.

But it is unclear if the Rucellai *loggia* was ever used for clan gatherings, and when members of the Strozzi returned from exile after 1494 the new palace was not in fact home; Filippo had intended the building for his own lineal descendants and his more distant relations did not challenge his wishes. However, rather than insisting on one interpretation of the family in Renaissance Florence choosing between the 'household atoms' and 'lineage molecules' of some social historians,[44] at the present state of research it may be more prudent, and probably more accurate, to suggest a varied picture. At one extreme, the family could count for nothing; if the economic and political power of the Martelli of Florence or the Eustachi of Pavia did depend heavily on 'family effort', Francesco Datini was a self-made man. Families did not conform to one pattern of behaviour. Even the simple conjugal household could change over time: for example by growing in wealth and numbers before declining in both as daughters were married off, sons set up their own homes and the family assets were divided – a process completed on the death of the household head. Relative poverty kept the family of Piero Guicciardini (1378–1441) living together, but as the fortunes of individual members improved, so they set up their own households. The same point can be made from the example of poor Venetian families. The subsidised housing built in the city was designed to provide the poor conjugal family with privacy as well as accommodation, but it also took account of differences of wealth and family size.[45] If commerce and business were no longer as closely linked to the family as they had been in the thirteenth and fourteenth centuries, Italian merchants, especially when working abroad, still turned readily to family and kin in the search for partners and agents, as the records of Tudor London reveal.[46] Some common interests could survive to check the decline of clan solidarity, as with the Buondelmonte of Florence, whose jointly held rights of ecclesiastical patronage delayed the break-up of what had once been a powerful and wealthy *consorteria*.[47] Lastly the awareness of the wider family, the sense of kin, could increase with years; the will of Ugolino, oldest member of the Rucellai clan in 1456, contained bequests to the various chapels associated with the Rucellai as well as the request to be buried in one of them.

As that case suggests, relations with the wider family could vary. Sentiment might be stronger than political reality, as is suggested by the example of Giovanni Rucellai's *loggia*; whereas the Peruzzi, jealous of the Medici and nervous of their own position, fell back on their own resources. Challenging the Florentine oligarchy in the 1420s, the Medici themselves had proved more cohesive than many of their more established opponents. Filippo Strozzi, trying to recover his fortunes in exile, turned to members of his family – among others – in his business dealings, but with success his independence of action increased. As Bullard has shown, the marriage in 1508 of a later Filippo Strozzi to Clarice de' Medici, daughter of the exiled Piero, caused concern among his kin, as Filippo himself was well aware. Not only were they unhappy with an alliance to a family traditionally regarded as rivals, but they sought to dissociate themselves from a house that was suffering political disgrace – that is, until the potential advantages of the match came to outweigh the possible dangers.[48] If Burckhardt was wrong to imply that individualism as personified by a Leon Battista Alberti or a Leonardo da Vinci was·typical of Renaissance society as a whole, it would also be wrong to replace his vision with too strict a 'model' of a more 'structured' society. Sentiments and instincts are as much part of social history as contracts and business partnerships.

NOTES AND REFERENCES

1. W. Altmann (ed.), *Die Urkunden Kaiser Sigmunds*, in *Regesta Imperii*, vol. xi (Innsbruck, 1896).
2. G. Brucker (ed.), *Two Memoirs of Renaissance Florence* (New York, 1967), pp. 71–2; B. Preyer, 'The Rucellai palace', in Giovanni Rucellai ed il suo Zibaldone, vol. ii, *A Florentine Patrician and his Palace* (London, 1981), pp. 198–201. We are grateful to James S. Grubb for letting us consult a draft of his paper on late medieval patriciates in the Veneto, presented at the conference *Istituzioni, Società e Potere nella Marca Trevigiana e Veronese* (Treviso, September 1986).
3. D. Queller, *The Venetian Patriciate* (Urbana and Chicago, 1986), p. 129; R. C. Mueller, 'Sull'establishment bancario veneziano' in G. Borelli (ed.), *Mercanti e Vita Economica nella Repubblica Veneta*, vol. i (Verona, 1985), pp. 61, 64.
4. Società Editrice Storia di Napoli, *Storia di Napoli*, vols ii and iii (Bari, 1975–76).
5. A. Ventura, *Nobiltà e Popolo nella Società Veneta* (Bari, 1964), pp. 353–4.
6. Ventura, op. cit., pp. 157–61.
7. R. C. Trexler, *Public Life in Renaissance Florence* (New York and London, 1980).
8. L. Martines, *The Social World of the Florentine Humanists* (London, 1963), pp. 18–84.
9. M. King, *Venetian Humanism in an Age of Patrician Dominance* (Princeton, 1986), pp. 92–205; Mueller, loc. cit., p. 90.
10. P. Tafur, *Travels and Adventures*, ed. M. Letts (London, 1926); A. Ventura, 'Il Dominio di Venezia', in *Florence and Venice*, vol. i, ed. S. Bertelli *et al.* (Florence, 1979), p. 168.
11. 'Araldica', in the Enciclopedia Italiana; J. d'Arcy Boulton, *The Knights of the Crown: the monarchical orders of knighthood in late medieval Europe* (Woodbridge, 1987).
12. R. Goldthwaite, 'The empire of things', in *Patronage, Art and Society in Renaissance Italy*, ed. F. W. Kent and P. Simons (Oxford, 1987).
13. On guilds, J. N. Najemy, *Corporations and Consensus in Florentine Electoral Politics* (Chapel Hill, 1982); R. Mackenney, *Traders and Tradesmen: the World of the Guilds in Venice and Europe* (London, 1987).
14. F. W. Kent, 'The making of a Renaissance patron of the arts', in *Giovanni Rucellai*, op. cit.; idem, 'Ties of neighbourhood and patronage in quattrocento Florence', in *Patronage, Art and Society*, op. cit.
15. R. Gaston, 'Liturgy and patronage in S. Lorenzo Florence', in *Patronage Art and Society*, op. cit.; J. Heers, *Family Clans in the Middle Ages* (Amsterdam, New York and Oxford, 1977).
16. D. Herlihy and C. Klapisch-Zuber, *Tuscans and their Families* (New Haven and London, 1983). Many of the latter's contributions to social history have been published together in translation as *Women, Family and Ritual in Renaissance Italy* (Chicago and London, 1985).

17. M. King, 'Caldiera and the Barbaros on marriage and the family', *Journal of Medieval and Renaissance Studies*, vol. vi (1976).
18. C. Klapisch-Zuber, 'An ethnology of marriage in the age of humanism', in *Women, Family and Ritual*, op. cit.
19. R. Finlay, *Politics in Renaissance Venice* (London, 1980), p. 82.
20. P. J. Jones, 'Florentine families and Florentine diaries in the fourteenth century', *Papers of the British School at Rome*, vol. xxiv (1956); L. Pandimiglia, 'Giovanni di Pagolo Morelli e la Ragion di Famiglia', *Studi sul Medioevo Cristiano offerti a R. Morghen*, vol. ii (Rome, 1974); J. K. Hyde, 'Some uses of literacy in Venice and Florence', *T.R.H.S.*, ser. v, vol. xxix (1979); S. K. Cohn, *The Labouring Classes in Renaissance Florence* (New York and London, 1980); F. Levy, 'Florentine Ricordanze in the Renaissance', *Stanford Italian Rev.*, vol. iii (Spring 1983).
21. M. Wackernagel, *The World of the Florentine Renaissance Artist* (Princeton, 1981); E. H. Gombrich, 'Apollonio di Giovanni', in *Norm and Form* (London, 1966); H. Wohl, 'Domenico Veneziano studies', *B.M.*, vol. cxiii, no. 824 (1971); C. Klapisch-Zuber, 'The Griselda complex; dowry and marriage gifts in the quattrocento', in *Women, Family and Ritual*, op. cit.
22. F. W. Kent, 'The making of a Renaissance patron', op. cit., esp. pp. 66–86.
23. V. d'Alessandro, 'Per una storia della società siciliana alla fine del medio evo', *Archivio Stor. per la Sicilia Orientale*, vol. lxxviii (1981), p. 194; A. Luchs, 'A note on Raphael's Perugia patrons', *B.M.*, vol. cxxv, no. 958 (1983).
24. Throughout his study, Finlay stresses the influence of noble families including that of the ducal family: *Politics in Renaissance Venice*, op. cit.; S. Bertelli, 'Machiavelli and Soderini', *Ren. Q.*, vol. xxviii (1975), p. 10; A. Sorbelli, *Francesco Sforza a Genova* (Bologna, 1901), pp. 262–3.
25. R. F. E. Weissman, *Ritual Brotherhood in Renaissance Florence*, (New York, 1982), p. 141.
26. Review by R. Manno Tolu of L. Sandri, *L'Ospedale di S. Maria della Scala di San Gimignano* (Florence, 1982), in *Bull. Senese di Stor. Patria*, vol. lxxxix (1982).
27. Apart from the works of Herlihy and Klapisch-Zuber already cited, the following studies have proved valuable: R. Goldthwaite, *Private Wealth in Renaissance Florence* (Princeton, 1968); idem, 'The Florentine palace as domestic architecture', *Am.H.R.*, vol. lxxvii (1972), and 'Organizzazione economica e struttura famigliare', *Atti del III Convegno di Studi sulla Storia dei Ceti Dirigenti in Toscana* (Florence, 1980); F. W. Kent, 'The Rucellai family and its loggia', *J.W.C.I.*, vol. xxxv (1972); idem, *Household and Lineage in Renaissance Florence* (Princeton, 1977); idem, 'Courtly and family interest in the building of Filippo Strozzi's palace', *Ren. Q.*, vol. xxx (1977) and with D. V. Kent, 'A self-disciplining pact made by the Peruzzi', *Ren. Q.*, vol. xxxiv (1981).
28. L. Martines, 'A way of looking at women in Renaissance Florence', *J. of Med. and Ren. St.*, vol. iv (1974).
29. M. King, 'Book-lined cells: women and humanism in the early Italian Renaissance', in P. H. Labalme (ed.), *Beyond their Sex. Learned Women of the European Past* (New York and London, 1980).
30. S. K. Cohn, 'Donne in piazza e donne in tribunale', *Studi Storici*, vol. xxii (1981); J. Kirshner, 'Wives' claims against insolvent husbands in later medieval Italy', and J. Day, 'On the status of women in medieval Sardinia', in J. Kirshner and S. F. Wemple (ed.), *Women of the Medieval World* (Oxford, 1985); J. C. Brown, 'A woman's place was in the home: women's work in Renaissance Tuscany', in M. W. Ferguson *et al.* (eds), *Rewriting the Renaissance* (Chicago and London, 1986).

31. S. Chojnacki, 'Patrician women in early Renaissance Venice', *Studies in the Ren.*, vol. xxi (1974), and 'Dowries and kinsmen in early Renaissance history', *Journal of Interdisciplinary Hist.*, vol. v (1974–75).
32. Klapisch-Zuber, 'The Griselda complex', op. cit.
33. *The New Catholic Encyclopedia* (New York, 1967).
34. C. Klapisch-Zuber, 'The "Cruel Mother": maternity, widowhood and dowry in Florence in the fourteenth and fifteenth centuries', in *Women, Family and Ritual*, op. cit.
35. P. Lanaro Sartori, 'Radiografia della soglia di povertà in una città della terraferma veneta', *S.V.*, n.s., vol. vi (1982).
36. O. Logan, *Culture and Society in Venice* (London, 1972), pp. 20–29; R. Goffen, *Piety and Patronage in Renaissance Venice* (New Haven and London, 1986), pp. 27–9.
37. Heers, op. cit.; D. O. Hughes, 'Kinsmen and neighbours in medieval Genoa', in *The Medieval City*, ed. H. A. Miskimin *et al.*, (New Haven and London, 1977); idem, 'Urban growth and family structure in medieval Genoa', in *Towns in Societies*, ed. P. Abrams and E. A. Wrigley (Cambridge, 1978); M. Scarlata, 'I Chiaromonti a Palermo nel secolo xiv', *Bull. dell'Ist. Stor. It. per il Medio Evo*, vol. xc (1982–83).
38. Giovanni di Donà (ed.), *Cronaca Bellunese* (1383–1412), (Belluno, 1873).
39. G. Vitale, 'La formazione del patriziato urbano nel Mezzogiorno d'Italia', *A.S.P.N.*, ser. iii, vol. xix (1980); R. Bizzocchi, 'La dissoluzione di un clan familiare; i Buondelmonti di Firenze', *A.S.I.*, vol. cxl (1982).
40. Goldthwaite, 'The Florentine palace', op. cit.
41. B. Preyer, 'The "chasa overo palagio" of Alberto di Zanobi', *Art B.*, vol. lxv (1983).
42. M. Berengo, *Nobili e Mercanti nella Lucca del Cinquecento* (Turin, 1965), pp. 83–107.
43. Klapisch-Zuber, 'Griselda complex', op. cit.
44. P. Burke, review article in *Historical Journal*, vol. xxii (1979), p. 977.
45. We are grateful to G. Gianighian and P. Pavanini for information on this point; cf. the review of their exhibition *Dietro i Palazzi* by M. Whitely in *Bulletin of the Society for Renaissance Studies*, vol. iii, no. 1 (1985).
46. M. E. Bratchel, 'Italian merchant organization and business relationships in early Tudor London', *J. of European Ec. Hist.*, vol. vii, no. 1 (1978).
47. Bizzocchi, loc. cit.
48. M. M. Bullard, 'Marriage, politics and the family in Florence; the Strozzi–Medici alliance of 1508', *Am. H.R.*, vol. lxxxiv (1979); Klapisch-Zuber, 'State and family in a Renaissance society', in *Women, Family and Ritual*, op. cit., p. 21.

CHAPTER FOUR

The *contado*

INTRODUCTION

Until comparatively recently the countryside has tended to be ignored by historians of Renaissance Italy, and Philip Jones's pioneering work attracted relatively few disciples among non-Italian students of the period.[1] The reasons for this neglect are not hard to find. The cultural achievements of the Renaissance are obviously associated with the concentration of activity, wealth and patronage in the towns, even if many of the key figures originated from 'up country': Leonardo came from Vinci in the Florentine countryside and Titian from Pieve di Cadore north of Venice. The religious life of the Peninsula appears to have been focused on the towns in terms of its architecture, its cults, its organisation and its movements for reform,[2] and it is significant that the Waldensian heresy in Piedmont was above all a rural expression of dissent. Elsewhere the spiritual hegemony of the towns was less directly challenged. The commune of Vicenza ordered the subject communities of the Vicentino to send representatives and candles to increase the solemnity of its Corpus Domini celebrations. The influential Franciscan Bernardino of Siena (1380–1444) reached his audiences in towns, while cities like Venice and Rome continued to owe much of their fascination for visitors to their large collections of relics. Pius II's attempt, between 1459 and 1464, to transform his rural birthplace Corsignano failed; though furnished with a cathedral and a bishop's palace, Pienza – as it was renamed – deep in the Sienese countryside, remained a backwater. The sanctuary of Loreto near Ancona appears to have been one of the few examples of a flourishing, widely recognised but rurally based cult.

If the inhabitants of the *contado* appeared to be further from the bosom of the Church, they certainly were more acutely exposed to natural and man-made disasters, thus swelling the numbers of the jobless and abandoned children as well as the ranks of women prepared to enter prostitution or domestic service – often the next worst thing. As described elsewhere (p. 81 ff), famine often drove *contadini* into towns looking for relief, while the countryside was regarded as a legitimate – and soft – target by both enemy forces and unscrupulous soldiery. Ladislao I of Naples, campaigning in Tuscany in 1409, was nicknamed 'king of the harvest-destroyers', while roaming bands in Piedmont earned a reputation as the 'consumers of villeins'. The *contadini*'s defences against such onslaughts were generally too lightly fortified or too run-down to be of any use. This gave force to Francesco Sforza's threat in 1452 : that if rural communities continued to aid his Venetian enemies, they would be sacked until nothing was left. It explains why in 1509 Machiavelli tried to persuade representatives from the Pisan *contado* to come over to the Florentine side by pointing out that it was they, and not the citizens of Pisa, who were suffering in that city's war of rebellion.[3]

Moreover, the economic activity of the towns long monopolised the attention of economic historians as signs of progress and even 'modernity', associated with a dynamic and forward-looking bourgeoisie. The countryside, by contrast, is represented as static, 'feudal' and 'medieval'. Rural industries, although far from unknown, were small-scale when compared to those in the towns, while analyses of trade, as for mid-fifteenth-century Rome, reveal a small role for the rural merchant. The 'progressive' characteristics of urban civilisation appeared to be confirmed by political developments worked through from the twelfth to fourteenth centuries, and involving the conquest of the country by the town. The city asserted its authority over the *contado*, the county or jurisdiction outside its walls, and broke the power of feudal lords as it suppressed the autonomy and controlled the economic life of rural communities.

Such arguments for urban superiority were not invented by later historians. An arrogance can easily be detected in the contemporary outlook of the citizen towards the *contadino*. For example, the status of citizenship was a privileged one, conferring on its holders such advantages as access to public office and freedom from such demeaning and demanding burdens as the labour services imposed on country districts in peace and war. Disputes between citizens and *contadini* were tried in urban tribunals in the light of urban statutes, which explains the readiness of landowners to refer such cases to court. In fifteenth-century Verona citizen notaries could practise in town and country, and had favoured access to certain public offices; rural notaries could practise only in the *contado*. In general, access to citizenship remained severely restricted, and *contadini* applying for the status often had to meet tougher requirements in terms of entry payments and undergo closer scrutiny by investigating officials than foreigners. 'Rural citizens' who demeaned their new status by working the land lost their citizenship, while in the course of the period the conditions facing aspiring citizens were toughened as the need felt by city governments to restore their populations after plague outbreaks became less acute. When, on 6 May 1499, the commune of Pisa opened its citizenship to *contadini* to win their support in the war against Florence, it stood out as a remarkable concession, the product of desperate circumstances.[4]

Hardly surprisingly, the attitude revealed in law can be found elsewhere. In cities like Rome even the urban poor expected wheaten bread, so leaving the rural population with coarser and less nutritious grains, or such substitutes as chestnuts and beans. The evidence of fifteenth-century Florence suggests that the daughters of immigrants could expect to marry into the poorest levels of Florentine society, although marriages between the families of newcomers and townsmen were relatively rare, even in those urban parishes closest to the *contado* or straddling the city walls.[5] More generally, the vernacular drama and literature of the period tended to represent the country-man as a figure of fun: as a 'country bumpkin'.[6] In early sixteenth-century Siena, companies of *'rozzi'*, or 'rustics', staged farces to delight their urban audiences, and the wealthy Sienese banker Agostino Chigi (1465–1520) paid for such entertainments in Rome. In the Veneto in the same period the most famous producer of such plays or farces was the Paduan actor-manager Angelo Beolco (1496–1542); known as 'il Ruzzante', he drew on slapstick and played on dialects to amuse his urban audiences. Satire of this type was not without some sympathy for the plight of the *contadini*, but harsher attitudes can be found. In 1421 the Florentine patrician Gino Capponi claimed that the country was a dwelling-place for beasts rather than men; a Lucchese notary in the early sixteenth century observed that the children of *contadini* 'grew up without being watched, like wandering beasts'. By 1504 many citizens of Pisa regretted the alliance made in 1499 with the *contadini*, 'men without reason', and went over to Florence.[7]

But to be satisfied with evidence of this nature would be to exaggerate the hostility between town and country, and could lead to a serious under-estimation of the importance of the *contado* for Renaissance Italy. The most telling corrective to the general urban emphasis comes with a recognition that Italian society was predominantly rural. Most of the population lived and worked in the countryside. Not only was this true of the islands and south, as well as of the more mountainous regions of the north like Piedmont and the Trentino; it was also the case with those areas often assumed to be urban in character: Tuscany, Lombardy and the Veneto. Of course the ratio of urban to rural population varied, but even in Florence the rural population outnum-bered the urban by three to one in 1427.

Moreover, by far and away the majority of Italian towns were relatively small and their inhabitants were not immured by what are often thought to be such essentially urban activities as finance and industry but were in fact closely involved with rural life as landowners, tenants, labourers, craftsmen and – above all – consumers. A study of the population of the Lombard commune Voghera in the early fifteenth century reveals that about half of its tax-paying population was involved in agriculture in various ways – which means that the proportion involved was probably higher still.[8] Even the greater concentrations of population had a rural character. Large areas of Flor-ence within its third circuit of walls remained as fields and orchards despite incentives offered by the commune to build there. In the fifteenth century the walls of Rome enclosed a larger extent of fields, orchards and vineyards than 'built-up' areas, and the streets and squares were regularly thronged with livestock. The tax records of sixteenth-century Verona reveal that agriculture was the largest employer after the textile industries and that a considerable amount of agricultural activity went on within the walls.[9] Even Venice, perhaps the most intensively built-upon city, had its rural aspect in the form of the game and fishing resources of the lagoons and its cultivated islands and *lidi*, while from the city itself the hinterland and the Dolomites were massively in evidence through as yet unpolluted air.

In view of the omnipresence of the countryside it is hardly surprising that attitudes to the *contado*, and even towards its inhabitants, were more varied and could be more sympathetic than those suggested by the record of satire and contempt. The merchant of Prato Francesco Datini (*c.* 1335–1410) surprised a correspondent with his generous treatment of his estate workers. During debates on the impoverished state of the Florentine *contado* in 1417 the government was reminded that the welfare of its *contadini* was as important for the republic as that of its citizens.[10] Vasari recorded that Donatello was a good landlord, leaving his farm to its workers. Satire and abuse could be balanced by sympathy, as in the sermons of Bernardino da Siena or in the poetry in the Paduan dialect of the years around 1500 which lamented the sufferings of the country from the scourges of war, plague and famine. In 1509, during the War of Cambrai, Venetian patricians heeded the urgings of the government and provided poor relief for the refugees flooding into the city from the war zones on the mainland.[11] In a much more gentle and romantic vein, an enthusiasm for the country can be seen in the pastoral theme which runs through the Renaissance period; this was encouraged not only by the facts of life but by the conventions of chivalric literature and the tastes of such influential writers of the classical and more immediate past as Virgil, Pliny and Petrarch – as well as by the fashion for taking health cures at spas like Caldiero in the Veronese.

If Alberti, in his *Della Famiglia*, could mock the stupidity and warn against the evil disposition of the peasant, he could also stress the idyllic and healthy aspect of country living – and as Alberti wrote, the fashion for villas grew. In the 1450s the Florentine architect Michelozzo transformed the Medici property at Careggi from a fortress to a country residence, and the taste for rural retreats developed elsewhere. In 1487 another Florentine, Giuliano da Maiano, worked on the villa of Poggioreale for Alfonso Duke of Calabria. In the later fifteenth century the Veronese properties of the Cipolla family inspired one of their number, Antonio, to celebrate the delights of country life in Latin hexameters.[12] Related was the interest in nature shown by artists, and presumably by their patrons. Medieval genres like 'The Labours of the Months' continued to find favour. Around 1400 the bishop of Trent, Giorgio di Liechtenstein, had one of the towers of his castle decorated with frescoes representing the months with scenes from rural life. The same theme runs through the frescoes painted around 1470 by Francesco Cossa and others for the suburban palace, the Schifanoia (or 'Banish-care') of Borso d'Este of Ferrara. Moreover, at this time painters appear to have been increasingly drawn to – and fascinated by – the landscape, a development particularly striking in the work of the Venetian artists of the late fifteenth and early sixteenth centuries. Giovanni Bellini (active *c.* 1460–1516), one of the most acute observers of the rural landscape of the Veneto, was himself a landowner.

Such interest in rural life may appear rather precious and superficial, a product of the tastes of a rather narrow section of society. But evidence of a broader-based and deeper-rooted attachment can be seen in the way immigrants to the towns often proudly preserved their rural place of origin in their names. The Kents have shown how the Temperani of mid-fifteenth-century Florence actively maintained their ties with their country kin, while Bartolomeo Scala, the chancellor of the city (1465–97), had an emotional attachment to – as well as investments in – his birthplace of Colle di Val d'Elsa.[13] Still less sentimental, but again a clear indication of the importance of the *contado* to town life, is the way urban statutes and the deliberations of urban councils are full of references to the surrounding countryside, covering a wide range of issues from questions of land tenure to the problems of tax-gathering. The weight of this evidence is such that every Italian city has spawned a rich and still more local historiography of rural communes and distinctive areas of its *contado*.[14] The history of the city of Verona is enriched by studies of smaller centres like Sirmione and Soave, as well as of regions like the Valpolicella and the Garda shoreline. Less parochial investigation of the wealth of evidence available on the *contado* has encouraged recent historians like Jones, Cherubini and Chittolini to reassess the relationship of town and country, and to suggest a much more important and positive role for the latter.[15]

THE EXPLOITATION OF THE *CONTADO*

This point of view would not necessarily have surprised contemporaries. In 1449 Modena wrote to its overlord Leonello d'Este that 'it is understood that any city without the obedience of its diocese or *contado* will disappear'. As that quotation suggests, the value placed on the *contado* can been seen in the way cities struggled to defend or extend their jurisdictions. When Verona surrendered to Venice in 1405 it hoped to preserve its traditional frontiers, but was disappointed by the loss of authority over rural communes rewarded with autonomy – like Cologna Veneta – or granted to the republic's Gonzaga ally – like Peschiera on Lake Garda. Orvieto, under the lordship of Ladislao of Naples in 1414, hoped to recover territory lost to its rivals; in 1455 Calixtus III ordered his representatives in Orvieto to treat favourably the commune's petition to be recognised as 'caput' over the 'membra' of the *contado*. Similarly Catanzaro wanted its Aragonese rulers to increase its territorial jurisdiction, its citizens associating this closely with their own prosperity.[16] What were the grounds for this belief, and how did urban interests in the *contado* express themselves?

For individual citizens the *contado* presented various opportunities for self-advancement and profit. Citizen status opened the door to *contado* office. Vicariates – as they were often called – in the *contado* did not enjoy the prestige, powers of jurisdiction or salaries of the more central offices of a commune. They did, however, carry local prestige, as well as some salary and powers of jurisdiction. For the vicar who was also a local landlord, the office increased his authority over his tenants and his neighbours. The Veronese Maffei family invested heavily in the Valpolicella in the fifteenth century and frequently held the office of vicar in the area; when the commune of Siena sold off *contado* offices in 1511, local landowners were often the purchasers. To the unscrupulous the office also opened the door to acts of local tyranny and extortion, provoking – as in the case of the Bolognese in the fifteenth century – distressed appeals to the communal government for redress and protection from the *contadini*. In 1497 the vicar of Illasi in the Veronese was prosecuted for speculating on the local grain market at the expense of the inhabitants.[17] The *contado* could also provide the landlord with the manpower to increase his political and military clout. The strength of the Roman or Neapolitan nobility could be measured in the size of the retinues drawn from their estates, while the *condottiere* rulers of the Romagna recruited men locally. In Florence, following the *Ciompi* uprising of 1378, citizen families drafted in their estate workers to defend their property. In the confrontation between the Medici and the Albizzi in 1433/4, both sides called on supporters from their *contado* estates.[18]

More generally, however, and for a wider section of the population, the *contado* was valued as a source of food and revenues in cash or kind; local studies on the Vicentino in the fifteenth century suggest that rents tended to remain in kind nearer the urban centre of consumption, while further from the city they were more likely to be in cash. The commercial life of most towns depended on the *contado* for the basic items of trade, towns like Cosenza in Calabria being in essence markets for local produce. The surrounding countryside was also essential for the support of urban industries. On Sicily timber was vital for the growing sugar industry; everywhere timber for construction and fuel came from the countryside, as did charcoal for such processes as glass-making and iron-smelting. The *zattere* district of Venice takes its name from the rafts of timber brought down the rivers of the hinterland for construction and fuel. In his *Craftsman's Handbook* of the 1390s the Florentine painter Cennino Cennini advised that the best colours came from the *contado*. The countryside was quarried for building stone; the ubiquitous presence in town buildings of marble from Istria, Carrara and Verona is testimony to a vigorous investment in the exploitation of such natural resources. The major urban industry, textiles, depended on the wool, flax, silk and dyes produced in the Italian countryside. L'Aquila in the Abruzzo was as famous for its saffron as for its wool, and the city asked Charles VIII that its adherence to the French cause in January 1495 be kept secret until the transhumance flocks had returned from Apulia.[19] But it would be wrong to separate industrial activity from the *contado*, seeing it solely as a supplier of raw materials. Textiles were processed or entirely manufactured in the *contado*, though generally on a small scale and under the jealous control of the urban guilds. Mills were located in the country, while on his estate at Cafaggiolo in the later fifteenth century

Lorenzo di Pierfrancesco de' Medici encouraged the production of high-quality majolica.[20]

It would also be a mistake to attempt to categorise too rigidly the attractions of the *contado* for the citizen. A villa could be at one and the same time a prestigious place of retreat and the centre of agricultural production. Hunting, an understudied aspect of the social and economic life of Italy, could be a fashionable form of relaxation, a valuable source of food and furs and a necessary check to predators on man and beast. Though frowned upon by canon law, sporting and social considerations were sufficient to make hunting a prominent aspect of the villa life of the papal court.[21]

These points help to explain the importance of the country to the town in general and why, more particularly, townsmen were eager to invest in the land. That subject has often been treated by social and economic historians as a 'problem', largely because of an artificial distinction drawn between the expected activities of the bourgeoisie and those of the nobles and peasantry. Investment in land had always presented itself as a natural activity for the townsman.[22] Local studies from Sicily to Piedmont, however, suggest that the period sees an increased flow of urban capital into land, leading to a decrease in rural landownership. It would be a mistake to exaggerate this trend. Immigration to the town, particularly heavy after the repeated plague attacks of the later fourteenth century, probably resulted in a shift of landownership in the sense that wealthy *contadini* acquired citizen status. Moreover, historical attention is naturally drawn to the documents. Not only was landownership more likely to be recorded in wills and tax returns than other forms of investment, but the fuller, more accessible and better-organised archives tend to focus attention on wealthier citizen families buying into better land nearer the towns, or on the estate management of such record-conscious institutions as hospitals and monasteries.

But while it is necessary to guard against an exaggerated picture of a massive and precipitous transfer of wealth from trade, finance and industry, all the available evidence does point to an increase in landed investment by townsmen. In some cases special circumstances provide the explanation. The Venetian conquests on the mainland, particularly from 1404, accelerated Venetian investment in land, and a similar phenomenon can be detected after the fall of Pisa to Florence in 1406. In 1461 the Florentine Riccardi were able to lease on favourable terms some of the properties of the Carthusian house at Pisa after it had mismanaged its estates.[23]

Other causes are more fundamental. The heavy losses of population in the late fourteenth century placed much land on the market, and encouraged a redistribution of ownership. This can be seen clearly in the estates of hospitals and monasteries; ecclesiastical communities, badly disrupted by attacks of plague and loss of continuity in personnel and expertise, also lost control of their estates.[24] For example, in Lombardy and the Veneto ruling families like the della Scala of Verona and the Visconti of Milan took advantage of their political ascendancy and the organisational weaknesses of some of the ecclesiastical institutions under their lordship. Relatives, clients and allies became abbots and abbesses as a preliminary to the distribution of ecclesiastical estates on favourable terms to family, friends and retainers. In this fashion, many of the lands and jurisdictions of an ancient foundation like the Benedictine house of S. Zeno in Verona were transferred to the della Scala, Visconti, Carrara and Venetian rulers of the city, and through the last to very largely citizen purchasers. Of course, not all ecclesiastical institutions were so badly served by their inmates or their lay patrons. The property of the Sienese house of Monte Oliveto Maggiore was greatly increased from the late fourteenth century through gifts and purchases. In the late fifteenth century reformed institutions like S. Giustina in the Padovano and S. Maria in Organo in the Veronese attracted bequests and able administrators, increasing their landed holdings and managing their tenants more watchfully. A similarly effective estates management can be detected in the great Milanese hospital, the *Ospedale Maggiore*, in the late fifteenth century.[25] None the less, the weight of evidence, from regions like the Roman *campagna* as well as the north, suggests that the redistribution of ecclesiastical land was a principal reason for the increase in citizen investment in the *contado*.

A further explanation can probably be linked to another major crisis in Italian social and economic life. It is generally agreed that the commercial and financial horizons of Italian bankers and merchants became more restricted in the period. In some cases this was due to the mismanagement of individual firms. Historians have agreed with Machiavelli that Lorenzo de' Medici's less effective management of the family firm was a reason for increasing investment in – and dependence on – land and stock in the Pisano and elsewhere. More fundamentally, Italian economic difficulties were due to increasingly effective competition abroad. The Venetian diarist and merchant Girolamo Priuli (1476–1547) lamented the shift he could detect among his fellow-nobles away from maritime commerce, the traditional source of Venetian wealth and greatness, towards the land (see below, pp. 263–4). The Venetians, in common with other Italian merchants, were finding that their markets were being steadily encroached upon by northern and 'Atlantic' Europeans, as well as by the Ottoman Turks.

But if Priuli, like many conservatives, exaggerated the degree of change for the worse, he certainly underestimated the difficulties facing the landowner. In this he has not been alone, for the assumption has often been that land was a 'soft option', one that was not remarkably productive but was safe, and increasingly preferable to the high risk encountered in the banking and commercial worlds. Indeed, the profits could be high, as was well realised by the stock-raisers of Rome or the Sicilian nobles who benefited from the 'colonial economy' of the island, developing their yields in sugar and wheat and building the ships to export their produce. In Lombardy, whose agricultural wealth astonished Commynes at the end of the fifteenth century, profits could be as high as 15 or 20 per cent. But profitability demanded effort, vigilance and investment. Landowners faced the perils of climatic disaster, disgruntled peasantry and the armies of friend and foe. According to Vasari, Brunelleschi joked at the troublesome investments in the *contado* of his rival Ghiberti, and it is hardly surprising that it was not only the religious houses that saw their estates crumble. In the course of the fifteenth century the Caetani of Rome were forced into the vicious spiral of selling and pawning land to cover their losses, and proved unable to check depopulation from their estates and the encroachment of malarial marsh (see below, pp. 208–9).

In general, however, the evidence points to the potential profitability of land investment, and the opportunities to make profits were probably enhanced as the population of Italy gradually recovered and increased in the course of the fifteenth and sixteenth centuries, while agricultural improvements were neither radical nor widespread enough to banish the spectre of famine. This provided an obvious and positive incentive to invest in land, and undoubtedly good management and land improvement could pay off. In the course of the fifteenth century such far-sighted landlords as the Este of Ferrara appear to have appreciated this increasingly, and it was appropriate that in 1447 the humanist Guarino da Verona suggested to Leonello that the muse of agriculture be included in the scheme of decoration for his rural palace at Belfiore. Around 1474 Giovanni della Rovere, Lord of Senigallia in the Romagna, encouraged immigration from Albania, the drainage of marsh and the management of woodland to boost the prosperity of the area. Lorenzo de' Medici's investments in the contado were accompanied by land improvements, and the introduction of such new forms of production as dairy farming and the cultivation of the mulberry. Moreover, the increasing adoption of short-term commercial contracts allowed the ambitious and informed landlord to manage his tenants more rigorously, and tailor his rents and yields more closely to the marketplace.

Behind these developments were certain basic advantages to encourage the urban landowner. The jurisdictional supremacy claimed by the town over the *contado* assisted him. Statutes and decrees tended to support the citizen's claims over his tenants, insisting on regular rent payments and punishing protests and trespass. Distraint was a weapon favoured by urban courts, threatening the *contadino* with the loss of his stock and equipment; the *contadino* in debt could be obliged by the courts to pawn some of his property or produce. A recent study of the Bresciano in the fifteenth and sixteenth centuries has suggested that the area within the city's jurisdiction was so heavily taxed that the *contadino* was increasingly forced to sell up to the urban buyer.[26] Other circumstances could place the *contadino* at the mercy of the townsman. Flooding, drought and freak weather could ruin his livelihood for more than the immediate future as reserves of seed corn and precious livestock were consumed. Disease could weaken his major resource, his own muscle-power, and could undermine the health, size and effectiveness of his family. Rarely did he have the cash reserves to tide him over such disasters, let alone to invest in the future. Faced with the bleak alternatives of flight or starvation, the *contadino* often had recourse to borrowing, opening up an avenue for urban investment in the *contado*; from Florentine evidence of the early fifteenth century it appears that this dependence could be expressed in interest rates as high as 40 and 50 per cent. Remaining in Tuscany, a recent study of the land investments of the rich Lucchese Michele Guinigi (1405–61) has shown how a well-placed citizen with capital, a positive assessment of the return offered by the *contado* and a nose for a bargain could amass tenancies through the indebtedness of *contadini*. With advances in cash, equipment, stock and seed to both tenants and independent peasant farmers, his expanding role as a landlord can be measured in more than legal titles.[27]

The growth of urban investment had considerable consequences for agricultural activity, at least in the richer and more accessible areas of the *contado* attractive to urban capital. Commercial contracts – and especially sharecropping contracts like the *mezzadria* (or 'halves') system – encouraged a greater involvement on the part of the landlord.[28] This was expressed in the growing number of leasebooks and rentals that record the march of urban capital and interest in the *contado*. Contracts themselves began to reveal a greater concern with the crops planted and the animals raised. A consequence of this was the introduction of more profitable crops and improvements to stock. Studies by Pinto of Tuscan contracts in the fifteenth and sixteenth centuries reveal landlords who were aware of the profits to be made in the urban market from such produce as wheat, fruit, olives and wine;[29] some landlords also appear to have been aware of the dangers of soil exhaustion and the advantages of diversification. The period sees the spread of sugar plantations in Sicily and the south, and the introduction of the mulberry and rice to Lombardy. Families like the Sforza of Milan and the Gonzaga of Mantua set about improving the quality of the horses bred on their estates. Related were attempts to reorganise and concentrate production in farms, tenants being housed on redrawn estates often under the direct eye of the resident landlord or his factor. Finally, greater investment and interest in the land encouraged the writing of agricultural treatises. The Perugian Corniolo della Cornia wrote his *Divina Villa* in the early fifteenth century; in 1516 Antonino Venuto da Noto dedicated a treatise on agriculture to Federico Abatellis Cardona, Count of Cammarata in Sicily.[30] Of course the impact and practicality of such works can often be doubted, and it is unlikely that the verse *De Agricultura* of the Florentine Michelangelo Tanaglia (1437–1512) had more than a marginal influence on farming methods. Of greater consequence were the hydraulic studies of engineers like the Sienese Mariano Taccola (c. 1381–c. 1453) and Francesco di Giorgio Martini (1439–1502), whose works were sources for the yet more inventive Leonardo da Vinci.

So far the emphasis has been on the interest of the individual citizen in the *contado*. But the city, whether independent or subject, also had interests in the countryside which can be loosely grouped under the headings of manpower and revenue. The oldest obligations placed by the city on the *contado* took the form of labour services, *corvées*; these ancient and statutory burdens received a new lease of life in a period which ensured that they would remain worth exacting for the city and worth avoiding for the communities of the *contado*.[31] They fall into military and civil categories. Within the first they could involve work on permanent or temporary fortifications, providing support for the armed forces in the form of transport, supplies and billets and contributing militia or pioneers closer to the front line. For some of these obligations, those *contadini* directly involved were entitled to payment or compensation from the soldiery or from those *contado* communities that had remained untouched.

However, the suspicion is that payment or compensation was slight, delayed or nonexistent; this is suggested by the insistence of the citizen community that· these burdens fell properly and exclusively on the *contado*, as well as by efforts to spread them across the rural communities. This conclusion is further encouraged by the evidence of the resentment of those affected, and by such occasionally candid observations as a Venetian report on the Padovano in 1502 that 'the burden is proving insupportable for the poor *contadini*' or the contemporary admission of the Florentine patrician Francesco Vettore that Florence governed her *contado* 'tyrannically'. The civil burdens included labour services on roads, bridges and dykes. Once again the avowed intention was to spread the burden across the *contado*; once again – from the complaints and ceaseless litigation provoked, as well as from the determination of the citizen community to remain exempt, even when its members lived outside the walls – it is clear that these burdens fell exclusively, though unevenly, on the *contado*.

On top of these traditional burdens came that of direct taxation, an imposition of more recent origin but one well established by the start of the period. Citizens were not exempt, but their privileged position can be seen from the way the tax burden was divided and assessed. Most studies – on cities as diverse as L'Aquila, Perugia, Florence, Pavia and Padua – agree that a disproportionate burden of direct taxation was placed on the *contado*; of course the rural population was always greater, but wealth was concentrated in citizen hands while the growing rural holdings of urban dwellers were assessed with the town rather than with the *contado*. It comes as little surprise that the allocation of the tax burden was determined by citizen councils and that their representatives carried out the method of assessment, often referred to as the *estimo*.

In the city, assessment was generally based on households, while rural communes were normally presented with a less carefully measured allocation which these communities then had to subdivide among their inhabitants. In theory this system might appear to create few grounds for resentment, but in practice the privileged position of the city was glaringly apparent. Not only were allocation and assessment in citizen hands, but the *estimo* of the *contado* was much less frequently carried out. This often meant that little immediate account was taken of such important changes in the economic and social circumstances of a rural community as the immigration of wealthy *contadini* to the city, or the impact of man-made or natural calamities. The Sienese *contado* was assessed in 1436, 1485 and 1525, and that last review was carried out by a communal government aware of the level of resentment felt in the *contado* and anxious to demonstrate its opposition to all the forms of tyranny associated with the previous Petrucci regime.[32]

It is only to be expected that this imbalance caused resentment, and a clear insight into the inequitable distribution of the tax burden and the attitude of the city towards the *contado* is provided by a document of 1475 prepared by a Veronese lawyer with extensive family holdings in the countryside, Gianfrancesco Cipolla.[33] Cipolla had been dispatched by his commune to Venice, the ruling city, to answer a mounting tide of complaint from the communities of the Veronese. The latter's delegates had been arguing the case for a single *estimo* to embrace both town and country. Cipolla's counter-arguments were evidently accepted by Venice, for no such radical reform was attempted. He argued that a single *estimo* would depopulate the city, whose citizens faced the greater burden of living 'civilmente'. Behind the arrogance of Cipolla's case, which evidently struck a chord in Venice, there did lie some economic substance. He also argued that *contadini* lived for free, meaning that they could gather their food and drink without paying the indirect taxes facing townsmen. This was not strictly true, since indirect taxes were levied on the *contado* as well as being collected at the gates of Verona and the larger rural communities. His point was that these could be more easily avoided in the less strictly governed *contado* where, moreover, the bulk of the food supply was produced. What he did not mention, however, was that in the Veronese, as elsewhere, the *contadini* faced the additional burden of the state monopoly of that vital commodity, salt – as well as those impositions discussed above. The salt monopoly affected citizen purchasers, but in the *contado*, to counter the temptations of contraband, individuals had to collect fixed quotas at controlled prices at determined intervals. Moreover, the obligation did not fall only on the *contadini* themselves; in view of the value of the commodity as a preservative and as a 'lick' to improve the health of livestock, their sheep and pigs were also assessed. In 1414 the Venetian republic ordered that every two months *contadini* were to collect the salt quotas, not only for themselves and for their sheep and pigs, but also for their children over the age of three. This policy reveals a basic contempt for the inhabitants of the *contado*; it also explains why in 1448 the republic was right to acknowledge that the burdens facing the rural areas of its state were greater than those facing the cities.[34]

THE RESISTANCE OF THE *CONTADO*

With admissions of this kind it may appear that the argument has come full circle to justify the view outlined initially – that the *contado* was subjected to and exploited by the city – and to support the views of those historians who are comforted by the evidence for exploitation in history. However, while the city did try to profit from and dominate the countryside, the fuller picture is more complex. In 1431 Parma wrote to its overlord, Filippo Maria Visconti, choosing an image familiar to medieval political thought, and already cited in the context of Orvieto, to express its relationship with the Parmigiano: 'the body without its limbs cannot long survive'.[35] In 1442 the

Venetian republic argued the same point in a letter to its subject city of Verona:

citizens, whether laymen or clerics, should conduct themselves with honour so that they can live in peace with the *contadini*; and the *contadini* with them, because for good or ill, things are so conjoined that citizens cannot live without *contadini* and vice versa.

Certainly the city believed in its superiority, but it was often prepared to acknowledge a vital relationship with the *contado*. Moreover, this relationship was a complex one and it would be wrong to see the *contado* and its inhabitants as constituting a single unit or a homogeneous society, totally under urban control and equally exposed to the relentless and selfish exploitation of the citizenry.

The interests of citizen and *contadino* could coincide, as is suggested by the well documented and researched case of Verona. In 1414 the Veronese persuaded the Venetian republic that it was inhuman and tyrannical to make all *contadini* from the age of three liable to the salt tax. The age limit was raised to six, and the city continued to press for the impact of the salt monopoly on the *contado* to be softened. In the late fifteenth century Veronese landlords and their tenants eagerly combined to clear forest and drain marsh to the alarm of the Venetian government, which saw such waste areas as a natural frontier defence. Again Verona, in common with the other subject cities of the Venetian mainland state, was persistent in its efforts to resist or reduce the consequences of the republic's policy of 1529, requiring fixed quotas of cattle to be sent to the capital.[36]

Moreover, while the investment of urban wealth in the *contado* can be detected throughout Italy, it was neither all-conquering nor always radical in its impact; nor was its effect on the status and condition of the *contadino* always negative. The attention understandably paid by historians to the investments of larger ecclesiastical institutions and richer urban landlords tends to obscure the fact that a characteristic of the *contado* was the tenacious survival of the small proprietor, rural as well as urban. The pace and penetration of urban investment was not uniform; it was concentrated in the more fertile and accessible areas like the *Sei Miglia*, the belt of good land immediately outside the walls of Lucca.[37] By the end of the fourteenth century, between 70 and 80 per cent of the land outside the walls of Siena was in citizen hands, but urban capital was not nearly so marked in the poorer and more remote areas, like the Tuscan *Maremma*. Also, an analysis of land transactions can reveal prosperous pockets of local ownership, like Bussolengo in the olive-growing area of the Veronese. Wealthier *contadini* in the Parmigiano could profit from the sale of rights and land made by the Sforza treasury in 1466. The contractual relationship between landlord and tenant was not always expressed in aggressively commercial terms. Sharecropping contracts, like the *mezzadria* contract, were in a minority in the fifteenth century, familiar outside the walls of Florence but virtually unknown outside those of Vicenza. Even when *mezzadria* contracts were arranged they could introduce an element of greater stability to the relations between landlord and tenant; indeed, they could favour the latter, with the evidence from Piedmont and the Pisano sometimes revealing that the rents due from the *contadino* were less than half.

Furthermore local studies, in the Vicentino and Pisano, point up the diversity of the legal, social and economic condition of the *contadini*, many of whom might work under little direct supervision from landlords, and many of whom might combine a patchwork of tenancies with some property of their own. And in Ferrarese territory, in the valley of the Po, the mobility of the rural workforce was not always a product of hard times but was also encouraged by a sustained demand for labour.[38] Even areas of traditionally high urban investment, like the productive hill slopes of the Veronese, reveal the vigorous survival of older forms of tenancy and a mosaic of holdings rather than the dominance of exacting commercial contracts and the concentration of estates into centrally supervised farming units. Even 'new' landlords were not necessarily ruled by the profit motive alone. Cosimo de' Medici appears to have been popular with his tenants, while a study of the estates of Santa Maria in Organo, Verona, reveals a body of prosperous peasants living in recently and soundly constructed houses, able to muster the labour and call on the livestock necessary to win good yields from rich land. And as that case suggests, the distinctions of wealth were as varied in the *contado* as in the town. Tax assessments of fifteenth-century Florence reveal prosperity as well as destitution in the *contado*, while the jaundiced remarks of Gianfrancesco Cipolla in 1475 and the careers of men like Bartolomeo Scala in Florence confirm the fact that the *contado* continued to produce an exodus of prosperous migrants to the town, modestly summed up by Scala's coat of arms depicting a ladder and the motto 'step by step'.

If the status and conditions of *contadini* could vary, the *contado* itself cannot be seen to have had a single character. For example, in the Venetian state the contado of Vicenza was relatively compact and subject to the city's jurisdiction, but its inhabitants had easier recourse with their petitions and complaints to Venice itself. Approaches of that nature were more difficult for the *contadini* of the Bresciano directly governed by the city, but in this case Venice had endorsed and encouraged the fragmentation of Brescia's larger *contado* into feudal jurisdictions and privileged communities.[39] Geographical, climatic, political and administrative circumstances all helped to create distinctions between rural communes and provided them with inexhaustible ammunition with which to bombard the city government or its overlord. For some communities it was their adverse conditions and poverty which lay behind claims for special treatment. Sirmione on Lake Garda could draw on privileges dating back to the emperor Frederick II and arising out of its alleged poverty to secure tax privileges and a greater autonomy of administration. Also in the Veronese, the commune of Vigasio won tax concessions in 1436 because of the damage caused to its crops by local bad weather. The following year Lomello in Lombardy asked for a 40 per cent cut in its tax assessment because of a drastic fall in population after a plague attack.[40] Other rural communes claimed special treatment for more positive reasons, due to their economic or strategic positions. Both applied to the federation of communes which made up the Valpolicella on the northern approaches to Verona. Similarly strong cards were held by the valley communities in the hinterland of Como and Bergamo: communities like the Valtellina, whose mountainous location and the virtual absence of citizen landlords tended to intensify the sense of a distinct corporate identity. Political circumstances could also favour individual or associated communes. In 1518 the Venetian republic took the remarkable step of admitting *contado* representatives to the parliament of Friuli, partly to foster their loyalty and partly to check the hegemony of the cities and nobles.[41]

That example introduces another aspect of city–*contado* relations which upsets the stereotyped picture of an oppressed and supine *contado*. Where a city came under the rule of another commune or lord the opportunity presented itself to remove, reduce or destroy the demands of urban government through petition and appeal. Remaining with Friuli, from 1458 the Venetian republic intervened to prevent landlords seizing the agricultural equipment of tenants in arrears with their rents. In 1440 the commune of Verona was alarmed at the efforts of *contadini* from Illasi and Soave to secure Venetian intervention to suspend rent payments. Such initiatives and interventions were hardly unique and the whole gamut of city–*contado* relations, from tax assessment to the control of waterways, reached the superior government. The territory around L'Aquila did not hesitate to petition the crown against the city's attempts to control rural industries and the distribution of the tax burden.[42] Attempts by the guilds of Milan to control rural textile production were thwarted by the accessibility and generosity of the Visconti and Sforza dukes. The rural communes of the Florentine *territorio* were ready to bypass Pisa or Pistoia and appeal to the republic directly.

Moreover, such appeals were not only the work of individual communes or *contadini*. At times, as the Veronese evidence clearly shows, large numbers of rural communities could band themselves together to appeal to the superior power, and even to lobby and bribe its councillors. Cipolla's defence of Veronese claims in 1475 was made in the face of an organised attempt by an association of rural communes to win the support of the republic on matters of such importance as the distribution of the tax burden and the status of *contado* immigrants in the city. If the issues were fundamental, that particular alliance of rural communes was *ad hoc*. Other associations were more permanent, as in the case of the 'community' of the communes from the shore of Lake Como who received fiscal and administrative privileges from their Visconti and Sforza rulers.[43]

However, the reaction of *contadini* and rural communities to the demands of landlords and cities did not always stop at petition and complaint. If there was no *Jacquerie* in the Italian countryside, violence and the threat of violence were certainly present and the level of disorder could become intense. Both the circumstances and the extent of violence varied, but in the more remote and mountainous areas of the Peninsula – and 37 per cent of the country can be defined as mountainous – violence was virtually endemic. This can be seen in the Apennines, in the Romagna and the jurisdiction of Bologna, although vendetta, rustling and kidnapping were not aimed exclusively at citizens and their property but could characterise relations within the *contado* itself. In the sixteenth century the level of brigandage in the hinterland of Lucca was such that a virtual siege mentality can be detected in the city. Generally fear of the 'mountain men', widely known for their independence of outlook and contempt for authority, was widespread and lies behind much of the savagely satirical literature written against them in the towns.[44]

But violence could also be controlled and aimed, with the urban landlord, his agents and his property as frequent targets. Some incidents were spontaneous and localised. In 1425 the Veronese humanist Guarino – himself a landlord – was shocked at the news of the murder of a Venetian noble on his estates in the Vallagarina; subsequently a vicar of the commune of Verona was killed as he tried to negotiate with angry *contadini*, and two other officials were attacked but managed to escape.[45] In 1461 enraged tenants in the Veronese attacked their Venetian and Veronese landlords, again with loss of life as well as damage to property, suggesting greater co-ordination and deeper resentment among the peasantry. This applies to the disturbances of the *tucchini* of Piedmont and Savoy in the period 1386–1390.[46] It can also be detected in Friuli in the early years of the sixteenth century when attempts by members of the feudal nobility to insist on a vigorous interpretation of their lordship, together with the burdens placed on the region by the Venetian government, provoked a series of rural revolts. In 1501 there were reports of friars urging the oppressed *contadini* to defend their rights. The threat was recognised by the nobility in parliament in 1503. By 1510 serious unrest had become a reality, with the countryside further disturbed by the conflicts of the War of Cambrai. Talk of a 'Sicilian Vespers' was in the air, and attacks on noble families like the Colloredo sent many feudatories fleeing to Venice for safety.[47]

As events in Friuli show, revolt in the *contado* could be triggered off or exploited in the course of wider political disturbances. Throughout the period instances can be found where *contadini* tried to take advantage of the political weaknesses revealed by the arrival of foreign armies to challenge the authority of the city and their landlords. In 1418 the citizens of Verona complained that years of political instability had resulted in many estates returning to the wild, while others suffered an even worse fate, falling into the hands of 'malevolent countrymen'. The dynastic conflict between the Aragonese and the Angevins in the *Regno* encouraged rural revolts in Calabria in the 1420s and again in 1459. Rumours of the death of Francesco Sforza triggered off revolts in the Piacentino in 1462.[48] Invasion could produce similar reactions. The Florentines, facing the threat of a Visconti attack in 1402, expected the *contado* communities to join the enemy. In 1405 and 1406, as the republic prepared to conquer Pisa, these communities were won over to the Florentine side with promises of greater autonomy under Florentine rule.

In 1452 Francesco Sforza was told that the *contadini* of the Cremonese were withholding their rents in the hope that Venetian conquest would free them from these obligations.[49] In 1475 Gianfrancesco Cipolla reminded the Venetian government that the *contado* communities had shown themselves to be more protective of their own skins than of the republic's dominions in the event of invasion; but a converse situation arose during the War of Cambrai when, to the amazement of outsiders like Machiavelli and Louis XII's councillor Claude de Seyssel, the *contadini* of those areas of the Venetian state under foreign occupation supported their erstwhile rulers. To account for this the Venetian diarist Girolamo Priuli was not unjustified in claiming that the loyalty of the *contadini* was due to the republic's record in mitigating their condition, but for both sides immediate issues were probably more responsible for the alliance. The *contadini* were alienated by the plundering ill-discipline of the invading armies; they also seized on the chance to attack the authority of the cities and citizen landlords who had welcomed foreign rule. These aims the republic did much to encourage, also granting its followers remission of taxes and a moratorium on debts. Venice actively recruited *contadini* as militia and the resultant bands, or *cernide*, played an important part in the republic's survival and the recovery of its territories. Machiavelli's dispatches from imperially held Verona in 1509 record the alarm felt in the city at the scale of the *contado*'s espousal of the Venetian cause.[50]

It is true that rural reaction, on whatever scale or in whatever circumstance, rarely altered the jurisdictional and economic ascendancy of the city, or halted the advance of urban capital. It is also true that rural communes could be used by the city as instruments of government; Florence's encouragement of the rural communities of her *territorio* in the early fifteenth century was intended to create local institutions responsible to the republic's demands in such areas as public order and tax allocation. It was not a disinterested exercise in local self-government, and Florence appears to have been unusually strict in monitoring the local statutes of its subject communities. However, it is also true that rural communities could challenge and obstruct city government and that political circumstances could bring benefits to such communes, singly or in association. The ready acceptance of Venetian rule by the Valpolicella before the surrender of Verona in 1405 did serve to preserve and enhance the privileges already enjoyed by this federation of rural communes, and similar gains were made by the rural communities that surrendered on terms to Francesco Sforza before he entered Milan and assumed the duchy in 1450.[51].

Such opportunism was both cause and effect of a deeply rooted local autonomy which challenged the authority of the city and found expression in careful collections of charters and privileges. Moreover, the evidence of reaction to urban rule – whether based on precedents and defended through appeal or provoked by exploitation and expressed in violence – shows clearly that the *contado* was not cowed into submission in the period. It explains the significance of the prayer devised or relayed by the Florentine priest Arlotto Mainardi (1396–1484): 'My Lord Jesus Christ, save me from the anger and the hands of the *contadini*.'[52] It explains why the 'second sack' of Rome, as *contadini* followed the mercenary armies into the city in 1527, was as terrifying as the first.

FEUDAL LORDSHIPS IN THE NORTH

When describing the social complexity of the countryside and assessing the attempts made by individuals and governments to draw on its resources, there is a tendency to overlook an element whose importance for the north in the Renaissance period has not yet been sufficiently acknowledged: the existence of feudal jurisdictions. Discussing the late thirteenth and early fourteenth centuries, Waley has rightly asked if 'medieval Italian history has been seen in focus' and has suggested that if it were, 'it might present the appearance of great stretches of feudalised territory with the towns fitted merely into the interstices.' Fasoli has also lamented the neglect of the subject. Examining the policy of the Venetian republic towards feudal tenure and lordship in its mainland territories, she has observed that 'a long historiographical tradition has habituated us to fix our attention on the cities, to make them the centres of gravity for our research.' Historians interested in feudalism and the Italian nobility have concentrated on the earlier Middle Ages. For the later period Fasoli has detected the assumption that feudal institutions had crumbled and noble families had lost status under pressure from hostile city governments, governments responsible for what has been called the 'shipwreck' of thirteenth-century Italian feudalism.[53]

This view has had a long and influential history, running at least from Burckhardt to Baron. Moreover, it has some foundation. From the thirteenth century many of the communes of northern and central Italy introduced statutes and passed decrees against various aspects of noble power in town and country; these often remained in force into the Renaissance period. For example, in 1386 Giangaleazzo Visconti passed a decree against the nobility using their retinues to intimidate officials. His son Filippo Maria drew on expert legal opinion to launch *quo warranto* inquiries into claims to fiefs and lordships. In 1444 the commune of Urbino asked its new lord, Federigo da Montefeltro, to cancel all privileges and immunities enjoyed by noble families. In the sixteenth century the statutes of Modena still included clauses introduced in 1306 to ban nobles and their clients from civic government.

Moreover, such policies did not always remain confined to paper. The commune of Florence clung to its traditional suspicion of noble power, rooting out with exceptional relentlessness lordships, first in its *contado* and then in its wider dominions. The commune was reluctant to follow the practice favoured by the Visconti, the Venetian republic, the crown of Aragon and other governments: that of rewarding reliable *condottieri* with lordships. When threatened, it destroyed the holdings of long-established families. The adherence of many branches of the Ubertino clan to the cause of Giangaleazzo

Visconti led to their downfall on the duke's death in 1402; a similar fate awaited the counts of Poppi in 1440 after they had supported Filippo Maria Visconti. From the mid-fifteenth century the republic followed similar policies in the Lunigiana, reducing the power of the Malaspina clan. This background helps to explain Machiavelli's hostile attitude towards the feudal nobility in Lombardy, the Papal States and the south, condemning them as sources of disorder and weakness for the state.[54]

It would, however, be wrong to exaggerate the impact of anti-magnate legislation or to generalise from the Florentine example. In the Italian countryside, fiefs were common and lordships were a prominent element. This was especially the case in the south and the islands, where relatively few cities had any effective jurisdiction or control of the territory beyond their walls; L'Aquila in the Abruzzo was unusual in having a *contado*. The same is true in the far north, for example in Piedmont and the prince-bishopric of Trent. Moreover, it is becoming increasingly recognised that this also applied in those regions where it has been too often assumed that fiefs and lordships belonged to a 'medieval' past. For the duchy of Milan feudal maps are as yet to be compiled but it is becoming clear how, for example, the city and *contado* of Piacenza remained dominated by the landed, political and military muscle of great families like the Anguissola and the Scotti – the latter claiming an ancient Scottish ancestry further to enhance their power.[55]

In expressing their growing awareness of the extent of feudal power in the north, historians have often had recourse to the term 'refeudalisation'. This has some validity. For example the Visconti, the Este and the Venetian republic formally confirmed the lordships of loyal supporters, as the Visconti did for the Pallavicini of Parma in 1438, the Este for the Cesi of Modena in 1416 and Venice for the noble castellans of Friuli between 1418 and 1420.[56] They also made new grants. Reliable *condottieri* were rewarded, like Giacomo dal Verme (*c*. 1350–1409), who earned the gratitude of both the Visconti and the Venetian republic in land and lordships. 'Newer' families and curial officials also benefited in this way. The favour enjoyed by the Pompei family of Verona allowed them to secure tax immunities for their estates round Illasi in 1469 and 1474, and their loyalty to Venice was capped by the award of the title of count in 1509.[57] Officials of the Visconti and Sforza, like the chancellor Cicco Simonetta (*c*. 1410–80), benefited from the dynasties' ability to dispose of lands and rights properly belonging to ecclesiastical institutions as well as those more directly available to their treasuries.[58]

'Refeudalisation' is, however, a misleading term if it is taken to mean that the grant of fiefs and lordships had ever been suspended or curtailed, to be subsequently resumed. In some cases the evidence suggests that there was a greater emphasis placed on defining and recording grants; this was a feature of Visconti policy, especially after the acquisition of the ducal title from the emperor Wenceslas in 1395 – a grant which greatly enhanced the dynasty's jurisdictional position in relation to the feudatories of its territories. Again, new grants could mean the confirmation and extension of existing holdings: the lordships of Giacomo dal Verme in Visconti and Venetian territory built on grants made earlier in the fourteenth century. For political reasons rulers could shift the direction of their patronage. This was the case in Aragonese and papal territory. In the north Giorgio of Liechtenstein, prince-bishop of Trent (1390–1419), enfeoffed followers from beyond the Alps to counter the insubordination of his vassals in the Trentino (see below, pp. 231–2). Lastly, financial pressure could force governments into bouts of generosity, as in the Sforza duchy after 1480. However, none of these circumstances was altogether new, and the evidence does not suggest that feudalism had to make 'a new start' in the period.

Another related reason why the subject of feudalism in northern Italy has been relatively neglected lies in the acceptance of generalisations often made in hindsight and too coloured by the demonology of the *ancien régime*: that feudalism was an anachronism, a foreign and regressive element in the civilisation of Renaissance Italy. In economic terms the nobility are often represented as absentee landlords, content to squeeze the maximum from their tenants, neglectful of the well-being of both men and the soil and ignorant of those sections of the economy that lay behind Italian greatness: commerce, finance and industry. But not all landlords were cynical and grasping *rentiers*, and it is artificial to divorce the economy and society of the countryside from those of the town. As has been mentioned, the towns depended on the countryside for their survival and their prosperity. The nobles of Genoa had a shrewd eye for the marketplace. The vassals of the prince-bishop of Trento were as anxious to be enfeoffed with tolls as with lands. In the early fifteenth century a market flourished in the lordship of the Pallavicini in the Parmigiano, in part due to its freedom from the jealous fiscalism of the city.

Again the nobility is often depicted as an anarchic, disruptive element, much given to feuding and contemptuous of the public good. This is the view conveyed by the anti-magnate legislation on the statute books of many Italian communes and by chronicles composed by nervous or hostile townsmen. It is the impression given by judicial records which by their very nature tend to record instances of *prepotenza* and thus point up the lawlessness of the nobility. It has a foundation in fact, as the relentless rivalry of the noble families of the Romagna or those of the commune of Genoa and its hinterland indicates. The geographical and jurisdictional extent of lordships could owe much to force and opportunism. The vassals of the prince-bishop of Trento, lords like the counts of Arco, took advantage of weak overlordship in the later fourteenth century. Similarly, in the chaos following the sudden death of Giangaleazzo Visconti in 1402, the noble houses and enfeoffed *condottieri* of Lombardy sought to increase their holdings through seizure, purchase and grant, as well as accepting land in pawn from the beleaguered government. Even in relatively well-ordered states, the disruptive character of the feudal nobility can be seen. In the Sforza dominions, the extensive lordships of a family like the dal Verme could provide a haven for tax-dodgers and outlaws, while the 'muscle-power', the *prepotenza*, of such families could be flexed by their clients and retainers, as the duke's officials reported nervously from Piacenza in 1484.

The ambitions of feudal families could provide a real threat to the government, and an opportunity for its enemies. In 1437 Count Alvise dal Verme was exiled from Venetian territory after abandoning the republic's cause for the greater rewards offered by its Visconti and Gonzaga enemies. With long-held lordships in both Visconti and Venetian territory, the dal Verme illustrate the temptations and dangers placed before an ambitious and strategically well-placed noble family.[59] The loyalty to the dukes of Milan of the lordship of Borgonuovo was not even secured by investiture of one Francesco Sforza's many illegitimate children, Sforza Secondo; on the accession of his half-brother Galeazzo Maria, he briefly went over to the Venetian republic.[60]

But there is another side to the picture. If some lands and rights were appropriated by force, others were held with a legitimacy and from an antiquity that rivalled or surpassed those of the governing power. Hence the Visconti felt more secure in investigating the claims and titles of the landed nobility after they had acquired an imperial dukedom in 1395, and the need felt to 'outrank' their subjects helps to explain the value placed by ruling dynasties on imperially granted feudal titles. Moreover, feudal rights and lordships would not have been so readily confirmed or granted – and especially not to *condottieri* – had they been inextricably associated with disloyalty. As is discussed elsewhere, in the Aragonese lands and the Papal States the award and recognition of fiefs and lordships were accepted means to reward and secure support. The same appears to have been true in the north. In 1404 and 1405 the Venetian government was prepared to recognise the lordships of Giorgio Cavalli in the Vicentino because of his acknowledged power and influence in the area and because of his apparent readiness to support the Venetian cause.[61]

Further, if the number of specifically feudal obligations owed by a vassal to his lord had diminished, the sense of obligation had not disappeared, even in the north. The vassals of the republic of Venice or the Sforza no longer owed their lords defined periods of military service, but they were expected to support and defend the regime. Nor were governments always resigned to treating their vassals with kid gloves. In 1437 Filippo Maria Visconti decreed those forms of taxation from which even immunities could not escape; by and large his vassals were liable to direct forms of taxation. In 1441 Filippo Maria affirmed the right of appeal from feudal jurisdiction to the ducal courts.

Lastly, if the feudal nobility is often caricatured as a source of discord and rebellion, a similarly unbalanced judgement is often given on their treatment of their own subjects. In fact this issue reveals most clearly the shortcomings of research to date into the nobility of northern Italy in the Renaissance. Genealogists have explored the ramifications of family history. Political and diplomatic historians have charted the shifting alliances and allegiances of noble houses. Economic historians have studied the patterns of land-holding. Archaeologists have at last begun to investigate their castles. But a central element of their lordships, the relationship between the lord and his vassals, tenants and retainers, has been largely unexplored. It is to be hoped that the work of historians like Chittolini, free from the more antiquarian enthusiasms often attending histories of noble families and reading between the lines of the state's authority, will be brought further to bear on the internal organisation of feudal power.

Despite the relatively slim evidence, there are grounds for seeing the nobility as tyrannical exercisers of authority over their subjects. In the *Regno* and the islands communities could resent being granted out in fief, and the conduct of individual lords could be a matter for grievance. The northern evidence can point in a similar direction. When the Venetian republic ended Giorgio Cavalli's lordship in the Vicentino for suspected treason in 1406, the commune of Schio was told that it had been freed from 'the yoke of servitude and subjection'. In 1407 Trent and some of the surrounding valley communities rose against the lordship of the prince-bishop. In the fifteenth and sixteenth centuries the Este frequently received petitions from *contado* communities against the impositions of their lords in matters like castle-guard and labour services.[62] Friuli was the scene of violent attacks on the feudal nobility between 1509 and 1511 from *contadini* fearful lest servile conditions be reimposed.[63]

However, such examples are not always such clear-cut instances of anti-feudal revolt as may at first appear. The rebellion in the Trentino in 1407 was led by a disgruntled feudatory of the prince-bishop, Rodolfo Belenzani. The uprisings in Friuli a century later were fomented by one of the great feudatories of the region, Antonio Savorgnan, eager to weaken his enemies among the nobility. Moreover, lords could be sustained by their subjects. Although it is easy to accept the stereotype suggested by Braudel when he refers to the 'anachronistic' character of the Sienese Maremma and the 'crushing presence of the feudal landlords who dominated the country', an inquiry carried out by the commune of Siena in 1404 into the jurisdiction claimed by the Cerretani family in the region produced willing witnesses drawn from a wide social range prepared to defend the lordship – as they did, successfully.[64] Similarly, an investigation authorised by Filippo Maria Visconti in 1424 into the rights of the marquises of Pallavicini heard charges of force, tyranny and intimidation levelled against them by the commune of Parma, anxious to control its *contado*, but the accusations could not be substantiated and the marquises' subjects were ready to support their lords. Even more striking is the evidence produced by Filippo Maria Visconti s inquiry into the lordships of the Anguissola in 1438; it appears that *contado* communities could invite the protection and lordship of such a powerful local family, seeking to extend its lordship beyond its strictly legal limits.

A similar conclusion can be reached from the evidence of communities situated within lordships and anxious to maintain their separate identity, even after their lords' fall from grace. The rural communes of the dal Verme lordships in the Veronese were reluctant to be merged with the rest of the *contado* on the exile of the count in 1437, and threats of violence deterred prospective purchasers of his confiscated property. It would be a mistake to ignore the presence of genuine affection and loyalty in the attitudes of such communities; the *de facto* lordship of the Anguissola was in part based on the 'love' of their subjects, as the Visconti inquiry recorded. However, other considerations were less emotional. The inhabitants of a lordship could be sheltered from the full force of the fiscal and labour burdens imposed by the governing lord or republic. Alvise dal Verme had secured for his subjects exemption from direct taxation and a reduced commitment to such labour-intensive projects as maintaining the dykes on the banks of the Adige. Similar explanations have been offered for the acceptance of feudal lordships in Emilia; for example, the courts of such jurisdictions could frustrate the claims made by citizens against *contadini*. While serving the Venetian republic as a *condottiere* in the early years of the War of Cambrai, Antonio Savorgnan frequently interceded with the government on behalf of his peasantry. Of course his subjects had to pay for a lord's protection, for access to his courts as well as for the use of his mills or his castles. Nevertheless, when assessing the vigorous survival of feudalism in northern Italy during the Renaissance it would be a mistake to ignore the fact that 'good lordship' could be understood in terms of protection from the state.

CONCLUSION

Ambrogio Lorenzetti's famous *Good Government* frescoes in the council hall of the Palazzo Comunale in Siena (1337–39) give a good indication of the nature of the relationship between town and country in the Renaissance period. The town is accorded greater prominence and its inhabitants and their activities are depicted more boldly and in greater detail and variety; but equal space is given to the *contado*, the links between them are stressed and the message is clear: that good government brings harmony and prosperity to two inter-related communities.[65]

Modern research is making increasingly clear the importance of the countryside in the Renaissance, and stressing that its value was as great for the 'urbanised' areas of the north as it was for the south and the islands. It was the major source of livelihood for the majority of the population as well as a potential source of profit for citizen investors and a prized source of men, materials and money for all forms of government. Moreover, there are signs that the relative importance of the countryside increased in the period. In part this was for negative reasons. The demands made by war became increasingly heavy as states moved in the direction of standing armies which required billeting and supplies, and as armies adopted more expensive and elaborate tactics and defences that necessitated the support of militia as well as of pioneers to move and position artillery. Furthermore, military budgets placed a growing and disproportionate share of the tax burden on the *contado*. Secondly, as Italian merchants, bankers and manufacturers faced stiffening competition abroad, they began to devote a relatively larger share of their capital and energy to the land. However, positive reasons for the growing interest in the land should also be recognised. A path to greater profits had been opened up through commercial contracts, land improvements and the reorganisation of holdings into more manageable farms. Villa life became more desirable for reasons of pleasure and prestige as well as for the better management of country estates. These elements came together in the writings of the mid-sixteenth-century Venetian patrician Alvise Cornaro, who signalled the greater store put on villa and agriculture by a society which before the start of the period had perhaps the least direct involvement in the land.[66]

But there were yawning gaps between potential and reality, and the 'conquest of the *contado*' by citizens, whether as officials or landlords, was only partial. The burdens placed by the city on the *contado* – to maintain dykes on such dangerous rivers as the Adige, or to support the war effort in men, materials and cash – provoked petitions and litigation and were subject to delay and avoidance.[67] The weight of *contado* business in communal statutes and in the minutes of communal councils should not be read automatically as a testimonial to urban supremacy, but rather to the difficulties faced in implementing that supremacy; the disproportionate tax burden placed on the *contado* was in part the product of urban self-interest, but it was probably also a deliberate overassessment in anticipation of the difficulty to be faced in securing a return. For the individual or the religious institution, land was never an easy investment; its return could be destroyed by freak weather, flooding, hostile or 'friendly' forces, disease or resentful peasantry – as the problems facing some ecclesiastical and noble landlords make clear.

The problems presented by alienated *contadini* also introduce the fact that the society of the *contado* was not made up of one cowed and homogeneous class. Serfdom still existed in parts of Liguria, and its recent memory haunted the *contadini* of Friuli. Round the cities in particular there were great numbers of landless labourers desperate for work. But the *contado* also contained peasants who might not have been well off when measured against the capital accumulated by some urban families, but who had their own parcels of land, while working the scattered holdings of a number of distant urban landlords. The *mezzadria* 'system', on paper appearing to favour the urban landlord, required strict supervision to do so in practice, and such contracts may not have proved so oppressive to a canny and conservative peasantry, especially in a period of labour shortages and land investment.[68] The extensive mountain areas of Italy preserved peoples of fierce independence who followed their flocks, harvested their chestnuts and prepared their charcoal with little direct contact with the townsman or communal official.

Moreover, the countryside should not be thought of in terms of 'open country' alone, but as also containing small towns with their own relatively prosperous elites, their own industries and their own liberties and institutions to defend. This history of the prosperous commune of Legnago, situated on the Adige in the Veronese, was dominated by running disputes with the theoretically superior authority of Verona over the distribution of taxation, the duties and privileges of Veronese citizens living and owning property in the area, and the degree of jurisdictional autonomy enjoyed by Legnago. The impression increasingly given by recent research is that the society of the *contado* was more varied over more gradations than used to be assumed. Individuals can come into focus who defy easy categorisation. Pietro Faccio emerges from the small rural commune of Chiesanuova in the mountainous Lessini district above Verona in the 1480s; he was well travelled between the communities of the Dolomites, a man who made a living from trading as well as from crops and livestock, and who acquired a good reputation in the administration of his commune.[69]

Finally if the social and economic history of the *contado* was more complex than was once thought, so too was the political, jurisdictional and administrative map. Governments had to deal with a variety of individual and associated rural communities ready to plead their special cases, often with considerable resourcefulness and tenacity. At times, too, they were prepared to turn from arguing from precedent and lobbying to using force or resorting to rebellion. Perhaps even more effective in thwarting the aspirations of the 'Renaissance state' were the feudal nobility who were prominent, even dominant, in the countryside in all regions of Italy except central Tuscany. It is unfortunate that historiographical prejudice, with a pedigree almost as ancient and exalted as those claimed by such noble houses themselves, has for so long hindered the objective study of their rule.

NOTES AND REFERENCES

1. P. J. Jones, 'Italy', in *The Cambridge Economic History of Europe*, vol. i, ed. M. M. Postan (Cambridge, 1966); 'La Storia Economica', in *Storia d'Italia* (Einaudi), vol. ii (Turin, 1974); 'Economia e Società nell'Italia medievale', *Storia d'Italia–Annali*, vol. i (Turin, 1978).

2. D. M. Webb, 'Penitence and peace-making in city and *contado*', *Studies in Church History*, vol. xvi (1979). For a perceptive assessment of the hegemony of the city in respect of cults and religious festivals, R. C. Trexler, *Public Life in Renaissance Florence* (New York and London, 1980), pp. 3, 7 and 275.

3. F. Fossati, 'Nuove spigolature d'archivio', *A.S.L.*, ser. viii, vol. vii (1957), p. 378; I. Cervelli, *Machiavelli e la Crisi dello Stato Veneziano* (Naples, 1974), p. 348.

4. J. E. Law, 'Venezia, Verona e il Contado nel '400', *A.V.*, ser. v, vol. cxvi (1981), p. 46; R. Bizzocchi, 'La dissoluzione di un clan familiare: i Buondelmonte di Firenze nei secoli xv e xvi', *A.S.I.*, vol. cxl (1982), pp. 7–10.

5. S. Cohen, *The Labouring Classes in Renaissance Florence* (New York–London, 1980), p. 42.

6. G. Romano, *Studi sul Paesaggio* (Turin, 1978).

7. R. S. Lopez, review of M. Berengo, *Nobili e Mercanti nella Lucca del Cinquecento* (Turin, 1965), in *Speculum*, vol. xlii (1967), pp. 517–18; M. Luzzati, *Una Guerra di Popolo. Lettere privati del Tempo dell'Assedio di Pisa* (Pisa, 1973).

8. D. Romagnoli, 'Voghera: popolazione e società nella prima metà del xv secolo', *Boll. della Soc. Pavese di Storia Patria*, n.s., vol. xxxiii (1981).

9. P. Lanaro Sartori, 'Radiografia della soglia di povertà in una città della terraferma veneta', *S.V.*, n.s., vol. vi (1982), p. 60.

10. G. Brucker, *The Civic World of Early Renaissance Florence* (Princeton, 1977), p. 401 ff.

11. Cervelli, op.cit., pp. 404–6 and *passim*.

12. G. M. Varanini, 'Le campagne veronesi del '400', in G. Borelli (ed.), *Uomini e Civiltà Agraria in Territorio Veronese*, vol. i (Verona, 1982), p. 236.

13. D. V. and F. W. Kent, 'Two vignettes of Florentine society in the fifteenth century', *Rinascimento*, ser. ii, vol. xxiii (1983); A. Brown, *Bartolomeo Scala Chancellor of Florence* (Princeton, 1979), pp. 5–6.

14. For example, G. M. Varanini, *Il Distretto Veronese nel Quattrocento* (Verona, 1980) and 'Un esempio di ristrutturazione agraria quattrocentesca', *Studi Storici Veronesi*, vols xxx–xxxi (1980–81); C. Povolo (ed.), *Lisiera, Storia e Cultura di una Comunità Veneta*, vol. i (Vicenza, 1981).

15. P. J. Jones, 'From manor to mezzadria', in N. Rubinstein (ed.), *Florentine Studies* (London, 1968); G. Cherubini, *Signori, Contadini, Borghesi* (Florence, 1974) and 'Le campagne italiane', in *Storia d'Italia* (U.T.E.T.), vol. iv (1981); G. Chittolini 'Città e contado nella tarda età comunale', *Nuova Rivista Storica*, vol. liii (1969); 'La crisi della proprietà ecclesiastica fra quattrocento e cinquecento', *R.S.I.*, vol. lxxxv (1973); 'Alle origini delle grandi aziende della Bassa Lombarda', *Quaderni Storici*, vol. xiii (1978); E. Sereni, *Storia del Paesaggio Agrario Italiano* (Bari, 1979). We have made particular use of a valuable collection of essays: *Contadini e Proprietari nella Toscana Moderna, Atti del Convegno di Studi in Onore di G. Giorgetti* (Florence, 1979), henceforth *Giorgetti*.

16. R. Valentini, 'Braccio di Montone e il comune di Orvieto', *Boll della Dep. di Storia Patria per. l'Umbria*, vol. xxv (1922), pp. 108–10; G. de Vergottini, 'Il papato e la comitatinenza nello stato della Chiesa', *Atti e Mem. della Dep. di Stor. Pat. per le Provincie di Romagna*, n.s., vol. iii (1951–53), pp. 157–8; E. Pontieri, 'La "Universitas" di Catanzaro nel quattrocento', *Studi di Storia Napoletana in Onore di M. Schipa* (Naples, 1926), p. 289.

17. Varanini in *Uomini e Civiltà Agraria*, p. 213; A. K. Isaacs, 'Le campagne senesi fra quattrocento e cinquecento', in *Giorgetti*, p. 402.

18. D. Kent, *The Rise of the Medici* (Oxford, 1978), pp. 20, 266, 301, 324, 337.

19. E. Pontieri, *Il Comune dell'Aquila nel declino del Medioevo* (L'Aquila 1979), p. 289.

20. G. Cora, *Storia della Maiolica*, vol. i (Florence, 1973), pp. 18–19.

21. D. R. Coffin, *The Villa in the Life of Renaissance Rome* (Princeton, 1979).

22. P. J. Jones, 'Florentine families and Florentine diaries', *Papers of the British School at Rome*, n.s., vol. xi (1956), pp. 183–205; R. Goldthwaite, *Private Wealth in Renaissance Florence* (Princeton, 1968), pp. 246–51.

23. P. Malamina, 'La proprietà fiorentina e la diffusione della mezzadria nel contado pisano', in *Giorgetti*.

24. C. M. Cipolla, 'Une crise ignorée. Comment s'est perdue la propriété ecclésiastique dans l'Italie du nord', *Annales*, vol. ii (1947); Chittolini, 'La crisi'.

25. G. Piccinini, *Mezzadri e salariati sulle terre di Monte Oliveto Maggiore* (Milan, 1982); Chittolini, 'Alle orgini'; Varanini, 'Un esempio'.

26. J. M. Ferraro, 'Proprietà terriera e potere nello stato veneto', *Civis*, vol. viii (1984).

27. S. Polica, 'An attempted "reconversion" of wealth in fifteenth century Lucca: the lands of Michele di Giovanni Guinigi', *Journal of European Econ. Hist.*, vol. ix (1980).

28. For a recent discussion of *mezzadria*, J. Brown, *In the Shadow of Florence. Provincial Society in Renaissance Pescia* (Oxford, 1982), pp. 94 ff.

29. G. Pinto, *La Toscana nel Tardo Medioevo* (Florence, 1982), and 'Mezzadria podarile, contadini e proprietari', *Società e Storia*, no. xii (1981).
30. C. Trasselli, *Da Ferdinando il Cattolico a Carlo V. L'Esperienza Siciliana* (Messina, 1982), vol. i, p. 360; L. Bonnelli Conenna (ed.), *La Divina Villa* (Siena, 1982).
31. J. E. Law, *The Commune of Verona under Venetian Rule* (D.Phil. thesis, University of Oxford, 1974), pp. 277–89.
32. Isaacs, loc. cit., pp. 379 ff.
33. Law, 'Venezia, Verona'.
34. Law, *Commune of Verona*, pp. 215–32.
35. G. Chittolini, 'Il particolarismo signorile e feudale in Emilia', *Il Rinascimento nelle Corti Padane* (Bari, 1977), p. 31.
36. B. Pullan, 'The famine in Venice and the new poor law, 1527–9', in Pullan (ed.), *Crisis and Change in the Venetian Economy* (London, 1968).
37. Berengo, op. cit.
38. E. Guidoboni, 'Terre, villagi e famiglie del Polesine', *Società e Storia*, no. xiv (1981); L. Chiappa Mauri, 'A proposito di due recenti pubblicazioni sulle campagne toscane', *Soc. e Stor.*, no. xix (1983); M. Luzzati, 'Toscana senza mezzadria', in *Giorgetti*.
39. M. Knapton, 'Il Territorio vicentino nello stato veneto', *Civis*, vol. viii (1984); Ferraro, loc. cit.
40. C. M. Cipolla, 'Per la storia delle epidemie in Italia', *R.S.I.*, vol. lxxv (1963).
41. P. S. Leicht, 'La rappresentanza dei contadini', in *Studi e Frammenti* (Udine, 1903).
42. Pontiere, *L'Aquila*, p. 187 and *passim*.
43. L. Prosdòcimi, 'Problemi sulla formazione del territorio di Como', *Atti e Mem. del II Congresso Storico Lombardo* (Milan, 1938).
44. G. Cherubini, 'La società dell'Appennino settentrionale' in *Signori, Contadini*; J. Larner, 'Order and disorder in Romagna', in L. Martines (ed.), *Violence and Civil Disorder in Italian Cities* (Berkeley–Los Angeles–London, 1972). pp. 40–41.
45. Law, 'Venice, Verona'.
46. Marie-José (ex-Queen of Italy), *La Maison de Savoie*, vol. i (Paris, 1956), p. 299.
47. P. S. Leicht, 'Un movimento agrario nel cinquecento', *Scritti Vari di Storia del Diritto*, vol. i (Milan, 1943).
48. F. Cusin, 'Le aspirazioni stranieri sul ducato di Milano', *A.S.L.*, n.s., vol. i (1936).
49. P. Ghinzoni, 'Informazioni politiche sul ducato di Milano', *A.S.L.*, ser. ii, vol. ix (1892), p. 864; Fondazione Treccani degli Alfieri, *Storia di Milano* (Milan, 1953), vol. vii, p. 30.
50. Cervelli, op. cit., p. 344 and *passim*; M. E. Mallett and J. R. Hale, *The Military Organisation of a Renaissance State* (Cambridge, 1984), pp. 349–50.
51. G. Chittolini, 'I capitoli di dedizione delle comunità lombarde a Francesco Sforza', *Studi di Storia Padana in Onore di G. Martini* (Milan, 1978).
52. Cherubini in *Storia d'Italia*, vol. iv, pp. 418–37.
53. D. Waley, 'The army of the Florentine republic', in *Florentine Studies,* p. 94; G. Fasoli, 'Lineamenti di politica e legislazione feudale in terraferma', *Rivista di Storia del Diritto It.*, vol. xxv (1952); G. Chittolini, 'Signorie rurali e feudi alla fine del medioevo', in *Storia d'Italia* (U.T.E.T.), vol. iv; T. Dean, 'Lords, vassals and clients in Renaissance Ferrara', *E.H.R.*, vol. c (1985), pp. 106–19.
54. M. E. Mallett, *Mercenaries and their Masters* (London, 1974). R. Bizzocchi suggests that feudal families could use ecclesiastical benefices to express and shore

up their local authority: 'Chiesa e aristocrazia nella Firenze del quattrocento', *A.S.I.*, vol. cxlii (1984), pp. 201 ff.

55. D. M. Bueno da Mesquita, 'Ludovico Sforza and his vassals', in E. F. Jacob (ed.), *Italian Renaissance Studies* (London, 1960), pp. 184–206.

56. G. Barni, 'La formazione interna dello stato visconteo', *A.S.L.*, n.s., vol. vi (1941), pp. 17–27; G. Chittolini, *La Formazione dello Stato Regionale e le Istituzioni del Contado* (Turin, 1979), and 'Il particolarismo'; Dean, loc. cit..

57. For Veronese feudalism, Varanini, *Il Distretto*.

58. G. Chittolini, 'Un problema aperto: la crisi della proprietà ecclesiastica fra quattro e cinquecento', *R.S.II* vol. lxxxv (1973).

59. Law, *Commune of Verona*, p. 338.

60. L. Cerri, 'I conti Sforza-Visconti e il feudo di Borgonuovo', *Archivio Storico per le Provincie Parmensi*, n.s., vol. xv (1915).

61. J. E. Law, 'Venice, Verona and the della Scala', *Atti e Mem. della Accademia di Verona*, ser. vi, vol. xxix (1977–78), pp. 159–60.

62. E. V. Bernadskaja, 'La questione dei tributi imposti ai contadini dell'Italia settentrionale', *Studi in Onore di A. Sapori*, vol. ii (Milan, 1957).

63. A. Ventura, *Nobilità e Popolo nella Società Venetà del '400 e '500* (Bari, 1964), pp. 195–204.

64. F. Braudel, *The Mediterranean and the Mediterranean World in the Age of Philip II*, vol. i (London, 1972), p. 76; G. Cherubini, 'La signoria dei Cerretani', in *Signori, Contadini*.

65. U. Feldges-Henning, 'The political programme of the Sala della Pace', *J.W.C.I.*, vol. xxxv (1972).

66. Cervelli, *op. cit.*, pp. 187 ff.

67. G. Borelli (ed.), *Una Città e il suo Fiume*, 2 vols (Verona, 1977).

68. C. Klapisch-Zuber, 'State and family in a Renaissance society: the Florentine *catasto* of 1427–30', in *Women, Family and Ritual in Renaissance Italy* (Chicago and London, 1985). p. 15.

69. G. M. Varanini, 'Spunti di vita economica e società nelle montagne veronesi', extract from *La Lessinia–Ieri Oggi Domani, Quaderno Culturale* (1983).

CHAPTER FIVE

The state: authority, famine and war

INTRODUCTION

Historians have long been interested in a transformation in the character of the Italian state which is thought to have occurred in the fifteenth and sixteenth centuries.[1] In general this is understood to have meant a marked increase in the effective authority of central government. In military terms it is seen to mean the acceptance of professional standing armies – and even of permanent navies – while developments are advanced in fortress design. These measures are taken by the state not only to counter its external enemies but to outclass the retinues and castles of its greater subjects and to discourage insurrection. To support its greater military commitments, the state is seen to increase the efficiency and burden of its taxation while indulging in 'proto-mercantilist' policies to boost its economy. In more strictly civil terms, the new state makes its legal authority run more effectively throughout its territories, challenging the 'medieval' liberties of noble families, the Church, subject communities and guilds, subordinating local statutes and 'levelling' all its subjects before a more centralised rule. Behind these advances a new bureaucracy is identified, served by a growing number of professional men, increasingly educated in the disciplines of law and the humanities.

Because this transformation appears to coincide with the demise of many, though not all, of the smaller city-states of Italy and the emergence – or re-emergence – of such larger units as the Venetian empire and the Papal States, historians have often labelled the change as the rise of the 'territorial' or 'regional' state. Alternatively they have chosen the expression 'the rise of the modern state', inspired by the way Italy appears to have heralded some later European developments, for example in the use of resident ambassadors, heed-less of Haskins's warning that it is not the job of the historian to award prizes for 'modernity'.[2] Alternatively the states of Italy have sufficiently impressed their historians with their greater strength to earn the accolade of the capital letter as 'the State'. Lastly, the expression 'Renaissance state' is used to convey, however vaguely, the sense that something both new and significant happens to the Italian state in the period.

This last concept owes much to a tradition dating back to Burckhardt, who described the Italian state of the fifteenth and sixteenth centuries 'as the outcome of reflection and calculation, the State as a work of art'. What Burckhardt was attempting to do was to relate developments in government to changes he detected in other significant aspects of the culture of Renaissance Italy. Rulers, like artists and men of letters, were freed from the constraints allegedly imposed on them by the medieval world's sense of order and hierarchy. Being less restricted, they became more creative. In discussing this creativity Burckhardt mentions their dedication in the pursuit of ends, their centralisation and their growing mastery of the resources and techniques of government. Anticipating by a century the arrival of the computer in Italian historiography, he is impressed by the statistical information assembled by such governments as the republic of Florence. However, doubts as to the validity of his general picture suggest themselves as he deals with individual examples. If he is impressed by the pathfinding achievements of Venice in the control of the Church and the management of state finance, his treatment of the Visconti and Sforza lords of Milan is anecdotal, dwelling on the rulers' personalities rather than on their policies or the institutions of their state.

Since Burckhardt, the subject has been considerably advanced by historians drawing on the rich archival evidence left by the various Italian governments. On the one hand the conclusions suggested by Burckhardt appear to have been confirmed, and distinctive aspects of government emerge, if not always for the first time then certainly more strongly. For example, in the course of the fifteenth century the workings of government, from the management of armies to the conduct of diplomacy, can be shown to become increasingly the business of professional state servants. Again, a central preoccupation of government, the collection of revenue, can be shown to have attracted increasing effort and ingenuity in its imposition, assessment and collection. Detailed examples can be cited to support Burckhardt's general picture. In 1453 Alfonso I of Naples chastised an embassy from Barcelona by claiming that their privileges and liberties thwarted his attempts to administer justice in Catalonia – a disadvantage not suffered by his Neapolitan subjects, who benefited in this respect from the wider powers of the crown.[3] In the same year, Lodovico Duke of Savoy (1434–65) appointed to his council a clerk renowned for his expertise in the workings of other Italian governments, while in 1460 the Venetian republic ordered its rectors on the mainland to draw up maps of their areas of administration.

On the other hand, modern research can cast serious doubts on the validity of the view of Burckhardt and his followers. The archival record can reveal the strength and resilience of the privileges enjoyed by the nobility, by the clergy both regular and secular, by corporations – whether economic or devotional – and by urban and rural communities. It can reveal the extent of corruption and delay in all aspects of administration, with venality as common a characteristic of public life as was the reluctance to serve the state. Officials can be shown to have been influenced by family and personal interests, as well as by the need to grant and the desire to receive favours. Again, specific examples can readily be found: in 1453, for instance, Francesco Sforza was told that the variety and extent of immunities and privileges claimed by the nobility of Parma was such that his lordship was more nominal than real.

The theme of this chapter will be that neither of these lines of interpretation can be taken to represent the prevailing characteristic of the Italian state throughout the period. Some supportive arguments can be found in the chapters dealing with the *contado* and the political histories of northern, Papal and southern states. Here the discussion will concentrate on the political vocabulary in use between governors and governed; the response of the state to the natural disasters of famine and disease; the military needs of governments, with their implications for fiscal and economic policies; and the distribution of public office. At the close of the chapter is a discussion of the territorial states created, largely in this period, by Venice and Florence. The intention is to show that important changes did take place in the nature of the Italian state, but that these changes were neither the invariable consequence of the state's own initiative nor firm steps on a road towards a greater and more centralised authority.

THE COMMUNICATION OF GOVERNMENT

The self-consciousness of the Italian states in matters of authority will be seen in later chapters in the way the issues of sovereignty and legitimacy featured so largely in their dealings with the traditional overlords of pope and emperor. A related self-consciousness can be detected in their domestic policies, and more particularly in the methods adopted to communicate their aims and authority to their subjects or fellow-citizens. Some forms of propaganda were traditional, and of these the most direct was the personal intervention of the ruler or of high officials. On occasion the very effectiveness of such appearances lay in their spontaneity: on 27 June 1458 Ferrante I showed himself to the people of Naples as a vital step in securing the succession. But such appearances could also be well planned and ritualised, funerals, coronations, weddings, entries and progresses often providing the occasion for state propaganda.[4]

All states made use of ceremony, the republic of Venice, the papacy and the southern monarchies perhaps having the more exalted and elaborate vocabulary of pageantry and ritual to draw upon, commensurate with their sovereign or royal status; when Francesco Sforza entered Milan in 1450 he is reported to have refused to ride in a chariot, as such a dignity belonged properly to monarchs. By contrast the iconography of ducal processions in Venice, with the doge heralded by silver trumpets and processing under a ceremonial umbrella, or baldachin, was not spectacle alone but was designed to express the authority of the republic, while the several annual celebrations linked to the cult of St Mark expressed the city's association with an evangelist and apostle who could 'rival' St Peter.[5] In Rome the religious and the secular could combine in the ceremony of the *possesso*, when a newly elected pope processed through the city as an expression of his lordship. A sacred quality also invested the anointed kings of Naples. When Ferrante I entered Bari on 7 January 1463 he wore canonical robes, as did Alfonso II at his coronation in 1494. However, the use of ceremonial by the state was common throughout Italy. In 1444 Leonello d'Este ordered ten days of public holiday to mark his marriage to Maria of Aragon, while in 1456 the commune of Florence decided to appoint a public herald to manage the republic's ceremonies. The celebrations ordered by the commune of Genoa in 1502 to welcome Louis XII as its overlord consisted of processions, the sounding of bells and trumpets and gun salutes, but were particularly distinguished by the monarch's readiness to touch those afflicted for the 'king's evil' (scrofula), a power traditionally credited to the kings of France.

Public proclamation was the normal method of conveying the wishes of government to its subjects, with town criers making announcements from designated public places, in many cases after a trumpeter had alerted passersby; in 1413 the commune of Verona paid the trumpeters and pipe-players who heralded news of a truce between Venice and the king of the Romans. Conversely, governments tried to ban slogans which endangered their authority. Giangaleazzo Visconti forbade the cries of 'Guelf', 'Ghibelline' and '*popolo*' as invitations to faction-fighting. In 1450 a Milanese was arrested for shouting 'Marco! Marco!' in support of the republic of Venice which had contested Francesco Sforza's bid for Milan, but he was released after insisting that he had really been crying 'Duca! Duca! Sforza! Sforza!'

But the decisions and workings of government could be given a more ritualised form to make a greater impact. The swearing-in of magistrates often took place in public; the Florentine militia ordinance of 1528 ordered that the public swearing-in of men be accompanied by a discourse on duty. The processes of law enforcement were exploited to convey a government's authority.[6] In Venice the punishment of serious offenders was frequently carried out in public and preceded by the parading and humiliation of the guilty. The Este had the captured ringleaders of a rebellion in 1385 dragged through the streets of Ferrara before being hanged. Nor did absence necessarily mean escape from the humiliation of public punishment. In 1412 John XXIII had the *condottiere* Muzio Attendolo depicted hanging upside down on the gates and bridges of Rome.

Nevertheless, governments could be anxious that their actions, achievements and virtues be given a more positive and lasting memorial. Coats of arms and *imprese* – personal devices – were carved, embroidered and painted to express authority. When Florentine magnates formally accepted the authority of the republic, they were expected to adopt the red cross on a white ground of the Florentine *popolo*. In the 1430s and 1440s Alfonso I commissioned Sicilian workshops to prepare banners demonstrating in heraldic terms his claim to the Neapolitan throne. Despite his humble family background, Nicholas V had his arms prominently displayed on the secular and ecclesiastical buildings advanced in his pontificate. In December 1509 Machiavelli reported to his government that as Venice retook cities from her enemies, the Lion of St Mark was represented as armed, with a sword in its paw rather than a book. And as that example perhaps suggests, victories could be celebrated by abusing the arms of the enemy. After John XXIII had defeated Ladislao in May 1411 he had his standard paraded and then humiliated in Rome.

Finally, artists and artisans could be employed to celebrate the achievements of rulers and officials on a grander scale, even if such projects were not always realised. In April 1393 the commune of Perugia considered erecting a statue to its lord, Biordo Michelotti, in emulation of the ancient Romans. In 1413–14 the commune of Siena commissioned Taddeo di Bartolo to decorate its palace with frescoes expressing the virtues and achievements of the republic.[7] Giovanna II of Naples had a funeral monument erected in the church of S. Giovanni in Carbonara to celebrate the virtues and triumphs of her brother Ladislao. And ceremony and permanence could come together, as when Alberto d'Este laid the foundation stone of the castle of S. Michele (now the Castello Estense) in the centre of Ferrara in 1385.

However, the period witnessed an enrichment of the already wide and varied forms of traditional state propaganda. For example, coinage continued to be used as a means of propaganda; accompanying the acquisition of a mainland state in the fifteenth century, the republic of Venice suppressed local mints and tried to protect the circulation of her own coins in part to express her lordship. To this traditional medium the Renaissance added the medal, keenly appreciative of its use in ancient Rome. Rulers like Filippo Maria Visconti in the north and Alfonso I in the south employed Pisanello to proclaim their achievements and virtues in this succinct and prestigious form, even if the circulation of medals was very limited when compared to that of coins or seals.

Similarly Renaissance taste added the classically inspired inscription to the more traditional coat of arms, perhaps the most famous being the statement 'Decreto Publico Pater Patriae' placed on the tomb of Cosimo de' Medici, designed by Verrocchio. Again, processions were familiar spectacles in Italian cities; increasingly their devisers drew on the Roman triumph to enhance their impact. In 1442 Alfonso I entered Naples in triumph, adorned with the attributes of his many kingdoms, drawn in a chariot and accompanied by floats celebrating such appropriate virtues as justice, and the event was preserved in the triumphal gateway built subsequently for the Castel Nuovo in Naples.[8] Lastly, if proclamation remained a method of communication, in Latin and weighed down with classical allusions it could emerge as the humanist oration, with skilled practitioners, like Bartolomeo Scala the chancellor of Florence, being enthusiastically applauded if not, we must assume, greatly understood. However, the printing press added a new and more effective dimension to the means of instruction and propaganda. Ferrante I had printed and circulated the confessions of the principal baronial rebels of 1487.

Unqualified, the weight and variety of such evidence could easily create a picture of the self-conscious Renaissance state, deliberate and skilled in the expression of its authority; such an impression would be misleading. Some projects, like the statue to Biordo Michelotti, were never realised. Expenditure on propaganda could be considerable and resented. The money lavished on the state visit of the duke of Milan to Florence in March 1471 angered many Florentines. Ceremonies themselves could be the occasion for acrimony, revealing divisions which the events were intended to heal or conceal. Alfonso I's triumphal entry into Naples offended some members of the aristocracy, while Ferdinando the Catholic's arrival in the city in 1506 provoked squabbles over precedence.

Moreover, the state had no monopoly of the means of propaganda; indeed, the dividing line between the exaltation of public authority and of the individual provoked dispute and caused anxiety. For example, Venice was apprehensive lest the ceremony attending the arrival and departure of its representatives in its subject cities might enhance their personal prestige rather than the republic's authority, and similar disquiet was aroused when Doge Francesco Foscari adopted the royal 'we' and Niccolò Marcello preferred gold to crimson on his state robes. The survival of local or private mints could circumscribe the authority of the state. In the 1460s the prince of Taranto exercised the privilege of a private mint at Lecce which produced coins bearing his own image, while in the Venetian state in the 1490s the principal subject cities were allowed to reintroduce their local patron saints to the coinage. And governments were not always able to control the enthusiasm of their supporters. In 1499 the inn of the Florentine ambassador in Lucca was smeared with excrement – an underrated form of political expression in Renaissance Italy – and a coffin was placed outside.

Lastly, it is appropriate to ask how widely noticed and understood the propaganda of governments and rulers was. *Imprese* were often intentionally ambiguous or difficult to decipher, and it is hard to believe that Alfonso I d'Este's (1505–34) device of a bombshell and the words 'Loco et Tempore' was appreciatively understood by the majority of his subjects to mean that the duke would choose the just moment to throw off restraint and explode into violence. On the other hand, not all devices were as inaccessible. In 1513 the Medici and their supporters adopted the *imprese* of the diamond and the reviving laurel branch to recall Lorenzo the Magnificent, who numbered the diamond and the laurel among his devices, and to signal the Medicean restoration.

But most convincing of all is the fact that opponents of the state and its representatives appreciated the power of propaganda and turned many of the proclamations of authority into expressions of dissent. The memory of the Sicilian Vespers of 1282 could be used to stir up sedition in Udine in 1511 and French-ruled Lombardy in 1516. The emblems, slogans and dress associated with the *Ciompi* kept alive their challenge to the order of Florentine society; the Venetian republic punished those who verbally insulted the state and its officials. If street theatre could be used in Florence by the Medici, it could be turned against them; scenes enacted outside their palaces in 1498 induced members of the family to flee the city.

Direct action could be an effective way of challenging the state and rallying support. On the flight of Innocent VII to Viterbo on 6 April 1405 the Vatican was sacked, its archives were pillaged and the papal arms destroyed or covered with filth. Indeed, the records and buildings of the state were favourite targets: the Visconti chancery and their castle at the Porta Giovia in Milan were attacked on the death of Filippo Maria in 1447. Dissent could also be expressed and broadcast in written form. On 14 December 1479 Cardinal Francesco Gonzaga reported that leaflets were scattered in Florence denouncing the tyranny of Lorenzo de' Medici, and in 1528 the walls of Lucca were festooned with placards attacking the city's tyrannical rulers. Angry *contadini* were the authors of subversive literature circulated in the Veronese in 1499. Better-placed dissidents were probably behind an allegorical picture found near the Rialto in 1505, depicting Venice as the Virgin, lamenting to St Mark the tyranny and dynasticism of the doge, Leonardo Loredan. Lastly, authorities did not have a monopoly of the symbols of justice. In January 1463 Paolo di Campofregoso, Archbishop of Genoa, had a gallows erected to hint to his cousin Lodovico that he should resign the dogeship. He did!

Whatever the authors and audiences, such propaganda was not produced in a vacuum; motives ranged from the desire of a community to proclaim its piety to the determination of a dynasty to demonstrate its accomplishments. The phenomenon should also be seen in the context of the growth of the state; much of the propaganda described above was designed to express its aims, authority and achievements. It should be read against a background of mounting demands on the resources and loyalty of subjects and citizens. However – as can be inferred from the evidence, and seen more clearly in the propaganda of protest and dissent – the state did not enjoy an uncontested initiative. Moreover, a closer examination of some of the principal areas of state intervention suggests that its demands could be the consequence of the challenges presented to it by both nature and man.

FAMINE AND DISEASE

Hunger and disease were probably the most severe and abiding threats posed to the society of Renaissance Italy. Both count as natural catastrophies but both, as contemporaries well realised, could be exacerbated by man, and particularly in wartime; the terrible conjunction of war, plague and famine was recognised as causing flight and heavy loss of life in Brindisi in 1528 and Barletta in 1529.[9] Of course the threats were far from new, but it is likely that the memory of the Black Death of 1347–48 and the impact of recurrent outbreaks of plague made society as a whole – and governments in particular – more aware of the need to recover from, or better still to prevent, such disasters.[10]

Throughout Italy, governments encouraged immigration. In part this can be explained in terms of a traditional concern to attract expertise in the persons of lawyers, doctors of medicine, skilled craftsmen and even teachers and students. But in this period, and above all in the late fourteenth century, the effort of many governments to attract manpower in general betrays an enhanced concern to maintain the population. Settlement in town and country was encouraged by tax concessions and reduced residence requirements for naturalisation or citizenship. Government intervention can also be seen in attempts to reduce or ward off the impact of food shortages. In this direction, efforts were prompted by the realisation that hunger could provoke social disorder; in 1383 Florence decided to keep the full extent of a food shortage a secret.

Administrative measures were taken to counter such threats. In Milan an *Ufficio di Provisione* was established; the optimistically named *Abbondanza* was set up in Rome in the mid-fifteenth century. Attempts were made to gather relevant information. In 1411 the commune of Verona conducted a survey of food production, while censuses in early-sixteenth-century Rome were in part designed to discover the likely level of food consumption. Efforts were made to encourage imports from friendly neighbouring states. The success of the Sienese grain office in this respect in 1456 found eloquent expression in a painting by Sano di Pietro (1406–81) showing the Madonna commending Siena to Pope Calixtus III as mule trains, carrying grain from the Papal States, make their way to the city.[11] Especially in time of famine governments intervened, preventing the export of grain, raising taxes and loans to buy food and trying to fix prices while preventing hoarding. In 1423 the Venetian government ordered its merchants trading in grain to bring their cargoes to the city, and in 1455 Venetian landowners were required to bring the yields from their mainland estates to Venice; more generally, tax incentives were used to stimulate imports.[12] More ambitiously, governments could try to encourage food production. The popes from Sixtus IV in 1476 tried to stimulate arable farming in the environs of Rome, even favouring small proprietors to check the preference of the larger landowners for stock-raising.

Governments were also aware of the dangers posed by plague and disease, and not only because of the severe disruption which they caused to society and the economy. To governments themselves the cost in terms of emergency payments to doctors, the suppliers of food and medicine and grave-diggers could be considerable, as Trent discovered in 1509 and as Siena had suggested poignantly by having the *Triumph of Death* painted on the covers of its account books in the plague year of 1437.[13] Moreover, plague outbreaks could be so severe that government could be suspended; this happened in Pisa in 1464 when a combination of malaria and plague prompted officials as well as private citizens to flee the city.

However, governments did not regard themselves as powerless, even if their efforts to preserve public health seem woefully inadequate and ill-conceived by modern standards. Rulers patronised medical experts: in the late fourteenth century Pietro da Tossignano dedicated an investigation into the plague to Giangaleazzo Visconti. Governments appointed public doctors to care for the sick, a practice well established in such larger centres as Venice by the late fourteenth century, but adopted by smaller cities in the course of the fifteenth.[14] Specialised magistracies were established to preserve public health; in Milan they seem to have been permanent from the early fifteenth century. Among the measures such officials attempted to enforce were those involved the banning of suspected plague-carriers; in 1382 the commune of Ferrara endeavoured in vain to stop the spread of plague into its territories.

Related were efforts to confine suspects, a famous early example being the *Lazzaretto* of Venice established in 1423, although other cities on trade routes like Milan and Trent were quick to adopt similar measures. Merchants were not the only mobile elements of the population to alarm the authorities in such circumstances. Venice in 1490 and Florence in 1504 tried to restrict the movement of prostitutes to check the spread of plague. A growing awareness of the importance of public hygiene can also be detected, if measures generally remained either too ambitious or too slight. A plague outbreak in Milan in 1484–5 prompted Leonardo da Vinci to advocate radical town planning to lessen the chances of infection – at least for the better-off. During an epidemic in Saluzzo in 1522 the marquis ordered the suspension of rice-farming in the *contado*.

Hospitals also received the attention of governments. In 1429 the commune of Palermo, with the encouragement of Alfonso I, decided to institute a single large hospital to replace a number of smaller and inadequate institutions – even if the commissioning of a large and vivid mural of the *Triumph of Death* cannot have encouraged a sense of physical well-being among its inmates.[15] Similarly in Milan in 1456 Francesco Sforza initiated the construction of the *Ospedale Maggiore*; in 1460, after gathering information on such longer-established hospitals as S. Maria della Scala in Siena, he approved the ambitious but careful design of the Florentine architect Antonio Averlino (Filarete).[16] Last – but by no means least – when confidence faltered in man's efforts to cope with such natural disasters, secular authorities joined in the invocation of divine mercy. In 1458 the council of the Viterbo commissioned an altarpiece of the *Madonna of Mercy* for its chapel, the councillors being portrayed gathered under the Virgin's protective mantle.

It would be a mistake, however, to draw on the evidence for government action in the face of natural disasters to give an exaggerated impression of the growing role and effectiveness of the state. Most obviously, such calamities were beyond the knowledge and resources of the governments of the day. Moreover, the efforts which were made can often be shown to be flawed in themselves, undermined by inefficiency and inconsistency. Papal policies to husband the food resources of the Roman hinterland did not prevent the granting of export licences. Harsh measures taken by officials in Cremona to deal with a severe famine in 1528 had such unanticipated consequences as the scaring-off of grain importers and the using up of the seed corn in the *contado*. When the commune of Bitonto appointed a public doctor in 1451 he was accorded tax immunity, a house and the right to quit the city in time of plague! Such crises could reveal the opportunism of individuals as well as narrowness of vision on the part of the state. The Este of Ferrara, like other signorial dynasties, profited from the urban market's dependence on the resources of their estates. The great Friulian noble Antonio Savorgnan built up a following in Udine in 1504 by posing as a champion of the poor against racketeers in the sale of flour, while in Venice in 1523 the doge Andrea Gritti celebrated his election by distributing wheat from his private granaries.

Nevertheless, the shortcomings and limitations of the state's actions have a positive side – however paradoxical that assertion may appear. Precise figures are not available, but it seems reasonably certain that the bulk of charity and relief was provided by the Church, confraternities, guilds and individuals, though often with the encouragement of the state. In Brescia in 1447 a central hospital was founded by the laity with the encouragement of the bishop and the Observantist orders of friars. The foundling hospital of the *Innocenti* of Florence, instituted in 1419, received the patronage of the guild of silk weavers, while in 1425 two lay confraternities combined to run more effectively the hospice of the Bigallo in the centre of the city. Charity, generally towards their own members, was among the functions of the flagellant confraternities in Florence and *scuole* in Venice. In Rome the hospital of S. Salvatore benefited from gifts of cash from the count of Anguillara in 1462 and property from Cardinal Stefano Nardini in 1483.[18] A fresco painted on the walls of the *Luogo Pio della Carità* of Milan in 1486 showed citizens distributing bread to the poor, while around 1520 the famous hospital of S. Maria del Ceppo in Pistoia commissioned a frieze in glazed terracotta depicting the seven acts of Corporal mercy.[19] In 1502 Christopher Columbus offered the commune of Genoa a tenth of his revenues from the New World to reduce the level of taxation on basic foodstuffs.[20]

WARFARE ON LAND[21]

From certain perspectives, it would appear inappropriate to discuss military matters in the context of the state. Throughout the period warfare was dominated by mercenary captains, *condottieri*, leaders of mercenary companies which were brought together and employed through a system of contracts, or *condotte*. To many historians in the nineteenth and twentieth centuries these armies appeared as unscrupulous and unreliable, fighting or avoiding battle to secure their own advantage, bereft of any sense of loyalty or obligation to their employers of the moment, in the eyes of whose subjects they appeared as rapacious foreigners. Their licence was in part the product of a weakness in society itself. Civilians no longer had the stomach or the training to fight for themselves. Knighthood and chivalry were a sham, and militia forces were low on commitment, equipment and training. The battles the *condottieri* fought on behalf of their employers were often little more than manoeuvres, inconclusive and bloodless, with the generals on both sides anxious to avoid losses and husbanding their resources for future advantage at the expense of other luckless and defenceless employers. Even historians who admired the *condottieri* tended to stress qualities of heroic individualism – verve, decisiveness, ruthlessness – rather than search for evidence of their usefulness as servants of the states of Italy.

However, this prevailingly negative assessment was firmly rooted in the period itself. Most especially in moments of defeat, contemporaries could be outspoken in their criticism of mercenary armies and their leaders, and the range of opinion included not only armchair strategists but experienced observers like Flavio Biordo (1392–1463), who had been chancellor of the papal captain Giovanni Vitelleschi in 1432, and Antonio Giacomini, a Florentine commissioner who had witnessed the failure of the republic's *condottieri* to retake the rebel city of Pisa in the early sixteenth century. An articulate tradition of military thinking runs through the period lamenting the lack of patriotic commitment which it was believed had inspired the armies of the Roman republic. By contrast, *condottieri* armies were condemned for their lack of discipline and reliability. They were accused of being more anxious to avoid a fight than to engage the enemy and of a lack of military professionalism; in these respects they were rated by their critics as inferior to other European armies, and battles like Agincourt stunned Italians with their ferocity and casualties.[22] Of all writers who took up these themes none was more influential than Machiavelli, whose views were in part shaped by his study of Roman history and in part by his own experience.[23] As a representative of the Florentine republic he negotiated with a number of mercenary captains, he was acutely aware of the disastrous campaigns undertaken to recapture Pisa (1495–1509) and he became a champion of a militia army as the answer to the republic's military needs.

It is, in fact, easy to light on incidents to give credence to the negative picture left by Machiavelli and endorsed by many later historians. In 1394 the mercenary captain and lord of Perugia, Biondo Michelotti, wrote to Siena with the news that his men were short of money and might turn their attention to the Sienese *contado* to remedy the situation; indeed, the records of Siena for the later fourteenth century are full of laments for the damage done to rural communities by the two 'plagues' of disease and mercenary soldiery. In 1450 Francesco Sforza, Duke of Milan and one of the leading soldiers of his day, was told that the dispatch of troops to prevent disorder round Alessandria was like sending wolves to guard sheep. To rid themselves of such ruthless men, governments could in turn be ruthless. In 1391 Andrea Tomacelli, brother of Boniface IX and rector of the March of Ancona, had the troublesome mercenary Boldrino da Panicale murdered at a banquet. In 1465 Ferrante I had the *condottiere* Giacomo Piccinino arrested, accused of treason and executed.[24]

However, to fasten on such melodramatic incidents and to follow the views of critics like Machiavelli too closely would be to misread the evidence and to produce an unbalanced picture. To illustrate this point from one famous incident, Machiavelli in his *History of Florence* described the Battle of Anghiari on 29 June 1440 between a Florentine-papal army and the troops of Filippo Maria Visconti as bloodless, yet it was hard-fought and left around three hundred dead. Between 1502 and 1503 Leonardo da Vinci was commissioned by the republic to paint a fresco of the battle for its council hall, a fact which indicates that Machiavelli's contemporaries could celebrate their military triumphs and applaud successful generals. Indeed, the Florentine republic, for all its rather dismal record in dealings with *condottieri* generals, was on occasion prepared to flatter them and celebrate their achievements. In 1436, Paolo Uccello was commissioned to paint a fresco for the cathedral to celebrate the achievements of Sir John Hawkwood, one of the city's more reliable and successful generals. The Medici commissioned the same artist in the 1450s to commemorate Niccolò da Tolentino's victory at San Romano in 1432. For all his earlier criticism of mercenary soldiers in his *De Militia* of 1421, Leonardo Bruni, as chancellor of Florence, delivered an oration in praise of the same Niccolò.[25] More celebrated still, in Italy as a whole, was Francesco Sforza, Duke of Milan from 1450, whose contemporary admirers were not drawn from his own retinue or dominions alone. Among the tributes was the *Sforziade* written by the court humanist Francesco Filelfo to celebrate his military career.

That there were two sides to the debate on the reputation of the *condottieri*, and that neither was free from exaggeration and rhetoric, serves to introduce the point that mercenary soldiers and their leaders were not alien beings inflicting themselves on Italian society. It is true that non-Italians fought in Italian armies. This was particularly the case in the later fourteenth century when a lull in the Hundred Years War had encouraged foreigners, among them the celebrated Hawkwood, to seek employment and fortunes in the rivalries of Italian politics. A century later, around 1485, Brunelleschi's biographer Antonio Manetti recorded that the sculptor's father served as a recruiting agent for the Florentine republic and noted that: 'in those times, and especially in Italy, soldiers from beyond the Alps were usually employed.' In the fifteenth century, the republic of Venice began to recruit large numbers of *stradiotti*, light cavalrymen from Dalmatia, Greece and Albania. With the Italian Wars, companies of Swiss, German and Spanish troops became increasingly employed. But for the most part mercenaries and their leaders were Italian, and foreigners only in the sense that Italy was a divided country.

That was also the case in the *Regno*. In 1444 or 1445 Borso d'Este, brother of the lord of Ferrara, advised Alfonso I to employ only Italian captains to defend his newly won kingdom,[26] and whether as a result of this advice or from independent political and military judgement Alfonso drew most of his troops from the Peninsula, and only a few from other Aragonese lands like Sicily and Sardinia.[27] Availability might have been another factor. A large proportion of Italian mercenaries and their leaders came from the poorer and more mountainous regions of the south, where the low rates of pay accorded to mercenary soldiers could still appear attractive and where lordship could still be measured in terms of castles and retinues. One such *condottiere* was Cola di Monforte, Count of Campobasso, who served the duke of Burgundy before entering Venetian pay from 1477 to 1478. The same is true for the Papal States where baronial families from the Roman Campagna, like the Orsini, and signorial dynasties from the Romagna, like the Malatesta, acted both as recruiting agents and as captains. Further north the Gonzaga of Mantua and the marquises of Monferrat represented the same phenomenon: lords who sought employment for their subjects and for themselves the prestige, revenues and political support coming from alliance and employment with greater powers. Furthermore, an analysis of one such *condottiere* company, that of Francesco Sforza's cousin Michelotto Attendolo from 1425 to 1448, reveals not an anarchic conglomeration of cosmopolitan looters but a well-organised, well-documented and remarkably stable force, largely of Italians and displaying considerable continuity.[28]

If *condottiere* companies were a much more intrinsic and stable element of society than their detractors would suggest, the civilian population was also much more familiar with warfare than was implied in the remark attributed to Hawkwood in an exchange with a Florentine commissioner: 'go and make cloth and let me manage the army'. After all, the attacks made by the likes of both Bruni and Machiavelli on mercenary armies reveal the pressing interest military matters had for contemporaries. Castiglione urged his courtier to be as familiar with the sword as with the pen, and if the author of *The Courtier* saw little active service himself, he came from a family of lesser *condottiere*.[29] An interest in military affairs is indicated by the number of treatises on the art of war, like those addressed to Ferrante I by Orso degli Orsini in 1477 and Diomede Carafa in 1478; neither man was an amateur, both had had active military careers. Familiarity with military matters can be demonstrated in other ways. Tournaments and other forms of military exercise, if often attracting pageantry and spectacle, are now seen to have been much more a part of Italian city life and to have been taken rather more seriously than used to be thought. For example, with the accession of Alfonso I the 'noble citizens' of Sulmona in the Abruzzo revived jousting with armour and lance.

Regular practice with the crossbow had long been part of Venetian life, and from 1490 the republic encouraged training and competitions with the arquebus to further familiarity with the new weapon. Nor had the feudal obligation to bear arms entirely disappeared. In Piedmont the feudal obligation of lords and communes remained the basis of the army of the house of Savoy, while castle-guard survived among the lordships of the Trentino. Finally, militia service was maintained and even developed as a duty facing the civilian population. True, measures taken in this direction were not always successful. The efforts of Machiavelli and others to give Florence a viable militia army met with some success in forcing the surrender of Pisa in 1509, but were too rushed and ill-directed to resist hardened Spanish infantry at the siege of Prato in 1512. In Venetian territory, however, the militia contingents, or *cernide*, received much more considered attention and achieved much greater success. Of course, they too suffered disasters. In 1452 four thousand Veronese militia were defeated with heavy losses by two hundred and fifty Mantuan cavalry, but in 1438 militia forces had defended Brescia against Filippo Maria Visconti's professionals. Later Turkish raids through Friuli galvanised the republic into improving the preparedness of local forces, and units of *cernide* under the command of the Friulian nobleman Antonio Savorgnan proved their worth for the republic between 1508 and 1511 against the Habsburgs.

But a growing familiarity with military affairs can also be detected in the way most of the principal states tried to manage the *condottiere* armies in their pay. By the start of the period, most governments had come to accept that there could be no viable alternative to hiring professional soldiers grouped in mercenary companies. With many *condottiere* captains being themselves rulers or aspiring to lordship, and with the majority of the soldiery being Italian, mercenary companies had become well and truly part of the landscape, and their employment by one state had meant their use by others. Moreover, as the principal states – and particularly those of the north – sought to expand and defend their frontiers from the late fourteenth century, the need for trained armies increased, to the point when soldiers were not only needed in a crisis but were required on a more permanent basis.

The consequences for the employing states were several and considerable. Companies at one time hired for no more than three months were, in the course of the fifteenth century, retained on a more permanent basis, with *condotte* of one or two years or even longer, and with defined wartime and peacetime strengths. In 1467 the duke of Milan offered Federigo da Monte-feltro, Lord of Urbino and one of the leading *condottieri* of the day, 60,000 ducats a year in peace and 80,000 ducats in war. In 1481 Ercole d'Este of Ferrara was retained at 50,000 ducats in peace and 80,000 ducats in war. To support this policy governments sought to flatter their more reliable and effective captains, rewarding them with titles, estates and desirable marriages. For example, Giangaleazzo Visconti Lord of Milan rewarded one of his most successful generals, the Veronese Giacomo dal Verme, with lordships in the Visconti state. His son Filippo Maria tried to win the loyalty of Francesco Sforza by allowing him to marry his daughter, Bianca Maria, in 1443, as well as by investing him with lordship of Cremona.

To carry out their policies, governments required experienced civilian commissioners to work with the *condottieri*, relaying instructions and watching over the interests of the state. They also needed administrators to hold musters and to supervise payments, billeting arrangements and the supply of fodder and provisions. Clearly the financial impact of increasingly perma-nent armies and a growing civilian administration were considerable, and represented the largest item on the budget of Italian states in the period. Moreover, costs rose, not so much due to a rise in the rates of pay, but rather because the size, as well as the permanence, of the forces increased, and the new artillery arm had a mounting impact on costs and organisation as well as on tactics. Related to the development of field and siege artillery was the growing employment of field fortifications, a tactic which was expensive in labour and required the drafting of pioneers.

These are general trends. Not all states were able or needed to follow these developments in full. As mentioned, the dukes of Savoy were still much dependent on the feudal obligations of their subjects, and their ability to hire mercenaries was linked to the cash payments made by their vassals in lieu of military service. In 1444 the paper strength of Alfonso I's army was over 20,000 men; its actual strength was only a quarter of that. The military strength of Venice was one of the most substantial and most highly organised in the Peninsula. The reasons do not lie only in the republic's relative wealth. Ruling a greatly enlarged territorial state in the fifteenth century, her lordship contested by the formidable duchy of Milan and her long frontiers crossed by some of the principal invasion routes into Italy, Venice was forced to strengthen her landward defences. The period sees a rapid growth of the size of Venetian armies to levels of around twenty thousand men in the early fifteenth century, and around forty thousand in 1509. These were maximum wartime strengths, and they included militia, but behind these exceptionally high figures was a peacetime strength of between eight and ten thousand professionals. The move towards a standing army can also be seen in the *condotte* between the republic and its captains. In the early fifteenth century, *condotte* were normally for three- or four-month periods with a clause giving the republic the option to renew the contract; by the 1440s the length of time had increased to one or two years or even longer, and *condotte* included clauses on peacetime strengths.

Related to these contractual developments was the republic's tendency to reward those *condottieri* who had proved their worth with bonus payments, with lands and lordships, with palaces and even with honorary Venetian nobility. In 1388 Giacomo dal Verme was rewarded with a palace in the city and membership of the nobility; later his lordships in the Veronese and Vicentino were confirmed and extended. Still more conspicuous was Venice's cultivation of Bartolomeo Colleoni, its commander-in-chief from 1454. The castle of Malpaga was the centre of a number of lordships granted to him in the Bergamasco, while the republic acceded to a request in his will that an equestrian statue in his memory be erected in a public place in Venice; from 1479 to 1488 Andrea Verrocchio worked on the bronze monument to the *condottiere* that dominates the square outside the church of Ss Giovanni e Paolo.

The republic's general aim was well articulated by the Senate in 1421 – 'it is always our policy to have good men available in both peace and war' – but these policies were also appreciated by the *condottieri* themselves. They looked for permanent employment, honours and security and they came to form a group of captains, nicknamed the *Marcheschi*, the followers of the banner of St Mark. Lastly, to manage the army, Venetian noble *provveditori* were elected for short terms of office, but often accumulated considerable experience of military affairs. On a more permanent basis were the *collatorali*, functionaries of lower status but of crucial importance who supervised such matters as billets and pay. In this respect the republic was particularly well served by a Vicentine noble, Belpetro Manelmi, who first appears as *collatorale* in Verona in 1416 but whose experience of – and influence on – military administration grew with the Venetian army until his death in 1455.

As has already been mentioned, however, the Venetian example is not typical and, as Michael Mallett has pointed out, Venetian practice and experience contrasted with that of Florence, a republic whose more agitated internal politics made her a less generous paymaster and a less considerate employer, wary of the dangers posed to civic life by military power. Florentine forces in both peace and war tended to be half the strength fielded by Venice. The Tuscan republic failed to build an atmosphere of trust with most of its captains, whose hire Florence often shared as part of an allied effort rather than employing them directly. A tradition of mistrust was created which tended to be self-perpetuating and affected both parties. In government circles this was fuelled by the yearning for an effective and patriotic militia. Among *condottieri*, the attitude did little to attract reliable soldiers to Florentine service or to inspire them when they drew the republic's pay; the decision taken in 1424 to have public portraits of Niccolò Piccinino and other unreliable *condottieri* painted hanging upside down can hardly have advanced good relations. Moreover, the hiring of *condottieri* and their supervision were conducted on a much more *ad hoc* basis than in Venice. The contrast emerges clearly around 1500. Florence was falteringly engaged in a protracted struggle to subdue Pisa, relying on *condottieri* she could not trust; Paolo Vitelli's lacklustre conduct of the siege was ended with his arrest and execution on 1 October 1499. Venice, on the other hand, could draw on a corps of captains who had served her through a number of campaigns and whose long service gave the republic's armies something of the 'national character' for which Machiavelli yearned as a key element in achieving military *virtù*.

While it is clear that the Italian states varied in the management of *condottiere* armies, it is also clear that the employment of mercenaries remained fraught with difficulties and that the most determined supervision had its limitations, and could break down badly in practice. Most obviously, even the most experienced and reliable of captains could not always guarantee military success. The generals Venice sent into action against the allies of the League of Cambrai were tried and tested men, but they lost the Battle of Agnadello on 14 May 1509, and with it virtually all the republic's mainland state. Moreover, even a judicious blend of control and flattery could not create loyalty. Alvise dal Verme, son of the much celebrated and rewarded Giacomo dal Verme, continued in Venetian service and favour until 1436, when the promises made by Filippo Maria Visconti and the prospect of a state of his own encouraged him to change sides. In 1509, after the disaster of Agnadello, Venetian militia forces were sent to guard the strongpoints of Padua and Treviso, revealing the republic's doubts as to the dependability of mercenaries to hold these last mainland cities against superior odds. In the following year the Venetian diarist Girolamo Priuli described *condottieri* in terms that would have pleased Machiavelli: as 'beastly men' who 'stood about scratching their bellies'.[30]

The general management of armies in terms of pay, supply, billeting and discipline was punctuated with abuses and disputes involving the *condottieri*, their civilian overseers and the local population. Belpetro Manelmi was hated by troops in Venetian pay for his strictness. Borso d'Este advised Alfonso I that Filippo Maria Visconti would prefer to unleash his *condottieri* on other states than keep them in billets and on the defensive because of the damage they would do. The damage inflicted by Colleoni's company in 1450 was such that the view was expressed in the Venetian Senate that he be asked to leave the republic's service since he contributed 'nothing to our state other than the complete desolation of its subjects', and in 1451 the Senate endorsed a Veronese arrangement to make rural communities not directly involved in the support of mercenary troops compensate those who were and who suffered. It is hardly surprising that in 1458 the Brescian commune of Palazzolo paid Colleone not to billet his men in its territory.[31]

From incidents such as these it seems clear that even the most determined of governments failed to master their mercenaries completely, and that Florentine distrust and Venetian care point to a shared and basic apprehensiveness. In the sixteenth century a Ferrarese chronicler, Giacomo Marano, chose to describe the raiding of Genoese troops in neutral Ferrarese territory in 1379 as 'the practice of soldiers who are paid to do evil'.[32] That attitude was widely and understandably shared throughout the period – except by the soldiers themselves, whose low rates of pay, often subjected to delays and stoppages for weapons and equipment, frequently lay at the root of these acts of 'evil'.

FORTIFICATIONS

Fortifications never became the total preserve of the state in the period, and in pronouncedly feudal areas like the Ferrarese men were still bound to pay for, work on and man their lords' castles, as well as looking to them for protection.[33] However, the aspiration of the state can be detected from the duchy of Milan to the kingdom of Sicily in the way governments attempted to license castle-building and tried to insist that private fortifications had to contribute to overall defence. More markedly, the aims of the state can be seen in the growing concern felt by governments to build, maintain and improve their own fortresses and town walls; this meant burdening their subjects with taxes and labour services, not only for construction and repair but also for the purchase and clearance of civilian property.[34]

The disturbed political condition of Italy was in itself enough to ensure that fortifications made heavy demands on state budgets. If in the fifteenth century Venice preferred on the whole to rely on the mobile and flexible defence offered by its armies and fleets, other governments poured money into the building or improvement of fortifications. From 1436, and for most of his reign, Alfonso I lavished resources on the defence of Gaeta, his bridgehead for the conquest of the *Regno*. In the following year Sigismondo Malatesta underlined his lordship in Rimini with the construction of the Castel Sismondo.

In Italy as a whole, however, conditions were to change and governments had to accept that defence would make heavier technological, financial and political demands. The Ottoman Turks posed a mounting threat. Their raids into north-eastern Italy forced Venice to undertake ambitious schemes along the Isonzo in the 1470s, and the heavy fortification of Gradisca in 1481. Further south, growing Ottoman naval strength and their capture of Otranto in 1481 stimulated the coastal defence of the *Regno* in the 1480s and 1490s, the castle of Monte Santangelo in the Gargano being a conspicuous example of the response to this 'scare'. From the 1490s a renewed impetus to fortify was created by the invasion of Italy by other European powers – above all by the French, who brought with them highly mobile, hard-hitting artillery.

As this suggests, technological developments centering round improvements in artillery were a further force for change. In the course of the fifteenth century, cannon not only became more manoeuvrable; with improvements in casting and the manufacture of gunpowder they increased their range, accuracy and destructive power. The changes worked on the conduct of siege warfare in turn stimulated developments in the design of fortifications, with architects finding a growing demand for their skills and ingenuity in military engineering as patrons and paymasters struggled to keep abreast of changes in theory and practice. A good example of the growing demand for military architects is provided by the Sienese Francesco di Giorgio Martini (1439–1502), who worked for the duke of Urbino, the Orsini and the kings of Naples, as well as for his native city. Some of his buildings – like the castle of Sassocorvaro built in the 1470s for the first of these, Federigo da Montefeltro – should probably be seen as exercises in ingenuity and innovation, similar to the intricate fortress designs found in his *Treatise* written in the 1490s, but a more impressively practical design executed in the same period for the same discerning patron can be seen in the castle of San Leo.[35]

The new practices in military engineering increasingly followed from the mid-fifteenth century and entailing heavy expenditure, whether in building from new or in modifying older structures, strove for 'ballistic shaping', designing defences to resist or deflect cannon fire. Walls and towers were lowered, thickened and scarped, and the defences were masked from enemy fire by a sloping area of ground, the *glacis*. The *glacis* also provided the defenders with a clear field of fire and points to another important development. The counterattacking quality of artillery was promoted by the construction of level platforms, and flanking fire was increased from round towers and then angled bastions. However, change was gradual. Most obviously, this was because of cost; the foundation stone of a new circuit of walls was laid in Naples on 3 July 1484, but the project took many years to complete. Moreover, the survival of earlier fortifications probably discouraged or postponed change and expense; the imperial walls of Rome, patched by successive popes, continued to serve as the city's principal defence. The period was one of transition, with siege artillery making no sudden, universal or revolutionary impact. Furthermore, due to its earlier lack of manoeuvrability, the initial contribution of artillery was probably to strengthen defence and so encourage the postponement of radical reconstruction.

Nevertheless, by the sixteenth century the combination of political and technological change was such that most states had embarked on ambitious building programmes. For example, the War of Cambrai (1509–17) persuaded even Venice to invest money and effort in the defence of such central mainland cities as Padua and Verona, and the need to protect her neutrality after that war led to what was tantamount to a sustained campaign to modernise the fortifications of her mainland and eastern dominions, as well as of the lagoons themselves. But the innovative work of architects of the calibre of the Veronese Michele Sanmicheli (1484–1559) and the fact that Renaissance Italy pioneered the style of fortress design followed down to the nineteenth century by the rest of Europe can too easily obscure the great difficulties all governments found in fully realising their plans and then maintaining, supplying and garrisoning the finished fortresses. Machiavelli aligned himself with a long tradition when he doubted the efficacy of fortresses. He voiced his scepticism by referring to Roman and contemporary examples. The governments of his day appreciated the problem on more mundane but nevertheless vital levels: those of the encroached-upon *glacis*, depleted stores and inadequate manning.

WAR AT SEA

The Italian states fully appreciated the value of sea power, even if their attempts to secure a command of the sea appear modest in the light of the naval thinking that has evolved since the eighteenth century.[36] With that appreciation went the belief that a naval command brought honour and the prospect of distinction and advancement. Venetian galley commanders paid for the decoration of their vessels and artists could be employed to commemorate naval events. Francesco Francia painted his *Minerva and Neptune* in 1512 to celebrate the appointment of the Genoese admiral Andrea Doria to defend the papacy against France.

Such attitudes are not surprising. In the cases of Genoa, the Aragonese empire and Venice, their economic well-being, their overseas possessions and their own defence had long been linked to their naval strength. Hence Alfonso I, after his acquisition of the *Regno*, expanded the dockyards of his capital and other cities and embarked on a programme of naval construction.[37] But perhaps the grasp of sea power can be most readily seen in Venice, where a long familiarity with the sea, combined with a continuity in government, produced an articulate and well-documented appreciation of naval strength. On a ceremonial level this can be seen in the annual *Sposalizio*, the Ascension

Day ritual when the doge cast a ring into the Adriatic – as a sign, not of dependence or partnership, but of lordship. Less flamboyant but equally clear statements can be found in the records of Venetian government. In 1400, the Senate recalled that 'our forefathers were always attentive to maritime affairs, knowing them to be the cause of the growth of our state and, above all, the means of holding it secure',[38] while in 1483 the council observed that 'the principal foundation of our state is our sea-going fleet'.

Such sentiments, however, would not have been incomprehensible to the more landlocked states, none of which was far from the sea and all of which realised the economic importance of seaborne trade. Lastly, it should be realised that the rivers and lakes of northern Italy, particularly of Lombardy and the Veneto, lent themselves to water transport and hence to amphibious warfare. The series of territorial wars beginning in 1426 between Venice and Filippo Maria Visconti witnessed intensive operations by river and lake squadrons, the Visconti fitting out fleets in such 'inland' cities as Pavia and Cremona. Some of these actions were spectacular. Drawing on Genoese expertise, a Visconti squadron destroyed a Venetian fleet on Lake Garda in 1439 – a fleet which had been dragged overland from the river Adige. In 1440 the Republic recaptured the lake with a replacement fleet of prefabricated vessels.[39]

As such engagements suggest, the cost of naval warfare was considerable.[40] Sailing ships and galleys were expensive to build and maintain. Venetian naval power rested to a great extent on her Arsenal, a walled-in area of dockyards, factories and warehouses which impressed contemporaries and which modern economic historians reckon to have been the largest concentration of labour in pre-industrial Europe.[41] Its workforce of *arsenalotti* were trained specialists, rewarded with houses within the Arsenal, relatively high wages and such privileges as acting as the ducal bodyguard. It produced expert galley-designers, like Leonardo Bressan in the late fifteenth century, and it is revealing that in 1500 the Turks took a captured Venetian vessel as a model for their own galleys

But war fleets were not only expensive to build and maintain; they were also expensive to run. Galleys in particular required large crews and a consequently heavy expenditure on food and wages; a standard Venetian light galley needed between one hundred and fifty and one hundred and sixty oarsmen as the basis for its crew. Moreover, the burden of naval warfare increased in the period. The reasons were partly political with the impact of the larger navies of the Ottoman Empire and the northern European powers being increasingly felt in the Mediterranean. They were also technological, with gunpowder having a growing influence on naval warfare and design from the fifteenth century. Symptomatic of these changes was the enlargement of the Venetian Arsenal in 1474 to allow the republic to build and maintain large fleets, and to develop the new skills connected with gunfounding.

The high costs involved had consequences for naval operations in particular and naval policies in general. Governments and commanders, through a mixture of choice and necessity, often tried to economise or delay in the distribution of pay and rations, making the recruitment and retention of crews difficult. True, there were some attractions to galley service. It could mean tax exemption or escape from debt and destitution; it could bring rewards in the form of booty and merchandise. Some commanders were scrupulous in matters of pay, rations and the division of spoils. But the general impression is that galley service was hard and dangerous, with crews often suffering as much at the hands of arrogant or niggardly commanders as from the weather and the enemy. Hence war fleets were often undermanned. Venetian squadrons generally left port seriously below strength, hoping to enlist Dalmatian oarsmen en route; in the fleet that confronted the Ottoman navy off the west coast of Greece in 1499 no more than a third of its manpower came from Venice, which probably had consequences for morale and discipline. To remedy the shortfall in voluntary enlistment the republic had recourse to conscription, demanding contingents from the guilds and confraternities of the city as well as from its subject communities. These measures, however, were of limited success. In 1413 the inhabitants of the Venetian colony of Negroponte fled to avoid galley service. Plans to recruit six thousand oarsmen from the Venetian mainland in 1522 had a poor response, and those who did turn out suffered badly from the weather and from their Dalmatian crew-mates.

As these expedients suggest, hard-pressed governments tried to spread the burden of naval expeditions, requiring their subjects to furnish warships. The towns of Sicily were expected to contribute to Aragonese naval forces, while Venice counted on contingents from its colonies in Istria, Dalmatia, the Aegean and Crete; in 1425 only eight vessels in a fleet of twenty came from Venice itself. Naval forces could rarely be kept for long on a war footing. Thus Calixtus III (1455–58) tried to build a papal navy to carry his crusade to the east. In 1455 an arsenal was established on the banks of the Tiber, its operations in part being paid for by the ornamentation stripped from the fine bindings of books in the Vatican Library.[42] This ambitious and costly programme was not continued under his successor, Pius II. Even Venice, the Italian state with the most consistent awareness of the value of sea power, scaled down her war fleets rapidly once a crisis had passed. In the years following the War of Chioggia with Genoa (1378–81) the republic's anxiety to recoup her past losses and minimise further ones resulted in a reduced naval force and a hesitant naval policy; the squadron to patrol the Adriatic had a theoretical strength of around ten and an operational strength of around five galleys. During the first French invasion of Italy, the republic's war fleet reached thirty-five galleys; by 1498, after the withdrawal of the French, the active fleet had been cut to thirteen units.

Lastly, the burdens imposed in the search for naval power were such that governments turned to their own greater subjects or to foreign fleets for assistance. Antonio Grimani, made Venetian captain general in April 1499, advanced 20,000 ducats for operations against the Turks, doubtless hoping that success at sea would advance his political career at home. One of the privileges of the grand admiral of Naples was to license privateering, while

Ferrante I turned to the wealthy merchant Francesco Coppola for ships to drive the Turks from Otranto in 1481, rewarding him with the title Count of Sarno. Indeed, the economic and political standing of some great lords enabled them to maintain private navies without government control while privateering, once encouraged, readily became unchecked piracy. The Sicilian nobleman Manfredo Chiaramonte, *de facto* lord of Palermo, was the moving spirit and force behind an international attack on the Barbary pirates in 1388. The piracy engendered round the coasts of Sardinia by the long conflict between Aragon and Genoa for the island became endemic.[43] But a more conspicuous and influential example of private navies can be seen in the case of Genoa itself, where naval power rested not with the commune but with great Genoese families who operated as sea *condottieri*, hiring their fleets to foreign powers as well as using them in the struggle to control the city of Genoa itself. No success story is clearer than that of Andrea Doria (1466–1560), who switched his naval services in 1528 from Francis I to Charles V, paving the way for his own ascendancy over the Genoese republic.

NOTES AND REFERENCES

1. P. J. Jones, 'Communes and despots: the city state in late medieval Italy', *T.R.H.S.*, ser. v, vol. xv (1965); L. Martinès, *Lawyers and Statecraft in Renaissance Florence* (Princeton, 1968), ch. 10; G. Chittolini, *La Formazione dello Stato Regionale e le Istituzioni del Contado* (Turin, 1979); A. I. Pini, 'Dal comune città-stato al comune ente amministrativo', in *Storia d'Italia* (U.T.E.T.), vol. iv (Turin, 1981); J. E. Law, 'Verona and the Venetian state in the fifteenth century', *Bulletin Inst. Hist. Research*, vol. lii (1979).

2. Cited by J. R. Strayer in *Comparative Studies in Society and History*, vol. vi (1963–64). pp. 321–4.

3. M. del Treppo, 'La "Corona d'Aragona" e il Mediterraneo', *Atti del IX Congresso di Storia della Corona de Aragon*, vol. i (Naples, 1978), pp. 330–31.

4. R. Filangieri, *Una Cronaca Napoletana Figurata del Quattrocento* (Naples, 1956); R. Trexler, *The Libro Cerimoniale of the Florentine Republic* (Florence, 1978); idem, 'The Florentine Theatre', *Forum Italicum*, vol. iv (1980); B. Mitchell, *Italian Civic Pageantry in the High Renaissance: a descriptive bibliography* (Florence, 1978); idem, 'The triumphal entry', *Forum Italicum*, vol. xiv (1980). Trexler's *Public Life in Renaissance Florence* (New York, 1980) is an imaginative and detailed study of ritual and ceremony, if it is often the case that more layers of meaning are suggested than the evidence can support.

5. E. Muir, *Civic Ritual in Renaissance Venice* (Princeton, 1981).

6. S. Y. Edgerton, 'Icons of justice', *Past and Present*, no. lxxxix (1980). Edgerton has expanded his ideas and evidence in *Pictures and Punishment. Art and Criminal Prosecution during the Florentine Renaissance* (New York and London, 1985).

7. N. Rubinstein, 'Political ideas in Sienese art', *J.W.C.I.*, vol. xxi (1958); E. C. Southard, 'The frescoes in Siena's *Palazzo Pubblico*', (New York, 1979).

8. E. Callmann, 'The triumphal entry into Naples of Alfonso I', *Apollo*, vol. cix (1979), and below.

9. V. Vitale, 'L'impresa di Puglia', *N.A.V.*, vol. xiii (1907), pp. 19–20; vol. xiv (1907), p. 185.

10. J. N. Biraben, *Les Hommes et la Peste*, 2 vols (Paris, 1975–76).

11. N. Guglielmi, 'Le groupe cathédral dans le paysage urbain en Italie', *J. of Medieval Hist.*, vol. vi (1980), p. 88; P. Brezzi, 'Il sistema agrario nel territorio romano', *Studi Romani*, vol. xxv (1977): D. Herlihy and C. Klapisch-Zuber, *Tuscans and their Families* (New Haven and London, 1985), pp. 261–2.

12. L. del Pane, 'La politica annonaria di Venezia', *Giornale degli economisti e annali di economia*, n.s., vol. v (1946).

13. L. Cesarini Sforza, 'A Trento nei primordi della Lega di Cambrai', *Archivio Veneto-Tridentino*, vol. xvii (1935).

14. B. Pullan, *Rich and Poor in Renaissance Venice* (Oxford, 1971), esp. pt ii; Comune di Venezia, *Venezia e la Peste* (Venice, 1979).

15. F. Bologna, *Napoli e le Rotte Mediterranee della Pittura* (Naples, 1977), pp. 12–14.

16. L. Grassi, 'Note sull'architettura del ducato sforzesco', in *Gli Sforza a Milano e in Lombardia* (Milan, 1982); F. Leverotti, 'Ricerche sulle origini dell'Ospedale Maggiore di Milano', *A.S.L.*, ser. 11, vol. vi (1981); 'L'Ospedale senese di S. Maria della Scala', *Bulletino Senese di Stor. Pat.*, vol. (1984).

17. H. Saalman, *The Bigallo* (New York, 1969).

18. P. Partner, *Renaissance Rome* (Berkeley–Los Angeles–London, 1979), pp. 104–9.

19. L. Vertova, 'A dismembered altarpiece', *B.M.*, vol. cxi, no. 791 (1969). The Pistoian hospital founded around 1277 became the richest religious corporation in the city by the fifteenth century. The frieze was largely the work of the Florentine della Robbia workshop: B. Pullan, op. cit., p. 201; F. Gurrieri, *Il Fregio Robbiano dell'Ospedale di Pistoia* (Pistoia, 1985).

20. H. Sieveking, 'Studio sulle finanze genovesi nel Medio Evo', *Atti della Soc. Ligure di Stor. Pat.*, vol. xxxv (1905–06), p. 176.

21. Crucial for this subject are: M. E. Mallett, 'Venice and its *condottieri*', in J. R. Hale (ed.), *Renaissance Venice* (London, 1973); *Mercenaries and their Masters* (London, 1974); 'Preparations for war in Florence and Venice', in S. Bertelli (ed.), *Florence and Venice*, vol. i (Florence, 1979); 'L'Esercito Veneziano in terraferma nel quattrocento', in *Armi e Cultura nel Bresciano* (Brescia, 1981); M. E. Mallett and J. R. Hale, *The Military Organization of a Renaissance State* (Cambridge, 1984).

22. G. Zancaruolo, *Cronaca Veneta*, Biblioteca Nazionale della Marciana, cl. VII It 1275 (9275), f. 484v; R. Walsh, 'Vespasiano da Bisticci, Francesco Bertini and Charles the Bold', *European Studies Rev.*, vol. x (1980).

23. J. Larner, 'Cesare Borgia, Machiavelli and the Romagnol militia', *Studi Romagnoli*, vol. xvii (1966).

24. F. Cusin, 'Le aspirazioni straniere sul ducato di Milano', *A.S.L.*, n.s., vol. i (1936), pp. 295–6; G. Franceschini, 'Biordo Michelotti e la dedizione di Perugia al duca di Milano', *Boll. della Deputazione di Stor. Pat. per l'Umbria*, vol. xlv (1948), p. 103; P. Partner, *The Lands of St Peter* (London, 1972), p. 376.

25. C. Bayley, *War and Society in Renaissance Florence* (Toronto, 1961).

26. C. Foucard, 'Proposta fatta dalla corte estense ad Alfonso I', *A.S.P.N.*, vol. iv (1879), p. 717.

27. A. Ryder, *The Kingdom of Naples under Alfonso the Magnanimous* (Oxford, 1976), ch. viii.

28. M. del Treppo, 'Gli aspetti organizzativi economici e sociali di una compagnia di ventura italiana', *R.S.I.*, vol. lxxxv (1973).

29. J. R. Hale, 'Castiglione's military career', *Italian Studies*, vol. xxxvi (1981).

30. R. Finlay, *Politics in Renaissance Venice* (London, 1980), p. 131.

31. J. E. Law, *The Commune of Verona under Venetian Rule* (D. Phil. thesis, University of Oxford, 1974), pp. 278–89; C. H. Clough, 'Per una storia civile di un comune minore nel pieno rinascimento: Palazzolo sull'Oglio', *Memorie Illustri di Palazzolo sull'Oglio (1968)*, pp. 25–6.

32. *Principio et Origine della Città di Ferrara*, Biblioteca Civica Ariostea, Ferrara, cl. I, no. 534, vol. ii, f. 153r–v.

33. E. V. Bernadskaja, 'La questione dei tributi imposti ai contadini dell'Italia settentrionale nei sec. xv e xvi', *Studi in Onore di A. Sapori*, vol. ii (Milan, 1957).

34. L. Beltrami, 'Un disegno originale del progetto delle fortificazioni di Milano', *A.S.L.*, ser. ii, vol. vii (1890).

35. J. R. Hale, *Renaissance Fortification: Art or Engineering* (London, 1977); idem, *Renaissance War Studies* (London, 1983); I. Hogg, *The History of Fortification* (London, 1981), pp. 68–75, 96–121; G. Volpe, *Rocche e Fortificazioni del Ducato di Urbino* (Fossombrone, 1982).

36. Sea power is a relatively neglected subject, but see: C. Manfroni, *Storia della Marina Italiana*, vols ii and iii (reprinted, Milan, 1970); J. F. Guilmartin, *Guns and Galleys* (Cambridge, 1974); above all F. C. Lane, 'Naval actions and fleet organization, 1499–1502', in *Renaissance Venice*, op. cit.; 'Venetian seamen in the nautical revolution of the Middle Ages', in A. Pertusi (ed.), *Venezia e il Levante*, vol. i (Florence, 1973); 'Wages and recruitment of Venetian galeotti, 1470–1580', *S.V.*, n.s., vol. vi (1982).

37. Ryder, op. cit., ch. x.

38. C. Manfroni, 'La battaglia di Gallipoli', *Ateneo Veneto*, vol. xxv (1902); C. Massa, *Venezia e Gallipoli* (Trani, 1902), pp. 12–13.

39. Mallett, *Mercenaries*, pp. 172–6.

40. J. R. Hale, 'Men and weapons: the fighting potential of sixteenth century Venetian galleys', *War and Society; a Yearbook of Military History*, ed. B. Bond and I. Roy (London, 1975).

41. R. Romano, 'Economic aspects of the construction of warships in Venice in the sixteenth century', in B. Pullan (ed.), *Crisis and Change in the Venetian Economy* (London, 1968).

42. P. Paschini, 'La Flotta di Calisto III', *A.S.R.S.P.*, vols. liii–liv (1930–32).

43. E. Putzulu, 'Pirati e corsari nei mari della Sardegna', *IV Congreso de Historia de la Corona de Aragón*, vol. i (Palma, 1959).

CHAPTER SIX

The state: finance and administration

PUBLIC FINANCE

The costs facing governments were both considerable and growing, with military expenditure forming the largest and most inflationary item on the budgets of Italian states. For example, the Florentine public debt rose from $\frac{1}{2}$ million florins in 1345, to 3 million florins in 1395, to 4 million florins in 1433, largely as a consequence of wars of expansion and defence. During the War of Chioggia the Venetian public debt rose from 3 million to 5 million ducats and the market value of its shares plunged; in 1512, during the War of Cambrai, Venetian military expenditure went from 60,000 ducats a month to a record of 84,000 ducats a month.

Hence the subject of public finance is central to the study of the state, a claim endorsed by the fact that the collection and expenditure of revenue generated much of the material found in the archives of Italian states. Of this probably the best-known and most thoroughly studied example is the Florentine *catasto*, or assessment, of 1427–30. Born out of a deepening political and financial crisis accelerated by war with Milan, the *catasto* survey of the city, its *contado* and the Florentine dominions was copied from Venetian practice and based on previous fiscal records as well as on a careful up-to-date assessment. Described by its most recent historians as a 'monument' to Florentine determination and financial skill, its compilation bears out Burckhardt's favourable impression of the republic's appreciation of statistical information – now frighteningly referred to as 'raw data'. But other governments shared an awareness of the need to monitor and increase their revenues, if their efforts do not appear to be so well documented. In 1477 Sixtus IV instituted the first of a series of budgetary reviews. In 1517 conscientious and long-suffering Belgian Charles Leclerc was dispatched to the *Regno* to investigate the collection – and loss – of revenue for Charles V.[1]

However, if the demand for revenue grew, and along with it a concern for more regular and precise information, the principal sources available to governments had been established earlier in the Middle Ages. Some derived from particular properties, rights and monopolies claimed by the state. From

Piedmont to Sicily Jewish communities were liable to special taxes. The property of rebels passed to the state; when Francesco Sforza took the duchy of Milan he confiscated the assets of his political opponents. Governments commonly exercised the right to license the exploitation of mineral resources, and of these the one which affected most Italians was the state's monopoly of the production and sale of salt. For example, the Aragonese rulers of Naples exercised the right to insist that their subjects collect a minimum quota of salt each year at a fixed price. The crown also claimed the right to license the movement of sheep and cattle, the transhumance traffic from summer pasture in the Abruzzo and Apennines to southern winter grazing in Puglia. From 1443 Alfonso I placed the Aragonese Francesco Monlober in charge of rescuing this regalian right from the usurpations of communes and feudatories; based on the royal city of Foggia, Monlober made this form of revenue one of the most important, and disliked, in the kingdom.[2]

Further north the papacy also licensed and drew profit from transhumance, while one of the most valuable of its monopolies were the mines at Tolfa where alum – a mineral used in the dying of cloth – was discovered in 1462. As is discussed elsewhere, the value of the papacy's temporal lordship over the lands of St Peter increased as its spiritual revenues from Christendom as a whole declined; long before the windfall discovery of alum the papacy claimed a census, or tribute, from subject communes and *signori*; from those areas more directly subject to its authority, like the commune of Rome, the papacy drew on such substantial and less nominal sources of income as taxes on the movement, processing and sale of goods.

Indirect taxes probably represented the largest item among the 'ordinary' revenues collected by Italian states with the great commercial city of Venice, in years of peace, drawing over 1 million ducats a year from such sources, a high level of return which gave strength and resilience to the republic's public finance well into the sixteenth century. But the return from indirect taxation declined sharply when it was most needed, in times of war, plague and famine; Italian governments had recourse to other forms of revenue which had once been regarded as 'extraordinary' but which had become an integral part of government finance by the start of the period. The most widely favoured was direct taxation, which in the signorial states of northern and central Italy was imposed on the subject population, while in the feudal principalities like Piedmont and the southern and island monarchies the procedure of consultation through parliament was still observed. Before parliament some levies of direct taxation were justified by the lord's right to traditional feudal aid; more frequently emergency and the defence of the realm were cited. For example, Alfonso I asked his subjects for aid to cover the expenses of his coronation and the marriage of his children as well as for a direct hearth tax. In 1500 the parliament of Sardinia voted Ferdinand a *donativo* of 45,000 lire over three years, and an aid to cover the marriage of his daughter Joan.[3]

No such consultation was followed by the central and northern signorial states, nor by the republics of Florence and Venice when they imposed direct taxation on their subject cities. In the case of their own citizens, however, both republics preferred the imposition of forced loans – called *prestanze* in Florence and *imprestiti* in Venice – to direct taxation, believing that the high yield from indirect taxation and subject communities would allow interest payments to be met, if the principal could no longer be paid off. Moreover, as shares in the public debt were negotiable in both republics, this method of public finance appealed at least to the wealthier among the state's creditors, who could regard their holdings as secure if modest investments. In Florence in the 1430s shares in the funded debt, the *Monte Comune*, traded at between 25 and 30 per cent of their face value and paid interest of between 3 and 8 per cent; the interest rate of the Venetian *Monte Nuovo* was fixed at 5 per cent in the late fifteenth century. But even the less well-off could have interests to protect; one of the reasons the extremists among the Florentine *Ciompi* lost popular support was their threat to the public debt and the interest payments on *prestanze*.

The range of basic resources available to governments, along with the increasing efforts made to monitor and maximise them, might suggest that the history of public finance confirms the growing authority of the state in the period, especially since the general trend of the tax burden was upwards. However, that is not the case. In the first place the state was unable to control all forms of revenue and sources of taxation. In periods of political confusion its control was weakened or lost. When Ferdinand I of Aragon began the reconquest of Sardinia in 1412 the crown collected no revenue from the island; royal lands had been usurped along with the income from mines and the sale of salt. It took three years for the crown to identify the sources of income to which it was entitled, and although royal revenue on the island would cover expenditure in peacetime and when carefully administered, it never made a substantial contribution to the Aragonese exchequer. Alfonso I found similar difficulties after his conquest of the *Regno*, with trade passing through ports held by his feudatories and so avoiding royal customs, and with salt pans and ironworkings in baronial hands; mindful of the political risks involved, the king did not attempt to recover all the lost lands and rights.

Even in more settled conditions revenue was lost through contraband. Venetian attempts to route trade from its mainland cities through the capital to the benefit of its customs were evaded on a large scale, as were attempts by the Neapolitan crown to direct commerce through designated *passi*, or crossings, on its long land frontier. In common with other states, neither government had the resources to patrol its boundaries closely. Lastly, some sources of revenue remained outside the public domain or outside the control of central government. Private tolls remained, even in areas like the Veneto where public authority might be expected to have eliminated them. Alfonso's acceptance of the gains made by his feudatories has been mentioned; on 8 January 1446 the tax on Jewish communities in the duchy of Calabria was granted in fief. Within the larger states, subject communes enjoyed varying degrees of fiscal autonomy. For example in papal territory, if Viterbo was subject to more direct rule, the larger and more distant communes of Ancona and Bologna had greater control over their financial affairs. Finally, in all the

Italian states the question of immunities remained, with spasms of investigation and vigilance being followed by bouts of generosity and acceptance.

If the states of Italy did not have a monopoly of all forms of revenue, neither did they achieve a strict control over the sources available to them. The amount of business devoted to the collection and allocation of resources, the paperwork generated by surveys like the Florentine *catasto*, can create an exaggerated impression of the state's competence and efficiency. Tax collectors could fail to keep accounts, increasing the difficulties experienced gathering revenue and pursuing debts, as the commune of Verona discovered in 1425 when proclamations had to be made reminding collectors of their duty to submit accounts. As this suggests, the administration of public revenues was open to corruption.[4] In 1447 Francesco d'Aquino, Grand Chamberlain of the *Regno*, was found guilty of maladministration and of not paying the hearth tax, and was forced to resign. One of the reasons for the unpopularity of Piero Soderini, *gonfaloniere* of Florence between 1502 and 1512, was his attack on abuses in the financial administration. In 1524 the Venetian Council of Ten ordered the public mutilation of a dishonest collector of the valuable wine tax. Moreover, the budgets of all Italian states were characterised by what has been called 'expediency financing'. Proposals of 1449 to centralise the revenue and expenditure of the house of Savoy were rejected by the dukes as too radical. Even in the relatively efficient Venetian state budgets were not carried out on a regular basis, and sources of revenue were allocated to items of expenditure in *ad hoc* fashion.[5] The assessment of taxation was rarely carried out with sufficient regularity to ensure accuracy and efficiency; on Sardinia in the sixteenth century taxation was being raised on the basis of an assessment of 1485. The monumental Florentine *catasto* of 1427, like the Domesday Book of 1086, has been used more by historians than it was by contemporaries. It was a remarkable one-off effort, a point of reference which was neither completed nor repeated.

Furthermore, governments were short-changed through the practice of tax farming. This was adopted as the normal means of collection, especially for indirect taxation and the salt monopoly, partly to save on manpower but, more important, to secure ready cash for the state. Taxes were usually auctioned on a short-term basis, the highest bidder making a down payment to the needy government and then paying the balance by instalments. For example, in 1445 Alfonso I farmed out the tax on the export of grain and foodstuffs from Puglia for 20,000 ducats over a twenty-eight-month period, but with a down payment of 10,000 ducats. Many of the customs officials of the *Regno* were in fact the crown's creditors. By 1525 the principal sources of papal revenue were in the hands of Roman and Tuscan bankers. The weakness of the system lay in the fact that in poor years the fetching price would fall, or bidders would not come forward at all; in good years the state could not enjoy the full potential of the tax; in all conditions tax farmers were liable to fall behind with their payments. The state also lost direct control, finding it hard to check favouritism and extortion. But despite such drawbacks the search for cash and credit could force the state to surrender taxes for a large number of years, even in perpetuity. Of this perhaps the most striking and institutionalised example is provided by Genoa, where most sources of revenue were given over to the commune's creditors organised in the Bank of St George.[6]

/These do not exhaust the difficulties the state faced in the collection of revenue. In his *Della Famiglia* Alberti might have paid tribute to the idea of the wealthy citizen contributing to the well-being of the state, but taxation was rarely paid with a will and obstruction and delay were standard in its assessment and collection. The Venetian government had on frequent occasions to cajole its subject cities into meeting their fiscal obligations, pleading with the 'limbs' to help the 'head', but the republic was unable to dismiss persistent Veronese complaints that warfare had so damaged the economy that the city was deserving of tax reductions; the level of direct taxation was reduced from 18,000 ducats a year in 1438 to 6,000 ducats a year in 1449.[7] Requests for revenue in the Aragonese kingdoms were met with delay. When the viceroy of Sardinia asked parliament for a *donativo* in 1481, negotiations over the grant were protracted. The estates wanted to secure favourable responses to their petitions. The urban representatives were unsure of their mandates; parliament moved its location on the island, and even attended the king in Castile.[8] Disputes were frequently protracted over the share of the tax burden to be met by the clergy, the city and the *contado*, as were arguments over the level of the tax threshold. For example, in Verona dispute over the definition of poverty lasted from 1439 to 1443 and revealed the difficulties both of collecting revenue and of achieving an accurate and equitable assessment.[9] Foreign residents and property-owners represented a constant difficulty for tax collectors and fruitful grounds for grievance from taxpayers, as did citizens with *contado* properties and wealthy immigrants from the *contado* to the city.

Of course, complaints at the imposition of taxation could be of a ritualistic nature. But indebtedness exacerbated by taxation could also debar Florentine guildsmen and members of the Venetian nobility from public office, while the evidence from Tuscany and the Veneto reveals how the tax burden could compound the misery of the poor, especially in the *contado*. The imposition of direct taxation by Venice on its subject cities was followed in the 1420s by the institution of official pawnshops to enable the poorer members of the urban and rural communities to find the ready cash to meet their tax bill.[10] It is hardly surprising, therefore, that resentment and hardship could threaten or explode in violence. In Ferrara in 1385, after an increase in the level of indirect taxation and the introduction of a more exacting *estimo*, the fiscal records of the government and the officials responsible were savagely attacked. Immediately after the murder of Galeazzo Maria Sforza in 1476 the level of taxation was reduced, while the authority of Lodovico Maria Sforza was undermined by the rumour that the subjects of the king of France paid taxation only if they had agreed to do so.[11] In 1522 the opponents to Charles V's tax demands attended the parliament at Messina armed.

It is therefore clear why the imposition and collection of revenue were among the greater burdens facing Italian governments, and it is unlikely that contemporary Tuscans would have said that the '*catasto* scans the land like the rays of a summer sun'; the city of Volterra resisted its inclusion in the survey until 1430.[12] It is true that Commynes was astonished at the apparent readiness with which the Venetians paid their taxes, and the duke of Ferrara's betrayal of Venetian interests in 1495 was so unpopular in the city that its taxpayers were prepared to pay extra to finance an attack on the duchy.[13] But these impressions and outbursts should be taken as exceptional; probably more typical is the attitude of the Venetian merchant Martino Merlini during the War of Cambrai: he reconciled patriotism with a determination to avoid paying taxes.[14]

Moreover, if all governments hoped for a surplus from the more ordinary sources of income to cover the costs of administration, to support the court and its expensive marriage alliances or to service the public debt, the political, military and financial circumstances rarely allowed them this comparative luxury. Finally, the moral as well as the technical and political difficulties of tax collection could be acknowledged. At war with Naples in 1409, the Florentine government asked itself how long it would be forced 'to take bread from the mouths of widows, orphans and impoverished persons'. Venetian nobles returned from office in the republic's dominions could be critical of the government's fiscal policies; in 1425 Giorgio Corner, ex-*podestà* of Padua, unsuccessfully urged the Senate to remove the burden of direct taxation from the city. In 1446 Filippo Maria Visconti agonised over the impositions he had placed on his subjects and sought justification for his actions. Lodovico Maria Sforza told Ferrante I of Naples that it was 'better to have one *carlino* and the love of your subjects than 10 *carlini* and their hatred'. Although he gave similar advice to Alfonso II, when Lodovico himself was driven into exile by the French he protested that he had reduced the burden on his subjects and had raised taxation only to defend the duchy.[15]

But the difficulties of tax collection can be seen even more clearly in the expedients to which governments had recourse to meet their pressing needs for ready cash and further credit. The pawning of jewellery was regularly resorted to. In 1409 Pandolfo Malatesta pawned jewels in Bologna; Lodovico of Savoy and Lodovico Maria Sforza pawned jewellery in Venice in 1462 and 1495 respectively. In the War of Cambrai Venice itself pledged jewels from the treasury of San Marco to the Sienese banker Agostino Chigi.[16] In the Renaissance, as now, education could suffer in the scramble for revenue. In 1433 Eugenius IV cut into the budget of the University of Rome to meet defence costs, and the Florentine *studio* suffered in the same way in 1452. Salaries were another casualty of military expenditure. For example, once Venice had taxed the salaries of its officials in 1434, the policy resurfaced as an 'expedient' with increasing regularity in the form of a cut, a suspension or a tax. Offices could be exploited in other ways to raise revenue. By 1521 the papal administration included over two thousand venal offices, representing a capital of $2\frac{1}{2}$ million florins and an annual interest payment, in the form of salaries, of 300,000 florins. Governments also borrowed money from their subjects and from foreign bankers. The lavish lifestyle and gambling of Ferrante Duke of Calabria forced him to pawn jewels with Catalan and Neapolitan bankers; his father had pawned his crown in 1443. Alfonso also granted office, titles and immunities to bankers like Giovanni Miroballo of Naples, while in 1461 Lodovico of Savoy settled debts with his chancellor Antonio di Romagnano in a similar fashion.[17]

Even in Venice and Florence, where public borrowing was a central part of state finance, the government had recourse to short-term, high-interest loans from wealthy citizens. The political ascendancy of Cosimo de' Medici was partly based on the large sums he had advanced; according to Guicciardini, Cosimo and Averardo de' Medici claimed that 'the only time when one could become great was during war, by providing for the military needs of the city, lending money to the commune.'[18] In an attempt to find a more permanent and manageable source of finance, the Florentine commune instituted the *Monte delle Doti*, or Dowry Fund, in 1425.[19] Fathers were invited to invest sums which would enable them to afford appropriate dowries for their daughters. After a slow start, the fund became a popular form of investment for the wealthier citizen, preying as it did on a common anxiety; by 1470 the annual interest owed by the *Monte* accounted for over half the commune's revenues. For its continuing success the fund depended on the death rate and celibacy of Florentine girls and the confidence of its creditors. The latter was challenged as early as the 1430s when payments became delayed and were made in instalments; by 1478 payments were so far in arrears that they were made only in part. The fact that the fund continued to attract investment is an indication of the close identity between the state's creditors and its governors.

A similar situation prevailed in Venice, where the government also struggled to keep faith with its creditors, most of whom were members of the nobility. Interest payments were suspended during the War of Chioggia (1380–81), but then resumed and the size of the public debt reduced. But that policy could not be sustained; the republic was increasingly unable to meet in full both the interest on its debts and the demands of war. Thus in 1482 a *Monte Nuovo* was set up which paid 5 per cent interest until the crisis of 1509, when the bonds were redeemed at a low market value and a new fund was established, the *Monte Nuovissimo*. Such moves tried the patience and hit the pockets of Venetians like the banker and diarist Priuli, who was left with his 'hands full of flies'.[20]

Priuli also recorded that many believed that 'when the *Monte Nuovo* was ruined, so too was the city of Venice'. Earlier, in Florence, the importance of the *Monte Comune* was signalled by its description as 'the heart of this body which we call the city'. Both cities displayed considerable financial ingenuity and economic resilience, but in both the return and market value of shares declined, largely under pressure from war finance. At moments of severe crisis interest payments were interfered with and new funds were established, and both cities reluctantly came to accept the need to tax their own citizens directly: Venice from 1439 and Florence from 1495.

POLITICAL ECONOMY

According to the Venetian diarist and historian Marino Sanudo (1466–1536), Doge Tommaso Mocenigo addressed members of the Senate in April 1423, opposing further conquests on the Italian mainland and urging them not to elect the expansionist Francesco Foscari as his successor. Doubt has been cast on the authenticity of the speech attributed to the doge but historians have upheld the accuracy of one of its central elements, a survey of the Venetian economy which includes information on the direction and balance of Venetian trade and on the number and output of its industries.[21] Burckhardt was impressed by this document, and even if its historical context may be open to doubt it helps to show how the mounting demands of war finance and the problems of taxation made Italian governments more acutely aware of the importance of economic prosperity. This perception was far from new, but if the response was rarely as imaginative or heroic as during the 'commercial revolution' from the eleventh to thirteenth centuries, it was heightened by the economic difficulties deepened by the Black Death and successive plague outbreaks. One response has already been mentioned. Italian governments were anxious to encourage immigration. In the fifteenth century Florence introduced tax concessions to encourage settlement in its subject communes of Pisa and Pescia. The policy was so successful that later in the century the commune began to tax and discourage immigration, at least by the less qualified. In the course of the century Siena also moved from all-out encouragement to selective discouragement.[22]

Governments also tried to defend home industries against foreign competition. In the late fourteenth century Florence erected tariff barriers against cloth imports and in the fifteenth did little to encourage the rival woollen industry of Pisa. In the course of that century Venice repeatedly legislated to protect its silk industry from foreign competition, both in its subject territories and in the city itself.[23] A more positive aspect to the same policy can be seen in the way the Sforza could use court expenditure to boost local manufactures.[24] But protectionism did not necessarily mean the exclusion or discouragement of foreign merchants. Ferrante I was ready to encourage them to settle in Naples; good relations with that monarch helped the exiled members of the Florentine Strozzi family to rebuild their fortunes.[25] The Sforza tried to win German importers away from Venice, where their activities were both encouraged and controlled through the *Fondaco dei Tedeschi*, the depot for central and east European merchants adjacent to the Rialto, the commercial heart of the city. On the other hand, there was a readiness to advance the interests of native merchants and to defend them from aggressive foreign competition. In the 1390s Venetian embassies to Sicily sought to improve on the privileges enjoyed by their merchants, while seeking compensation for acts of piracy suffered by them. In response the Sicilian crown tended to drag its feet, although in 1406 Sicilians were ordered to take reprisals on the subjects of Ladislao of Naples for losses experienced at their hands by merchants from Trapani.[26]

As can be inferred from such incidents, the struggle for economic advantage could lead to acts of violence and on a larger scale to war and conquest. The history of the Aragonese empire is inextricably linked to the commercial and financial interests of Catalan merchants from Barcelona–Naples, for example, providing a profitable market and the *Regno* a valuable source of grain, oil and wool. Catalan merchants and bankers tended to be favoured by the crown, which in turn depended heavily on their credit. In 1451 Alfonso I legislated to further what del Treppo has characterised as the 'colonial' economy of his Italian lands, to protect cloth exports from Barcelona, grain exports from the *Regno* and the construction of merchant vessels by his subjects.[27] In the late fourteenth and early fifteenth centuries the republic of Venice embarked on a series of wars of expansion on the Italian mainland, largely to protect her trade routes and her role as an entrepôt between Europe and the Mediterranean. Less successfully, in 1406 Florence fulfilled a long-entertained ambition to control access to the sea by acquiring the rival city of Pisa (see below, p. 112 ff.). This set in train the rather overambitious scheme to launch state-operated trading galleys on the Venetian model, while many Pisan merchants preferred exile to the enterprise of the Florentine industrialists and landowners seeking to profit from their city's ascendancy. Finally, the profits of war could be pursued in a less declared fashion. Privateering was licensed and practised by the kings of Naples. Similarly, in war and peace the royal admirals and vice-admirals of Sicily sanctioned and profited from the privateers operating from the island's strategically placed anchorages.

Governments also tried to maximise their resources, and this included their manpower. Such rulers as the Malatesta of Rimini and the Gonzaga of Mantua brought employment for their subjects and revenues for themselves by raising mercenary armies for the service of their larger and richer neighbours. The importation and production of vital raw materials and articles of manufacture were encouraged. In the early fifteenth century Venice drastically reduced the duties on the rafts of timber descending the rivers of the mainland to furnish her shipyards and construction industries. Later in the century the republic intervened increasingly to protect the forests of her mainland state and in 1487 ordered that all larger vessels had to be built in Venetian yards. Venice also exploited her virtual monopoly of salt – principally imported from the Mediterranean and the Adriatic – to raise revenues, organising its distribution and sale at fixed prices and even enforcing regular quotas on rural districts.[28] The duchy of Milan, in common with most governments, licensed the prospecting and extraction of minerals. The Milanese arms industry was one of the finest and most productive in Europe, partly through ducal encouragement.

Similar policies were directed at the agricultural sphere, not only for food production but also in respect of industry and exports. As mentioned, one of the first acts of Alfonso I on securing the *Regno* was to reform the *Dogana delle Pecore*, and while the taxation and encouragement of the transhumance of sheep and cattle earned the disapproval of later historians for its alleged Spanish origins and impoverishment of southern agriculture, at the time it produced a sharp boost to royal revenues as well as to the commercial activity of the *Regno*. Finally, governments were anxious to enlarge upon their natural resources. This could take the form of developing the waterways of their territories, and canal-building was a prominent aspect of state encouragement of trade in the north, favoured by low-lying land and the availability of rivers. In 1466 the duke of Savoy initiated the building of the *Naviglio* from Ivrea to Vercelli, a work completed in 1479.[29] The construction of locks on the more advanced network round Milan was one of the technical problems undertaken by Leonardo for Lodovico Maria Sforza. The Sforza dukes also encouraged the production of silk and its manufacture into cloth; in 1470 Galeazzo Maria Sforza ordered his subjects to introduce the mulberry to their lands. From the late fifteenth century the Venetian republic established the cultivation of hemp near its subject city of Vicenza to lessen the dependence of its cordage industry on imports from the Black Sea.[30]

Such examples of economic planning have encouraged historians to describe the state of the Italian Renaissance as mercantilist or proto-mercantilist. However, as in other areas, the effectiveness and role of the state should not be exaggerated. Most obviously, economic policies did not always work. Venetian efforts in the early fifteenth century to channel the cloth exports of her mainland cities through her own port failed as merchants continued to use cheaper and more direct routes; equally unsuccessful were the republic's attempts to route the commerce in metals exclusively through Venice.[31] Attempts by the crown in 1452 and 1453 to encourage the exploitation of mineral deposits in the *Regno* failed. Insistent Sforza legislation to safeguard the Milanese woollen industry from foreign competition is as suggestive of failure as repeated Venetian measures to protect her silk industry. Again, government policy could lack continuity. The Visconti supported the economic and jurisdictional ascendancy of the merchants' guild of Milan; the Sforza appear to have spread their patronage more widely across the various guilds.[32] The Malatesta of Rimini did try to favour the local economy by, for example, establishing fairs. However, their efforts were piecemeal and did not solve the principal problem by curtailing Venetian influence.

Another important area where the power of government tends to be exaggerated is in relation to trade and industrial guilds. While in most of the cities of Italy these institutions had lost the political role they had exercised in the thirteenth and fourteenth centuries, their influence over the social and economic lives of their members was probably still considerable. This is often obscured by the fact that guild statutes were regularly presented to the government for confirmation, giving the impression that the state initiated often quite minute reforms or exercised a close supervision over guild activities. Of course that could be the case; in 1519 the Venetian Council of Ten appointed a commission of nobles to review the statutes of the ailing silk guild with a view to increasing its competitiveness. But the confirmation of the statutes of the Milanese guild of furriers in 1466, 1480 and 1483 probably represents less the watchfulness of Sforza and more the activity of the guild itself.

A similar point can be made in slightly different contexts. Despite the importance of the raw materials, Venetian policy towards prospecting for and exploiting minerals appears almost passive or *ad hoc*, responding to the requests for licences from individual companies; and when the Council of Ten drew up more exacting regulations in 1488 to govern the organisation and taxation of mining it drew on German practice – as generally in Europe. Again, the Renaissance papacy is often credited with stimulating the building industries of Rome with policies amounting to an urban renewal; but while it is true that the popes did initiate projects themselves, and did encourage others to do likewise, behind their example and the granting of privileges lies the preparedness of Roman families, and native and foreign churchmen to invest in building.

More generally, the role of private and corporate enterprise was encouraged by the state's acute dependence on external and internal allies and by its need for credit; in view of the practice of farming taxes and the desperate need felt by most governments for ready cash and credit, it is difficult to trace longer-term, ambitious economic 'strategies' from the key area of indirect taxation. Enterprise also thrived on the inadequacies of the state's powers of supervision and control, and the presence of favouritism in public life. The commune of Florence placed the administration of its mint in the hands of the guilds of bankers and merchants of foreign cloth, both vitally interested in the condition of the currency.[33] In this desperate search for ready revenue, the papacy invested the alum mines at Tolfa with Florentine, Genoese and Sienese bankers. Finally, the limitations to the Renaissance concept of public authority can be illustrated from the self-interest of the state itself, whether in its republican or princely forms. Florence and Venice, while clearly not seeking to impoverish their subject communities, tended to favour the 'capital' over the 'provinces'. The Neapolitan crown used its authority to speculate in the markets for grain, oil and wool; on his accession Alfonso II abandoned the practice of exploiting these markets as a gesture to win over native and foreign merchants, and to placate the crown's creditors.[34]

ADMINISTRATION

A telling way to illustrate the predicament of the Renaissance state is through its administration. Some historians have been encouraged by the evidence to view it as a self-conscious institution purposefully developing the machinery of government and deliberately employing more highly trained and professional servants. For example, not only do the records of government survive in greater abundance from the period, but their range expands and their degree of specialisation increases. New archival series reflect the proliferating concerns of government; in the case of Venice the state's documentation became more specialised as the republic's rule advanced on the Italian mainland. Governments also became more careful of their archives. Bartolomeo Scala, as chancellor of Florence, had the commune's records reordered and in 1484 had copies made of key items of legislation. A similar awareness can be found in subject cities nervously defensive of their liberties; in the later fifteenth century the communes of the *Regno* began to collect the privileges granted to them by past rulers into 'Red Books'; Trani's collection was made in 1502.[35]

Related to these developments in record-keeping was a growth of special-isation in government as well as a multiplication in the number of public offices. One area of change, long recognised as being of particular significance, was the growth of a more professional diplomatic service in all the principal states of Italy.[36] More recently historians have detected a similar change in the civilian personnel in charge of the payment, billeting and general super-vision of *condottiere* armies; the republic of Venice appears to have increasingly drawn its diplomats and military *provveditori* from the one group of experi-enced members of the nobility.[37] At the centre of government, movements in the same direction can be seen in the chanceries of the various states. Conditions of appointment were tightened in the attempt to create a more loyal and cohesive bureaucracy. In Venice in the course of the fifteenth century membership of the chancery became increasingly confined to native citizens, and rules governing training and conduct became more exacting.[38] A drive for greater efficiency and integrity among chancery officials can be detected in the reforms of Cicco Simonetta, the Sforza chancellor, in 1453 and 1469; Simonetta was also anxious that his chancery observed the correct form in addressing correspondence to other Italian and European states. Such internal developments were mirrored by an increasing interest in describing the organisation of government; for example, in the Milanese context the humanist Tristano Calco (1455–1515) wrote an account of the Sforza admin-istration.[39] Lastly, the chanceries of most of the Italian states began to place a greater premium on a higher level of training for their personnel, especially since it was becoming increasingly expected that the more formal of diplo-matic correspondence should be couched in fashionably elegant Latin. One of the reasons Antonio Beccadelli rose to prominence in the service of Alfonso I was his command of humanist Latin.[40]

Taken too much at face value, however, such evidence can give an exag-gerated impression of the state's competence, efficiency and sense of direction; it can also tempt historians into an anachronistic eagerness to characterise the administrators of Venice, Florence, Naples or Milan as 'civil servants' or 'bureaucrats'. In the first place, the careful accumulation and ordering of the archives of government was not pursued everywhere with the same attention. If the Renaissance papacy enjoyed a relatively greater degree of political stability conducive to the preservation of records, the court of the duke of Savoy was itinerant and had the Alps to face when transporting itself between Piedmont and Savoy. Secondly, where more complete archives do survive it is neither necessarily nor entirely a consequence of greater governmental efficiency. The better-preserved archives of Verona after 1405 reflect the greater political stability experienced under Venetian rule as much as the care and conscientiousness of chancery officials. Moreover, the greater attention that could be paid to preserving the archival record could constitute a challenge to government. Subject cities like Verona or the maritime communes of the *Regno* were made more aware of the need to conserve such documentation as the privileges issued to them by previous rulers to provide them with the precedents to withstand the demands of the current regime. This relates to a point discussed earlier as well as in the chapter on the *contado*: that where the workings of government are well recorded they tend to reveal the pressures experienced and the obstacles faced rather than standing as unambiguous testimonials to the will and initiative of the state.

Furthermore, the proliferation of offices could not only generate confusion over areas of competence but could be prompted by motives other than the desire for efficiency. Perhaps the most conspicuous example of this is the multiplication of venal offices at the papal court, a practice which grew virtually unchecked from the pontificate of Pius II and which was designed to raise revenue and reward clients. What had begun as an expedient became permanent; and the same was true with other Italian states, like the county of Montferrat and the republic of Venice, as they had increasing recourse to the sale of public office.

Public office could also be viewed as a form of reward or relief for loyal or needy subjects; indeed, the appetite for public office probably increased as a means to supplementing or replacing other sources of wealth. Not only could this lower the standards of administration, especially in the case of appointments in subject communities, further from the control and scrutiny of central government; it could also heighten the political temperature by engendering tension and jealousy over the distribution of patronage. The Venetian republic attempted to circulate the less important castellanships of its empire among needy members of the nobility and loyal subjects; the probable results of this policy were the weakening of the defences of the state while stimulating the traffic in public office – practices and spectacles which alarmed and disgusted more traditionally minded patricians.[41]

But the practice of patronage was not due only to an increased appetite for office. A traditional obligation on the good ruler was to reward and advance his deserving subjects, and this was as much a feature of republican governments as it was of signorial regimes. In Florence the *familia* of the *Signoria* – the corps of servants, guards, messengers and musicians employed by the commune's executive and enjoying relatively good pay and security of tenure – was an area of patronage and favouritism, as the term *familia* suggests.[42] Higher up the social and political scale, the panegyricists of the Medici were often on the lookout for public office in Florence or its dominions. In 1465 Sforza Maria Sforza made a clean sweep of the officials of his duchy of Bari, ignoring the letters of commendation held by the occupants from Ferrante I, in order to advance his Lombard followers.[43]

The effort to still resentment over the distribution of public office was frequently made, but long-term solutions were rarely produced. In January 1437 the commune of Orvieto asked its overlord Eugenius IV to delegate

Stefano Porcari – at that stage renowned as an impartial administrator – to reform the method of allocating office.[44] However, the elaborate measures instituted on 18 February accepted the existence of factions within the commune and sought only to balance the shareout of office between them. As that example suggests, the record of reform can often offer insights into the formidable difficulties facing governments rather than their successes. Alfonso I was faced with petitions for a general pardon when he sought to check maladministration and corruption in the governments of the *Regno* and Sicily in 1455 and 1456. If Lodovico of Savoy cited divine inspiration in his attempts in 1460 to secure good laws and honest magistrates for his subjects, his reforms had little impact in practice.[45] The itinerant officials dispatched by Venice to inspect the conduct of its representatives in its overseas and Italian dominions used to be cited as a sign of the republic's efficiency and even-handedness. They certainly reveal Venetian good intentions, but the record of their circuits shows them to have been spasmodic, rarely productive of tangible reforms, often bewildered by the range of complaints and petitions presented to them, unfamiliar with local conditions and anxious to 'let sleeping dogs lie'.[46]

It would, however, be wrong to conclude that the shortcomings in the administrations of Renaissance states stemmed from the scramble for office alone. Further difficulties flowed from a contrary tendency: a reluctance to accept appointments, especially if they involved the costs, dangers and inconveniences which could be experienced while serving away from home. On his deathbed in 1429 Giovanni di Bicci de' Medici warned his heirs to shun public office and to avoid the *Palazzo della Signoria* unless summoned to attend.[47] In 1479 Florentine legislation listed all the external offices of the republic and the fines incurred by those who refused to accept them.[48] The high reputation of Venetian diplomacy in the Renaissance can hide the fact that many nobles were extremely reluctant to serve abroad, and had recourse to constitutional chicanery and a variety of excuses to avoid such duties. The avoidance of public office, like its pursuit, shows how far private interest compromised and controlled the administration of the Renaissance state.

THE 'TERRITORIAL STATES' OF VENICE AND FLORENCE

As mentioned in the introduction to Chapter Five, a feature of the period is the creation of territorial states by the republics of Venice and Florence. For the former the more important acquisitions were: Treviso (1389), Vicenza (1404), Verona and Padua (1405), Friuli (1420), Brescia (1426) and Bergamo (1428). Florence extended its dominion over Prato (1350), Pistoia (1351), Volterra (1361), Arezzo (1384), Pisa (1406), Cortona (1411) and Livorno (1421) (see maps). In general terms, the phenomenon was far from new. The Italian states had long pursued expansionist policies; Venice had held Treviso between 1339 and 1381 as well as ruling territory in Istria, on the eastern shore of the Adriatic and in the Byzantine Empire. Nor were the underlying motives new; the two republics extended their dominions to pre-empt rivals, to protect earlier gains and to defend their trade routes. Lastly, the aims of the ruling states and the interests of their citizens had precedents. The governments of Venice and Florence sought security, a balance of income over expenditure, easier access to supplies of food and other raw materials and markets and trade routes to stimulate their economies. Their citizens hoped for opportunities to invest in land and in commercial and industrial ventures, as well as for privileged access to the better offices in Church and state.

These are general characteristics. The attempt to be more specific in the cases of Venice and Florence is frustrated by the fact that until relatively recently historians have tended to neglect the relations between ruling and subject cities, and to ignore the histories of the latter. To date only one monograph has been published in English on a subject city, Judith Brown's study of the commune of Pescia under Florentine rule from 1339.[49] More fundamentally, this comparative neglect can be explained by the fact that the chronicle tradition of many of the subject cities – of Verona, Pisa, and Arezzo – becomes, at least temporarily, thinner and more disjointed when compared to that of Venice or Florence.[50] Moreover, contemporary political thinkers and historians concentrated on the principal states of Italy, showing relatively little interest in how they governed their subject territories. Nevertheless, despite the lacunae in the historiography of the subject, attempts have been made more recently to characterise the states created by Florence and Venice. As mentioned in the introduction, some historians, working most often from the records of the central government, have chosen to stress the initiative of the state, seeing the new territorial states of Venice and Florence in terms of an imposed authority which increasingly governed the 'provinces' in the interests of the 'capital'.

In the case of Venice the terms of the debate have been largely set by Angelo Ventura in a general study of the republic's mainland state. For Ventura the republic was determined to assert and exploit its authority, and he rejects the older interpretation of the *stato di terra* as a federation and the newer view that it was a mosaic of autonomies.[51] He stresses how completely the republic denied the citizens of its subject cities participation in anything more than local government. The *Serenissima*'s authority was expressed and its interests upheld by a few noble officials chosen by and from the *Maggior Consiglio* and dispatched to govern the subject cities and their *contadi*. More fundamentally, to carry out its policies the republic created closed oligarchies in its own image in the subject communes. These administrative and social changes paved the way for Venetian demands for foodstuffs, taxation and labour service; while individual Venetians, generally from the nobility, were in a privileged position to pursue ecclesiastical and secular office and to invest in land.

Closer examination suggests that this interpretation is too theoretical, or owes too much to hindsight. The *stato di terra* was not created according to a grand design. The first cities (Treviso, Vicenza, and Padua) were taken to thwart a dangerous enemy, the Carrara of Padua, who were threatening to create a state of their own with the potential to blockade Venice and strangle its trade routes. Friuli was occupied for similar reasons, and to protect recent conquests as well as Venetian territory in Istria. Only with the conquests in Lombardy associated with the doge Francesco Foscari did Venetian frontiers extend decisively beyond a coastal region and a traditional sphere of influence, and the republic embrace a more openly expansionist policy. This did not only alarm other Italian and European powers; it also fuelled doubts within the city itself as to the wisdom of pursuing the role of a major land power.[52]

Not unrelated to this often rather *ad hoc* increase in territory is the fact that the republic did not normally choose to base its claim to lordship on the right of conquest. Not only was there no attempt to dismantle or deny imperial overlordship, but the republic's claims were not even incorporated in the titles of the doge or the commune. Rather than be taken by assault, communities were allowed to surrender and present petitions designed to protect or enhance their liberties. Venice appears to have cultivated the impression that its subject cities had accepted its rule by their own free will; the official Veronese surrender in the Piazza San Marco in July 1405 was devised as an occasion for mutual rejoicing, with the doge observing: 'the people that walked in darkness have seen a great light'. Further evidence of the republic's care or restraint in interpreting its authority can be seen in the way it did not radically alter the statutes and institutions of its subject cities, and generally allowed them to continue to administer the terms of their own citizenship.[53]

The republic's caution was due to practical as well as to jurisdictional considerations. Its Italian empire was extensive and contained a number of major cities with independent political traditions. Verona, for example, was a city of considerable industrial, commercial and agricultural importance. In the fourteenth century it had been the capital of an expanding state and the seat of a brilliant court. In the early fifteenth century its population had fallen to around 14,000 against Venice's approximately 85,000 but by the early sixteenth century the gap had narrowed, with Verona having about 42,000 inhabitants to about 100,000 in Venice. In governing the *stato di terra*, comprising such formidable cities, the republic had neither the means nor the political conceptions to carry out policies as fundamental as those suggested by Ventura. At the centre the government of the mainland state had to compete with a wide variety of other matters for the attention of the members of the *Maggior Consiglio*, the Senate and the *Collegio*, and even when the Council of Ten began to take an increasing role, from the later fifteenth century, its initiative was countered by pressure of business.[54]

It is true that a large number of specialised offices were created, generally in the areas of defence and taxation, but they were usually made in response to a crisis and on a short-term basis; the lack of continuity in Venetian administration was compounded by its dependence on the generally reluctant co-operation of the councils and officials of its subject communities. On the ground the few permanent Venetian representatives were also elected for a short term, around sixteen months, and rarely served again in the same posting. The impression given of the tours of duty of such rectors, or *rettori*, in larger cities like Brescia is one of powerlessness in the face of unfamiliar problems and formidable local oligarchies.[55] On the whole, *rettori* seem to have been anxious to steer clear of confrontation and controversy, and where they did seek to strike a higher profile as governors it was to adopt the posture of the friend and protector of the community. In 1407 the noble Zaccaria Trevisan wrote to his successor as *capitano* of Padua: 'The special traits of a Venetian governor are a sense of humanity and clemency, to make yourself loved, whereas other lords rule cities from the heights of their citadels.' When Francesco Barbaro served, unusually, for a second term as *podestà* of Verona in 1441 he was welcomed as 'pater patriae' and modestly urged the Veronese to see him as their 'father, guardian and perpetual defender'.[56]

For these reasons it is difficult to accept that the republic ever contemplated reshaping the oligarchies in its subject cities on the model of the Venetian nobility. In fact, where Venetian interference was greatest, in Treviso – close to the lagoons and for long an area of Venetian influence and investment – the result was not the fostering of a local oligarchy but an end to the consultative assembly of the commune and the introduction of more direct Venetian rule.[57] Treviso was an exception, but the oligarchies which largely dominated the councils and offices in the other mainland cities were the product of local circumstances rather than of Venetian legislation. Moreover, far from being creatures of Venetian rule, the leading families of the principal subject cities were often a source of opposition. Cultivating an increasingly exclusive and aristocratic outlook, they generally distanced themselves from the Venetians who continued to regard trade as compatible with noble status. They resented being used as cat's-paws for unpopular fiscal and military policies. They were jealous of the privileged position of the nobility in the pursuit of the better ecclesiastical benefices. They disliked the republic's apparent readiness to hear appeals from the *popolo* and from *contado* communities. Yearning for a greater political role, they were liable to collaborate with the republic's enemies; many of the principal families of Verona and Padua welcomed the emperor Maximilian with enthusiasm after the republic's defeat at Agnadello in 1509.

It is therefore clear why Venice could not afford to be indifferent to the composition and conduct of the local oligarchies. Where they seemed to further Venetian interests they could be supported, as happened in Udine and Dalmatia after 1511 when popular revolts were thought to challenge the republic's rule. On the other hand, Venice was prepared to intervene against local families of dubious loyalty; the suspicion that members of some leading families of Verona had collaborated with the republic's Gonzaga and Visconti enemies in 1439 prompted deportations and investigations by the Ten, while the hostility of the leading citizens of Padua in the aftermath of Agnadello led to the temporary suspension of the city's constitution once the city had been retaken.

As these moves suggest, it would be wrong to claim that Venetian rule had no impact on its subject cities. Promises to respect the petitions accepted on their surrender could be ignored. In May 1353 the Istrian commune of Pola complained that its Venetian governor 'pisses over our statutes and ordinances'.[58] In 1498 Padua offered to renounce the privileges it had secured in 1406 as a sarcastic comment on the republic's capacity to ignore its liberties. Local compilations of statutes might have retained their validity in theory, but they became increasingly superseded by Venetian practice and legislation. In general terms the demands for men, money and materials increased, and although military expenditure thwarted Venetian hopes that revenue would exceed expenditure and that the mainland would be able to pay for its own defence, the imposition, distribution and collection of the fiscal burden provoked disputes and resentment.[59] In 1442 a manifesto appeared in Verona denouncing the Venetian *podestà* and the level of the tax burden, to the contrived horror and shame of the city's council. In 1514 Sanudo reported that anger at exactions in Friuli ran so high that leaflets were scattered in the capital denouncing the Venetians as thieves and tyrants. In 1530 the Friulian noble Roberto Spilimbergo lamented in his diary at the burdens consequent on 'this perpetual servitude.[60] Moreover, as the state was forced to raise its demands and as its knowledge of and interference in the *terraferma* grew, so the appetite of Venetians as individuals developed for office in Church and state, and their investments in land increased. Abuses and resentment followed. In the opening years of the sixteenth century the Venetian noble Domenico Morosini warned against the dangers of corrupt officials and absentee bishops, while the government was constantly made aware that Venetian landowners on the mainland were managing to escape both local and Venetian taxation.

But the repressive and negative aspect of Venetian rule should not be exaggerated. In the first place its impact varied considerably and was obviously most intense in the cities nearest the lagoons, Padua and Treviso. More generally, and as has been pointed out elsewhere, the defence of liberties and the resistance to demands could be tenacious and effective. For example, when in 1462 the Council of Ten increased the powers of the Venetian *podestà* in Verona to control election to office and to secure a more loyal administration, the Council was bombarded by petitions, supported by its local representatives, until it was forced to abandon the reform.[61] In the aftermath of the War of Cambrai very few of the leading families of the mainland cities had shown themselves to have been so hostile to Venice as to be unable to recover their ascendancy.

Moreover, the accessibility of Venetian councils and magistracies to appeal and petition from individuals and communities was undoubtedly one of the major reasons for the growing impact of the republic's rule in such areas as the administration of justice, the distribution of taxation and the allocation of office; for too long historians have neglected the interests and opportunism of the subject in examining reasons for the growth in the state. Lastly, the greater stability conferred by Venetian rule and the easier access to the Venetian market probably contributed to the economic revival which can be detected in the mainland cities in the fifteenth century. These reasons, together with the republic's restrained interpretation of its authority, suggest that the Venetian claim that it ruled with the consent of its subjects was not without some justification. They also help to explain the remarkable degree of loyalty and support the republic could draw on from the *popolo* and the *contadini* during the War of Cambrai, to the astonishment of such critical contemporaries as Machiavelli (above, p. 63).

This reputation does not appear to have been shared by Florence, whose enemies were quick to claim that the republic's concern for liberty did not extend to its neighbours. In 1375 Gregory XI observed that the Florentines 'reduce the liberty of their neighbours to serfdom where they can'. In 1388 for the Lucchese and Sienese the Florentines were the wolves of Tuscany, while in 1497 the Pisans were urged to stand firm against the republic's 'injuries, tyrannies, damages, exactions and acts of violence and extortion', an assessment of Florentine rule endorsed by Commynes.[62]

Like the Venetians, the Florentines themselves could doubt the wisdom of their wars of expansion. On 5 September 1412 the view was expressed in a debate that Florence had been stronger before it had acquired such cities as Arezzo and Pisa.[63] Machiavelli was probably thinking of the plight of Pisa when he observed in his *Discorsi* that 'of all forms of harsh servitude, the harshest is experienced when you submit to a republic'; certainly the history of the Florentine territorial state in the period is marked by a number of rebellions which were far more serious in terms of local support and determination than anything Venice had to face. Pisa's exploitation of the invasion of Charles VIII in 1494 and its tenacious defence of its liberties down to 1509 is the best-known example. Similarly damaging for the reputation of Florence – and of Lorenzo de' Medici – was the revolt of Volterra, provoked by Lorenzo's attempts to exploit the commune's alum deposits and ended by a violent sack at the hands of mercenaries under the command of Federigo da Montefeltro (1472).

Some insight into the grounds for anti-Florentine feeling can be gathered from the republic's attitude to its authority. While Venice appears to have been content that its subject cities sent embassies to congratulate each newly elected doge and that they observed St Mark's Day as a festival, Florence seems to have been much more insistent that its ascendancy be recognised more explicitly in ritualistic terms. The subject cities had to send representatives to Florence on St John's Day and honour the city's patron saint with gifts of candles, and in some cases with a pallium; in 1391 Pescia had to borrow money to pay for its candles. Arezzo and Pistoia were ordered to observe the same religious festivals as Florence, while Pisa had to send a monthly tribute to the cathedral as well as honouring St John. Its guilds had to adopt the patron saints of their Florentine counterparts.[64]

But the republic appears to have been as anxious to exercise as to express its authority; in Pistoia the gathering momentum of Florentine rule can be charted from the fourteenth to the sixteenth centuries, not simply in ceremonial but in the reform of offices and the supervision of the commune's statutes.[65] More generally, the republic tried to ensure that its political ascendancy was reflected in the ecclesiastical hierarchy and organisation of its dominions. If Venice secured for its bishop the dignity of patriarch in 1451 and proposed the candidates for vacant benefices, in 1409 the see of Florence was elevated to an archbishopric, with the bishops of Fiesole, Arezzo, Pistoia and Volterra as suffragans.[66] The *catasto* of 1427–30 was an attempt, unique to northern Italy, to incorporate the whole state in the one tax assessment. Whereas Venice attempted to govern its mainland state through its over-worked general councils and a plethora of magistracies, Florence approached the administration of its principal subject city, Pisa, in a much more single-minded fashion.[67] If Venice had had no aspirations to rule her neighbours in the years preceding their acquisition, Florence had long hoped to take Pisa, to subdue a rival and to gain access to the sea. On the Pisan side, the city's fall to Florence in 1406 was followed by an exodus – on a scale never approached in the Venetian state – of Pisan merchants preferring exile to Florentine enterprise. On the Florentine side the city was heavily garrisoned, citizens regarded as a threat were deported, the commune's jurisdiction in the *contado* was weakened and the office of the Sea Consuls was created in 1421 to supervise the city's guilds and develop a Florentine galley fleet. Taking advantage of the conquest, the exile or deportation of so many Pisans and the depressed state of the city's economy, leading Florentine families like the Medici, the Capponi and the Rucellai were quick to invest in land in the Pisano. As elsewhere in the Florentine dominions, high ecclesiastical office was sought to add to or restore family fortunes; Alamanno Adimari acquired the prestigious archbishopric of Pisa in 1406.

The particular case of Pisa helps to explain why some modern historians like Marvin Becker have seen the history of the Florentine territorial state in terms of centralisation and exploitation,[68] but while these characteristics are probably more pronounced than in the Venetian case, neither they nor the scale and efficiency of Florentine policies should be exaggerated. In the first place the size, wealth and economic activity of Florence gave it an in-built predominance over its subject communes for which little constitutional or legislative endorsement was needed.[69] Despite this, Florentine expansion was less single-minded and ruthless than is often suggested, and imperial over-lordship was not denied. At least initially her ascendancy over some communes took the form of a protectorate rather than of direct rule. This was so with Volterra in 1361, Florence proclaiming her anxiety to preserve the freedom of the city; in 1385 the citizens of Volterra were told that 'our predecessors took your town under the protection of our commune at a time when it was shaken by the discord of tyranny'.[70]

Elsewhere, as at Pescia, the subject community was allowed to present petitions and, as in the Venetian state, the fiction was preserved that it had surrendered on terms, as if a treaty had been entered into by equal partners. In the case of Pisa, conquest was only one of the options considered by Florence in the years before 1406 and the Florentine chronicler Goro Dati could portray his city as a reluctant user of force, anxious to free Pisa from tyranny.[71] Further, Mallett has argued that Florence had no intention of destroying the Pisan economy and took positive steps to encourage immigration, to develop the commercial and agricultural activity of the city and its *contado* and to boost the prestige and well-being of the city by reviving its university. Lastly, not all leading Pisans supported the city's rebellion against Florentine lordship after 1494.

Taking this line of argument still further, Judith Brown has claimed that the relatively small and unimportant commune of Pescia probably benefited from Florentine rule. It was allowed considerable autonomy, and although its legislation had to be submitted to Florence for approval, little of it was ever modified. The greater security allowed the commune to develop its agriculture and particularly the cultivation of the mulberry, while argument and obstruction repeatedly allowed Pescia to default on its fiscal obligations and progressively to reduce its tax burden. The picture offered by Brown of a comparatively powerless community exploiting Florentine rule is sufficiently close to the examples studied in the Venetian dominions to suggest that the territorial state created by Florence was not as compact, centralised or supine as some historians have tried to claim.

As will be argued in the contexts of the Papal States and the Aragonese empire, the history of the territorial states, like that of the Renaissance state in general, has too often been written from the centre, from hindsight or from an artificial perspective. Too little attention has been paid to the realities in 'the provinces' and to the aspirations, opportunism and bloody-mindedness of the subject populations – not to mention the pragmatism, indifference and exhaustion of their governors. The sources that survive from even the smaller subject communities show greater commitment to autonomy and less deference to 'central' authority than historians of the Renaissance state often allow.[72]

NOTES AND REFERENCES

1. A. Molho, *Florentine Public Finance in the early Renaissance* (Cambridge, Mass., 1971); D. Herlihy and C. Klapisch-Zuber, *Tuscans and their Families* (New Haven and London, 1985); C. Bauer, 'Studi per la storia delle finanze papali durante il pontificato di Sisto IV', *A.S.R.S.P.*, vol. i (1927); P. Partner, 'Papal financial policy in the Renaissance and Counter-Reformation', *Past and Present*, no. 88 (1980); P. Gentile, 'Lo stato napoletano sotto Alfonso I', *A.S.P.N.*, n.s., vol. xxiii (1937) and vol. xxiv (1938); P. Pedio, 'Il regno di Napoli ed il suo bilancio', *Annali del Mezzogiorno*, vol. viii (1968); A. Ryder, 'Cloth and credit: Aragonese war finance in the mid-fifteenth century', *War and Society*, vol. ii (1984).

2. A. Ryder, *The Kingdom of Naples under Alfonso the Magnanimous*, (Oxford, 1976), pp. 359–62.

3. C. Bellieni, review of A. Era, *Il Parlamento Sardo* (Milan, 1955) in *Studi Sassaresi*, ser. ii, vol. xxvi (1956).

4. J. E. Law, *The Commune of Verona under Venetian Rule*, (D. Phil. thesis, University of Oxford, 1974) chs vii and viii.

5. M. Knapton, 'Il fisco nello stato veneziano di terraferma', in G. Borelli *et al.* (eds), *Il Sistema Fiscale Veneto* (Verona, 1982).

6. H. Sieveking, 'Studio sulle finanze genovesi nel Medio Evo', *Atti della Soc. Ligure di Stor. Pat.*, vol. xxxv (1905–06).

7. G. M. Varanini, 'Il bilancio della Camera Fiscale di Verona', in *Sistema Fiscale Veneto*.

8. G. Todde, 'Un donativo straordinario', *Studi Sardi*, vol. xvii (1959–61).

9. P. Lanaro Sartori, 'L'esenzione fiscale a Verona nel '400 e '500', in *Sistema Fiscale Veneto*.

10. G. M. Varanini, 'Tra fisco e credito: note sulle camere dei pegni nelle città venete del quattrocento', *Studi Storici Veronesi*, vol. xxxiii (1983).

11. D. M. Bueno de Mesquita, 'Ludovico Sforza and his vassals', in E. F. Jacob (ed.), *Italian Renaissance Studies* (London, 1960), p. 213; R. Fubini, 'Osservazioni e documenti sulla crisi del ducato di Milano nel 1477', in S. Bertelli and G. Ramakus (eds), *Essays presented to M. P. Gilmore*, vol. i (Florence, 1978), pp. 101–2.

12. Herlihy and Klapisch-Zuber, op. cit., p. xxiii.

13. R. Finlay, *Politics in Renaissance Venice* (London, 1980), p. 33, pp. 49–50.

14. I. Cervelli, *Machiavelli e la Crisi dello Stato Veneziano* (Naples, 1974), p. 304.

15. D. M. Bueno de Mesquita, 'The conscience of the prince', *Proc. British Academy*, vol. lxv (1979), pp. 420, 433–4; P. Ghinzoni, 'Don Celso Maffei da Verona e Ludovico il Moro', *A.S.L.*, ser. i, vol. vi (1879), pp. 603–4; G. Brucker, *The Civic World of Early Renaissance Florence* (Princeton, 1977), p. 235; Law, op. cit., p. 254.

16. F. Gilbert, *The Pope, his Banker and Venice* (Cambridge, Mass., 1980).

17. F. Saraceno, 'Due anni di regno di Lodovico duca di Savoia', *Curiosità e Ricerche di Storia Subalpina*, vol. ii (1876), p. 530.

18. A. Brown, *Bartolomeo Scala Chancellor of Florence* (Princeton, 1979), p. 333.

19. L. F. Marks, 'The financial oligarchy in Florence under Lorenzo de' Medici', in *Italian Renaissance Studies*, op. cit.; J. Kirshner and A. Molho, 'The dowry fund', *J. of Mod. Hist.*, vol. l (1978).

20. G. Luzzatto, 'Il debito pubblico nel sistema finanziario veneziano', *Studi di Storia Economica Veneziana* (Padua, 1954); Finlay, op. cit., pp. 264 ff.

21. H. Baron, 'The anti-Florentine discourses of doge Tommaso Mocenigo', *Speculum*, vol. xxvii (1952); G. Luzzatto, *Storia Economica di Venezia* (Venice, 1961), pp. 165–8.

22. A. Fanfani, 'L'azione dei Visconti e degli Sforza per richiamare forestieri a Milano', *Atti e Mem. del III Congresso Storico Lombardo* (Milan, 1939).

23. R. Broglio d'Ajano, 'L'Industria della seta a Venezia', in C. M. Cipolla (ed.), *Storia dell'Economia Italiana* (Turin, 1959).

24. G. Barbiere, 'Gottardo Panigarolo mercante e spenditore sforzesco', in *III Congresso Storico Lombardo*, op. cit.; idem, *Economia e politica nel Ducato di Milano* (Milan, 1938).

25. R. A. Goldthwaite, *Private Wealth in Renaissance Florence* (Princeton, 1968), pp. 52–73.

26. F. Giunta, *Aragonesi e Catalani nel Mediterraneo*, vol. i (Palermo, 1953), pp. 224–8; C. Trasselli, *Mediterraneo e Sicilia all'Inizio dell'Epoca Moderna* (Cosenza, 1977).

27. M. del Treppo, 'The "Crown of Aragon" and the Mediterranean', *J. of European Ec. Hist.*, vol. ii (1973).

28. Law, op. cit., pp. 213–52; M. Knapton, 'Il Consiglio dei Dieci nel governo della terraferma', *Atti del Convegno Venezia e la Terraferma* (Milan, 1981), pp. 250–51; J.-C. Hocquet, *Le Sel et la Fortune de Venise*, vol. i (Lille, 1978).

29. M. C. Daviso di Charvensod, *La Duchessa Iolanda* (Turin, 1935), pp. 146–9.

30. F. C. Lane, 'The rope factory and the hemp trade', in *Venice and History* (Baltimore, 1966).

31. P. Braunstein, 'Le commerce du fer à Venise', *Studi Veneziani*, vol. viii (1966).

32. M. F. Mazzaoui, 'L'industria lombarda del cotone e politica economica dei duchi di Milano', *Milano nell'Età di Lodovico il Moro* (Milan, 1983).

33. H. Saalman, *The Bigallo* (New York, 1969) p. 4.

34. P. Gentile, Lo stato napoletano', op. cit., *A.S.P.N.*, n.s., vol. xxiv (1938), pp. 21–5; I. Schiappoli, 'Il conte di Sarno', *A.S.P.N.*, n.s., vol. xxii (1936); F Catalano, 'La crisi italiana alla fine del secolo xv', *Belfagor*, vol. xi (1956), pp. 410–12.

35. Brown, op. cit., esp. ch. vii; F. Carabellese, *La Puglia nel secolo xv*, vol. ii (Bari, 1907).

36. G. Mattingly, *Renaissance Diplomacy* (Harmondsworth, 1965).

37. M. Mallett, Diplomacy and war in late fifteenth century Italy', *Proc. British Academy*, vol. lxvii (1981), pp. 273–5.

38. M. Neff, 'A citizen in the service of the patrician state: the career of Zaccaria dei Freschi', *S.V.*, n.s., vol. v (1981).

39. E. Motta, review of L. Pelissier, *Documents sur la première année du règne de Louis XII* (Paris, 1890) in *A.S.L.*, ser. ii, vol. vii (1890), pp. 955–6; J. E. Law, 'Un confronto fra due stati "rinascimentali": Venezia e il dominio sforzesco', in *Gli Sforza a Milano e in Lombardia* (Milan, 1982), p. 403. Central to the study of Milanese administration is the work of C. Santoro; cf. V. Ilardi, 'The Visconti-Sforza regime of Milan: recently published sources', *Ren. Q.*, vol. xxxi (1978).

40. A. Ryder, 'Antonio Beccadelli: a humanist in government', in C. H. Clough (ed.), *Essays in Honour of P. O. Kristeller* (Manchester, 1976).

41. J. E. Law, 'Lo stato veneziano e le castellanie di Verona', in G. Cracco and M. Knapton (eds), *Dentro lo 'Stado Italico': Venezia e la Terraferma fra Quattro e Seicento* (Trent, 1984).

42. G. Brucker, 'Bureaucracy and social welfare in the Renaissance: a Florentine case study', *Journal of Mod. Hist.*, vol. lv (1983).

43. N. Ferorelli, 'Il ducato di Bari sotto Sforza Maria e Ludovico il Moro', *A.S.L.*, ser. v, vol. i (1914), pp. 411 ff.

44. L. Fumi, 'Il governo di Stefano Porcari in Orvieto', *Studi e Documenti di Storia e Diritto*, vol. iv (1883).

45. Saraceno, loc. cit., pp. 528–9.

46. Law, 'Verona and the Venetian state', pp. 15–17.

47. G. Holmes, *The Florentine Enlightenment* (London, 1969), p. 139.

48. V. Promis, 'Tasse per rifiute a diverse cariche nella repubblica fiorentina', *Misc. di Storia Italiana*, vol. xvi (1877).

49. J. Brown, *In the Shadow of Florence. Provincial Society in Renaissance Pescia* (New York–Oxford, 1982). Two recent collections are: Centro Italiano di Studi e d'Arte, Pistoia, *Egemonia fiorentina ed autonomie locali nella Toscana nord-occidentale del primo rinascimento* (Pistoia, 1979), henceforth *Egemonia fiorentina*; Cracco and Knapton (eds), *Dentro lo 'Stado Italico', Venezia e la Terraferma fra Quattrocento e Seicento* (Trent, 1983), henceforth *'Stado Italico'*.

50. R. Fubini, 'Antonio Ivani da Sarzana, un teorizzatore del declino delle autonomie

comunali', in *Egemonia Fiorentina*, p. 115; J. E. Law, 'Venice, Verona and the della Scala', *Atti e Mem. della Accademia di Verona*, ser. vi, vol. xxix (1977–78), pp. 157–8.

51. A. Ventura, *Nobilità e Popolo nella Società Veneta del '400 e '500* (Bari, 1964); 'Il dominio di Venezia nel quattrocento', in S. Bertelli (ed.), *Florence and Venice* (Florence, 1979), vol. i; 'Introduzione' to '*Stado Italico*'.

52. N. Rubinstein, 'Italian reactions to terraferma expansion in the fifteenth century', in J. R. Hale (ed.), *Renaissance Venice* (London, 1973); Cervelli, op. cit., *passim*.

53. Law, 'Verona and the Venetian state', op. cit.; J. S. Grubb, 'Alla ricerca delle prerogative locali: la cittadinanza a Vicenza', in '*Stado Italico*'; contributions by G. Cozzi and C. C. Lopez in G. Cozzi (ed.), *Stato, Societa e Giustizia nella Repubblica Veneta* (Rome, 1980).

54. Knapton, 'Il Consiglio dei Dieci', op. cit.

55. J. M. Ferraro, 'Proprietà terriera e potere nello stato veneto: la nobilità bresciano del '400–'500', in '*Stado Italico*'.

56. Law, *Commune of Verona*, pp. 374–6.

57. M. Knapton, 'Venezia e Treviso nel trecento', *Tomaso da Modena e il suo Tempo. Atti del Convegno Internazionale di Studi* (Treviso, 1980).

58. We would like to thank Michael Knapton for this telling reference.

59. M. Knapton, *Capital City and Subject Province: Fiscal and Military Relations in the Late Fifteenth Century* (D.Phil. thesis, University of Oxford, 1978). p. 234; C. G. Mor, 'Problemi organizzativi e politica veneziana nei riguardi dei nuovi acquisti di terraferma', in V. Branca (ed.), *Umanesimo Europeo e Umanesimo Veneziano* (Florence, 1967).

60. P. S. Leicht, 'Un movimento agrario nel cinquecento', *Scritti Vari di Storia del Diritto Italiano*, vol. i (Milan, 1943), p. 74.

61. On Venetian influence on the constitution and composition of the Veronese councils, J. E. Law, 'Venice and the "Closing" of the Veronese council in 1405', *S.V.*, n.s., vol. i (1977) and G. M. Varanini, 'Note sui consigli veronesi', *A.V.*, ser. v, vol. cxii (1979).

62. M. Berengo, review of M. Luzzati, *Una Guerra di Popolo. Lettere Private del Tempo dell'Assedio di Pisa* (Pisa, 1973) in *R.S.I.*, vol. lxxxvii (1975), p. 172.

63. Brucker, *Civic World*, op. cit., p. 344.

64. P. Silva, 'Pisa sotto Firenze', *Studi Storici*, vol. xviii (1909–10); M. Wackernagel, *The World of the Florentine Renaissance Artist* (Princeton, 1981), pp. 193–4; R. C. Trexler, 'Ritual behaviour in Renaissance Florence', *Medievalia et Humanistica*, n.s., vol. iv (1973), p. 135; idem, *Public Life*, pp. 5, 361–2, 506–7.

65. E. Altieri Magliozzi, 'Istituzioni comunali a Pistoia prima e dopo l'inizio della dominazione fiorentina', *Egemonia Fiorentina*.

66. R. Bizzocchi, 'Chiesa e aristocrazia nella Firenze del quattrocento', *A.S.I.*, vol. cxlii (1984), pp. 245–53.

67. On Pisa, Silva, loc. cit.; Luzzati, op. cit.; M. Mallett, 'Pisa and Florence in the fifteenth century', in N. Rubinstein (ed.), *Florentine Studies* (London, 1968); E. Fasano-Guarini, 'Città soggette e contadi nel dominio fiorentino: il caso pisano', in *Ricerche di Storia Moderna*, vol. i (Pisa, 1976); G. Petralia, 'Ricerche prosopografiche sull'emigrazione delle famiglie mercantili pisane a Sicilia', *Boll. Stor. Pisano*, vol. 1 (1981).

68. M. Becker, 'The Florentine territorial state, in *Florentine Studies*; idem, *Florence in Transition*, vol. ii, 'Studies in the rise of the territorial state' (Baltimore, 1968).

69. A major theme of Herlihy and Klapisch-Zuber, op. cit.
70. N. Rubinstein, 'Florence and the despots', *T.R.H.S.*, ser. v, vol. ii (1952).
71. A. Molho, 'A note on the Albizzi and the Florentine conquest of Pisa', *Ren. Q.*, vol. xx (1967); A. P. McCormick, 'Goro Dati and the Roman origins of Florence', *Bibliothèque d'Humanisme et Renaissance*, vol. xlvi (1984), p. 34.
72. E.g., R. Witt, 'Coluccio Salutati and the political life of the commune of Buggiano', *Rinascimento*, ser. ii, vol. vi (1966).

CHAPTER SEVEN

The Church and religious life

Visually churches impose themselves on any visitor to Italy, even if his interests are confined to the paintings that adorn their walls and altars. Even the
paintings in galleries – and not only in Italy – often began as sacred decorations of sacred buildings. May we infer that the Church and religion played
a larger part in the lives of Italians as a whole than they did in other parts
of Christendom? It may be suspected that the answer to this question is
complicated. For one thing, the Italian clergy are displayed in their own
records (which are plentiful if patchy, and remain largely unexplored) as just
as wicked as laymen often were, and additionally culpable of many of the sins
from which the clergy were specifically prohibited – the lewd thoughts and
actions which the laity tolerated in themselves, whatever they may have been
expected to do by earnest preachers. Besides the faults enumerated in church
records, the laity had for centuries mounted hostile criticism of men in orders
who did not practise what they preached. These critics, from Dante and
Boccaccio onwards, were more scathing than were non-Italian laymen of the
clergy in France or Germany, for example, if only because many Italian lay
writers were handling a vernacular more sophisticated than others, and
perhaps had a larger lay readership. Such lay vituperation extended well into
the sixteenth century, and beyond.[1]

The attempts to reform the moral behaviour of clergy and laity are
discussed later in this chapter; it will begin, however, by surveying briefly
the Church and the clergy before going on to attempt some speculation as
to the state of religion, a much more difficult subject. In dealing with the
clergy it is easiest to begin with the senior ranks in the hierarchy, if only
because they are in general relatively easy to identify and because they have
already been much discussed by historians.

RENAISSANCE POPES AND CARDINALS

When discussed of old this topic was dealt with almost exclusively in constitutional terms and it has long been a complaint that historians, both in and

out of Italy, have tended to treat the subject by dealing mainly with the popes. The character of individual popes and their administrations are, however, useful indicators of the tempo and direction of church life in Italy in the period. This begins with the Great Schism of 1378 which led to two popes emerging, one an 'Italian' (if a Neapolitan can be so described), the other a Frenchman (if this covers Robert of Geneva); a later attempt to solve the problem led to the adoption of a Greek – Filargi, Archbishop of Milan – in 1409 at the so-called Council of Pisa. The Neapolitan was succeeded by Italians, as was Filargi, Alexander V. By 1414 there was Benedict XIII, of Aragonese background, with a redoubtable base in Peñiscola near Valencia, and two Italian rivals, John XXIII and Gregory XII. This division of authority had devastating effects everywhere in Latin Christendom, but its consequences for Italy were perhaps especially damaging. The two Italian popes freely promoted their adherents to sees which were already occupied and it took a generation before this tangle was more or less unravelled, since it was extremely difficult to take his office away from a bishop who had been legitimately consecrated. The confusion of rival bishops was most evident in north Italy, but in the kingdom of Naples the Aragonese Benedict XIII played the same game, if on a smaller scale.

It is, of course, fair to add that Italy was already endowed with a superfluity of bishops, so that the addition of a few more did not signify much; in any case, Italian bishops – like bishops everywhere at this time – were not notable for their residence in their sees, or for their zealous performance of pastoral duties. If most bishops set a poor example, what may be said of the popes themselves? Those who lived through the Schism were, in the 'Roman' line, Urban VI (d. 1389), Boniface IX (1389–1404), Innocent VII (1404–06) and Gregory XII (1406–resigned 1415); the two 'Avignon' pontiffs were Clement VII (1378–94) and Benedict XIII (1394–deposed by the Council of Constance in 1417); after the deposition of the others by the Council of Pisa, the 'conciliar' popes were Alexander V (1409–10) and John XXIII (1410–deposed at Constance in 1415). Pastor and others have discerned some merits in one or two of these men,[2] but for the greater part of their time they were clinging desperately to office and buying support internationally by craven concessions to the princes of their 'obedience'.

The result was an increasing impatience in the Church and a general acceptance of the call to a council at Constance. This important assembly, besides deposing John XXIII and Benedict XIII and receiving the resignation of Gregory XII, took two important decisions, both intended to reduce the pope to the position of a constitutional monarch. In 1415, when John XXIII tried to kill at birth the Council he had unwillingly summoned, the Council, in the decree traditionally called 'Sacrosancta', declared the authority of a general council in matters of doctrine and discipline to be superior to that of a pope. And in 1417, just before the election of the Roman Martin V as pope over an undivided Church, it adopted the canon 'Frequens' by which another council would meet in five years, another seven years after that and thereafter every ten years. The restored papacy never accepted conciliar supremacy; although they never had the effrontery to deny 'Frequens', the popes had the devious achievement of ignoring it by administrative means.

If the popes of the Schism were concerned mainly with saving their own positions, this was to a large extent an Italian matter. What is remarkable about their successors in a united Roman Church was that they too were fairly narrowly Italian in their interests. There were compelling, if not noble, reasons for this. The income of the papacy in the thirteenth and fourteenth centuries had been substantially drawn from 'spiritual' payments from all over Christendom – mainly annates and common services, taxes levied on parochial and episcopal revenues respectively. After the Schism these sources of revenue diminished and the popes had to rely more and more on their seignorial rights in the States of the Church, supplemented as the fifteenth century drew to an end by an increase in even more dubious methods such as the sale of offices in the departments of the Curia, a practice which was, in effect, largely restricted to Italians who saw in their investment a form of life annuity (see Chapter Six).

Martin V, elected at Constance in 1417 by a conclave which included representatives of the five 'nations' into which the Council was by then divided for deliberative and legislative purposes, had to make good his claims to the Papal States and Rome itself. This had been more or less accomplished by his death in 1431. His impetuous successor, a Venetian who styled himself Eugenius IV, aroused so much opposition that he had to leave the city ignominiously; he resided in Florence from 1434 to 1443 – an important moment from a cultural point of view, for it led the pope to recruit more humanists to his staff and exposed the intellectuals in the Curia to the influence of the early Renaissance in its Tuscan manifestations. Martin V at least had made papal control more effective in papal territories; his successor Eugenius undid much of this and also alienated the Fathers at the Council of Basel, held under the terms of the decree 'Frequens'. It is true that Eugenius succeeded in negotiating, at his own Council of Ferrara-Florence (1438–39), the ill-starred union of the Greek and Roman Churches; but the unrest he provoked in Rome led many subsequent popes to fear revolutionary activity in the city.

Apart from Nicholas V (1447–55) and Pius II (1458–64), both men who rose from the ranks by way of a mastery of humanist styles (see Chapter Twelve, below), the other popes of the period were a lamentable lot, certainly as spiritual leaders. They were also increasingly elected by conclaves in which secrecy was slight and outside political pressure considerable. The Venetian Pietro Barbo, Paul II (1464–71), was a nephew of Eugenius who, so the papal librarian Platina tells us in his *History of the Popes*, switched from a mercantile career to the Church when he realised that he would have help in high places. This was more or less the start of a series of popes who were clever, but – to outward appearances – gave little attention to either genuine reform at large or the very real problems of the Church in Italy. Their names all too often bear the taint of corruption.

Calixtus III (1453–58) was a Borja, a Catalan who had achieved promotion owing to the papal acceptance of Alfonso I as *de jure* ruler of the kingdom of Naples; henceforth the family will be referred to in the Italian form of Borgia.[3] Like the other popes of the period, their earlier careers give little indication of the degree to which the Vatican ambience twisted them into cunning and intrigue – the Lateran was no longer the Roman headquarters of the popes. Calixtus was a learned canon lawyer. His vows had been taken as a Franciscan; his behaviour would have horrified the saint buried so securely at Assisi. Sixtus IV was the title chosen by della Rovere (1471–84). His career involved the Pazzi conspiracy against the Medici, as well as the formal inauguration of the Vatican Library (see Chapter Twelve, below). But as with many of the popes of the period, a principal aim was the territorial enrichment of his previously undistinguished family. After Innocent VIII (1484–92) there was a still more horrendous succession of power-seekers.

It is hard to find anyone with a good word to say for Rodrigo Borgia, at any rate in respectable society. He called himself Alexander VI (1492–1503) and unquestionably deserves the ill reputation he has earned, which is well documented by his master of ceremonies, the Strasbourgeois Johann Burckard; the *sang-froid* with which the latter recorded his master's sexual proclivities is itself a commentary on the Rome of the early years of the sixteenth century. If Alexander VI was ruthless in supporting his family (see Chapter Ten, below), his successor Julius II (della Rovere) was both a great patron of the arts and a soldier who did much to further the somewhat fortuitous subjugation of the Romagna and the Marches by his predecessor's son Cesare Borgia. The patronage of the arts and an even more devious public policy characterises the pontificates of the two Medici popes Leo X and Clement VII, who were separated by the brief reign of Hadrian VI (1522–23), who had been tutor to Charles V. The foreign policy of the Medici popes saw their relatives restored to Florence but failed to prevent the horrors of the Sack of Rome in 1527, described in the next volume in this series.[4]

As stated above, it is merely to indicate the tone of the Curia and the sort of men who became 'servants of the servants of God' that the popes have been introduced at the beginning of this chapter. This may have been an oversimplified approach, but who chose these pastors whose charge, before Luther, was Christendom, but whose immediate preoccupations were mainly Italian? These were the cardinals who assembled in conclave for the election, who in consistory formed the Pope's highest advisory body and who as a college had a share in some papal revenues.[5] As the popes of the *quattrocento* became increasingly involved in the internal politics of the Peninsula, so the leading rulers in the states of Italy – the Gonzaga, Sforza, Medici and so forth – found it worth their while to secure cardinals' hats for members of their families. Over the years this could have striking effects; it undoubtedly ennobled and enriched many otherwise not very impressive clans, like the della Rovere. It was to result in the Medici being returned in 1530 as the rulers of Florence.

It also meant that – with papal encouragement – the patronage of the cardinals helped to make Rome if not the cultural, then at least the architectural and artistic capital of Italy. There were many 'good' cardinals, and there were many hardworking ones: men such as Albergati, Capranica and Bessarion. As the mention of the last, a Greek, indicates, there were also a number of non-Italian members of the College, of whom one or two – such as the English cardinal Bainbridge – lived in Rome, unlike Bainbridge's contemporaries the other English cardinals Warham and Wolsey.[6] Put another way, just as Italian states found it useful to have a voice near the pope, so did many European governments. But despite their influence and background, the cardinals had more or less been cowed by the papacy – although not in the interregna between pontificates. This indeed was one of the main consequences of the Great Schism, when the College had tried to achieve recognition as the supreme power in the Church, and had failed. Used as legates and as governors of papal territories, frequently in a position to influence the direction of papal favours, the cardinals were not an important administrative, let alone spiritual, element within the Church. They found increasing compensation in high life, palaces, villas and ostentation of all kinds.

EPISCOPAL, PAROCHIAL AND CATHEDRAL CLERGY

While it is relatively easy to find out about popes and cardinals, the problem of gauging the character of Italian clergy at a lower level becomes more difficult. In effect the popes nearly always appointed bishops, albeit occasionally only after prolonged haggling with the local government.[7] The Venetians, for example, were sometimes extremely recalcitrant over particular papal nominations, and most governments felt that for a bishop to be appointed who was not a native of the state in which his diocese was situated was a way of deflecting revenue away from the locality to the coffers of the popes. Of course the doctrine that the bishop was elected, or chosen, by the clergy of the diocese was not abandoned, and exceptionally – as with Albergati at Bologna in 1417 – actually occurred. But virtually all bishops were in practice or theory directly subject to the pope, and on the whole were hardly noted as spiritual leaders. There were many of them, especially in Naples and Sicily where Christianity had first established itself. These southern sees were often poverty-stricken and it was hard, and perhaps pointless, to fill them with able men. In the north the bishoprics were larger, more nearly like transalpine dioceses, though many of them were impoverished by such long- and short-term catastrophes as fluctuations of the Po delta and war. Some of the fourteenth-century sees were virtually eliminated by the sixteenth century.

The curious system of papal nomination under political pressures of all kinds did not preclude the emergence of some remarkable figures of whom the archbishop of Florence Antonino (1389–1459), scholar, reformer and saint (from 1523) is perhaps one outstanding example. But Antonino was one of only a handful of prelates who resided in their dioceses and tried to supervise the parishes, clergy and laity for whom they were responsible. The majority were probably pluralists and/or absentees, their supervisory role being carried out by underpaid deputies, often bishops of impoverished southern sees, or friars. But before considering the evidence of the visitation records we should note briefly the characteristics of diocesan organisation in Italy.

The basic unit was the parish, before Trent not in any significant way an administrative unit. The parish consisted of the baptismal church, where the *parroco* was the senior priest among a group which included priests from dependent chapels. The 'rectors' were often beginning to find themselves in control of baptismal churches, as the 'chapel of ease' (as it was called in England) itself blossomed into a full-blown baptismal church. The process is found all over Europe, but one has the impression that it was slower in Italy than elsewhere, and the surviving baptistries in the larger towns of central Italy are a reminder of this. The parish priest of the diocese of Pisa, for instance, had to go to the cathedral once a year to get the necessary chrism, although the habit of baptising only in the cathedral or its baptistry was declining. Baptism in this period of plague and uncontrollable disease was often too urgent to be postponed even for a few hours, and of course then, as now, in an emergency anyone can baptise; a priest and the chrism are not of the essence. In fact the only sacraments for which an ordained priest was and, in the Roman Catholic Church, is still necessary are the Eucharist – by canon law required of all, preceded by confession, at least once a year – and Supreme Unction, the comfort of communion on the deathbed. For the rest, marriage, although a sacrament, was (before Trent) the trysting of the parties with the priest as a desirable witness, and most men died without the local priest being either desired or available.[8] Two other sacraments needed a bishop: the ordination of priests – and the consecration of bishops themselves – and the confirmation of the laity, which was seldom performed in this period.

These ceremonies were supervised theoretically by the diocesan bishop or 'ordinary' or by someone delegated by him if he was non-resident, as was frequently the case in the wealthier Italian sees. Supervision was supposed to be ensured by regular episcopal visitations, when the bishop inquired into the spiritual state of both clergy and laity and the material condition of church property and possessions. Habitually such visitations were pretty routine affairs. Here, for example, are the questions put by the bishop of Piacenza to priests in a visitation of his diocese early in the sixteenth century.[9] Is the church served by a curate exercising cure of souls? Is Mass said daily? Are the chrism and the holy elements kept with a lamp? Do parishioners attend Sunday service and Easter communion? Are there any notorious sinners in the parish – usurers, blasphemers, heretics, adulterers, men maintaining concubines or incestuous relationships, persons married within the degrees prohibited by the Church? Do the bells ring the 'Ave Maria' in the morning and evening? Does the priest bless the holy water each Sunday, asperge the people and announce future feast days? Are sacraments provided without charge? To go into the detailed responses to such interrogation at Piacenza or elsewhere would take too long; the general picture is of a mechanical view of their office by the bishops of Piacenza, who held only three or four visitations, mostly of churches in Piacenza itself, between 1476 and 1559. And the majority of the bishops of Piacenza were absentees. After such visitations, bishops were supposed to issue a set of remedial injunctions. A few of them did this. They make depressing reading, and the author on whom the above account is based finds throughout the period 'the same climate of slow decline'. Although many other examples lie buried, especially in notarial archives, other bishoprics have been studied and are readily available for comparison. Two generalisations may be allowed: the parochial clergy were of low quality; we know hardly anything about parishes not in or near the larger towns.[10]

In the larger cathedral cities the number of the clergy was greater, although many of the members of the cathedral chapters were absentees. Such churches often had schools, although it seems that the aspirants to priesthood attending them were usually boys from the town hoping for a comfortable berth in the cathedral. Parochial clergy outside such favoured places were instructed by apprenticeship to a local clergyman, often ill-trained himself, whom they served at the altar and to whom they said the responses. It was no different elsewhere in Latin Christendom, and the situation did not really change until the early nineteenth century.

The clergy attained their posts in various ways. In the greater cathedrals the chapter tended to be monopolised by the scions of local notables, who neglected the prescription for a collegiate life and corporate discipline. Many livings were in the gift of corporate bodies such as cathedral chapters and convents, but very many of the smaller livings were – and this was unusual outside Italy – filled by election of the people of the parish.[11] In practice 'the people' meant the important handful of prominent men in a community, often in turn swayed by one of their number or by the local *signore*. However appointed, parochial clergy and the patrons who nominated them and the secular and ecclesiastical authorities who taxed them regarded the parish 'as an economic rather than as a social or religious entity'.[12] It may be added that there were large numbers of unbeneficed clergy, usually in minor orders and many with jobs of a relatively unclerical kind (for example certain officers in universities) who consequently enjoyed some kind of clerical and privileged status.

So far only the secular clergy have been considered. The distinction between them and members of religious orders is blurred; from popes down to parish clergy we find men who were – and in some sense remained – members of religious orders, and many members of orders were also ordained priests. But the distinction is nevertheless, important.

THE RELIGIOUS

The technical phrase used for members of orders as a group was 'the religious', the source of much – often scurrilous – humour. Alternatively they are referred to as 'regular clergy': clergy living according to a rule. Religious orders were composed of groups of clergy, with constitutional and corporate regulations approved by the pope at their commencement, who lived according to the vows they took when finally fully professed. One may securely venture another generalisation. There were surely more religious in Italy than elsewhere, just as there were more orders. The orders themselves may be divided into two broad categories: the monastic – virtually all in some way derived from the Benedictine monachism as laid down in the Rule established by St Benedict of Nursia at Monte Cassino in the early sixth century – and the mendicant orders dating from the thirteenth century. As regards the first, in the course of time some of the original Benedictine houses (like Monte Cassino itself) thrived exceedingly. These monasteries were directly responsible to the pope, in a kind of feudal dependence; Monte Cassino is again an illustrious example. Situated in the kingdom of Naples, it formed in effect a large enclave of papal territory and both diplomatically and militarily complicated papal relations with the *Regno* down to and including the fifteenth century. It need hardly be said that the black monks in Italy, as elsewhere, by the end of the Middle Ages were in many ways lukewarm observers of the Rule of their founder, protecting themselves from its rigours by papal graces affecting the Order as a whole and privileges accorded to individual houses. Monasteries in a diocese came under the oversight of the bishop, but Benedictine houses in all their variety were exempt, and when they were also manifestly corrupt the bishop had to obtain a papal commission to investigate.

In the late Middle Ages the normal way of reforming or controlling religious houses was by encouraging them to amalgamate in loose federations called 'Congregations'; this had been tried with the Benedictines, but was more or less a failure in Italy until the congregation of S. Giustina of Padua was formed in 1409 largely due to the influence of devout Venetian patricians such as Ludovico Barbo (*c.* 1382–1443).[13] In 1504 the houses in this Congregation merged with the reformed group dependent on Monte Cassino and Subiaco, and since these were St Benedict's own houses the reformed Congregation was called after Monte Cassino: Cassinese. The notion behind the Congregation was that convents could support each other in reform, but with the strong individuality of Benedictine houses the Order was slow to move in that direction. An essential cause for the corruption of many monasteries – especially in Italy, where there were more hungry prelates than elsewhere – lay in the practice of granting abbeys *in commendam* to clergy who took the income and did not reside. Houses thus suffered a disastrous drop in income and became physically dilapidated; the monks, deprived of leadership, often became dissolute and ignorance prevailed as well as indiscipline. All of this seems to have gone further in the Peninsula than elsewhere in Christendom, until reform gradually got under way at the end of the fourteenth century.

Flowing from the same Benedictine impulse, several other orders developed in the eleventh century: Camaldolese, the Carthusians and the Cistercians.

Camaldolese, called after Camaldoli near Arezzo, was very informal in organisation and placed its emphasis on the fervour of retreat from the world: on the eremetic element in the Benedictine tradition. It was and remained the only specifically Italian variant of the Benedictine Rule, although by the fifteenth century its houses were in practice becoming more conventional, leaving a heritage of tension between Camaldolese monks who were in practice conventual in organisation and others with an attachment to the hermit tradition. The greatest Camaldolese of this period was Ambrogio Traversari (1386–1439), who was also a humanist and has since been beatified.[14] Just how lax this once austere group of monks had become may be seen in the remarkable letters Traversari wrote about his attempts at reform when he became minister-general of the Order in 1431.[15] Another eleventh-century offshoot of Benedictinism was the Order of Vallombrosa, named after its mother house near Florence. This Order was also virtually entirely Italian, and had also suffered a decline from its earlier ideals by this period.

The other two great orders had many houses in Italy, although both had been founded in Burgundy. Deriving their name from their original foundation at La Grande Chartreuse, the Carthusians were even more eremetical and contemplative than the Camaldolesi. They still retained in Italy, as elsewhere, something of their original fervour, attracting much secular support and as a result indulging in some spectacular building. The charterhouse, as a convent of the Order was called, consisted of a collection of individual cells, since the monks gathered and broke silence only for services; buildings were arranged so that servants could attend the monks without disturbing them, through a window that faced the cloister. A number of monuments survive from the late Middle Ages to commemorate this relatively incorrupt group of monks: the Certosa (Charterhouse) of S. Martino above Naples founded by the Angevins in the fourteenth century; the Certosa of Pavia, begun by Giangaleazzo Visconti in 1396 and the burial place of the dukes of Milan; and the Certosa of Ferrara, the consequence of Este patronage in the mid-fifteenth century. But despite its relative austerity, the Order in Italy was not prolific of great men; one has been mentioned: Niccolò Albergati (1375–1443), who became bishop of Bologna in 1417 and was made a cardinal by Martin V in 1426.

The Cistercian Order (so named after Cîteau) sought isolated sites and tried to avoid contact with corrupting influences. As a result, its austerity attracted wealth and by the end of the Middle Ages the monks were by no means models of respectable abstinence, nor were their conventual buildings stark and undecorated. What had once been a thriving and influential Order had lost its impetus. The same may be said in even greater degree of the Augustinian canons, who claimed to derive their rule from St Augustine but who constituted an economical form of monasticism, with the monks largely supported by parochial duties. Underfinanced and badly led, the Augustinians were in serious decline by the fifteenth century. Their canons regular, following a rule, are mainly to be found in Italian towns and their most famous establishment was the Lateran, which as a community was far from decrepit and which pursued its way independently of papal attempts to reform them in this period. All these offshoots of Benedictine monachism had suffered from the repeated outbreaks of plague, as well as from grants *in commendam* and absentee abbots. The exceptional history of the so-called Lateran Canons is touched on below.[16]

The most conspicuous regular clergy in Italy were not monks but mendicant friars. Even more clearly than the monks, they illustrate the desire for detachment from the world and the difficulties of achieving it. Vowed to absolute poverty, both individually and corporately, at the start they lived by begging; this attitude commanded such admiration that the laity showered wealth upon them, and for this and other reasons poverty gradually evaporated. The first mendicants were followers of St Francis of Assisi (d. 1226), who secured papal approval in 1209. The next mendicant body had a non-Italian founder, the Spaniard St Dominic (d. 1221), whose Order, greatly influenced by Franciscan practices, was founded in 1220 and became extremely numerous in Italy. Both sets of friars were soon equipped with convents and had to devise complicated ways round their rule of poverty in order to enjoy their wealth without possessing it.

On the whole the Dominicans managed this better than the Franciscans, who almost from the start were divided into two groups: the Spirituals, who aimed for a strict adherence to the original vision of the founder; and the Conventuals, who accepted the frequent papal modifications to the Rule. The fourteenth century witnessed repeated quarrels between extremists on both wings of the Franciscans; finally, just before the period covered by this volume, an attempt was made to reform the Conventuals by insisting on the strict observance of the Rule – not very taxing, as it had been greatly softened since the days of St Francis. Thus three types of Franciscans have to be distinguished, especially in Italy: the Spirituals, living rough and ascetic lives in emulation of their founder; the Conventuals, content to be very little different from enclosed orders of monks, save that they relished the liberty of movement implicit in their vows; and the Franciscans of the strict observance, or Observants. There was, in effect, civil war in the Order and popes were under constant pressure in the fifteenth century to concede victory to one side or the other; all were against the Spirituals, who had virtually disappeared by the end of the century. In 1517 priority was conceded by the papacy to the Observants and there were thus (and remain) two Franciscan Orders, but by this time a further variety had emerged, founded in Calabria in 1452 by S. Francesco di Paola (1416—1507; canonised 1519). At first known as the Hermits of St Francis, from 1492 they took still further the terminology of humility adopted by the Franciscans, the Friars Minor, and became known as the Minims, the 'least' in the household of God; they quickly spread all over Europe. After the severance of the Order yet another descendant of Franciscan idealism emerged in the Capuchin Order, established in 1529 and again stressing early Franciscan practices which made the new friars unpopular with the established Franciscans but popular with the laity.[17]

The Dominican Order, although it copied the Franciscans' vow of poverty, did not aim, as St Francis and his closer followers had done, at 'sancta simplicitas'. Dominic's aim was the overthrowing of heresy; the Dominicans sought to be learned and made for the universities to master the techniques and truths of learning and theology. These Black Friars were also known as the Order of Preachers and rapidly established houses in the universities, though less so in Italy, where theology was not cultivated at the larger universities and was sometimes provided only – and then by the late fourteenth century – in a few Dominican houses attached to the *Studia Generalia*; Padua and Ferrara are cases in point. Bologna too made available the theology of the Order of Preachers, and it was from that centre that Savonarola ultimately gravitated to the convent of San Marco in Florence, becoming its prior in 1491. If Italian Dominicans still had to go to Paris or Cologne for sophisticated training in theology, what is noticeable in *quattrocento* Italy was in fact the outstanding preaching of some Observant Franciscans: S. Bernardino of Siena (1380–1444; canonised 1450), S. Giacomo della Marca (1393–1476; canonised 1726), S. Giovanni di Capistrano (1386–1456; canonised 1724) and Bernardino da Feltre (1439–94).[18] It was of course true that Dominicans were prominent preachers, as can be seen from the case of Savonarola; another Dominican of great importance was Florentine archbishop Antonino; earlier still, Giovanni Dominici (1357–1419) was a leading opponent of the new learning, as the next chapter will show. Yet despite the dramatic if temporary effects of their great men, of whom only a few have been mentioned, the Dominican Order in Italy was in decay in the later Middle Ages. It too had its attempts at a strict observance, but these were of a mitigated rigour and seldom successful. In 1475, as part of a series of measures to enhance the status and underline the privileges of the mendicant order, the Franciscan Sixtus IV eased any remaining Dominican consciences troubled by the problem of poverty by revoking the prohibition on property-holding.

For many Dominicans before the action of Sixtus IV the idea of no longer being 'mendicants' was horrific, however comfortable – even rich – many of them were. Mendicancy was tremendously evocative in a world where the few were well off, the majority poor. This relish in being technically poor is also revealed in the other orders established in Italy: the Carmelites, the Augustinian hermits, the Servites and others. The Carmelites, founded at first on Mount Carmel before Christians were expelled from the Holy Land, by our period were gradually sinking into a torpid state from which they were not to be roused until the later sixteenth century. The Augustinian friars or hermits – Luther belonged to one of the reformed friaries of the Order – went through the cycle of reform and relapse rather like the Dominicans, whom they resembled in their rule and original aims. The Servites, or Order of Servants of the Virgin Mary, were thoroughly Italian in origin: their mother house is near Florence, and their founders in the thirteenth century had been well-to-do Florentines. The Order went into decline, although one of its famous sons was Paolo Sarpi (1552–1603), a Venetian critic of the papacy and one of the first freethinkers in European history.

Nearly all these orders of monks and friars developed second Orders

composed of fully professed nuns,[19] so called even when they were members
of a mendicant order and also in theory enclosed, even if the friars to whom
they were affiliated were not. The mendicant orders also developed third
orders. The tertiaries, or members of the Third Orders, were initially laity
under light vows, but the pressure to conform led to the establishment of
houses of enclosed Tertiary nuns, under strict rules and subject to strict vows.
In all cases Tertiaries were particularly devoted to works of mercy, and were
prominent in hospitals and work for the needy. But here again, in the last
decades of the Middle Ages the orders of nuns, both regular and Tertiary,
were often in bad repute. The canons of the general chapters of the orders
record repeatedly that monks or friars charged with entering such nunneries
– to say Mass, for instance, or to hear confession – must be chaperoned by
another monk or friar and frequently replaced. Many nuns had joined an order
because the entrance fee or dowry paid by their families on entry to a convent
was substantially less than the dowry that would have to be paid to secure
a husband.

Moreover, the relatively late age at which young men got married meant
not only that prostitutes flourished and homosexuality became sometimes a
major social problem, but also that nuns became attractive alternatives,
especially those with no sense of vocation (see Chapter Three, above). The
problem of keeping nuns from leaving their houses unauthorised and keeping
out young gallants led civic authorities to step in – much to the annoyance
of the ecclesiastical hierarchy, which claimed sole jurisdiction, although it was
unable to do anything effective without the force of the lay arm. There was
trouble, for instance, in Florence in the fifteenth century. The *Signoria* established a secular commission to supervise nunneries in 1421, and disobeyed
Eugenius IV's direction fifteen years later that it should be disbanded.[20] Of
course in a few places – Venice, Genoa, Messina – very wealthy nunneries
harboured upper-class ladies who, however immoral, were protected by the
patricians who ran the city and were accused by some contemporaries of
enjoying the favours of the nuns. Besides, both monks and nuns were now
accustomed to being allowed to visit their families for long periods. This,
of course, did not happen to men and women in well-regulated convents.

All in all the picture sketched above is rather dispiriting: popes intent for
the most part on promoting the interests of their families; monks and friars
with rules which had for the most part become so diluted as to present little
discipline; nuns many of whom neglected claustration along with other vows.
Yet many lay people were are least outwardly virtuous and devout. Before
we turn to them we should, however, note that such sentiments, together
with the desire to organise sympathisers for mutual support, led to the
development of fresh forms of regular religion. Many of these developments
were to take place after our period, but they undoubtedly owed much to the
confraternities which emerged in large numbers in Italy in the late Middle
Ages. By 1400 we find such companies of laity – men and women, who
appointed priests as their chaplains – in most Italian towns. They practised
regular churchgoing and went to confession and attended Mass more

frequently than the obligatory Easter ceremony. They also resorted to 'discipline', which, when strictly interpreted, meant flagellation, although this tended to be frowned upon if performed in public in more than a ritualistic fashion. Some secular authorities could be alarmed at the activities of such groups, which could be anonymous, meet at night and in other respects appear potentially conspiratorial.[21] But they multiplied, and began to adopt such titles as the 'Confraternity of Divine Love'. We even find in the Milan of the 1460s a pious company of priests, while in Rome the membership of the Oratory of Divine Love in Trastevere contained a high proportion of clergy; here we are approaching the emergence of the typical new orders of the sixteenth century – the Oratorians, the Jesuits and others – composed of priests who in effect were unenclosed, at any rate at first.

RELIGION AND THE LAITY

One has the impression that there were proportionately more clergy, including nuns, in Italy than elsewhere, but few figures exist at present to verify this guess. For early-fourteenth-century Florence, we have the well-informed picture given by Giovanni Villani in his *Chronicle*, which K. J. Beloch in his study of Italian populations summarises as: 80 monks, 700 friars, 500 nuns and 200 or more priests.[22] This gives a total of 1,480 clergy out of a total population of 92,000, but the proportion of the clergy is higher when all those in minor orders and enjoying clerical privileges are taken into account. For sixteenth-century Venice, with priests and regular clergy making up perhaps 3 per cent of the population, the proportion appears to have been even higher.[23] A further indication of the large numbers and impact of the clergy is provided by the multitude of churches and religious buildings of all kinds, including hospitals, surviving from this and earlier periods. This, together with the maintenance of a large number of clergy, testifies to the loyalty of most Italians to the Church as an institution, just as it goes far to explain frequent criticism of and hostility to the clergy and serious lapses in the moral standards of the clergy themselves.

Needless to say, Italian laymen and women hated having to pay money to the Church. The instance of a Visitor asking if money was charged for sacraments has been quoted above. It certainly often was, but beyond this there was in Italy, as elsewhere, the tithe in its various forms. This was a perpetual source of friction among the laity, who had to face the increasing weight of taxation and other burdens imposed by the state and who resented the exemptions from lay levies which the clergy traditionally claimed and often succeeded in enjoying – albeit taxed, of course, by the Church itself (see Chapter Six). Normally the civil authorities did not tax ecclesiastical property, although Venice occasionally did so with papal concurrence. And throughout Italy we find prohibitions of gifts of land to clerical corporations and churches, analogous to the mortmain provisions found in northern

Europe and evaded as frequently in Italy as elsewhere. Illogically, the laity's piety often endowed monks and friars to the point where they were regarded as contemptible layabouts – which they often were.

Money also came into the relations of clergy and laity through the illegality of usury according to canon law. This canonical condemnation was, of course, attenuated in many ways which enabled men of business, and especially bankers, not to be incommoded in their activities. But it was, all the same, a worry; in his multitudinous papers the merchant of Prato Francesco di Marco Datini has left plenty of evidence both of his usurious practices and of his occasionally troubled conscience. One consolation for troubled bankers was to open an account, usually modest, in their ledgers for the credit of God, 'il conto di Messer Domeneddio'. Bankers and other persons profiting from this pre-capitalistic world of currencies and commodities also gave lavishly to charity, adorned or built sacred buildings and bought, as they trusted, security in the afterlife by funding Masses by chantry priests for themselves or their families. The well-to-do faced with financial crisis could, of course, borrow from a bank on the security of their valuables and even, if necessary, on their land. This was far from being as easy for the less well-off and was very hard for the poor.

The poor were particularly vulnerable, and raised money with small pledges – furnishings, tools, clothes and so on. Such accommodation for small borrowers had for long been provided for by moneylenders who were often Jews; but even in Italy, where the papacy's protection of the Jews was to a certain degree more effective – especially in Rome and the Papal States – than in other parts of the Latin west, there was growing hostility towards them. Lending to the poor was, of course, a risky business and the lender tried to cover his risk by high interest rates, just as the wealthy bankers and merchants did in dealing with princes and the rich. But the poor suffered severely and, like all who borrowed in this way, were involved in a usurious transaction and were in consequence committing a serious sin.

Hence the readiness with which the Franciscans and other mendicants took up a fierce anti-Jewish and anti-usury position and welcomed the establishment of civic-controlled pawnshops, *Monti di Pietà*. The first of these seems to have been established in 1462 at Perugia following the preaching of an Observant. But the apostle of the pawnshop was Bernardino da Feltre. So insistent was he in preaching on behalf of the setting-up of *Monti* that he has probably been credited with more of such establishments than he actually promoted in person; there were eighty-eight towns with *Monti* by 1515. But in his sermon on the *Monte* at Pavia, which was established in 1493, there is a full account of the moral problems of borrowing and lending and of the practical problems of establishing the pawnshops in a sensible and secure way, controlling the charges to the level necessary for the operation of what were very complicated arrangements to control the pledges, house them, maintain serious supervision, and so forth. The initial capital to start the enterprise – and to raise this was the aim of many Observant sermons, especially those of Bernardino – came from acts of charity by the rich, contributing to a common pool of cash. Strictly managed in this way, pawnbroking could not make a man rich; but it allowed those who had money to help those who had not with a means of lending and borrowing that avoided breaking the law of the Church.[24] Venice, however, was less impressed by the *Monti* and continued to rely on her large Jewish community to provide moneylenders for the poor − at least as far as the city of Venice itself was concerned.

Another prominent and sensitive area for charitable activity was the provision of dowries. In Florence, to a certain extent, this became institutionalised in the *Monte delle Doti*, a publicly managed fund in which fathers could invest for the future well-being of their daughters (see Chapter Six).[25] But charitable gifts to provide dowries for the poor are found all over Italy, their intention being to give the daughters of poor or relatively poor families enough money to acquire a husband or enter a nunnery; in the latter case the dowry was intended as capital to finance a girl when she entered a cloister. Around 1500, the surplus of the *Monte di Pietà* in Venice − where the 5 per cent interest rate was more than enough to cover the administration of the pawnbroking establishment − was often given to the 'donzelle', maidens, of Venice and towns in the Veneto.[26] It was also a favourite charity to contribute to establishments for 'convertiti', reclaimed fallen women.

A complication regarding poverty, found in many areas but particularly in Italy and Spain, derived from the inability of gentlemen to work for a living; they forfeited their status if they did. These were the 'poveri vergognosi', who derived their name from the parable of the 'unjust', or perhaps inefficient, steward in Luke chapter xvi, verse 3, who when dismissed by his master said: 'I cannot dig; to beg I am ashamed'. One of the functions of many confraternities like the Florentine 'Good Men of St Martin' was the relief of such well-born poor, and since honour was essential to these shamefaced indigents, their alms had to be distributed at night by confraternities devoted to this activity.

The laity were also attracted to serve in the hospitals of Italian towns. These had for long been remarkably well developed, as can be seen from the case of the great foundation in Rome of Innocent III in 1198, the *Arcispedale* of S. Spirito in Sassia (from Wessex, since the adjoining church had been founded by King Ine in the eighth century). From 1471 this was rebuilt and greatly extended by Sixtus IV, and came to cater not only for the old miseries of plague and leprosy but for the new scourge of syphilis.[27] The hospital of S. Spirito also cared for foundlings and foundling hospitals are found in all the large Italian towns, one of the most remarkable being the Innocents' hospital in Florence, designed by Brunelleschi (1419–26), with its long portico decorated by the roundels of Andrea della Robbia; appropriately, it is now flanked by a maternity hospital. In Venice the foundling hospital established in the fourteenth century had the more sinister name of the Ospizio degli Esposti − the hospice of exposed or abandoned children − now better known as S. Maria della Visitazione or della Pietà. In this period, those hospitals offered an outlet for female charitable impulses. Luther's surprised admiration for the gently born veiled ladies taking their turn in

Italian hospitals will be recalled, along with their clean sheets and clean dishes for food and drink.

These institutions were direct reflections of a religion which listed among the seven corporal acts of mercy feeding the hungry, visiting the sick and burying the dead (see Chapter Five). Unfortunately, scholarly work in this area – beyond the study of local institutions – is only just beginning, and apart from saying that Italy probably took a lead in the later Middle Ages with confraternities, hospitals and other philanthropic developments, it is hard to go much further without the basis of more solid comparative evidence. But for an earlier generation the evidence of Italian religion is more self-evidently displayed in the relatively large number of Italian saints. Even when Pastor wrote his famous chapter on the 'true renaissance', as he called it, and contrasted with the 'pagan renaissance', it was to the Italian saints that he turned for evidence of the 'innately religious temperament of the Italian nation'. He enumerated eighty-eight saints and *beati* between 1400 and 1520 in his *History of the Popes*[28] and he also tabulated the hospitals and 'foundling asylums', together with other charitable institutions in Italy founded before 1399 and from 1399 to 1524 – a quite staggering number:

	Up to 1399	1400–1524
Hospitals and foundling asylums	13	103
Almshouses	12	—
Orphanages	14	9
Relief of the poor	92	53
Dowries	6	53
Education	9	7
Various	5	—

The large number of hospitals and dowry endowments in the fifteenth century was for the most part a feature of the large towns where wealth and social ills tended to be concentrated, but measured as a yardstick of practical piety the Italian scene – despite its corrupt clergy and massive prostitution, despite the turmoil of war and invasion and the ravages of plague and syphilis – comes out of any comparison with other lands remarkably well.

Nor is there lack of evidence for the enthusiasm of Italians for certain religious observances. This is the era when the Pax, or Osculatorium, was increasingly used during the celebration of Mass, the practice being encouraged by the Franciscans in particular. A small plate of wood, ivory or some other material, often decorated with the Crucifixion and mounted on a handle, was kissed by the presiding priest and handed to the server to extend the 'kiss of peace' to the congregation; the ceremony was more elaborate in larger churches with more clergy present. It is also the age when the Dominicans, closely associated with the cult of the Virgin, promoted the Rosary, the beads by which the Virgin's cult was stimulated. Already such devotions were encouraged in Italy, as elsewhere, by bells tolling the Angelus in the morning and evening to signal the repetition of the 'Ave Maria'; in the fifteenth century, a midday Angelus was added in Italy.

Those who were able to attend the papal blessing of the 'Agnus Dei' regarded themselves as especially privileged if they obtained this object; this was a small cake of wax, stamped with the emblem of the Lamb and Flag; Martin V undertook to bless a supply of these tablets every seventh year of his pontificate. With these observances we should link the Lenten devotion to the Stations of the Cross, fourteen pictures or carvings placed round the nave of a church. This reminder of Christ's progress to Calvary was itself a distant echo of the devotions of pilgrims in Jerusalem at the time of the Crusades; but it became extremely popular in the late Middle Ages, again encouraged by the Franciscans. A final example of devotion – again associated with the Franciscans, but in this case specifically Italian in origin – was focused on the Holy Name of Jesus. Launched by the preaching of S. Bernardino of Siena, this cult found expression in the monogram IHS, and like all these aids to religious observance had consequences for the arts and architecture and in the decoration of chapels of families, guilds and confraternities, as well as of churches.[29]

By the standards of modern Roman Catholicism the observances just described may sometimes appear quaint, magical or superstitious. Certainly there were no incentives to partake of the Eucharist more than the statutory occasion at Easter. Men who communicated more often were regarded with some suspicion and women who confessed and communicated frequently – say four times a year – were regarded as peculiarly devout. The services in the bigger churches were becoming more vivid and ritualised. The elements now had to be kept on the altar with a candle, and in the Eucharist were elevated so that all the congregation could see Christ. It was a good attendance at Mass that Visitors to a parish inquired about, and their presence at Mass was a 'proper' way for the laity to commemorate Sundays and holy days – although there could be complaints if Mass on these occasions was celebrated too late in the morning, as that cut into the sociable holiday atmosphere! The church was very much the House of God, and many churches could also boast the possession of the body of a saint or other relics. These ancient magnets for the devout, believed to work miracles sometimes of a specialised kind, were also attractive because for many churches, especially the larger ones, they were associated with processions to avert disasters or celebrate holy days – a subject increasingly studied in recent years – and with indulgences.[30]

Indulgences – the careless or cynical promise of these was to set ablaze the bonfire of Lutheranism – granted the remission of the penalties of sin on earth and after death, in purgatory, provided that the sinner had truly repented and been forgiven. The theology of this concept – depending on the inexhaustible merits of Christ, the Virgin Mary and the saints, the Treasury of Merit – was often preached to simple folk in the period as readily acquired by pilgrimage, by visiting the privileged churches or by cash down to a 'pardoner'. It was frequently expressed by the remission of so many years in purgatory and could be intended for the individual qualifying for the indulgence on behalf of someone else, so that the devout could hope in this way to ease the pain of dead relatives. Much the same was believed to result from Masses for the dead, frequently financed in the wills of the dying and – in the case of the rich – leading to incredible numbers of services, frequently performed in the chapels built at the side of the nave or in the aisles – chantry chapels. These are found multiplying everywhere in late medieval Europe, but in Italy they were further encouraged by their connection with confraternities, which organised large-scale propitiatory devotions for past members.

With the large number of confraternities, with bells ringing the Angelus, with crucifixes at street corners and crossroads (themselves emblematic of the choices before man, and the proper way to choose between them), with ordinary men and women as well as the rich and powerful crossing themselves in a gesture of protection and perhaps prayer, one can readily arrive at the conviction of Italian devotion, or at worst religiosity. There is, however, another picture, heavily emphasised by older writers like Burckhardt and Pastor. This is a dark view of the violence, immorality and cynicism of the Italy in the two centuries before the Reformation. For Burckhardt this was the price the Italians paid for their cultural leadership of Europe: for having housed the Renaissance before it crossed the Alps. Pastor accepted this, for he distinguished, as explained earlier, between a true or Christian renaissance and the pagan or classical renaissance which he regarded as pestilential, the culture of the period being redeemed only by large numbers of saints, very large numbers of sacred pictures and buildings and a handful of virtuous friars and bishops.

The difficulty of coming to an assessment of Christian belief in the Italy of the later Middle Ages and Renaissance is that views such as those summarised above are based almost exclusively on urban evidence, and indeed frequently on written records and literature of various kinds. What were the views and practices of the illiterate masses, especially in rural areas? Scanty visitation records in rural Tuscany in the fifteenth century suggest that even in the neighbourhood of towns like Florence and Pisa there were villages without priests, where birth, marriage and death occurred without ceremony; and a Jesuit a century later found that in a small commune near Fano, an episcopal town in the March of Ancona, more than half of the inhabitants had never communicated in their lives, and a larger proportion did not know how to make the sign of the cross or understand to what it referred. The bishops of Fano were often non-resident, and were able to hand the see to a relative.[31] Another Jesuit found the peasants of the Abruzzo – a region close to Rome itself – and those of Apulia and Calabria in such a state of religious barbarism that he talked of an 'Italian India', awaiting conversion. This evidence is late, post-Reformation, but it recalls Machiavelli's bitter observation in the *Discorsi*: that one should 'look at those people who live in the immediate neighbourhood of the Church of Rome, which is the head of our religion, and see how there is less religion amongst them than elsewhere.[32]

It is indeed true that in urban settings there were confraternities such as the Misericordia in Florence whose members devoted themselves to burying the dead, or of S. Giovanni Decollato in Rome which deputed two brothers to accompany criminals to their execution with comforting words; these, together with the endless processions bearing relics, were visual reminders of Christianity's power of persuasion to perform good works.[33] But spectacles, often less evidently of religious interest, were also provided, especially when the pontificate of Paul II saw the carnival introduced to the centre of Rome. Even the papal procession across Rome from Vatican to Lateran, or similar gestures in other towns, were little different from the magnificent displays undertaken by princes, and by republican governments where they still existed. Jousting was not unknown in wealthier monasteries as a *divertissement*. It is hard to believe that devotion was promoted by these parades – nor was it by the miracle or mystery plays which, as in all countries, were found in Italy; the *sacre rappresentazioni*, as they were called, were often well written by their Italian authors, but as elsewhere they contained burlesque as well as holy scenes. Rodocanachi says that the carnival was introduced to avoid grosser Roman amusement. It is harder to imagine anything grosser than the carnival by the early sixteenth century, when racing took place in the Roman *Corso* – which thus acquired its name – instead of being mainly at Monte Testaccio, a place of medieval merriment.[34]

For Machiavelli, in the chapter to which reference has already been made and in other passages of his writings, the papacy was responsible directly for the lamentable political state of Italy as well as for the appalling corruption of the Italian clergy. His view was shared by Guicciardini, not least in the famous maxim in the *Ricordi* where he hopes – and knows it to be in vain – to see three things in his lifetime: Florence well governed, Italy free of foreign occupation and an end everywhere to the 'tyranny of those wicked priests'.[35] One cannot, of course, regard these two remarkable Florentines as representative. But both, by different routes, end up with an anticlericalism which is extraordinarily aggressive. The vernacular plays of Machiavelli should be remembered, with their contemptuous view of the clergy; but Guicciardini may well appear the more remarkable when it is remembered that he rose high in papal service.

No papal governor – like Guicciardini – nor, indeed, any authority with extensive powers in Italy could avoid becoming entangled in the profoundly difficult Church–State relations which characterised the Peninsula. Authority over public morality and over the priesthood and the religious of all kinds lay with the representatives of the Church. Even a government with such strong claims to independence as Florence or Venice or the larger principalities was faced with a challenge to its authority when trying to enforce order. Florentine attempts to regulate nunneries, which so incensed Eugenius IV when he was in the city, have been referred to (see above, p. 135).[36] Ironically, conflicts of authority also occurred in the subject communes of the Papal States, where the pope appointed both governor and bishop and where both were in a direct way dependent on the Curia. The temporal authority clashed with the spiritual authority, especially when the papal governor attempted to maintain his jurisdiction over priests. This ambiguity sprang directly from the double authority of the pope – 'sovrano e pastore', to quote an apt phrase of Paolo Prodi.[37] From the fifteenth century onwards, the pastor was succumbing to the prince. Whatever the political consequences of this, it confused the hierarchy and diminished the educated layman's respect for religion. He – and the uneducated layman also – relished the pomp and circumstance. He resented having to pay for it.

One last point should be made regarding heresy in Italy. With the exception of the Waldensians – the first 'Protestant' Church in Christendom, but by the period largely confined to the mountainous area of Piedmont – heresy had more or less been obliterated, with the extermination of the last *Fraticelli*, the heirs of the Spiritual Franciscans, in Florence in the 1460s. But the total exclusion of heresy, by an indifferent public and an occasionally active Inquisition, was again put to the test as the new ideas from Germany began to percolate into the Peninsula. This was largely through Venice, with its large colony of German merchants and its cosmopolitan 'Latin Quarter' at the University of Padua. Perhaps less obviously, a history of devotion among a small number of the Venetian patriciate, like the reformer Ludovico Barbo, not only inspired Catholic reform but also created the ambience from which was to emerge, in the early sixteenth century, a book later judged to be in serious conflict with the teaching of the Church. This was the *Beneficio di Cristo*, which has recently attracted the attention of scholars interested in the pre-Tridentine Church in Italy. This, with its Calvinistic allusions, was not printed in Italian – or at all – until the Venice edition of 1543, a few years after the first publication of John Calvin's *Christianae Religionis Institutio* (Basel, 1536). The matter has been much discussed and still retains elements of mystery; nor is it the first 'Protestant' work in Italian, a priority recently claimed for the *Alfabeto Christiano* of Juan Valdés, a Spanish Erasmian who had settled in Naples and wrote in the late 1530s what has been called 'the first manifesto of Evangelism in Italy'.[38] Benedetto di Mantova (or Fontanini), the author of the *Beneficio*, was a member of the Benedictine Congregation of S. Giustina at Padua, and its house in Venice, and was an intimate of many leading and perfectly orthodox clergy: Gregorio Cortese (later a cardinal), Cardinal Pole and similarly minded and serious men. The rest of the story of the influence of Valdés, Bernardino Ochino and others lies beyond the scope of this volume and indeed largely outside Italy, for it spread into northern Europe and greatly affected the development of the Anabaptist movement.

It fittingly concludes this survey to indicate that a number of Italians – in the Veneto, perhaps also in Naples and elsewhere – were aware of an alternative to traditional Roman Catholic religion, even if governments, in Italy, unlike some across the Alps, were unwilling to lead civil authority to a new direction in belief.

NOTES AND REFERENCES

1. For example, in the *Ragionamenti* or *Dialogues* of Pietro Aretino (1492–1556).
2. L. Pastor, *The History of the Popes*, ed. and trans. F. I. Antrobus, vol. i (London, 1891); A. Esch, *Bonifaz IX und der Kirchenstaat* (Tübingen, 1969).
3. M. Mallett, *The Borgias. The Rise and Fall of a Renaissance Dynasty* (London, 1969).
4. Also, J. Hook, *The Sack of Rome* (London, 1972); A. Chastel, *The Sack of Rome* (Princeton, 1983).
5. D. Hay, *The Church in Italy in the Fifteenth Century* (Cambridge, 1977), pp. 36–7; cf. Gregorio Penco, *Storia della Chiesa in Italia, I. Dalle Origini al Concilio di Trento* (Milan, 1977). On the predicament of signorial families with representatives in the college, D. S. Chambers, 'The housing problems of Cardinal Francesco Gonzaga', *J.W.C.I.*, vol. xxxix (1976); idem, 'Francesco "Cardinalino"', *Atti e Mem. dell'Accademia Virgiliana di Mantova*, n.s., vol. xlviii (1980).
6. D. S. Chambers, *Cardinal Bainbridge in the Court of Rome* (Oxford, 1965).
7. For example, L. Fumi, 'Chiesa e stato nel dominio di Francesco I Sforza', *A.S.L.*, ser. vi, vol. i (1924); L. Prosdocimi, *Il Diritto Ecclesiastico nello Stato di Milano* (Milan, 1973); C. Cenci, 'Senato Veneto: *probae* ai benefizi ecclesiastici', in C. Piana and C. Cenci, *Promozioni agli ordini sacri a Bologna e alle dignità ecclesiastiche nel Veneto nei secoli xiv-xv* (Florence, 1968).
8. At the twenty-fourth session of the Council of Trent (11 November 1563) the canons regarding matrimony made marriage by a priest essential. On late medieval marriage ritual: C. Klapisch-Zuber, 'Zacharias or the Ousted Father: nuptial rites in Tuscany between Giotto and the Council of Trent', in *Women, Family and Ritual in Renaissance Italy* (Chicago and London, 1985). The traditional seven sacraments (besides confirmation and ordination mentioned later) also include penance, taken seriously, it may be supposed, in convents, but only momentarily by the laity.
9. F. Molinari, 'Visite e sinodi pretridentini a Piacenza', *Italia Sacra*, vol. ii (1960).
10. A contemporary estimate of the ignorance of the clergy is provided by the *Libellus ad Leonen X* by the Venetian Camaldolese monks Giustiniani and Quirini. They reckoned that between two in a hundred and ten in a thousand clergy had learnt Latin, and few of these who had a smattering of Latin grammar had studied it systematically. This aside in their desolating study deserves to be pondered: J. B. Mittarelli and A. Costadini (eds), *Annales Camaldolese*, vol. ix (Venice, 1773), col. 676. More generally, D. Hay, *Italian Clergy and Italian Culture in the Fifteenth Century*, The Society for Renaissance Studies, Occasional Papers No. 1 (London, 1973).
11. For Venice, N. S. Davidson, 'The clergy of Venice in the sixteenth century', *Bulletin of the Society for Renaissance Studies*, vol. ii, no. 2 (1984).
12. P. A. Linehan, *The Spanish Church and the Papacy in the Thirteenth Century* (Cambridge, 1971), p. 267.
13. Hay, *Church in Italy*, p. 148; B. Collett, *Italian Benedictine Scholars and the Reformation* (Oxford, 1985).
14. L. Martines, *The Social World of the Florentine Humanists* (London, 1963), pp. 311 –12.
15. G. G. Coulton, *Five Centuries of Religion*, vol. v (Cambridge, 1950), chs xxvi–xxxiii.
16. Hay, op. cit., pp. 77–8, 89–90.

17. The Capuchins were founded by Matteo di Bassi of Urbino (d. 1552) and adopted a hood, or 'cappuccio', in memory of St Francis. Some valuable insights into the history of the Franciscan Order in fifteenth-century Italy can be found in, R. Goffen, *Piety and Patronage in Renaissance Venice* (New Haven and London, 1986).

18. Bernardino da Feltre took his name from his predecessor from Siena. He was beatified in 1654. B. Pullan, *Rich and Poor in Renaissance Venice* (Oxford, 1971), pp. 455–66.

19. The Cistercian nuns were not regarded as a separate order. Probably the most influential Dominican nun in the period was St Catherine of Siena (1347–80), canonised by the Sienese pope Pius II in 1461. For insights into her considerable cult in Italy, F. Hall and H. Uhr, 'Aureola super Aureum: crowns and related symbols of special distinction for saints in late Gothic and Renaissance iconography', *Art B.*, vol. lxvii, no. 4 (1985), pp. 578–83.

20. G. Brucker, *Renaissance Florence* (New York, 1966), pp. 191–3.

21. Pullan, op. cit., pt i; R. F. E. Weissman, *Ritual Brotherhood in Renaissance Florence* (New York, 1982).

22. K. J. Beloch, *Bevölkerungsgeschichte Italiens* (Berlin–Leipzig, 1937–61), vol. ii, p. 132; G. Villani, *Cronaca*, ed. G. Aquilecchia (Turin, 1979), bk xi, ch. 94.

23. Davidson, loc. cit.

24. Pullan, op. cit., pt iii.

25. J. Kirshner, *Pursuing Honor while Avoiding Sin. The Monte delle Doti of Florence* (Milan, 1978).

26. Pullan, op. cit., pp. 605 ff.

27. E. Lee, *Sixtus IV and Men of Letters* (Rome, 1978), pp. 137–43.

28. Pastor, op. cit., vol. i, pp. 35–56; vol. v (London, 1950), pp. 86–8.

29. Fragile examples of such religious art are the banners of confraternities, e.g. C. M. Kauffman, 'Barnaba da Modena and the Flagellants of Genoa', *Victoria and Albert Museum Reprints*, 20 (London, 1971); F. Dabell, 'Domenico Veneziano in Arezzo', *B.M.*, vol. cxxvii, no. 982 (1985).

30. For example, E. Muir, *Civic Ritual in Renaissance Venice* (Princeton, 1981).

31. F. Ughelli, *Italia Sacra*, 2nd edn by N. Coleti, 10 vols (Venice, 1717–22, reprinted Bologna, 1972–74), vol. i, cols 668–9; P. Tacchi-Venturi, *Storia della Compagnia di Gesu in Italia*, vol. i, pt i, 2nd edn (Rome, 1951), p. 327.

32. *Discorsi*, bk i, ch. 12; *Machiavelli, the Chief Works*, trans. A. Gilbert, vol. i (Durham, North Carolina, 1965), p. 228.

33. The Roman confraternity was founded in the late fifteenth century by Florentine merchants, as an offshoot of the Florentine confraternity of the *Misericordia*: S. Y. Edgerton, *Pictures and Punishment* (Ithaca, 1985), p. 179, n.11, pp. 165–92.

34. E. Rodocanachi, *Le Carnaval à Rome au XVᵉ et XVIᵉ siècles* (Amiens, 1890).

35. F. Guicciardini, *Opere Inedite*, ed. G. Canestrini, vol. i (Florence, 1857), p. 154, no. 236; translation from *Maxims and Reflections of a Renaissance Statesman*, trans. M. Domandi, intro. N. Rubinstein (Philadelphia, 1965).

36. Cf. C. Cipolla, *Chi ruppe i Rastelli?* (Bologna, 1977), for another Florentine example.

37. *Il Sovrano Pontifice* (Bologna, 1982), the title of ch. 2. Trans. Haskins (Cambridge, 1987).

38. P. McNair, *Peter Martyr in Italy* (Oxford, 1967), pp. 39–40. The most recent full analysis of the problems surrounding the *Beneficio di Cristo* is by C. Ginsburg and A. Prosperi, in *Eresia e Riforma, Miscellanea* I (Florence–Chicago, 1974), pp. 137–204.

PART THREE

Political histories

CHAPTER EIGHT

Italy and Europe

INTRODUCTION

Detailed historical maps of Renaissance Italy are hard to find, and those that are available tend to be on a regional rather than on a 'national' basis. This is unfortunate, because the three major political divisions of the Peninsula are the products of history rather than of geography: the kingdom of Italy, part of the Western Empire, embraced most of the north and Tuscany; the Papal States ran, roughly, diagonally from the Adriatic to the Tyrrhenian seas; in the south was the *Regno*, the kingdom of Naples. Around the Italian coasts, a series of islands were barely considered by contemporaries as forming part of Italy: Sicily, which in the period became firmly associated with Naples under the same Aragonese dynasty, as did the Lipari and Maltese groups; Sardinia and Corsica, battled over by the Aragonese and Genoa; over the islands of the Dalmatian coast Venice extended her rule, as she did over parts of Greece and some of the Greek islands until they were overrun by the Ottoman Turks. But the basic distinctions – between the north, the Papal States and the *Regno* – owed their existence to centuries of warfare between the empire and papacy.

If one tries to picture the Peninsula at the start of the period covered by this volume, the broad regions outlined above and followed in the chapters below are evident enough; but the moment one descends to a detailed analysis of each area one is at once confronted by the multiplicity of smaller states. Some of them were small only in comparison with the great kingdoms outside Italy. Within Italy itself Venice and Milan were dominant in large measure over their neighbours, and there has always been a temptation to write Italian political history in terms of these large and often aggressive units, along with Florence and Naples. But in fact such divisions of Italy do less than justice to the reality of the smaller centres of power. These are particularly prominent in the Papal States. Rome was economically weak compared with the cities mentioned above; and its authority as a 'capital' city could be weakened still further when rebellious subjects of the Papal States appealed to the doctrine which made a general council the ultimate source of authority in the Church.

On the other hand, Rome had a tradition depending not only on the power of the papacy but on the saints it harboured and the privileges it could confer through jubilees, held ever more frequently as the fifteenth century advanced. The papacy also claimed overlordship of the *Regno* and the greater islands, and the growing power of Aragon in the region was hindered by the support the popes could give to a rival dynasty with claims in the region, the French house of Anjou.

Hence it is difficult to follow, in Italy, the pattern suggested by northern and Iberian states in terms of the steady emergence of central government, and in the succeeding chapters, although the broad divisions indicated above will be followed, the picture to emerge will include many lesser states of a variety of types – feudal, communal and 'despotic'. This divided and sub-divided land was the scene of extraordinarily tenacious struggles for power which, as suggested in Chapters Five and Six could both strengthen and weaken the authority of the state. The story begins at the end of the four-teenth century and ends, so far as this volume is concerned, in the third decade of the sixteenth. By then the outside pressures had changed. The Habsburg emperors were now also the rulers of a unifying Spain, which controlled – or was in the process of controlling – much of Central and South America. The years of the French invasions of Italy coincided with the arrival of silver and gold from across the Atlantic, and the economic picture for the Peninsula, as for Europe as a whole, was to be transformed. Finally, the whispers of criticism of the old Church which had already been faintly heard in Italy culminated in the storm of Luther, and gave added significance to the Sack of Rome in 1527.

The century and a half between the outbreak of the Great Schism and the Sack of Rome (1378–1527) saw a gradual build-up of international rivalries of which Italy became increasingly the centre. These replaced the older struggle between empire and papacy which had once set the whole Peninsula in the international arena; that contest had virtually faded from the Italian scene and the traditional party labels of Guelf and Ghibelline were now used with even less discrimination as factional names, without reference to more general principles of political organisation or loyalty. As a result, the tangled internal politics of Italy can appear to lack coherence beyond the struggle for territory, commercial advantage and autonomy between states, and the struggle for authority within them. In northern and central Italy some 'shape' can be given to Italian politics by historians convinced of a conflict between 'communes and despots', between republican governments and lordships of various kinds; but if that was ever a real political issue, rather than a matter of political and diplomatic rhetoric, it ceases to serve as a description of – let alone an explanation for – the nature of Italian political life beyond the early fifteenth century, and its area of possible application is geographically limited. It cannot be applied to north-western Italy, nor to the south and the islands.

This incoherence, it is often argued, was arrested by the Peace of Lodi (9

April 1454), followed by the creation of the Italian League. The accuracy of this will be considered shortly; the events of 1454–55 certainly ushered in a somewhat different pattern for Italian politics and provide a suitable break in this chapter. They also represented one of the rare instances when Italian governments showed awareness of the dangers of foreign attack as well as of their own internal weakness. On the first point, it is remarkable that there was virtually no realisation on the part of the Italians that their states, relatively small in terms of area, population and resources, were increasingly exposed to challenges of a totally different order of magnitude from those once posed by the emperors Frederick I and Frederick II. There were hints of such an awareness in the mid-fifteenth-century crisis but it is hard to find the raw facts, based on comparisons of scale, explicitly referred to by Italian or indeed by northern observers. Only a few fugitive allusions go beyond the traditional platitudes that the Alps sheltered Italy from barbarism – beyond the use by a few literate persons (literate meaning in Latin) of 'barbarism' as a cultural term to describe and dismiss Italy's northern neighbours.

UP TO LODI

Today, with the advantage of hindsight, it is hard for a non-Italian – and perhaps even for an Italian – not to find the sharpest of contrasts between the peninsular world and the rest of Europe where, during this period, the 'nation-states' were forming. It is true that Germany was as divided – or even more divided – than Italy, but it formed the central part of an empire theoretically under the leadership of the dynasties of Luxembourg and then of Habsburg and it was emotionally, and sometimes physically, given a greater sense of unity by fear of the Ottoman Turks. The Spanish kingdoms and the bulk of transalpine Europe offered, so it might seem, a pattern for political development which Italy was not to follow until the *Risorgimento*, or even later. A telling account of the confrontation between the multiplicity of Italian states and the major European powers has been left by the contemporary Venetian diarist and historian Marino Sanudo, but these catastrophic events drew the attention of many other writers at the time.

Yet it would be a mistake and an anachronism to exaggerate the Italian–non-Italian contrast as it existed at the end of the fourteenth century. If at that time Italy was entering a period of even more intensified division, the future 'great powers' were almost as enfeebled, if not so formally divided. France, the future centre of autocratic rule, did not arrive at that position until much later and the reign of Louis XIV; for much of the earlier period covered by this book the country was divided by a bitter civil war, traditionally referred to as the struggle between Burgundians and Armagnacs, as well as experiencing the threat and reality of foreign invasion. England witnessed the upheavals of Richard II's reign – an introduction, as it proved, to the so-called 'Wars of the Roses' of the mid-fifteenth century. Aragonese royal power was checked by assertive consultative assemblies, the *Cortes*, as well as being dispersed in the political ambitions of its expansion in the western Mediterranean. The Castilian crown was beset by an ambitious nobility, and remained preoccupied with the completion of the *Reconquista* of Moslem Granada. Nothing in the general European scene in the decades around 1400 could have suggested a marked contrast between weak powers in Italy and strong states on its frontiers. It has already been pointed out (in Chapter Two above) that Italians saw themselves as dwelling in a land of towns, and in this they differed from an England of counties and a France where provincial life survived with vigour. But disorder and disobedience were endemic in every part of Christendom; for the most part such unrest was political in character but it could also have social and economic roots, not so very different from those that produced the brief *Ciompi* rebellion in Florence in 1378, the year in which this picture of the political history of the Italian states and their relations with the European powers will open.

1378 was notable not only for rioting in Florence but also for an occurrence which was to have longer-term and more widely spread repercussions. This was the year in which the Great Schism began, tearing the Church apart and complicating the ecclesiastical organisation of Europe as a whole and of Italy in particular. That it harmed the Church needs no further emphasis (see above, Chapter Seven), but the political effect on Italy was all the greater because a pope now resided, or attempted to reside, in Rome and became increasingly dependent on the Italians of his obedience. Earlier, from 1308 to 1376, the papacy had been based at Avignon and had rarely resided in Rome for a century before that. Moreover, in the Avignon period all the popes had been Frenchmen, while Frenchmen predominated in the college of cardinals and the papal administration, the *Curia Romana*. Not that the absentee or French popes had neglected Italy or their States there, which ran diagonally across the Peninsula from south of Venice to north of Naples, an impossible frontier to hold against the ravaging armies of invasion or passage. Rome itself was threatened by the kingdom of Naples, which almost encircled it and found ready allies in the contumacious and opportunistic baronage of Umbria and Lazio. This kingdom, now in the hands − one could hardly say control − of the last of the Angevins imported in the late thirteenth century by the papacy as allies and as a counterweight to the Hohenstaufen, aimed to expand in two areas: to the north of Italy and in the Balkans. This was perhaps the first non-Italian influence to make itself felt. But south of Naples, and detached from it since 1282, lay 'Trinacria' or the kingdom of Sicily ruled by Aragonese princes, who were able to establish themselves in Naples from 1442 and in this way to forge a link between the fortunes of Italy and Spain which was to endure for centuries.

The small political units which comprised the Papal States during the absence of the popes at Avignon had in many ways emancipated themselves from the control of popes who in turn were reluctant to see their remaining territorial revenues in Italy eaten up by the need to bribe obedience or to employ mercenaries to enforce it. It was during the Avignon residence that a score of small states established themselves. Among the states that thrived during the period of papal absence and weakness some attained greater coherence and stability, such as that of the Malatesta, based on Rimini but comprising other towns in the Romagna and the March of Ancona. The hiatus of papal authority in central Italy, combined with the fact that the emperors Henry VII (1308–13) and Lewis IV (1314–46) ceased to do more than fish in the troubled political waters of the Peninsula, favoured the consolidation and expansion of the Visconti of Milan in Lombardy and beyond; the Papal States were as attractive to the Visconti from the north as they were for the Angevins from the south. The other larger states of Italy were generally content with more local ambitions, at least as far as the Peninsula was concerned. Florence slowly extended her influence and authority in Tuscany. Venice was anxious for the security of her immediate hinterland, while her commercial lifelines encouraged more expansionist policies in Istria, Dalmatia, the Balkans and the Levant. Genoa struggled to extend her trade in both the eastern and the western Mediterranean, but territorial expansion nearer home was compromised by internal political weakness as well as by the presence of an increasingly powerful neighbour, the counts of Savoy–Piedmont.

Even this tangled picture does not do full justice to the complicated political situation in fourteenth-century Italy. It omits the ambitions and fortunes of the Carrara family at Padua, the Este at Ferrara, the Gonzaga at Mantua and many smaller lordships and towns which were often anxiously dependent on the patronage and alliance of powerful neighbours. In general, lordships – *signorie* – had become the predominant form of government in northern and central Italy, but the ruling families, whether of recent or ancient origin, tended to avoid radical change. Feudal ties were exploited or reintroduced in rural areas; towns, provided they paid their taxes and proved loyal, were allowed a considerable degree of self-government; in neither was the order or composition of society much altered.

But in Italy as a whole divisions were exacerbated by the Schism. Divisions could also lead to non-Italian intervention in the affairs of the Peninsula; indeed, such intervention was hardly surprising given the bitterness that could characterise the rivalry between the Italian states. For example, the struggle between Venice and Genoa for commercial advantages in the east culminated in the War of Chioggia (1378–81), with the Genoese securing the alliance of the Carrara of Padua as well as of the king of Hungary, with whom Venice disputed Dalmatia, and the Austrian Habsburgs. Although the republic narrowly avoided defeat, Venice had to make concessions, surrendering Treviso to the archduke of Austria in 1381 and Dalmatia to the Hungarian crown. Again, the imperial overlordship of northern Italy, although often dormant, was never forgotten. If Charles IV (1347–78) had come to Italy to do little more than secure a full imperial coronation (1355) and exploit the political divisions of the country, his second son Sigismund, first as king of Hungary (from 1386) and then as king of the Romans (undisputed from 1411), was prepared to intervene to alter the balance of power in the north-east, especially at the expense of Venice. Finally, the Schism provided further encouragement to foreign intervention. To win support, Clement VII in 1379 offered the kingdom of Adria, to be carved out of the Papal States, to Louis of Anjou.[1] This scheme came to nothing, but in 1382 Clement allied himself again with Louis, again unsuccessfully, but this time in the attempt to wrest the kingdom of Naples from Carlo 'della Pace' King of Hungary, of the rival Angevin line of Anjou-Durazzo.

As has already been mentioned, Giangaleazzo Visconti, who was lord of the entire Visconti inheritance from 1385 and who purchased the title of duke from the emperor in 1395, was also drawn to the Papal States as a way of encircling his principal enemy, Florence, as well as of extending his dominions southwards. After his sudden death in 1402 his ambitions were taken up by Ladislao of Naples, who appeared not only poised to dominate Rome in the south of the Papal States but ready to extend his power north-wards through Umbria into Tuscany and the Romagna. The threat he posed prompted another pope, Gregory XII from the Roman line, to sell him the Papal States as a whole. The fact that this surrender produced no lasting political and territorial realignment was due less to any immediate recovery of papal authority and more to the fragility of the king's authority in the Lands of St Peter, a fragility revealed by the ambitions and opportunism of *condottieri* and baronial families and confirmed by the complete collapse of Neapolitan power following Ladislao's sudden death in 1414.

Sudden death had previously brought about the disintegration of the Visconti lordships in the north; Filippo Maria Visconti gradually began to re-establish his father's state, but he was never in a position to threaten Florence as seriously as Giangaleazzo had done due to an effective alliance secured in 1425 between the republic and Venice, the latter now firmly embarked on a policy of expansion on the Italian mainland. For Venice the Florentine alliance and her Italian acquisitions represented more than an adjustment in diplomacy; they were the outcome of a critical debate between policies of aggressive westward expansion on the mainland, the *terraferma*, and the maintenance of her possessions and commercial interests overseas, in the Adriatic and the Levant. Conventionally, the two points of view have been seen as polarised round the doge Tommaso Mocenigo, a leading proponent of the old way, and the younger Francesco Foscari, who was to succeed his rival in 1423 and whose aggressive anti-Milanese policies were to prevail. The result was that from 1425 Venice and Florence, the greatest of the surviving Italian republics, were in alliance, producing a new alignment in northern Italy which seriously impeded Filippo Maria's plans to restore his father's state.

But the extent of the shift in Venetian policy should not be exaggerated. Far from being abandoned, her Adriatic and eastern possessions were added to, if they were not always held for long in the face of the expanding Ottoman Empire; Dulcigno (modern Ulcinj in Albania) was acquired in 1423 and lost in 1571, but Salonika fell to the Turks in 1430 after only seven years of Venetian rule. Moreover, Venice had long appreciated the islands and territories in the immediate vicinity for water and food supplies, as well as for her commercial and political security. Thus from an early date the republic's authority had been established over the *dogado*, the area of the doge's jurisdiction; Treviso and its territory were held from 1339 to 1381 and from 1389, while the collapse of the Visconti state led to the acquisition of such important mainland cities as Verona (1405). Mocenigo himself had been no 'isolationist' as doge; by 1420 the republic's lordship was established in Friuli and Dalmatia. Thus when Filippo Maria Visconti began to pick up the threads of the state that had disintegrated in 1402 he was faced with a much stronger and more aggressive Venice; to the south Florence had also expanded in Tuscany, taking Pisa in 1406; to the west Amadeo VIII of Savoy–Piedmont (1391–1451) had also extended his territories at the expense of the Visconti.

As Simeoni has stressed, the alignment between Venice and Florence against Filippo Maria dominated and shaped the political life of northern Italy from the 1420s to the 1440s.[2] Especially in Florence, the policy was dignified in terms of *libertà*, less in the sense of broadly based or republican government and more in terms of the survival of independent states, above all of Florence itself. Less articulate in presenting their policies to the outside world and later historians, but as closely involved, were such lesser neighbouring powers as the Gonzaga of Mantua and the Este of Ferrara, who looked to the major protagonists for protection, alliances and employment as *condottieri*. The series of wars also fuelled the ambitions of those mercenary captains anxious to acquire territory, lordships and titles in emulation of the Gonzaga and Este. One of the most outstanding was Francesco Bussone, better known as Carmagnola (*c.* 1385–1432), who proved to be one of Filippo Maria's most successful generals, retaking such central Lombard cities as Monza, Lodi and Alessandria for the Visconti and massively defeating an invading Swiss army near Bellinzona in 1422. But Carmagnola's military achievements fed political and territorial ambitions which aroused the suspicion of his employer, whom he deserted for Venetian service in 1425. Further victories followed, and for the republic Carmagnola took Brescia and Bergamo; but Venice also came to fear his motives and duplicity, and summarily executed him for treason in 1432.[3]

Another leading *condottiere* of the northern wars was Francesco Sforza (1401–66), whose equally opportunistic but much more successful career was to have a longer-lasting effect on the balance of power. Francesco had worked his military and political apprenticeship in the *Regno* before entering the service of Filippo Maria and earning the promise of the duke's illegitimate daughter but only heir, Bianca Maria, in 1432. But the promised match did not secure the *condottiere*'s energies and loyalty for the Visconti state, and a period of Venetian service preceded his marriage to Bianca Maria in 1441. Then, on the death of Filippo Maria intestate in 1447, Francesco Sforza emerged as a leading claimant to the duchy. The others, in descending order of credibility, were: the emperor Frederick III; the house of Orléans, from the marriage of Valentina Visconti to Louis of Orléans in 1389; the house of

Savoy, from the marriage of Maria of Savoy to Filippo Maria in 1427; and Alfonso I of Naples, on the slender basis of an alleged testament in his favour. In fact, Visconti rule in Milan was followed by that of the Ambrosian republic – so called after St Ambrose, the patron saint of Milan – an oligarchic government which struggled to preserve the city and its hegemony in Lombardy from the house of Savoy in the west and Venice in the east. Once again Francesco Sforza switched allegiances between the Venetian and the Ambrosian republics before exploiting Milanese exhaustion and his own military might to secure his claims, being accepted by the Milanese as duke on 11 March 1450.

As mentioned, Francesco Sforza had begun his military career in the *Regno*, where dynastic entanglements and rivalries were the cause and effect of foreign intervention and internal disunity. Giovanna II of the Anjou–Durazzo line succeeded her brother Ladislao in 1414. Although twice married, she had no direct heir and instituted as her successor first Alfonso of Aragon in 1421 and then Louis III of Anjou–Provence in 1424. Louis's claims passed to René ('le bon roi René', as he was to be remembered in France) in 1434, but on Giovanna's death in 1435 it was her earlier protégé Alfonso who was in the better position to assert his claims, already in possession of the Aragonese dominions of Sicily and Sardinia and able to draw on the considerable commercial and naval strength of Barcelona. Nevertheless the war of succession was long-drawn-out. Genoa, the rival of Barcelona in the western Mediterranean, entered the war on the Angevin side and defeated – and captured – Alfonso at the naval battle of Ponza in 1435. Only in 1442 was the king was able to enter Naples in triumph without, however, having forced René to surrender his claims to the Neapolitan throne.

The following year Alfonso was also able to legitimise his conquests by securing a bull of investiture from his overlord Eugenius IV. That this was seen as more than a formality was due to the fact that the papacy had supported the claims of René and that papal authority in the Lands of St Peter was making a recovery from the dark days of the Schism, if that recovery was both halting and slow. The quarrel between Eugenius and the Council of Basel had given the pope's opponents a pretext for resisting him, and Eugenius had even been driven from Rome in 1432. But in exile in Florence, Eugenius's fortunes changed. The warlike *condottiere* cardinal Giovanni Vitelleschi began to reimpose papal authority around Rome; the Council of Ferrara-Florence (1438–39) raised papal prestige in Christendom as a whole.

This recovery encouraged Eugenius's successor Nicholas V to play the part of the peacemaker in Italy. The alliance between Venice and Florence had foundered, largely due to fears in Florence as to the extent of Venetian expansion at the expense of Milan; now Francesco Sforza found an ally – and creditor – in Cosimo de' Medici. To counter Venice and preserve his newly won duchy, Francesco was also ready to accept the dangerous alliance of France, but it was not only the threat of French intervention that disposed the papacy and the principal Italian powers towards peace moves, but the fall of Constantinople to the Ottoman Turks on 29 May 1453. This not only shocked Christendom but brought home the threat the Turks posed to the commercial and territorial interests of a number of Italian states, especially Venice, Genoa and the *Regno*. Peace negotiations launched by the papacy in November 1453 were unsuccessful but they did lead to direct and secret agreements between Venice and Milan, which emerged as the Peace of Lodi on 9 April 1454. Its terms included some territorial adjustments – notably the cession of Crema to Venice – as well as agreements to encourage trade. But its major significance lay in the fact that it envisaged the adherence of the other principal Italian powers, aiming to secure the Sforza dynasty through a general pacification. Sforza diplomacy subsequently engineered the support of Florence in August 1454 to what came to be called the Italian League. Nicholas V agreed to join in November, and Alfonso – with some reservations – on 26 January 1455. The League was blessed by the pope on 25 February, celebrated in Rome on 2 March and announced in the principal cities of Italy on 25 March.

Initially the League was to last for twenty-five years. Other than preparing Italy to face the Ottoman challenge, a principal goal was to keep France out of the Peninsula. To achieve this the League aimed to secure the internal peace of the country and to prevent the internecine wars of the Italians themselves. The territorial *status quo* was to be recognised. None of the contracting powers was singly to wage war, declare peace or enter into alliance. The members of the League were to support each other in the event of attack. The main contracting parties were to keep on a military footing soldiers to achieve these aims; Venice and Milan (and later Naples) were each to have forces of six thousand horse and two thousand foot in time of peace, and eight thousand horse and four thousand foot in time of war. As mentioned, the League was to last for twenty-five years, but although it was subsequently renewed it did not bring peace to Italy. However, it did do something to limit the warring potentialities of the member states and to encourage diplomacy as a permanent feature of the Italian scene.[4] On the first point it is interesting to observe the alliances of the larger Italian states and their various forms of association with their smaller neighbours in the mid-fifteenth century. Here are the lists of 'amici', 'collegati', 'aderenti' and 'raccomandati' as they appear in the final document:

Venice: 'amici' – Savoy, Este, Monferrat, the bishop of Trent, Sigismondo Malatesta of Rimini, Malatesta Novello of Cesena, Federigo da Montefeltro of Urbino and Sigismund of Habsburg, Archduke of Austria; 'collegati' – Siena, Lucca, Bologna, Ancona: 'raccomandati' – Giovanni Count of Gorizia, the Ordelaffi of Forli, the Correggeschi counts of Correggio in Reggio Emilia, Giovanni Count of Veglia and Segna in Dalmatia, Carlo Gonzaga and the lords of Lodrone, Graziadio da Campo, Elisabetta di Greste (widow of Federico Castelbarco) – all in the Trentino.

Florence: 'amici' – the two Malatesta lords, Emanuele Appiano Lord of Elba and Piombino; 'collegati' – Bologna, Lucca, Perugia; 'raccomandati' – the

Manfredi of Imola and Faenza, the Malaspina marquises of the Lunigiana and other communes and lords.

Milan: among other 'collegati' and 'aderenti' – Genoa, Bologna, the Este, the Gonzaga, Ancona, the two Malatesta, Alessandro Sforza Lord of Pesaro, the Manfredi, the Swiss Confederation.

Naples: 'amici' – Savoy, Siena, Lucca, Federigo da Montefeltro, Emanuele Appiano, the Del Carretto marquisate of Finale in Liguria, the Malaspina, the Correggeschi, Rodolfo Varano Lord of Camerino and the Orsini, Colonna and Farnese.

Simplified though they are, these lists give a sufficiently clear indication of divided Italy. It is noteworthy that several of the smaller states figure in more than one grouping (for example Bologna), and it is also clear that the four *potentia* had zones of influence – the use of the word 'powers' in the agreements is not without significance. Venice's region was the Romagna, Dalmatia and Istria, the Trentino; Milan's Genoa, the Romagna and the March of Ancona; that of Naples included some towns in Tuscany, the Papal States; Florentine influence ran in the Papal States as well as in Tuscany. But the zones of influence did overlap and provide a potential source of friction; and non-Italian powers were involved, the Habsburgs and the Swiss.[5]

FROM LODI TO THE SACK OF ROME

When Guicciardini began his *Storia d'Italia* with an idyllic picture of Italy before the death of Lorenzo de' Medici in 1492, some historians have been tempted to attribute this state of peace to the Italian League, while admitting that it crumbled. In fact both the twenty-five years of its initial duration and subsequent confirmations of its conditions witnessed many infractions. But the League did have certain positive consequences and encouraged an awareness of the two persistent dangers which constantly threatened the stability of what historians, with hindsight, have often termed the 'balance of power' in Italy.[6] The first danger lay in the inherent rivalry of the Italian states themselves, which produced an atmosphere of wary suspicion and a climate of conspiracy not allayed by the ancient practice of sending political opponents into exile (see below, p. 164).[7] The second was the perpetual danger of foreign intervention, in a sense recognised by the League itself with the inclusion of the Habsburg Sigismund Archduke of Austria, of the Swiss Confederation and, most obviously, of Alfonso I, but with the total exclusion of France. On the other hand – and more positively – by committing themselves to co-operation the principal powers of the Peninsula and their clients also committed themselves for the first time to a sense of *Italianità* in a political and military dimension. One consequence of this was a vast increase in diplomatic activity on, one might say, a more professional or permanent basis; and related to this was a more articulated sense of the balance of power.

These developments encouraged the sense of an Italian political entity and – though it ultimately proved vain – make one view the underlying strategy of the League, to keep Italy free from invaders from 'barbarian' Europe, as its most important aim. And perhaps for a time this was its most successful aspect, for disaster did not strike Italy until 1494. But for this there were many fundamental reasons extraneous to the defensive provisions of the League. Louis XI of France (1461–83) had not only the threat of possible English attack to contend with – although that was diminished by dynastic conflict in England – but more seriously and immediately he faced a challenge from his greater vassals, in particular from the duke of Burgundy, Charles the Bold (1467–77). It is worth stressing the internal situation in France, because long before the League had been formed, France had been a major factor in Italian politics. The house of Savoy had interests on both sides of the Alps and its history, certainly in this period, belongs as much to France as to Italy. The French crown had had eyes on Genoa; Charles VI had attempted to rule the city from 1396 to 1409. From the marriage of Valentina Visconti to Louis I of Orléans in 1389 the city of Asti had passed to the French dynasty, which thus also acquired claims to the duchy of Milan. The Angevins never renounced their claims on Naples. A few statesmen of the skill and perspicacity of Francesco Sforza and Lorenzo de' Medici were fully alive to the dangers posed by France, as well as the distractions caused by its troubles at home.

By around 1490, however, the situation had changed, with momentous consequences for the European balance of power and the states of Italy. The great appanages had ceased to pose a challenge to the French crown; indeed, Burgundy from 1477 and Brittany from 1488 were united to the crown, which also came to combine claims to Naples and Milan. The only foreign embarrassments facing the French king were the possibilities of an English invasion or an attack from the Iberian peninsula, where royal authority was also beginning to enjoy renaissance. The danger to the smaller states of Italy was therefore steadily growing greater as the fifteenth century drew to a close; but as has been mentioned, while Italians were fully alive to the threat of attack from abroad and while the flow of diplomatic information was remarkably astute and detailed, there is little evidence that contemporary Italians were fully aware of their relative weakness in respect of the emerging greater powers of Europe.

This can be seen most clearly in the League's failure to end the internecine strife of Italy; indeed, in some respects the League itself had been an agreement to differ in detail. This certainly applies to Alfonso I, whose terms for adhering to the League had left him free to attack Genoa. The grounds for antagonism are instructive in respect of later developments and amounted to more than commercial competition between Genoa and Barcelona or the long-standing rivalry over Corsica. As the Battle of Ponza indicated, the Ligurian city was an obvious staging-post for any Angevin, or French, attack on the *Regno*, and could to some extent depend on French help if threatened by the Aragonese. This happened in 1455 when an Aragonese naval attack was launched which, though unsuccessful, had the effect of driving the Genoese and doge Pietro Campofregoso to place the city under the protection of the French crown in May 1458. This in turn made it easier for the Angevins to pursue their claims to the Neapolitan throne, as they were encouraged to do when Alfonso died on 27 June 1458, to be succeeded by his bastard son Ferrante; the rest of his dominions, including Sicily, Sardinia and Malta, going to his brother and legitimate heir John.

Ferrante's attempts to dislodge the French from Genoa in 1459 failed, but so too did the Angevin cause in the south. Pius II, anxious for a Neapolitan alliance and hostile to Angevin intentions, recognised Ferrante as king in 1459. The unruly baronage of the *Regno* were as disloyal to the Angevins as they were to the Aragonese, and although Ferrante failed to enlist Italian support in the terms of the League, he decisively defeated his enemies at Troia on 18 August 1462, which ended — at least temporarily — Angevin and French pretensions in the south. But the Neapolitan upheaval had undoubtedly pointed the way to an enlargement of an Italian crisis. The intrigues of Louis XI, the attempts by Francesco Sforza to outflank these by prompting the Yorkists in England to attack France, portended the sixteenth-century situation in which Italy became a fulcrum of European diplomatic activity. In the words of Ilardi:

Italian affairs in the second half of the fifteenth century had already become an important factor in the struggle for power among the rising national monarchs, anticipating the large-scale Franco–Spanish rivalry for control of the Italian peninsula in the following century.[8]

The unstable situation of Italy after Lodi was not the work of the greater powers and foreign intervention alone. *Condottieri* had been listed among the allies and clients included in the League, and as the need for mercenary soldiers remained, so too did their ambitions and the destabilisation that followed from them. One such was Jacopo Piccinino, who had entered Venetian service after long years of employment with the duke of Milan. Although he reached the rank of captain general of the republic's forces by 1454, his hopes for rewards in the familiar forms of lands, lordships and titles were unrealised; moreover, his record of Milanese service and his unruly soldiery did not persuade Venice to retain him in its scaled-down army after 1454. Thereafter his ambitions were directed towards Siena and the Papal States, and although he had been supported by Alfonso I he joined the Angevin cause against Ferrante. He was reconciled after the defeat of the Angevin cause at Troia, and his career prospects appeared to blossom with the marriage to one of Francesco Sforza's illegitimate daughters, Drusiana, in 1464 — with a generous dowry to match — and with the promise of office and military command in Naples. This, however, led to one of those incidents that have helped to cast a lurid light on the political morality of Renaissance Italy in general and on the careers of the *condottieri* in particular. Though honourably received in Naples, he was murdered in prison on 14 July 1465, presumably as a drastic precaution against further acts of treachery.[9]

Better known, or more notorious, was Sigismondo Malatesta, Lord of Rimini from 1432. He encouraged the criticisms of his enemies by his public passion for his mistress, Isotta degli Atti (whom he married in 1456), and by his alleged rape of the duchess of Bavaria in 1450. A more permanent memorial to his controversial career is the *Tempio Malatestiano*, the church of San Francesco in Rimini which Sigismondo had rebuilt from 1447 as a monument to himself, to Isotta, to his classical tastes and – at least for his enemies – to his paganism. The bitter hostility of Pius II led to his denunciation in that pope's *Memoirs*, his excommunication in 1459 and, uniquely, his inverted canonisation to hell in 1462. Behind the vituperation and propaganda lay the restless ambition of an able *condottiere*-prince, anxious to defend and extend his state while securing profitable employment. His desertion of Alfonso I earned him the implacable hostility of that ruler; Sigismondo's victories over the king were celebrated in the *Tempio*. His resistance to his overlord Pius II and his bitter rivalry with his neighbour and fellow-*condottiere* Federigo da Montefeltro lay behind his excommunication. By 1463 he had lost most of the Malatesta lands other than Rimini. The *Tempio* remained incomplete and he sought compensation for his losses in land and reputation in Italy by fighting for Venice in southern Greece against the Turks (1464–66).

A final *condottiere* to illustrate the disturbed state of Italy after the Peace of Lodi is Bartolomeo Colleoni. He first entered Venetian service in 1431 and despite deserting the republic on two occasions, in 1442 and 1451, his skill as a soldier led him to hold the position of captain general from 1455 to 1476. Colleoni was flattered and well rewarded by the republic. He was enfeoffed with lands in his native Bergamasco, around Malpaga, where he established a court in a princely style and was posthumously recognised, as noted earlier, by the erection of a bronze equestrian monument, designed by Verrocchio, outside the church of Ss Giovanni e Paolo in Venice. But his relatively settled career, at least in its latter stages, did not prevent him from invading Florentine territory in 1467 at the instigation of those Florentine citizens opposed to the continuance of the Medici ascendancy in the city. In this case, however, the Italian League did come into at least partial operation; the invasion was repulsed at the Battle of La Molinella on 25 July by Florentine forces reinforced by Milan and Naples and led by Federigo da Montefeltro.[10]

Opposition to the ascendancy of the Medici provides a further and better-known illustration of the dangerous political divisions of Italy: the Pazzi conspiracy of 1478. The ringleaders, Francesco, Girolamo and their father Jacopo de' Pazzi, came from an ancient Florentine family, jealous of the influence of Lorenzo, whom they planned to assassinate along with his brother Giuliano while they attended Mass in Florence Cathedral on 26 April 1478; they anticipated support from a general uprising against Medici tyranny in Florence. In the event only Giuliano was killed, the people did not rise in revolt, and execution and exile were swiftly meted out to the conspirators and their accomplices. But this affair had an Italian dimension. Sixtus IV, hostile to Lorenzo because of Medici attempts to thwart the ambitions of his nephew Girolamo Riario in the Papal States, had switched the papal account from the Medici to the Pazzi bank. His precise role in the conspiracy itself – and more particularly in the assassination attempt – remains unclear, but with the archbishop of Pisa as a leading conspirator and then victim of the pro-Medici backlash, papal involvement became conspicuous; Sixtus excommunicated Lorenzo and brought his vassal Ferrante into the conflict. Although the pope tried to weaken the Medici position in Florence further by distinguishing between Lorenzo and the commune, Florence faced invasion and defeat and was saved largely by Lorenzo's dramatic personal embassy to Ferrante in December 1479, securing peace by March of the following year.

This crisis almost reached a European dimension, with Louis XI inclined to intervene on Florence's behalf. The menace of foreign intervention came even closer in the War of Ferrara (1482–84), which revealed how dangerous for the Peninsula its restless, shifting alliances could be. The war is named from the campaigns Venice fought, initially in alliance with Sixtus IV and ultimately unsuccessfully, to acquire Ferrara, a papal fief. Apart from the republic's desire to increase its control over the important waterway of the Po, the occasion for the war was the Pope's hostility towards another vassal, Ferrante, with whom the Este were allied and against whom the papacy sought Venetian naval aid. But the republic's successes and the support for Ferrante from Milan, Florence and Spain persuaded Sixtus to join the counteralliance and to transform it into the Most Holy League against Venice. The republic precipitated peace by encouraging the Angevin claim to Naples and the Orléanist claim to Milan.

Although the terms of the Italian League were reaffirmed in 1484, its failure to end the internecine struggles of the Italian states is highlighted not only by the threatened or actual intervention of other European powers but by the growing challenge posed by the Ottoman Turks, whose capture of Constantinople in 1453 had encouraged the search for peace in Italy. Their conquests had continued in the Balkans and in 1480 they had threatened the island of Rhodes, held for Christendom by the Knights of St John. However, the threat came nearer home for the Italian powers with raids into Venetian territory in Friuli in 1469 and in the 1470s, followed in August 1480 by an expedition from Valona across the Adriatic to attack, sack and hold the Apulian city of Otranto. This massive assault on the *Regno* caused temporary panic in Italy. Nearly half of the inhabitants of Otranto were taken into slavery, and Christian churches were desecrated. Much criticism was levelled at Venice for the inactivity of its war fleets, but the republic had just fought a long and exhausting war with the Ottomans (1463–79) and no real help in resisting the invaders was forthcoming until September 1481, when galleys from the papacy, with a few from Aragon and Portugal – the pitiful response to a call from Sixtus for a massive European crusade – joined the Neapolitan forces to prevent reinforcements assembled at Valona from crossing the Adriatic and forced the Turks in Otranto to withdraw, by no means defeated. What really saved Italy at this juncture was not military and naval force or political resolve but the death of Mohammed II 'the Conqueror' in 1481 and his succession not by one son – the intention of the Ottoman institution of fratricide – but by two: Bayezid II (1481–1512) and Djem. The latter, having failed to oust his brother, fled to the west, where he was held by various princes – and by the papacy from 1489 – as a threat and a bargaining counter. He died in 1495, but while he was alive the Turks were nervous of his employment by the west as the pretext for attack or as the leader of an internal insurrection.

With the last decades of the fifteenth century, the political climate of Italy darkened. The political situation within the country grew tenser and a number of profoundly altered circumstances began to affect Italy's neighbours. The internal situation was shaped by both short-term changes and longer-term developments. Obvious examples of the first would include the death of Lorenzo de' Medici (1492) and Ferrante of Naples (1494), as Lodovico Maria 'il Moro' assumed power in Milan after the mysterious and controversial death of his young nephew Giangaleazzo Maria Sforza on 22 October 1494.

One of the most important elements in the second category was the gradual emergence of the territories ruled by the pope as a papal state in an increasingly meaningful and secular sense. With a more or less united Church, the popes began to adjust with growing confidence to the newer princely character of Italy and, indeed, of Europe. It used to be common to attribute this development to Alexander VI and to his son Cesare Borgia, but the process was much earlier in origin and can be seen clearly by the pontificate of Pius II (1458–64). Pius demonstrated his leadership of Christendom by summoning the Congress of Mantua in 1459 in an attempt to confront the Italian and European powers with the gravity of the Ottoman threat and the need to launch a crusade. The rout of the conciliar threat to papal authority was expressed in his 1460 bull *Execrabilis*. He also demonstrated a determination to rule the Papal States and Rome effectively, in 1460 successfully confronting disorder in the city that had adopted the dangerous slogans of Roman republicanism. But the impact of reconstructed papal authority on Italian politics was not always the product of positive policies. Papal elections were in the hands of a body of cardinals whose membership considerably reflected the secular interests and ambitions of other Italian powers; the choice of popes of advanced years provided another destabilising element, compounded by the eagerness of the elderly heirs of St Peter to do the best for their families in what was necessarily likely to be a short period of years. 'Nepotism' – if that is not always strictly the right word and relationship – was a characteristic of most of the Renaissance popes, but especially so with the della Rovere Sixtus IV (1471–84), the Borgia Alexander VI (1492–1503) and the Medici Leo X (1513–21) and Clement VII (1523–34).

A further reason for the intense jungle of Italian politics and for the ready involvement of non-Italian powers was certainly not new: far more than in northern Europe, Italian governments had recourse to the legal or illegal exile of their enemies or critics, usually involving the confiscation of their lands and property and sanctions of more or less similar ferocity directed against their kin and allies. Genoa, so crucial to the balance of power in the western Mediterranean and access to Italy from the north-west, was a dramatic example of a city ringed by mountain strongholds in the hands of such alienated, vengeful and dangerous persons and their retainers, alert for any changes in *lo stato* within the city or the wider political situation to facilitate their return.

An even greater threat to such territorial integrity as Italy possessed was the export of malcontents to courts beyond the Peninsula. Intrigues were stimulated by courtiers who had fled from Aragonese Naples and Sforza Milan. Charles VIII's attack on the *Regno* in 1494 was urged by exiled members of one of the leading clans of the kingdom, the Sanseverino, and in particular by Antonio di Sanseverino, Count of Marsico and Prince of Salerno and once Ferrante's grand admiral, but from 1484 living in exile at the French court. The Milanese noble Gian Giacomo Trivulzio deserted Lodovico Maria to serve Charles VIII and commanded the forces of Louis XII against Milan in 1499. Giuliano della Rovere, the future Julius II, fled to the French court in 1494 to conspire against his rival Alexander VI. And it was not only the principalities that suffered from the hyperactivity of influential exiles. Piero de' Medici looked to Louis XII for assistance; the family was reinstated in Florence in 1530 largely thanks to an imperial army. An exception is provided by the Venetian republic, whose nobility was remarkably cohesive and loyal to the state; but during the War of the League of Cambrai (1509–17) disaffected and opportunist citizens from its subject communes found refuge and encouragement at the imperial court. Leonardo Trissino, from a leading Vicentine family, found service with the emperor Maximilian after being exiled for murder from the Venetian state.[11]

Related, and again not at all new, was the readiness with which cities could surrender and adjust themselves to new rulers. The formula behind their calculations consisted of positive and negative elements: the opportunities for advancement and the settling of old scores; the fear of sack and reprisals. Familiar examples of pragmatism and opportunism are provided by Pisa, which eagerly surrendered to the French king Charles VIII and rejected Florentine rule in 1495; and by the Venetian subject city of Treviso, which decided not to surrender to the emperor Maximilian in June 1509 because it doubted the strength of his forces and was impressed by the tax concessions offered by the republic. Both cases suggest how the state could not take the loyalty of its subjects for granted, and how the choice between foreign and native rule was a matter for calculation rather than blind patriotism.

None the less, it would be wrong to conclude that Italian statesmen were indifferent to relations with their European neighbours. As has been stressed, the likelihood of foreign intervention was taken very seriously throughout the fifteenth century, and the possibility became reality with the French invasions of Charles VIII in 1494 and Louis XII in 1499. The first was encouraged by the deaths of two leading Italian statesmen, Lorenzo de' Medici and Ferrante I. To the kingdom of Naples Charles had a legal claim. Lodovico Maria Sforza, whose rule in Milan was tainted by usurpation and was also threatened by a French claim, urged Charles to attack Naples in 1493; this the king did, seeking further justification for his mission by representing it as the necessary preparation for a crusade against the Turks (Tables 3 and 8).

The military operation astounded contemporaries. The French army reached Asti on 9 September 1494. Thereafter Charles enjoyed a royal progress through the Peninsula; the element of surprise experienced by all parties is graphically captured by Charles's counsellor Commynes in a valuable non-Italian account of what Guicciardini was bitterly to term the 'calamità d'Italia'. After a perfunctory encounter with the pope, to whom Charles pledged his loyalty as head of the Church, the army marched on and, after some desultory skirmishing around Naples, Charles received the submission of the city on 2 February 1495, scarcely six months after the invasion had begun. On 12 May he was crowned king of Naples; the rapidity of his final advance had been expedited by divisions among the baronage of the *Regno* and by a general reaction against Aragonese rule.

Yet the very success of the French led to their undoing. Their troops, scattered and ravaging the land, were virtually out of control; the *Regno* was too vast an area to 'occupy' and the lines of communication and supply were tenuous. Moreover, at last the powers of Italy realised that they must concert their defences in the spirit of the League, though without the participation of Florence, allied to France, and with Charles's European rivals. This was the background to the alliance of Italian states with Spain and the Empire signed at Venice on 31 March 1495. The allies confronted the retreating French at Fornovo on the river Taro in the northern Apennines on 6 July, and although the French suffered fewer casualties and broke through the Italian formations, their adventure was over. Charles reached Asti and recrossed the Alps in mid-July.

His return had been complicated by tortuous negotiations to secure the escape of Louis Duke of Orléans, bottled up in the Lombard city of Novara. His retreat was accomplished by a treaty between Charles and the duke of Milan on 9 October 1495. Louis, soon to succeed Charles as king, had been pressing the Orléanist claim to the duchy of Milan, a claim which was to lead to a later invasion of the Peninsula. Louis inherited the kingdom of France in 1498 on the death of Charles on 7 April. By that date all the latter's conquests in Italy had been lost; Louis's invasion was therefore to mark a new beginning for the miseries of Italy. It also introduced the most tortuous phase of what later historians were to call the 'Italian Wars'. Louis's invasion of Milan in 1499 met with success and the capture of Lodovico in 1500. It coincided with Borgia attempts to secure their domination of the Romagna and the Marches. That plan collapsed when the Borgia pope died in 1503 and Cesare, ill and unable to intervene to protect his gains, was eventually forced to flee Italy to imprisonment and death in Spain.

Spain was also an interested party to the dismemberment of Italy, planning to acquire the *Regno* as well as Sicily, Sardinia and Malta. These ambitions were disguised by the Treaty of Granada (11 November 1500) between Ferdinand the Catholic and Louis XII to partition the *Regno*. In the event, Ferdinand outwitted the French and Spanish troops were masters of the kingdom by January 1504. Although it could not be recognised at the time, this was a critical turning point, the moment when Italy ceased to be an area of small states over which expansion by internal or external powers could be made piecemeal. It was steadily to become the centre of a much larger competition for domination between Habsburg and Valois. The story is familiar enough. Aragon and Castile had been united by marriage; the heir of that union conveyed it again by marriage to the emperor Maximilian's grandson, Charles. Charles, elected emperor in 1519, ruled the lands of the Aragonese crown – including Sicily, Sardinia, Malta and Naples – as well as Castile, which was soon to be mistress of the New World, and the Habsburg territories in Burgundy, the Netherlands and Austria. Italy then became the main route between Habsburg-controlled lands in the Mediterranean and the north.

The equation which was to shape Italian political history was finally completed when Louis XII was succeeded by Francis I. Francis inherited all the family claims in Italy and added to these youth, a certain flair for politics and a great deal of personal ambition. Much of his energy was directed at retaking the duchy of Milan, which Louis had lost to the Sforza in 1512 and which Francis managed to hold between 1515 and 1521 and again between 1524 and 1525. As these events show, the subsequent arithmetic of Italy is hardly to be distinguished from the political history of Europe as a whole, and the balance of power the Italian states had perceived and tried to maintain by the terms of the League of 1455 was now largely outside their control. These conditions were to prevail for centuries, although a convenient line can be drawn across the Italian story at the Treaty of Cateau-Cambrésis (August 1559), which confirmed Spanish hegemony in the Peninsula.

But a more dramatic indication of the changed circumstances, and one felt acutely by Italians themselves, was the Sack of Rome on 6 May 1527. The Sack and its consequences are dealt with in the following volume of this series, but it is worth emphasising here that the disaster should not be viewed only in terms of the terrible loss of life, the damage to the fabric of the city and the eclipse of Rome as the capital of humanist letters. An imperial army, largely made up of Protestant soldiers, had humbled the papacy in Italy, as in Christendom as a whole. Of the great powers that had joined the Italian League of 1455, only the republic of Venice remained undefeated and unconquered, preserving its traditional form of republican government. In fact, of the indigenous Italian states, Venice remained the only one left with a realistic claim to great-power status towards the end of the period, and as a result had been confronted by an alliance of European and Italian states, the League of Cambrai of 10 December 1508. The subsequent war lasted until 1517, and although the republic survived it became increasingly overshadowed by its European and Mediterranean neighbours in the course of the sixteenth century.

If the Italian League and the Italian Wars gave a great impetus to diplomacy they have also supplied much material for the diplomatic historian, to the extent that the history of Renaissance Italy can become submerged by a chess game of escalating ingenuity and scope, sustained by the wealth of diplomatic reports and bewildering succession alliances. Moreover, a story that ends with the Sack of Rome and Habsburg hegemony may appear a negative way of concluding a study of the states where the Renaissance was born. The negative impression can appear emphasised by the fact that the states of Italy, seen by Burckhardt and others as masters of their own destinies, appear as pawns in the international arena at the end of the period, and even earlier they had been preoccupied by questions of legitimacy and status *vis-à-vis* the empire and papacy. Even Florence, once thought of as the torchbearer of a new independent, resourceful and entrepreneurial state, can be shown to have been overawed by the glamour and authority of old hierarchic order of Christendom, of empire, monarchy, nobility and chivalry.[12] A period which begins with the confidence of the civic humanists ends with the disillusionment and anxiety of Machiavelli and Guicciardini, and the nostalgia of Castiglione.

But it would be wrong to accept such a conclusion without considerable reservations. Devastating and disruptive though the wars of Italy could be, both before and after 1494, their impact should not be exaggerated. Italy had not existed as a nation-state, and Italy was not 'occupied' by foreign armies in the nineteenth- or twentieth-century sense. The nature, role and authority of the state were not as important in the Renaissance as they were to become, perhaps by the *Risorgimento* and more certainly later. Moreover, the wars of Habsburg and Valois did not eradicate the Italian state system completely. The papacy recovered from the disaster of 1527 and re-established its authority in Rome and the Papal States. A Medici principate replaced the Florentine republic in Tuscany. The enduring quality of the Venetian republic became a commonplace of European political thought. The house of Savoy weathered the threats from France, Spain and the Swiss Confederation. Nor were the smaller states and lordships eliminated. The Malaspina lordships in the Lunigiana survived the encroachments of Genoa and the Medici as direct feudal dependencies of the empire until the French Revolution. The Appiano lords of Elba and Piombino preserved their lordships, however precariously, down to the seventeenth century. The Este duchy lasted to the end of the sixteenth century, the Gonzaga marquisate into the eighteenth. The commune of Lucca preserved its republican, if oligarchic, constitution until the French Revolution.

And not all contemporary observers were as plagued by doubts and disappointments as the great Florentine historians. Giorgio Vasari saw the history of the fine arts in terms of progressive excellence, capable of continuation even beyond the supreme achievements of Michelangelo. Indeed, the arts were to a considerable extent stimulated by the unsettled state of Italy in terms of both patronage and subject matter. In 1472 Bartolomeo Colleoni commissioned the Lombard sculptor Giovanni Antonio Amadeo to execute the lavish Capella Colleoni in Bergamo as both a funeral chapel and a memorial. However flawed the Italian victory at the Battle of Fornovo,

Francesco Gonzaga, the allied commander, commissioned Mantegna to paint the masterpiece known as the *Madonna della Vittoria* in celebration of the French defeat. Moreover, the Italian Wars which that battle did so little to prevent led to a diaspora of Italian talent, creating an indebtedness to and a fascination for Italian culture which finds a later manifestation in the Italian Renaissance studies of the nineteenth and twentieth centuries.

NOTES AND REFERENCES

For more detailed bibliography on the various Italian states, see Chapters Nine to Eleven. The genealogical tables should also be consulted. The basic narrative of events is clearly set out in L. Simeoni, *Le Signorie*, vols i and ii (Milan, 1950). The 'plight' of Italy and its relations with foreign powers are discussed by P. Pieri, *Il Rinascimento e la Crisi Militare Italiana* (Turin, 1952).

1. For the later history of this proposal, D. M. Bueno de Mesquita, *Giangaleazzo Visconti* (Cambridge, 1941). ch. xii.
2. Op. cit., vol. i, p. 462.
3. A. Battistella, *Il Conte di Carmagnola* (Genoa, 1889). The best recent account of the *condottieri* is M. Mallett, *Mercenaries and their Masters* (London, 1974).
4. G. Mattingly, *Renaissance Diplomacy* (Harmondsworth, 1965). Recent editions of the source material include: P. M. Kendall and V. Ilardi, *Dispatches with Related Documents of Milanese Ambassadors in France and Burgundy*, vol. i (Athens, Ohio, 1970–); Lorenzo de' Medici, *Lettere*, gen. ed. N. Rubinstein, vol. i (Florence, 1977–) E. Sestan (ed.), *Carteggi Diplomatici fra Milano Sforzesco e la Borgogna*, vol. i (Rome, 1985).
5. Simeoni, op. cit., vol. i, pp. 515–16. The various categories of alliance and association reflect degrees of independence and dependence *vis-à-vis* the major powers. The best account of the Peace of Lodi and the Italian League is G. Soranzo, *La Lega Italica* (Milan, 1924).
6. Mattingly, op. cit., chs viii and ix; E. W. Nelson, 'The origins of modern balance-of-power diplomacy', *Medievalia et Humanistica*, vol. i (1942).
7. L. Martines, 'Political conflict in Italian city states', *Government and Opposition*, vol. iii, no. i (1968).
8. V. Ilardi, 'The Italian League, Francesco Sforza and Charles VII', *Studies in the Renaissance*, vol. vi (1959), p. 165.
9. Anticipating the laconic press statements of later regimes, Ferrante explained that Piccinino had fallen from a prison window.
10. B. Belotti, *Vita di Bartolomeo Colleoni* (Bergamo, 1923).
11. C. Clough, review of A. Ventura, *Nobilità e Popolo nella Società Veneta del '400 e '500* (Bari, 1964), in *S.V.*, vol. viii (1966).
12. R. C. Trexler, *Public Life in Renaissance Florence* (New York and London, 1980).

CHAPTER NINE

The south and the islands

REALMS, RULERS AND RIVALS

To treat the kingdoms of Corsica, Sardinia, Sicily and Naples together may appear contrived, most obviously when a relief map or questions of distance are considered but also when independence emerges as a prominent feature of their individual histories. However, certain themes are common to these separate kingdoms. In the first place, the papacy claimed lordship over the south of Italy and the islands based on the alleged Donation of Constantine. Secondly, all these territories had a strategic importance in the Mediterranean. This, combined with their agricultural resources in such basic commodities as grain and wool, their potential as markets and sources of revenue, and the opportunities they offered for advancement and patronage, made them desirable in the eyes of foreign powers, merchants and adventurers. Finally, foreign claims and ambitions challenged and fuelled a strong spirit of independence which emerges as a further common characteristic of their separate histories and historiographies.

Partly for that reason, there can be a temptation to undervalue, or even ignore, papal claims of overlordship.[1] For example, the tribute demanded from the kings of Naples had a symbolic quality which did not realistically reflect the true value of that southern kingdom. The payment of a census and a white palfrey often fell into arrears or was neglected. On occasion such payments were waived by the papacy itself as it tried to foster good relations with its powerful neighbour and vassal. More important, the loss of prestige and authority experienced by the papacy during the Schism (1378–1417), together with its slow and only partial recovery, might suggest that papal overlordship had become nominal, if not defunct. However, conclusions along these lines would be misleading. The Schism coincided with, and helped to encourage, political divisions on both the islands and the mainland. Moreover, the issue of papal overlordship remained very much alive throughout the period.

Such overlordship presented a potential challenge to the ruling houses and a possible source of support and legitimacy for rivals and rebel subjects. For example, Martin V excommunicated Giovanna II of Naples soon after her coronation in 1419, and assigned the succession of the kingdom to the rival branch of the house of Anjou. In 1485, when the commune of L'Aquila in the Abruzzo joined in the baronial rebellion against Ferrante of Naples, its mint struck coins to celebrate both its new-found liberty and its recognition of the direct lordship of Innocent VIII.[2] No more telling indication of this point can be found than Lorenzo Valla's denunciation of the *Donation of Constantine* in 1440. Historians of Renaissance humanism have traditionally celebrated Valla's mastery of history, philology and Roman Law. Less appreciated is the fact that Valla's patron was Alfonso I, whose claim to the throne of Naples had not yet been recognised by the pope, Eugenius IV. Still less recognised is the fact that however telling and substantial were Valla's arguments, papal overlordship survived. Alfonso himself was eager to come to terms with the papacy, securing the investiture of his new kingdom from Eugenius on 14 June 1443.[3] On 17 July 1486, Ferrante I agreed to pay Innocent VIII an annual tribute and present him with a palfrey every three years; in 1521 the Habsburg emperor Charles V promised to pay an annual tribute and present a palfrey each year in exchange for the investiture of the kingdom of Naples.[4]

The survival of papal lordship as a real political issue in the histories of the islands and the kingdom of Naples was also due to the intervention and rivalries of external powers. Some had little more than passing political importance. For example, the French house of Narbonne had claims through marriage to rule Sardinia as justiciars of Arborea; that ancient and hereditary office could bring its holder some prestige and authority as champion of Sardinian rights and autonomy.[5] On the extinction of the native dynasty in 1407, those Sardinians opposed to the claims and expansionist designs of the crown of Aragon offered the office to William III of Narbonne in 1408. He assumed the title, and with Genoese help tried to muster resistance to the Aragonese. However, he faced a formidable opponent, while his own resources and political support were unreliable. Moreover, William's own commitment to the cause of Sardinian autonomy was opportunistic; by 25 May 1414 he was prepared to sell the justiciarship to the Aragonese crown for 153,000 florins. Nonpayment of the agreed sum brought him back to the struggle in 1417, but the hopelessness of his cause persuaded him to settle for the more modest sum of 100,000 florins in August 1420. Payments were made in instalments until his death in 1424.

Much more tenacious in their opposition to the Aragonese were the Genoese, Corsica providing one focus for their rivalry (see below, Chapter Eleven, pp. 244–5).[6] Both the Italian commune and the Aragonese crown claimed the lordship of the island. At different times, both were encouraged in their claims by papal investiture. Both appreciated Corsica's strategic importance, as well as its potential value as a market for manufactured goods and a source of raw materials. Aragonese claims appeared the more likely to be made good, thanks to the ability of their General Vincentello d'Istria, viceroy for the Aragonese crown from 10 February 1418. By 2 February 1420,

Alfonso V of Aragon was confident enough to summon a parliament to secure the homage of his Corsican subjects. But resistance on the island, aided by Genoa, continued, and Alfonso's parliament met as his forces tried to reduce the city of Bonifacio. Thereafter, other and potentially more rewarding commitments on the mainland of Italy distracted the Aragonese; the Genoese continued to fuel resistance and in 1434 were able to capture and execute Alfonso's viceroy. While the republic never dominated the island, its citizens continued to try, and not without success, to exploit its economic potential.

Essentially similar motives prompted the other great maritime and commercial city of Venice to secure the coastal towns of Apulia in the kingdom of Naples.[7] These ports had considerable strategic importance at the entrance to the Adriatic, and their permanent acquisition could have protected and favoured Venetian commerce. Moreover, Venetian merchants had long realised their value as markets and as a source of such vital commodities as grain, wool and oil. The first attempt to transform the privileged trading position enjoyed by its merchants into direct Venetian rule was made in 1484 in the course of a war between the republic and Ferrante I. The opportunity presented itself again in the aftermath of the French invasion of the southern kingdom in 1495. The republic was able to take the ports of Polignano, Mola and Monopoli; Trani, Brindisi, Otranto and Gallipoli she acquired as pledges for the naval and financial aid she advanced to Ferrante II. Again Venetian rule was brief; in 1509 the republic was forced to surrender the ports to Ferdinand the Catholic. Furthermore, the towns were costly to maintain and their commercial value declined with their detachment from the agricultural resources of the hinterland. Nevertheless their strategic and commercial potential induced the republic to exploit a further phase in the conflict over the Neapolitan kingdom, acquiring the Apulian ports for a final brief period from 1528 to 1530.

However, the main struggle to acquire and govern the southern and island kingdoms involved branches of the French Angevin dynasty and the crown of Aragon, held until 1410 by the house of Barcelona and then, after a two-year interregum, passing to the Trastamara. Angevin rule dated from the thirteenth century, when the papacy had invested the dynasty with the Sicilian crown and a kingdom which encompassed not only the island of Sicily but also the mainland of southern Italy. In 1282 they had been deprived of Sicily by the Aragonese, but the Angevins continued to call themselves kings and queens of Sicily, although their capital was fixed at Naples and their authority was confined to the mainland. With the death of the childless Giovanna II on 2 February 1435 the direct line came to an end, but the Angevin claim to the throne was taken up vigorously by René of another branch of the dynasty, and subsequently by the French royal house itself.

Dynastic intricacy is also a feature of their rivals. At the start of the period the claims to Corsica and Sardinia were exercised by the kings of Aragon, while the Sicilian throne was held by a cadet branch. It too then passed to the main royal line through the marriage of Maria of Sicily to Martino 'the Younger' on 29 November 1391. He died on 25 July 1409 and the throne passed to his father, Martino 'the Elder'. With his death on 31 May 1410 Sicily experienced the interregnum common to all the Aragonese dominions, until the succession passed to the Trastamara. The reign of Alfonso V of Aragon (Alfonso I of Sicily and Naples) saw the kingdom of Naples, known familiarly as the *Regno*, added to the Aragonese empire. However, on his death the Neapolitan succession passed to his illegitimate son Ferdinando I (better known as Ferrante), while the islands and Aragon itself were ruled by Alfonso's brother John until 1479. This divided succession continued, the throne of Naples being contested by the cadet branch of the Aragonese crown and Charles VIII and then Louis XII of France. Finally, in 1503, the kingdom of Naples was reunited with the other Aragonese dominions under Ferdinando II (the Catholic) until 1516, when the succession passed to the Habsburg emperor Charles V.

THE PLACE OF THE DYNASTY

Although the genealogies of the southern and island crowns can appear bewildering, it would be a mistake to underestimate their relevance. Family interest was a powerful force, and such dynasties as the Angevins and the house of Barcelona were pursuing aspirations felt and recognised throughout society – albeit on a much grander scale. Further, in the pursuit of their aims, the rival dynasties had a considerable impact on the histories of the areas concerned. Finally, certain themes can be drawn out of these dynastic entanglements and confrontations which can give them a greater coherence, while helping to explain their wider impact.

In the first place, the physical presence of royalty, long recognised as a critical aspect of medieval kingship, retained its importance in the dynastic and political histories of the islands and the south. This can be seen in the elaborate ceremony attending the entry to Naples of Alfonso I on 26 February 1433, an event commemorated in the sculptured triumphal arch subsequently placed round the principal entrance to the Castel Nuovo (see below, Chapter Thirteen, p. 307). That entry was followed more immediately by a parliament of the king and his secular vassals on 28 February, when the Neapolitan barons were prompted to ask that Alfonso acknowledge his son Ferrante as Duke of Calabria, the title traditionally enjoyed by the heir to the throne.[8] The request was granted and after a further procession through Naples Ferrante was invested with a gold crown, a jewelled sword and his arms as duke on 3 March. On Alfonso's death on 27 January 1458, Ferrante seized the initiative and rode round the capital to the cry of 'Ferro' from his supporters. Between 1460 and 1464, during his first war with the Angevins and the first baronial rebellion, Ferrante toured his kingdom in person, exacting homage and fealty from his subjects in carefully planned and recorded ceremonies. On his death on 25 January 1494 his son, Alfonso Duke of Calabria, rode round Naples with his supporters, trumpeters and the regalia, shouting 'Long live Alfonso' – 'to comfort the people', as a contemporary chronicler put it.[9]

An equally striking theme is the sense of common family interest shared by the various members of a ruling house. This can be seen in the way a dynasty rarely surrendered its rights or claims. In 1372 Federico III of Sicily came to an agreement with Giovanna I of Naples. She recognised his right to the island and the right of his daughter Maria to succeed him; he acknowledged the feudal superiority of Giovanna and the right of the Angevins to succeed to Sicily in the event of Maria dying without heirs. However, this attempt to resolve the rivalry between Aragon and Anjou not only helped to earn Federico the nickname of 'the Simple'; it also angered Peter IV of Aragon, as it threatened both to compromise the house of Barcelona's hold on the Sicilian crown and to jeopardise the succession. More generally, dynastic rights were defended and pursued tenaciously, as the wars between the royal houses of Valois and Trastamara over the kingdom of Naples bear witness.

Moreover, members of a family could be used as instruments of policy, to represent the crown and personify the ruling dynasty. When René of Anjou, imprisoned in Burgundy, was unable to further his claims in person to the kingdom of Naples, his wife Isabella of Lorraine acted as regent with considerable effect between 1435 and 1438. However, the sense that the interests of the crown were a collective responsibility shared by all members of the ruling house is perhaps more clearly seen in the case of the Aragonese. Again, Sicily can provide a good example. To preserve the Aragonese inheritance while respecting Sicilian autonomy, on 11 June 1380 Peter IV of Aragon ceded his claim to the island to his second son Martino (later called 'the Elder'). After Martino's son, Martino 'the Younger', had married Maria in 1391 and was crowned in 1392, Martino 'the Elder' was referred to as 'helper' of the queen and 'administrator' of the king. When he became King of Aragon on 8 May 1398, official documents issued in Sicily styled Maria and the two Martins as joint rulers.[10] Later a less elaborate solution was attempted to solve the problem of respecting local autonomy while preserving dynastic interests when Ferdinand of Aragon sent his son John as viceroy to the island between 1415 and 1416. In this context – of the solidarity of family interest – Alfonso I's decision in 1442 to leave Naples to his illegitimate son Ferrante, while his brother succeeded to the other kingdoms, does not appear as divisive or as careless of family interests as some later historians have argued.

If members of a royal house could be used as representatives of the crown or as co-rulers, more familiar and more common is the use of marriage alliances to defend royal rights, to open up the possibility of new dominions, to secure foreign allies and to draw powerful families more closely to the crown. Anxiety lest the kindom of Sicily pass through marriage out of Aragonese hands explains the determination of the crown of Aragon to win papal consent to the marriage of Martino 'the Younger' to Maria despite the fact that the marriage was within the prohibited degrees. After Maria's death in 1402, the two Martins considered a marriage alliance between the widower and Giovanna of Naples as a means of reconciling the two dynasties while opening up the possibility of an Aragonese succession on the mainland and the reconstruction of the ancient kingdom of Sicily. In 1415 proposals for a marriage between Giovanna, now queen of Naples, and John viceroy of Sicily reached the stage of a contract being drawn up and a dowry determined.[11]

Marriage alliances were also used to win a dynasty the support of other Italian powers or of its own more powerful subjects. Alfonso I of Naples, after completing the conquest of his new kingdom, was glad to secure a marriage alliance with one of the oldest ruling houses of Italy, the Este of Ferrara; his illegitimate daughter Maria married Leonello d'Este in 1443, while in 1473 that particular alliance was cemented with the marriage of Eleanora, daughter of Ferrante, to Ercole I. Within the kingdoms themselves, marriage was a way in which the royal house tried to win baronial families to its cause. In 1452 Maria, the illegitimate daughter of Ferrante, married the Sienese nobleman Antonio Piccolomini, who was awarded the duchy of Amalfi in 1462. His loyalty to the ruling house was expressed in his adoption of the name Aragon and his decision, taken on his wife's death in 1470, to bury her in the Neapolitan church of S. Maria Monteoliveto, much favoured by Alfonso, Duke of Calabria and heir to the throne (see below, Chapter Thirteen, p. 323).

Lastly, the value of family connections can be seen in one instance where these ties were based on neither blood nor marriage, but adoption. On 8 July 1421 Giovanna II, surrounded by external and internal enemies, adopted Alfonso V of Aragon as her heir. This was a political expedient unrelated to any bonds of affection, but Alfonso used it as the basis of his claim to the *Regno*. He referred to Giovanna in official documents in terms of filial piety; he dated his regnal years from Giovanna's death in 1435; he adopted the Angevin coat of arms. Yet however tenaciously asserted, Alfonso's claim through inheritance by adoption was contrived and insecure. Giovanna, indeed, had quickly regretted her decision and had adopted Louis III of Anjou on 1 July 1423. Alfonso's attempts to persuade the queen to readopt him failed, and a document showing that he had succeeded was a forgery.[12]

But there is no need to dwell on such an unusual case to see how wrong it would be to interpret the dynasty in exclusively positive terms, as a means of extending and defending royal power. The reverse side of the coin reveals the family, and the individuals within it, as a potential source of political embarrassment and weakness to royal authority. The dynasty was not necessarily characterised by cohesion and a sense of shared responsibility. The last years of the reign of Giovanna I of Naples were disturbed by a struggle over the succession between the two branches of the Angevin house: Carlo III of Durazzo and Louis I of Provence, Giovanna's adopted heir. Carlo was successful, but the dispute was intensified by the Schism, with Clement VII supporting Louis; Urban VI invested Carlo on 1 June 1381, but he later excommunicated him and tried to exercise a direct lordship over the kingdom, as well as proving to be of more than passing effect. The death of Carlo III on 24

February 1386 and the succession of his son Ladislao at the age of twelve gave new encouragement to the Angevins of Provence, and they continued to pursue their claims beyond the death of Giovanna II, the last of the Durazzo line, into the Aragonese period. Though much less pronounced, the threat of family rivalry also stalked the Aragonese. It seems likely that Ferdinand of Aragon came to doubt the wisdom of sending his second son Giovanni to rule Sicily as viceroy in 1415. The cities of Messina and Syracuse urged Giovanni to have himself crowned, thus preserving a clearly distinct Sicilian crown. In the event Giovanni's loyalty to his father outweighed Sicilian persuasion, but the threat the latter posed probably contributed to the abandonment of a policy of granting the title of viceroy to members of the ruling house.[13]

No more were marriage alliances guaranteed sources of support. The marriage of Alfonso Duke of Calabria to Ippolita Maria Sforza in 1465, and that of his daughter Isabella to Giangaleazzo Maria Sforza in 1489, did not prevent Lodovico Sforza from supporting the claims of Charles VIII in 1494. Nor was marriage an invariably effective way of securing the loyalty of powerful noble subjects. To strengthen his hold on the Neapolitan throne and to secure the succession of Ferrante, Alfonso I married two of his children into leading baronial families. In 1443 Ferrante himself married Isabella di Chiaramonte, an heiress in her own right but also the niece of Giovanni Antonio di Balzo Orsini, Prince of Taranto. A daughter, Eleanora, married Marino Marzano, the eldest son of the Duke of Sessa. Although both marriages appeared to achieve their political ends during Alfonso's lifetime, on his death both noble families were among the leaders of the baronial revolt which challenged Ferrante's succession and supported the Angevin cause.[14]

If marriages with the families of tenants-in-chief could fail to create secure alliances, foreign claims could also prove illusory as sources of prestige and support. Carlo III of Anjou–Durazzo, once he had conquered the *Regno* in 1382, turned his attention to the kingdom of Hungary, losing his life in that enterprise in 1386. His wife Margherita tried to hide the news of his death until she had mustered her forces to support their son Ladislao. As that situation well illustrates, if the presence, personality and ability of a ruler could prove an asset to a royal house, so such personal factors could be a source of weakness. Ladislao's minority helped to plunge the *Regno* into another bout of faction and foreign intervention.

Moreover, weakness in the chain of succession, the lack of an adult male heir with an incontestable claim on the throne, appears to have been particularly conspicuous in the histories of the southern and island kingdoms, especially in the late fourteenth and early fifteenth centuries. From 1377 to 1391 the minority of Maria of Sicily allowed the leading baronial houses of the island virtually to put the crown into commission. Foreign powers, such as the republic of Venice, found it much more practical to negotiate with these baronial houses than with the crown. Artale d'Alagona, the vicar general of the kingdom and one of Maria's guardians, considered marrying his ward into the Visconti family of Milan as a device to preserve Sicilian autonomy and his own influence while thwarting the ambitions of the house of Aragon.[15] From 1414 to 1435 Giovanna II of Naples, for all her determination to preserve the crown's authority and her own freedom of action, was unable to save her kingdom from foreign intervention, internal faction and the ambitions of overmighty favourites — difficulties all related to her sex, her childlessness and her previous lack of experience in government. For example, her reliance on the support of the Colonna pope Martin V as a valuable foreign ally and as the authority needed to sanction her coronation led to the rapid advancement of other members of the Colonna clan in lands, lordships and titles in her kingdom.[16]

THE PATRONAGE OF THE CROWN; THE EXPECTATIONS OF ITS SUBJECTS

Giovanna's advancement of the Colonna was part of the price she had to pay for her coronation on 21 October 1419, but it illustrates more than the special predicament of the house of Anjou–Durazzo. Her concessions point to another important characteristic of the mainland and island kingdoms: the crown was crucially dependent on support, both from its own subjects and from foreign allies and adventurers. As suggested above in Chapters Five and Six, the growth of the state depended on the acquiescence, self-interest and ambitions of the ruled as well as on the efforts and initiatives of their rulers. This is often in danger of being overlooked, especially when the history of the south and the islands is seen too exclusively in hindsight, in terms of the more or less remorseless march of the Aragonese Mediterranean empire, a late-medieval preparation for the emergence of the Habsburg empire in the 'modern' period.

Throughout, the strength and success of the crown was related to its ability to engage the interests of its subjects. In trying to achieve this the crown had an important inherent advantage as a source of patronage. For example, it had the power to grant titles, as when the Martins of Sicily tried to flatter Guglielmo Raimondo Moncada by investing him with Malta in 1396 and then promoting that fief of the Sicilian crown from a county to a marquisate.[17] The crown could endorse or examine doubtful titles to reward or discipline its subjects. Giovanna II empanelled a committee of jurists to ensure that her favourite, Sergianni Caracciolo, inherited the county of Avellino through his wife over the claims of her uncle.[18] In 1524 the imperial administration of Charles V sought to question the royal charters held by Bona Sforza to the duchy of Bari, and although a direct appeal from the duchess led to her investiture on 17 December, it did not preclude the right of other parties to challenge her title in the future.[19] The crown could dispose of the lands of declared rebels to win allies and reward friends, as the steady enfeoffment of Spanish families on Sardinia, Sicily and the mainland shows. As a gesture of mercy or reconciliation the crown could choose to restore confiscated lands to contrite rebels, or their heirs, in whole or in part. In July 1398 Ladislao of Naples came to terms with Niccolò Ruffo, Count of Catanzaro and erstwhile supporter of Louis II of Anjou, recognising his many Calabrian titles and making him viceroy in 1399.[20] After the seizure of Giovanni Caracciolo Duke of Melfi at a tournament in Naples for his part in the second baronial rebellion, on 6 July 1487 Ferrante granted his son Troiano part of the Caracciolo patrimony.[21]

However, neither of these concessions succeeded in securing the unswerving loyalty of those concerned, which suggests that the crown's exercise of patronage was not always a source of strength. It certainly was not in every case a result of royal initiative, and it would be wrong to interpret the plethora of feudal titles – in the *Regno*, for example – as an expression of royal authority. In the first place, generosity was seen as more than a pleasing personal virtue in a monarch. Conventional wisdom placed open-handedness firmly among the obligations of a ruler. The good deeds of Alfonso I 'the Magnanimous' as recorded by his admirers can appear as spontaneous and even eccentric acts, but his magnanimity had a political dimension which went beyond the generosity prompted by occasional encounters with needy peasants or in response to the more mannered requests from his circle of retainers and scholars. Even before he had entered Naples Alfonso had signalled his intention of being conciliatory and generous towards the baronage, assigning them the great offices of the realm. In the opening parliament of his reign, from February to March 1443, the king's willingness to recognise the extent of baronial lands and jurisdictions again reveals an anxiety to win support.

Secondly – and as Alfonso's actions suggest – the possibility of the intervention of the papacy as overlord, or of rival claimants to the throne, could pressurise and compromise the exercise of royal patronage. In 1390 Boniface IX sought to encourage Sicilian resistance to the Aragonese by appointing the island's four leading barons – Andrea Chiaramonte, Antonio Ventimiglia, Guglielmo Peralta and Manfredo d'Alagona – as papal vicars. In January 1460 John of Anjou secured the alliance of Onorato III Caetani – most of whose lordships lay in the Papal States, but who had some holdings in the *Regno* – by promising that in the event of victory over Ferrante I he would grant his vassal the lands and offices in the royal household held by his kinsman Onorato II, one of Ferrante's staunchest supporters.[22] Again the commune of L'Aquila turned at various times to the papacy, the Angevins and Charles VIII, as well as to the Aragonese, and found them all prepared to recognise its privileges. Thus the commune coupled its adherence to the cause of Charles VIII with a series of requests aimed at enhancing its autonomy, and ranging from freedom to elect all its officials to tax exemptions for thirty years – requests which Charles accepted in their entirety on 24 April 1495. Such generosity attached L'Aquila to the French cause for rather longer than might have been thought wise, but the return of its obedience to the Aragonese in September 1496 was accompanied by generous terms aimed at conciliation rather than reprisals.

Furthermore, the exercise of royal patronage could prove self-defeating in the sense that it could be divisive. The privileges granted by the Martins to

Messina in 1396 and 1410 – accepting that the court should reside there virtually permanently, that the city should house the royal courts, archives and mint and that its citizens should enjoy the same trading rights as Aragonese – contributed to the alienation of Palermo, the traditional royal capital. Again, the favour shown by Giovanna II to her Grand Seneschal and lover Sergianni Caracciolo sparked off or exacerbated rivalries and culminated in Sergianni's murder on 19 April 1432. The crown's distribution of offices, pensions and benefices in Sicily may have been designed to build up support, but it also produced resentment and complaints at royal favouritism.

Lastly, as the history of communes like Messina and L'Aquila or of noble families like the Caracciolo make clear, the monarchy faced in its subjects an insistence on their real or pretended rights, privileges and liberties; Alfonso I's execution in 1446 of a secretary, Giacomo Scorza from Eboli, for falsifying royal privileges is suggestive of the difficulties facing the crown. In the case of a family like the Caracciolo, this insistence was manifested in a dynasticism quite as determined as that found in the royal line, a determination to restore the fortunes the dynasty had attained under Sergianni (1372–1432).[23]

THE CASE OF SICILY

Family pride and local patriotism are salient themes in the history of Italy, but in Sicily the defence of rights and liberties could concern a wider community, that of the island realm itself, especially when the monarchy appeared to fail in its responsibilities towards its subjects.[24] Although championed at times by the great baronial houses of both Sicilian and Spanish descent and by the larger cities, the sense of Sicilian identity appears to have run deeply through the island's history. The vernacular chronicle tradition and the more formal records of kings, churchmen, nobles and communes show that Sicilian patriotism stemmed in part from the belief in a golden age when the island flourished under its wise and resident Norman and Hohenstaufen rulers.

Patriotism was heightened by the island's long resistance to foreign oppression, its particular moment of glory being the revolt of the Sicilian Vespers (1282), which led directly to the expulsion of the tyrant Charles of Anjou and the invitation to the house of Barcelona to assume the throne. The xenophobia provoked by the Spanish nobles and merchants brought in the train of the Aragonese intensified the sense of autonomy, although the cause did attract adherents of foreign origin. During the Schism, Sicilian patriotism was given a religious dimension as the island chose the Roman allegiance, while the crown of Aragon followed Avignon; the bishop of Catania led rebellions against the Aragonese in 1392 and 1394. Lastly, resistance to the Aragonese produced new martyrs and heroes: Andrea Chiaramonte, executed outside his palace in Palermo on 1 June 1392, and his kinsman Enrico, who led the city's subsequent rebellion.[25]

In political terms, the aims of the Sicilians appear to have been a resident and independent monarchy – though of the Aragonese royal line – and a generous respect for Sicilian rights and privileges. Such aims lay behind the meeting of the baronage at Castronovo in July 1391 at the prospect of the succession to the throne, being determined in Aragon-Catalonia. They emerge more clearly at a parliament meeting at Syracuse on 3 October 1398 when, largely on the initiative of the urban representatives, the crown was asked to put its house in order in a number of key respects ranging from the maintenance of the royal domain to the defence of the rights of all loyal Sicilians. They were expressed again in May 1411 when the city of Messina proposed that a general parliament be held to resolve the crisis provoked by the death of Martino 'the Elder'.

Nor should the issue of Sicilian liberties prominent in the island's history around 1400 be regarded as a passing awareness prompted by the successive succession crises. It explains the experiment of appointing a member of the ruling house as viceroy from 1415 to 1416, why the request for a resident monarchy was never entirely abandoned and why kings, viceroys and the Sicilians themselves continued to take the institution of parliament seriously. In 1458, on the death of Alfonso I, a parliament was assembled at Caltagirone which asked that the eldest son of the king of Aragon should be made viceroy. King John turned down the request but did promise that parliament would be consulted on matters of taxation, that the military obligations of his vassals would be reduced and that only Sicilians would be allowed to acquire lands and lordships on the island.

The fact that 'Sicilian alternative' was not produced is in large measure due to divisions within the island. More powerfully motivated by a narrower sense of liberty, the nobility was rarely able to co-operate for long and the greater cities of Palermo, Catania and Messina vied for primacy. These forces emerge clearly in a series of protests against the burdens of Spanish rule, spilling over into open rebellion in Palermo in 1517. The opportunism and lack of cohesion of the nobility, and the rivalry between Messina and Palermo, undercut any collective attempt to assert the island's liberties. Moreover, although the revolts in Palermo were partly inspired by the news of the death of Ferdinando II in 1516, the collective defence of Sicilian liberties also failed because the island had no native royal house to challenge the crown of Aragon or – as in this case – the Habsburg succession.[26]

The jealous defence of liberties which motivated the communes and noble families of the *Regno* and the islands and which in the case of Sicily could also be associated with the wider community of the realm did not deny royal authority; that would have challenged the prevailing view of society as a hierarchy of relationships in which self-interest implied the acceptance of a chain of reciprocal responsibilities. But it did encourage towns and nobles, as well as foreign adventurers, to bargain with their loyalty. It meant that throughout the period and throughout the area royal power had to be earned before it could be exercised.

FOREIGN ADVENTURERS AND ROYAL PATRONAGE

The fact that none of the contenders for the throne in the *Regno* and the islands came from native royal houses makes it hardly surprising that the crown depended extensively on foreign supporters. Giovanna II advanced the Colonna to secure an alliance with Martin V, but the policy was far from being unprecedented. Both Carlo III and Ladislao III had favoured the Prignani and the Tomacelli to win the support of Urban VI and Boniface IX respectively. Under the Aragonese, Ferrante drew on the assistance of the Albanian chieftain George Castriota (better known as Skanderbeg) to suppress the first baronial revolt of 1459–62. Castriota was rewarded with lands and his son John became a committed supporter of the king, being granted lands and the titles of marquis and duke in 1474.

Rather less successfully, help was sought from foreign *condottiere* captains, men anxious to find work to keep their reputations and their companies on the increase, while also hoping for profitable and prestigious lands and lordships from their employers. The opportunities for such advancement were increased by political confusion; hence it is hardly surprising that the reign of Giovanna II, characterised as it was by disputes over both the throne and the succession as well as by the factiousness of the nobility, attracted the opportunism and ambition of *condottieri*. On 24 February 1417 the queen made the young mercenary captain Francesco Sforza count of Ariano and 'legitimised' him to allow him to succeed to the lands granted previously to his father, her grand constable, Muzio Attendolo. This did not guarantee his loyalty, and from 1420 Francesco was acting as viceroy for Louis III of Anjou in Calabria with a salary in cash and rents. Francesco's position in Calabria was whittled away only with the Aragonese conquest of the duchy between 1435 and 1442.[27]

If such foreign adventurers rarely achieved more than transitory success, on an altogether more permanent and influential level was the Spanish penetration of the island kingdoms and the *Regno*.[28] This took several forms. The Aragonese monarchy tended to advance and reward those on whose military and naval skill they had relied to conquer and make good their Italian realms. For example, Aragonese attempts to rule Sardinia were accompanied by the extensive enfeoffment of Catalans and Aragonese families to defend and sustain the monarchy. Alfonso I secured the *Regno* by granting key military commands to Catalans. After the first rebellion of the Neapolitan barons, Ferrante rewarded the Aragonese admiral Galcerano de Requesens by selling him cheaply the county of Avellino, seized from Giacomo Caracciolo.[29]

Still more prominent were the large numbers of Spanish – and more particularly Catalan – merchants and administrators who accompanied and sustained the spread of Aragonese royal power. This is hardly surprising in view of the commercial activity of the port of Barcelona and the interests its merchants had in securing favourable markets for such manufactured goods as cloth, as well as privileged access to such basic raw materials as grain, salt, oil and wool. To these commercial interests were added financial and administrative concerns as the crown turned to members of the mercantile community for loans and rewarded them with such offices as the receivership of customs. Making credit available to the crown could lead to social advancement, the award of a knighthood and investiture with lands and jurisdiction.

The presence of large numbers of Spaniards as merchants, financiers, soldiers, courtiers and landowners could cause resentment. In late 1444 or 1445 the Este warned Alfonso I against favouring Catalans at the expense of his Italian subjects, and their warning seemed justified in view of the anti-alien riots that broke out in Naples in 1444 on rumours of the king's death.[30] However, the presence of such resentment, and the eventual decline in the status of the island and mainland kingdoms to provinces of the Habsburg empire from the sixteenth century, should not lead to an exaggeration of the speed and density of Spanish penetration. In the first place, the degree and character of Spanish settlement varied considerably. On Sardinia, the level of immigration from Valencia, Aragon and Catalonia was so great that the towns of Alghero and Cagliari became fortified enclaves in which the foreign settlers alone enjoyed the privilege of citizenship. Native Sardinians remained excluded from all three estates, or *bracci*, of the island's parliament.[31]

However, settlement on that scale and with that exclusive character was repeated neither on Sicily nor on the mainland, and the rate of Spanish penetration varied. Alfonso's dependence on Spaniards to staff his household and finance his government appears to have been exceptionally acute, possibly in view of his long struggle to conquer the *Regno* – and even his own inability to master Italian. Under Ferrante, ruler of Naples alone among the Aragonese dominions, the Spanish nature of the court and branches of the government was less pronounced. Furthermore, Spanish families could 'go native', marrying into native dynasties and thoroughly identifying themselves with local issues. Alfonso's viceroy during the conquest of Calabria was Antonio Centelles-Ventimiglia of Aragonese-Sicilian descent. His marriage to the heiress Enrichetta Ruffo led to the acquisition of the county of Catanzaro and the marquisate of Crotone until his rebellion in 1444 led to exile and the loss of his fiefs.[32] On Sardinia the Aragonese noble Leonardo Alagon inherited the marquisate of Oristano through marriage in 1470. Provoked into rebellion by the counter-claims of the island's viceroy, Leonardo became the leader of Sardinian resistance to foreign rule until his defeat by the crown in 1479.[33]

Earlier in that revolt, on 12 January 1478, the city of Cagliari had written to Barcelona for assistance against the rebel islanders, and while this does underline the connection maintained between the mainland and Spanish communities overseas, the closeness of these links should not be exaggerated. Indeed, at times a distancing can be detected. For example, despite the large number of Spanish families settled in the course of the fourteenth century in both Sardinia and Sicily, the parliament or *Cortes* of Aragon refused to allow these kingdoms to send representatives to discuss the succession crisis that followed the extinction of the house of Barcelona in 1410.

However, the clearest indication that it would be mistaken to exaggerate the Spanish presence in particular or the foreign presence in general can be seen in the way the crown continued to draw on and bargain for the support of its indigenous subjects. If Spaniards formed Alfonso I's closest advisers in his household, Italians still predominated in the other offices of the crown, as well as in the lower echelons of the household itself. If Catalan merchants and financiers were much turned to by that same monarch, so was Giovanni Miroballo. He was a Neapolitan merchant who had welcomed Alfonso's entry to the city in 1443. The following year, as the administrator of the city's customs, he advanced money to the crown. By 1448 he had proved so valuable that his bank took on the royal account. During Alfonso's reign he was knighted, invested with lands and appointed to high office. From 1459 he was master of the royal mint.[34]

AN ARAGONESE 'EMPIRE'?

In 1419, before he had begun his Neapolitan enterprise, Alfonso had made Antonio Fardella of Trapani vice-admiral of the kingdom of Sicily. In the early fifteenth century Fardella was a leading figure in the life of his native city through a combination of a large clan and wealth derived from land, trade and piracy. His prominence was further aided by the service he was able to render the crown. When he died in 1450 – aged around a hundred – the Fardella faction dominated the life of Trapani to the point of eclipsing its communal autonomy.[35] Such exploitation of royal patronage is commonplace in the histories of the islands and the *Regno*. The chancery of Charles VIII during his brief rule in Naples in 1495 was besieged by petitions: from his own followers seeking reward, from his new subjects seeking the confirmation or extension of their privileges, as well as from those trying to exploit the political confusion and the exile of many supporters of the Aragonese to further vendettas or secure pensions and favours.[36]

Evidence of this kind at once raises questions about the extent of royal authority in the area – questions which are encouraged by the traditional interpretation of its history as one of transition from 'medieval' to 'modern', and as a struggle between crown and baronage from which the crown eventually emerged triumphant.[37] In the case of the island and mainland kingdoms these issues can be focused on a discussion of the nature of the Aragonese empire, on the extent to which the crown was able or even sought to weld together its various realms, separated by geography as well as by distinct traditions. In the first place, the royal titles to the various kingdoms were preserved as distinct, even when – as in the case of Alfonso the Magnanimous or Ferdinand the Catholic – they were all exercised by one man. The separate identities of the various crowns was expressed both in the title of the rulers and in the use of the office of viceroy to represent royal authority. If Alfonso I could present himself as the reviver of the previously united kingdom of Sicily, and style himself 'Rex Siciliae Citra et Ultra Fanum' (meaning king on both sides of the straits of Messina), he also came to adopt the title of king 'of the Two Sicilies', a title which established itself because it more accurately reflected the political and administrative situation.[38] Except in Sardinia, where the sense of belonging to a kingdom with a single identifiable ruler had never taken root, this was certainly desired by their subjects; but the physical absence of the king and his court, the centres of patronage and advancement, did cause resentment and disappointment and explains the anxiety of the towns and nobles of Sicily around 1400 that a monarch should reside on the island, and the hopes of the Neapolitan nobleman Tristano Caracciolo that Ferdinando the Catholic would reside in Naples.

If the institution of monarchy itself did not formally challenge the separate identities of the kingdoms of the region, neither – by and large – did the institutions through which the crown expressed its authority. One way in which it has been argued that the Aragonese dynasty attempted to unify its dominions was through the institution of parliament.[39] This appears most plausible in Sardinia, where there was no history of consultative assemblies. There the settlement of Aragonese and Catalan noble and merchant families had been particularly heavy.[40] The settlers were used to such institutions and many of them continued to attend the *Cortes* of Aragon.[41] As late as 1484 Ferdinand felt able to summon the parliament of Sardinia to attend him at Córdova and Seville. Moreover, aspects of the procedure of the Sardinian parliament resembled the *Cortes* in Aragon–Catalonia; after Alfonso's first Sardinian parliament of 1421 a committee of three, one representative from each estate, was chosen to collect the tax voted. A similar committee was elected in the Sicilian parliament of 1446, but consultative assemblies on the island had a long and active history which makes it difficult to see them as Aragonese imports. That also appears to have been the case in the *Regno*, although parliaments had almost ceased to be called under the Angevins and Alfonso does appear to have deliberately revived the institution, extending its representative character to include the royal towns as well as the tenants-in-chief. Moreover, the business of all three parliaments was essentially the same. The king sought grants of taxation, while the estates of parliament presented petitions.

However, such similarities of a general and even of a procedural nature are outweighed by differences stemming from the particular histories of each kingdom. On Sardinia, where the sense of belonging to a kingdom was weak, where there was no history of consultation between crown and subjects before 1421 and where the political climate was turbulent, parliament met infrequently. On Sicily, where a greater sense of cohesion prevailed and where there was a parliamentary tradition, parliaments were called at regular intervals. Not only were meetings of parliaments unsynchronised within the Aragonese empire, but there were institutional differences, again reflecting local conditions. In the *Regno* only two estates were summoned, the clergy being exempt from taxation, whereas three estates were called in Sardinia and Sicily. Lastly, the business of the three parliaments was different in all-important detail. The petitions presented to the king or his representatives reflected local rather than imperial issues. If the Aragonese monarchy did make use of parliamentary assemblies on the islands and in the *Regno*, and if in general their business was similar, the actual record of their meetings and their individual histories reflect the particular circumstances of each kingdom rather than any unifying policy initiated by the crown.

If the history of parliament suggests a unity that was more apparent than real, an examination of other examples of 'centralisation' or 'unification' does little to qualify that picture – at least in the period under consideration. Spanish legislation was not automatically extended to the other kingdoms, as the 'common law' of the Aragonese empire. On Sardinia, with its relatively dense Aragonese and Catalan settlement, a procedure for applying Spanish legislation did exist, but even there it was at the request of the crown's subjects rather than on the initiative of the crown itself, and ancient indigenous Sardinian legal procedures continued to be drawn upon and exploited by parties in dispute. The crown could initiate legislation applicable – at least in theory – throughout the empire, on such matters as barring foreigners from ecclesiastical benefices, but measures of this kind were generally in response to local aspirations and complaints and had, in any case, to be enacted separately for each kingdom.[42] On balance, law remained traditional and 'provincial' rather than becoming standardised and 'imperial', while the development of an imperial appeal court, as in the *Sacrum Consilium* initiated under Alfonso I, was probably in response to the needs and litigious natures of the crown's subjects rather than an exercise in centralisation. Ryder has charted the tenacity of plaintiffs like Emilia Capice, widow of Tommaso di Sanseverino and Countess of Marsico and San Severino, whose efforts to secure her dowry took her to the high court in Naples before reaching a successful conclusion in the *Sacrum Consilium* in 1444.

Clearer royal initiative can be detected in the appointment of officials to defend royal rights throughout the empire, like the humanist Antonio Beccadelli, in the service of Alfonso I as a diplomat and administrator from 1444.[43] But as with negotiations over grants of taxation, the real business of watching over the crown's domains and interests was carried out by delegated officials working in an intensely local political and jurisdictional setting. This could produce administrators more sympathetic to local conditions than the imperial government, as Galasso has shown in examining the quandaries experienced by the early Habsburg viceroys of Naples.[44] Conversely, appeals could be directed to the imperial government against the rigours of its representatives. The scrutiny of Bona Sforza's title to the duchy of Bari in 1524 was the work of Charles V's officials in Naples rather than of the imperial bureaucracy. On her appeal, the emperor chose to respect rather than dismiss her claims to the fief.

The point of such illustrations is not to suggest that the Aragonese and later the Habsburg monarchy was careless of or lacking in authority. Nor is it to ignore the fact that its subjects could exploit the empire as a path to a career, a form of speculative investment or an opportunity for litigation and appeal. However, what the history of a fief like the duchy of Bari does help to demonstrate is the fact that throughout the period a striking characteristic of the histories of the islands and the *Regno* is the survival of a strong sense of autonomy. To some extent this was understood collectively to embrace the individual kingdoms, as has been shown in Sicily, but to a greater degree it was upheld by baronial houses and urban communes that remained their more powerful and articulate political constituents.

THE CROWN AND THE NOBILITY

The historiography of the island and mainland kingdoms has tended to present the nobility as virtual caricatures of feudalism, that word being applied in its more emotive and pejorative guise. Towards the subject population the nobility is presented as grasping and exploitive, as absentee landlords administering their estates and jurisdictions through agents concerned with short-term profits rather than the welfare of their tenants. Towards the monarchy and the state the nobility is generally depicted as similarly selfish and short-sighted, prone to faction and concerned with dynastic advantage and exploiting the generosity and weakness of the crown. This negative and critical assessment grows all the more bleak as Spanish followers of the Aragonese crown become more established, first on Sardinia, then on Sicily and finally in the kingdom of Naples.[45]

Undoubtedly much of this assessment has to stand. The progressive enfeoffment of its Spanish followers by the crown did lead to an increase in the number of absentee landlords whose estates were administered by agents more interested in profit than in good lordship.[46] On Sardinia the obligation of the crown's vassals to reside in their fiefs came to be ignored. On Sicily the peasantry of the large estates, or *latifunda*, became increasingly subjected to the economic and jurisdictional control of their lords. Moreover, in all the kingdoms there is evidence that communities could dread being parted from the royal domain and granted in fief. When Alfonso I granted the Sardinian town of Villa di Chiesa (Iglesias) to the Catalan Arnaldo Ruggero de Pallars in exchange for the service of two hundred men, the commune energetically upheld its right to inalienability in the parliament of 1421. Malta asked repeatedly to remain directly subject to the Sicilian crown, while the Sicilian community of Vizzini purchased its return to the royal domain seven times. In the *Regno* in 1419 there was an uprising on Capri on the news that the island was to be granted in fief. When the government of Charles V considered selling the communes which had escheated to the crown on the death in 1528 of Giovanni d'Aragona, many of them were prepared to increase their tax contributions to stay in the royal domain.[47]

Towards the crown itself the nobility displayed calculating self-interest more readily than unswerving loyalty. The Sardinian families granted fiefs on Sardinia to buttress royal authority became increasingly neglectful of such obligations as military service. Opportunism and self-interest also coloured the attitude of the Neapolitan nobility. If Troiano Caracciolo, Duke of Melfi, was apparently so close to Ferrante II as to be grief-striken at his sovereign's death in 1496, and if his loyalty to the Aragonese cause might seem to be underlined by his being chosen as one of the barons sent to invite Federico to assume the throne, disappointment that the new king was not prepared to respond favourably to his requests led him to desert to the French cause.

However, contemporaries – and most obviously the nobility themselves – did not always come to such critical conclusions. The tomb monument of Diego I Cavaniglia Count of Montella, who died in 1481, celebrated his virtues. The Neapolitan humanist Giovanni Pontano claimed that the many lordships of Roberto di Sanseverino, admiral of the *Regno* from 1460, were justly and generously administered. Around 1506 Tristano Caracciolo, kinsman of the Duke of Melfi, dedicated to him a work which celebrated the heroic character and deeds of their ancestor Sergianni (1372–1432), grand chamberlain and favourite of Giovanna II (see above, p. 178) and for many historians the epitome of political opportunism and self-interest. Later Tristano dedicated to the duke's son a treatise on the lines of a mirror for princes, placing before him the model of the good lord: learned, responsible and caring, watchful against the abuses of officials.[48]

Of course, both works reflect the shared family pride of the Caracciolo as well as the gratitude felt by the humanist Tristano towards his generous and more powerful kinsman. However, both also reveal a positive view of the nobility which serves to alert the historian against becoming too slavishly the 'king's friend' – a danger perhaps even more present for students of the *Regno* and the islands than for those of medieval England or France. That feudalism did not necessarily mean anarchy is further suggested by the fact that Naples emerged as one of the principal centres in Europe for the study of feudal law. Moreover, to see the history of the area too exclusively in terms of a right/wrong confrontation between the crown and the nobility over such imposed issues as 'the growth of the modern state' would be as misleading as to see the nobility's relations with both its subjects and the crown in a completely negative light.

In the first place, the higher nobility did not exist in a social and political vacuum, but needed the support and co-operation of other sectors of the population to maintain its wealth and influence. Unfortunately, in the present state of research that suggestion is made largely in the light of studies of other nobilities. Historians have readily accepted the importance of the 'reguli', or 'kinglets', as contemporaries could call the leaders of baronial families; but for all the emphasis placed on the role of the nobility in the histories of the islands and the south little analysis appears to have been done on the nature of their lordships and the social, territorial and jurisdictional realities behind their often bewildering array of titles.

A good example is provided by Giovanni Antonio di Balzo Orsini, Prince of Taranto, Duke of Bari, Count of Lecce and Count of Conversano. He was described by a contemporary as the most powerful man in Italy after the duke of Milan. In the description of the *Regno* prepared for the Este in 1444 it was claimed that he was the lord of four hundred castles and that he could ride from Naples to Taranto through his own estates, without crossing the royal domain. Of the one thousand, five hundred and fifty fiefs in the kingdom he held three hundred, and within them controlled seven archbishoprics and thirty bishoprics. He was the immediate overlord of three times the number of communes in the royal domain. His protection in 1438 of the royal town of Monopoli from the Angevins turned into a *de facto* lordship. He had his own mint, was addressed in the Roman imperial manner as 'serenissimo' and claimed that he ruled 'by grace of God'. His political and military power is clear enough. He played a crucial part in securing the throne for Alfonso I, and as grand constable was duly awarded a special place in Alfonso's triumphant entry to Naples, sitting at the king's right hand in his first parliament of 1443. His pointed absence from Ferrante's coronation at Barletta on 4 February 1459 gave notice of his desertion of the Aragonese cause. But until a more detailed feudal map is available, and until the ties of clientage have been explored, it is difficult to assess clearly the roots of the power wielded by a family like the Balzo Orsini.[49]

Despite this serious lacuna it is possible to show that the higher nobility were not socially and politically detached, by the adherence of other groups to a nobleman's cause. In the *Regno* a family like the Camponeschi, counts of Montorio, owed their influence in L'Aquila in part to the large number of their clients. Rather more rarely certain issues could unite a wider section of society, as when Ferdinando the Catholic was forced in 1513 to abandon the attempt to introduce the Inquisition on the Spanish model to Naples in the face of an alliance between the feudal nobility, the urban patriciate and the *popolo*.[50] Moreover, if some communities dreaded the prospect of seigneurial government, other evidently welcome it, finding their lords powerful in the protection and advancement of their subjects. When Alfonso I declared in 1445 that Catanzaro had returned to the royal domain on the revolt of Antonio Centelles-Ventimiglia, the commune asked not only that clemency be shown but also that its former lord be reinstated. Its citizens probably feared that the prestige and economic benefits their city had enjoyed as the capital of a lordship would be lost.[51] When Troiano Cavaniglia, Count of Mantello, was a ward of Ferrante I his vassals rebelled against the royal officials in 1487, resentful at their own treatment and fearful for their lord's safety.[52] Lastly, when Lodovico Maria Sforza was confirmed as duke of Bari in 1479, the news was greeted with cries of 'Sforza' and the wearing of Sforza insignia to express relief that the threat of direct royal rule had passed.

If it would be a mistake to see the relationship between the nobility and its subjects exclusively in terms of antagonism, the same would be true of the relationship between the nobility and the crown. As has been mentioned, throughout the period the crown tried actively to encourage the loyalty of the nobility by favouring them with office, lands, titles and royal marriages. Such policies could succeed. Onorato II da Caetani, Count of Fondi, was a loyal supporter of Alfonso I before his conquest of Naples.[53] He was later a close adherent of Ferrante, lending him money and following the royal lead in palace-building and church patronage in Naples. His services were acknowledged and encouraged by the award of high office, membership of the Order of the Ermine (1464) and the grant of the Aragonese arms. When Pietro Bernardino da Caetani joined the second baronial rebellion in 1487, he was disinherited by his father. Ferrante acknowledged this gesture by acting as guardian for Onorato's grandson when he succeeded to the county in 1491. The Cavaniglia, a family of Valencian origin who had followed Alfonso to Naples, were also conspicious in their loyalty. When Diego I, Count of Mantello died in 1481, leading his own retinues against the Turks in Otranto, Ferrante invested his young son Troiano and waived relief payments. Troiano remained loyal to – and well rewarded by – the Aragonese and Habsburg cause until his death in 1528; Charles V assisted his purchase of Troia in 1521 by halving the price.

However, as representatives of the higher nobility these men were remarkable for their constancy; indeed, for all the favour shown him in his youth by Ferrante I, Onorato III da Caetani joined the French in 1495. But the disloyalty so often shown to both the Aragonese and their rivals raises the question of the aims of the baronage. It never went so far as to contemplate abolishing the crown. Rumours circulating towards the end of the reign of Giovanna II that her three most powerful vassals planned to surrender Naples to Eugenius IV while ruling the rest of the kingdom as papal vicars probably reflects their power and influence in the *Regno* rather than a definite policy.[54] Furthermore, the baronage rarely seem to have been able to combine in attempts at reform or to secure for themselves a greater voice in royal government. Only in Sardinia does parliament appear to have been seen as a possible means of organising baronial opposition to the crown, possibly because of the island's close connections with Aragon and Catalonia, where the *Cortes* by tradition had great influence. From 1446 the nobles making up the *braccio militare* struggled to obtain the right to convene on their own initiative, but the irregular meetings of the Sardinian parliament and the divisions within the nobility itself weighed against them. In Sicily the *braccio militare* was the largest estate but, as has been seen, here again it was rarely cohesive enough as an estate to compromise royal power.

In the *Regno* concerted opposition to the crown took place outside parliament. In December 1459 and January 1460 an alliance of the baronage presented Ferrante with a series of requests before coming out in open rebellion under the Angevin banner. Some of their petitions were intended to benefit the realm as a whole by, for example, lessening the burden of the salt tax by the free distribution of salt rather than its imposition on the population through a system of fixed quotas. But most of the requests turned on the interests of the baronial houses themselves: the search for *condotte*, for land, for a moratorium on debts, for a share in the revenue of the realm. The barons in league against Ferrante in 1486 claimed to be reacting against the tyranny of the king and of his son Alfonso, Duke of Calabria, but their claim to be acting as champions of the kingdom and its overlord Innocent VIII against the bad government of the Aragonese shallowly disguised their fear of a more authoritarian and demanding royal government and their hopes to benefit from the intervention of the papacy and the Angevin pretender, John of Lorraine. In general, and during the Barons' War in particular, the Neapolitan nobility appears to show scant interest in political ideas compared to that preoccupation which they shared with the crown – the protection and advancement of their dynastic interests. What made Giovanni Caracciolo, Duke of Melfi, abandon an uneasy neutrality to support the baronial cause in 1486 was the promise of high office, military command, an advantageous marriage with the Balzo Orsini and further lordships.[55]

The wavering loyalty of the nobility raises questions not only of its own motives but also of those of the crown. Why and to what extent did the crown tolerate such inconsistency? Some historians have seen its policy in essentially negative terms, the crown having to 'put up with' the nobility until the opportunity arose to strip it of its titles, lands and jurisdictions. Concessions, as when Alfonso I accepted the wide powers of jurisdiction granted to baronial families in the *Regno* by the Angevins, were means to buy time for an eventual reassertion of royal authority.

Of course, when the opportunities presented themselves the crown did try to exercise and increase its authority. After the second baronial rebellion Ferrante I tried to ban the formation of alliances among the baronage against the crown. When it had gained the upper hand, the crown could prove ruthless towards its enemies. After the defeat of the first baronial rebellion at the Battle of Troia in April 1462, Giovanni Antonio di Balzo Orsini appeared to succeed in making his peace with Ferrante. However, he died in mysterious circumstances on 15 November 1463, almost certainly murdered on royal orders, and his many lordships were quickly seized. Similarly dramatic was the fate of Francesco Coppola, Count of Sarno. Although he was of noble birth, it was as an entrepreneur that he owed his rise to power in the *Regno*. His business interests ranged from prospecting for minerals to the manufacture of soap; from investments in land to handling the crown's business interests as both agent and partner. The reason for his desertion of Ferrante in the second baronial rebellion is unclear; possibly his very success and prominence made him distrustful of the king. Whatever his motives, their consequences were disastrous. The rebellion failed and although Ferrante feigned to forgive the count he was seized, tried and executed. His goods were confiscated by the crown.[56]

Ferrante had the confessions of the baronial conspirators of 1486 published, spelling out their intention to desert the court, fortify their castles and support the Angevin cause.[57] But despite the gravity of that threat to royal power and the severity of the crown's response, it is difficult to argue that the crown ever had a sustained 'anti-feudal' policy. A revealing illustration of this point can be seen in the complaints brought to Alfonso I by the communes and vassals subject to the Calabrian lord Carlo Ruffo, Count of Sinopoli. By his manipulation of the wine market to secure higher prices for his own produce, and by the generally high level of the exactions facing his subjects, families were allegedly forced to flee their homes. One noble vassal described the count as a 'wilful and vicious lord', a judgement which was brought closer to home for the king when he had to stop Ruffo interfering with the trade of the royal town of Scilla. Yet despite the complaints against bad lordship and the infringement on the rights of the crown, Alfonso confirmed the count in all his lands and rights on 10 April 1454. Again, in 1513 Ferdinando helped the count of Sanseverino to suppress a rebellion of his vassals.[58]

As has already been mentioned – and as these last examples help to confirm – royal policy towards the nobility appears to have been characterised less by a search for confrontation and more by the attempt to create or maintain allies: through marriage, the award of titles, offices and honours and the granting of lands and jurisdictions. Only conspicuous or persistent rebellion seems to have led to the kind of fate suffered by Francesco Coppola, and even then the crown sought rather to reward its more loyal supporters than to increase its own domains. Thus Ferrante drew on the lands that had come to the crown on the death of the prince of Taranto to enfeoff Sforza Maria Sforza as duke of Bari in 1465, and further lordships, confiscated from rebellious baronial houses, were granted to Lodovico Maria Sforza in 1487. Under Ferdinand and Charles V it was the repeated failure of conciliation and the survival of the Angevin cause that led to the progressive enfeoffment of the Spanish followers of the monarchy, rather as the house of Barcelona in the fourteenth century had rewarded Aragonese and Catalan families on Sardinia to defend its authority and punish its enemies on the island.

THE CROWN AND THE TOWNS

As potential allies the towns did not offer the crown support that was any more or less reliable than that of the nobility; nor did the crown take such support for granted. This was not so much due to their relative economic and political weakness when compared to such exceptional centres of finance, industry and trade as Florence, Milan and Venice. The city of Amalfi suffered badly in the political divisions experienced by the *Regno* in the later fourteenth and early fifteenth centuries.[59] Its commercial role was restricted to the coastal trade between Palermo and Rome, and its imports and exports were increasingly in the hands of the Genoese. As Amalfi shows, the economies of the southern and island cities had been thoroughly penetrated by foreigners: Catalans, Florentines, Venetians as well as Genoese. Foreign involvement was encouraged by frequently rehearsed royal privileges, and grants to those prepared to advance money to the crown. On the other hand, the picture is not one of unrelieved decline and the relative economic importance of some of the cities was considerable. The commercial growth of Messina was assured by its position and reflected in its aspirations to capital status as well as in the extensive land purchases made by its citizens on both shores of the Straits. The economic and political importance of L'Aquila was acknowledged by Innocent VIII when he promised the city on 6 October 1485 that he would treat it as the equal of Bologna if it recognised his direct lordship.

A more important reason why the towns never conformed to the classic role as firm allies of the crown lies in the fact that a clear distinction did not exist between the urban patriciate and the nobility, and although cities can be found in conflict with the feudal power of individual lords this was not part of a confrontation along ideological lines. On Sicily nobles acquired citizen status, town palaces and properties and civic office, while successful members of the urban patriciate pursued ecclesiastical benefices, appointments under the crown, fiefs and titles of nobility on the basis of their wealth from trade and land. As mentioned, the nobility was often linked by ties of clientage to townsmen, and a good example of such connections is provided by the career of Simone Caccetta of Trani, a successful notary, merchant and taxfarmer. Further encouraged by the grants of fiefs and a knighthood, Caccetta challenged the city's oligarchy in the late 1450s with the opportunistic backing of the prince of Taranto. This dangerous alliance led to the parties becoming embroiled in the Angevin–Aragonese dispute, the death of Caccetta and the intervention of Ferrante in support of the city's oligarchy.[60]

In general the crown appears to have supported the restricted urban government of landowners, merchants and lawyers. It could take steps to encourage the economy. In 1466 and 1483 Ferrante ordered the removal of all illegal tolls introduced by lay and ecclesiastical landlords on the movement of goods and livestock, but these measures were intended 'to rebuild the kingdom' rather than to play townsmen against the nobility.[61] Finally – and as has already been mentioned – the crown was quite prepared to grant royal towns in fief, the number of towns 'lost' to the royal domain in Sardinia, Sicily and the *Regno* increasing in the Aragonese period.

In view of the policies of the crown in their regard it is hardly surprising that the towns of the kingdoms could be as opportunistic, as calculating in their loyalty and as jealous of their privileges as the nobility. The nobility and the leading citizens, the *popolani*, of Naples, however otherwise divided by faction, shared the belief that their city deserved a privileged voice in the government of the *Regno*. The sense of being a capital stemmed from the fact that Naples, as one of the most important markets of the Mediterranean, was so much larger than the other southern cities, its population rising from about 40,000 in 1400 to about 120,000 in 1494. Moreover, it enjoyed such privileges as exemption from direct taxation and representation on the royal council, as well as the prestige and the more material benefits of being a seat of royal – and, under Alfonso I, imperial – government. It is not surprising, therefore, that the nobility and *popolani* attempted – especially at moments of royal weakness – to gain a still greater say in their own affairs, and even in those of the realm. On the accession of the minor Ladislao I in 1386 the city elected eight deputies – six nobles and two *popolani* – as the 'Eight of Good Government'. They demanded such concessions as an amnesty, greater control of the city's revenues and the dismissal of unpopular royal advisers. Going still further, they rejected the authority of the regent Margherita and swore homage to Louis II of Anjou on 14 April 1390. The turbulent ascendancy of the Eight came to an end only with the failure of the Angevin cause in the *Regno* and Ladislao's re-entry to Naples on 10 July 1399.

On the accession of Giovanna II, Naples presented her with a broader and more balanced committee 'of good government', made up of ten nobles and ten *popolani*, to secure administrative and financial concessions. These constitutional experiments to increase the city's autonomy and its influence in the kingdom were neither long-lasting nor very effective in view of the factiousness of Neapolitan society and in the face of the royal prerogative and the power of the feudal nobility. But the city's sense of importance did not dim. A high proportion of the petitions accepted by Ferdinando the Catholic in the parliament of 1507 were related to the privileges and special status enjoyed by Naples.[62]

CONCLUSION

Over the period both the political map and the balance of power appear to have changed substantially. Around 1380 the position of the crown on the islands and the mainland was compromised by disputes over the succession and by the virtual hegemony enjoyed by its 'overmighty subjects'. By 1530 the Habsburg monarchy appears to have defeated both internal and external challenges. Three royal lines had been replaced by one; and whereas once Naples and Palermo had been centres of royal government, now the Italian kingdoms of the Habsburg empire were administered by viceroys and were becoming provincial in all but name. The social composition of the nobility, which had presented the leading internal challenge to royal authority, had changed; not simply through natural causes but through the repeated failure of rebellion with its attendant deaths, exiles and executions, as well as through the steady influx of the crown's Spanish supporters. Only Corsica escaped both the establishment of Spanish royal authority and the large-scale settlement of its followers.

The crown's success is undoubtedly in part due to the personal ability and determination of a number of rulers. The remarkable number of treatises and memoranda on the practice of government addressed to the Aragonese by humanists, royal ministers and fellow-rulers, though in part a reflection of the difficulties they faced, is also an indication that they took the role of kingship seriously. Thus it is reasonable to suggest that an acute sense of responsibility made Alfonso II abdicate on 23 January 1495; plagued by self-doubt and overwhelmed at the prospect of the French invasion, he retired to a Sicilian monastery.[63] But his was a unique gesture, and Alfonso's earlier career as Duke of Calabria had shown him to be a forceful military and political leader and an able defender of his father's crown. Alfonso's career also emphasises a point made earlier: that the Aragonese drew considerable strength from their own relative unity, a unity which was encouraged by the fact that they were a foreign dynasty.

Moreover, the crown had certain inherent sources of strength which not even the weakness revealed by the succession of a minor or a woman could remove. Some derived from traditional feudal rights. For example, the crown never totally abandoned its right to ask its vassals for feudal aid, it continued to use parliament to secure additional revenues, it exploited the right of wardship and certainly from the time of Charles V the payment of relief became a matter for much closer scrutiny. More generally, the crown had a *raison d'être* as a source of patronage which its subjects recognised and sought to foster. This preserved its authority even at such moments of extreme weakness as the accession of Maria of Sicily or Ladislao I of Naples; indeed, it is remarkable in view of the agitated political histories of the various kingdoms that no ruling monarch lost throne or life to a rebellion. In 1381 Giovanna I was deposed and then murdered in prison in 1382, but on the instigation of her Angevin rival, Carlo III. Federico I of Naples was deposed in 1501 but once again by a rival to the throne, his kinsman Ferdinando the Catholic.

The crown found another source of strength in the divisions of its subjects. For example, the commune of Sulmona in the Abruzzo looked to the Aragonese to end the factionalism which had divided the town since the Angevin period. Although neither Alfonso I nor Ferrante was able to supply or impose a solution, the very fact that petitions seeking royal intervention were presented built up a relationship between the crown and its subjects which earned Sulmona frequent royal visitations and such privileges as a mint and the cession of royal land, while the crown gained a valuable ally.[64] Finally – and still more positively – the crown, at least under the Aragonese, had much greater resources to draw on relative to those available to even its more powerful subjects; the formidable resources of the southern monarchy were remarked upon by such informed observers as Guicciardini.[65] Moreover, the naval power at its disposal allowed it to muster and deploy its resources more effectively than its internal or external enemies were normally able to achieve.

It would, however, be a mistake to exaggerate the strength of the crown or to let hindsight hasten the introduction of Spanish absolutism. Between 1527 and 1529 a further French invasion plunged the *Regno* into precisely the kind of turmoil which rebellion linked to foreign intervention had provoked so easily and so often in the past, while more generally the effectiveness of royal authority on Sardinia must be open to serious doubt. Moreover, to draw up a balance sheet of the relative strengths and weaknesses of the crown and its subjects presupposes that their relationship was determined by latent or actual hostility. To some extent that was true, as the reign of Ferrante I makes clear. Soon after his accession his tenants-in-chief are reported to have said that as long as 'the king faces war and other troubles our security and prosperity are well assured'. In 1487 Ferrante observed in connection with baronial power that 'in this realm all the inhabitants should be equal', and that 'we do not want our subjects to be despoiled and unjustly burdened'.[66] Such sentiments could be translated into political action. The arrest of Luigi Camponeschi, Count of Montorio, in 1485 was presented by Ferrante as a justifiable move against a local tyrant who had defied both royal authority and the liberties of L'Aquila, the centre of his power. Alienated members of the Neapolitan nobility saw his arrest as a further indication of the crown's hostility to their status, while the commune of L'Aquila — or at least a faction within it — saw the arrest as the confirmation of its fears that Ferrante was prepared to ignore its privileges.

But the presence of political differences and grievances, even when they exploded into rebellion and reprisals, do not mean that the crown had an anti-feudal policy any more than they mean that the nobility and the larger communes sought the abolition of the monarchy. Even when the crown was particularly protective of its authority, as under Ferrante, there is no evidence of a policy to wear down, curtail or cancel the privileges of its subjects, or to abandon rewarding loyalty with lands, titles, offices and immunities. Neither does the crown appear to have exploited such anti-feudal revolts as flared up in Calabria, the Abruzzo and Basilicata between 1512 and 1515.[67] Returning to L'Aquila, the Camponeschi, back in royal favour, contributed to the recapture of the city in 1486, as well as to Ferrante's efforts at reconciliation through the issue of an amnesty and the confirmation of privileges. Just as its subjects continued to hope for a generous and accessible monarchy, so the crown continued to believe in its ability to engender and retain loyalty. To have turned off the tap of patronage would have been to surrender one of the most fundamental and acceptable attributes of monarchy. Seeing this, Francesco Guicciardini, to the surprise of some later historians, chose to explain the relations between the Aragonese crown and its greater subjects in terms of personalities rather than policies.

NOTES AND REFERENCES

1. Relations between the papacy and the south were so close, especially during the Schism, that the standard histories of the papacy are of relevance. A valuable up-to-date work of reference is the *Storia di Napoli* of the Società Editrice Storia di Napoli, vols ii and iii (Bari, 1975–76). The following more specialised studies are of particular value: G. Romano, 'L'origine della denominazione "Due Sicilie" e un'orazione inedita di L. Valla', *A.S.P.N.*, vol. xxii (1897); G. Fasoli, 'L'Unione della Sicilia all'Aragona', *R.S.I.*, vol. lxv (1953); F. Giunta, *Aragonesi e Catalani nel Mediterraneo*, vol. i, *Dal Regno al Viceregno di Sicilia* (Palermo, 1953); R. Moscati, *Per una Storia della Sicilia nell'Età dei Martini* (Messina, 1954); A. Boscolo, 'Isole Mediterranee, Chiesa e Aragona durante lo Scisma d'Occidente', in *Medioevo Aragonese* (Padua, 1958). The maps and genealogical tables below should be consulted.
2. E. Pontieri, *Il Comune dell'Aquila nel declino del Medioevo* (L'Aquila, 1979), p. 154.
3. A. Ryder, *The Kingdom of Naples under Alfonso the Magnanimous* (Oxford, 1976).

4. G. Lioy, 'L'abolizione dell'omaggio della Chinea', *ASPN*, vol. iii (1882); B. Croce, *Prima del Machiavelli, Una Difesa di Re Ferrante I* (Bari, 1944).

5. A. Caldarella, 'La Sardegna dopo la morte di Martino I', *Studi Sassaresi*, ser. ii, vol. xiii (1935); A. Boscolo, 'L'impresa di Martino il Giovane in Sardegna' and 'L'attività storiografica sulle figure di Ferdinando I d'Aragona e di Alfonso il Magnanimo', *Medioevo Aragonese*; L. d'Arienzo, *Documenti sui Visconti di Narbonna e la Sardegna*, vol. i (Padua, 1977). A valuable survey of Sardinian studies is contained in *Archivio Storico Sardo*, vol. xxxiii (1982). We are grateful to Professor d'Arienzo for her guidance on Sardinian bibliography.

6. A. Marongiu, 'La corona d'Aragona e il regno di Corsica', *Arch. Stor. di Corsica*, vol. xi (1935).

7. A. Zambler and F. Carabellese, *Le Relazioni Commerciali fra la Puglia e la Repubblica di Venezia*, vol. ii (Trani, 1898); V. Vitale, 'L'impresa di Puglia', *N.A.V.*, vols xiii and xiv (1907); G. I. Cassandro, 'Contributo alla storia della dominazione veneta in Puglia', *A.V.-T.*, vol. xvii (1935).

8. E. Pontieri, 'La giovanezza di Ferrante I d'Aragona', *Studi in Onore di R. Filangieri*, vol. i (Naples, 1929).

9. L. Volpicella, 'Un registro di ligi omaggi al re Ferdinando d'Aragona', *Studi di Storia Napoletana in Onore di M. Schipa* (Naples, 1926); R. Filangieri, *Una Cronaca Napoletana Figurata del Quattrocento* (Naples, 1956), p. 82. This is an excellent source for the presentation of royal authority. We would like to thank Dr A. Antonovics for the reference.

10. A. Flandrina, 'Capitoli di pace tra i due Martini e la regina Maria con Francesco ed Enrico Ventimiglia', *Arch. Stor. Siciliano*, vol. xi (1886), pp. 142–5.

11. A. Boscolo, 'Progetti matrimoniali aragonesi per l'annessione del Regno di Napoli', *Studi Medievali in Onore di A. de Stefani* (Palermo, 1956).

12. *Storia di Napoli*, vol. ii, pp. 334–40, 391.

13. Giunta, op. cit., pp. 319–30; Fasoli, loc. cit..

14. Pontieri, 'La giovanezza', pp. 569, 593; E. Nunziante, 'I primi anni di Ferdinando d'Aragona', *A.S.P.N.*, vols xvii (1892), xix (1894), xx (1895) and xxi (1896).

15. G. Romano, 'I Visconti e la Sicilia', *A.S.L.*, ser. iii, vol. v (1896).

16. E. Pontieri, 'Muzio Attendolo e Francesco Sforza nei conflitti nel Regno di Napoli', in *Divagazioni Storiche e Storiografiche*, vol. i (Naples, 1960): p. 103.

17. A. Luttrell, 'The house of Aragon and Malta', *J. of the Faculty of Arts of the University of Malta*, vol. iv (1970).

18. For biographies and bibliographies on baronial families, consult where possible the *Dizionario Biografico degli Italiani*; G. Vitale, 'Le rivolte di Giovanni Caracciolo duca di Melfi e di Giacomo Caracciolo conte di Avellino', *A.S.P.N.*, ser. iii, vols v–vi (1966–67), p. 48.

19. On the Sforza lordship of Bari, L. Pepe, *Storia della Successione degli Sforzeschi negli stati di Puglia e Calabria* (Bari, 1900): N. Ferorelli, 'Il ducato di Bari sotto Sforza Maria Sforza e Lodovico il Moro', *A.S.L.*, ser. v, vol. i (1914).

20. E. Pacella, 'Un barone condottiere della Calabria, Niccolo Ruffo', *A.S.P.N.*, ser. iii, vol. iii (1963).

21. Vitale, loc. cit.

22. Moscati, op. cit., p. 76; F. N. Arnaldi *et al.*, 'Fondi e la Signoria dei Caetani', in *Il Quattrocento a Roma e nel Lazio* (Rome, 1981).

23. G. Vitale, 'L'umanista Tristano Caracciolo ed i principi di Melfi', *A.S.P.N.*, ser. iii, vol. ii (1963).

24. A valuable introduction to the history of Sicily is D. Mack Smith, *A History of Sicily*, vol. i (London, 1968); also H. G. Koenigsberger, 'The parliaments of Sicily and the Spanish empire', in *Estates and Revolutions* (Ithaca, 1971).

25. G. Lagumina, 'Enrico di Chiaramonte in Palermo', *Arch. Stor. Sic.*, vol. xvi (1891); L. Boglione, 'L'ambasciera di Enrico Chiaramonte . . . al re Martino', *Arch. Stor. Sic.*, vol. xv (1890).

26. C. Traselli, *Da Ferdinando il Cattolico a Carlo V, l'Esperienza Siciliana*, 2 vols (Palermo, 1982).

27. Pontieri, 'Muzio Attendolo'.

28. B. Croce, 'La corte spagnola di Alfonso il Magnanimo', *Atti Accad. Pontiana*, vol. xxiv (1894); V. d'Alessandro, 'Per una storia della società siciliana alla fine del medioevo', *Arch. Stor. per la Sic. Orientale*, vol. lxxciii (1981). From a study of the dress in the famous Palermo *Triumph of Death*, J. Bridgeman has suggested that the society of the city had become 'provincial' followers of Spanish fashion: 'The Palermo *Triumph of Death*', *Burl. Mag.*, vol. cxvii, no. 868 (1975).

29. Vitale, 'Le rivolte', p. 28.

30. C. Foucard, 'Proposta fatta dalla corte estense ad Alfonso I', *A.S.P.N.*, vol. iv (1879).

31. Caldarella, loc. cit.

32. E. Pontieri, *La Calabria a metà del secolo xv e le Rivolte di Antonio Centelles* (Naples, 1963).

33. A. Era, 'Storia della Sardegna durante il regno di Ferdinando il Cattolico', *V Congreso de Historia de la Corona Aragon* (Saragossa, 1954).

34. Ryder, op. cit., *passim*.

35. C. Traselli, *Mediterranea e Sicilia all'Inizio dell'Epoca Moderna* (Cosenza, 1977).

36. E. O. Mastrojanni, 'Sommario degli atti della cancelleria di Carlo VIII', *A.S.P.N.*, vol. xx (1895).

37. G. Galasso, 'Momenti e problemi di storia napoletana nell'età di Carlo V', *A.S.P.N.*, n.s., vol. xli (1961). Ryder's study is subtitled: 'The Making of a Modern State'.

38. Pontieri, 'Alfonso V d'Aragona nel quadro della politica italiana', *Divagazioni*, pp. 250–51.

39. On parliaments in general, A. Marongiu, *Medieval Parliaments* (London, 1968) and H. G. Koenigsberger, 'The Italian parliaments', *Journal of Italian Hist:*, vol. i (1978).

40. On Sardinia, A. Marongiu, *I Parlamenti Sardi nella Storia e nel Diritto pubblico* (Rome, 1932); A. Boscolo, 'Parlamento Siciliano e parlamento sardo', in *Mélanges Antonio Marongiu*, (Brussels, 1968), and 'Il braccio reale nei parlamenti sardi', in *Medieovo Aragonese*; B. Anatra, 'Parabola della preminenza feudale', in *Problemi di Storia della Sardegna Spagnola* (Cagliari, 1975).

41. Trasselli, *L'Esperienza*, pp. 308–9.

42. Caldarella, loc. cit., p. 155; G. Santini, 'Il diritto spagnolo come diritto sussidario nel Regno di Sicilia', and C. Giardina, 'Unione personale o unione reale fra Sicilia e Aragona e fra Sicilia e Napoli durante il regno di Alfonso', both in *Atti del Congresso Int. di Studi sull'Età Aragonese* (Bari, 1972); R. Brown, 'The Sardinian *Condaghe* of S. Michele di Salvenor in the sixteenth century', *Papers of the British School in Rome*, vol. li (1983).

43. A. Ryder, 'Antonio Beccadelli: a humanist in government', *Essays in Honour of P. O. Kristeller*, ed. C. H. Clough (Manchester, 1976).

44. Galasso, loc. cit.

45. F. Carabellese, *La Puglia nel secolo xv*, vol. i (Bari, 1901); P. Gothein, *Il Rinascimento nell'Italia meridionale* (Florence, 1951), pp. 3–5; N. Cortese, *Feudi e Feudatari Napoletani della prima metà del Cinquecento* (Naples, 1931); B. Croce, *Storia di Napoli*, 3rd edn (Bari, 1944); P. Pieri, *Il Rinascimento e la Crisi Militare Italiana* (Turin, 1952), pp. 130–31; E. Pontieri, 'La Puglia nel quadro della monarchia degli Aragonesi', *Atti . . . sull'Età Aragonese*; G. Galasso: 'L'Ultimo feudalesimo meridionale nell'analisi di G. M. Galanti', *R.S.I.*, vol. xcv (1983).
46. A. Boscolo (ed.), *Il Feudalesimo in Sardegna* (Cagliari, 1967), pp. 1–24.
47. Boscolo, 'Parlamento siciliano', p. 52; N. Faraglia, 'Studi intorno al regno di Giovanna II', *Atti Accad. Pontaniana*, vol. xxiv (1894), p. 5; Luttrell, loc. cit., p. 60.
48. F. Scandone, 'I Cavanigli conti di Troia', *A.S.P.N.*, n.s., vol. ix (1923); C. de Frede, 'Roberto Sanseverino principe di Salerno', *Rassegna Storica Salernitana*, vol. xii (1951), p. 33.
49. L. Beltrani, 'Gli Origini di Lecce e di Taranto', *A.S.P.N.*, n.s., vol. xxxvi (1956); C. Foucard, 'Fonti di storia napolitana', *A.S.P.N.*, vol. ii (1877); G. Papuli, 'Documenti editi ed inediti sui rapporti tra le università di Puglia e Ferdinando I', *Studi di Storia Pugliese in Onore di N. Vacca* (Galatina, 1971); M. Viterbo, 'Aragona, Orsino del Balzo e Acquaviva d'Aragona nella contea di Conversano', *Atti del Congresso Internazionale di Studi sull'Età Aragonese* (Bari, 1972).
50. Galasso, 'Momenti', p. 52.
51. E. Pontieri, 'La "Universitas" di Catanzaro nel quattrocento', *Studi . . . M. Schipa*.
52. Scandone, loc. cit., pp. 153–4.
53. P. T. Quagliarella, 'Uno stemma del secolo xv nella chiesa del Carmine Maggiore di Napoli', *A.S.P.N.*, n.s., vol. xli (1961).
54. Beltrani, loc. cit., p. 120.
55. Vitale, 'Le rivolte'.
56. I. Schiappoli, 'II conte di Sarno', *A.S.P.N.*, vol. lxi (1936).
57. C. Frede, 'Il conte di Lauria nella congiura dei baroni', *Atti Accad. Pont.*, n.s., vol. iv (1950–2).
58. Pontieri, 'La Calabria', pp. 143–51; Galasso, 'Momenti', p. 52.
59. M. del Treppo, A. Leone, *Amalfi Medioevale* (Naples, 1977).
60. G. Cassandro, 'Il comune meridionale nell'età aragonese', *Atti . . . Età Aragonese*; G. Vitale, 'La formazione del patriziato urbano nel mezzogiorno d'Italia: ricerche su Trani', *A.S.P.N.*, ser. iii. vol. xix (1980).
61. Croce, *Storia*, p. 85.
62. A. Marongiu, 'Pagine dimenticate della storia parlamentare napoletana', *Studi in Onore di R. Filangieri*, 3 vols (Naples, 1958), vol. ii; G. d'Agostino, 'Il sistema "politico-rappresentativo" interno del Regno di Napoli', *A.S.P.N.*, ser. iii, vol. xvi (1978).
63. G. L. Hersey, *Alfonso II and the Artistic Renewal of Naples* (New Haven and London, 1969), p. 119.
64. G. C. Rossi, 'Sulmona ai tempi di Alfonso', *A.S.P.N.*, ser. iii: vol. iii (1963).
65. C. de Frede, 'Francesco Guicciardini come storico di Napoli', *A.S.I.*, vol. cxl (1982).
66. Croce, *Storia*, p. 72; M. Jacoviello, 'Relazioni politiche tra Venezia e Napoli', *A.S.P.N.*, ser. iii, vol. xvii (1978).
67. C. de Frede, 'Rivolte anti-feudali nel Mezzogiorno d'Italia durante il Cinquecento', *Studi in Onore di A. Fanfani*, vol. v (Milan, 1962).

CHAPTER TEN

The Papal States

INTRODUCTION[1]

In view of their long joint frontiers, running tortuously through often mountainous country, it is hardly surprising that relations were both close and complex between the vassal kingdom of Naples and the 'Lands of St Peter' over which the papacy claimed a direct lordship. Their economies were interrelated by both short-term ventures and more permanent connections. Ferrante of Naples was anxious lest the alum mines of Tolfa, in papal territory, would drive from the market alum produced in the *Regno*, and from 1470 to 1472 a single company was established to exploit both sources, until the superior quality of the Tolfa alum made the Neapolitan deposits unprofitable. More fundamentally, the transhumance sheep runs, so important to the economies of both states and to the revenues of their governments, crossed the border. Between Rome and Naples there was an important trade in such basic commodities as wine and grain.

Connections were also close in the political sphere. Lords of the Roman hinterland, families like the Colonna, the Orsini and the Caetani, held lands and titles in the *Regno*. In 1418 Giacomo Caetani decided to divide the family estates, with his second son inheriting the lands in the *Regno*, while the principal line retained the ancestral lordships in the papal provinces of the Campagna and Marittima. But, as has been mentioned (see above, pp. 187–8), that distribution was not entirely determined by the frontier, and disputes over the inheritance did recur. Nor was it only native Roman families whose interests transcended the border. Papal relatives could hope to benefit during periods of good relations with the king of Naples; on 11 May 1494 Jofrè Borgia, one of the sons of Alexander VI, married Sanchia, illegitimate daughter of Alfonso II, securing from his father-in-law the principality of Squillace, a generous *condotta* and one of the ceremonial offices of state.

Furthermore, just as the papacy could intervene in the *Regno* to support or oppose the reigning monarch, so too the kings of Naples could champion or challenge papal authority in Rome and beyond. Of this a clear example is provided by Ladislao of Naples, who was identified by Boniface IX as an essential ally and was duly crowned by a papal legate in May 1390. During Boniface's pontificate Ladislao did indeed prove to be a reliable ally, buttressing the pope's authority in Rome and the Papal States. But such a policy, aiming at mutual support, was neither pursued nor experienced as consistently by Boniface's successors. On 25 April 1408 Ladislao seized Rome and Gregory XII was forced to recognise his *de facto* lordship over the city by paying him 25,000 florins. Again, in 1413 Ladislao took advantage of papal weakness to send his troops into Rome. He virtually ruled the city and much of the Papal States until his death on 6 April 1414.

If the histories of the Papal States and the *Regno* were closely linked, they also display some important common characteristics. For both governments the area to administer was formidable, a problem enhanced by the mountainous nature of much of the terrain. Secondly, as with Naples, Rome was not a centrally placed capital, owing its status to powerful historical and religious traditions rather than to its geographical position. It is true that the road system, largely based on the ancient Roman network, did ease the problem of communication, but for the papacy this could prove a mixed blessing, conveying invading armies or roaming bands of mercenaries as easily as merchants, pilgrims and papal officials. Rome's off-centre position within the Papal States might partly explain why Boniface IX moved the papal Curia to Perugia between 1392 and 1393.

The problems presented by geography were heightened by the Schism which, if it proved disruptive in Sicily and the *Regno*, certainly challenged the pope's authority in the Papal States. The rival popes, Urban VI and Clement VII, fought to control the city itself, but even after the latter had returned to Avignon in June 1379 his adherents, or those who exploited his cause, contested the authority of his Roman rival. One of the earliest supporters of the Clementist allegiance was Onorato I Caetani, Count of Fondi; indeed, it was in the cathedral of San Pietro at Fondi on 20 September 1378 that Clement was crowned pope. Onorato was extensively rewarded. In exchange for the obligation to present Clement with a white horse each year, he was made count of Campagna and Marittima provinces and the title was made hereditary for three and then four generations. He was allowed to nominate candidates for the ecclesiastical benefices in his territories. Lastly, his lordships, some seized from rival kinsmen, were confirmed.

Onorato's allegiance to the Avignon cause was in large measure due to self-interest but he continued to encourage opposition to the Roman papacy, allied with other noble families like the Colonna and the Savelli as well as with disaffected elements in Rome itself, until Boniface IX launched a crusade against him on 2 May 1399. When Onorato died in April 1400, he had lost through conquest and desertion all the towns and most of the castles which had once acknowledged his lordship. To the north, in Umbria, the *condottiere* Biordo Michelotti built up a lordship based on Perugia and Orvieto and challenged Boniface's authority from 1393 until his murder by local rivals in 1398. Even after the Schism, challenges to the papacy from within the Church could be exploited by its secular enemies. In 1433, as the *condottiere*

Francesco Sforza seized lordships in the March of Ancona, he was accused by Eugenius IV of supporting the Council of Basel, while the commune of Rome, in rebellion in 1434, sought that Council's protection.

In 1433 Sforza had tried to justify his action by claiming to be attempting to secure a passage to his lands in the *Regno*, and this serves to point to another similarity between the Papal States and the southern kingdom. The large area and the long frontiers involved, combined with the internal disruption provoked by the Schism, made papal territory appear a tempting prize for more powerful neighbours. The case of Ladislao of Naples has already been mentioned, but threats also came from the north. In 1392 Giangaleazzo Visconti, Lord of Milan, considered creating a kingdom out of the Papal States for his son-in-law, Louis of Orléans. That plan – to strip the papacy of its temporal authority – had a long tradition and although it came to nothing, its failure did not deter Giangaleazzo from acquiring lordships in Umbria and the Romagna, over Perugia in 1400 and Bologna in 1402. Later, the republic of Venice acquired a number of Romagnol towns, places of commercial and strategic importance like Ravenna (1441–1509 and 1527–29) and Rimini (1503–09).

The problems faced by the papacy within the states of the Church can be subdivided geographically. First, there was Rome itself. For historical and religious reasons, the city was clearly identified as the appropriate residence of the papacy; after all, the pope was the bishop of Rome. However, the long residence at Avignon, though bitterly resented by the Romans themselves, had strengthened the autonomous institutions and expectations of the commune of Rome, to the point where the Romans could no longer be considered as acquiescent subjects of papal lordship.

Secondly, in the hilly hinterland of Rome, beyond the city's immediate *contado*, families like the Caetani, the Colonna, the Orsini, the da Vico and the Anguillara were entrenched. Although often referred to as 'feudal nobles', none of these families held feudal titles within the Papal States – except for the counts of Anguillara, whose principal estates lay to the north of the city, near Lake Bracciano. Their unique title helps to explain why Alexander VI tried to challenge the sale of ex-Anguillara land to Virginio Orsini on 3 September 1492. As feudal overlord, he claimed the right to annul the sale of a papal fief and managed to secure 35,000 ducats from the Orsini in return for his grudging consent. It was rare, however, for the nature of papal lordship to be focused in such feudal terms, and it is difficult in consequence to be sure of the precise relationship between the baronage and the papacy in respect of rights and obligations. What is much more certain is that the baronage enjoyed considerable *de facto* authority as lords of townships and castles dominating the Roman countryside and commanding key communication routes; the scope of their authority is suggested by the efforts of Guglielmo Caetani in 1510 to secure the legal opinion that his lordship at Sermoneta was independent of both pope and emperor.

Lastly – and further afield in the provinces of the Romagna, the Marches and Umbria – the local political map was complicated by the presence not only of lordships but also of communes of some size and importance as markets and manufacturing centres. By the late fourteenth century, most of these communes had lost their independence to powerful local families who drew their economic and military strength from their estates, their role as mercenary captains, and their retainers in town and country; thus Urbino had long been dominated by the Montefeltro dynasty, as Rimini had by the Malatesta. However, a minority of the communes — Bologna, Perugia, Ancona — were able to sustain at least a spasmodic independence under papal overlordship, although their periods of republican government were generally dominated by the feuds and ambitions of powerful local families aspiring to hegemony.

To compartmentalise these areas too strictly would be misleading; their political histories were closely interrelated. On 5 March 1392 the commune of Rome and Boniface IX formed an alliance to wage war on Giovanni Sciarra da Vico, whose lordship lay to the north of the city in the region of Viterbo. In 1465 Paul II employed Federigo da Montefeltro, Count of Urbino, and Napoleone Orsini in a decisive campaign against another turbulent family in the north, the Anguillara. In 1492 and 1511 the Colonna and the Orsini joined with the commune of Rome to seek concessions from Innocent VIII and Julius II. The Borgia and other popes used nepotism to further their authority in the district of Rome and the more distant provinces. However, behind these episodes, chosen to illustrate the variety of the political relationships within the Papal States, one central and general theme emerges. Throughout the Schism and beyond, the economic importance of the Lands of St Peter to the papacy grew. As papal authority weakened in western Christendom and as its 'spiritual' sources of revenue were reduced in consequence, so the importance of that area over which the papacy could claim a direct lordship and from which it ·could anticipate temporal revenues increased. Indeed, not only did temporal revenues represent the largest item of income, but within its own territories the papacy could hope to increase such revenues, as well as to manage the supply of basic commodities needed by the papal court, ranging from firewood to foodstuffs. Such fundamental fiscal and economic realities help to explain the efforts made by all the popes in the period to defend and extend their authority over Rome and the provinces beyond the city's walls.

THE COMMUNE OF ROME

Writing of the 1390s, Gregorovius remarked that 'the condition of Rome offers but a barren subject for the historian'. This negative judgement was based in part on the allegedly unremittingly secular pontificate of Boniface IX (1389–1404). It was also inspired by the sorry economic and disturbed social condition of Rome and its surrounding countryside. Finally, the factionalism and political inconstancy of the Romans themselves appeared to complete this depressing picture. Gregorovius was not alone in coming to such conclusions; his views were shared by other 'Ghibelline' historians in the nineteenth and twentieth centuries who regretted the failure of the Roman commune to resist the Renaissance papacy. Still more significantly, such views were expressed by contemporaries contemplating the decline of Rome from its ancient greatness, the erosion of the liberties of the commune or the appalling social, economic and political consequences of untrammelled faction. In 1398 the north Italian humanist Pier Paulo Vergerio wrote: 'Rome, which was host of every virtue, master of just aims and sacred laws, now is a den of evil thieves; now rules not discipline, not reason, but vice.' Nor did the Romans themselves shrink from such conclusions. In August 1511 the patrician Marcantonio Altieri addressed an oration on the Capitol to representatives of the citizens and the baronial families of the countryside rehearsing the damage caused by faction and stressing the benefits which would flow to the commune from peace and concord.[2]

There is certainly an element of exaggeration in both contemporary and later descriptions of the sorry state of Rome. To lament the decline of the city and moralise on its fall from greatness were popular political and literary themes before the Schism, and remain so to this day. Moreover, recent research on the social and economic history of the city in the allegedly darkest days between the Avignon residence of the popes and the pontificate of Nicholas V (1447–55) has suggested that the economy was much more buoyant than is allowed by the more traditional, negative picture.[3] Some of this buoyancy is associated with the merchants, professional men and artisans of the city, but to a much greater extent it is linked to what is now thought to have been an aggressive exploitation of the *contado* by wealthier Roman citizens, often at the expense of inefficient baronial and ecclesiastical land-lords, to profit from the potential of the land in cereals, wine and livestock.

Of the communes of Italy, Rome appears to have been unique in having a guild for those entrepreneurs involved in farming the *contado* for crops and livestock; this *Ars Bobacteriorum*, or guild of stockbreeders, was one of the principal elements in the alliance of interests which governed the commune in the fourteenth and early fifteenth centuries.[4] Its statutes of 1407 and its role in the religious rituals of the city confirm its members' prominence in the economic, political and social life of Rome, a prominence far greater than that of any of the other guilds. Seen in the light of their activities, the live-stock reported by outraged humanists and startled travellers to be grazing amid the ruins of ancient Rome – as well as the exploitation of these same ruins for building materials and lime – might be an indication of the econ-omic resilience of the city, albeit on the level of a market town, rather than a graphic pointer to its decline.

However, the older view should not be discarded, for all its elements of exaggeration. Political disorder in the *contado* exacerbated economic difficulties by disrupting commerce and the pilgrim traffic. The warfare of the period, a matter of raiding rather than set-piece engagements, contributed to the abandonment of villages and may have even inclined agriculture away from arable farming towards stock-raising, the former being more acutely dependent than the latter on a settled rural population and peaceful conditions. It seems undeniable that the city suffered economically from the prolonged absence of the pope, the Curia and the college of cardinals; indeed, without important industries and off the main trade routes, it probably depended on its role as a capital even more acutely than such commercial centres as Naples and Palermo.

This dependence was perceived by both Romans and popes, and helps to explain much of the history of the Roman commune and its relationship with the papacy. From the return of Gregory XI from Avignon in 1377, the commune of Rome was anxious to retain both the papacy and its own autonomy, so that while the commune was prepared to celebrate the pope's return and acknowledge his overlordship, it was at the same time anxious to preserve its liberties. The dual authority which resulted can be traced especially in the relations between the commune of Rome and papacy with the communes and lordships beyond the city's walls. For example, Gregory XI made peace with Francesco da Vico, whose lordship lay to the north of Rome, in April 1377 while the commune accepted a treaty only in November. In September 1389 the commune of Velletri to the south accepted the lordship and protection of Rome, not of Boniface IX.

But this balance between two distinct authorities could not be sustained; the areas of conflict were too many and too central. The popes believed in an authority that came from God and which was expressed by man in the Donation of Constantine, in theoretical and historical arguments which placed the bishops of Rome as heirs to the Caesars and even in the acknowledgement, however reluctant, of the Roman commune itself. They wished to express that authority by appointing senators to represent them and to oversee the administration of the commune. They wanted to realise the potential of their lordship by establishing fiscal and judicial privileges for the members of the papal Curia. They wanted to control certain strongpoints in the city, most obviously the Castel S. Angelo and the district of the *borghi* in the neighbourhood of St Peter's and the Vatican, as well as to be able to introduce and station their troops within the walls. Finally, they were anxious to profit from the tax revenues collected by the commune from such sources as the sale of salt, the taxation of the *contado* and the tolls collected at gates, bridges and at the port of Rome.

Against such pressures the commune of Rome and Romans themselves did offer resistance. Partly this was encouraged by the lords of the Roman Campagna and foreign powers anxious to exploit the grievances of the population to the embarrassment of the papacy. In 1377 the Florentine chancery, and Florentines living in Rome, harped on the subject of the ancient liberties of the commune to weaken the authority of Gregory XI.[5] In 1398 a coalition of the Colonna, Caetani and Savelli families tried to prompt an insurrection against Boniface IX. In 1404 Ladislao of Naples acted as a mediator between the commune and Innocent VII, as a result of which the commune's autonomous administration was restored, along with its palace on the Capitol.

Moreover, the liberties of the commune were preserved by the wider difficulties confronting the papacy as well as by the varying characters and abilities of the popes themselves. Boniface IX became pope at the remarkably early age of thirty-three, and the records of his pontificate not only show him to have been resident in Rome for long periods, but also reveal him to have been determined and resourceful as well as authoritarian and ambitious. He was followed by men whose pontificates were short (Innocent VII, 1404–06; Gregory XII, 1406–09; Alexander V, 1409–10; John XXIII, 1410–15), who were frequently absent from the city and who were confronted by the conciliar movement as well as by the antipopes. Martin V's entry to Rome on 28 September 1420 ushered in another period of stable residence by an able pope whose membership of the Colonna family made him no stranger to Roman politics, as well as giving him powerful local support. However, any attempt to date the establishment of papal authority in the city from 1420 would be misleading. His successor, the Venetian Eugenius IV (1431–47), had to flee the city on 4 June 1434, his authority shaken by his attempts to reduce the Colonna so favoured by Martin as well as by the military successes of ambitious *condottieri*, above all Francesco Sforza, in the Papal States. It was only with the pontificate of Nicholas V (1447–55) that the Romans became faced with the longer-term implications of living in the papal capital.

Although the survival of the commune's autonomy was assisted by such external events, as well as by discontinuity in papal residence and in the papal succession itself, it would be a mistake not to acknowledge the more positive efforts of the Romans themselves. Their seizure of the Castel Sant'Angelo on 27 April 1379 and the subsequent heavy damage inflicted on the tomb of the Roman emperor Hadrian on which the papal fortress was built is often seen in terms of mindless vandalism, but it should be realised that the castle did appear to the Romans as direct a threat to their liberties as its guns were to their lives and property. Nevertheless, the repair of the castle under Boniface IX serves as a reminder that the autonomy of the Roman commune was steadily eroded.[6] The signs of this are many, if few of them were as explicit as the refurbishing of the Castel S. Angelo. Some were abrupt. In 1398 Boniface IX curtailed the status of the Society of Crossbowmen and Shieldbearers which had not only defended the commune's authority in the past, but had even participated in its government with a standing akin to that of a powerful guild. After 1398 its role was reduced to that of a civic militia, and in 1408 it was abolished altogether.[7]

Other indications of growing papal authority are more gradual, even halting. Members of the Curia came to enjoy legal and fiscal privileges. Communal offices went increasingly to papal nominees; even when Nicholas V allowed the commune greater liberty to appoint officials, their eligibility was scrutinised. Communal officials began to work increasingly under papal direction. The revenues, administration and staffing of the university of Rome came under papal control and supervision.

In part, this growth in papal authority was due to clear-cut military or political victories such as the failure of conspiracies in 1398 and 1400. It was also due to political and social divisions within Roman society, the autonomy of the commune being compromised on the one hand by popular unrest and on the other by the *prepotenza* of noble families and their retainers. Thus fear of disorder following the flight of Eugenius IV quickly convinced the commune to accept the government of Giovanni Vitelleschi, whose pastoral authority as a bishop was less conspicuous than his ability as a general and his ambitions as a member of a magnate family from Corneto (now Tarquinia) in the Papal States. He was governor of the city in 1435, and the commune's acceptance of his effective rule in Rome and its *contado* is suggested by a decision taken in 1436 to erect an equestrian statue to him on the Capitol, hailing him as one of the fathers of the city.

Vitelleschi was eventually disowned by Eugenius IV and when, in 1440, he was fatally wounded it was probably to the pope's relief, if not on his actual orders. But his work had prepared the way for Eugenius's return, and it points to the principal reason for the commune's failure to maintain its authority against that of its overlord. Christendom in general and the Romans in particular believed that Rome was the proper residence of the papacy, fitting in the religious sense that the pope was in direct apostolic succession to St Peter, the first bishop of the city. That gave the papacy an indisputable authority in the city; but in the Middle Ages authority tended to carry with it obligations, and to the Romans these included the residence of a court which would confer prestige, draw pilgrim traffic, and generate wealth and employment through the presence of the Curia and the cardinals' households. Moreover, it was hoped that papal residence would bring greater political security to the city and its hinterland. Such expectations reveal a basic dependence of the city on the papacy which can be seen clearly in the repeated petitions sent by the commune to the popes at Avignon soliciting their return. Subsequently it can be seen in the way the papal decision whether or not to hold a Jubilee or to withdraw from Rome could be held over the heads of the commune and a populace torn between resentment and profit. The threat to cancel the Jubilee of 1390 led to the public humiliation of the communal leadership before the pope. On 6 August 1405 a delegation from the commune sent to negotiate peace with Innocent VII was brutally attacked by the pope's nephew, Lodovico Migliorati. Although this provoked an uprising and the ignominious flight of the pope to Viterbo, on 13 March 1406 he returned, begged to do so by the commune.

However, although the pontificate of Nicholas V did mark a turning point in relations between the papacy and the Romans, it did not impose a sudden end either to challenges to papal authority or to ideas of communal autonomy. One of the most dramatic and celebrated threats to papal power followed close on the Jubilee of 1450, which in certain respects had been a clear celebration of the re-established authority of the bishop of Rome. The leader of the revolt was Stefano Porcari, from a Roman family long prominent in the administration of the commune and with a personal career of distinction in government both within the boundaries of the Papal States and beyond.[8] Porcari's experience of such cities as Florence and Siena, his family background and an enthusiasm for Rome's past greatness resulted in an ambitious plan to free the Roman commune by seizing the pope, the cardinals and the Castel S. Angelo.

However, the conspiracy was betrayed on 5 January 1453, Porcari was hanged in the Castel S. Angelo and his fellow-plotters on the Capitol on 9 January. The revolt was easily suppressed and had no opportunity to gather popular support, but it was sufficiently serious to be reported at length by foreign ambassadors as well as by contemporary chroniclers and historians. Its gravity can be gauged from the pope's prompt decision to have a statue of the Archangel Michael placed on the summit to the Castel S. Angelo; the previous monument to the warrior saint who had driven the rebel angels from heaven had been destroyed by the Roman mob when the castle had fallen in 1379. Later, in 1468, Paul II thought he had discovered a plot to kill him on the part of a small group of scholars fired by an antiquarian enthusiasm for ancient Rome, a modish dabbling in paganism and personal grievance at the pope's reduction of the number of posts available in the Curia; the fact that the reprisals taken against the members of the so-called Roman Academy were not savage suggests that their schemings had amounted to a 'scare' rather than a serious conspiracy.[9]

Subsequent challenges to papal overlordship were not so melodramatic, if they do indicate that the issue of communal autonomy was not dead. They normally occurred between pontificates or during moments of papal weakness when the commune attempted to claw back some of the fiscal, jurisdictional and administrative autonomy which it had lost. On the death of Sixtus IV in 1484, the commune petitioned the college of cardinals to restore its control of civic offices and its jurisdiction in the Roman *contado*; after his election, Innocent VIII ignored these concessions. On 26 August 1511, during the serious illness of Julius II, the leading baronial families and representatives of the commune bound themselves together with an oath of unity to recover lost liberties and privileges, but while the pope was prepared to make some concessions, they did not significantly alter the balance of power in the city.

This had in fact swung heavily in favour of the papacy. Most of the popes of the later fifteenth and early sixteenth centuries were concerned to tighten their control of communal courts, magistrates and revenues. Julius II even altered the traditional composition of the papal guard, replacing recruits from noble and citizen families with Swiss mercenaries. The only clear exception to this tendency was Paul II (1464–71), who appears to have tried to win over Roman opinion on a popular level by indulging in public displays of magnificence and generosity, and on a more institutional level by strengthening the authority of the commune and its courts; but this papal retreat' was completely reversed by his successors, and in no way can this be seen more clearly than in the projects in town planning and construction directly sponsored or indirectly encouraged by the papacy.

Rather in keeping with his conciliatory attitude towards the commune, Paul II had his private palace in Rome (now called the Palazzo Venezia) built close to the traditional seat of the Roman commune, the Capitol.[10] Other popes naturally did not ignore that district of town. Nicholas V had the communal buildings on the Capitol repaired and enlarged – itself a good indication as to how far the commune had become an administrative arm of the papacy. Otherwise, papal initiatives were directed elsewhere – most obviously towards St Peter's, the Vatican and Castel S. Angelo, but also towards districts outside the medieval centre, like the *borghi* between St Peter's and the Tiber. Although aesthetic considerations were not absent, such schemes had distinctly practical ends. They helped to express papal authority in an obvious way; they also helped to house the ever-increasing number of members of the papal household, as well as the merchants, bankers, inn-keepers and artisans who supplied the papal Curia, the households of the cardinals and the large number of pilgrims and ecclesiastics drawn to the papal city.

Precise figures are impossible to obtain, but it is clear that the city's population rose from around 17,000 at the end of the fourteenth century to around 35,000 in the mid-fifteenth century, to peak possibly as high as 85,000 in 1517, before declining to about 54,000 in 1527.[11] It is also clear that this overall growth was due largely to immigration stimulated by the residence of the papacy in Rome rather than to the natural increase of the indigenous population. Evident too are the political consequences of this trend and the town planning and construction that accompanied it. The Roman patriciate whose wealth and political muscle had figured so largely around 1400 was progressively swamped by immigrants, a process which occurred at every level of society, from the courtier to the prostitute and the artist to the artisan. Furthermore, these communities of immigrants were acutely dependent on the continuity of papal residence, and formed an obvious buttress to the maintenance of papal authority – although Leo X complained at the flood of petitions for office and favours from fellow-Florentines which followed his elevation in 1513. The dependence on papal overlordship which had weakened the autonomous Roman commune earlier in the period took on an added dimension by its end, inspiring the Roman patrician Marcantonio Altieri to lament the swan song of the Roman commune, the last cries of a beautiful but dying creature.[12]

THE BARONIAL FAMILIES

The barons of the Roman hinterland, like those of the *Regno* with whom they were often closely related, are often represented as a dangerous anachronism, a turbulent threat to law and order in Rome and its countryside and a stumbling block to the advance of papal government. This unflattering reputation is far from being undeserved, even if the pillorying of the baronage by some contemporary and later commentators is excessive. When Innocent VII fled from Rome in August 1405 the Romans hailed Giovanni Colonna as Pope John XXIII, while he did nothing to dissuade them from kissing his feet and sacking the Vatican. The coronation of Calixtus III on 20 April 1455 was disrupted by violent street-fighting between the houses of Orsini and Anguillara. On 20 September 1526 the Colonna, in rebellion against Clement VII, sacked the Vatican once more.

Fully aware of the danger posed by the baronage to its government, the commune of Rome banned them from public office. Similar fears and sentiments could be expressed elsewhere. On 20 August 1380 the commune of Segni to the south of Rome stipulated exemplary punishment for anyone favouring the authority or influence of any lord in its jurisdiction. In 1387 the people of Viterbo, exhausted by the wars in which they were involved by their lord Francesco da Vico, rose in rebellion, murdered Francesco and submitted the commune to the Church.[13] Nor did the period see any tempering of the fears provoked by the prospect of baronial power. Contemporary chroniclers peppered their narratives with laments at the disorder and insecurity associated with baronial houses and their retinues. On 10 February 1489 the Roman commune forbade the cries of 'Orso' and 'Colonna' from the carnival celebrations. Pacts arranged in 1492 and 1511 during the illnesses of Innocent VIII and Julius II were partly designed to forestall faction-fighting between the retinues of such families. It is hardly surprising, therefore, that the papacy, whose prolonged residence at Avignon had been in part an escape from the threat of baronial intimidation, can also be found taking measures to curb baronial *prepotenza*. On 22 September 1466 Paul II issued a bull in the vain attempt to curb vendetta, a practice Sixtus IV legislated against on 12 April 1481. Sixtus and Alexander VI tried to balance the baronial families represented in the college of cardinals; Julius II elevated no member of a Roman house to the cardinalate. Moreover, the popes and their agents were prepared to resort to less restrained tactics; the entire period is punctuated by wars against the various families of the Roman hinterland. In 1436 Eugenius IV's legate Giovanni Vitelleschi directed a ruthless campaign against the Colonna, who had been largely responsible for the pope's ignominious flight from Rome in 1434. When their stronghold at Palestrina fell on 14 August, Vitelleschi ordered that the town be destroyed and had its cathedral bell carried off in triumph.

The Colonna had been struggling to maintain the gains in land and privileges secured under Eugenius' predecessor, Martin V; as a member of the clan, he had been prodigal in favouring his kinsmen with estates, tax exemptions and strategic marriage alliances. The cold wind they experienced on his death might seem to confirm the view of historians who see the baronial families of Rome and its hinterland as very much on the defensive·in the period, their aggressive behaviour being both the effect and the cause of the measures taken against them by the commune of Rome and then by the papal government. Their difficulties are seen partly in economic terms. Early in the period they are represented as retreating before the business acumen of the landowners and merchants who largely made up the Roman ruling class; later the inroads into their position are seen to be the work of the Tuscan bankers and merchants who gravitated to the Roman Curia. One consequence of the economic pressure is said to be the gradual transfer of property in town and country to Roman or foreign entrepreneurs, and of this a telling example is provided by Onorato III Caetani, Lord of Sermoneta and other places to the south of Rome. His ill-calculated support of the Angevin cause in the *Regno* after 1460 forced him to pawn and sell property to the extent that on his death in 1477 his remaining estates were heavily encumbered with debts.[14]

As that case well illustrates, economic weakness could be linked to other reverses. If the Roman baronial families had hopes to manipulate the papacy on its return in 1378, their efforts met with mixed results. Only one pope – and it is perhaps significant that he was elected at Constance – came from the Roman nobility. Increasingly such families had to combat the influence of foreigners at the papal court, and frequently they were in direct competition with ambitious papal dynasties advanced through the nepotism practised by most of the holders of the papal see. In 1490 Innocent VIII invested his son Franceschetto Cibo with the lordship of the dispossessed counts of Anguillara. Better known is the aggressive nepotism of the second Borgia pope, Alexander VI, who in 1501 created duchies for members of his own family out of estates confiscated from the Caetani and the Colonna.[15] It is tempting to conclude with a picture of the Roman nobility losing their hold on the land, as their hopes for advancement through offices, benefices and *condotte* at the hands of the papacy were increasingly disappointed; the da Vico would appear to present themselves as fitting confirmation of this picture of decline and fall. They held the hereditary office of prefect of Rome, but by the end of the fourteenth century their political restlessness had resulted in their effective banishment. Their real power, however, rested in the lordships they controlled to the north-west. On his return to Rome in 1376, Gregory XI feared attack from the prefect by sea and land. The potential challenge the da Vico presented to the papacy was maintained down to 1431 when they joined the Colonna revolt against Eugenius IV; but they were unable to resist the ruthless generalship of Vitelleschi, who drove them from their lordships and executed the head of the house, Giacomo II, in 1435.

It would, however, be a mistake to concentrate on the difficulties facing the Roman nobility, or to see the turbulent decline and fall of the da Vico as typical. In the first place, the weakness of the da Vico was not the consequence of adverse economic and political circumstances alone. Like the counts of Anguillara, another baronial family from north of the city, the da Vico were a small family whose fortunes rested too precariously on a few members.[16] Larger clans like the Orsini, the Colonna or the Caetani proved much more resilient. Secondly, and more positively, it would be a mistake to underestimate the inherent strength of the baronial families. Most obviously this stemmed from the castles and lands they controlled in the hills of the Roman hinterland. Too often glibly dismissed as belonging economically and socially to the 'backwoods', their fortifications commanded the routes taken by merchants and pilgrims to Rome, while their lands produced a variety of crops and sustained livestock, again vital to the provisioning of the capital. The account given by Flavio Biondo of a visit to the Colonna lordships around

Genazzano in the 1420s reveals a prosperous and populous community.[17]

Moreover, those baronial families held formidable concentrations of property in Rome itself, where their retainers were grouped and which they were ready to defend with fortifications, men and artillery – which helps to explain Biondo's description of Rome in 1443 as being 'like a wood of castles and towers'. One such concentration was that of the Orsini around their palace on the Monte Giordano, and its existence points to another source of strength.[18] Like the Neapolitan baronage, they drew much of their political muscle from their retainers and clients, and while such ties of interest demand more investigation by historians, their presence can be recognised from the evidence at present available. If Francesco da Vico was killed in a popular revolt in Viterbo in May 1387, his kinsman Giovanni Sciarra was swept to power by a faction in February 1391. On 25 May 1436, during the minority of Onorato III Caetani, his subjects in Sermoneta banded together to protect his rights from ambitious kinsmen. In Rome the reason why the faction-fighting associated with baronial houses was so disruptive lay in the involvement of their clients and supporters. The conflict between the Colonna and the Orsini in 1480 enmeshed two powerful Roman families, the Santa Croce and the della Valle, allied to the rival baronial houses.

However, the della Valle were allied to Sixtus IV as well as to the Orsini, while their enemies supported Ferrante I of Naples as well as the Colonna. This points to another source of strength which could be drawn upon by the Roman nobility. Because of their castles and retinues, and the strategic position of their lordships on the roads to Rome and on the frontiers of the Papal States, they presented themselves as likely allies or *condottieri* to foreign powers. This can be traced throughout the period. In 1376 Francesco da Vico was allied to Florence, apprehensive at the consequences of the papacy's return to Rome. The Orsini secured powerful marriage alliances with the Aragonese and the Medici, Giangiordano marrying Cecilia, natural daughter of Ferrante I, in 1487 while in 1488 Alfonsina married Piero de' Medici. Of course, marriage alliances did not always create indissoluble ties and the Orsini deserted their allies to serve Charles VIII in 1494, although that move in itself confirms both the opportunity for and the value of foreign alliances for the Roman nobility.

A final reason why it would be a mistake to see the history of the baronial families exclusively in terms of decline is that it would be to subscribe too readily to the stereotype often found in histories of Renaissance Italy: that of a central government purposefully gathering its strength and crushing such sources of opposition as the 'feudal nobility'. In the first place, without a hereditary principle of its own, the papacy found it difficult to outlast its opponents. After the death of Eugenius IV the Colonna were able to rebuild Palestrina; on the death of Alexander VI the Orsini, Caetani and Colonna, who had all suffered at his hands during the later years of his pontificate, recovered their lordships. Related to this is the fact that policies were rarely pursued unswervingly towards individual families or the baronage as a whole; and not only between pontificates, but even during the rule of a single pope.

This can be seen in the case of Boniface IX, perhaps the ablest and most determined of the popes during the Schism. If early in his pontificate he joined with the Roman commune in its traditional hostility towards the da Vico, in 1395 the pope's brother Andrea Tomacelli married into the family. Again, on 14 May 1400 Boniface responded to a Colonna attack on Rome by excommunicating the family, launching a crusade against them and securing an alliance with Ladislao of Naples as well as with the commune of Rome. Although the allies were successful in the field, the Colonna were allowed to beg forgiveness and censure on them was lifted in 1402.

As the Tomacelli–Vico marriage shows, popes were prepared to look for allies among the baronial houses, and part of the reason for Vitelleschi's determined actions on behalf of Eugenius IV against the da Vico and the Colonna is that he himself came from such a family in the neighbourhood of Corneto. It was to his new palace confronting the main entrace to the town that he took the columns symbolically seized from the Colonna residence at Palestrina.[19] Moreover, after Giovanni's death Eugenius faced members of the Vitelleschi clan as determined to maintain their position as the Colonna had been on the death of Martin V. More successful beneficiaries of the fall of the da Vico were the Farnese, whose share of confiscated lands helped their rise towards the Roman and European prominence they enjoyed in the sixteenth century. Even Alexander VI, often represented as hostile to all the Roman baronial houses, found it necessary to secure alliances with them; in 1503 the Borgia pope granted *condotte* to the Savelli to assist him in his struggle with other families.

Finally, and as the case of Alexander VI clearly shows, however hostile the popes were towards individual families or to alliances of families, they were not hostile to the social or political values they represented. Since Machiavelli, the Borgia pope has been seen as an implacable enemy of the Roman nobility. But this was not a consistent characteristic of his pontificate, and when it did emerge more clearly with the excommunication of the Colonna, Savelli and Caetani on 20 August 1501, or with Cesare Borgia's dramatic seizure of his enemies from among the baronage at Senigallia on 31 December 1503, it was in the context of efforts to install the Borgia dynasty in the kind of lordships its enemies had previously enjoyed. Borgia ruthlessness, like the dynasticism which was in large measure its cause, was not unprecedented, but it did take papal hostility towards baronial families to extremes neither reached previously nor surpassed subsequently. As has been mentioned, however, confrontation was not a consistent feature of Alexander's pontificate, and one of the reasons members of the Orsini allowed themselves to be trapped at Senigallia in 1503 and Rome in 1504 was that they counted on an alliance with the Borgia.

It would be wrong, therefore, to conclude that the relationship between the papacy and the Roman nobility was one of permanent antagonism, let alone one characterised by ideological incompatibility. It is true that all the popes were jealous of their authority. They objected to baronial houses which openly flouted papal overlordship, disrupted trade and pilgrim routes and provoked or sustained disorder in Rome. On the other hand, they were prepared to win over such families through marriage alliances, the grant of lands and privileges, the award of *condotte* and the bestowal of cardinals' hats. Similarly the noble families, if resentful of challenges to their ambitions and privileges, continued to look to the papal court for rewards and advancement. In the Papal States, as in Europe as a whole, it was impossible to arrive at a settlement permanently acceptable to all parties. But the picture of a changing balance of power between the various baronial families and the papacy should not obscure the fact that there also existed a perceived, if wary, reciprocity of interest which was probably more typical of their relations than such occasional dramatic incidents as Vitelleschi's execution of Giacomo II da Vico on 28 September 1435. The evidence of the surviving correspondence between Onorato III Caetani and Cardinal Lodovico Trevisano for the 1450s is perhaps a more accurate reflection of normality. This shows the papacy anxious to secure a reliable and watchful ally on the crucial road between Naples and Rome. The lord of Sermoneta, for his part, valued the friendship of an important patron in the capital.

THE OUTLYING PROVINCES

Papal overlordship also had implications for the provinces of the Papal States further from Rome: the Patrimony of St Peter, the March of Ancona, the Duchy of Spoleto and the Romagna. Here, only the busy Adriatic port of Ancona presented the papacy for most of the period with a republican form of government ruled by a citizen oligarchy. Elsewhere local families struggled more conspicuously to achieve ascendancy and lordship over both rural communities and the larger towns.

But if the prevailing form of government tended to be lordship, *signoria*, in practice or in the making, the origins, nature and circumstances of family power varied considerably. Some families, like the Este of Ferrara, had ancient local origins, and an influence or ascendancy dating back to the thirteenth century.[20] Others were outsiders, achieving power through military and political strength, as when the *condottiere* Francesco Sforza conquered the March of Ancona between 1433 and 1434, or Cesare Borgia overwhelmed the Romagna and the March between 1499 and 1502.[21] Other foreign rulers acquired lordships through powerful family connections, as when Giovanni della Rovere was assigned the vicariate of Senigallia in the March in 1474 by his uncle Sixtus IV. Some lordships were intensely personal in character; much of the strength of Federigo da Montefeltro's lordship in Urbino (1444–82) lay in the accessibility of the ruler.[22] Other *signorie* were exercised at a distance through representative officials, as with Visconti rule in Perugia from 1400 to 1404. As will be shown, some families enjoyed a title to govern, from their subjects or from the papacy. Others, like the Bentivoglio of Bologna or the Baglioni of Perugia, had the status of *primi inter pares*, influencing but not directing policy and sharing power more or less equally with other prominent families.[23] Lastly, some families could draw on considerable revenues from estates and investments, as well as from the states they ruled, while others existed in much more 'straitened circumstances'. Small lordships in relatively poor country, like that of the Varano over Camerino in the March, contrasted with those based on considerable centres of population supported by flourishing trade, agriculture and local industries, like that of the Este of Ferrara. Radical changes in fortune and resources could also be experienced by the one dynasty. This can be seen clearly in the case of the Malatesta of Rimini, who were among the more prosperous lords of the Romagna around 1400 but whose dependence on outside protection and service as *condottieri* had increased by the end of the century as their state declined in extent and suffered economically from war and foreign competition.[24]

But it is not only the variety of origins and character that makes it difficult to generalise about the nature of family power; the problems are increased by a prevailingly unsympathetic historiography.[25] To champions of the Papal States, these local dynasties appeared as usurpers and rebels; to liberal and secular historians, their often violent seizure and exercise of power was equally distasteful. Perhaps only the Este of Ferrara and the Montefeltro of Urbino were seen by nineteenth-century historians as exceptions, as 'princes of the Renaissance' rather than as warlords or tyrants. By the fifteenth century neither dynasty was parvenu, and both appeared to enjoy the general support of their subjects. Moreover, both acquired the added prestige and legitimacy of hereditary ducal titles, the Este in 1471 and the Montefeltro in 1474; indeed, the Este enjoyed the additional lustre of a ducal title for the imperial city of Modena from 1452. Most obviously of all, both led highly cultivated courts.

But the generally adverse reputation of the *signori* was not the creation of later historians. Their contemporary enemies were numerous, and of these the papacy had both the grounds and the means to discredit those families who challenged its overlordship. Here an extreme example is provided by Sigismondo Malatesta's rebellion against his overlord Pius II. The pope seized on Sigismund's rather unconventional private life and his alleged indifference to Christianity to enhance the charge of treason, and went beyond excommunication in 1461 to arrange for the lord of Rimini an inverted canonisation to insure his place in hell. Less spectacularly and more generally, the opponents of the *signori* accused them of tyranny on the grounds either of their lack of a proper title to rule or of their contempt for the common good of their subjects as manifested by the violence and self-interest of their government. These criteria were wide and testing, and it is hardly surprising that they could be applied with effect to virtually all the ruling dynasties of the Papal States. In 1506 Julius II claimed to be restoring to the Bolognese their 'liberty' by ridding them of the 'tyranny' of the Bentivoglio, but accepting the plausibility of the charge of tyranny should not absolve the historian from the need to investigate the nature of lordship in the Papal States to a greater depth and with less prejudice.

In the first place, it is important to note that most *signori* were sensitive to the charge of tyranny and anxious to project an image of virtue and legitimacy. Borso d'Este had himself portrayed under the word 'Justice' in the frescoes decorating his Schifanoia palace in Ferrara (*c.* 1470). Acknowledgement by the crowned heads of Europe was also much prized. In 1460 Sante and Giovanni II Bentivoglio secured the title of counts palatine from the emperor Frederick III, while in 1469 Giovanni was granted the privilege of incorporating the imperial eagle in his coats of arms. In 1474 the obliging king of Denmark was lavishly entertained in Bologna, while Federigo da Montefeltro was proud of the Order of the Garter awarded him by Edward IV in the same year.

When it came to achieving a more specific legality, not all families were able to acquire a title to govern. This can be seen most clearly in the case of the Baglioni of Perugia in the later fifteenth and earlier sixteenth centuries. While chroniclers tended to fasten on their deeds and accentuate their authority, and while the Baglioni certainly could influence the government of the commune, the practical administration of the city and its *contado* was shared between papal representatives and communal councils of leading citizens, including the Baglioni but not in overwhelming numbers or with distinct authority. The situation was somewhat similar in Bologna, with the Bentivoglio holding the position of *primi inter pares*, although Giovanni II – thanks to the powerful support in 1463 of the Sforza, the king of Naples and the papacy – was granted the communal office of standard-bearer of justice for life. However, in the majority of cases where the ascendancy of a dynasty went beyond the exercise of influence to lay claims on a more explicit lordship, efforts were made to obtain titles to govern, to avoid one of the contemporary definitions of tyranny.

The most readily available source of a title was from the lord's own subjects, and when a *signore* came to power the occasion was generally marked by a ceremony in which the commune presented lists of petitions to the lord or his representatives and, on their acceptance, formally acknowledged the new regime. The substance of such ceremonies can often be doubted. The lists of petitions generally have a *pro forma* quality, rehearsing requests for tax exemption or reduction, asking that the commune's *contado* be preserved, if not extended, and seeking to maintain the political influence and wealth of those prominent members of the community who had normally drafted the petitions in the first place. Moreover, they were generally presented in circumstances where the political and military realities had been decisively tilted in favour of the incoming *signore*, as when the communes of the March of Ancona surrendered to Francesco Sforza in 1433. Lastly, the petitions were not always accepted in full and were often subsequently ignored. After its conquest by Sforza in December 1433, the commune of Montolmo asked for twenty-five years' tax exemption but was granted only ten, and even that concession was not respected.[26]

On the other hand, it would be a mistake to dismiss such petitions as always without substance. They could be presented even when the lord's power was overwhelming, as when Perugia surrendered to Giangaleazzo Visconti Lord of Milan in 1400, and even the triumphant progress of Cesare Borgia through the Romagna and the March from 1499 was marked by the acceptance of communal petitions and statutes. The petitions and their response were carefully kept in the commune's archive and were often appended to its statutes, providing the precedents and legal ammunition for further petitions in such areas as tax relief and the communes's jurisdiction over its *contado*. And often specific requests – for the reduction of taxation levels, for a moratorium on debts, for urgent supplies of food, for the removal of billeted soldiery – could be met. After the commune of Montolmo returned to papal rule in 1443 it secured tax concessions, as well as an amnesty, the promise to respect communal autonomy and the cancellation of debts. Lastly, most incoming *signori* appear to have seen the value of trying to win over rather than alienate their new subjects. This was most clearly the case when the succession was uncertain, as when the illegitimate Federigo da Montefeltro accepted the petitions presented to him by the commune of Urbino on 23 July 1444, as he succeeded to his murdered brother Oddantonio. Not only do these petitions reveal the surviving extent of communal autonomy, but their tone is closer to that of a treaty between equal partners than to a document of surrender.[27]

However seriously the procedures of petition and acceptance were taken by the *signori* and their subjects, they did not carry the juridical or even the political weight necessary to remove the need for a title granted by the ultimate overlord of all these communities, the papacy. The form of recognition increasingly applied by the papacy from the fourteenth century was the grant of the title of papal vicar. It used to be thought that such grants invariably represented a capitulation on the part of the largely theoretical power of the papacy in the face of the real power of their overmighty subjects, especially in more distant provinces like the Romagna. Certainly there were instances where that was true. In 1419, with the nadir of papal fortunes in the Papal States at the end of the Council of Constance, Martin V was forced to grant a vicariate to the powerful Perugian *condottiere* Fortebraccio which covered most of the communes of Umbria. In 1434 Eugenius IV's grants of the titles of marquis of the March of Ancona and standard-bearer of the Church to Sforza represent a desperate attempt to come to terms with a successful *condottiere* who appeared to be sweeping all before him.

However, papal grants of vicariates are not necessarily a sign of weakness and a loss of initiative. During the Schism Boniface IX made extensive use of such grants; they could represent an acceptance of uncomfortable political and military realities, as when he was forced to recognise the lordships accumulated by Biordo Michelotti in Umbria on 25 March 1396.[28] But they could also be used as bargaining power to win allies, and in 1397 Pandolfo Malatesta, another papal vicar, was serving Boniface IX as captain general against Michelotti. Again, in 1447 Nicholas V ceded Iesi to Alfonso I, partly for the payment of 35,000 ducats but largely because of his successful campaigns against the Sforza in the March. The award of the title of vicar was not a licence to absolutism. It took precedence over any grants secured by the *signore* from his subjects; it committed a lord to the payment of an annual census, to upholding the welfare of his subjects, to providing his overlord with military aid and to attending parliament.

Moreover, the title was not hereditary; at most it was awarded for two generations. As mentioned, hereditary titles were granted to the Este and Montefeltro, but such concessions were extremely rare, and in these cases they were bestowed on families whose lands were distant from Rome and who had a record of loyalty to the papacy as allies and *condottieri*. Furthermore, if the feudally based obligations to provide military service and counsel in parliament were largely obsolete, papal recognition re-emphasised papal sovereignty and provided specific grounds for intervention, the replacement of a ruling family and even the introduction of direct papal rule. The census arrears of the Manfredi of Imola by 1473 provided Sixtus IV with the pretext of removing them in favour of his nephew Girolamo Riario;[29] similarly census arrears gave Alexander VI the grounds for launching Cesare Borgia against the lords of the Romagna in 1499. Lastly, the non-hereditary quality of vicariates strengthened the hand of the papacy at moments of weakness in a signorial dynasty; in 1463 Paul II employed Federigo da Montefeltro to prevent the illegitimate Roberto Malatesta succeeding his uncle Malatesta Novello in Cesena.[30] In 1504 Julius II persuaded the childless Guidobaldo da Montefeltro to adopt his nephew and the pope's kinsman, Francesco Maria della Rovere, as his heir to the duchy of Urbino.

The search for titles shows that the ruling families of the Papal States were sensitive to the charge of tyranny in terms of 'defect of title'; it also emphasises how external events could have a direct bearing on the internal affairs of the communes of the Papal States and the ascendancy of their leading families. As has been mentioned, it used to be believed that there was a direct correlation between papal weakness and the flourishing of the *signori*; in general the *signori* did flourish longest in those areas furthest from Rome, but the relationship between papal weakness and signorial strength can also be seen in particular cases. Following the death of Alexander VI on 18 August 1503 and the subsequent collapse of the authority of his son Cesare, families like the Varano, Sforza and Montefeltro returned from exile to their lordships in Camerino, Pesaro and Urbino. Conversely, strong and determined popes like Sixtus IV, Alexander VI and Julius II could challenge the authority and autonomy of hostile signorial dynasties.

But it would be wrong to create too simple a formula linking signorial strength to papal weakness, and vice versa. Some popes actively encouraged and supported signorial families as positive manifestations of their authority, and this can be seen most clearly in those dynasties whose ascendancies were the product of papal nepotism, like the della Rovere and Riario (Sixtus IV, 1471–84 and Julius II, 1503–13), the Borgia (Calixtus III, 1455–58 and Alexander VI, 1492–1503) and the Medici (Leo X, 1513–22 and Clement VII, 1523–34). Moreover, it is important to realise that papal–signorial relations were not simply bilateral, existing in a vacuum. Geography could encourage the ambitions of foreign powers. The Este of Ferrara long remained tied to the commercial and political interests of Venice, while the province of the Romagna was particularly exposed to intervention, being more accessible from Florence, Milan and Venice than from Rome. In 1441 Ostasio III da Polenta, long a client of Venice, left his lordship of Ravenna to the republic.

This helps to explain why the *signori* of the Papal States should not be seen as independent powers; indeed, with the growing hegemony of the larger Italian states and the growing impact of the European powers on Italian politics, the balance of economic and military resources grew steadily less favourable to them and their roles as the *raccomandati*, or clients, and *condottieri* of more powerful external protectors hardened. The dependence of the Bentivoglio on their neighbours the Sforza can be poignantly illustrated by the fact that when Giovanni II succeeded his kinsman Sante as head of the family in 1464, he inherited not only his ascendancy in the affairs of the commune but also Sante's wife Ginevra, niece of the duke of Milan. From 1523 to 1538 Francesco Maria della Rovere, Duke of Urbino, welcomed the political protection as well as the salary following from his position as commander-in-chief of the Venetian army.

However, in 1488 the citizens and *contadini* of Faenza refused to let Florence exercise the guardianship of the young Astorre III Manfredi; to concentrate on the *signori*'s dependence on other powers would be to create the misleading impression that the needs and attitudes of their own subjects were not of much importance. Such an impression was frequently created by older historians who stressed the role of force in the acquisition and retention of power. Force, indeed, could be present. In 1385 the Este began the construction of a fortress in the centre of Ferrara in the aftermath of a prolonged period of popular unrest against the burden of taxation. In 1437 Sigismondo Malatesta began rebuilding the castle of Rimini, and named it after himself to impress his subjects with the strength, presence and permanence of his authority. The sack which the commune of Montolmo suffered in 1433 at the hands of Francesco Sforza dissuaded other communes in the March of Ancona from resisting him.

But if the threat or exercise of force could certainly be present in a lord's acquisition, retention and loss of power, other less dramatic but perhaps even more fundamental elements could be involved. In the first place, if many *signori* were able to enjoy a substantial and even a lion's share of the tax revenues of their states, they needed resources of their own on which to build and sustain their ascendancy. Most obviously this would take the form of land and property in the city and its *contado*, from which the ruling dynasty could draw cash revenues, food supplies and manpower and to which it could retreat if its political situation in town deteriorated. Thus the Baglioni of Perugia drew much of their political muscle from the various lordships they held in the *contado*, where their castles were situated and from which they could draw on retainers and revenues, as well as the food supplies so vital to the political and economic life of a medieval urban society.

However, no leading family could long enjoy an effective authority on no more than its own resources or foreign protection, and historians are becoming more aware of the dependence of the *signori* on the support, collusion or at least the acquiescence of others. For that reason, it is increasingly recognised that the longer-lasting dynasties did not operate as distant dictators but were associated with an oligarchy of other prominent local families, and made extensive use of patronage to create a following. Successful dynasties appreciated the value of marriage alliances and understood the importance of circulating secular, and where possible ecclesiastical, offices. Studies of individual signorial families like the Malatesta of Rimini and the Este of Ferrara reveal their awareness of the value of patronage, and the concession of office and privilege: the rise in the course of the fifteenth century of the Romei family of Ferrara in Este service and favour is a good example of this.[31] Even implanted foreign dynasties could appreciate this fact. Girolamo Riario, Lord of Imola from 1474 to 1488, for all his powerful papal and Sforza backers, did not fundamentally challenge the institutions and personnel of communal government and the resultant dual government, or 'diarchy', meant that prominent local families continued to taste power and wield influence. In view of their reputation for ruthlessness and bloodletting encouraged by Romantic historiography, the *signori* were remarkably tolerant of the numerous and prominent vicars of Bray among their subjects. The lawyer Girolamo Vanni could serve Guidobaldo da Montefeltro, Duke of Urbino, switch his allegiance to Cesare Borgia in the autumn of 1502, support Guidobaldo's brief return to power, survive Cesare's counterattack in December and weather the Borgia fall and the Montefeltro restoration of 1503.[32]

Furthermore, by establishing generous and lavish courts or households, they brought prestige to their communities as well as to themselves, while also creating employment and circulating wealth. By serving as *condottieri*, they increased the opportunities for employment among their subjects. Lastly, the *condotte* and alliances they could secure as the *accomodati* or friendly foreign powers could afford their subjects some protection from external and internal enemies. Thus, on the assassination of Girolamo Riario in 1488, the councils of Forlì were forced to admit that the commune could no longer risk its independence and had to accept the regency of his widow, the strong-minded and well-connected Caterina Sforza. It is hardly surprising, therefore, that the more successful *signori* of the Papal States can be shown to have responded to the needs and expectations of a wide cross-section of their subjects. Federigo da Montefeltro was a much-sought-after *condottiere* who knew how to conserve his manpower. He was accessible to his subjects, and brought them a period of relative peace and ordered government. The court and palaces he created brought prestige and employment to his dominion; his observance of religion was generous and conspicuous and measured up to the pious expectations of his subjects. Recognised by his overlord the papacy, and accepted by his subjects, Federigo was not regarded as a tyrant.

The fact that most *signori* could not avoid that charge is not simply a comment on the exacting contemporary criteria of good government but is also a reflection of the difficulties of acquiring and maintaining power. Employment as a *condottiere* was not a guarantee of success and warfare was not always waged profitably in foreign parts. The creation of a clientele of trusted and able supporters was essential, but this very act could foment jealousy and unrest. As mentioned, in the course of 1385 the Este faced a number of challenges to their lordship, in part fuelled by the reliance they had placed on a foreign advisor, Tommaso da Tortona, while in 1482 the wealthy and well-placed Trotti family of Ferrara became scapegoats as the city suffered from Venetian attack. From such cases, it is clear why Castiglione in his *Courtier* was at pains to stress that his courtier's anxiety to win his lord's favour should not appear too obvious or deliberate.

Furthermore, the ruling dynasty itself, the core of a family's power and influence, could prove a source of weakness if it provoked rivalry and jealousy. As Galeotto Manfredi, Lord of Faenza, admitted to Lorenzo de' Medici in 1488, no *signore* could avoid the hatred of at least some of his subjects. In Bologna, the ascendancy of Giovanni II drove his erstwhile allies, the Malvezzi, into opposition and then exile, where they encouraged Julius II in his resolve to restore Bologna to direct rule.[33] Moreover, the opportunities for creating a sense of loyalty or acceptance as the 'natural' ruler of a city could not be achieved overnight, and it was rare that a foreign lord created any degree of loyalty beyond the level of acquiescence. Support for the Malatesta was stronger in Rimini, the ancient centre of their hegemony, than in any of the other subject communes. The lordships amassed by the *condottieri* Biordo Michelotti in Umbria (1393-98) or Francesco Sforza in the March from 1433 could not be called states. The subject communes were called upon for tribute in men, money, provisions and billets. Beyond that there was little expectation on the part of ruler or ruled that more profound changes would be made, or a new focus for loyalty created.

The difficulty of gathering and maintaining a wide and consistent body of support did make these signorial families susceptible to the attention of external powers, and of these none was more crucial than the sovereign authority of the papacy. As has already been discussed in the contexts of Rome and its district, historians have tended to see papal monarchy in terms of a progression towards a strong and centralised state; from a period of divisions, weakness and concessions during the Schism to one of steadily increasing direct rule of a more authoritarian kind. The papacy valued the Papal States, and their economic and political importance increased as the international standing of the papacy declined. Within these broader terms the popes were anxious to achieve financial and political security, with loyal subjects and the opportunity to reward and advance supporters and kinsmen. However, in pursuit of these aims the papacy did not follow consistent policies. This was partly due to force of circumstance and papal relations with other Italian and European states. It was also a consequence of the fact that the papacy was not a hereditary monarchy, and the abilities and interests of successive popes could vary.

It would therefore be a mistake to see the papacy moving steadily towards the defined goal of a more centralised and authoritarian state; none of the Renaissance popes launched an all-out attack on signorial power. Pius II attacked the Malatesta but not the Montefeltro; Alexander VI drove out the lords of the Romagna and the March of Ancona but married his daughter Lucrezia to Alfonso d'Este in 1503. The papacy could award titles to loyal families, and papal relatives were married into such families. In 1424 Martin V married his kinswoman Caterina Colonna to Guidantonio da Montefeltro and in 1474 Federigo da Montefeltro was not only made duke, but his daughter was married to Giovanni della Rovere, nephew of Sixtus IV. Throughout, nepotism was seen as a way of extending and defending papal authority; Boniface IX made his nephew Andrea Tomacelli duke of Spoleto and rector of the March of Ancona, and Alexander VI made his son Cesare duke of the Romagna. However, as the papacy was not a hereditary monarchy, such a policy created new generations of local dynasties potentially hostile to papal claims, with the beneficiaries and appointments of one pontificate becoming threats to its successors. The stronger and more centralised government Cesare Borgia introduced to the Romagna threatened to challenge papal overlordship. Francesco Maria della Rovere, nephew of Julius II and Duke of Urbino, was deprived of the fief in 1516 by the Medici pope Leo X in favour of his own nephew Lorenzo, but Francesco Maria was able to re-establish himself on the pope's death in 1521.

Moreover, it is important to realise that papal successes and intervention were not always consequences of papal initiatives. The papacy could find itself the beneficiary of events beyond its control; the death of Giangaleazzo Visconti (1402) and of Fortebraccio (1424) brought many of the communes of Umbria back under direct papal lordship. As overlord, the papacy could find itself drawn into local disputes. For example, growing papal intervention from the later fifteenth century in the compilation of lists of citizens suitable for public office in Perugia was not simply a pure exercise in papal overlordship but was invited by the local resentment caused by too narrow, inequitable or partisan a distribution of office. This serves to underline the fact that the extent of papal authority was conditioned, at least in part, by its interaction with the local community. When local or papal families were toppled from power and their dominions were returned to a more direct dependence on the papacy, the new regime was not necessarily characterised by a greater centralisation or authoritarianism and the displacement of local oligarchies and institutions.

In fact, the extent of local autonomy could be respected or even increased from the position attained under the more immediate and watchful eye of a local *signore*. On the death of Pius II in 1464, the commune of Senigallia rebelled against his nephew, Antonio Piccolomini, and sought a return to the direct rule of the Church; the communes of Ravenna and Cervia soon repented submitting to the more exacting protection of Venice on the collapse of papal authority that followed the Sack of Rome in 1527. The papacy's relations with its subject communes could be conditioned by their distance from Rome, their economic importance and the intervention of foreign powers; Innocent

VIII was alarmed when the strategically and economically important port of Ancona contemplated submitting to the protection of Matthias Corvinus, King of Hungary, in 1488.

Papal relations with subject communes could also be shaped by such variables as the character of papal officials; the popularity and ability of the papal legates and vice-legates governing Perugia varied. Of course, the impact of more direct papal rule could be obvious and heavy; in 1532 a new castle was built in Ancona and the archives of the previous republican regimes were destroyed. But in the majority of cases it seems more likely that the local patriciate welcomed the introduction of more direct papal lordship in anticipation of a less immediate and interfering government, one more susceptible to appeals and petitions and hence more exposed to long-drawn-out arguments from accumulated privileges. For example, when Cesena returned from the rule of the Malatesta to direct papal lordship in 1466, there was no dramatic change in the institutions and personnel of government. There was resentment at such aspects of papal government as demands for taxation and the quartering of troops, but these were standard grievances and probably did not cancel out the greater autonomy enjoyed in such areas as the distribution of offices and even in financial administration since the ending of signorial rule.

A further suggestive example supporting this hypothesis is presented by the commune of Ascoli Piceno in the March. In 1482 the papacy granted it certain privileges strengthening its autonomy, the news reaching the commune on 25 March, the feast of the Annunciation.[35] In commemoration the commune commissioned Carlo Crivelli to paint an altarpiece of the Annunciation; the work, dated 1486, depicts the commune's patron saint, Emidius, holding a representation of the town and kneeling alongside the Archangel Gabriel, while the altarpiece bears the inscription 'Liberty under the Church' and the arms of pope and bishop. Even if fiscal pressures in the course of the sixteenth century gradually reduced the autonomy of the more accessible and richer communes like Perugia, the process was gradual and local oligarchies long retained an influential role in the government of their cities.

CONCLUSION

Between 1461 and 1465 Cardinal Lodovico Trevisano commissioned from the Mantuan medallist Cristoforo di Geremia a portrait medal which celebrated on its reverse his triumphant achievements towards the restoration of the Church.[36] In many ways this expresses both the aims and the accomplishments — as well as the style — of the Renaissance papacy. Both during and after the Schism the relative importance of the Lands of St Peter increased, and the popes of the period all sought to defend their authority there and realise its potential. In this they appear to have been assisted by the fact that the theoretical basis of their temporal authority remained largely unchallenged by their political enemies. This is remarkable. Both the authenticity and the validity of the Donation of Constantine, from which papal claims in large measure derived, had been increasingly questioned, most famously by Lorenzo Valla in 1440.[37] Machiavelli made no mention of the Donation in the eleventh chapter of *The Prince*, on ecclesiastical principalities; rather cursorily, he attributed the strength of papal temporal power to its divine sanction.

He was more forthcoming, however, when describing the difficulties faced by the papacy in the practical exercise of its authority, and it would be a mistake to see successive popes working steadily and progressively towards the perceived goal of a more unified and centralised state. It would also be a mistake to attempt to characterise the Renaissance papacy with excessive simplifications and generalisations, making the various pontificates conform to a standard type. This would be to ignore the scale of the geographical difficulties facing them, as well as the changing internal and external political circumstances. It would also be to overlook the personal and dynastic priorities of the individual popes. It is true that by the end of the period papal authority was more firmly established and faced fewer formidable internal enemies, but progress in that direction had neither been even nor unchecked, and further from Rome the achievements appeared less solid. Moreover, the extent of papal initiative should not be exaggerated. The expectations of the popes' subjects and dependants, flocking to Rome and the Curia, advanced the workings of papal authority.

Lastly, the achievement of direct papal lordship did not mean the introduction of absolutism, or increased centralisation at the expense of local autonomies; partly for this reason it remains appropriate to refer to the 'lands' or 'states' of the Church in the plural. Possibly only in the commune of Rome were the more authoritarian implications of papal rule increasingly experienced and perceived by end of the period. More generally, no new administrative machinery was introduced to unify or centralise government, and the smothering of the Roman commune and the metamorphosis of the city from dilapidated market town to papal capital should not be taken as typical for the Papal States as a whole. Certainly by the end of the period the papacy, as Italian prince, was worth more than the farthing the corner-boys of Florence left ringing in the ears of Martin V in 1419, but as that Colonna pope's own descendants were to remind Clement VII when they sacked the Vatican in 1526, the achievements of the Renaissance papacy were not secure. Nor had the papacy succeeded in protecting the Lands of St Peter from the depredations of foreign enemies, as the Sack of Rome cruelly demonstrated in the following year.

NOTES AND REFERENCES

1. The most useful general studies are: J. Guiraud, *L'Etat Pontifical après le Grand Schisme* (Paris, 1896); F. Gregorovius, *History of the City of Rome in the Middle Ages*, trans. A. Hamilton, vol. vi, pt ii–vol. viii, pt ii (London, 1898–1902);

L. Pastor, *History of the Popes*, ed. F. Antrobus and B. Kerr, vols i–x (London, 1891–1938); P. Paschini, *Roma nel Rinascimento* (Bologna, 1940); P. Partner, *The Papal State under Martin V* (London, 1958), and *The Lands of St Peter* (London, 1972); M. Caravale and A. Caracciolo, *Stato Pontificio nell'Età Moderna*, in *Storia d'Italia* (U.T.E.T.), (Turin, 1978); P. Prodi, *Il Sovrano Pontefice* (Bologna, 1982), now available in English.

2. C. Gennaro, 'La "Pax Romana" del 1511', *A.S.R.S.P.*, ser. iii, vol. xc (1968). The best introductory evocation of the city is P. Partner, *Renaissance Rome* (Berkeley–Los Angeles–London, 1979). We are particularly grateful to Guy Boanas for advice on the bibliography of Renaissance Rome.

3. C. Gennaro, 'Mercanti e bovattieri nella Roma della seconda metà del trecento', *Boll. dell'Ist. Stor. It. per il Medio Evo*, vol. lxxviii (1967); A. Esch, 'Dal medioevo al rinascimento: uomini a Roma dal 1350 al 1450', *A.S.R.S.P.*, ser. iii, vol. xxv (1970–71); L. Palermo, *Il Porto di Roma* (Rome, 1979); J.-C. Maire-Vigueur, 'Les "carati" des églises romaines à la fin du moyen âge', *Mélanges de L'Ecole Française de Rome–Moyen Age*, vol. lxxxvi (1974); 'Classe dominante et classe dirigeante à Rome à la fin du moyen âge', *Storia della Città*, vol. i (1976); *Les Pâturages de l'Eglise et la Douane des Bétails dans la Province du Patrimonio* (Rome, 1981).

4. G. Ricci, 'La "nobilis universitas bobacteriorum urbis"', *A.S.R.S.P.*, vol. xvi (1893).

5. R. Trexler, 'Rome on the eve of the Great Schism', *Speculum*, vol. xlii (1967); A. Esch, 'La fine del libero comune di Roma nel giudizio dei mercanti fiorentini', *Boll. dell'Ist. Stor. It. per il Medio Evo*, vol. lxxxvi (1976–77).

6. C. d'Onofrio, *Castel San Angelo e Borgo* (Rome, 1971).

7. A. Natale, 'La Felice Società dei Balestieri e dei Pavesati', *A.S.R.S.P.*, vol. xlii (1939).

8. A recent contribution to a long bibliography is M. Miglio, '"Viva la libertà et populo di Roma"; oratoria e politica a Roma: Stefano Porcari', *A.S.R.S.P.*, ser. iii, vol. xxviii (1974).

9. R. J. Palermino, 'The Roman Academy', *Archivum Historiae Pontificae*, vol. xviii (1980).

10. M. Miglio, 'Il leone e la lupa', *Studi Romani*, vol. xxx (1982); more generally, T. Magnusson, *Studies in Roman Quattrocento Architecture* (Rome–Stockholm, 1958); L. Spezzaferro, 'La politica urbanistica dei papi e le origini di via Giulia', in *Via Giulia* (Rome, 1973); C. W. Westfall, *In this Most Perfect Paradise* (University Park–London, 1974).

11. D. Gnoli, '"Descriptio Urbis" e censimento della popolazione di Roma avanti il sacco borbonico', *A.S.R.S.P.*, vol. xvii (1894).

12. Gennaro, '"Pax Romana"', p. 30.

13. C. Calisse, 'I prefetti di Vico', *A.S.R.S.P.*, vol. x (1888); G. Falco, 'I comuni della Campagna e della Marittima', *A.S.R.S.P.*, vol. xlix (1926).

14. P. Pavan, 'Onorato III Caetani: un tentativo fallito di espansione territoriale', *Studi sul Medioevo Cristiano offerti a R. Morghen*, vol. ii (Rome, 1975).

15. M. Mallett, *The Borgias* (London, 1969); C. Shaw, 'Alexander VI, Cesare Borgia and the Orsini', *European Studies Review*, vol. xi (1981).

16. V. Sora, 'I conti di Anguillara', *A.S.R.S.P.*, vol. xxix (1906).

17. Guiraud, op. cit., p. 52.

18. W. A. Simpson, 'Cardinal Giordano Orsini as a prince of the church and as a patron of the arts', *J.W.C.I.*, vol. xxix (1966); A. Cavallaro *et al.*, *Bracciano e gli Orsini nel '400, Il '400 a Roma e nel Lazio* (Rome, 1981).

19. C. W. Westfall, 'Alberti and the Vatican palace type', *Journal of the Soc. of Architectural Historians*, vol. xxxiii (1974). We would like to thank Dr David Whitehouse for information on this point.

20. On the Este, L. Chiappini, *Gli Estensi* (Varese, 1967); W. L. Gundersheimer, *The Style of a Renaissance Despotism* (Princeton, 1973).

21. On the Romagna, J. Larner, 'Order and disorder in the Romagna', in *Violence and Civil Disorder in Italian Cities*, ed. L. Martines (Berkeley–Los Angeles–London, 1972).

22. On the Montefeltro, J. Dennistoun, *Memoirs of the Dukes of Urbino*, ed. E. Hutton (London, 1909); G. Franceschini, *I Montefeltro* (Varese, 1970); most recently, C. H. Clough, 'Federigo da Montefeltro: the good Christian prince', *Bull. of the John Rylands Library*, vol. lxvi (1984).

23. C. M. Ady, *The Bentivoglio of Bologna* (Oxford, 1937); C. F. Black, 'The Baglioni as tyrants of Perugia', *E.H.R.*, vol. lxxxv (1970) and 'Commune and papacy in the government of Perugia', *Annali della Fondazione Italiana per la Storia Amministrativa*, vol. iv (1967).

24. G. Franceschini, *I Malatesta* (Varese, 1973); P. J. Jones, *The Malatesta of Rimini* (Cambridge, 1974), and P. J. Jones et al., *Studi Malatestiani* (Roma, Istituto Storico del Medio Evo, 1978).

25. J. E. Law, *The Lords of Renaissance Italy* (London, 1981).

26. T. Valenti, 'Francesco Sforza e il comune di Monte dell'Olmo', *Atti e Mem. della Dep. di Storia Patria delle Marche*, ser. iv, vol. ii (1925).

27. G. Luzzatto, 'Comune e principato in Urbino', *Le Marche*, vol. v (1905); W. Tommasoli, 'Note politico-economiche su Urbino nei primi anni della signoria di Federico di Montefeltro', *Studi Urbinati*, vol. xlix (1975).

28. G. Franceschini, 'Biordo Michelotti e la dedizione di Perugia al duca di Milano', *Boll. della Dep. di Stor. Pat. per l'Umbria*, vol. xlv (1948).

29. I. Robertson, 'The signoria of Girolamo Riario in Imola', *Historical Studies*, vol. xv (1971).

30. Idem, 'The return of Cesena to the direct dominion of the Church', *Studi Romagnoli*, vol. xvi (1965).

31. G. Tagliati, 'Relazioni tra la famiglia Romei e la corte estense', in *Il Rinascimento nelle Corti Padane* (Bari, 1977).

32. C. H. Clough, 'The chronicle of Girolamo Vanni of Urbino', in *The Duchy of Urbino in the Renaissance* (London, 1981).

33. R. Patrizi Sacchetti, 'La caduta dei Bentivoglio', *Atti e Mem. della Dep. di Stor. Pat. per le Provincie di Romagna*, n.s., vol. ii (1950–51).

34. L. Mancini, 'Sinigaglia dai Malatesti ai Rovereschi', *Atti e Mem. della Dep. di Stor. Pat. per le Marche*, ser. iv, vol. iii (1926); J. Hook, 'The destruction of the new "Italia": Venice and the papacy in collision', *Italian Studies*, vol. xxviii (1973).

35. R. Weiss, 'The medals of Julius II', *J.W.C.I.*, vol. xxviii (1965), p. 165; M. Davies, *Carlo Crivelli* (London, 1972), pp. 28–9.

36. G. Hill, *Medals of the Renaissance*, revised and enlarged by G. Pollard (London, 1978), p. 68.

37. We are grateful to Dr J. Canning for making us aware of the extent to which Roman lawyers had anticipated Valla's conclusion.

CHAPTER ELEVEN

The northern states

INTRODUCTION

The Papal States were bordered on the north by the kingdom of Italy, part of the Holy Roman Empire, whose southern frontier followed the modern provinces of the Veneto, Emilia and Tuscany. As a factor in Italian history, the empire has been viewed even more negatively and critically than it has for the history of Germany, and it is true that within the borders of the kingdom the emperor's writ ran relatively rarely, even in theory. The most conspicuous island of independence was Venice, which refused to acknowledge imperial overlordship – at least for the city itself and its *dogado* – or jurisdiction, surviving even the challenge posed in 1509 during the War of Cambrai, when Maximilian announced his intention of reducing the republic to the status of an imperial free city. Another anomaly was presented by the temporal authority claimed by the patriarch of Aquileia in north-eastern Italy, in Friuli and Istria. Although his Istrian territories had been gradually eroded by Venice and although the republic overwhelmed Friuli between 1407 and 1420, the patriarch's claims were not surrendered without tortuous negotiations. In 1445 the patriarch acknowledged Venetian lordship in exchange for the recognition of his spiritual authority, the grant of 5,000 ducats a year and limited temporal jurisdiction over three minor communities.[1]

From her claims to independence Venice could just be categorised as one of the external powers threatening the integrity of the kingdom, acquiring a mainland empire which embraced not only Istria and Friuli but also the whole of the Veneto and eastern Lombardy, a process of expansion marked by the acquisition, through a mixture of force and connivance, of such principal cities as Treviso (1388), Vicenza (1404), Verona and Padua (1405), Brescia (1426) and Bergamo (1428), all previously under signorial rule. Later in the century the kingdom and these Venetian territories were menaced from the east by the Ottoman Turks, whose threat became increasingly clear after 1471. Later again a further incursion into the kingdom was made by the papacy seeking to profit from the redistribution of territory provoked by the Italian Wars, and trying to secure the ex-Sforza cities of Parma (1512–15;

1521–45) and Piacenza (1512–15; 1521–47), and the Este cities of Reggio (1512–23) and Modena (1514–27).

Of the external powers, the French crown had the greatest aspirations during the Wars, Francis I, for example, trying to detach the marquisate of Saluzzo from its traditional allegiance to the empire.[2] But French ambitions in the north were of longer standing and further reaching, encouraged by the claim to the lordship of Milan following from the marriage in 1387 of Valentina, daughter of Giangaleazzo Visconti, to Louis d'Orléans, brother of Charles VI. The French crown also aspired to the lordship of Genoa and succeeded in introducing its rule to that turbulent city at various times: between 1396 and 1409, 1458 and 1461, 1499 and 1512, in 1515 and finally between 1527 and 1528. Towards the duchy of Savoy it was French influence rather than direct lordship that threatened the kingdom of Italy, and the early years of Louis XI's reign show clearly the potential extent of French ambitions in Savoy and elsewhere. In September 1461 Louis offered to make Francesco Sforza a peer of the realm of France if he renounced his duchy's allegiance to the empire; that offer was rejected, but when Sforza acquired the lordships of Genoa and Savona he agreed to accept them as fiefs of the French crown in December 1463. In 1462, one of the aims that Louis pursued in intervening in a dispute between Lodovico Duke of Savoy and his ambitious and alienated son Filippo *senza Terra*, or 'Lackland', was to make the duchy a fief of the French crown rather than of the empire.

None of these threats permanently altered the frontiers of the kingdom of Italy. The republic of Venice obtained imperial recognition for some of its mainland territories in 1437, and agreed to purchase formal recognition for them all from Charles V in 1523 for 200,000 ducats; even papal rule in Parma, Piacenza and Modena was legitimised by imperial investiture.[3] However, if imperial overlordship remained intact in theory, it did not mean that the emperors were able to exercise a real authority in northern Italy; more important than the challenges posed by foreign powers was the long-established autonomy, bordering on independence, enjoyed by the various states of the region, states which for the sake of convenience can be grouped in three categories: feudal principalities, signorial regimes and city republics. In terms of historical treatment, by far the greatest attention has been paid to the last. It can therefore be difficult to recognise the fact that the surviving city republics of northern Italy were exceptions to the rule, in the Peninsula as in Europe as a whole, and that in terms of area and population the feudal principalities and signorial regimes were of greater importance.

SAVOY–PIEDMONT; MONFERRAT

In north-western Italy the three principal feudal states were the counties of Savoy and Piedmont, and the marquisate of Monferrat.[4] In 1418 Amedeo VIII of Savoy inherited Piedmont on the extinction of the cadet branch of

Savoy–Acaia, and the principal Savoyard line was successful in the late fourteenth and early fifteenth centuries in extending and legitimising its authority. For example, towards the west Amedeo VII took advantage of a succession dispute in the county of Provence to acquire the lordship of Nice. In the east the house of Savoy threatened the duchy of Milan, encouraged by the period of rebellion and civil war that followed the death of Giangaleazzo Visconti in 1402 and by Filippo Maria's long wars with Venice and Florence; playing Venice off Milan, Amedeo VIII was ceded the city of Vercelli by Filippo Maria in 1427. From 1413 the marquis of the small neighbouring principality of Saluzzo acknowledged the counts of Savoy as his immediate overlords. In 1416 Sigismund King of the Romans invested Amedeo VIII with the ducal title, if the enhanced dignity applied strictly to only Savoy and not to such territories as Piedmont and Nice. Amedeo also made territorial and jurisdictional gains at the expense of the branch of the Palaeologus dynasty ruling the marquisate of Monferrat. Between 1431 and 1434 Gian Giacomo Palaeologus, with his marquisate threatened by Visconti and Savoyard invasion, surrendered a number of towns, including Chivasso, to the duke of Savoy, and acknowledged his feudal superiority over others.

However, while Amedeo VIII was undoubtedly a ruler of great ability, he was also fortunate in that both his principal neighbours, Visconti Milan and Valois France, were too distracted by other challenges to restrain the ambitions of the house of Savoy. The prevailing judgement of historians, shaped as it is so often by the ideal of the 'strong, centralised state', tends to stress the weakness of these north-western feudal principalities in respect of both foreign powers and their own subjects. It is undeniable that in the period the authority of these dynasties was generally narrowly circumscribed and often closely contested, and the reason for this stems in part from their geopolitical situation.

Most obviously the territories of the house of Savoy were divided by the Alps and the personal authority of the ruling house has been rightly described by Daviso di Charvensod as 'seasonal' – unable to transcend that formidable natural barrier when the passes were closed – although the mountainous nature of much of the terrain impeded the exercise of authority throughout the year.[5] The house of Savoy tried to cope with these facts of life. The court remained peripatetic and although there were favoured residences, at Chambéry and Thonon north of the Alps and to a lesser extent Pinerolo to the south, no fixed ducal capital emerged. Towards Piedmont from 1424 the dukes tried to give a more personal expression to their authority by awarding their eldest son the title of prince of Piedmont, and greater administrative supervision by establishing a council with wide financial and judicial powers which settled at Turin from 1436. More ambitiously, in 1430 Amedeo VIII issued five books of statutes, the *Statuta Sabaudiae*, intended to apply to all his subjects, introducing Roman Law practices in place of localised customs and codifying the rights of the prince and the roles of his officials.

But the dictates of geography and climate protected and encouraged the autonomy enjoyed by the dukes' noble vassals, the communes of their dominions and those regions with a well-developed sense of identity, like the Val d'Aosta, which had amassed its own privileges and statutes; indeed, the Savoyard statutes of 1430 recognised the autonomy of the Val d'Aosta and other regions. More generally the dukes made very slow progress in the face of deeply entrenched noble franchises and the jealously guarded privileges of cities like Turin and Nice. Nor did they still the resentment felt by Piedmontese lawyers and noblemen towards their better-placed and more frequently favoured opposite numbers in Savoy. Moreover, the Savoyard dominions, though extensive, commercially well placed and rich in agricultural produce and raw materials, were not as remunerative for their rulers as those of their Valois and Visconti–Sforza neighbours. When carefully managed and kept in peace, as under Amedeo VIII, their return could allow the dukes to make occasional loans to the French crown, but more generally the duke's finances were in the red and his revenues did not match the fiscal potential of his more powerful neighbours.

These problems also confronted the marquises of Monferrat.[6] They too were jealous of their authority, and in 1473 Guglielmo II Palaeologus introduced measures intended to widen the jurisdiction of his courts by encouraging appeals and weakening noble franchises. In implementing such policies the barrier was less one of geography, but the small extent of their state and its relatively underdeveloped economy often made the marquises dependent on the protection of more powerful foreign powers, and obliged to take service with them as *condottieri*. This introduces the fact that both Monferrat and Savoy–Piedmont were in frontier zones; both were exposed to external influence as well as to the threat of invasion. As mentioned, sandwiched between Savoy and Milan, Gian Giacomo Palaeologus was forced to make territorial and jurisdictional concessions to Amedeo VIII in 1434, but the house of Savoy itself rarely held such a whip hand. In 1471 during the epileptic illness of Amedeo IX, and then after his death on 30 March 1472, his wife Iolanda depended on the support of Galeazzo Maria Sforza to establish her regency in the face of the rival claims of Amedeo's younger brother Filippo *senza Terra*, backed by Louis XI.[7] Later in her regency, Iolanda's unsuccessful efforts to steer Savoy through the rivalries of its neighbours provoked an invasion by the Swiss Confederation, her own seizure by Charles the Bold of Burgundy in 1476 and Louis's ascendancy over her young son, Filiberto I.

The difficulties presented by the geopolitical and economic nature of these states could be compounded, as the minority of Filiberto I shows, by moments of weakness in the ruling house. Dynastic succession was not always smooth, and the house of Savoy, particularly in the latter half of the fifteenth century, experienced a series of short reigns and a large number of minorities which necessitated councils of regency and opened the way to foreign intervention and internal disputes, as well as preventing continuity in government. Not only did Filiberto I succeed to the duchy at the tender age of seven, but he died in 1482, and was followed by his brother Carlo I, who was himself only fourteen. When he died in 1490, his son Carlo Giovanni was only a year old and died in 1496. On that occasion the succession passed to his father's uncle, Filippo *senza Terra*, whose career had been largely dominated by the desire to manage the affairs of the duchy in default of strong leadership from the holders of the title. It was therefore ironic that Filippo died the following year and that his son, Filberto II, was seventeen when he attained the title and survived only until 1504. It was with Filippo's third son, Carlo II (1503–53), that the house of Savoy regained some dynastic stability.

At least it survived, while the Palaeologi of Monferrat died out in the male line in 1533; the marquisate passed in default of heirs to the emperor Charles V, who assigned it to Federico II Gonzaga, husband of Margherita Palaeologus, in 1536. But if it survived, the Savoyard dynasty, in common with all ruling houses, experienced differences of character and ability, not always attributable to extreme youth and inexperience. This can be seen clearly in the contrast between Amedeo VIII and his son Lodovico. In 1434 Amedeo VIII, who had expanded the dynasty's dominions and strengthened its authority, retired to a monastery he had founded at Roncaglia, leaving his son as his lieutenant. Lodovico had not been prepared for government; his elder brother Amedeo Prince of Piedmont had died only in 1431. Moreover, Lodovico was unable to free himself of the influence of dominating personalities. His father continued to be involved in the government of the duchy, his authority increased – at least within its frontiers – when as Felix V he was made pope by the Council of Basel (1439–49). Secondly, in 1432 Lodovico married Anna, daughter of John II Lusignan, King of Cyprus; not only was she another powerful personality, but she brought with her a small but unpopular number of Cypriot courtiers. Aeneas Sylvius Piccolomini described Anna as 'a woman incapable of obedience' and her husband as 'a man incapable of command'; the duke's rule was punctuated by struggles for influence involving leading nobles as well as members of his own family, both encouraging the intervention of foreign powers.

A focus of imbroglio was the chancellorship, an office held from 1444 by Giacomo di Valperga, an ally of the dauphin of France, and disputed by Antonio di Romagnano, much of whose support came from the Sforza. In 1456, when the dauphin broke with Charles VII, Giacomo's position as chancellor became untenable and he fled the duchy while his lands were seized and his rival was granted the chancellorship. However, the death of Charles VII in 1461 brought Giacomo back into favour and office and forced Antonio into exile. There followed a brief period in which Lodovico ruled under the influence of Valperga and Louis XI, but this was broken when Lodovico's son, Filippo *senza Terra*, murdered the chancellor and ousted his followers. The duke appealed to Louis for assistance and the French king contrived the detention of Filippo in 1464, although this further coup did not prevent the return of Antonio di Romagnano as chancellor with the backing of Galeazzo Maria Sforza in 1466.

A perhaps less bewildering way of charting the difficulties of the house of Savoy, while gaining insight into the nature of its authority and dominions, is offered by the history of parliamentary assemblies which achieved prominence after the death of Amedeo VIII.[8] In some respects they illustrate the fragmented nature of the Savoyard state. Exempt as they were from taxation, the clergy and the higher nobility tended to stand aside from such assemblies, relying on bilaterial negotiations with their rulers. While there were estates general representing most of the duke's dominions, the estates of Savoy and Piedmont seem to have met more frequently as separate assemblies which could express quite distinct views on such matters as foreign policy. As was also the case with the estates of Monferrat, delegates could claim reluctance to travel and disclaim full powers of attorney when money matters were on the agenda.

On the other hand, representatives were ready to recognise the existence and integrity of the duke's dominions and were prepared to contribute to their government and preservation. As contemporaries noted, this emerged most clearly in the second half of the fifteenth century when the estates general attempted to fill the void created by the succession of minorities and regencies and to associate itself more positively with the government of the duchy. In 1456 the estates general refused to accept in its entirety a treaty between Lodovico and Charles VII; their objections resulted in a reduction in the financial and military assistance offered to the French king. In 1462 both Lodovico and Filippo *senza Terra* argued their cases before the estates general, which then attempted a reconciliation. In 1466, following the accession of Amedeo IX, the duke and his council took an oath before the estates to observe the liberties of the duchy. In 1468 the estates of Piedmont were allowed to nominate a committee to meet with the duke and his councillors, to conserve the duchy, protect the duke's patrimony and root out abuses, a right that was claimed again in 1476. In 1490 the estates general failed to persuade the regent, Bianca di Monferrat, to allow them to nominate three representatives from Savoy and three from Piedmont to meet with the council of regency, but in the years following more frequent meetings of the estates were convened.

In fact those years would seem to mark the high point in the history of the duchy's parliaments; like the estates of Monferrat those of Piedmont and Savoy never secured legislative powers, but they did establish the right to petition and advise. Some representatives chalked up what amounted to parliamentary careers; Lodovico Tagliandi represented Ivrea from 1473 to 1512 and advised Galeazzo Maria Sforza's ambassador on the place of the estates in the government of the duchy. As mentioned, foreign powers were aware of this role and would send ambassadors to attend meetings and win over delegates; in 1490 Lodovico Maria Sforza urged Bianca di Monferrat to handle the estates with care. This advice came from a ruler who was doubtless aghast at the prospect of having to consult representatives in a parliamentary forum, and it is clear that the estates could thwart ducal policy: in 1517 they rejected a request from Carlo II to finance a standing army of 10,000 infantry. On other occasions an element of bargaining entered the relationship between the duke and the estates; in 1487 Carlo I secured some of the *donativo*, or subsidy, he required but in return had to make concessions which limited the burdens he could place on his subjects in future. Lastly, as is indicated by the reconciliation ceremony of 1462 and the constitutional demands of 1490, the estates could envisage for themselves a positive role in preserving the authority and dominions of the house of Savoy.

This may suggest one of the principal reasons for the survival of the duchy of Savoy, a survival which can appear less remarkable when the anachronistic criteria of the 'strong, centralised state' are discarded. The dukes ruled over a feudal principality where the elements of consultation and consent were preserved – as Tagliandi informed the Sforza ambassador in 1476. Rather as in Sicily or the *Regno*, the court was seen as a source of patronage and legitimacy and as a means to advancement. The house of Savoy provided a focus and a sense of common interest for its greater subjects, the higher lay and ecclesiastical nobility and the lesser nobility and merchants who dominated the government of the towns. This sense of common interest was not strong or disinterested enough to eclipse franchise and privilege; indeed, it was a product of precisely such forms of liberty. Nor did it create a sense of cohesion binding enough to prevent rebellion and the intervention of other states; in 1476 Tagliandi also admitted that foreign powers found it easy to bribe members of the estates. But together with the prestige deriving from the ancient origins, royal connections and enhanced ducal status of the ruling house, it contributed to the maintenance of this conglomeration of lordships and immunities straddling the Alps.

ECCLESIASTICAL PRINCIPALITIES: TRENT AND AQUILEIA

The decentralisation of authority was also marked in north-eastern Italy in the prince-bishopric of Trent and the patriarchate of Aquileia. As in the north-west, geopolitical circumstances contributed to the political fragmentation. Both these states lay on international frontiers and straddled important trade routes between Italy and central Europe. Certainly in the case of the former, the configuration of the landscape on the northern shores of Lake Garda and in the valleys of the Adige and its tributaries militated against the effective exercise of central authority. In neither could hereditary succession make even a slight contribution in terms of continuity to the authority of the ruler.

In the prince-bishopric of Trent, real authority had largely devolved to – or had been usurped by – the bishop's lay vassals, families like the Castelbarco in the Vallagarina or the lords of Arco near the north shore of Lake Garda.[9] Trent was not a capital in any real sense, although as the largest town in the region it did have some influence over the smaller communities, at least when they came to revise their statutes. The fact that the bishop's authority was not eclipsed altogether was due to the sheer fragmentation of power. Rivalries between and within families were exacerbated by external intervention, for example by the Visconti of Milan or the della Scala of Verona, securing adherents among the Trentino nobility with offers of protection, *condotte* and pensions. Reminiscent of the Anglo–Scottish border, castles clùng to the rocky landscape, the products of a restless and feuding frontier society. Even within his lands and jurisdiction a lord's authority over his vassals might be far from authoritarian. The statutes of the small rural commune of Bondone, drawn up in 1401, reveal a considerable degree of autonomy for its immediate lord, Pietro di Lodrone, while in 1420 the commune can be found taking the initiative to the extent of asking the bishop to invest his sons with the family's fiefs.[10] Where signorial power was weakened, as in Venetian-held territory in the Vallagarina in the fifteenth century, the smaller communes showed themselves eager to defend and extend their degree of autonomy.

It is therefore not surprising that the lay power which eventually achieved a permanent ascendancy over the prince-bishopric could draw on considerable outside resources. On 23 January 1363 the county of the Tyrol passed to the Habsburgs, and with it the hereditary advocacy, or protectorate, over the prince-bishopric. One consequence was that all subsequent bishops came from north of the Alps, and most were closely identified with the Habsburgs. Further consequences can be gauged from the agreement between Rudolph of Habsburg and the prince-bishop on 18 September 1363 by which the latter not only pledged himself and his successors to the Habsburgs but committed his vassals to the support of the Austrian dynasty, and agreed to place reliable representatives in the castles and towns of the principality.

However, the absorption of the area into the Habsburg sphere of influence was neither immediate nor uncontested. The prince-bishop George of Liechtenstein (1390–1419) did try to renounce the agreement of 1363 and reassert his secular authority and freedom of action, but his policy of enfeoffing retainers from north of the Alps provoked rebellion in 1407 among some of the privileged valley communities and more centrally in the city of Trent, where Rodolfo de' Belenzani, a landowner and merchant, led a revolt to secure greater autonomy for the commune, and possibly his recognition as *signore*.[11] These disturbances gave the Habsburgs the opportunity to intervene, strengthening their authority by on the one hand suppressing the revolt, while on the other making concessions to the autonomous aspirations of some communities. Rural communities were invited to send representatives to the count's diet at Merano in 1423. Other challenges were external. In 1408 and 1409 Rodolfo de' Belenzani had considered enlisting the support and even the lordship of Venice, and the republic did pose a threat to Habsburg hegemony in the south of the principality. Following the acquisition of Verona in 1405, the republic inherited the lands of one of its adherents, a branch of the Castelbarco family, in 1411 and then pushed its frontier further north up the commercially important valley of the Adige to acquire Rovereto in 1416. In 1440 she seized the commune of Riva on the northern shore of Lake Garda. But these Venetian footholds in the Trentino were only temporary, and all these acquisitions were lost to the Habsburgs in the War of Cambrai.

The bishop of Trent was a suffragan of the patriarch of Aquileia who also exercised temporal jurisdiction near a frontier zone of great commercial importance, towards which outside powers had designs ranging from the exercise of influence to the conquest of territory. However, in the case of the lands granted to the patriarchs in the twelfth century the stakes were greater in that the area was economically more productive, cause and effect of a large-scale Tuscan and Florentine immigration since the late thirteenth century. As has already been mentioned, by the start of the period most of the coastal regions of Istria had fallen under Venetian rule although some communes, like Muggia, enjoyed the higher degree of autonomy afforded by the disjointed authority of the patriarchs, before surrendering to the republic in 1420.[12] Trieste represented a more tempting prize but one that was made more elusive by the city's own resources and by its citizens' determination to preserve a considerable degree of self-government. Revolts punctuated Venetian lordship between 1369 and 1380, when the city took advantage of the republic's virtual isolation and defeat in the War of Chioggia to surrender to the patriarch, Marquardo of Randek, on 26 June. The terms of surrender allowed him to appoint a representative, or captain, and enjoy some of its revenues, but the commune intended to retain its institutions, peg indirect taxation, control most of its revenues and send representatives to meetings of the patriarch's parliament when such matters as the raising of extraordinary taxation were considered. However, the death of Marquardo on 3 June 1381, disputes over the succession, the absence of real support from other subject communes and internal divisions within Trieste led the city to surrender to Leopold of Habsburg on 30 September.[13]

This did not end aspirations to a greater autonomy. The commune continued to be governed by its own statutes and to resist interference from the Habsburgs and their allies in the immediate vicinity, the Walsee lords of Duino; in 1461 Frederick III conceded to Trieste complete management of its revenues and control of the captaincy in return for 1,200 florins a year. However, Venetian designs on the city – always a potential commercial rival – and the activity within Trieste of a pro-Venetian faction brought an end to the city's virtual independence when the lords of Duino entered it in 1468 as champions of the Habsburgs and their local adherents. The communal constitution was abolished and restored only partially in the 1490s. Venice held the city briefly from 1508 to 1509, but Habsburg rule was then reimposed.

Communal autonomy was also a prominent issue in the history of Friuli and no more strikingly than in the case of its two principal cities, Udine and Cividale, rivals in the pursuit of privilege and influence in the affairs of the patriarchate, as well as over the control of its trade routes.[14] But they were not the only contenders. As in Piedmont–Savoy and the Trentino, the political stage was also dominated by a number of feudal families of whom the Savorgnan clan was the most assertive, establishing an ascendancy in Udine despite the fact that that commune's fourteenth-century statutes had banned such families from citizenship and communal office. The Savorgnan had a hereditary seat on the council and the eldest son of the family assumed the office of captain during vacancies in the patriarchate; their influence derived not only from their castles and estates but also from their commercial interests and the farming of tax revenues. But their ascendancy had its opponents and could be badly shaken. The murder of Federico Savorgnan by his enemies on 15 February 1389 left his young son Tristano saddled with debts and a ward of the commune. However, on 7 April 1391, at the age of fifteen, he took his place on the council, and by October 1399 the newly elected deputies on the commune's executive council were unwilling to serve without his approval.

But the vassal communes and lords did not eclipse the temporal authority of the patriarchs to the extent suffered by the prince-bishops of Trent; the counts of Gorizia, though advocates of the patriarchate, were not only its vassals but were unable to draw on the external resources available to the Habsburgs in the Trentino. On the other hand, as in the northern states so far discussed, the authority of the ruler was limited by his obligations towards and his dependence on his subjects, the constitutional nature of his authority being rooted in the feudal relationship and perpetuated by the political re-alities presented to the patriarch by his subjects and neighbours. This can be seen in the way patriarchs, certainly from the late fourteenth century, took an oath on entering office to preserve their subjects in their 'ancient and praiseworthy customs'. As in the duchy of Savoy, a strong and highly articulate belief in a collective interest, preserving the ancient liberties of the *Patria* of Friuli, characterised relations between lord and vassal, impressed itself on foreign powers and emerged in institutional terms in meetings of parliament.

Assemblies of higher clergy, the nobility and townsmen were well estab-lished by the fourteenth century, and their role grew with disputes over the succession and the patriarchs' increasing need for financial and military support.[15] Though summoned on the initiative of the patriarchs, parliament had achieved the right not only to petition its overlord but to participate in a wide range of business, from diplomatic relations and defence to voting on subsidies and hearing appeals. It had been associated with the patriarchs in the codification of the constitution of Friuli between 1366 and 1386. Its meetings were frequent and between sessions it was represented by a council elected to act with the patriarch. It is therefore understandable why the sixteenth-century Friulian political theorist Girolamo da Porcia could say that in the fourteenth century the *Patria* resembled a republic rather than a prin-cipality; twentieth-century historians like Leicht and Koenigsberger have stressed the prominent share in government acquired by the parliament in the fourteenth century.

To survive, this level of constitutional participation needed continuity in the patriarchate itself and the absence of interference from external powers. In fact, in the late fourteenth and early fifteenth centuries the rivalries and self-interest of the communes and lordships of Friuli were heightened by a series of disputed appointments, fuelled by foreign involvement; ultimately they put an end to the independence of the *Patria* and compromised its jeal-ously guarded liberties. The internal struggle for influence tended to polarise around the rival communes of Cividale and Udine, the latter generally dominated by the Savorgnan. In the period Udine and the Savorgnan tended to look to Venice for support, and the republic's concern to keep open the trade routes, to prevent a hostile power from dominating the hinterland and to secure a patriarch tolerant of Venetian holdings in Istria ensured that Venice would welcome allies in the area.

The inevitability of the Venetian conquest of Friuli was stressed by nationalist historians in the nineteenth and twentieth centuries, but it is more probable that the option came to be accepted by the republic only gradually – although she was certainly concerned to secure allies and influence in the *Patria*. In 1385 the Savorgnan were made honorary and hereditary members of the Venetian nobility and the republic regarded them as adherents, advancing them pensions and employing them as *condottieri*. In 1408 Venice claimed to have spent 300,000 ducats to 'preserve the liberty and peaceful state of the *Patria* of Friuli', without which the area would have fallen under 'the yoke of tyrants'.

Such protestations did not impress Cividale, which was generally a prominent member of the opposite camp and sought the support of powers hostile to Venice, like the Carrara of Padua in the 1380s. But the seesaw of influence became markedly more pronounced when Sigismund, King of Hungary and from 21 July 1411 King of the Romans, decided to contest the Venetian occupation of Hungarian territory in Dalmatia and imperial territory in Italy with an invasion through Friuli. His aims appeared to be furthered when John XXIII elevated the pro-Venetian patriarch Antonio Panciera to the cardinalate on 5 June. Most of the *Patria* and even, briefly, the Savorgnan acknowledged Sigismund's overlordship, and the Venetian republic was hard put to it to defend its own territories south of the Livenza river. The Savorgnan were driven into exile and the chapter of Aquileia elected the pro-imperial Lodovico of Teck as patriarch. Hostilities were suspended by a truce from 1413 to 1418 but the threat to her influence and interests in the *Patria* decided Venice on a policy of conquest which was executed between 1418 and 1420. To celebrate this triumph, the embassy of surrender from Udine was persuaded to reveal the whereabouts of the – supposedly – original gospel written by St Mark. This highly prized relic was paraded through Venice by a large body of the clergy and placed in the treasury of the city's patron saint.[16]

Thereafter Friuli remained under Venetian rule, except during the War of Cambrai – a war which had been partly provoked by the republic claiming the right of escheat to Gorizia on the death of Count Leonardo without heirs in 1508, a claim contested by the emperor Maximilian.[17] However, the survival until then of the county of Gorizia as a Venetian fief points to the fact that the republic's rule did not introduce radical social or constitutional changes to the *Patria*; the fact that Friuli remained in 'Italian hands' has meant that its degree of autonomy has been more carefully studied and more fully recognised than that of cities like Trieste or Trent which fell under foreign Habsburg rule.[18] The larger centres – like Udine and Cividale – and the more important families – like the Savorgnan – increasingly chose to deal directly with the republic, but the concept of the *Patria* as a community survived and found continuing expression in its parliaments.

Indeed, it could be argued that the comparative stability afforded by Venetian rule, coupled with the republic's mounting demands for men and money, positively encouraged the survival of the institution, and its representative character was increased with the summons of spokesmen from communes subject to feudal jurisdictions. Though no longer enjoying the eminence it had attained in the fourteenth century, excluded from the issues of war, peace and diplomacy and no longer a court of final appeal, the parliament met frequently and continued to have a role in such critical areas as the defence of local privileges, legislation and the distribution of the tax burden. It was in regard to the last that Cividale reminded the Venetian *luogotenente*, or representative, in 1491 of the Roman Law maxim so often cited in the context of late medieval parliaments: that 'what concerns all should be approved by all'.

SIGNORIAL REGIMES

On 13 January 1400 an Udinese notary recorded that Tristano Savorgnan was addressed as 'magnifico', and observed that that title was generally associated with the lords and tyrants of the Italian cities'.[19] As has been mentioned, many of the cities ruled by *signori* lay in the Papal States; there were far fewer of such small, autonomous lordships in the kingdom of Italy, and only two ruling dynasties survived: the Este in Reggio Emilia and Modena and the Gonzaga in Mantua.

For much of the period, however, the heart of the kingdom was dominated by the lordships based on Milan and Pavia of the Visconti down to 1447, and then the Sforza from 1450. In territorial terms, the Visconti state was already well advanced by 1380.[20] The agricultural, industrial and commercial resources of Lombardy, and the relative accessibility of its principal cities from Milan, gave the Visconti the incentive and the wherewithal to build up a collection of lordships which embraced lakes Maggiore, Lugano and Como in the north, the western shore of Lake Garda in the east, the cities of Alessandria, Asti and Tortona in the west and Parma in the south. A further wave of expansion ensued after Giangaleazzo Visconti had acquired the entire Visconti inheritance after imprisoning his uncle Bernabò in May 1386.[21] To the east, in 1387 and 1388, Giangaleazzo acquired the della Scala lordships of Verona and Vicenza, and the Carrara cities of Belluno, Feltre and Padua; the last was recaptured by Francesco Carrara 'the Younger' in 1390, but Belluno and Feltre remained in Visconti hands until 1404. To the south, as part of his campaign to isolate Florence, Giangaleazzo added Siena between 1389 and 1392 (and again from 1399) and Pisa in 1399, before moving into the Papal States to take Perugia in 1400 and Bologna in 1402.

However, this conglomeration of lordships proved fragile. On Giangaleazzo's sudden death in 1402, his widow Caterina and his two sons, Giovanni Maria (aged fourteen) and Filippo Maria (aged ten), were unable to maintain its frontiers. In part they were assailed by vengeful dynasties; the della Scala retook Verona in 1404, only to be betrayed by their ally Francesco Carrara. In other cases subject cities reinstated republican governments, as in Siena. Elsewhere *condottieri* took advantage of Visconti weakness to acquire lordships for themselves; Pandolfo Malatesta ruled Brescia from 1403 to 1421 and Bergamo from 1408 to 1419. Finally rival powers, and particularly the republics of Venice and Florence, grasped the opportunity or saw the necessity of intervening, the former acquiring Vicenza, Belluno and Feltre in 1404 and Verona in 1405, while Florence took Pisa in 1406.

Eventually Filippo Maria Visconti was able to stem this process of disintegration, but Venice had now become a committed mainland power and not only denied him the cities of eastern Lombardy and the Veneto, but advanced towards Milan by taking Brescia (1426) and Bergamo (1428). Filippo Maria's death in 1447 without a direct male heir ended Visconti lordship, although the city of Milan, now ruled by the oligarchic Ambrosian republic, attempted to preserve a hegemony over its neighbours. However, the threat from foreign powers proved too great and Milan was forced to accept the lordship of Francesco Sforza, who claimed the Visconti inheritance by virtue of his marriage to Bianca Maria, the illegitimate daughter of the last Visconti duke, but in fact because of his skill and resources as a *condottiere* general. Francesco and his heirs were able to reassemble Filippo Maria's state.[22] They also pursued his ambition to rule Genoa, with periods of success: from 1464 to 1478 and again from 1487 to 1499. However, they were unable to retake the cities held by Venice; nor were they able to withstand the military force of Louis XII and the claims of the French crown inherited through the house of Orléans and dating from the marriage of Valentina Visconti to Louis of Orléans in 1389. The Sforza were reinstated – in 1500, from 1512 to 1515, from 1521 to 1524, in 1525 and lastly from 1529 to 1535 – before Milan fell finally to the Habsburgs.

In trying to describe the signorial states of northern Italy – and especially the central and dominant lordship of the Visconti and Sforza – the historian comes across problems of interpretation similar to those encountered in the context of the Papal States. In 1388 the Florentine patrician Donato Acciaiuoli described Giangaleazzo Visconti as 'a *signore* with an appetite for conquest', and because of their record of expansion the *signori* created enemies, though in this case their reputations have had to withstand the attacks less of the papacy and more of the contemporary and latter-day champions of republican regimes threatened by signorial ambitions.[23]

Republican arguments were largely inspired by a patriotic belief in independence and self-government. They were opposed to tyranny, which was understood to mean the violent seizure and retention of power, the lack of a legitimate title to govern and a contempt for the common good. To this more traditional political vocabulary, newer ideas and a more original form of expression were added, and in this respect the lead was taken by the humanists associated with the chancery of the Florentine republic, in whom the repeated Visconti threat stimulated an increasing familiarity with the moral and political ideas of the late Roman republic. From around 1410 the new rhetoric and enhanced repertoire of political discussion, increasingly inspired by classical as well as by more contemporary examples, appear to have permeated the councils of the republic, and from Florence they began to influence discussion and expression elsewhere in Tuscany, as well as in Genoa, Venice and the short-lived Ambrosian republic.

The political and social values of 'civic humanism' its attack on tyranny and its emphasis on the right and duty of the citizen to participate in government and society, have had a great appeal for democratic and liberal opinion – as has the moving picture painted by Hans Baron of Florence's lone stand against Visconti tyranny in 1402, as a precursor to Britain's defiance of Hitler in 1940. The ascendancy of the republican interpretation of north Italian history, and the dangers involved in questioning it, make the task of describing signorial governments all the harder. Giangaleazzo Visconti is supposed to have claimed that the pen of Coluccio Salutati, the humanist chancellor of Florence (1375–1406), was a mightier weapon than a company of cavalry. Historiography has proved him right.

However, in the blackening of their reputations some of the *signori* required little contemporary or posthumous assistance. On 12 July 1381 Antonio della Scala had his elder brother Bartolomeo murdered to gain sole control of the *signorie* of Verona and Vicenza.[24] As mentioned, Giangaleazzo Visconti seized his uncle in 1385 to similar ends, and Bernabò's sudden fall from power became a popular subject for moralising on the caprice of fortune. Attempts to educate rulers away from tyranny could fail spectacularly. In 1408 Carlo Malatesta, governor of the Visconti state, urged the young Giovanni Maria on the need to cherish the common good, and in 1457 Francesco Sforza advised his heir Galeazzo Maria on the conduct becoming a true prince.[25] In 1410 and 1476 respectively, both fell to assassins; the idealistic champions of tyrannicide who dispatched Galeazzo Maria received unexpected endorsement when his widow, Bona of Savoy, interceded with Sixtus IV on behalf of her husband's soul, and confessed to the duke's acts of tyranny.[26] The actions of their successors could be viewed in a similarly unfavourable light. In 1412 Filippo Visconti married Beatrice, who was both much older than himself and widow of Facino Cane, who had been one of the most dangerous *condottieri* threatening the Visconti state; in 1418 Beatrice was executed for adultery in circumstances that appealed to the nineteenth century's taste for melodrama, inspiring a play, a ballet and an opera by Bellini. Galeazzo Maria's young heir, Giangaleazzo, was overshadowed by his uncle Lodovico Maria, and when the young duke died in 1494 there was talk of poison.[27]

But as in the Papal States, the northern *signori* were sensitive to their reputations and employed their own propagandists, whose arguments could be as conveniently supported from fitting classical examples as those of their republican adversaries. Writers like Antonio Loschi and Andrea Biglia in

Visconti service could present the dynasty as pacifiers and unifiers, the scourgers of tyrants, bringing order and justice and defending the Peninsula from barbarian invaders north of the Alps, often in Florentine pay.[28] The same is true of the Sforza court. Doubts as to the legitimacy of their hold on the duchy of Milan stimulated the patronage of writers and artists by the first duke and his heirs to advertise their virtues as rulers – with the emphasis placed on Francesco and his achievements both before and after his succession to the duchy. For example, Giovanni Simonetta (1410–92) wrote a eulogistic history of his patron Francesco, which was translated into Italian by Cristoforo Landino and dedicated to Lodovico Maria in 1489, before being printed in Milan in 1490. Vellum copies, beautifully illuminated and hailing Francesco as 'Pater Patriae', were ordered by Lodovico Maria and his nephew Giangaleazzo.[29] Aiming at a wider audience, Galeazzo Maria contemplated the construction of a mausoleum to commemorate the deeds of his father, and both he and Lodovico Maria favoured celebrating Francesco's achievements with a larger-than-life-size bronze equestrian monument.[30]

Moreover, the defence of the *signori* and the attacks of their enemies were focused on the issue of legitimacy; and in the north, as further south, the idea that authority was bestowed by the commune continued to survive even when the political and military realities might seem to have compromised the principle.[31] When Antonio della Scala was driven from power by the forces of Giangaleazzo Visconti on 18 April 1387 his authority reverted to the commune of Verona, which negotiated its surrender on the following day. Again, when Francesco Sforza entered Milan on 22 March 1450 the ceremonial was designed to demonstrate that his authority, including even the title of duke, was granted to him by a grateful and willing commune.[32]

But, as in the Papal States, the acknowledgement of popular sovereignty was felt to be either insufficient or else too compromising, and signorial dynasties sought other sources of legitimacy. Possibly the most obvious was that of hereditary right; the Gonzaga benefited from the absence of succession disputes and outside pretenders to attain the position of 'natural' rulers of their native city, Mantua. In other cases the right of succession was more contrived. One of Francesco Sforza's principal claims to the duchy of Milan stemmed from his marriage to Bianca Maria, illegitimate daughter but sole heiress of Filippo Maria Visconti; to strengthen this aspect of his claim, forged documentation was prepared to demonstrate that Filippo Maria had granted him the succession on 10 November 1446. Hereditary succession was proclaimed in other ways. In 1463 Bianca Maria and Francesco rebuilt the church of San Sigismondo in Cremona, scene of their marriage in 1442, and the foundation stone bore the Visconti and the Sforza arms.[33] But as such manoeuvres suggest, a claim based on hereditary right could be challenged. Giangaleazzo's seizure of the entire Visconti dominion was subsequently threatened by Bernabò's children.[34] Most damaging of all, the claim to the lordship of Milan which passed to the French royal house through the marriage of Valentina Visconti and Louis d'Orléans, haunted the Visconti and the Sforza and contributed to the overthrow of Lodovico Maria in 1499.

Again like their counterparts in the Papal States, the northern *signori* looked to their overlord for a legitimate title. In this case the traditional title in demand was that of imperial vicar, and in October 1387 Antonio della Scala secured the recognition of the emperor Wenceslas in an unsuccessful bid to thwart Giangaleazzo Visconti's intention to acquire Verona and Vicenza. However, for its recipients the unsatisfactory nature of the title lay not only in the unpredictability of imperial support but also in the fact that it was non-hereditary; for reasons of both prestige and political practicality, the *signori* sought more illustrious and hereditary titles from the empire. The pace was set by Giangaleazzo Visconti, who paid 100,000 florins for investiture as duke on 5 September 1395; later it was rumoured that he was seeking the crown of the kingdom of Italy. More modestly in 1433 Gianfrancesco Gonzaga acquired the marquisate of Mantua from Sigismund, and in 1452 Borso d'Este was made duke of Modena by Frederick III. But once again such grants failed to make watertight the juridical status of the northern *signori*. Imperial grants could be questioned: the imperial electors disputed the right of Wenceslas to elevate Giangaleazzo to ducal status. This challenge contributed to the deposition of Wenceslas on 20 August 1400 and the precedent, together with the strategic and jurisdictional importance of Milan, urged caution on later emperors. Francesco Sforza's recognition as duke by the commune of Milan was not accepted by Frederick III. Galeazzo Maria failed in his bid for imperial recognition of the ducal title, let alone his quest for a royal crown. It was only in 1493 that Lodovico Maria secured imperial investiture as duke for the inflated sum of 400,000 ducats.[35]

The difficulties of the *signori* with all these sources of legitimacy help to explain why they, like the lords of the Papal States, were eager to associate themselves with the royal and princely houses of Europe. In some cases practical political considerations lay behind such alliances, as when Galeazzo Maria married Bona of Savoy in 1468. Again, marriage alliances could be related to the acquisition of titles. Gianfrancesco Gonzaga not only obtained the title of marquis from Sigismund, but his heir Lodovico married the emperor's granddaughter, Barbara of Brandenburg (1433). In other cases, however, the alliances secured or pursued were too careless of geography to be anything other than an investment in prestige. Lucia, sister-in-law of Giangaleazzo Visconti, appears to have been selected for an English match. In 1398 there were rumours that she was the intended bride of Henry Bolingbroke; in 1407 she married Edward Holland, Earl of Kent. A sister, Anglesia, married the king of Cyprus in 1400. In 1524 a marriage was contemplated between Federico Gonzaga and a daughter of the king of Poland, before Federico made the more practical and productive marriage to Margherita, heiress of Monferrat, in 1531.[36] Finally prestige was obviously present in the way the *signori* displayed the honours bestowed on them by royal and princely houses. When Francesco Gonzaga attended the marriage of Valentina Visconti to the duke of Orléans in 1389 he was granted the right to wear the French royal livery. In 1416 Henry V permitted his son Gianfrancesco to wear the English royal livery, a privilege confirmed by Henry VI and celebrated by the prominent display of that livery in the Arthurian tournament scenes painted by Pisanello in the Gonzaga palace at Mantua.[37]

But the pursuit of such honours, titles and alliances was too demanding in diplomatic effort and financial outlay to be explained in terms of theoretical justification and prestige alone. In a period when monarchy was both the most common and most often praised form of government, the closer the *signori* could approach the status, the more confidence they could have in their authority at home and abroad. When Henry VI confirmed the Gonzagas' right to wear the royal livery, Gianfrancesco's reputation was doubtless enhanced by the grant and by being addressed as a blood relative of a king; but his authority was also increased by the privilege of allowing fifty of his adherents to wear the livery. Titles to govern could promise more substantial benefits, and the pursuit of ducal and even royal dignity by the Visconti and the Sforza had aims beyond protocol, the principal being to thwart rival claimants who themselves could look to the empire for sanction; in 1473 Galeazzo Maria Sforza was told that the republic of Venice was trying to secure imperial investiture for the duchy of Milan. On that occasion Frederick III reportedly would have preferred to invest the Ottoman Turks;[38] but imperial support could sustain exiled pretenders. If the della Scala failed to recover the lordships of Verona and Vicenza after 1404, the recognition and support they received from Sigismund as king of the Romans (from 1410) and emperor (from 1433) allowed them to haunt the diplomacy and threaten the frontiers of the Venetian republic to considerable effect.[39] Again, imperial backing periodically resuscitated Sforza hopes to recover the duchy of Milan after 1499.

The acquisition of imperial titles could also strengthen the internal authority of the *signori*. As Chittolini and others have made clear, the lords and communes of the kingdom of Italy were eager to lay claim to rights and privileges in such matters as land, jurisdiction and the exaction of services and taxation – claims for which they were often ready to assert ancient and imperial origins.[40] In such circumstances the possession of the title of duke or marquis could increase the opportunities and powers of the *signori* themselves: to make grants and enfeoffments, to initiate *quo warranto*-style inquiries; to favour loyal vassals with lesser titles. Such activity appears to have been encouraged when the *signori* were in receipt of juridically impressive titles from the empire, and it helps to explain why historians have seen the fifteenth century as a period of 'reinfeudation'. For example, Chittolini has shown how Filippo Maria Visconti investigated the rival claims to jurisdiction and territory advanced by the marquises of Pallavicini and the commune of Parma in 1424. In 1427 he found in favour of the former, but their disloyalty led to the seizure of their holdings in 1428 to the benefit of the ducal exchequer rather than of Parma. Also in 1428 Sigismund ordered the great families of Malaspina, Fieschi and Campofregoso in Genoese territory to be loyal to his representative, Filippo Maria.

However, the *signori* did not use their enhanced authority only to suppress or dispossess their subjects. Filippo Maria's investigation into the rights claimed by the Anguissola in the Piacentino led to the confirmation of some of their lordships, and the elevations of others to county status in 1438; the acquisition of the Pallavicini lordships allowed the dukes to reward loyal followers. In general the process of reinfeudation so marked in the fifteenth century should be seen in terms of the exercise of patronage, and as in the Papal States the effective use of patronage was fundamental to the success of a signorial regime.

This interpretation contrasts with the more traditional view which sees signorial power in authoritarian terms. Of course, the *signori* were jealous of their authority; in subject communes the *podestà*, intended to be a foreign and neutral head of the judiciary, became a signorial nominee, and communal autonomy could be infringed in other ways. Signorial decree increasingly superseded local statute and signorial intervention could modify the composition of government, as when Francesco Sforza altered the membership of the Council of Vigevano in 1463.[41] Again, the more traditional view often sees the acquisition and retention of power in terms of force, and it is true that force could be threatened or used. The fifteenth century sees a considerable increase in the corps of troops guarding the person of the Visconti and Sforza dukes. Many of the smaller, as well as the larger, communes of the Visconti–Sforza state were dominated by castles. Following his acquisition of Verona, Giangaleazzo Visconti began the construction of a *cittadella*, a fortified barracks area within the walls, on 7 March 1390. This, involving the appropriation of land, houses and churches, contributed to a Veronese rebellion in June, which was duly crushed as reinforcement reached the garrison through the new fortifications. It is hardly surprising that on the ending of Visconti rule in 1404 the Veronese began the demolition of this fortress in their midst, just as the Milanese set about the destruction of the Visconti castles in the city in 1447.[42]

These incidents suggest that force alone could not maintain signorial rule – if Machiavelli exaggerated when he argued that Francesco Sforza's rebuilding of the Visconti fortress at the Porta Giovia in Milan led ultimately to the fall of his dynasty.[43] Moreover, in practice such fortresses could not be kept on a war footing, and in many instance – as in Mantua or Pavia – their aspect and use were residential rather than repressive; indeed, it was his exercise of patronage rather than his powers of policing that was key to a *signore*'s relationship with his subjects. This was readily recognised by contemporaries, for whom accessibility and generosity were well-accepted attributes of the good ruler. Granting a fief to a follower in 1454, Francesco Sforza explained that it was 'proper and natural for lords to be liberal to everyone, and especially to those who serve them with the greatest loyalty, devotion, care and diligence in all circumstances', and in 1457 the duke defended his claim to control the distribution of ecclesiastical benefices in his dominions by citing his obligation to reward his followers.[44]

The granting of fiefs and the provision of benefices were two of the more obvious avenues for patronage. Others could include: the award of office; the recognition or granting of privileges to individuals, families or communities;

the advancement of new men to positions of trust; the recommendation of clients to friendly governments. But the exercise of patronage was far from being straightforward or a panacea for~all political ills. To begin with, the *signori* did not always hold the initiative, whatever the official record of his acts might suggest to the contrary. The older view of the *signori*, encouraged by Burckhardt, as dictatorial and absolutist figures does not acknowledge the fact that they were besieged by petitioners and that many of their acts were in response to requests presented by their opportunistic, ambitious or litigious subjects.

Students of signorial policy, especially if they work from calendared records, have often concentrated on the conclusions rather than on the pre-ambles of chancery documents, thus accentuating the *signore*'s will without taking due account of his subjects' interests. On the other hand, to focus on the preamble or opening clauses to other categories of evidence, such as guild or communal statutes, can also distort the evidence by casting the *signore* more in the role of ruler than ratifier. The statutes of Verona of 1393 owe far more to the Veronese and to previous editions than to the lordship of Giangaleazzo Visconti. Francesco Sforza's march on Milan was as marked by his conciliatory reception of petitions from subject communities as it was by his skill as a *condottiere*; and shortly after his acquisition of the duchy he was encouraged by a supporter in Pavia to continue to reward his adherents.[45]

Following from this is the fact that the support encouraged by patronage was often partisan. Francesco Sforza's Pavian adviser was asking him to square the circle when he urged him both to reward his friends and to eschew faction along Guelf and Ghibelline lines; in 1461 an investigation into the allegiances of his subjects revealed to Francesco just how partisan his support was. Earlier Petrarch had warned Francesco Carrara 'the Elder' that too exclusive a favour-itism would alienate those left unsatisfied.[46] The much-rewarded loyalty of Cicco Simonetta, chancellor of Francesco and Galeazzo Maria Sforza, made him increasingly the target of the jealousy and suspicion traditionally directed at upstart and alien confidants of princes, and brought about his downfall and execution in 1480 as well as the overthrow of the regency of his patroness, Bona of Savoy.[47]

In general it appears likely that the *signori* could not take for granted the loyalty of their subjects; if signorial regimes could earn acceptance, they could not draw on a deep-rooted loyalty. This predicament was acute in the case of the Visconti–Sforza state, as was demonstrated when Giangaleazzo's amalgam of lordships largely fell apart on his death, or when Lodovico Maria Sforza's subjects showed themselves more prepared to accept foreign rule than to rally to the Sforza cause. In 1499 Lodovico could protest to his critics that his subjects were devoted to him, but the French invasion had in fact revealed their traditional skills at self-preservation, and an overenthusiastic belief in the rumour that the subjects of the French king were free from taxation. The commune of Vigevano, one of the Sforza's favourite residences where the dukes had lavished attention on improvements in town and country, did not hesitate to accept French rule.

Possibly the greater extent of the Visconti–Sforza state made the task of rulers whose titles, by any contemporary standard, were uncertain all the more difficult when it came to stimulating a sense of loyalty among their subjects. But the same conclusions can be drawn from the smaller *signorie*, where the role of one family over generations might suggest that it had been accepted as the 'natural rulers'. The Veronese and Vicentines quickly deserted Antonio della Scala in 1387, and although pretenders from that native dynasty showed considerable enterprise in exile, the body of positive support they could rely upon was slender. Such conclusions make the achievements of the Gonzaga of Mantua all the more remarkable. Their success was probably due to a number of factors: the relatively defensive location of Mantua itself; the good fortune of an uninterrupted and undisputed succession; the acquisition of prestigious titles to govern, and supportive marriage alliances; a pragmatic foreign policy which generally avoided risky wars of expansion in favour of protective and profitable alliances. These circumstances and achievements allowed the Gonzaga to present to their subjects a lordship characterised by continuity and familiarity as well as by a relatively benign and accessible patronage.

GENOA

The fact that so few signorial governments survived helps to explain why Machiavelli's attempt to relate practice to theory in *The Prince* appears so urgent. In May 1414 another Florentine, Agnolo Pandolfini, put forward an explanation for the relative instability of such regimes: 'The states of *signori* are not as secure as those of communes, for death does not destroy a community as it does a *signore*'.[48] The contrast must have appeared plausible in the light of Florence's conflict with the Visconti, but the claims it made for republican stability or continuity are called at once into question by the case of Genoa, which Commynes described as a city 'ever prone to revolution', and where the republican government was frequently subordinated to foreign and non-Italian lordship.[49] At least two Genoese regimes lasted for only a matter of hours – those of Antonietto Adorno on 17 June 1378 and Battista Campofregoso on 24 May 1437 – and while these are extreme examples the city's history of *coups d'état* and foreign intervention, combined with its relatively unimportant contribution to the cultural achievements of Renaissance Italy, explains why the Genoese state remains one of the least studied.[50]

The political weakness of Genoa was reflected in its subject territories, over which its rule could be extremely tenuous.[51] For example in 1378, constrained by financial and military difficulties, Genoa leased Corsica to a consortium, or *maona*, for an annual tribute. In fact the *maona*'s authority was challenged by Corsican resistance, Aragonese intervention and the ambitions of one of its shareholders, the Lomellini, to secure the lordship of the island. By 1406 Lionello Lomellini had squeezed out most of his partners, sworn fealty to Genoa's then overlord, Charles VI of France, and acquired the title of count. But his failure to control the island and his inability to pay the tribute persuaded the commune to try to restore its own direct lordship in 1407. This in turn proved unsuccessful, and faced by Corsican rebellion, threats from Aragon and the designs of prominent Genoese families, above all the Campofregoso, Genoa ceded the island in 1453 to a more powerful consortium, the Bank of St George. The transition was neither smooth nor final. The Corsicans were unimpressed. The ambitions of the Campofregoso were not abandoned. From 1468 to 1482 the Sforza, as overlords of Genoa, tried to impose their authority, but with only fleeting effect.

The weakness of the commune, the vigorous survival of local autonomy, the jealous dynastic interests of leading Genoese families and the designs of foreign powers were also present in the case of Sarzana.[52] That commune had been ceded to the Campofregoso in 1421, but it continued to enjoy privileges acknowledged by previous French and Genoese administrations. The Campofregoso attempted to use their lordship as the base for further expansion, as well as for political influence in Genoa itself, until pressure from Florence – seeking to extend its dominion and influence on the Ligurian coastline – as well as from Florence's allies within Genoa hostile to the Campofregoso, forced them to surrender the commune in 1468 and again in 1484.

The spasmodic and ineffective quality of Genoese authority in Corsica and Sarzana reflected the instability of Genoa itself. From 1339 public office had been divided equally between the nobility and the *popolo*, among whom the wealthier and longer-established families – the *popolo grasso* – had achieved an ascendancy which extended to the monopoly of the office of doge and of the executive, the council of *anziani* or 'elders'. The distinction between the nobility and the *popolo grasso* is difficult to discern. Families could intermarry, while political allegiances and foreign alliances did not follow class lines. The economic concerns of both groups were similar, with land and lordships beginning to play an increasingly important part among a diversity of economic interests. A few noble families, like the Malaspina and the Carretto with lordships in Genoese territory, did appear to stay aloof from trade and the Genoese political arena, but the same cannot be said for the rest of the nobility. Families who appear distant from the commercial and political concerns of the city, like the Grimaldi and the Spinola of Luccoli, protected and advanced their interests through more urban-based clients and kin. The distinction between the nobility and the *popolo grasso* should perhaps be seen in terms of family tradition – expressed vividly when nobility and *popolo* squabbled over precedence on the entry of Louis XII in 1502 – rather than real differences in economic activity, political aspirations and social attitudes.

Similar difficulties are experienced when trying to identify categories within the *popolo*, but the majority of the population – the shopkeepers, the poorer notaries, the craftsmen, the artisans and the proletariat – were denied a prominent place in government. Although in theory they were entitled to half the *popolo*'s quota of public office, the poorer elements appear to have lacked the resources and organisation to exploit the potential of their share of power. Occasionally they did demand a wider share of public office. In 1401 the threat they posed led to efforts to disarm the artisans and weaken the authority of the guilds. More dramatically, in 1507 widespread unrest, fuelled by a repressive French regime and set against a background of plague, famine and economic difficulties, swept a silk-dyer, Paolo da Novi, briefly to power as doge (10–18 April) and granted the *popolo minuto* a greater but short-lived share of public office.

More generally the influence of the *popolo minuto* on government was indirect, as the clients, adherents, employees and partisans of noble and *popolo grasso* families. Their hold on power was far from harmonious, if the origins of discord lay less with class divisions or party lines and more with restless family rivalries. The families of Genoa who ruled, or aspired to do so, were organised in *alberghi* which might be translated as 'houses', but which are better understood as clans.[53] *Alberghi* varied in size and resources; in 1448 the Grimaldi (with sixty male members) and Ceba (with eight) merged, with the latter abandoning their name and coat of arms in return for full membership of the larger clan. But they resembled each other closely in aims and character. They consisted of the kin, clients and neighbours of a family, sharing the same surname and coat of arms by birth or by adoption. New blood could be recruited so that ancient family names might mask the presence of relatively recent immigrants. Members of *alberghi* were grouped together in neighbourhoods; whatever estates, fiefs and commercial interests members of an *albergo* had beyond the walls or frontiers of Genoa, this neighbourhood association was the core and measure of their power in the city itself. Their often fortified houses dominated a *piazza*, where their church, *loggia* – or meeting-place – warehouses and bathhouse could also be found. The *albergo* owned property in common and conducted its affairs by its own statutes. It managed marriage alliances, political strategy and the pursuit of public office. Such occasions as weddings and funerals expressed the *albergo's* identity.

However, the *alberghi* themselves could split, and the faction which characterised Genoese political life was a product of both internal and external rivalries. It was also one of the causes for foreign intervention and rule; the strategic and economic potential of Genoa and its overseas possessions made it a tempting target, and its disturbed government whetted the appetites of the houses of Valois, Savoy, Monferrat, Visconti–Sforza, Aragon and Habsburg. For example, in 1396 Antonietto Adorno surrendered the lordship of Genoa to Charles VI, partly to protect the city from Giangaleazzo Visconti and partly to defend himself and the Adorno from rival dogal families.[54] In 1421 the Adorno in exile supported Filippo Maria Visconti's acquisition of the city to oust their rivals the Campofregoso, but in 1463–64 divisions among the Campofregoso themselves helped pave the way for Francesco Sforza's conquest of the city; the duke of Milan was also assisted by the Adorno and by a general yearning for peace.[55]

However, if the ambition and factionalism of the leading *alberghi* facilitated the introduction of foreign rule, they could also overturn it. Tommaso

Campofregoso led moves to put an end to Visconti rule in 1436 and Paolo Campofregoso, Archbishop of Genoa, was among the leaders of the revolt which ended the *signoria* of Charles VII. Secondly, whatever the ambitions of foreign powers, the *alberghi* certainly tried to exploit powerful external backers, as is suggested by the examples already given but most dramatically by Andrea Doria, whose espousal of the Habsburg cause secured his own hegemony in the city in 1528.

Such incidents might suggest that the disturbed state of Genoa has been exaggerated, and even the commune can be found demonstrating greater resilience and continuity than is often allowed. When Florence attempted to negotiate with Genoa in 1413 over territorial disputes, it was not clear who represented the commune; but this apparent evidence for fundamental political and administrative confusion should not obscure the fact that Florence was forced to make the major concessions.[56] Again, for all the commune's turbulent political history, the humanist Giacomo Bracelli was prominent as a diplomat and chancellor of the republic from 1411 to 1465, when he surrendered his office in favour of his son.[57] And as his career suggests, foreign lordship did not always threaten fundamental change. For example, in 1396 Charles VI was hailed as the defender of Genoa, and initially his rule did not appear to challenge the city's liberties; the legal and institutional developments that occurred were the products of Genoese needs and efforts, like the compilation of statutes in 1403 and the foundation of the Bank of St George in 1407. The terms Andrea Doria reached with Charles V at Madrid on 10 August 1528 allowed wide autonomy to the city and explain why the doge could be hailed as 'Restorer of Liberty' and 'Pater Patriae'.

Lastly, the city was not always so fundamentally divided as to prevent the moderation or suspension of faction and the assertion of the common interest. In 1409 the tyranny of the French governor, Boucicault, and the burdens and infringements of liberty associated with foreign rule provoked a successful insurrection, which the archbishop of the city justified in a letter to Charles VI. By 1473–57, the insensitive and demanding government of Galeazzo Maria Sforza and his plans to strengthen the fortresses of the city stimulated conspiratorial meetings and the circulation of propaganda appealing to the leadership of the *alberghi*, the support of the people and the slogan 'St George and Liberty' to drive out Sforza rule. A 'Lament' addressed to the duke reproached him for treating Genoa like a slave and not a wife; a delegation to him is reported to have aptly compared the city to the basil plant, giving off a sweet aroma if well treated, but harbouring scorpions if abused. In 1528 the history of foreign intervention and popular disturbances persuaded the traditional ruling families to redefine Genoese nobility to create a closed and institutionalised ruling class to achieve a greater political stability.[58]

The reform was less radical than it may at first appear, designed as it was to guarantee a place in government to the noble and popular *alberghi* who had held office before the unrest of 1507. This introduces the fact that continuity in the history of Genoa, as well as its military and economic resilience, did not depend solely on the relatively fragile institutions of the commune and moments of intense republican and communal spirit. The *alberghi* have already been mentioned. Another source of power and order beyond the state was the Bank of St George. This had been instituted in 1407 to administer the republic's funded debt. Political instability and the demands of government insured that the role of the Bank increased to the point of indispensability. It acquired control of virtually all public revenues, and gradually moved into communal buildings. As mentioned, it was granted the administration of Corsica; but if the Bank illustrates the weakness of the commune, it also reveals the resilience of Genoese society and the existence of an alternative government. It is significant that Louis XII promised to respect its interests in 1499, and even more telling that the Bank paid the French king the indemnity due from Genoa after its rebellion in 1507.

FLORENCE

Introduction

Machiavelli described the Bank of St George as a state within a state[59] and, reflecting this distribution of power, historians of Genoa have tended to concentrate more on its economic and social history and less on the commune itself. That is not true of Machiavelli's Florence, whose political and institutional history has long been a subject for research, making the city one of the most studied in Renaissance Europe. The cultural achievements of the Florentines have been another major inspiration for generations of students, but the fascination of the city for historians has been sustained by the wealth, range and nature of the surviving documentary evidence.[60] The most familiar sources are those of the historians and political thinkers of the early sixteenth century, outstanding among them being Machiavelli and Guicciardini. But they should be understood as the most accessible representatives of a long and articulate tradition of political commentary and reflection. Around a century earlier, Giovanni Cavalcanti (1381–1450), in his *Istorie Fiorentine*, provided a vivid if idiosyncratic account of factional politics and the rise of the Medici. In 1479 another patrician, the scholar Alamanno Rinuccini (1419–99) – whose historical interests were inherited from his father and passed on to his son – wrote a *Dialogue on Liberty* attacking the ascendancy of Lorenzo de' Medici.

Works of this nature were probably aimed at a relatively small circle. Even more intimate but still extremely informative are the diaries (*ricordi, ricordanze*), letters and memoranda including observations on affairs of state and advice on political conduct as well as material of a more domestic nature. The early-fifteenth-century *Ricordi* of Giovanni Morelli lie between chronicle and diary; as Dale Kent has shown, the private letters which form an important part of the surviving Medici archive are an invaluable source for the study

248

of their political alliances and patronage. Other sources preserve the record of political debate. Most obviously this was conducted in the place of government, the *Palazzo della Signoria*, and nowhere is such discussion more vividly preserved than in the *Consulte e Pratiche*, the minutes of commissions of leading citizens summoned to advise on important matters of policy. This type of source, apparently limited to Florence and her Tuscan neighbour Lucca, preserves not only proposals and resolutions but much of the content and spirit of debate; as Gene Brucker has shown, a historian can chart from these minutes the changing or consistent 'positions' of members of the regime, and analyse the language and content of their rhetoric.[61] However, as Cavalcanti caustically observed, political debate was not confined to the *Palazzo* but could often be conducted with more consequence in private palaces. Something of the atmosphere and substance of such discussions is preserved in the debates of a circle of pro-Medici conservatives, associated with the patrician-scholar Bernardo Rucellai and meeting in his gardens, the *Orti Oricellari*, during the exile of the Medici in the opening years of the sixteenth century.[62]

There are dangers in arguing from relative silence, or in drawing conclusions from unevenly directed research, but the remarkable wealth of Florentine political discussion and observation is not an illusion created by the surviving evidence or a longer historiography. Explanations have been sought in the influence of antiquity – and of Roman history and political thought in particular – on impressionable Florentine citizens; but while the impact of Roman republicanism can be traced in debate, diplomatic correspondence and political literature, its contribution comes too late, has too variable an impact on the different genres and reaches too narrow a circle to constitute by itself a satisfactory explanation. Again, the activity of chroniclers, diarists and commentators was to a considerable extent self-generating, most evidently where history-writing was a family tradition, as in the case of the Rinuccini or of Neri Capponi (d. 1457), who reworked a chronicle composed by his father on the conquest of Pisa. However, the fundamental explanation probably lies in the agitated internal and external history of Florence itself, a phenomenon which long predates the period but which also characterises the commune during the Renaissance.

The revolt of the Ciompi[63]

The disturbed tenor of Florentine political life can be seen at its most extreme in the summer of 1378, when the failure of a *coup* launched on 24 June by a number of patrician families provoked a series of increasingly radical protest movements from the *popolo minuto*. These are normally referred to under the heading of 'the revolt of the *Ciompi*' – a word deriving from the French 'compères', meaning companions, while the section of the *popolo minuto* who adopted it came from the least skilled and unenfranchised proletariat. However, for all its impact on contemporaries and future generations, the causes of the unrest and the aims of the *Ciompi* and others are still open to debate: it remains unclear, for example, how far the *Ciompi* were 'infected' by the 'contagion' of unrest which characterised the social history of Europe in the fourteenth century and which had manifested itself in the neighbouring city of Siena.

However, high among the causes must come the war which Florence had fought with the papacy between 1375 and 1378. Psychologically this proved damaging, as it overthrew a traditional and profitable alliance and brought with it spiritual penalties. Materially the city suffered some disruption to trade and food supply; but more seriously the level of taxation became so high that many of the poorer taxpayers were pushed into debt. Behind these immediate hardships lay longer-term political and economic grievances. The *sottoposti* of the *popolo minuto*, those who worked for and were ruled by the guilds of the city, were not allowed to form associations of their own, while the better-off, organised into 'lesser guilds' or *arti minori*, struggled for influence in government against the patrician members of the *arti maggiori*; the attempted *coup* of 24 June was partly prompted by these traditional antagonisms, exacerbated by an expensive, inconclusive and damaging war. Furthermore, a large number of the *popolo minuto* worked in the cloth industry, and while this central element in the Florentine economy was probably not as depressed as economic historians once assumed, its growth had been checked by the war and the threat of social disturbance while its profits had tended to benefit the skilled workforce rather than the *Ciompi*, whose hopes for an improved standard of living were dashed in the years before 1378.

By 21 July the aims of the insurgents, apart from settling old scores and looting, appear to have centred on acquiring guild status and hence representation in government. Following from this, they hoped for an assurance against lay-offs in the textile industry as well as the redistribution of public office and a reform of the taxation system, whose dependence on forced loans, *prestanze*, tended to favour the commune's wealthier creditors. Initially they were successful, with the creation of three new guilds to incorporate the unenfranchised workers of the *popolo minuto*, but the radical implication of their other proposals, the abiding hostility of most of the patriciate and the increasingly revolutionary utterances and behaviour of extremists forced open divisions in the ranks of the *popolo minuto* – never a homogeneous 'class' – and led to the disbandment of the *Ciompi* guild on 31 August. A broader-based regime, still including the remaining two newly created guilds, survived until it collapsed under the weight of faction and hostility in January 1382, leading to the abolition of the new guilds and a progressive swing of power away from the *arti minori* towards the *arti maggiori*.

Some recent historians have criticised those who dismiss the revolt of the *Ciompi* as an aberration or as just another manifestation of factional struggle, and it is remarkable that the conference held to celebrate the last centenary of the revolt missed the event by a year. The aims of the *Ciompi* reveal the presence of deep social and political grievances, and the unrest of summer 1378 was not unprecedented. Their ability to organise, their sense of identity in August as the 'People of God', suggests that they were not a mindless and directionless mob, even if their opponents could liken them to plague or describe them as 'ruffians, malefactors, thieves . . . useless men of base condition'. The revolt long haunted the collective political memory of the Florentines.

On the other hand, the revolt was an aberration in the sense that Florentine political conflict was not generally organised along class lines. As in Genoa, the family, though not as institutionalised, was generally the focus of political activity. By 1378 this traditional orientation had been weakened, due in part to the tensions aggravated by the war of 1375–78 but also to the disturbed social climate of the city. Repeated and severe visitations of the plague had damaged social cohesion, not only through loss of life but also because of the large numbers of immigrants – generally from the *contado* – who had high expectations of city life, untrammelled by more traditional ties. After the violence and repression of 1378 and the setting-up of a powerful security magistracy, the *Otto di Guardia*, political conflict became once again a manifestation of faction and a product of family rivalries and loyalties. Most of the smaller-scale disturbances and revolts of the years that followed did not so much mirror the social antagonisms of the *Ciompi* rebellion as represent the efforts of alienated patricians to draw on the support of exiled or aggrieved members of the *popolo minuto*; such is the nature of the conspiracies of 1411 and 1412, directed from Bologna by exiled members of the Alberti clan and attempting to exploit popular dissatisfaction provoked by war and the natural calamities of plague and famine.

Oligarchic rule[64]

Some studies of the period following 1382 can appear almost apologetic, as if constrained by a need to defend Florence from the anachronistic charge of failing to realise a democracy. In fact, in certain respects participation in public life was relatively wide. The *parlamento* continued to be called, and hence to preserve at least the appearance of popular sovereignty. Lot continued to determine the final selection of candidates for most offices: there were over 3,000 such offices to be filled annually; this number grew in absolute terms with the frontiers of the Florentine state in the fifteenth century, and relatively as the total population continued to fall due to onslaughts of the plague. The level of participation appears even higher when it is realised that these offices had to be filled from an adult male population of around 10,000 in the first quarter of the century, and only by guild members, aged twenty-five, from families with a record of residence, tax contribution and loyalty to the regime.

Of course, not all offices were of equal importance, but even in respect of the small thirty-seven-man executive, the *Signoria*, the number considered eligible rose from around 600 in 1393 to over 2,000 in the 1420s. It is true that extraordinary commissions, or *balìe*, were established to deal with crises, and they could eclipse the larger consultative and legislative assemblies of the commune. But the *balìe* neither usurped the authority of the *Signoria* nor achieved permanence; they did not even forsake the practice of wider consultation. A *balìa* of eighty-one, established in 1393 in the face of an Alberti conspiracy and retained to expedite affairs of state during the Visconti wars, was duly abolished in 1404. Against this background, Florentine civic humanism, with its stress on the participation of citizens, appears more than a posture, and Salutati's claim that 'the foundation of our government is the parity and equality of all the citizens' sounds more than propaganda.

On the other hand, closer examination reveals a more narrowly oligarchic regime. Meetings of the *parlamento* were stage-managed. Not only were the two new guilds disolved in 1382, but the role of the fourteen lesser guilds in government, their share of public office, was gradually reduced. The entry of newer families to the lists of those eligible for higher office probably decreased after 1390. The numerical increase in those eligible for such appointments probably reflects more an equitable distribution among established families than the admission of newcomers. However large and increasing the number of public offices, the cynical view of a contemporary, Cavalcanti, and the patient research of Rubinstein, Brucker and Kent suggest that in the 1420s the core of the regime, or *reggimento*, consisted of around sixty to seventy families and that its presence and influence were more accurately reflected in those regularly called to take part in the advisory *pratiche* than in those holding the more formal offices.[65] It is to them that the language of civic humanism had meaning, although their sense of status was probably more demonstrably gratified by the greater pomp and ceremony that entered Florentine public life from the close of the fourteenth century.

However, the problems of defining membership of the regime's inner circle have proved as tantalising for historians as they were for contemporaries. This is largely because the Florentine 'ruling class' was not defined as such; if it was characterised by a more aristocratic outlook, it was not an aristocracy in a formal sense. Its growing exclusivism was not accompanied by legislation but was an accelerating process stimulated by a fear of threats from abroad and within. Historians in pursuit of greater precision by instinct tend to make connections, to exaggerate the definition of the *reggimento*, encouraged to do so by the fact that chroniclers were naturally drawn to the more prominent individuals. Thus the period between 1382 and 1434 used to be explained in terms of the ascendancy of the Albizzi family, partly because they were prominent and partly because the confrontation between Rinaldo degli Albizzi and Cosimo de' Medici, which came to a head in 1433 and ushered in the period of Medici predominance, suggested that their rivals had previously controlled the oligarchy. In fact, the Albizzi were only one among several outstanding families in the *reggimento*; they did not manage the regime or direct its policies, and among the factors which gave such a family prominence were some which made it difficult for a family to act alone.

In part, prominence was a product of wealth, with the *reggimento* largely made up of bankers, merchants and industrialists, together with a few lawyers, notaries and *rentiers*. However, membership of the *Signoria* was not the monopoly of the wealthiest Florentines. It could also be related to

252

successful office-holding in Florence, its dominion or abroad. Less tangibly, but probably more important, it was related to the status of the individual family: its size, the depth of its Florentine roots, its skill at side-stepping lost causes and its ability to secure marriage alliances among social equals, while creating ties of clientage with potential supporters. These considerations help to explain the agitated character of Florentine political life in the period.

For some leading families these years came to be viewed in retrospect with nostalgia, as a golden age for those with a claim to prominence in the *reggimento* and as a period of consensus and exemplary statesmanship. But in the main this was a reaction to the Medici, while at the time the degree of unity achieved was largely a product of the *Ciompi* revolt and the repeated threats from abroad. Looked at more closely, the restlessness of Florentine politics is more striking than its harmony, and in the 1420s politicians and chroniclers claimed to view with alarm the proliferation of illegal assemblies, of *sette* and *conventicule*, which denunciation or investigation did little to inhibit. Public debate and argument might be nominally concerned with such issues of principle and public concern as foreign policy, methods of taxation and the preservation of the common good, but Florentine internal politics were more profoundly shaped by the preoccupations of its leading families – and their supporters – with status and influence. Of this there is no more fully documented and more closely studied example than that of the Medici, and their associated 'party'.

The rise of the Medici[66]

The very weight of evidence has created problems of interpretation. From the ascendancy of Cosimo (1434–64) the Medici were aware of the value of propaganda while adopting the posture of self-effacing but patriotic citizens. However, with the creation of two Medici popes, Leo X (1513–21) and Clement VII (1523–34), and with the acquisition of the title of duke in 1532, their propaganda became at once more forthright and retroactive. As a consequence, the rise of the Medici to power was made to appear inevitable and the family itself unique – an impression which many later biographies and monographs serve to heighten. However, recent historians, among them Brucker and Dale Kent, have suggested some correctives to this image embellished in hindsight. Few contemporary chroniclers appear to have been aware of a Medici bid for power. Possibly their suspicions were lulled by Giovanni de' Medici (1360–1429), who built up the family's economic and political fortunes but whose relative respect for the republican constitution and blameless conduct in public life led to him being overlooked as founder of the dynasty in favour of his son Cosimo. Still earlier, the family had not been conspicuously wealthy, and in the fourteenth century the political reputation of the Medici had been unsavoury. They were associated with acts of violence; Salvestro de' Medici had had a prominent role in the earlier stages of the *Ciompi* rebellion.

In fact, these disadvantages probably help to explain the Medici's later success. Though certainly an ancient family, as challengers to the inner circle of the *reggimento* the Medici could more readily attract the alliance and support of up-and-coming families; they even proved sympathetic to *contadini* and the inhabitants of the subject cities of the Florentine *dominio*. Their enemies tried to turn these links with the *nouveaux riches* and the people against them. A poem of 1426, ascribed to the oligarch Niccolò da Uzzano, denounced challenges to the *reggimento* from below, while Cavalcanti assigned to the same year a rally addressed by Rinaldo degli Albizzi alerting the noble houses of Florence to the threat posed to their ascendancy by the lesser guilds, the 'new men' and the people.

This might suggest that the Medici were the leaders of a clearly defined party, and various overlapping ties of association can be identified. Other than from their own family, the Medici drew support from *parenti* linked to them by marriage. Others worked for the Medici bank, or were beholden to the Medici for loans and advances. A high proportion of their supporters were concentrated in the Medici quarter of San Giovanni, where Medici influence in the *gonfaloni*, or neighbourhood organisations, told in the assessment of taxation and the pursuit of public office. Finally, the surviving correspondence records individuals and families turning to the Medici for favours, ranging from help in meeting tax bills to support in the search for office. However, it would be a mistake to see a Medici 'party' in too rigid terms. It had no ideology. Cosimo allied with other leaders of the *reggimento* to support the disastrous war with Lucca (1427–33), and Cavalcanti's claim that he championed a more equitable form of taxation does not appear to be supported by his contribution to debate. If many newer families were linked to them, the Medici had close associations with such aristocratic houses as the Bardi – in that particular case as banking partners.

It is difficult to provide a definitive description of their body of support. Some families, like the Guicciardini, were divided in their loyalty, and the degree to which Florentines remained neutral or pragmatically exploited the patronage of the faction leaders of the city should not be underestimated. Nevertheless, the Medici 'party' did have an identity. This derived from family, marriage, neighbourhood and clientage, and its aim was the protection and advancement of its influence. Moreover, its cohesion was probably strengthened by the growing alarm and hostility of other families more deeply entrenched in the oligarchy. Individually they were organised and connected like the Medici, but collectively – and even separately – they appear to have been more fragmented; leading opponents of the Medici challenge, like the Strozzi and the Albizzi, were themselves divided.

A further major reason for the Medici rise to ascendancy lay less in the general political and social circumstances. From the 1390s the heads of two closely related branches of the family, Averardo and Giovanni, began to rebuild their economic fortunes in banking, in particular through branches in Rome which began to handle an increasing volume of papal business.[67] This gave them the wherewithal to employ and reward family and friends.

It also allowed them to secure allies abroad, and not least the papacy; the support of Eugenius IV, himself exiled and resident in Florence, helped to sustain the Medici cause and promote their return in 1434. Their wealth also gave them the resources to adopt an increasingly prominent profile in the city in such prestigious projects as the rebuilding of their parish church of San Lorenzo (from 1421) and commissioning from Donatello and Michelozzo the tomb monument to John XXIII in the baptistry (1425–27).[68] Lastly, their wealth made them increasingly essential creditors to the state, as wars with the Visconti and Lucca proved long and expensive.

Another asset was less of their own choosing. Increasingly alarmed by Medici influence in such sensitive areas of public life as state finance and the distribution of office, their enemies, led by Rinaldo degli Albizzi, took advantage of the election of a *Signoria* on balance hostile to the Medici to send them into exile in October 1433. For some members of the family this proved as disastrous as had been intended. Averardo's branch never recovered from the financial losses it incurred, compounded by the illness and death of Averardo himself (5 December 1434). For Cosimo, however, the setback proved short-lived. While studiously not conspiring against his native city and having abandoned the idea of using force, he allowed himself to be feted abroad, particularly in Venice, to the embarrassment of his enemies and the encouragement of his friends. His financial assets were sufficiently well spread and secured to allow him to weather the storm, and his supporters remained sufficiently numerous to sustain him with their news and their votes. Lastly, his enemies were not ruthless enough in rooting out the Medici 'party' or successful enough at managing the affairs of Florence. Their failure to prevent the election of a pro-Medici *Signoria* in August 1434 led to the triumphant return of Cosimo from exile on 6 October.[69]

The Medicean ascendancy: strengths and weaknesses[70]

Cosimo's return from exile marks the beginning of the ascendancy of the Medici, an ascendancy which was interrupted by two further periods of exile (1494–1512, 1527–30), when less compromised republican regimes were restored. For reasons that have already been discussed, it is tempting to describe the Medici as the 'rulers' of Florence. Increasingly in the eyes of the Florentines and of the rulers of other states they had the attributes of lordship. In 1471 the Sforza believed that 'the affairs of the city have reached the point where everything depends on a word from Lorenzo, and nobody else counts for anything'. In 1479 Bartolomeo Scala, Chancellor of Florence and an enthusiastic Medicean, described Lorenzo as his 'sun', 'leader' and 'pole star'. Moreover in 1481, after the conspiracy of the Pazzi, who had attempted to kill Lorenzo and had succeeded in murdering his brother Giuliano, the commune defined future attempts on his life as *lèse majesté*. But none of the Medici in this period held the lordship of Florence. On the other hand, the Medicean form of ascendancy, which political thinkers described as a 'veiled tyranny', was not unique. The Bentivoglio managed the government of

Bologna in the fifteenth century, but held no title to do so; the same applies to the Petrucci of Siena between 1502 and 1525.

In part the Medici maintained themselves in power through the same resources and connections which had allowed them to challenge the previous *reggimento*, but they sought to go beyond acceptance by their own allies and clients and to identify themselves with the regime. They made themselves accessible to petitions from the *contado* and the subject cities of the *dominio*. Important Florentine marriages were increasingly celebrated in the Medici palace. Faithful and informative clients in the chancery – like Bartolomeo Scala, chancellor from 1465 – were encouraged in their careers and rewarded.[71] They commissioned works of art to celebrate Florentine successes; Paolo Uccello's *Rout of San Romano* (1455), painted for the Medici palace, commemorated a victory over Siena on 1 June 1432 in which an ally of the Medici, the *condottiere* Niccolò da Tolentino, had played a prominent part.[72] By the death of Piero in 1469, such policies appeared to be bearing fruit. An assembly of six hundred leading citizens asked his son Lorenzo to continue to direct the *reggimento*; as Lorenzo himself recorded, 'the principal men of the city and its government' had asked him to take on the 'guidance of the city and the regime'. Later Scala was to urge Lorenzo to act for 'your own preservation and for that of the regime which is associated with you, and for the preservation of the city which in turn is linked to the regime'.

However, the Medici also took more drastic measures to secure their position. In 1434 Rinaldo degli Albizzi and his supporters were exiled; in 1466 an unsuccessful challenge to Piero was similarly followed by the exile of his enemies. After the crisis of the Pazzi conspiracy of 1478 and the war with the papacy that followed, the Medici and their supporters created a new Council of Seventy which was intended to eclipse the authority of the more traditional legislative councils. Presented as a temporary measure, its five-year term was repeatedly renewed. Moreover, it was intended to be more reliably partisan, with its carefully picked members holding office for life and vacancies filled by co-option. More generally, the Medici aimed to influence the choice of personnel for such high offices as the *Signoria*. To do so, they focused on the *accoppiatori*, who had the role of filling the ballot bags with the names of those deemed eligible after the process of scrutiny. Under the Medici, sortition – the random element previously preserved as names were drawn from the ballot – was reduced. The *accoppiatori* chose the office-holders; furthermore, they also chose a number in addition who were as a consequence assured of an easier passage through future scrutinies and privileged access to other offices. The procedure was clearly intended to have a cumulative effect, with the spread of Miceleans into high office and their dominance of the scrutiny lists; revealingly, the *accoppiatori* were among the godparents present at the baptism of Lorenzo on 6 January 1449. Finally, the Medici also set out to reduce the influence of the *Parte Guelfa*, a wealthy institution which was trying to defend its traditional role as a guarantor of political rectitude and whose officials claimed the right to participate in scrutinies and *balìe*. After the anti-Medici plot of 1466 its role in government was reduced, while after the Pazzi conspiracy its assets began to be sold off, ostensibly to reduce the scale of the public debt.[73]

Related to these more explicit measures to remove challenges to their regime was the shrewd use of what today would be called propaganda to convey an impression of the Medici as pious, generous and patriotic citizens, Maecenases of the arts and literature and servants of the common good. Famous in this connection are the plans to parallel the work they were advancing on their parish church of San Lorenzo with the construction of their palace, close by on the Via Larga. Recent research would seem to confirm Vasari's claim that Cosimo backed away from a more grandiose plan put forward by Brunelleschi in favour of a less provocative design by his successor, Michelozzo.[74] However, some of their realised projects were unambiguous statements of the Medici presence. Around 1448 Piero commissioned an elaborate marble tabernacle for Ss Annunziata, boasting in its dedicatory inscription of its expense; the point was not lost on the Dominican friar Domenico Corella, who recorded Piero's generous piety, noted the presence of the Medici arms and described the patron as 'undoubted heir of Cosimo/His country's splendour, guardian of his house'.[75] Other steps taken more or less obviously to hold the public stage included their close association with the confraternity and cult of the Magi and the cult of the Medici saints of Cosmas and Damian.[76] They supported attempts to increase the size and improve the standard of the cathedral choir; after 1482 Lorenzo initiated remembrance services for members of his family in the principal churches of the city. Rather more secular, but equally subtle, was the creation of Cosimo's reputation as 'Pater Patriae'. This was not the work of Cosimo himself, but was launched after his death by Piero and leading Mediceans. Its earliest expression was the tomb marker designed for San Lorenzo by Verrocchio between 1465 and 1467, and bearing the inscription: 'Here lies Cosimo de' Medici, by public decree father of his country'.[77]

Lastly, the Medici appreciated the value of foreign allies. To secure them they used marriage alliances to link them to some of the indisputably noble and princely houses of Italy and Europe. Both Lorenzo and his son Piero married into the Orsini; a further son, Giuliano (1478–1516), acquired the duchy of Nemours through his marriage to Filiberta of Savoy. The Medici were also able to use their wealth as bankers. Francesco Sforza was heavily in debt to the Medici bank and both he and his son proved reliable allies; probably, like other rulers, they found it easier to deal with a 'prince' than with a relatively cumbersome, quarrelsome and public republican government.

The role of the Medici in the area of foreign policy was as influential as it is difficult to define with precision. It is revealed in the mass of diplomatic correspondence to and from Lorenzo[78] More specifically, it can be seen in the alliance established with the Sforza of Milan, which reversed Florence's traditional hostility to the signorial rulers of that city; Galeazzo Maria was prepared to come to the aid of Piero in 1466 and Lorenzo on his succession in 1469. It can also be seen in the way Lorenzo acquired a cardinal's hat for his son Giovanni, who was to prove instrumental in reintroducing the Medici to Florence in 1512; Lorenzo's nephew Giulio, as Clement VII, helped to secure their definitive return in 1530. Less dramatically but equally important, the Medici cardinals and popes created another valuable means of Medici patronage. In 1519 the Florentine Benedetto Buondelmonte wrote from Rome that he was reluctant to leave 'because here is my lord, here is my *patria* and here everything suits me perfectly'.[79]

However these methods of control were not fail-safe. They were tested by such inherent weaknesses in the Medici line as the point of succession. Thus Piero's succession in 1464, after the long 'reign' of Cosimo, precipitated a reaction against manipulation of the constitution and in favour of the return of government to its more traditional forms and home in the *Palazzo della Signoria*; a meeting of four hundred citizens held on 27 May 1466 pledged itself to the cause of free speech and election by lot. Behind such high-sounding statements of principle were other leading families seeking a greater say in the *reggimento*, as well as those aggrieved by Piero's decision to call in debts and offended by his less accessible and affable leadership – Piero was seriously handicapped by gout.

Again, the failure of the legitimate line of succession and the dependence of the Medici cause after 1519 on absent Medici popes and the illegitimate Ippolito and Alessandro weakened the dynasty and its effective hold over the loyalty of other leading houses, some of whom – like the Strozzi and the Salviati – were related to the legitimate Medici line. Lastly, the Medici's success depended very much on the personality and ability of individuals. Cosimo's political and social skills, combined with his successful management of the bank, contributed to his success, but were not equalled by his heirs. Lorenzo's other preoccupations in domestic and foreign policy proved more demanding than his supervision of the bank, and the decline of that institution through mismanagement and competition removed an important asset from the armoury of his influence. His son's brash inexperience did much to alienate the other families on whose co-operation the Medici depended.

This introduces a further key explanation for the difficulties facing the Medici. Studies of the pro-Medici *balia* of 1434 reveal that it had not been 'packed' with Miceceans, while research on the personnel in the *reggimento* before and after the events of 1433–34 suggests continuity rather than radical change, with the presence of large numbers of 'neutral' families in government. Consequently, in maintaining – as in acquiring – power the Medici needed to court the co-operation and acceptance of others. Moreover, not only did the number of Florentines eligible for office rise in the period, but the ideal of participation in public life remained undimmed and Medici attempts to win the hearts and minds of their fellow-citizens and to manipulate the constitution were far from totally successful.

For example, their patronage could cause offence, as when Cosimo's decision to rebuild and refurbish the convent of San Marco after 1438 for the Observant Dominicans led to the displacement of its previous occupants and the eclipse of the generosity of other benefactors. Individuals were not unreservedly loyal. Giovanni Cavalcanti became as disillusioned by the Medici as he had been by the Albizzi. Other families did not stand still or mothball their political ambitions. One such were the Pazzi, an ancient magnate family who were not sufficiently secured by ties of marriage to toe a Medici line. Their accumulation of wealth threatened the Medici, who further alienated their rivals by trying to block inheritance claimed by the Pazzi through a marriage to the Borromeo in 1461. Even the Medici house was not free from internal jealousy. Pierfrancesco de' Medici sympathised with the opposition to his cousin Piero in 1466; his children claimed that the principal line had defrauded them of part of their inheritance and later supported the republican revival of 1494.[80] Furthermore, institutions set up to buttress the regime tended to become progressively less reliable and their membership less compliant. By the end of his life Lorenzo had come to doubt the support of the Council of Seventy.

Lastly, the prominent part played by the Medici in Florentine diplomacy did not guarantee their position at home. Lorenzo's alienation of Sixtus IV led to the switch of the papal account from the Medici to the Pazzi and encouraged the latter in their attempt to eliminate their rivals in 1478. Piero's decision to negotiate with Charles VIII in person, but without a mandate from the commune, and the humiliating terms he accepted involving a tribute and the admission of French garrisons to many of Florence's subject towns precipitated the collapse of his political standing and his exile. The Sack of Rome and the imprisonment of Clement VII encouraged the republican revival of 1527.

The internal and external difficulties challenging the Medici naturally invite an explanation as to the failure of the revived Florentine republic of 1494–1512 and 1527–30.[81] It certainly did not fail due to apathy, if the enthusiasm for republicanism, reform and renewal which followed the fall of Piero and was expressed in the sermons of Savonarola was not long sustained. Such hallmarks of Medicean ascendancy as their coats of arms and the Council of Seventy were destroyed. More positively, both periods are characterised by intense political discussion, prominent in debate being the issue of how far the Venetian constitution was an appropriate model for Florence to follow. The political class was more clearly defined and expressed in a Great Council of all taxpayers aged over twenty-nine who had held or who had been considered eligible for high office, or who were the direct descendants of such citizens. The *Palazzo della Signoria* was renamed the *Palazzo del Popolo* and the hall of the Great Council followed the dimensions of that of the Greater Council of Venice. On 22 September 1502, Piero Soderini was elected head of state for life, with the title of *gonfaloniere* and with the office of the Venetian doge as a model. Moreover, the constitution introduced in 1494 and revived in 1527 was the most broadly based in the republic's history, admitting to the political class around 3,000 citizens (out of a population of around 90,000) and making provision for the regular admission of new members. Lastly, the Florentines could prove tenacious in defending their constitution, most notably during the siege of the city from October 1529 to August 1530.

The broader constitution failed, however, due to internal and external forces. There had been no ruthless purge of Mediceans in 1494 and once again the *reggimento* displayed continuity rather than drastic change. While the Great Council had its champions, patrician families like the Rucellai, with a more exclusive attitude to power, found the extent of participation distasteful and were alarmed by Piero Soderini's failure to favour a narrower regime. Secondly, the reputation of the government was undermined by its reverses and apparent weakness in foreign policy. Conspicuous here was its failure to recapture Pisa, which had seized the opportunity of the French invasion of 1494 to reassert its independence and which defended itself, through a combination of foreign assistance and determination, against spasmodic, ill-considered and underfunded Florentine attack until 8 June 1509. Thereafter, Soderini's commitment to a French alliance and his consequent support of the anti-papal council of Pisa (November 1509) swung Julius II in favour of a Medici restoration with the aid of Spanish troops; the sack of Prato on the outskirts of Florence brought about the fall of the republic on 29 August 1512.

Behind these failures is the fact that Florence no longer had the resources to deal on an equal footing with the great powers of Europe; and the persistent conjunction of foreign difficulties and internal dissension persuaded such Florentines as the historian Francesco Guicciardini to look back to the age of Lorenzo with growing nostalgia. It was the combination of the regime's internal and external weaknesses that resulted in the final return of the Medici, powered by an alliance struck in August 1529 between Charles V and Clement VII and cemented by the marriage of Charles's daughter Margaret to Alessandro de' Medici.

VENICE

The myth of Venice

In 1380, during the War of Chioggia when Venice was besieged by a formidable coalition of Italian and foreign enemies, an anonymous letter was allegedly found in the Venetian camp addressed to the king of Hungary and reproaching him for joining the city's adversaries. The letter was registered by the Venetian chancery as a propaganda document. It celebrated the antiquity and longevity of the city, its long association with freedom, its devotion to Christianity and St Mark, its respect for justice and peace and its military triumphs.[82]

The letter belongs to a long tradition of writings in praise of the republic and creating what historians have called the 'myth of Venice'.[83] This was not the work of Venetians alone, anonymous or otherwise. From an early date foreigners enthused on the nature of its government and the character of its society. Some, of course, were trying to please. In 1451 the Greek scholar

George of Trebizond wrote to his patron Francesco Barbaro that the early Venetians had closely modelled their constitution on the ideal set out in Plato's *Republic*. Others were more disinterested. Florentine statesmen, while often wary of Venetian imperialism in mainland Italy, came to acknowledge Venice's enviable stability and security. Even before the constitutional discussions which followed the expulsion of the Medici in 1494, Venice had presented itself as a model. In 1411 Filippo Corsini pointed out that the respect for the law in Venice had assured its survival; in 1426 the poem attributed to Niccolò Uzzano explained the longevity of Venice by its aristocratic government.[84]

The celebration and discussion of the virtues of Venetian society and the strength of its constitutional arrangements accelerated from the close of the period as Venice emerged as one of the few Italian states to survive foreign invasion, and as the stability of Venetian society appeared to contrast with the upheavals experienced in the rest of sixteenth-century Europe. These themes were embraced by nineteenth- and twentieth-century historians impressed by the related Venetian achievements of prosperity, independence and internal peace. For Molmenti, 'Amid the countless revolutions of Italy, harried, enslaved, torn and spoiled by foreign arms, Venice alone continued to enjoy a glorious and vigorous independence'; while for Horatio Brown – the pioneering British historian of the city – 'Venice was the virgin child of Italy's ruin . . . from invasion she alone escaped, pure and undefiled'.[85]

Of course, the chorus of celebration has been upset by discordant voices and the historian who – even after a lifetime's work on Venetian material – persists in coming to positive conclusions runs the risk of denunciation.[86] The enthusiasm of a Molmenti or a Brown was not shared by Enlightenment historians, who saw Venice as a sinister oligarchy. After his experience attached to the French embassy in Venice in 1743 Rousseau singled out the Council of Ten as 'a tribunal of blood, an object of horror to patricians and people alike'.[87] This is the ruthless, secretive city of Verdi's *I Due Foscari* (1844), based on Byron's verse-drama of the same title, but the darker side of the coin was familiar to contemporaries. Benedetto Molin, a fifteenth-century diarist, signalled the presence in his text of the security magistracy, the Council of Ten, by a marginal illustration in which the Roman numeral ten was represented as a dripping dagger.[88] Pius II rejected the city's reputation for justice by asking contemptuously what fish knew of law, while a sixteenth-century proverb observed that 'Venetian law does not last a week'.

Such jibes would have been readily endorsed by those of the republic's subjects on the mainland for whom Venice was the city of the 'three thousand tyrants'. This was a view shared by Louis XII's minister Claude de Seyssel (1450–1520), who saw in the republic's exclusive nobility a source of disorder and weakness; in 1525 the Florentine Roberto Acciaiuoli could praise Venice for its security and stability while complaining of the arrogance of the nobility.[89] But the republic itself could be made painfully aware of its own weaknesses, and as the diarist Molin suggests, the Venetian nobility itself could experience bouts of self-doubt and self-criticism. After the capture of Padua in 1405 it was discovered that Carlo Zen, hitherto one of the city's military and naval heroes, had been among the nobles in receipt of gifts from the enemy, Francesco Carrara. In 1483 the Ten was informed that the duke of Ferrara was kept well up to date with Venetian plans, thanks to the gossiping of noble senators. In the aftermath of the stunning defeat at Agnadello inflicted on Venice by the allies of the League of Cambrai on 14 May 1509, chroniclers, diarists and the councils of the constitution increasingly agonised as to whether the republic had deserted its ancient virtues, with its nobility scrambling for offices of profit and neglecting the character-building traditions of sea and trade for the debilitating delights of country estates. Further reverses in that war piled on the agony: in 1513 the news of a defeat at La Motta reached the city on 8 October, one of St Mark's feast days and normally the occasion for confident celebration. The segregation of the Jewish community in the ghetto in 1516 was part of an attempt by the republic to placate God's wrath and turn the tide of the war.[90]

Steering a course between myth and anti-myth, the historian encounters a further problem in the source material. The humanist Giovanni Conversini of Ravenna (1343–1408), who had taught in Venice, complained that Venetians were interested in material gain rather than in such cultural activity as the study of history. Another foreign teacher and historian of Venice, the Roman humanist Marcantonio Sabellico (1436–1506), complained that when he tried to talk to his noble pupils about politics he was faced by a wall of silence.[91] Put in a more positive light, such exaggerated observations are related to the aspect of the myth that stressed the unity of the nobility and its loyalty to the state. But for the historian discretion can be frustrating, which may help to explain why so many of the principal themes of Venetian history remain unexplored.

Certainly the Venetian archives do not preserve sources that are as revealing on the nature of political discussion as the *Consulte e Pratiche* of Florence, and the Venetian chronicle tradition includes a remarkable number of anonymous writers and copyists. They portray a society that had experienced greater order and continuity than that of Florence or Genoa, and whose greater confidence – or complacency – might help to explain why contemporary discussions of Venetian government were attempted more often by foreigners than by Venetians. However, Venetian archival and chronicle resources are extensive and well preserved, and in more recent years both have been subjected to an increasing volume of research which reveals that the Venetians and their government were far less complacent and reticent and far more self-critical and outspoken than was once assumed. For example, historians are now beginning to mine the unique source provided by the diaries of Marino Sanudo, which cover the period 1496 to 1533 in fifty-eight volumes. Sanudo failed in his ambitions to attain high office and to be commissioned to write the republic's official history, but his jaundiced, minute and well-informed record has increasingly allowed historians like Finlay to scrutinise the myth of Venice from the inside.[92]

The site of Venice

The explanations most readily offered by contemporary and later historians for the survival and strength of Venice are related to its situation. The lagoons protected the city from attack and obviated the need for city walls. Giangaleazzo Visconti is reported to have observed that to take Venice its lagoons would first have to be drained, while in the sixteenth century the Venetian Senate referred to them as the 'sacred walls of the fatherland'. Modern historians concur with that view, although the defence of the city was not entrusted to nature alone. During the War of Chioggia the posts marking the navigable channels were pulled up; the great dockyard of the *Arsenale* was protected by battlemented walls; in the sixteenth century fortresses on the *lidi* – the narrow islands separating the lagoons from the Adriatic – were updated. But the republic's enemies rarely mustered the land and naval forces necessary to threaten the city's water defences; when they did so during the War of Chioggia, with a coalition centring round the Carrara of Padua and the republic of Genoa, they posed the most serious threat to the republic's existence in the period.

The city's location at the headwaters of the Adriatic and close to the mouths of such vital trade routes as the rivers Adige and Po also made a contribution to its economic prosperity; but modern historians are less prepared to accept the moral dimension some contemporaries attached to their economic observations. As has been mentioned (p. 54 above), some conservatives, like the diarist and merchant Girolamo Priuli (1476–1547), regarded seafaring as character-building as well as profitable, and hence beneficial to the individual as well as to the state. The Venetian noble Gasparo Contarini (1483–1542) made the same point in his account of the constitution when he explained the practice of encouraging young nobles to serve as crossbowmen on the republic's trading galleys.

But the debate between the respective values of sea and land ran throughout the period. In the aftermath of the traumatic War of Chioggia, Chancellor Raffaino Caresini urged Venice to 'cultivate the sea and shun the land, for honours and riches abound with the former while the latter is the source of scandal and error.' In the early sixteenth century Andrea Mocenigo regretted the change in policy which he saw as following on the death of his ancestor the doge Tommaso Mocenigo in 1423: the republic had become increasingly embroiled in mainland wars which had distracted her from the true source of her greatness, the sea. The same point could be made by the republic's enemies. In the aftermath of Cambrai Jean Lemaire a spokesman for Louis XII, claimed that the twelfth-century mystic Joachim of Fiore had foretold that the Lion of St Mark would suffer if the sea was deserted in favour of the land; Machiavelli was to argue a variant of the same theme: that while the Venetians had fought their own battles at sea the republic had prospered, but its dependence on *condottieri* for the defence of its landward interests spelled disaster.[93]

Although modern historians prefer to discuss the issues of sea and land in terms of security and economic interest, the more moralistic stance adopted by contemporaries underlines the importance of the debate as well as its social and political dimensions. The republic's relative detachment from Italian politics before the fifteenth century had sheltered her from the full force of such sources of discord as the Guelf–Ghibelline vendetta. The acquisition of a mainland empire increased the demands placed on the republic's government, while introducing a subject for inexhaustible debate. Moreover, as individuals Venetians became more exposed to influence and lobbying from the mainland. The disgrace attending the latter years of Francesco Foscari (1373–1457) was in part due to the fact that both his son, Jacopo, and his son-in-law, Andrea Donà, had received presents from Francesco Sforza. Less treasonable but probably more common was the acceptance of gifts from subject communities pressing a case in Venice; in 1461 the commune of Verona was alarmed to hear that a number of *contado* communities had presented a Venetian noble with a large consignment of wheat as part of their campaign to reduce their tax burden. In the attempt to counter such pressures the republic forbade its doge to receive gifts from the *terraferma*, reminded its local representatives of the need for probity and repeatedly tried to limit the size of the embassies sent by its subject cities to the capital. Another source of anxiety – and one close to the concerns of Priuli – was the fact that expectations of public office increased with the frontiers of the mainland empire, and encouraged competition within the nobility.

Lastly, in their considerations of the remarkable site of Venice contemporaries could recognise the significance of its 'environment' for the day-to-day life of the city. In the description of Venice which the Welshman William Thomas included in his *History of Italy*, published in 1549, stress is laid on the importance of gathering fresh water supplies in cisterns, as well as on the heavy expenditure regularly required to keep the all-important lagoons from silting up. From earlier in the Middle Ages magistracies had been established to preserve the navigation channels in and around the city, as well as to protect the *lidi* which sheltered the lagoons from the Adriatic; in 1415 and 1439 steps were taken to gather together and preserve in one archive all measures concerned with the lagoons, the *lidi*, the channels of navigation and the city's anchorages. Greater recognition is now being given to the 'environmental legislation' of medieval Italian and European cities, but historians like Pavan are right to emphasise the man-made and artificial quality of Venice. The intense and constant effort needed to maintain the precarious fabric of the city and its site probably contributed towards a precocious acceptance of public authority, as well as a heightened sense of identity and common interest among the Venetians themselves.[94]

The constitution

The magistracies responsible for the environment were aspects of a constitution which in turn has been accorded a central role in the explanation of the republic's continuity and stability. Although evolved over centuries and never formally defined, from the late fourteenth century the constitution became increasingly the subject of description and analysis. Non-Venetians like Pier Paolo Vergerio, writing around 1400, and Venetians like Gasparo Contarini, writing between 1523 and 1531, claimed to see in it a balance between those forms of government preferred by political thinkers from antiquity: democracy, aristocracy and monarchy.[95] Democracy was not taken to mean the representation of the people as a whole in government; the popular assembly, or *Arengo*, had long been defunct before it was formally abolished in 1423, while the ceremonial attending the election of the doge was designed to dispel any impression that he had been popularly elected. The democratic element in the constitution was provided by the Venetian nobility, a hereditary aristocracy whose membership had been largely determined around 1300 and to which thirty new families were added in 1381 as a reward for their services in the War of Chioggia. Although a largely honorific nobility could be bestowed on friendly foreign princes and reliable *condottieri*, the rare proposals made to recruit new members on a more regular basis were turned down; the suggestion made in 1403 that when a noble house had died out it be replaced by a suitable citizen family was rejected. Nevertheless the size of the Venetian nobility grew steadily, from around one thousand five hundred in the mid-fourteenth century to over two thousand five hundred in 1500, when the total population of the city was probably around one hundred thousand. Its voice in the government was the Greater Council, the *Maggior Consiglio*, which all Venetian noblemen over twenty-five – and a few under that age – could attend by right of birth.

Sovereignty rested with the Greater Council, which could express that authority in debate and in election to the higher offices of state, but for practical purposes government was directed by much smaller bodies. Central was the *Consilium Rogatorum*, increasingly called the Senate by humanist writers, which had an original membership of sixty but whose size increased with additional and *ex officio* members to around three hundred. In turn much of its initiative had passed to its executive members, collectively called the *Collegio*, while throughout the period the Senate, like the *Maggior Consiglio* and other bodies, lost ground to the Council of Ten. That had been established in the early fourteenth century to protect the state from subversion, but – in a manner not unknown to other small, secretive security agencies – the Ten enlarged its competence into such important areas as defence and expenditure.

These smaller councils suited the aristocratic tendency within the constitution if membership was intended to be of short duration, with senators holding office for only one year at a time. The monarchical element was provided by the office of the doge. He was head of state and was often described as a prince in contemporary accounts. But during the period his powers, which had already been closely defined, were increasingly circumscribed. His salary was little more than an honorarium. He was no longer accorded the privilege of burial in his own chapel of San Marco, while from 1400 he was to be addressed by his fellow nobles as informally as '*messer lo doge*'. On the other hand, and as will be discussed below, the office was potentially influential and surrounded with ceremonial. The doge presided over all the councils of the constitution, and as one of the few life appointments provided an element of continuity in the conduct of government. It is hardly surprising, therefore, that the position was much sought after by ambitious leading families, and elaborate electoral procedures had to be evolved in the hope of preventing the choice of doge from becoming the cause and effect of faction.[96]

However, the apparent neatness with which democratic, aristocratic and monarchical elements can be identified within the constitution should not lead to an uncritical acceptance of a descriptive scheme applied relatively late in its history. The Venetian nobility was not formally segregated into categories. Authority was not distributed equally between the participating parts of the mixed constitution, nor was there any clear or consistent separation of powers between the various councils and magistracies. Moreover, while in theory there was equality within the nobility, most contemporary observers recognised that the aristocractic element predominated. Priuli argued that 'those who wish to preserve and maintain a good republic must above all preserve and maintain equality', and the principle was rehearsed during discussions in 1506 on electoral procedures that 'it has always been a characteristic of our state to promote equality, especially in the affairs of the Greater Council'; but behind both statements lay the recognition that an elite prevailed, not only through the greater role taken by the smaller councils but in political and social terms. As with Florence, an undefined inner group, the *primi della terra*, numbering between one and two hundred nobles, held a central position achieved through a variable formula based on family size, wealth, experience and political and military achievements. This predominance was expressed in repeated election to the Senate, the *Collegio* and the Ten as well as to sensitive embassies, the more important governorships within the empire and military and naval postings.

But the ruling elite was not defined and the constitution itself was not immutable. The growing role of the Ten was disputed by the councils and magistracies it threatened, while the power of the doge – like that of a pope or a prince – depended a great deal on the age, personality and ability of the individual. Francesco Foscari was in office for thirty-four years (1423–57) and appears to have had a considerable influence, especially in foreign policy – if the exact nature of his authority remains to be explored. Down to the election of Agostino Barbarigo in 1486, however, Foscari's successors held office for only a few years. Most of the doges appear to have been attentive to matters of ceremonial, but this characteristic could be more marked in some cases than in others. To commemorate his achievements Foscari began the celebrated 'Porta della Carta', the sumptuous Gothic entrance to the ducal palace. In 1485 Marco Barbarigo began the 'Scala dei Giganti', the ceremonial stairway leading from the inner courtyard of the palace to the state apartments and serving as the place of coronation; indeed, Marco introduced a new and more splendid coronation ceremony. These initiatives were followed by his brother Agostino (1486–1501), who ensured that the staircase celebrated the greatness of the Barbarigo dynasty as well as the triumphs and virtues of Venice. Marino Sanudo hailed this second Barbarigo in imperial terms and his capacity for hard work was acknowledged; but Agostino's practice of making visitors kneel and kiss his hand alarmed members of the Greater Council, which after his death appointed inquisitors to examine his actions and took steps to strengthen the controls on ducal power and modify the coronation and funeral services to check the growing princely appearance of the office.[97]

If the description of the constitution as 'mixed' has to be treated with care, the same applies to its corollary: that the mixed constitution contributed to the relative stability and peace of Venice. Not only were such issues as the role of the Ten and the authority of the doge recurrent matters of dispute, but the spirit of the constitution itself was under siege. The vetting procedures for admitting members of the nobility were difficult to enforce and probably abused, at least until the more thorough collection of records on the births and marriages of noble families; the Golden Books which permitted a closer monitoring of the nobility were begun only towards the end of the period with the registration of births from 1506 and marriages from 1526. The state was forced to violate its own rules by selling underage entrance to the *Maggior Consiglio* and the Senate to raise money in the aftermath of the War of Cambrai. From at least 1396 legislation had to be repeatedly and increasingly introduced to check the malpractices of *broglio*, a term applied to the soliciting of votes and the promising of favours. Queller has found ample evidence of the 'civic irresponsibility' of the Venetian nobility: for example in frantic attempts to avoid election to onerous and expensive foreign postings by expedients ranging from proposing others to feigning ill-health and absence from the city.[98] Poorer members of the nobility earned the nick-name of the 'Swiss' because of their readiness to sell their votes; to secure his election as doge Francesco Foscari spent over 30,000 ducats to provide dowries for the daughters of poor nobles. In 1492 two nobles were exiled for proposing that 70,000 ducats be made available each year to subsidise poorer members of the nobility; the Council of Ten considered that this would encourage clientage and the return home of as many as eight hundred nobles from the Venetian colony of Crete. Lastly, minute regulations failed to prevent fraud during ballots and the corruption of balloteers.

None the less, for all its imperfections and internal adjustments, the constitution did help to give continuity to the republic's government, and for this the explanation offered by such contemporaries as Vergerio and Contarini is not without some validity. The office of the doge was too circumscribed to present a serious challenge to the constitution, and the nobleman Bernardo Bembo (1433–1519) endorsed the observation of Aquinas that 'all the princes of Italy are tyrants except the doge of Venice'. Yet it was not a cipher. Contested between the leading families of the city and often held by men of considerable experience and ability, the office helped to give continuity to the business of government and was surrounded with sufficient ceremonial to make its holder a credible head of state, who certainly impressed foreign ambassadors and visitors.

An inner aristocracy might have had a lion's share of power and influence, but its ascendancy was not defined and high office could still be attained by relative outsiders. Andrea Gritti (1455–1538), who became doge in 1523, was seen by Sanudo and others as representing traditional Venetian values and devoting himself to the service of the state, but he did not come to prominence via a *cursus honorum*.[99] Much of his early life was spent as a merchant, largely overseas, and his political career was rather abruptly launched with a series of military, naval and diplomatic posts during the War of Cambrai. Moreover, as Gritti's early life suggests, the appetite for public office among the nobility should not be exaggerated. If, in around 1500, two thousand five hundred nobles were eligible to attend the *Maggior Consiglio*, the nobles present rarely reached one thousand seven hundred; in 1509 Priuli – for all his interest in political affairs – boasted of his own indifference to a public career.

If not all nobles were anxious to exercise their constitutional rights to the full, broader participation in government was afforded by the circulation of office and more basically by the fact that in theory all members of the nobility were equal; there was no hierarchy in the seating plan of the *Maggior Consiglio*. That body may have had little control of the day-to-day functions of government, but it did not follow the decline of the *Arengo*. The Council retained legislative, judicial and electoral powers and its members must have had rather more than the illusion of being close to the centre of power, while enjoying the prestige and security of belonging – as of right – to the sovereign institution of the constitution. Moreover, as Finlay and others have argued, the loopholes found in the constitution may have made a positive contribution to stability – possibly by making the ranks of the nobility not quite as tightly closed as is often thought; more probably by preserving the involvement of the rank-and-file nobility, if rarely in the inner councils and higher offices of state, then certainly in the *Maggior Consiglio* and through the practice of *broglio*.

The checks and balances which operated both because of and in spite of the constitution might also help to explain why faction did not prove as damaging in Venice as it did elsewhere, ballots – whether properly conducted or rigged – reducing the occasions for bloodshed. Divisions did of course exist over policies and appointments; they could also exist along apparently party lines, most obviously between younger and older members of the nobility. Contarini stressed the need to encourage and satisfy the young by giving them access to appropriate offices, but by appropriate he did not mean important. In fact, Finlay has described the government of the city as a gerontocracy and has calculated that between 1400 and 1500 the average age of the doges on election was sixty-nine; Francesco Foscari caused controversy from the start by securing office at forty-nine.[100] Entry to the Senate could be achieved at thirty-two and to the Ten at forty, but in practice the majority of the members of these councils were aged fifty. In Venice age was conventionally associated with wisdom and hence with the better government of the city, but it was not understood in these terms by those lacking years and rank and confined to the *Maggior Consiglio* and offices of lesser importance. In 1500 a disgraced naval commander, Antonio Grimani, hoped for trial among the elders of the Senate rather than before the 'youngsters' of the Greater Council, and when the War of Cambrai forced the republic to sell underage entry to both the *Maggior Consiglio* and the Senate, conservatives saw this as opening the floodgates to corruption and constitutional malpractice. But present research suggests that the quarrels between young and old did not take on an ideological dimension or polarise consistently around different policies and attitudes.

Governors and governed

One of the more prominent aspects of the myth of Venice to emerge was the stress placed on the theme of harmony, not only within the nobility but in society as a whole. For Sanudo,

This holy republic is governed with such order that it is a marvellous thing. She has neither popular sedition nor discord among her patricians, but all unite in promoting her greatness; and therefore, as wise men say, she will last for ever.

As regards the nobility, discord and jealousy were not eliminated. This is suggested by the fact that Venetian noble families, far from suppressing their individuality to achieve the 'singular unity' which so inspired Ruskin and his contemporaries, in fact projected and celebrated themselves through chronicles, palaces, funerary monuments and portraits. Moreover, rivalries could occasionally explode into violence, as when Andrea Contarini attempted to assassinate Francesco Foscari in 1426. Nevertheless it is true that faction never spilled over into the armed confrontation and street-fighting that drew in other sections of the population in Genoa or Florence.

As regards Venetian society as a whole, the archives of the councils of the constitution and of the magistracies responsible for law and order leave a record that is far from harmonious. In a large city, which was difficult to patrol and seal off, disorderly conduct was conspicuous, especially at night and often in the vicinity of brothels, bathhouses and inns.[101] Nobles as well as commoners were involved, but the problems of law and order were heightened by the fact that the city contained a cosmopolitan and mobile population. For example, in 1516 the Council of Ten was fearful lest the news of military reverses on the mainland might inflame a population swollen with refugees, many of whom were armed. During attacks of plague, when many of the wealthier inhabitants had fled, the authorities were anxious lest unguarded property might be looted. The measures taken and the officials appointed were unsuccessful in radically reducing the level of violence. The records of one of the principal police magistracies, the *Signori di Notte*, show the difficulties encountered in controlling violence and vandalism, while efforts to limit the disorder associated with prostitution by confining the activity to specified areas – like the *Castelletto* near the Rialto – were of little effect. More generally, the practice of public punishment reveals the difficulty of apprehending offenders as well as the republic's intention to set examples.

But while violence was prevalent, it appears to have been neither organised nor insurrectionist in character; the majority of the threats to the state investigated by the Council of Ten came from beyond the republic's frontiers or from its subject territories. The well-informed Vicentine diarist Luigi da Porto (1485–1529) recorded that following the defeat of Agnadello criticism of the nobility was voiced from within the city, but the numbers involved were small, and if rumours of unrest inspired Maximilian to encourage rebellion, the emperor's call was unheard.

The need felt by historians to explain the relative peace of Venice has not been sufficient to shift the direction of research away from the nobility itself – although as has just been suggested, the conduct of the nobility had implications for the rest of society. Indeed, it has recently been argued that the nobility's awareness of its responsibilities in this respect led them to encourage and participate in civic ritual; generally in the form of annual or extraordinary processions designed to stress the unity of the city and the divine favour within the grasp of its inhabitants. For example, St Vitus's Day on 15 June was celebrated annually to commemorate the defeat of a revolt led by two nobles, Marco Querini and Baiamonte Tiepolo, in 1310. The doge led a procession of officials, the clergy and the more important confraternities from S. Marco across the Rialto bridge to the church of S. Vito, where twelve large candles were presented in thanksgiving. But if the purpose of such ceremonies is relatively clear, and if they certainly made an impression on foreigners, their impact in terms of popular attitude and behaviour is harder to pin down.

Possibly making a greater contribution to the social peace of the city was the fact that the nobility, though 'closed', was not aloof. Marriage continued between noble and citizen families; the nobility did not withdraw from the rest of the population to its own districts, as happened increasingly in fifteenth-century Florence. Noble palaces remained scattered, and although they might dominate a parish and its *campo*, they were not detached from its society. The same point can be made for the nobility as a whole, containing as it did many gradations of economic and political fortune and hence liable to be much closer in experience and living conditions to the people than its legal status would suggest.

The barriers raised round the nobility by their hereditary and privileged status were weakened in other respects. Between them and the mass of the population there were the privileged *cittadini*, or citizens, whose ranks were not as closed as those of the nobility.[102] As elsewhere in Italy, citizen status could be acquired through attested residence in the city over a variable number of years as a law-abiding taxpayer. The award brought with it certain commercial privileges and the right to be treated in law as a Venetian rather than as a foreigner. The status also opened the possibility of public office in Venice and its dominions, while for 'original citizens' – those whose families had enjoyed citizen status over three generations and whose numbers roughly equalled those of the nobility – the state reserved some diplomatic postings and secretarial appointments attached to the more important offices and councils of the constitution and grouped under the chancery.

Such privileges have long been identified as making a positive contribution to the easing of tensions. In the aftermath of Agnadello the noble Antonio Loredan addressed a gathering of citizens in the Greater Council Hall, making the point that they had access to public office for life, whereas nobles could expect only short-term appointments, and that they provided an element of continuity in the conduct of government and the administration of justice. Contarini also argued that the privileged employment of *cittadini originarii* made a contribution to the stability as well as the good government of the republic, and later historians have tended to endorse the view. Its credibility is enhanced by the fact that citizens were also given a monopoly of office in the *Scuole Grandi*, the five largest, wealthiest and most prestigious confraternities in the city.[103]

If in the *Scuole Grandi* some of the divisions of Venetian society were muted if not removed, the same can be said of the much more numerous *Scuole Piccoli* – numbering over one hundred in the late fifteenth century – to which both nobles and commoners belonged. Moreover, both types of confraternity had a charitable as well as a more purely devotional function. Although the beneficiaries of their good works tended to be their own members, the confraternities did go some way towards alleviating poverty and distress: from the construction of subsidised housing to the management of small hospitals; from the payment of dowries to the provision of pensions for the war wounded. Of course there was nothing uniquely Venetian about devotional and charitable confraternities, and as has been suggested elsewhere, the state itself was acutely aware of the dangers presented by hunger and disease.

A more distinctive and perhaps more subtle role can be seen in the office of the procurators of S. Marco.[104] Appointed for life from the ranks of the nobility, these officials had the honour of supervising the upkeep and embellishment of the saint's shrine; they also acted as the saint's trustees in respect of the gifts granted him by the faithful. On to these original functions were grafted the role of acting as public trustees for Venetians anxious that their bequests to charities, institutions and individuals be properly administered. Although from 1516 the office of procurator began to be sold, it long carried great prestige and responsibility and was often regarded as a final stepping stone to the position of doge. The procurators have been described by Mueller as the 'executors and trustees of the commune's wealthier class', but it would be wrong to think of them as serving an elite of the wealthiest; their services were in increasing demand throughout the period, and both the number of procurators and the number of their citizen secretaries rose. Certainly their role in Venetian society was subtle and pervasive and rightly characterised as 'the best single expression of the identity of public and private interests' in Venice. For these reasons the office should also be seen as contributing to the

271

stability of society by linking the interests of individuals, families and institutions to the well-being of the state, and the good offices of its patron saint.

A final reason for the relative stability of Venice may initially appear more negative – the absence of industries employing large numbers of unskilled workers.[105] It is true that the *Arsenale* was probably one of the largest concentrations of workers in pre-industrial Europe, and that the *arsenalotti* could protest at their conditions of service. But within the walls of the *Arsenale* the workforce was distributed between clearly demarcated and specialised guilds and tended to be both privileged and peaceful; providing a bodyguard for the doge, the *arsenalotti* were probably seen as supporters of the state rather than as potential rebels. The other major employer was the fleet. Here again, oarsmen or *galliotti* can be found protesting against conditions of service and arrears of pay, and they were not allowed to form their own guild; but grievances do not seem to have coalesced into revolt and a threat to the state, probably because the nature of their employment prevented the *galliotti* from organising themselves and because an increasing number of oarsmen were recruited abroad.

Otherwise, for all the vigour of the economy, there were no large concentrations of unskilled workers in the city. Manufacture and retailing were carried out from small shops, or *botteghe*, and were subdivided among a large number of specialised guilds. This subdivision – together with the fact that the guilds were denied any role in government, while their statutes were approved and supervised by noble magistrates – might suggest that the Venetian nobility intended to both divide and rule the workforce – a hypothesis encouraged by the fact that so much of the city's commercial and financial activity was concentrated in relatively few noble hands. However, Mackenney has argued that their very exclusion from political power and lack of direct participation in major commercial and financial enterprises may have removed some of the grounds for social and economic tension from within the guilds themselves, with less of a gulf between masters and artisans and an avenue of appeal beyond the guild to the relatively disinterested city magistracies. And the fact that the majority of its workforce enjoyed the status and protection conferred by guild membership, as well as membership of related confraternities, spared the city from the threat posed by a large, unprotected and resentful proletariat.

To reach such conclusions, supportive of at least some of the elements of the Venetian myth, may seem an anticlimax, but it does help to explain why the republic – for all its enemies and critics – was unique among Italian states in that it came to be regarded as an exemplar. It also explains why Pullan has warned of the difficulties encountered in explaining the relative continuity and stability of the city in a period of turmoil: 'the motives of the silent are sometimes harder to discern than those of the vociferous are to disentangle.' Admirers of Venice have not always been as circumspect, and when human explanations have been sought for the republic's success they have tended to focus on the wisdom and character of the nobility. For Petrarch, Venice was rich with gold, but richer still in reputation; strong in her wealth yet stronger in her virtue; built on marble, yet more firmly based on civil concord; surrounded by the salt sea, but made safer by her saltier counsels.

At the end of the nineteenth century Molmenti argued from what he considered was a striking contemporary parallel: 'The Venetian aristocracy resembles the British aristocracy of today in its principle of hereditary statesmen who hand down the art, the secret, the tradition of government from father to son.'

Such explanations or characterisations are no longer regarded as acceptable. Not only was the Venetian nobility a minority of the population; in view of the differences in wealth and status and the evidence of faction and self-interest within its ranks, it is difficult to credit it with a collective character, let alone a collective wisdom. On the other hand, the nobility was an influential part of society and could be aware of a responsibility to lead by example, as well as of a need to earn the confidence of its subjects. In 1435 the *Maggior Consiglio* reminded itself that 'the principal foundation of our city and its singular ornament is justice, both at its heart and in its subject lands', but the exhortatory tone of such statements suggests that members of the nobility did not always share the confidence in their virtues proclaimed by their admirers. Although research has a long way to go in exploring Venetian society as a whole – let alone the nobility in particular – it would probably be reasonable to conclude with a hypothesis suggested above. The stability and continuity experienced by Venice derived from a sense of community and an acceptance of public authority, which came from the city's unique and precarious situation and was shared in but not monopolised by the nobility. Petrarch's explanations for the greatness of Venice should be reversed.

CONCLUSION

To treat the various states of the kingdom of Italy separately underlines distinctions noted by contemporaries and often expressed by them in the vivid if crude language of prejudice and *campanilismo*. In 1403 Carlo Malatesta Lord of Rimini announced his intention of protecting Pisa from that 'pigeon-colony of peasants', Florence. In 1413 Paolo Guinigi Lord of Lucca was told of his brother Giovanni's impression of the republican government of Siena, which was 'governed by a hundred tyrants – stocking-makers, locksmiths and other low types – who behave like pigs, so that when one shouts the rest come running.' Filippo Maria Visconti expressed his view of republican regimes:

that it is better to obey a prince or king, whatever his disposition, than submit to being governed by a rabble of artisans or by rulers of whom we cannot even tell who their fathers were.

Differences could also be expressed in more measured tones, as in the propaganda war between republican Florence and signorial Milan. When in 1397

Antonio Loschi denied the republic's pretended Roman origins and accused the Florentines of destroying the peace and well-being of Italy while visiting tyranny on their neighbours, Carlo Rinuccini answered that the Florentines were the true heirs of republican Rome and the champions of liberty, as well as arguing for the superiority of republican to monarchical forms of government.[106]

But such rhetoric could be seen through. If the Milanese humanist Andrea Biglia (1395–1435) thought it fitting to express Francesco Foscari's enthusiasm for a pro-Florentine, anti-Visconti alliance in 1425 in terms of a belief in republican liberty, Flavio Biondo – for all his Venetian sympathies – was more down to earth, representing Venice as reluctantly engaging in hostilities for reasons of security and self-interest.[107] Moreover, in general the history of Italian diplomacy is not one of confrontation between rival political systems, and the differences in government between states could be expressed in less emotive and more pragmatic terms. In 1391 Florentine ambassadors assured the lord of Pisa that the city intended to preserve its republican constitution and that the eminence of one citizen, Rinaldo Gianfigliazzi, would not develop into tyranny. The correspondence between the Sforza and Lorenzo de' Medici reveals an awareness of the delicate nature of the latter's ascendancy. In 1486 Lodovico Maria Sforza quizzed the Venetian ambassador about the nature of faction within the nobility, and the news of his interest alarmed the republic.

As mentioned, the distinctions between the states of the kingdom of Italy could be expressed in terms of liberty. Liberty was understood in two senses. With reference to the internal workings of a state, it referred to the right to participate in government; in the context of external relations, liberty meant freedom from foreign interference. In the first sense the concept did have real meaning, although participation in the government of the surviving northern republics was restricted, while the *signori* and princes did not rule as aloof dictators. In May 1413 the Florentine patrician Filippo Corsini argued that 'everyone should speak truly and honestly, even in disagreement . . . . We live in a free city and that which, among other things, promotes liberty is freedom of speech in the councils'; but Corsini was addressing fellow-members of the *reggimento* whose attitude towards broader participation is perhaps suggested by Francesco Bruni's proposal of 1384 that Florence should destabilise the more popular government of Siena: 'it is both necessary and desirable to restore the Sienese government into the hands of worthy men lest the idiots who now rule bring the whole country to ruin.'

In its second sense liberty had an even greater relevance because it could be understood in terms of autonomy by subject cities, while – at the other end of the spectrum – for Venice liberty meant independence. But if liberty in this second sense did have wider implications, the commodity itself was in diminishing supply. For all their differences in policy and constitutional arrangements, the internal affairs of the northern states were much influenced by external events, and in the course of the period that influence increased to the point of pressure and even conquest. The number of states diminished.

Of those that survived, the smaller and less economically powerful became more dependent on foreign alliances and protection. Finally, with northern and Spanish intervention, even the larger states began to succumb to foreign ascendancy or rule.

A telling example is provided by the Pio lords of Carpi in the Modenese. In the fifteenth century much of their energy was devoted to preserving their *signoria* from their immediate overlords, the Este of Modena, but in 1500 Ercole d'Este managed to secure half the lordship. To establish his hold on the entire Pio inheritance, Alberto III embarked on an international career as a courtier, diplomat and *condottiere*; but in gambling on the fortunes of the Empire and France, Alberto became a pawn rather than a force in European diplomacy and failed to prevent the Este from securing the investiture of the entire lordship from Charles V in 1527.[108]

A similar progressive shift in the balance of power can be seen in Tuscany, where Florence oscillated between policies of expansion and alliance in respect of her neighbours. Fully alive to the dangers, the republics of Siena and Lucca were ready to welcome foreign allies, and their instinct for self-preservation kept alive the imperial claim to overlordship – as is shown by Siena's enthusiastic reception of Sigismund in the winter of 1432–33. While the Empire remained relatively weak and preoccupied elsewhere, its intervention was little more than an occasional embarrassment for Florence; in 1403 its *Signoria* observed sourly that 'the policies of the Pisans are so variable that they change regimes whenever the emperor comes, and there is no stability to their government.' But when the Empire was in Habsburg hands the situation was transformed. Lucca, Siena and the rebel city of Pisa courted the support of Maximilian, and when Florence was besieged by an imperial army in 1529–30 the city found itself not only in rebellion but in a position of considerable weakness. On its surrender in August 1530 Charles V promised to respect its liberties, but the Medici were installed with his support.[109]

Florence had in fact acknowledged imperial overlordship on several occasions in the period. By contrast, the Venetian republic stated in 1381 that

> by the grace of God, our lordship and commune of Venice from the very beginning has never been a tributary to any king, prince, lord or commune in the world. That is how things stand now, and that is how they will remain in the future.[110]

Though forced to recognise imperial overlordship for her dominions in Italy and to pay tribute to the Ottoman Turks for her eastern possessions, for the city itself and its *dogado* that statement remained true until 1797.

NOTES AND REFERENCES

1. P. Paschini, 'Da medico a patriarca di Aquileia', *Memorie Storiche Forogiuliesi*, vol. xxiii (1927).

2. A. Tallone, 'Gli ultimi marchesi di Saluzzo', *Studi Saluzzesi*, vol. x (1901).

3. J. E. Law, 'Verona and the Venetian state in the fifteenth century', *Bulletin of the Inst. of Hist. Research*, vol. lii (1979).

4. The bibliography tends to concentrate on the diplomatic, political and dynastic histories of these states: F. Saraceno, 'Due anni di governo di Lodovico duca di Savoia', *Curiosità e Ricerche di Storia Subalpina*, vol. ii (1876); F. Gabotto, *Lo Stato Sabaudo da Amedeo VIII a Emmanuele Filiberto*, 3 vols (Turin, 1892–95); M. C. Daviso di Charvensod, *La Duchessa Iolanda* (Turin, 1935); G. Tabacco, *Lo Stato Sabaudo nel Sacro Romano Imperio* (Turin, 1939); Marie-José, *La Maison de Savoie, Amédée VIII*, 2 vols (Paris, 1962); F. Cognasso, *I Savoia* (Varese, 1981). Table 6.

5. M. C. Daviso di Charvensod, 'Considerazioni intorno ai Tre Stati in Piemonte', *Boll. Stor-Bib. Sub.*, vol. xlv (1947).

6. A. Bozzola, 'Appunti sulla vita economica . . . del Monferrato', *Boll. Stor.-Bib. Sub.*, vol. xxv (1923).

7. E. Bollati, 'La ribellione di Filippo senza Terra', *Misc. di Storia Italiana*, vol. xvi (1877); M. C. Daviso di Charvensod, 'La ribellione di Filippo senza Terra', *R.S.I.*, ser. iv, vol. vi (1935).

8. A. Bozzola, *Parlamenti del Monferrato* (Bologna, 1926); A. Tallone, *Parlamenti Sabaudi* (Bologna, 1928); A. Marongiu, *Medieval Parliaments* (London, 1968); H. G. Koenigsberger, 'The parliament of Piedmont during the Renaissance', in *Estates and Revolutions* (Ithaca, 1971).

9. For bibliography and background, as well as for useful material on the period: G. M. Tabarelli and F. Conti, *Castelli del Trentino* (Paderno Dugnano, 1974); M. Knapton, 'Per la storia del dominio veneziano nel Trentino', *Civis*, vol. viii (1984).

10. G. Papaleoni, 'Commune e feudatarii nel Trentino', *Atti dell 'Accad. di Rovereto*, ser. iii, vol. ii (1896).

11. *Dizionario Biografico degli Italiani*.

12. Fonti e Studi per la Storia della Venezia Giulia, ser. i, fonti iii, *Le Istituzioni di un Comune Medievale: Statuti di Muggia del sec. xiv* (Trieste, 1972).

13. L. Simeoni, *Le Signorie*, vol. ii (Milan, 1950).

14. One of the greatest contributions to the study of Friuli was made by P. S. Leicht; some of his most important articles were republished in *Studi di Storia Friuliana* (Udine, 1955). Also of value is P. Paschini, *Storia del Friuli*, 3rd edn (Udine, 1975).

15. P. S. Leicht, 'Il parlamento della Patria del Friuli', *Atti dell'Accademia di Udine*, ser. iii, vols x–xi (1903–04); 'Il parlamento Friuliano nel primo secolo della dominazione veneziana', *Rivista di Stor. del Diritto It.*, vol. xxi (1948); Marongiu, op. cit.; H. G. Koenigsberger, 'The Italian parliaments', *Journal of It. Hist.*, vol. i (1978).

16. G. Dolfin, *Cronaca Veneta*, Biblioteca Nazionale della Marciana, It. VII, 794 (8503), ff. 313v–314r; V. Marchesi, *L'Imperatore Sigismondo a Udine negli anni 1412 e 1413* (Udine, 1884); G. Cogo, 'La sottomissione del Friuli al dominio della repubblica veneta', *Atti dell'Accad. di Udine*, ser. ii, vol. iii (1896); F. Seneca, 'Alcuni appunti sulla situazione adriatica all'inizio del secolo xv', *Archivio Stor. Pugliese*, vol. vi (1953).

17. A. Ventura, *Nobilità e Popolo nella Società Veneta* (Bari, 1964), pp. 187–214.

18. P. S. Leicht, 'I confini della Venezia nella storia del diritto italiano', *Scritti Vari* (Milan, 1943).

19. Leicht, *Studi*, p. 35.
20. N. Valeri, 'Gli studi viscontei-sforzeschi fino alla crisi della libertà nell'ultimo ventennio', *A.S.I.*, vol. xciii (1935); Fondazione Treccani degli Alfieri, *Storia di Milano*, vol. vii (Milan, 1956); F. Cognasso, *I Visconti* (Varese, 1966).
21. D. M. Bueno de Mesquita, *Giangaleazzo Visconti* (Cambridge, 1941). Table 7.
22. C. Santoro, *Gli Sforza* (Varese, 1977).
23. N. Rubinstein, 'Florence and the despots', *T.R.H.S.*, ser. v, vol. ii (1952); D. M. Bueno de Mesquita, 'The place of despotism in Italian politics', in J. R. Hale *et al.* (eds), *Europe in the Late Middle Ages* (London, 1970); P. J. Jones, 'Communes and despots', *T.R.H.S.*, ser. v, vol. xv (1965); H. Baron, *The Crisis of the Early Italian Renaissance*, revised edn (Princeton, 1966); G. Brucker, 'Humanism, politics and the social order', in S. Bertelli *et al.* (eds), *Florence and Venice*, vol. i (Florence, 1979).
24. E. de Marco, 'Crepuscolo degli Scaligeri', *A.V.*, ser. v, vols xxii and xxiv (1938, 1939).
25. N. Valeri, 'L'insegnamento di Giangaleazzo, ed i consigli al principe di Carlo Malatesta', *Boll. Stor-Bib. Sub.*, vol. xxxvi (1934); D. Orano, *Francesco Sforza: 'I suggerimenti di buon vivere'* (Rome, n.d.).
26. V. Ilardi, 'The assassination of Galeazzo Maria Sforza', in *Violence and Civil Disorder in Italian Cities*, ed. L. Martines (Berkeley–Los Angeles–London, 1972).
27. On the self-doubt of Lodovico Maria Sforza, P. Ghinzoni, 'Don Celso Maffei di Verona e Lodovico il Moro', *A.S.L.*, ser. i, vol. vi (1879); D. M. Bueno de Mesquita, 'The conscience of the prince', *Proc. Brit. Acad.*, vol. lxv (1979).
28. G. Romano, 'Un giudizio di A. Biglia sulla funzione storica dei Visconti', *Boll. Stor. Pavese*, vol. xv (1915).
29. T. Kren (ed.), *Renaissance Painting in Manuscripts* (New York, 1983), pp. 107–12.
30. P. Ghinzoni, 'Statua equestre in bronzo di Francesco Sforza', *A.S.L.*, ser. i, vol. v (1878); H. W. Janson, 'The equestrian monument from Cangrande della Scala', in *Aspects of the Renaissance*, ed. A. R. Lewis (Austin and London, 1967).
31. F. Ercole, 'Comuni e signori nel Veneto', *N.A.V.*, n.s., vol, xix (1910).
32. A. Colombo, 'L'ingresso di Francesco Sforza a Milano', *A.S.L.*, vol. xxxii (1905).
33. D. Giampietro, 'La pretesa donazione di Filippo Maria Visconti a Francesco Sforza', *A.S.L.*, ser. i, vol. iii (1876); D. Biandra Trecchi, 'Le statue sforzesche del Museo di Vicenza', *Atti del III Congresso Stor. Lombardo* (Milan, 1939).
34. G. Romano, 'Giangaleazzo Visconti e gli eredi di Bernabo', *A.S.L.*, ser. i, vol. xviii (1891).
35. C. A. Vianello, 'Gli Sforza e l'Impero', *Atti e Mem. del I Cong. Stor. Lomb.* (Milan, 1936); Archivio di Stato di Milano, *Squarci d'Archivio Sforzesco* (Como, 1981).
36. G. Coniglio, *I Gonzaga* (Varese, 1967).
37. I. Toesca in D. S. Chambers and J. Martineau (eds), *Splendours of the Gonzaga* (London, 1982).
38. F. Cusin, 'I rapporti tra la Lombardia e l'Impero', *Annali degli Studi Economici e Commerciali di Trieste*, vol. vi (1934).
39. J. E. Law, 'Venice, Verona and the della Scala', *Atti e Mem. della Accademia di Verona*, ser. vi, vol. xxix (1977–78).
40. D. M. Bueno de Mesquita, 'Lodovico Sforza and his vassals', in *Italian Renais-*

sance Studies, ed. E. F. Jacob (London, 1960); G. Chittolini, *La Formazione dello Stato Regionale e le Istituzioni del Contado* (Turin, 1979).

41. F. Fossati, 'Rapporti fra una "terra" e i suoi signori (Vigevano e i duchi di Milano)', *A.S.L.*, ser. v, vol. i (1914).

42. A. Vincenti, *I Castelli Viscontei e Sforzeschi* (Milan, 1981).

43. *The Prince*, ch. 20.

44. J. E. Law, 'Un confronto fra due stati "Rinascimentali": Venezia e il dominio sforzesco', *Gli Sforza a Milano e in Lombardia* (Milan, 1982).

45. G. Chittolini, 'I capitoli di dedizione delle comunità lombarde a Francesco Sforza', *Studi di Storia Padana in Onore di G. Martini* (Milan, 1978); C. Magenta, *I Visconti e gli Sforza nel Castello di Pavia*, vol. iii (Milan, 1883).

46. B. G. Kohl and R. G. Witt (eds), *The Earthly Republic. Italian Humanists on Government and Society* (Manchester, 1978).

47. R. Fubini, 'Osservazioni e documenti sulla crisi del ducato di Milano nel 1477', in *Essays presented to M. P. Gilmore*, ed. S. Bertelli and G. Ramakus, vol. i (Florence, 1978).

48. G. Brucker, *The Civic World of Early Renaissance Florence* (Princeton, 1977), p. 387.

49. *Mémoires*, bk viii, ch. 22.

50. V. Vitale, *Brevario della Storia di Genova* (Genoa, 1955); J. Heers, *Gênes au XVe siècle* (Paris, 1961); P. Coles, 'The crisis of a Renaissance society: Genoa 1488–1507', *Past and Present*, vol. xi (1957). A recent survey of Genoese history can be found in A. Borlandi, '"Janua, janua Italiae": uno sguardo al '400 genovese', *A.S.L.*, vol. cxliii (1985).

51. H. Sieveking, 'Studio sulle finanze genovesi nel Medio Evo e in particolare sulla Casa di San Giorgio', *Atti della Soc. Ligure di Stor. Pat.*, vol. xxxv (1905–06); G. P. Balbi, 'I Maonesi e la Maona di Corsica', *Mélanges de l'Ecole Francaise de Rome – Moyen Age*, vol. xciii (1981).

52. F. Sassi, 'I Campofregosi in Lunigiana', *Giornale Storica e Letteraria della Liguria*, vol. xxix (1928); A. Ivaldi, 'La signoria dei Campofregosi a Sarzana', *Atti della Soc. Ligure di Stor. Pat.*, n.s., vol. vii (1967).

53. J. Heers, 'Urbanisme et structure sociale à Gênes', *Studi in Onore di A. Fanfani*, vol. i (Milan, 1962); E. Grendi, 'Profilo storico degli alberghi genovesi', *Mélanges E.F.R.*, vol. lxxxvii (1975).

54. D. Puncuh, 'Il governo genovese del Boucicaut', *Mélanges E.F.R.*, vol. xc (1978).

55. A. Sorbelli, *Francesco Sforza a Genova* (Bologna, 1901).

56. Brucker, op. cit., pp. 351–2.

57. *Dizionario Biografico degli Italiani*.

58. A. Neri, 'Poesie storiche genovesi', *Atti della Soc. Ligure di Stor. Pat.*, vol. xiii (1884).

59. *History of Florence*, bk viii, ch. 29.

60. The best recent introduction to the city is G. Brucker, *Renaissance Florence* (New York, 1969). A good account of the source material can be found in the introduction to D. Kent, *The Rise of the Medici* (1978).

61. Brucker, *Civic World*.

62. F. Gilbert, 'Bernardo Rucellai and the Orti Oricellari', *J.W.C.I.*, vol. xii (1949).

63. G. Brucker, 'The Ciompi revolution', in *Florentine Studies*, ed. N. Rubinstein (London, 1968); V. Rutenburg, *Popolo e Movimenti Popolari nell'Italia del '300 e '400* (Bologna, 1971); C. Cohen, 'Rivolte popolari e classi sociali', *Studi*

Storici, vol. xx (1979); Ist. Nazionale di Studi sul Rinascimento, *Il Tumulto dei Ciompi* (Florence, 1981); review articles by V. Hunecke in *Journal of Italian Hist.*, vol. ii (1979) and *Journal of Mod. Hist.*, vol. lv (1983).

64. A. Molho, 'The Florentine oligarchy and the Baliè of the late trecento', *Speculum*, vol. xliii (1968); and 'Politics and the ruling class in early Renaissance Florence', *Nuova Rivista Storica*, vol. lii (1968); R. G. Witt, 'Florentine politics and the ruling class', *Journal of Medieval and Renaissance Studies*, vol. vi (1976); N. Rubinstein, 'The political regime in Florence after the *Tumulto dei Ciompi*', *Journal of It. Hist.*, vol. ii (1979).

65. M. T. Grendler, 'The *Trattato politico-morale* of Giovanni Cavalcanti', *Travaux d'Humanisme et Renaissance*, vol. cxxxv (Geneva, 1973); A. M. Anselmi, 'Contese politiche e sociali nelle "Prime Storie" del Cavalcanti', *A.S.I.*, vol. cxxxiv (1976); D. Kent, 'The importance of being eccentric: Giovanni Cavalcanti's view of Cosimo de' Medici's Florence', *Journal of Med. and Ren. Studies*, vol. ix (1979).

66. A good introduction to the ascendancy of the Medici is J. R. Hale, *Florence and the Medici* (London, 1977). Among the more detailed studies of value are: D. Kent, 'The Florentine *reggimento* in the fifteenth century', *Ren. Q.*, vol. iv (1975) and *The Rise of the Medici*; A. Molho, 'Cosimo de' Medici: *Pater Patriae* or *Padrone?; Stanford Italian Rev.*, vol. i (1979); N. Rubinstein, 'Oligarchy and democracy in fifteenth century Florence', in *Florence and Venice*, vol. i. Table 8.

67. R. de Roover, *The Rise and Decline of the Medici Bank* (Cambridge, Mass., 1963); G. Holmes, 'How the Medici became the pope's bankers', *Florentine Studies* (n. 63, above).

68. E. H. Gombrich, 'The early Medici as patrons of art', in *Italian Renaissance Studies*, ed. E. F. Jacob (London, 1960).

69. D. Kent, 'I Medici in esilio', *A.S.I.*, vol. cxxxii (1974).

70. N. Rubinstein, *The Government of Florence under the Medici* (Oxford, 1966); 'Florentine constitutionalism and Medici ascendancy', *Florentine Studies*; 'Lorenzo de' Medici: the evolution of his statecraft', *Proc. of the British Acad.*, vol. lxiii (1977); 'State and regime in fifteenth century Florence', in *Per F. Chabod*, ed. S. Bertelli, vol. i (Perugia, 1980).

71. A. Brown, *Bartolomeo Scala Chancellor of Florence* (Princeton, 1979).

72. G. Griffiths, 'The political significance of Uccello's *Battle of San Romano*', *J.W.C.I.*, vol. xli (1978).

73. A. Brown, 'The Guelf party in fifteenth century Florence', *Rinascimento*, ser. ii, vol. xx (1980).

74. I. Hyman, 'Notes and speculations on S. Lorenzo, Palazzo Medici and an urban project by Brunelleschi', *Journal of the Soc. of Architectural Historians*, vol. xxxiv (1975).

75. C. E. Gilbert, *Italian Art 1400–1500* (Englewood Cliffs, 1980), pp. 148–151.

76. R. Hatfield, 'La Compagna de' Magi', *J.W.C.I.*, vol. xxxiii (1970); R. C. Trexler, 'Lorenzo de' Medici and Savonarola', *Ren. Q.* vol. xxxi (1978).

77. A. Brown, 'The humanist portrait of Cosimo de' Medici, "Pater Patriae"', *J.W.C.I.*, vol. xxiv (1961).

78. Lorenzo de' Medici, *Lettere*, general ed. N. Rubinstein, for the Istituto Nazionale di Studi sul Rinascimento (Florence, 1977).

79. R. Bizzocchi, 'Filippo Strozzi e i Medici', *R.S.I.*, vol. xciii (1981).

80. A. Brown, 'Pierfrancesco de' Medici', *J.W.C.I.*, vol. xlii (1979).

81. F. Gilbert, 'Florentine political assumptions in the period of Savonarola and

Soderini', *J.W.C.I.*, vol. xx (1957), and 'The Venetian constitution in Florentine political thought', *Florentine Studies*; N. Rubinstein, 'Politics and the constitution in Florence at the end of the fifteenth century', *Italian Renaissance St.*; S. Bertelli, 'Petrus Soderinus Patriae Parens', *Bibliothèque d'Humanisme et Renaissance*, vol. xxi (1969), and 'Pier Soderini "Vexillifer Perpetuus"', in *Renaissance Studies in Honor of H. Baron*, ed. A. Molho and J. A. Tedeschi (Dekalb, 1971); R. Devonshire-Jones, *Francesco Vettori* (London, 1972); R. P. Cooper, 'Pier Soderini: aspiring prince or civic leader', *St. in Med. and Ren. Hist.*, n.s., vol. i 1978); R. C. Trexler and M. E. Lewis, 'Two captains and three kings; new light on the Medici chapel', *St. in Med. and Ren. Hist.*, n.s., vol. iv (1981). Two recent contributions are: J. N. Stephens, *The Fall of the Florentine Republic* (Oxford, 1983) and H. C. Butters, *Governors and Government in early sixteenth century Florence* (Oxford, 1985).

82. D. Robey and J. E. Law, 'The Venetian myth and the "De Republica Veneta" of Pier Paolo Vergerio', *Rinascimento*, ser. ii, vol. xxv (1975), pp. 57–9.

83. W. J. Bouwsma, *Venice and the Defense of Republican Liberty* (Berkeley and Los Angeles, 1968), chs 1–3; B. Pullan, 'The significance of Venice', *Bulletin of the John Rylands Library*, vol. lvi (1974); E. Muir, *Civic Ritual in Renaissance Venice* (Princeton, 1981); E. O. G. Haitsma Mulier, *The Myth of Venice and the Dutch Republic* (Assen, 1980).

84. Brucker, *Civic World*, pp. 336–7.

85. Horatio Brown's major contribution is *Venice an Historical Sketch*, 2nd edn (London, 1895). His translation of Pompeo Molmenti's work appeared as *Venice*, 6 vols (London, 1906–08), pts 1 and 2 being relevant.

86. F. C. Lane, *Venice, a Maritime Republic* (Baltimore and London, 1973).

87. *The Social Contract*, bk iv, ch. 5.

88. B. Molin, *Diario*, Biblioteca Nazionale della Marciana, It. VII, 6759 (7667).

89. I. Cervelli, *Machiavelli e la Crisi dello Stato Veneziano* (Naples, 1974). p. 264; Devonshire-Jones, op.cit., p. 172.

90. R. Finlay, 'The foundation of the Ghetto: Venice, the Jews and the War of the League of Cambrai', *Proc. of the American Phil. Soc.*, vol. cxxvi (1982).

91. Burckhardt, op. cit., p.41; L. Lazzarini, 'Patriziato veneziano e cultura umanistica', *A.V.*, ser. v, vol. cxv (1980).

92. R. Finlay, *Politics in Renaissance Venice* (London, 1980). The most valuable recent introduction to Venetian politics and society is D. S. Chambers, *The Imperial Age of Venice* (London, 1970).

93. A. Tenenti, 'The sense of space and time in the Venetian world of the fifteenth and sixteenth centuries', in *Renaissance Venice*, ed. J. R. Hale (London, 1974); Cervelli, op. cit., *passim*.

94. E. Pavan, 'Venise et la mort à la fin du Moyen Age', *Mélanges E.F.R.*, vol. xciii (1981), and 'Recherches sur la nuit vénitienne à la fin du Moyen Age', *Journal of Medieval Hist.*, vol. vii (1981).

95. F. Gilbert, 'The Venetian constitution in Florentine political thought', *Florentine Studies*.

96. Finlay, *Politics*; Muir, op. cit., and 'The doge as "Primus inter Pares"', in *Essays presented to M. P. Gilmore*, vol. i.

97. On ducal patronage, D. Pincus, *The Arco Foscari: the building of a Triumphal Gateway in fifteenth century Venice* (New York, 1970); M. Muraro, 'La scala senza giganti', in *Essays in Honour of E. Panofsky*, ed. M. Meiss (New York, 1961).

98. D. E. Queller, 'The civic irresponsibility of the Venetian nobility', in *Essays in Memory of R. L. Reynolds*, ed. D. Herlihy *et al.* (Kent, 1969).

99. J. C. Davis, 'Shipping and spying in the early career of a Venetian doge', *S.V.*, vol. xvi (1974).

100. R. Finlay, 'The Venetian republic as a gerontocracy', *Journal of Med. and Ren. Stud.*, vol. viii (1978).

101. E. Pavan, 'Police des mœurs: société et politique à Venise à la fin du Moyen Age', *Revue Historique*, vol. cclxiv (1980).

102. B. Pullan, *Rich and Poor in Renaissance Venice* (Oxford, 1971), pt i.

103. In Venice, as in Florence, the activity of the confraternities was supervised by the state, but it is revealing that in the latter of the *Signoria* remained much more fearful of their potential as seedbeds of faction: R. F. E. Weissman, *Ritual Brotherhood in Renaissance Florence* (New York and London, 1982).

104. R. Mueller, 'The Procurators of San Marco', *S.V.*, vol. xiii (1971).

105. R. Mackenny, 'Arti e stato a Venezia', *S.V.*, n.s., vol. v (1981) and 'Guilds and guildsmen in sixteenth century Venice', *Bulletin of the Society for Renaissance Studies*, vol. ii, no. 2 (1984).

106. A. Molho, 'A note on the Albizzi', *Ren. Q.*, vol. xx (1967), p. 191; Brucker, *Civic World*, p. 33; P. J. Jones, 'Communes and despots', p. 78; R. Witt, 'Cino Rinuccini's *Responsiva alla Invettiva di Messer Antonio Lusco*', *Ren. Q.*, vol. xxiii (1980).

107. G. Ianziti, 'From Flavio Biondo to Lodovico Crivelli', *Rinascimento*, ser. ii, vol. xx (1980).

108. C. H. Clough, 'Francis I and the courtiers of Castiglione's *Courtier*', in *The Duchy of Urbino in the Renaissance*, pp. 41–4.

109. N. Rubinstein, 'The place of the Empire in fifteenth century Florentine opinion and diplomacy', *Bulletin of the Inst. of Hist. Research*, vol. xxx (1957), and 'Firenze e il problema della politica imperiale al tempo di Massimiliano I', *A.S.I.*, vol. cxvi (1958).

110. By the terms of the Peace of Turin (1381), Venice was obliged to pay the crown of Hungary 7,000 ducats a year on St Stephen's day in exchange for freedom of navigation in the northern Adriatic. The payments were made for a number of years; but the Republic denied that they represented homage. *Monumenta Spectantia Historiam Slavorum Meridionalium*, vol. IV (Zagreb, 1874), pp. 119–183; R. Cessi, *Storia della Repubblica di Venezia*, vol I (Milan, 1944), p. 328.

PART FOUR

Learning, the arts and music

CHAPTER TWELVE

The old learning and the new

For centuries the historians of European history and civilization have accepted that a revival of the ideals of Greek and Roman antiquity occurred in the period 1350–1600. At first this view was very largely confined to the history of the fine arts, where the Florentine architect and artist Vasari had used the Italian word *Rinascita* in 1550 in his *Lives*. It became clear, however, that even earlier the notion of such a rebirth had been voiced by writers who applied the concept to literature. The process of extending the new artistic attitude to *belles lettres* was generally accomplished by the seventeenth century, and by the eighteenth often seemed to usher in a world that was radically different in its outlook to the 'Middle Ages', as the period between antiquity and 'modern' times was beginning to be called. From this point it was a short step to regard the Renaissance as a period when Western Europe experienced a more or less total transformation, not just in art and letters but also in ideas and politics. The sciences of man and nature, so important in nineteenth-century progressive thought and action, were also traced back to the same time. Such a view of 'the state as a work of art' and 'the discovery of the world and of man', to quote the rubrics of two sections in Burckhardt's *Civilisation of the Renaissance in Italy* (1860), seemed entirely reasonable to the nineteenth-century world in which statesmen, scientists, church leaders were all products of the grammar school (*lycée*, gymnasium) where the basis of instruction was Latin grammar.

As indicated by the title of Burckhardt's book, this new world was itself Italian in origin, as was the word first used to describe the transformation. It must be appreciated, however, how slow and indistinct the change seemed in Italy, as later in Europe outside Italy; we are considering the views and practice of a handful of intellectual innovators and their critics. The large majority, even of the literate, was apparently indifferent to new modes of thought. It is also important to realise how much overlap there was between the declining status of the old learning and the rising status of the new. There was not always opposition between thinkers whom later writers were to identify as humanists and scholastics. The humanist (a word which emerged only in the argot of students towards the end of the fifteenth century) was an arts teacher, and we may guess that at Bologna or Padua or Pisa (where it seems *umanista* was first written down) was likely to be for the most part teaching youths whose further ambition was a degree in law or a career as a notary. Such students and such a further programme for the ambitious remained the norm in Italy for long enough, for they were the professions which it paid to belong to. Nor was a university degree essential to enter the ranks of the clergy or the lower ranks of the legal profession. The bulk of secular clergy were men whose training had been essentially an apprenticeship to a priest, and the solicitor's preparation was essentially derived from observing another practitioner at work, rather than a formal training in Latin.

Yet there can be no doubt that from the 'arts', however unreceptive most men were, came novel views which increasingly secured the support of influential Italians and gradually coloured public life. So much scholarly attention has been devoted to the humanists and the so-called 'humanist movement' in the last two generations that we are inclined to regard the period as mainly characterised by such developments, comparing the Italian scene as heralding the future, as many attitudes first found in the Peninsula gradually penetrated the continent of Europe as a whole and then its American (north and south) dependencies. But it must be remembered that there would have been little chance of the new learning crossing the Alps if there had not been similar trends there and if the fresh attitudes of Italians had not been enveloped in older traditions, conveyed by older institutional links in Church and state which evolved only slowly.

THE OLD LEARNING

In some important respects the environment of student and teacher did differ markedly in Italy from north European patterns. The most significant difference may be seen in the character of the Italian university, where the senior faculty was law and not theology. While there were a fair number of universities, only a few stand out in the European context. In the later Middle Ages these were Bologna, Padua and Pisa, and in almost all respects Italian universities followed the example of Bologna. The law curriculum involved, unless exemptions were granted, lectures and ultimately examinations on the principal texts of Civil Law (the various classical texts were known as the *Corpus Iuris Civilis*) over a period of about six or seven years; the professor dictated the texts and lectured on them and on the main commentaries on them, the glosses. The study of Roman Law in this way was theoretically an exercise in memorising the text and the principal glosses, the last mainly derived from the thirteenth and fourteenth centuries, and the school exercised the dialectical and logical capacities of the student in disputation and oral examinations.

The prize for those who stayed the course was the award of a degree which could not be made to men younger than twenty, again unless special dispensation was given, which it often was to the rich and well connected. Hard work or, for the well-to-do, a minimum of hard work together with judicious presents to important teachers, led to the degree of licentiate in Civil Law, or the more expensive and prestigious doctorate.

A growing number of civilians in the fifteenth and sixteenth centuries also took a degree in Canon Law. Here lectures and commentaries were based on Gratian's *Decretum* which, together with subsequent collections of church laws, mainly papal bulls, were known collectively as the *Corpus Iuris Canonici*. A long period of study was prescribed for this, but was truncated for those who had already acquired a degree in Civil Law. A man who had 'graduated', to use a modern term, in both Roman and Canon Law had the enviable title D.U.J., *doctor utriusque iuris*, doctor of both laws. Some older men took their licentiate or doctorate, but the ambitious and prosperous, eager to take up the practice of a very lucrative profession, were in their late twenties.

There were also courses leading to degrees in arts (Latin style or rhetoric) and higher degrees in medicine, the latter being, after law, a characteristic of some Italian institutions, as will appear shortly. In its emphasis on law Italy ensured for its centres of higher learning an extraordinary continuity with the public life of the major cities and the principalities, including the papacy on its return from Avignon in 1368. The connection of the law with civic life is particularly interesting and important. Whereas in the north great universities like Paris and Oxford struggled, on the whole successfully, to emancipate themselves from control of the Church (the local bishop) and the municipality, the reverse happened in Italy, as it did in one or two German towns. Despite an earlier period when the Italian *studia generalia* had gone their own way, defiant of pressure from other authorities, by the end of the fourteenth century the state was mostly in control; the position of the Church, represented by the archdeacon in Bologna and elsewhere, had been eroded and the citizens who paid the professors really controlled the doctors:

The general management of the *studium* in its relations to the state was eventually entrusted to a board known as the 'Reformatores Studii'. In the course of the fourteenth and fifteenth centuries such a body was established by the city government or prince in all Italian universities.[2]

The guild or *universitas* had been established initially in Bologna by the students. Student election of the rector withered away as a significant privilege. Bolognese citizens became entrenched in the system, which brought wealth and prestige to the town even if it cost money in higher salaries to prevent famous scholars being poached by other institutions.

The civic connection was extremely important for the law graduates of Italy. It opened the way to important careers as well as into the fat fees the more important practitioners could charge for their learned opinions (*consilia*). In both Church and state the possession of a law degree was necessary for certain administrative posts. In the cities the chief magistrate in civil cases, the *podestà*, was a lawyer who was not a native of the town, appointed with his suite for a period of years. In Florence this requirement covered also the

Captain of the People (at first with criminal jurisdiction), the Executor and for a long period in the fifteenth century the Appellate judge. This attempt to obtain dispassionate justice led to a *cursus honorum* which enabled a lawyer (a doctor or licentiate in civil law) to move from place to place and did much to consolidate the reality of an Italian sense of self-identity (see above, p. 9). Such a dominant position for judges of all kinds, usually chosen from 'foreigners', is found all over the Peninsula.

The doctor of law was, if able, in a position to exert considerable influence as he moved from town to town. It is true that even in republican cities the ultimate authority was increasingly in the hands of a patrician oligarchy by the end of the fifteenth century, but even then the citizens who monopolised power were frequently doctors of law and often obtained their degrees, usually by expensive short cuts, from Bologna, as Giovanni de' Medici, later to be pope as Leo X, did when he 'graduated' at the age of thirteen. Leo X employed another Florentine – Francesco Guicciardini, with a doctorate from Padua – in important administrative posts in his service; before going to Padua Guicciardini had read law in Florence and Ferrara, the later a 'cheap' university chosen by Francesco's father on grounds of economy, a recent biographer asserts.[3] In instancing the careers of two Florentines we are again using the many studies thrown up on all aspects of this city in the last thirty years. But governments everywhere needed men with ready tongues and the capacity to think securely and remember accurately, which was the hallmark of the well-trained doctor of civil law or D.U.J. The law, then, was the principal feature of the universities and, in general, it was Civil Law which led most certainly to lucrative *consilia*. Professor Martines has produced inventories of some of the manuscripts containing such material from the hands of Florentine lawyers for the period covered by the book (often earlier, for many learned opinions quote the views of previous jurists); it is a formidable list, enough to deter the toughest researcher.[4]

Canonists were of course advisers to popes, cardinals and bishops. As such they were also essential to the recruitment of certain departments of the papal Curia, although the evidence suggests that, as in other Italian principates, the civil lawyer was on balance more sure of a place, especially if he or his family had other connections with the central administration of the papal 'tribunals', to use a modern term for the church courts in Rome. The *quattrocento* saw these courts diversifying and the emergence of the *Segnatura Justiciae*, gradually separated from the *Segnatura Gratiae* (which dealt with legal disputes arising from the issue of papal favours, often stemming from the Penitentiary), becoming by the early sixteenth century the senior body. Older, but gradually losing its primacy, was the court of the *Rota*, which was in fact becoming a body which, it has been said, was 'a solemn tribunal of Roman Law'.[5] But every department of the Curia involved paperwork, processing supplications into due form, recording them in great ledgers, trying to avoid chicanery provoked by empty spaces in the folios which lay around before they were bound up. This work in the Camera, the Chancery, the Datary, was done by notaries, as in all aspects of Italian public life, but some who rose in the papal world were termed referendaries and were very important well-trained and well-rewarded men.

The canonists had a niche, then, in the corridors of ecclesiastical power, although the multiplication of D.U.J.s indicates the growing influence of the 'legist' as opposed to the 'canonist'. But just as the civilian was faced with practical and political problems in his work for city, prince, prelate or pope, so the canonist did not always live in the theoretical abstractions of the *Corpus Juris Canonici*. Not only was he faced with the tensions between jurisdictions, as between state and Church, especially acute when the representatives of both were prelates but, for the period from 1378 to 1442, the conciliar challenge to papal authority involved the lawyer in the discussion of problems which absorbed the whole fabric of authority. In these debates the lawyers of Bologna played a major part. As the Schism finally died away with the resignation of 'Pope' Felix V, elected at Basel in 1439, the influence it exerted on papal policy continued, as kings and even cardinals used the threat of the Council to bully the pope into sharing power and profit. This invocation of the legis-lation of Constance, reiterated at Basel, was met by the popes with a skilful avoidance of direct confrontation and of those conciliar canons which called for the regular assembly of councils. All this led to a very large theoretical literature which was to pave the way in later centuries for a fresh advance in political speculation. F. W. Maitland, in his translation of a part of Gierke's study, lists about a hundred publicists, legists and canonists whose commen-taries and tracts give some indication of the participation of lawyers in the public life of the last two centuries of the Middle Ages.[6]

It would thus be a mistake to regard Justinian, Gratian and the other old authorities studied at Padua, Bologna and elsewhere as precluding active involvement by lawyers in the problems of their own day. It is true that the greatest names, Baldus and Bartolus and their pupils, belong to an earlier period. But the future Pius II, who had reluctantly studied law at Siena, absorbed from this an immense amount of the literary and legal background which enabled him to follow the debates at the Council of Basel, which he was to record in his *Commentaries* on that assembly. There is, however, no doubt that the Italian universities were traditional and old-fashioned in their attitude to scholarship, and not unnaturally it was rare to find innovation in the senior faculty of law. Medicine — although it led a few scholars to desert the Averroist texts, as Pomponazzi did in the early sixteenth century — did not encourage an inventive intelligence; and theology, as it slowly made its way from Dominican convents into the universities of Italy, was based firmly on Aquinas and Scotus.

The art of composition in Latin was the province of the faculty of Arts, but one did not need to attend a university to acquire a facility in writing Latin: a good grammar school was enough. And it was from the grammar schools of the bigger towns that most Italian lawyers came. These were the humble notaries, created by emperor or pope or by those designated by them, a privilege worth paying for since in turn the notary paid to be entitled to the office. The office of notary was itself worth having, since the notary did most of the written legal work involved in conveyancing and certifying public acts of all kinds. The documents he drew up were registered by him and his papers formed a large and important legal record, which included not only documentation concerning the buying and selling of property, partnerships, marriage contracts and wills but also the vast range of formal undertakings before witnesses. Somewhat surprisingly to the northern student of the Middle Ages, the notaries were also employed in Italy to produce certified accounts of many ecclesiastical acts – notarial registers often include lists of ordinands, visitations by the bishop or his nominee, and the ensuing injunctions. All over Italy notaries proliferated, especially in the bigger towns, where they fulfilled important secretarial posts. It was their use in such a capacity (and many places insisted on employment of notaries in key jobs) that gave them the grip they evidently acquired on the machinery of government.

The *notaria* was based on the ability to write clear Latin, but not all notaries had this or really needed it. In practice the humbler members of the profession used the formula books prepared for their use, specialised *artes dictaminis* which remained more or less unchanged from the mid-thirteenth century onwards. Nevertheless, in the bigger universities the courses in rhetoric and dialectic, the main 'classical' elements in the Faculty of Arts (the liberal arts) did make an appearance, however unimportant their teachers were compared with those in the law faculty. Thus the young Italian who lived near or in a town like Venice, Genoa, Florence, Bologna or Milan could acquire from grammar masters of professors a skill in Latin which was sufficient to take him into a safe profession or into the higher fields of what would nowadays be called administration. It is much regretted that the actual teaching of arts subjects in 'secondary' schools in Italy has not been thoroughly studied, most works on *quattrocento* education giving in effect an account of educational theory found in a few distinguished treatises and neglecting the curriculum in ordinary grammar schools.[7] If Florence had no university, or had one only fugitively (see below, p. 299), the city had good schools and was reputed as a centre of training of notaries. So had many other places, Arezzo for example.

THE ESTABLISHMENT OF THE HUMANITIES

Traditionally, Petrarch (1304–74) has been regarded as the founder of the new Latin scholarship. His father was an exile from Florence, a lawyer who was in Arezzo when Petrarch was born, in Carpentras when Petrarch was a boy and before he was sent to study law at Montpellier and then Bologna. Destined to succeed his father as a notary, Petrarch needed good Latin and picked it up *en route* to a profession he came to loathe. His love was Latin literature and the moral teaching he found in Augustine and Cicero; his contemporary fame in Italy rested on his vernacular poetry, which he affected to despise. Petrarch's life of learning and leisure was made possible by his being technically a priest and thus able to hold church benefices, and by the protection and hospitality of popes in Avignon and princes in northern Italy. Despite his reverence for Cicero he could not in the end settle in republican Venice (where for a time he owned a house) or go back to Florence which, when he was famous, tried to persuade him to come. Polishing his Italian verses, collecting his letters – which were in Latin – and writing some remarkable essays of which the most interesting is the *Secretum*, a dialogue on Christian virtues in which the author debates with St Augustine, his reputation steadily grew.

Another of his Latin works must be mentioned: *On his Own Ignorance and that of Others*. This was in answer to the criticism of some Aristotelians from Padua who had deplored Petrarch's ignorance of the teaching and learning of the schools, the earliest example of an attack on the cultivation of the humanities by adherents of the old learning. In essence Petrarch's defence is a defence of moral philosophy; anyone who applies himself can be clever, but true wisdom involves striving 'for a good and pious will (rather) than for a capable and clear intellect'.[8] This ringing defence of eloquence caught the attention of other grammar-school boys who found in Cicero not only encouragement to virtue but also the advice on how to persuade and move others by the skilful employment of Latin cadences. It was, after all, a world that depended on the spoken word for public business, but also for diplomacy and the formal speeches that characterised contacts between rulers.

Christian and Ciceronian, admirer of the withdrawal from the world symbolised by the monastery (his brother was a monk) and by his own retreats to Vaucluse and Arquà, poet of idealised love of Laura and father of illegitimate children, Petrarch seems a bundle of contradictions. From him indeed were to spring contradictory elements in the literary and philosophical currents of Italians in the Renaissance. His admirers and followers fall into two groups. In one – perhaps the most long-lasting – were those who emulated his vernacular poetry, his *Trionfi*, his sonnets rather than the laborious Latin epic, the *Africa*. More immediately the Latin defences of 'love of wisdom' (philosophy) were to appeal to men who were to occupy important and influential positions in the political world of the next century.

Three such disciples stand out: Giovanni Boccaccio, Coluccio Salutati and Leonardo Bruni. Boccaccio (1313–75) had a career and an influence curiously similar to Petrarch's, although there are some sharp divergences. He too was pushed towards law by his father, once the latter had realised that his son would not make a businessman. Boccaccio too resented this and longed for a literary life, which he attained by writing Italian poems based on his experiences in Naples and later, after his return to Florence, the work he is chiefly remembered for, the *Decameron*, which was the first major and enduring creation in Tuscan – later what would be Italian – prose. If this suggests the programme of Petrarch, whom he greatly admired, in other respects we should note his faithfulness to Florence. He entered the Guild of Notaries and Justices and served the commune in administrative and ambassadorial capacities. He also compiled the *Genealogia Deorum Gentilium*, an encyclopaedia of the myths and legends of antiquity which was to be a reference work for generations. It also contained a forceful defence of the study of the Latin writers, especially the poets, which went beyond the patristic and medieval excuse of spoiling the Egyptians, which the canon lawyer would find in Gratian's *Decretum* when he discusses the education of the clergy, and Boccaccio elaborated the doctrine that the ancient poets enshrined truth hidden in allegorical form. All this is saved for the last two books of the *Genealogia*, in which Boccaccio lists the writers whom he regards as path-finders, notably the two Florentines Dante and Petrarch (the latter 'my lord and father'), and Barlaam and Leontius Pilatus, from whom the author had learned his Greek. The *Genealogia* also contains sustained passages proclaiming the author's Christian belief.[9]

Coluccio Salutati (b. 1331) did not add in his Latin writings, as Petrarch and Boccaccio had done, to the growing maturity of the Tuscan vernacular following in the wake of Dante in the *Divina Commedia*, but in a sense he did more. He gained for humanities, in the words of Georg Voigt, 'the right of citizenship' in Florence.[10] Here again we encounter another notary, but this time one who did not repine at a profession which was to carry him through a series of secretaryships and other administrative posts in small Tuscan communes to his appointment as secretary or chancellor of Florence in 1375, a post which he held until his death in 1406. Salutati had learnt his Latin grammar and rhetoric at Bologna, and it was for his skill in these as much as for his varied administrative experience that he was appointed chancellor: 'especially for his capacity in rhetoric and the *ars dictaminis*', as the citation read when the *Signoria* of Florence made him a citizen in 1400.

As chancellor Salutati handled personally the official correspondence of the government, especially with princes and states outside Florence. As time went on he had at his fingertips the correspondence of the principal magistrates, as well as of the *Signoria* – the governing body – whose membership changed every two months; he must have known more – indeed, he was expected to know more – than the members of the *haute bourgeoisie*, who after 1378 increasingly dominated the affairs of the republic. His classical learning imposed itself on the instructions given to captains, to ambassadors, to officials in the *contado*; his correspondence with the world outside Florence had an authority which impressed other secretaries, and frequently his propaganda took on a forcefulness which was clearly appreciated by the Florentines. He thus became not merely an able and influential official but the centre of the study of the humanities, a living demonstration of the relevance of letters to the cultural and civil life of the community. The chief evidence of this is his correspondence, his friendship with Petrarch and Boccaccio in their later years, and above all the way his career led the Florentine government to appoint further notaries as chancellors.

In all these aspects Salutati was edging towards a sympathy for and a defence of the *vita activa* against the *vita contemplativa*, of *negotium* as against *otium*, of Roman republicanism and the *vita civile* – all of which was to be absorbed by the portmanteau expression 'civic humanism'[11] to be applied to the Florentine thinkers of the early fifteenth century (and, where suitably evocative, to all sorts of other thinkers down to the eighteenth century, the value of the concept becoming, it may be argued, drained of its usefulness). If for Salutati the ideal seemed to be Brutus rather than imperial Caesar, republicanism rather than tyranny, he was yet capable of all sorts of hesitations and contradictions: in fact very much a man of his time, which probably goes some way to explain the trust and admiration of contemporary Florentine bigwigs; they could understand this able and mixed-up man and made no attempt to reconcile his various views, as later historians of ideas were to do.

After some years, when lesser notaries fulfilled the senior secretarial posts in the administration, the government in 1427 appointed Leonardo Bruni, a notary from Arezzo who had worked in the papal Curia (where he had for a brief time had Salutati on his staff). Over fifty when he was appointed, Bruni held the senior position in the chancery until his death in 1444. By then old and revered, Bruni had established himself in the tradition of Salutati, who had encouraged him to learn the revived Latin of the humanists and also Greek; his proficiency in the latter was remarkable and was reflected in many translations – not least from Aristotle, whose writings had been widely available in Latin since the early thirteenth century, but in a Latin considered by Petrarch and his literary successors to be barbarous. The new translations offended theologians and other scholars, who regarded the older versions of the works of the 'Master of those who are masters' (to paraphrase Dante) as almost as sacrosanct as holy writ.

Equally important and perhaps more original were Bruni's historical works, which mark a sharp break with earlier Florentine surveys and especially with the very good vernacular chronicles of Giovanni Villani (d. 1348) and his brother Matteo (d. 1363). Bruni's first narrative was a history of the Florentine people from the beginning down to 1404; his second a history of his own time, incomplete but covering the period 1378 to 1440. Both of these works were translated into Italian, the first by Donato Acciaiuoli on the instruction of the *Signoria*; and both set a new standard in style and in the use of documentary material, although for history Bruni stuck in the main to the narrative outlined by the Villani as far as it went, a procedure to be followed by other humanist historians. In his histories Bruni was a fervent and lucid exponent of the ideals of the city which had adopted him.

But many of the states opposed to Florence also had secretaries who had attacked Salutati and now attacked Bruni. Salutati replied in kind to an invective composed by a Visconti secretary, Antonio Loschi; and Bruni composed a sort of continuation of this in his celebrated *In Praise of Florence* (*Laudatio Florentinae Urbis*), which provoked Pier Paolo Decembrio to a 'panegyric' on Milan dedicated to Filippo Maria Visconti (1436). Such praise of a town and disparagement of its rivals were by no means unusual, nor confined to Florence and Milan. More interesting, as well as more revealing of Bruni's originality, was his vernacular life of Dante. In this he attacks the

traditional view that a poet must eschew the world, avoid politics and matrimony and any other distractions. After mentioning Dante's military service
and return to study, though maintaining his 'social and civic intercourse' he
goes on:

And here let me say a word in reproof of the many ignorant folk who suppose that
no one is a student except such as hide themselves away in solitude and leisure;
whereas I, for my part, never came across one of these muffled recluses from human
conversation who knew three letters. A great and lofty genius has no need of such
inflictions . . .[12]

He was thus in direct opposition to the views of Petrarch and Boccaccio.

The successful notary, with an increasingly confident training in the
humanities, continued to dominate Italian public life in the larger centres.[13]
In Florence after Bruni the significance of the chancellor diminished as the
ruling Medici moved ineluctably towards more autocratic government. Carlo
Marsuppini, who succeeded Bruni, was an elegant Latinist; his successor,
Poggio Bracciolini, was a luminous stylist with fifty years as a clerk in the
papal Curia but a sleazy personality, who hardly ever attended to his functions
in the Palazzo Vecchio – why should he, since he was seventy-three when he
was appointed? Thereafter came two Medici nominees; the self-satisfied and
extremely competent Benedetto Accolti (another native of Arezzo) was the
first chancellor with a doctorate in law. He died in 1464 and his negligible
successor, the miller's son Bartolomeo Scala, was a mere functionary, for the
power of the state now turned on the fulcrum of the Medici household.[14]
Niccolò Machiavelli, who was somewhat surprisingly nominated as second
chancellor in 1498 (the chancery had been divided and this was the
junior of the two posts), was not trained in the law either as a doctor or as
a notary, although his father had been a doctor and, despite straitened
circumstances, saw that Niccolò was instructed in Latin grammar and rhetoric
(he apparently had no Greek). We may be sure that he would not have been
appointed if the Medici had not been a clan temporarily without a Florentine
chief. When in 1512 they returned to power, Machiavelli was finished as a
politician. To this we owe the great works he wrote soon after his disgrace,
the *Prince* and the *Discourses on The First Ten Books of Livy*. It was ironic that
after Salutati had established the humanities as the heart of the communal
government, a position consolidated by Leonardo Bruni, the chancery was to
become increasingly void of significance in the political and cultural life of
Florence.

CRITICS OF THE HUMANITIES

The old learning produced spirited criticism of the new. As noted above, this
was not a new problem. The Church Fathers were aware that in using Latin
they were tempted sometimes to enjoy it for its own sake, and the education

of the clerks kept this issue alive. There had been earlier periods, baptised, we may say, as 'renaissances' by modern scholars, in the coterie round Charlemagne, in the perhaps larger number of literati associated with the schools of Chartres in the twelfth century. To such developments Carthusian and Cistercian mystics (the greatest being St Bernard) were implacably opposed. The monk had no need of the 'arts'; many of the early Carthusians and Cistercians were illiterate, as were many of the first followers of St Francis of Assisi.

Attacks on the cultivation of the humanities from the mid-fourteenth century were in some cases the confident dismissal of novelty by men accustomed to older ways; in others they suggest merely the pleasure of debate. One suspects that the Paduan Averroists who, it seems, greatly upset Petrarch were men affected by such motives. But Petrarch was a much admired poet in the *volgare*, as Boccaccio was in both poetry and prose. Petrarch's ethical stance – that philosophy meant love of wisdom – and Boccaccio's elaborate argument that poetry, including pagan poetry, was a way of conveying mystical truths both had relevance and were destined to fortify the advocates of educational reform.

There were several skirmishes, well rehearsed in histories of Italian scholarship. But the Dominican-dominated theologians and preachers of the *quattrocento* produced the most impressive reaction to the humanist position in Giovanni Dominici's *Lucula Noctis*, a tract composed in 1405. With the benefit of hindsight we can regard this laborious work, with its punning play on *Luciola* (firefly) and the name of Coluccio (from Nicolucci) Salutati, to whom the work was dedicated, as a failure from the start[15] Salutati died before he had completed his dignified reply, which gently demonstrated Dominici's bad Latin and failure to appreciate truth. Dominici, who became a cardinal and archbishop of Ragusa and died in 1419, was on the losing side in a battle in which good sense, backed by grammatical and orthographical propriety, was soon victorious.

St Antonino, archbishop of Florence from 1446 to his death in 1459, was a pupil of Giovanni Dominici; it was more important that he was a protégé of Cosimo de' Medici. Polymath by old-fashioned standards, Antonino was a good bishop by the lax standards of his own day.[16] But if he lived in a Dominican setting, he was surrounded by Medicean values. His convent at S. Marco (established so that Cosimo could have a branch of the Order of Preachers which was not part of the Lombard Congregation, as S. Maria Novella was) had many contacts with humanists and with the artists who were involved in re-building Florence and his own convent in the new manner. But by the end of the century S. Marco had recruited Girolamo Savonarola, the hellfire preacher and prophet from Ferrara, who was to turn Florentine life upside down for a few years. He was, so far as the new learning was concerned, another Dominici. It is true that Ficino's mystical theology, Platonic and hermetic, seemed to him compatible with Christian teaching and both he and his disciple Giovanni Pico della Mirandola frequented Savonarola's sermons. Yet for Savanorola the cultivation of the humanities was another vanity and it may well be questioned whether Ficino or Pico was a humanist, in any meaningful sense.

Marsilio Ficino (1433–99) was encouraged by Cosimo de' Medici and later by Lorenzo to translate Plato's works and related material really or supposedly bearing on Platonic ideas. The enormous work was more or less completed by 1492 and before that, in his *Platonica Theologia de Immortalitate Animarum* (Florence, 1482), he produced an account of Platonic speculation which was to be enormously influential, not least by encouraging later writers on Italian culture to suppose that in the field of philosophy Plato at this stage ousted Aristotle as the dominant intellectual force. His admirer Pico (1463–94) seemed to bear out this picture, as well as having a romantic aura through dying young and having been silenced by a nervous pope in 1487 when he had proposed to defend in public a number of theses, some of which the hierarchy judged to be heretical. In fact Ficino was in some ways trying to marry Platonic with Aristotelian principles, these last much tinged with Thomist interpretations and vocabulary. As for Pico, it should be remembered that his education involved study at Paris, the very centre of traditional thought. Much of this was offensive to thoroughgoing humanists. The Venetian scholar Ermolao Barbaro (1453–93) wrote a letter to Pico in which he accused him of defending an uncouth way of philosophising, barbarous and as fruitless as trying to make an Ethiopian white.[17]

Another deviant group of scholars was composed of the small number of men who were attracted to problems derived from older traditions in their Italian framework. The greatest was Pietro Pomponazzi (1462–1525), a Mantuan who taught at Padua from 1488 and later at Ferrara and Bologna. Padua had had a strong Averroist-Thomist tradition in its philosophy school in the *quattrocento*; it was one of the places where Pico had imbibed his admiration for Aristotle: and in the structure of the faculties at Bologna and elsewhere such metaphysical speculation was closely associated with medicine and what a later age would call natural science. Pomponazzi's argument that the immortality of the soul could not be proved by Aristotelian logic shocked many orthodox scholars, although he tempered it by saying that philosophical truths were not necessarily valid in religion. This doctrine was condemned at the Fifth Lateran Council (session VIII, December 1513).

The attacks launched against Aristotelian thinkers tended to lead nowhere, since they pounced on style and offered no fresh alternative understanding of the natural or philosophical order. In any event the theologians were to come into their own with the Lutheran challenge. Erasmus could criticise the overemphasis on Latin orthodoxy in language and style; but he was to become irrelevant as an influence on ideas by the mid-sixteenth century, when Protestants and Catholics turned against him. The *Ciceronianus* (1528) was especially directed against the possessive and arrogant stylists of Rome. It is curious that in a way the long-term victory lay with the new learning because of the pervasive effects of writing and printing. Erasmus wrote what we may loosely call an 'italic' hand.

The northern scholar worked for a time within the house of the Venetian printer Aldus Manutius (1450–1515), whose exquisite editions of the Latin and Greek classics set a new standard in the popularisation of accurate scholarship. The scripts of Italy in the Renaissance still dominate modern typography as 'roman' and 'italic'.[18] The influence of the new writing style was reinforced in another way. The birthplace of printing was the Rhineland; it spread very rapidly in Italy and for a time Italian presses dominated the world of scholarship and Italian handwriting dominated the chanceries of Europe.

All over Italy, but especially in Rome itself, there was another influence bearing on the evolution of script and print: the handsome capitals on monuments. Those of antiquity were particularly moving to men anxious to penetrate as far as they could into the ancient world. The inscription on the Pantheon invited similar advertisements and these were steadily exploited by popes and their supporters from the time of Eugenius IV onwards; in his pontificate the papal *breve* was increasingly written in the chancery cursive. The splendid monumental capital letters, both of Roman date and as revived by scholars and artists, gave the scripts of humanism some of their most characteristic features and offered the early printers a dramatic repertoire in which to display their wares.[19] Further, by the early sixteenth century handbooks intended to teach the beginner the mastery of chancery cursive began to appear. The first (1522) was by Ludovico Arrighi of Vicenza, who had been a printer as well as a scribe and a papal scriptor. Arrighi was encouraging a mode of writing which was reflected in the script of men of letters, men of fashion and scholars all over the Peninsula. The avidity with which the new technique was appreciated is proved by the frequent reprints of Arrighi and the production of similar works by others (notably Tagliente and Palatino).[20]

The writing-books bore the style over the Peninsula and beyond – so did the printers, like Aldus. And so did the papal briefs themselves, object lessons in the new art which involved governments in Italy and elsewhere in efforts to reply in kind. It is worth insisting on the essentially non-Florentine character of this development. In Florence, of course, the new cursive had exponents – the style of St Matthew by Ghiberti at Orsanmichele (1419–22) but this shows the saint with an open book on which the text is inscribed in antique roman capitals. But 'italic' and 'roman' are associated in the first instance with places where the values which have been characterised as civic humanism are either muted or altogether absent.[21]

THE HUMANITIES OUTSIDE FLORENCE

The term 'civic humanism' was coined to describe the republican sentiment which conditioned writers like Salutati and Bruni and their immediate followers. Republican it was in the strict sense, for it involved establishing, as Bruni did in his history of Florence, that the foundation of the city was to be ascribed not to Julius Caesar but to the establishment of a colony by some of Sulla's soldiers; it was, that is to say, not imperial Rome to which it owed its existence but the Roman republic. With this went a conviction (see above, pp. 292–3) of the superiority of the *vita activa* over the *vita contemplativa*. Much of this was fairly indigestible outside Florence, even in those republican centres which survived – Florence's as yet unconquered neighbours Siena and Lucca, or more distant Genoa and Venice. By the end of the fourteenth century, when Salutati was chancellor of Florence inaugurating the new principles of public life, the bulk of Italy was ruled by princes, including the curious prince with ill-determined claims to rule Christendom, the pope, and the only king in the Peninsula, ruler of the tumultuous and disloyal magnates of the Neapolitan state. Paradoxically, apart from Venice it was the princes who did most to encourage systematically humanist practices and principles.

This was to some degree a response to the diplomatic advantage enjoyed by Florence as a result of her early-fifteenth-century chancellors. The rulers of Milan also employed good Latinists, and some wordy warfare ensued. A distinguished series of writers was attracted to the Milanese court. Antonio Loschi (1368–1441), author of the invective against Florence to which Salutati replied in kind, provided a platform for Bruni's *Laudatio*. Later the Milanese chancery was to have a more distinguished servant in Pier Candido Decembrio (1392–1477). Decembrio survived the death of Filippo Mario Visconti and was an all-important figure in the short-lived regime that followed (the so-called 'Repubblica Ambrosiana', 1447–50); this flirtation with republican sentiment not unnaturally put him out of favour with Francesco Sforza when he became duke. Decembrio had to take to his travels, like the unpleasant Filelfo, who had intrigued against him.

Francesco Filelfo (1398–1481) is himself a curious witness to the prestige with which literature might endow an able exponent. Filelfo, who came from Tolentino in the Marches, had lived in Greece and returned to Italy at a time when fluency in Greek was a glamorous attribute. With his mastery of Latin and Greek, he felt that the world owed him a living. In Florence during the period when the Medici were expelled in 1434, he then spent the rest of his unsavoury career backing other losers; in Siena, in Bologna, and at Milan from 1434, he was consistent only in regularly attacking Cosimo de' Medici. Surviving the revolution in Milan, he promised to immortalise Sforza in an epic, the *Sforziad*, and was amply rewarded. Likewise it is significant af the times that he was well received by Nicholas V when he passed through Rome en route for Naples in 1453, as he was at Naples by King Alfonso. His poisonous letters and epigrams remind one of the way Aretino was later to try to bully his protectors. When he was finally called to Florence by Lorenzo, he died with nothing to be remembered by except scandal. This 'blend of pride and vileness, of hypocrisy and barefaced boldness, of cunning and violence'[22] was capable of affection only for his huge family: he had about two dozen children, legitimate (from three wives) and illegitimate. It seems extraordinary that he was given the chair of eloquence in the Roman university, the Sapienza, by Sixtus IV – or was that a comment on the care of popes for their university, which was indeed not remarkable?

Venice and Rome were somewhat outside the pattern established by the civic humanists in Florence, as they were in practice fairly indifferent to the threats and blandishments of the maverick scholars typified by Filelfo. Venice, as has been explained earlier (pp. 260–273) was a republic with a difference; the foreign affairs of the *Serenissima* were mainly in the hands of a small group of wealthy patricians – and the chancery, although in expertise and style it conformed to that found elsewhere, did not threw up figures like Bruni or Decembrio. In many ways the trend was conservative, but by the mid-fifteenth century a school in the humanities had been established near St Mark's, specifically designed to support the chancery. It had also, as noted earlier, a strong religious affinity towards the end of the fifteenth century, and in addition had the privilege of some fine collections of books. Cardinal Bessarion's library, given in 1468, suitably indicated the profound Greek influence among Venetian scholars and men of letters; Greek was also prominent in the production of the Aldine Press. These are some of the characteristics reflected in the work of Ermolao Barbaro, encountered on a previous page as a critic of Pico, who was a great philologist in the Valla tradition; his annotations on Pliny are in the grand manner, even if they are narrowly restricted to matters of style.[23] It is somewhat curious that a man like Barbaro – devout, in early life playing his part in the public life of a politician – should not have attempted to produce anything approaching the defence of *negotium* as opposed to *otium*. This is presumably a reflection not only of the Venetian constitution and social situation but of Barbaro's own temperament. In 1491 Innocent VIII nominated him as patriarch of Aquileia without the prior consent of the Venetian government, at this stage neurotically protective of its right of presentation to prelacies, and he died in Rome, an exile, in 1493.

In Venice there were plenty of schools, if only two senior establishments, supported by the government and therefore with a regular and continuing existence; and a course there was the Venetian 'quartier Latin', as Renan called Padua in a famous phrase already quoted. Much of the same availability of schoolmasters was true of most of the bigger and many of the smaller Italian towns, although they have not as yet been adequately studied. What is worth noting is the absence in Venice of a university as such; and much the same is true of Florence, despite the ephemeral appointment of great men from time to time. Pisa was (one might say) the 'quartier Latin' of Florence. Rome, on the other hand, was not entirely bereft of a university, but the Sapienza was almost at the bottom of the list of Italian institutes of higher learning; presumably its numerous scholars were teachers of the young aspirants to wealthy promotions in the offices of the papal Curia. But hungry men with good Latin flocked to Rome: partly for employment, partly because it was a centre of fascination for anyone with a training in the humanities, where the great monuments of Republic and Empire still stood around in the crumbling city, totally parasitic as it had always been. The penetration of the humanities into papal Rome is often stated to have begun with the ten years spent by Eugenius IV (1434–43) in Florence, but it should be remembered that Loschi, Bruni and Poggio were employed in the Curia at various times long before then, and Poggio gives an entertaining picture of the (presumably after-hours) storytelling among the *scriptores* in his *Facetiae* – somewhat fourth-form humour, but much to the taste of the last century's search after sex.

The enormous number of Latinists employed in Rome made the city by the end of the fifteenth century a kind of cultural capital of Italy, enhanced as it was by papal and ecclesiastical patronage of artists and architects. The significant popes in this evolution were Nicholas V (books snd buildings alone mattered to him, according to the Florentine bookseller Vespasiano da Bistici, although in practice what was to become the Vatican Library was his main monument, the building of the Borgo and the rebuilding of St Peter's remaining, one might say, on the drawing board) and, it may be supposed, Sixtus IV who, if not a scholar himself, was a patron of scholars and artists. Above all the Medicean popes Leo X and Clement VII, with their Florentine background, gave an air of Tuscan style to the papacy itself for nearly twenty years at the beginning of the sixteenth century. But it may be doubted whether the personality of the man wearing the tiara mattered very much by the second half of the *quattrocento*. The momentum of curial activity was such that it survived Paul II's suspicious attack on the Abbreviators, who had been made into a college (or a form of investment) by Pius II in 1463; he then imprisoned Platina, Pomponio Leto and other members of a coterie whom Paul assumed were members of a republican conspiracy. Likewise the humanist clerks and secretaries survived the bellicose pontificate of Julius II and the brief but austere reign of the Dutchman Hadrian VI (1522–23). In any case, even if the pope himself might frown on the humanists technically in his service, many of whom literally fed at his board, there were others in Rome who could use good Latinists and pliant servants. The 'office of a cardinal' (*De Cardinalatu*, 1510) was the subject of a celebrated book by the curialist Paolo Cortesi, which has been much discussed as recent scholarly attention to this period has shifted to Rome (see Chapter Ten, above).[24]

Despite this recent attention, one is left with the distinct impression that the Roman humanists were less significant figures, less original thinkers, than those of north Italy, let alone the Florentines. Some great and influential figures there certainly were such as the historian Platina, papal librarian from 1475, who died in Rome in 1481. Called Platina from his birthplace, Piadena, Bartolommeo dei Sacchi was an able writer and in his greatest work, the history of the popes, by no means uncritical of the pontiffs of his own day, if only by comparing them implicitly with earlier and less political leaders of the Church. His life of Paul II was extremely sharp: Platina had been one of the group imprisoned and tortured by this pope. But his views were on the whole balanced and it is symptomatic that until the nineteenth century the histories maintained acceptance not only in Roman Catholic but also in Protestant countries. Yet this work, while not as trivial as his other exercises in the new humanist manner, missed a chance to depict the evol-ution of an institution. A biographical approach such as Platina adopted was essentially old-fashioned and limiting. It should be remembered how Italian history was to be handled by Guicciardini. There are no problems in Platina, only personalities, and even these come to life only in his own day. This, it may be assumed, was a result of what has been called 'curial humanism'.

Flavio Biondo (1392–1463) was in all respects a more original scholar. The *Decades*, his history of Italy and of Christendom from the fall of Rome down to the 1440s, was in some ways a prosaic work, though it was plundered by later and more stylish Latinists like Pius II and remained the first history of the Middle Ages, as they were to be called later, and therefore indispensable for future generations. His antiquarian works on the antiquities, including the institutions of ancient Rome, anticipated the approach of a Muratori two hundred years later. But his most remarkable work was undoubtedly his survey of Italy, the *Italia Illustrata*, which has been discussed earlier (pp. 5 and 20). Unlike the pedantry and absurd attitudinising of Pomponio Leto and his followers in the so-called Roman Academy, Biondo's survey of Italy, though destined to be outdated within a century of its completion (1453), established a style of 'chorographical' investigation that was to thrive in Italy and elsewhere in Europe.

The Roman environment produced massive opportunities for employment, but carried with it some inhibiting influences. The first was the overwhelming dynasticism of popes, cardinals and prelates, which communicated itself to the secretaries and clerks in their employ. Just as there was a tendency for popes to be chosen from one family after Martin V and before the Reformation (two Rovere pontiffs, two Piccolomini, two Medici), so in humbler ranks there were curial families on the make. But this dynasticism operated in a clerical society which excluded matrimony for those who were in senior positions or aspired to acquire the plums that awaited the unmarried clerk. Rome was, it need hardly be said, not lacking in female company for its multitude of ambitious celibates; the prostitutes of the city were celebrated for their numbers and, in a few cases, for their wit and learning. But the promotion of the family in such conditions encouraged servility and clientage more pronounced than was to be found in republics or principates, although it is fair to remark that in the papal court such scrambling for office had a less destabilising effect than if often had in secular societies. Indeed, if the popes themselves had not become involved in the political intrigues of the Peninsula they might have reigned over one of the more tranquil regions, despite the vulnerable position of the Papal States, stretching as they did from the Adriatic to the Tyrrhenian Sea.

Besides the peculiar features already noted in the circumstances within which the humanities developed in Renaissance Rome, it must be stressed again that the Curia still attracted men from all over Christendom and, more to the point from the viewpoint of letters, from all over Italy. Biondo came from Forli, Platina, as has been observed, from a small town between Cremona and Mantua. Such recruits to the court of the pope were very common and lent it some claim to be an Italian centre in a way to which other courts could not pretend. Apart from the cultural rivalries to which allusion has been made (for example between Milan and Florence), Rome was still in a sense *caput mundi*, until at any rate the Lutheran revolt; and if that claim meant very little after Avignon and the Great Schism, it could still echo in Italy as a sentimental evocation of the roots of religion and culture.

A final condition which the scholars in Rome were obliged to accept was an inherent conservatism in thought. Reformers in the fifteenth century made the papal machine the object of criticism and by the early sixteenth the famous *libellus* of the Venetians Paolo Giustiniani and Pietro Quirini, to which reference has already been made, had appeared. The authors of this diatribe against the Italian clergy hit out in two directions. They criticised not only the vast bulk of the clergy who were totally unlettered, but also those few who were learned but who devoted their talents not to Scripture and commentaries on sacred texts but to vain studies of Latin and Greek authors for their own sake. To remedy this the monks proposed that in every place where letters were taught ('ubi studia litterarum vigent') there should be instruction in Christian theology. On the other hand, the authors made it plain that they had no time for the logic-chopping sophistry of the Parisian masters ('hanc Parisiensium cavillosiorem disciplinam').[25] Some such principles were accepted, albeit implicitly, in the educated circles of Rome. Many of the curial officials there were, of course, men who had been educated in the traditional universities of the north, where old-fashioned theology reigned supreme. But even the Italians were hesitant in following those like Lorenzo Valla who were prepared to jettison Aquinas, and proposed 'a completely new form of theology . . . that would utilise the rhetorical foundations of their own culture'.[26]

Thus the Roman situation was curiously stagnant – willing to encourage and promote the practitioners of the new humanities but hesitant to advance a radical reformation either of religious studies or of religion on such a basis. If we compare this inherent caution in letters and learning with the existing developments in the fine arts in the city at this time, the paradox is all the more striking. Moreover, Valla (1407–57), much the greatest of the Roman humanists and, of those referred to above, the only one to be born in Rome, posed further difficulties for the curialists. His vigorous mind and sharp tongue commanded the sort of competence in Latin to which hardly any of his contemporaries could aspire. This, displayed most fully in his elaborate *Opus elegantiarum linguae Latinae* (Rome, 1471), he was also able to display in a number of highly contentious works. It was Valla who ridiculed the language, even more than the historical improbability, of the 'Donation of Constantine' which had for centuries been one of the props of papal primacy, albeit not without its earlier critics. Valla also displayed a profound philo-sophical scepticism in several of his writings and in the *Elegantiae*, where he defended Quintilian's eclectic style against Ciceronian orthodoxy, he challenged (unavailingly) the method of 'imitation' by which curialists climbed the ladder of promotion as scriptors and secretaries. His most influential work was, however, to owe its celebrity to Erasmus, who printed Valla's *Adnota-tiones* on the New Testament in 1505 and from this beginning was to go on

302

to embark himself on a new translation, laying one of the eggs that Luther was to hatch.

But the Reformation lay in the future, as far as the humanists of Italy were concerned. Their victory was in the northern acceptance, quite remarkable in its rapid development, of the educational basis which they advocated. Much has been written on the theory of humanist education, for we have some remarkable essays on the subject and, despite the traditional revulsion of scholars for teaching, we have here some remarkable schoolmasters. The two most famous practical educators were Guarino de' Guarini of Verona (1374–1460) and Vittorino de' Rambaldoni of Feltre (1378–1446). With these two enormously influential figures we have left the republicanism of Florence for the princely audience of north Italy.

Guarino of Verona, who had learnt Greek in Greece with Crisoloras, taught briefly at Florence, then at Venice, and from 1429 at Este Ferrara, where he was both a professor in the university and had the responsibility of teaching the prince's children and others, the poor students being admitted gratuitously. His textbooks were old fashioned; his methods were novel, both in encouraging his pupils to master the texts of antiquity and in cultivating not only their minds but their social and physical resources. If anyone in the Renaissance had some conception of the 'universal man' it was Guarino, teacher of princes and of other schoolmasters. Vittorino da Feltre is a somewhat more shadowy figure because, unlike Guarino, he seldom put pen to paper, whereas his slightly older contemporary was an indefatigable letter-writer. As Guarino was patronised by the Este family, Vittorino was by the Gonzaga of Mantua. There, in 'La Casa Gioiosa' ('The Joyous House'), he taught the Gonzaga children, the children of other noblemen and of his friends, and boys from humble homes. The method was similar to Guarino's. Games and the pursuits of a gentleman were not forgotten; scholarship consisted of mastering Latin grammar and emulating Cicero, not least for moral instruction in public duty. Vittorino was himself a devout and earnest man who numbered among his intimates Ambrogio Traversari, the Camaldolese general who bridges so consistently the apparent gulf between the pagan classics and the Christian religion. 'As Cicero said,' to paraphrase a letter of Vittorino to Ambrogio, one of the few of his letters to have survived, 'all praise of virtue consists in the active life.'[27] To that extent the concept of *negotium* carries these humanists from their princely environment to a point of view closely similar to that of republicans like Salutati and Bruni.

NOTES AND REFERENCES

1. The topics touched on in this chapter have been extensively treated in many books devoted to the Renaissance in Italy. For those which lie behind the mid-nineteenth century see Wallace K. Ferguson, *The Renaissance in Historical Thought* (Cambridge, Mass., 1948). Modern scholarship begins with J. Burckhardt,

Civilization of the Renaissance in Italy, trans. Middlemore (London, 1929), and among its chief monuments are G. Voigt, *Die Wiederbelebung des classischen Alterthums* (3rd edn, Berlin, 1893); E. Garin, *L'umanesimo italiano* (Bari, 1952; in English, New York, 1966); Hans Baron, *The Crisis of the Early Italian Renaissance* (2nd edn, Princeton, 1966); P. O. Kristeller, *Renaissance Thought* (2 vols, New York, 1961). For further bibliography see Hay, *The Italian Renaissance in its Historical Background* (Cambridge, 1961).

2. H. Rashdall, ed. F. M. Powicke and A. B. Emden, *Universities of Europe in the Middle Ages*, vol. i, p. 212 (Oxford, 1936).

3. R. Ridolfi, *Life of Guicciardini*, trans. C. Grayson (London, 1967), p. 8.

4. L. Martines, *Lawyers and Statecraft* (Princeton, 1968), pp. 449–55.

5. N. del Re, *La Curia Romana* (3rd edn, Rome, 1970), p. 252n. Del Re deals with all the courts, with good references. See also John F. D'Amico, *Renaissance Humanism in Papal Rome* (Baltimore, 1983), p. 249nn.

6. Otto Gierke, *Political Theories of the Middle Ages*, trans. F. W. Maitland (Cambridge, 1900), pp. lxvi–lxxvi; cf. R. N. Swanson, *Universities, Academies and the Great Schism* (Cambridge, 1979).

7. G. Manacorda, *Storia della Scuola in Italia, I. Il Medioevo* (Milan, n.d.. = 1914) only reaches the fourteenth century.

8. Trans. H. Nachod, in E. Cassirer *et al.* (eds), *The Renaissance Philosophy of Man* (Chicago, 1948), p. 105; *De Ignorantia, sui Ipsius et Multorum* ed. L. M. Capelli (Paris, 1906), p. 70.

9. *Genealogia Deorum Gentilium libri*, ed. V. Romano, 2 vols (Bari, 1951), vol. ii, pp. 434f., 769–74., 769–74.

10. Voigt (above n.1), vol. i, pp. 159–61.

11. Hans Baron and Eugenio Garin (above, n.1).

12. *Early Lives of Dante*, trans. P. H. Wicksteed (London, 1904), pp. 119–20.

13. In general see Christian Bec, *Les marchands écrivains à Florence 1375–1434* (Paris, 1967) for the connection between Florentine society and culture.

14. E. Garin, *Scienza e Vita nel Rinascimento Italiano* (Bari, 1965), pp. 20–21.

15. *Lucula Noctis*, ed. E. Hunt (Notre Dame, 1940).

16. S. Orlandi, *S. Antonino*, 2 vols (Florence, 1960) and now David Peterson, *Archbishop Antoninus: Florence and the Church in the earlier Fifteenth Century* (University Microfilms International, Ann Arbor, 1985). The Ph.D. was presented to Cornell in 1985.

17. *Prosatori Latini del Quattrocento*, ed. E. Garin, (Milan, 1953), pp. 862–3; on p. 929 an account of Ficino's enormous scholarly production; and see also P. O. Kristeller, *Supplementum Ficinianum* (Florence, 1937).

18. There is another enormous literature on the questions posed by these terms. For a very stimulating recent work on a key Italian printer, see M. J. C. Lowry, *The World of Aldus Manutius* (Oxford, 1979).

19. Jiro Kajanto, 'Papal Epigraphy in Renaissance Rome', *Annales Academiae Scientiarum Fennicae*, ser. B, vol. 222 (Helsinki, 1982).

20. Reprints of these conveniently are gathered in *Three Classics of Italian Caligraphy*, ed. O. Ogg (New York, 1953): the works of Arrighi, Tagliente and Palatino.

21. James Wardrop, *The Script of Humanism* (Oxford, 1968).

22. The judgement is that of V. Rossi in the *Storia Letteraria, Il quattrocento* (Milan, 1938) p. 42, from which the above details are abstracted.

23. *Plinianae Castigationes* (Rome, 1493; Venice, 1494, etc.), a posthumous publi-

cation on which see V. Branca in *Renaissance Venice*, ed. J. R. Hale (London, 1973), pp. 223–4.

24. Note especially the various studies of David Chambers, especially 'The economic predicament of Renaissance Cardinals', *Studies in Medieval and Renaissance History*, vol. iii (1966), pp. 287–313. See too John D'Amico, above, n.5, and J. W. O'Malley, *Praise and Blame in Renaissance Rome* (Durham, N. Carolina, 1979).

25. *Libellus*, col. 678 (cf. above Chapter Seven, n.10.)

26. D'Amico, p. 146.

27. W. H. Woodward, *Vittorino da Feltre and other Humanist Educators* (Cambridge, 1897), p. 82.

CHAPTER THIRTEEN

The patronage of the arts and music

INTRODUCTION

No other aspect of the culture of Renaissance Italy has had a greater impact than the fine arts of painting, sculpture and architecture. Together with a wide range of closely related decorative arts and craft forms, they have attracted generations to the country and its civilisation and have stimulated scholarship in areas beyond the purely artistic. Moreover, their attraction shows no sign of diminishing; indeed, the appreciation of the various art and craft forms continues to grow, stimulated rather than discouraged by widening connoisseurship and deepening academic research. For example, the drawings which survive from the hands of Renaissance artists and the portfolios of their workshops can now be valued as works of art in their own right – a status they attained only rarely and towards the end of the period itself – but also as sources for workshop practice and the development of methods and ideas. It is possible to see how workshops like that of the Venetian Jacopo Bellini (c. 1400–70) built up a collection of compositional studies; how apprentices would practise rendering the folds of drapery from lengths of material stiffened in plaster; how artists increasingly experimented with chalks and charcoal to achieve subtler treatments of anatomy and the human face.[1]

Again, spurred by war damage, such natural disasters as the Venetian and Florentine floods of 1966 and the threat of environmental pollution, techniques have been advanced for the removal and restoration of frescoes, increasing awareness of the working practices of Renaissance artists and revealing traces of the preliminary sketch, or *sinopia*, on the prepared plastered wall. Such techniques have also been used to recover lost works, such as the Arthurian fresco cycle painted by Pisanello for Lodovico Gonzaga of Mantua around 1446. Cleaning and restoration can reveal details of an artist's technique and the evolution of his style, as has been the case since layers of overpainting, dirt and thick varnish have been removed from a succession of altarpieces by Giovanni Bellini (c. 1460–1516) in Venice.[2]

Not only have the works of art themselves been subjected to closer scrutiny; archival sources have been investigated for documentary evidence on the careers, status and workshops of artists and craftsmen, as well as for the contracts and correspondence linking them to their patrons.[3] Lastly, the forms and content of works of art have been studied with increasing care to achieve a greater awareness of religious and secular iconography, as well as of the significance of such features as dress, colour and gesture.[4] For example, it is becoming increasingly realised that the elaborate dress often given to the figures in religious paintings is not always a product of the artist's fancy, but can refer to specific costumes taken from religious plays and pageants. Perhaps a danger here lies in too great an ingenuity leading to unhistorical expectations as to the level and nature of contemporary reaction and appreciation. Many would have admired the triumphal arch Alfonso I built round the entrance to the Castel Nuovo in Naples from 1445.[5] It was intended to impress; but few would have been aware of its concentration of antique allusions and classical connotations. How many of his subjects knew of Alfonso's admiration for the 'Spanish' Roman emperor, Trajan, or shared his interests in the writings of the Roman architect Vitruvius?

Taking another related contemporary example, Alfonso was so impressed by what he had heard of Donatello's bronze equestrian statue of the *condottiere* Erasmo da Narni (Gattamelata) in Padua that in 1452 he asked the sculptor to execute such a monument for him in Naples. While Alfonso might well have been excited by the Roman, imperial connotations of such a work, it is likely that the majority of the statue's admirers were more struck by Donatello's technical and artistic mastery of an expensive material than by his informed use of classical forms and ideas. In some cases the erudition and ingenuity of the artist went beyond the grasp of his patron. On 12 March 1524 the Confraternity of Mercy in Bergamo commissioned Lorenzo Lotto to design *intarsia* (wood inlay) choir stalls for S. Maria Maggiore depicting Old Testament scenes. In a letter of 16 February 1528 Lotto tried to explain his use of hieroglyphics to his puzzled patrons.[6]

However, if the impact of the arts can be exaggerated or misrepresented, there is also the danger of not appreciating the full range and the contemporary context of the work of Renaissance artists and craftsmen. Much has been lost or damaged through natural and man-made causes. The *Fonte Gaia*, a public fountain commissioned by the commune of Siena from Jacopo della Quercia in 1409 to adorn the central piazza and celebrate the political virtues inspiring the government, became so damaged by the nineteenth century that its remains were moved under cover, to be replaced by a copy on a different site. The importance of the project has to be gathered from della Quercia's surviving drawings and the modifications introduced by both him and his employers over a ten-year period.[7] Even more complete has been the loss of the fresco cycle executed by Gentile da Fabriano and Pisanello between 1408 and 1422 for the Palazzo Ducale in Venice, where the damp conditions have been notoriously cruel to the achievements of generations of fresco-painters. Of course, the work of Renaissance artists and craftsmen was not always intended to last; this applies most obviously to the decorations, floats, costumes and machinery they produced for pageants, tournaments and festivals: in his *Commentaries* Pius II proudly described the lavish street decorations devised by himself and his cardinals to accompany the Corpus Domini procession in Viterbo in 1462. Giorgio Vasari (1511–74) bitterly regretted the loss of a machine designed by Filippo Brunelleschi (1377–1446) to represent Paradise for a celebration of the Annunciation; his determination to perpetuate its memory resulted in an account almost as long and detailed as that given to the cupola designed and supervised by the architect for the cathedral of Florence.

Vasari suggests that Brunelleschi's invention fell apart through neglect, but man's role in damaging the legacy of Renaissance Italy could be more deliberate. Tastes could change; Vasari claimed that work carried out by Piero della Francesca (d. 1492) for Borso d'Este and Nicholas V was destroyed by the building modifications of their successors. Lorenzo de' Medici's large collection of *objets d'art* in bronze and precious metals was in part melted down, even during his own lifetime; other items were dispersed through sale and gift. The moral crusading of the Dominican friar Girolamo Savonarola in Florence after 1491 led to the burning of 'vanities'.

Over the centuries there has been a massive redistribution of objects, making it difficult to see the arts and crafts of Renaissance Italy in their intended context. But, as the case of the Medici collection of *objets d'art* makes clear, the process had begun in the period. The shifts of political fortune meant that the furnishings and decoration of the Montefeltro palaces at Urbino and Gubbio can be appreciated only after a patient study of contemporary inventories and descriptions.[8] At least the palaces themselves have survived, and have not suffered the fate of the suburban residences of the Aragonese rulers of Naples; nothing remains of the villa built by Alfonso II at Poggio Reale, whereas the Palazzo Ducale in Urbino has been relatively well preserved and houses an impressive gallery, even if its exhibits can do little more than hint at the splendours of the late fifteenth century. Similar difficulties are encountered when trying to appreciate the more private collections of Renaissance patrons. As is made clear from her voluminous correspondence, Isabella d'Este (1474–1539) was an insatiable collector of genuine and reproduced antiques as well as of contemporary works, but disputes continue as to the extent and arrangements of her collection, disputes exacerbated by the stubborn emptiness of her purpose-built rooms in the Gonzaga palace at Mantua.

Dispersal continued, accelerating in the nineteenth century with the deconsecration of many religious buildings and the growth of an interest in and a market for the Renaissance period outside the Peninsula. This can be seen in the case of majolica, or 'Raphael ware' as it was misleadingly called in the nineteenth century. Thus the collections of *albaredi*, or glazed and elaborately decorated spice jars, once held in the royal spicery of the Castel Nuovo of Naples or by the Florentine hospital of S. Maria Nuovo, have been dispersed, a fate shared by majolica dinner services and tiles from Montefeltro and Gonzaga palaces (see below, p. 314).

Not only have such small-scale objects been moved from their original context; single large-scale works could be dismantled, as was often done with altarpieces made up of several panels. To meet the market for Renaissance art, many triptychs and polyptychs were dismantled and dispersed with the sacrifice of their elaborately carved and gilded frames, as well as of their overall design. This has been the fate of the altarpiece commissioned in 1437 from the Sienese painter Sassetta and placed in the church of San Francesco in Borgo San Sepolcro in 1444; dismantled in the early nineteenth century, its surviving panels are distributed between galleries in France, Britain and Italy, while its *predella* panels and its frame are lost. A similar fate befell many *cassoni*, or wedding chests, although occasionally the process could be reversed for the unwary collector with the marketing of 'identikit' *cassoni* made up of an amalgam of panels from several pieces. Even larger works of art could find their way outside Italy. For example, the Victoria and Albert Museum exhibits a reconstruction of the chancel of the Florentine church of S. Chiara. This was built at the expense of Jacopo di Ottaviano di Bongianni in 1493 to designs by Giuliano di Sangallo; such decorative features of the structure as the frieze of enamelled tiles from the della Robbia workshop were removed after its deconsecration. Of course, the movement of works of art can greatly assist in their preservation and study, but centuries of dispersal, loss and destruction make it all the more difficult to appreciate the role of the craftsmen and artists in the society of Renaissance Italy.

A further reason why it can be difficult to appreciate the artistic achievement of the period lies less with the accident of survival and the treacherous connoisseurship of the sale room, and more with the emphasis of art historical scholarship. For obvious and important reasons, attention has largely focused on 'renaissance' themes, and on the increasing impact made on many leading artists and their patrons by the real or imagined achievements of classical antiquity. Encouraged by survivals from the ancient world and by the exploration of classical literature by humanist scholars, artists and architects sought to increase their familiarity with the legacy of Rome and Greece. This was partly achieved through observation and discovery. The workshop drawings of a large number of artists, like those of the Venetian Jacopo Bellini or the Florentine Domenico Ghirlandaio (1449–94), reveal the interest shown in classical forms and themes. Vasari stressed the painstaking and almost archaeological examination made by Filippo Brunelleschi into the architecture and building techniques of ancient Rome. In 1525, the Venetian noble scholar Pietro Bembo noted the careful studies of antiquity undertaken by contemporary artists in the Veneto. Rather whimsically, the architect Francesco Grazioli designed the façade of his house at Asolo (*c*. 1530) to look as if it had been put together from antique fragments.[9]

Moreover, the corpus of examples was steadily enlarged with new discoveries; among the most dramatic and influential was the unearthing in Rome around 1490 of the Golden House of Nero. Its fresco paintings had an immediate impact, for example on the 'grottesque' decorative designs developed by the painter Pintoricchio working in the Vatican for Alexander VI between 1492 and 1495. Furthermore, this interest was encouraged by an accelerating fashion for collecting examples of the art of antiquity; the appetite of collectors spurred on the search for antiques and then facilitated their study. On 18 July 1472, Cardinal Francesco Gonzaga asked for the company of the painter Mantegna to divert him with discussion of his collection as he took the waters at Poretta. The Venetian cardinal Domenico Grimani (1461–1523) made an important collection of antiquities which he left to the Venetian state. Lastly, the interest of the humanists in classical literature increased familiarity with the theory and practice of the arts and architecture in antiquity, as well as enlarging the repertoire of secular themes for artists and their patrons. The scholar and architect Leon Battista Alberti (1404–72) shared with such fellow-Florentines as Brunelleschi a passionate interest in the surviving monuments of antiquity, but combined that with a knowledge of such authorities as the first-century Roman architectural theorist Vitruvius; these sources of inspiration were combined in such works of theory as his *De Pictura* (1435) as well as in his own designs. Later, a similar association of talents can be seen in the Veronese Fra Giocondo (1433–1515), who published an edition of Vitruvius in 1511.

The study of antiquity had multiple consequences for the practice and appreciation of the arts and architecture, but its influence was first and most profoundly seen in sculpture, for which classical models were relatively accessible and easily circulated. Thus the esteem attached to bronze sculpture was encouraged not only by the reputation of the few known Roman examples, but by Pliny the Elder's praise of this medium in his *Natural History*, as rehearsed in such treatises as the *De Sculptura* of 1514 by the Paduan scholar Pomponius Gauricius. Classical forms were revived. The Veronese painter Pisanello (1395–1455), virtually single-handed, re-established the medal, both as an art form and as a prestige item. The Florentine sculptor Donatello (1386–1466) created the first life-size, free-standing bronze nude since antiquity in his *David with the Head of Goliath* for the Medici palace between 1430 and 1433. Other sculptors, the Dalmatian Francesco Laurana (1430–1502) prominent among them, produced portrait busts, encouraged both by Roman example and by the demand from patrons. The influence of antiquity can also be detected in the execution of decorative detail. Around 1406, Jacopo della Quercia included *putti* with garlands to decorate the sarcophagus of Ilaria del Carretto, wife of the lord of Lucca. Lastly, such changes would not have been so noticeable had they not been accepted and encouraged by artists' patrons. Thus the Venetian Cardinal Zen, who died in 1501, urged in his will that the statues on his tomb in San Marco should be in bronze and as 'antique as possible'.

However, the significance of the revival of antiquity in the period can be distorted. In the first place, its arrival was not sudden. When the court painter Jean Bapteur included illustrations of the buildings of ancient Rome in the illuminated manuscript known as the *Apocalypse of the Duke of Savoy* (between 1428 and 1435), or when Masolino drew inspiration from the architecture of the Coliseum for his frescoes of 1431 for the chapel of cardinal Branda di Castiglione in the Roman church of San Clemente, they were both expressing a traditional admiration for the monuments of antiquity. Secondly, the period could show itself to be careless of the value of these same monuments. Even popes as responsive to the Roman past as Nicholas V and Pius II continued to license the destruction of classical buildings for lime, thus eating into the Roman heritage, while around 1500 Bramante quarried ancient buildings to build a palace for Cardinal Adriano Castellesi in the *Borgo* district. Indeed, it has been suggested that the Renaissance period, which witnessed so much building in Rome, was responsible for an unprecedented level of damage to the ancient city. This is supported by Raphael's observation to Leo X that 'the new Rome which we now see standing in all its beauty and grandeur, adorned with palaces, churches and other buildings, is built throughout with the lime obtained from ancient marbles'; and although Leo's interest in the classical city led him to commission the painter to map ancient Rome, as well as to order the preservation of all inscriptions, the building of St Peter's itself increased the demand for lime.

More important, the artists and patrons of Renaissance Italy absorbed a wider range of influences beyond those of a more specifically 'renaissance' nature, although one of the consequences of an excessively antiquarian approach to art history and a preoccupation with the classical tradition can be to relegate other sources of influence to the sidelines. For example, the impact of Flemish painting is receiving growing recognition.[10] The northern influence can be explained from its painters' mastery of the medium of oil-painting, their skill in expressive portraiture and detail and their ability to infuse interiors and landscapes with light. The reputation in Italy of such great northern painters as Jan van Eyck (d. 1441) and Rogier van der Weyden (1399–1464) is well known; when between 1461 and 1465 the Florentine architect Filarete advised Francesco Sforza Duke of Milan on the decoration of his ideal palace in the ideal city of *Sforzinda*, he paid tribute to the skill of the French painter Jean Foucquet (*c.* 1420–*c.* 1481) as well as to the two Flemish masters. In general, however, Flemish painting is often seen in terms of a few talented individuals largely incidental to the principal developments in 'renaissance' art. Their patronage by Italian clients tends to be cited to illustrate the catholic taste of a few collectors, some of whom can be accounted for by their business interests in the north. Thus Battista di Giorgio Lomellini, from a Lucchese family long prominent in Bruges, commissioned a much-admired triptych from Jan van Eyck around 1434 which, after 1444, was acquired by Alfonso I of Naples. When the Venetian Bernardo Bembo served as ambassador in Bruges between 1471 and 1474 he acquired a diptych from Hans Memlinc. Both were more fortunate than the Medici agent, Angelo Tani. He commissioned a *Last Judgement* from Memlinc, but it was seized by pirates en route to Italy in 1473.

Such examples could be multiplied. Their cumulative significance would appear all the greater if seen in relation to the activities and reputations of Flemish craftsmen as well as of artists in Italy. Tapestries were costly and much sought after, and Flemish weavers were seen as the masters of the medium. Flemish tapestries were imported to Venice as Flemish canvases were traded through Florence, and some of the leading fifteenth-century patrons employed Flemish weavers to produce the most expensive of all forms of wall decoration for their palaces – Nicholas V, Alfonso I and Federigo da Monte-feltro. Despite mounting evidence of this nature, however, there is still a tendency to underestimate the influence of the north and to submit to Michelangelo's views that:

They paint in Flanders only to deceive the external eye . . . . Their painting is of stuffs – bricks and mortar, the grass of the fields, the shadows of trees, and bridges and rivers, which they call landscapes, and little figures here and there, and all this . . . is in truth done without reasoning or art, without symmetry or perspective, without care in selecting and rejecting.

In general, Italian patrons and artists would not have shared that view, as is clear from the stir caused by the arrival in Florence in 1483 of the altarpiece ordered by Tommaso Portinari from Hugo van der Goes.

Finally, and not unrelated to the question of northern influence, the concentration on the revival of antiquity and the classical tradition tends to eclipse other important sources of inspiration. The Christian religion remained the prevailing influence but under-recognised is the popularity of themes drawn from chivalry, which tend to be placed by later historians among the quainter or more fanciful aspects of Renaissance art, or as stubborn but essentially backward-looking survivals from the medieval world. Chivalric literature and display remained extremely popular, and their popularity was not confined to court circles often characterised as outdated and nostalgic in their tastes and behaviour; it is hardly surprising, therefore, that chivalry had an influence on the arts. A good example is the fresco cycle in the castle of Manta in the Saluzzese (the modern province of Cuneo), painted in the early fifteenth century and inspired by a chivalric verse romance, the *Chevalier Errant* composed by the marquis Tommaso III of Saluzzo in 1394.[11] Chivalric themes were also favoured by the lords of the cities of the Po valley, as revealed in the Arthurian fresco cycle painted by Pisanello for Lodovico Gonzaga; these frescoes prominently displayed the English royal livery granted to the Gonzaga of Mantua in 1416 and confirmed by Henry VI in 1436.

A further reason why the artistic achievement of Renaissance Italy can be underestimated is again not unconnected to the concentration on the classical tradition. The art history of the period has been read traditionally with a Tuscan, and more precisely a Florentine, orientation. This is understandable in view of the conjunction and succession of highly innovative and influential artists and architects; the first half of the fifteenth century embraced such talented Florentines as the architect Brunelleschi (1377–1441), the sculptors Ghiberti (1378–1455) and Donatello (1386–1466), the painters Masaccio (1401–28) and Uccello (1391–1475). The Florentine achievement was quickly recognised; in the late fifteenth century Giovanni Santi from Urbino, poet, painter and father of Raphael, acknowledged the concentration of artistic talent associated with Florence; while around 1490 the duke of Milan was informed by his representative in the city of the qualities of the principal artists working there.

The Florentine emphasis in art history can also be explained from the record of the conspicuous patronage of the arts by Florentine institutions and families and by Lorenzo de' Medici's grasp of the fact that Florentine artists could be used for 'propaganda purposes': to broadcast the reputation of the city as well as the discernment and magnificence of its leading family. In 1480 Lorenzo recommended the architect Giuliano da Maiano to Ferrante I of Naples, and in 1488 secured for Filippino Lippi the commission to fresco the Carafa chapel in S. Maria Minerva in Rome. Furthermore, the pioneering art historian Giorgio Vasari (1511–71) was an adoptive Florentine patriot and a staunch adherent of the Medici; the emphasis of his *Lives of the Artists*, first published in 1550, stressed a progression of achievement by prevailingly Tuscan and Florentine artists and architects. Vasari's *Lives* are an invaluable and informed source, and they have understandably conditioned the appreciation of Renaissance art to this day; their message is given vivid credibility from the great concentration of works of art surviving in Florence.

Nevertheless, the dominance of the Florentine achievement is to be regretted to the extent that it has overshadowed other Italian schools and postponed their study. Of course, it is true that of the other schools perhaps only the Venetian produced such a concentration and continuity of talent, but when attention moves from less exclusively aesthetic considerations to address such problems as the role of artists and craftsmen, the motives for patronage or the place of the arts in society, then it would be valuable to be able to examine other Italian schools more on their own terms. There are difficulties in redressing the balance. The importance of the court of Alessandro Sforza at Pesaro (1445–73), another centre sympathetic to Flemish art, is difficult to appreciate due to the destruction and dispersal of its collection of paintings[12]. The attempt to study the patronage of the arts in Palermo, still one of the busiest ports in the period, has to deal with an extremely fragmented record in terms of both documentation and surviving works.[13] In other cases, however, well-documented and well-represented regional schools simply await full recognition. Friuli, for example, should receive more than local acknowledgement for its elaborate polychrome altarpiece in carved wood as produced by the workshop of Domenico da Tolmezzo in Udine (1462–1507).[14]

Lastly, new perspectives can be opened up after a fuller recognition of relatively well-documented and well-known examples. The Veronese artist Pisanello worked more extensively for the most important patrons of his day than most of his contemporaries, not only for the leading families of his adopted home town, Verona, but for the Venetian republic, Martin V and the courts of the Visconti, the Gonzaga, the Este and Alfonso I. His achievements were hailed by such contemporary men of letters as the influential humanist Guarino Veronese. Yet in many standard texts he remains a provincial figure, tied to the themes of the chivalry, courtly elegance and closely observed detail characteristic of the Gothic north. Only his achievement as a medallist earns him the kind of positive attention directed at such figures as Masaccio because he fulfils the role of a 'renaissance' artist, working in the classical tradition.[15]

The label of provincialism has been placed even more dismissively on the Venetian painter Carlo Crivelli (active 1457-95), largely because he spent most of his career in the Marches. As a result his work tends to be approached in a rather negative or condescending spirit and seen in terms of borrowings from other masters, archaisms like the continued use of gold leaf and a lack of substance as betrayed by his graceful figures and wealth of decorative detail. But Crivelli was knighted by the king of Naples and well patronised by Marcher families. Such contemporary acknowledgement should encourage a reassessment, and a more positive recognition of the virtuosity and inventiveness of his technique.

Finally, in general discussions of the role of the arts in Renaissance Italy, the concentration has been placed too exclusively on what are acknowledged today as the fine arts. By comparison, what might be called the decorative arts or even craft forms tend to be ignored, despite their evident importance for the embellishment of religious and secular buildings. The glazed terracotta sculpture of the highly productive Florentine della Robbia workshop is discussed in the context of the patronage of the fine arts, despite Vasari's comment that Luca della Robbia (1400–82) had become disenchanted by the hard work and low profits of marble and bronze sculpture, and had turned to glazed clay as an easier and more remunerative medium.[16]

However, Vasari's semi-smear does tend to relegate to more specialist studies the production of majolica tiles and vessels unless they be identifiably the work of a great workshop, like the ceiling tiles representing the seasons commissioned by Piero de' Medici from Luca della Robbia in the 1450s. In this case, the separation of the arts from the crafts is made despite the fact that the glazing techniques are similar, and that the market for majolica was a large and varied one, with tiles and vessels in the medium performing a decorative as well as a practical function in many contexts. Majolica was used to produce highly decorative table ware, as in the case of the commemorative service made by Niccolò da Urbino for the marriage of Federico II Gonzaga and Margherita Palaeologus of Montferrat in 1531. Glazed tiles formed a prominent element of the decorative scheme in chapels commissioned by the Caetani in the cathedral of Capua (c. 1440) and the Landi in S. Sebastiano, Venice (1510). With items in majolica serving as gifts and mementos, collections could be built up. The collection of the Neapolitan humanist Jacopo Sannazaro (1458–1530) was admired in 1519 by the Venetian connoisseur Marcantonio Michiel.

Similarly under-recognised is the work of masters in wood inlay or *intarsia*.[17] Once again this is partly due to Vasari, who tended to dismiss *intarsiatori* as plodding craftsmen; and here again the relative lack of interest flies in the face of the more contemporary evidence. In his commonplace book, the Florentine patrician Giovanni Rucellai (1403–81) claimed that contemporary masters of the medium rivalled the achievements of the ancients, and demonstrated 'such skill in perspective that one could not do better with a brush'. *Intarsia* panels, using different colours and grains of woods, could produce stunning *trompe l'œil* effects and brilliantly clear studies in perspective. The medium could attract the skills of leading artists, and Sandro Botticelli (1445–1510) and Francesco di Giorgio Martini (1439–1502) have been associated with the ingenious *intarsia* panels commissioned by Federigo da Montefeltro for his palace and its *studiolo* in Urbino; the panels in the *studiolo* convey the effect of open and closed cupboards and a carefully chosen display of armour, books and musical instruments. The choirs and sacristies of churches were often the context for *intarsia* work. Around 1500 Fra Giovanni of Verona designed the elaborate wood inlays for the choir stalls of the Veronese church of S. Maria in Organo – possibly influenced by the studies in perspective theory which the mathematician Luca Pacioli dedicated to the duke of Milan in 1498.

Close to the plight of the decorative arts is that suffered by what today might fall into the category of *objets d'art*. Here a good example is suggested by the miniature relief carvings in bone and ivory decorating boxes and mirrors as well as being assembled into larger works such as altarpieces. Outstanding in the medium in the late fourteenth and early fifteenth centuries was the workshop of Baldassare Embriachi, a Florentine entrepreneur who was driven into exile in Venice in 1395.[18] His fine carvings in bone and ivory found appreciative markets in the major centres of northern Italy and beyond the Alps. Around 1400 Baldassare completed a commission for the duke of Milan of an elaborate polyptych of twenty-four panels for the high altar of the Certosa of Pavia, depicting the lives of Christ and Mary as well as the *Journey of the Magi*. The meticulous craftsmanship of his contemporary Florentine Lorenzo Ghiberti (1378–1455) has long been recognised from the famous bronze doors he cast for the baptistry of Florence. When the mastery shown by Baldassare's craftsmen in the similarly expensive and prestigious medium of hippopotamus ivory receives its due recognition, our appreciation of the great range, versatility and role of the artists and craftsmen of the Renaissance will be both fuller and better balanced.

COLLECTORS AND COMMITTEES

In early-fifteenth-century Italy, the craftsmen of the Embriachi workshop were unusual in being much sought after abroad. Before the end of the century the appreciation of Italian art beyond the Alps was limited, and the pronounced taste of Matthias Corvinus King of Hungary (1440–90) for Italian majolica, sculpture and illuminated manuscripts was remarkable. A change came with the Italian Wars, when a large number of potential patrons from north of the Alps were repeatedly presented with the artistic achievements of the country, and Italian artists and craftsmen were invited abroad. Of this Leonardo da Vinci is a well-known example, but he was far from being unique. Guido Mazzoni (1450–1518), the Modenese sculptor of vividly life-like terracotta statues, followed Charles VIII from Naples to France in 1495.[19]

It would, however, be wrong to conclude from the long-established appreciation of foreign works of art in Italy and the relatively late impact of Italian art abroad that the Peninsula was 'provincial'; rather, the prevailingly one-way traffic was a consequence of the wealth, acquisitiveness and developed tastes of Italian patrons.

This introduces an explanation for the patronage of the arts which is familiar today. In the Renaissance there can be detected a growing appreciation of 'art for art's sake', a developing connoisseurship which encouraged patrons to collect works of art as objects of value and beauty in themselves. As has been suggested, this can be seen in the taste for northern works of art; in 1448 Giovanni de' Medici was in correspondence with an agent in Bruges on the subject of the tapestries seen at an Antwerp fair and their suitability for his private collection. Collecting did become increasingly fashionable, and among wealthier and more demanding patrons this often found a focus in the embellishment of their private apartments – in some cases with the establishment of *studioli*, rooms ostensibly set apart for study and reflection but often housing concentrations of works of art and elaborate schemes of decoration. From Nicholas V successive popes increasingly sought to leave the record of their patronage in the apartments of the Vatican palace and the Castel S. Angelo. Among secular patrons, Federigo da Montefeltro commissioned Justus of Ghent between 1472 and 1475 to paint representations of the *Liberal Arts* for the *studiolo* of his palace at Gubbio, and a cycle of *Famous Men* for the *studiolo* of his principal residence at Urbino; for the latter Federigo also bought tapestries depicting the Trojan War from Tournai in 1476.

Even better-known as a collector was Isabella d'Este, Marchioness of Mantua (1474–1539). As is revealed by her surviving correspondence, in her dealings with Giovanni Bellini – and still more so in her negotiations with Leonardo da Vinci – Isabella was more concerned to secure a finished work from these celebrated masters than to tie them to closely defined themes. Indeed, in the case of da Vinci she was even anxious to secure a sketch portrait from the artist, suggesting that material which once would have had little worth outside the artist's workshop was acquiring value in the eyes of some collectors. This was certainly true by 1500, but it is possible that around fifty years earlier Pisanello had been admired in court circles in Ferrara and Naples for his dexterity and inventiveness as a draughtsman.

However, talent-spotting and connoisseurship were not confined to court circles. The tapestry collection of Giovanni de' Medici has been mentioned; by the early sixteenth century there is also secure evidence for private collections in Venice which were clearly objects of pride as well as of personal interest for their owners. Gabriele Vendramin, the owner of Giorgione's *Tempesta*, said that his collection brought 'a little rest and quiet' to his soul. Andrea Odoni was a collector of antique statuary and contemporary paintings; his famous portrait by Lorenzo Lotto (1527) celebrates his antiquarian interests by placing the sitter proudly among items from his collection. Such activity aroused the admiration of contemporaries, and the descriptions compiled around 1530 by another Venetian, Marcantonio Michiel, are a principal source for the study of private collections and the nature of connoisseurship in the early sixteenth century. Such accounts are relatively rare, but from them and from the more common evidence drawn from inventories, wills and contracts the tastes of private collectors appear to have been catholic rather than specialised, a conclusion confirmed by the evidence of patrons for whom the curiosity, value, beauty and technical mastery displayed by works of art or by *objets d'art* were of growing importance. The Venetian Giuliano Zancaruol commissioned a painting of Christ from Giovanni Bellini, stating that cost was of no importance 'as long as it is beautiful'.[20]

As that quotation suggests, the period also reveals a growing aesthetic sensibility stimulated by particular works of art or by individual artists. For example, the humanist Bartolomeo Fazio (*c.*1400–57), in the chapter on artists appended to his *On Famous Men* of 1456, not only refers in passing to a number of contemporary collectors but also records what in all probability were the tastes and opinions current at the court of Alfonso I. Expressiveness, realism, mastery of detail and technical versatility are the qualities he ascribes to Gentile da Fabriano, Pisanello, Jan van Eyck and Rogier van der Weyden, while Donatello is praised for his technique, rivalling that of the ancients, and his ability to give the appearance of life to statues in bronze and marble.[21]

The increasing readiness of scholars to acknowledge the arts was in part a response to the prominence they were acquiring in the priorities of patrons. Rather more telling is the fact that the interest and knowledge of patrons can be increasingly detected from such relatively matter-of-fact source material as contracts and correspondence. A letter of 14 December 1464 from the commune of Bologna to the architect Aristotle Fieravanti begins with a disquisition on the importance of architecture before appointing him as city architect. In 1476 Galeazzo Maria Sforza wrote to his agent in Venice asking him to secure the services of Antonello da Messina because of his ability to draw from life. Around 1490 an agent of Lodovico Maria Sforza attempted to describe four leading painters working in Florence not so much in view of their availability, reliability or cost, but rather in terms of their character and style as artists.

Perhaps such expressions of interest could be seen as rather vague or general, but patrons can be found taking a minute interest in the details of a commission. On 15 September 1431 the Venetian noble Marino Contarini gave specific instructions to the painter Jean de France for the embellishment of his palace on the Grand Canal, the Ca' d'Oro, from 'the gilding of all the foliage on the two large capitals on the corners where the lions are placed' to having 'all the merlons veined in the manner of marble, with some black touches round the edges of the said merlons if it looks right'. On 8 June 1474 Galeazzo Maria Sforza was given a detailed report of the proposals in terms of cost, material and design from a team of artists bidding for the decoration of a chapel in his castle at Pavia. Lastly, it seems likely that Lorenzo de' Medici had an informed interest in architecture, encouraged by the experience of sitting on a commission in 1468 to discuss the completion of the cupola of

Florence's cathedral, by being shown the sights of ancient Rome in 1471 by Alberti and then by reading Alberti's *Ten Books of Architecture* in the 1480s.

The informed interest shown by patrons can be further detected in the growing fashion for presenting works of art as gifts. This could happen on a diplomatic level. In 1457 Filippo Lippi reported to Giovanni de' Medici on the progress he was making with a triptych for presentation to Alfonso I, while in 1518 a later generation of Medici commissioned Raphael to paint a *St Michael* and a *Holy Family* as gifts for Francis I and his queen.[22] It could also take place on a more personal level. The distinguished Florentine doctor Giovanni Chellini recorded for 27 August 1456 that Donatello,

of his kindness and in consideration of the medical treatment which I had given . . . gave me a roundel the size of a trencher in which was sculpted the Virgin Mary with the Child at her neck and two angels on each side, all of bronze and one the outer side hollowed out so that melted glass could be cast on to it and it would make the same figures as those on the other side.[23]

More important, the informed interest of patrons can be seen in the fashion for dedicating to them works of artistic theory. In 1498 the mathematician Luca Pacioli, in collaboration with Leonardo da Vinci, dedicated his *On Divine Proportion* to Lodovico Maria Sforza. In some case it can be doubted how real the dedicatee's interest was in the subject under discussion, as when the Sienese artist and engineer Mariano Taccola dedicated his work on war machines to the emperor Sigismund around 1432.[24] In other cases, however, a convergence of interest between author and patron can be detected, and no more clearly than in the relationship between Leonello d'Este and Alberti. Personal contact was probably first made during the Council of Ferrara in 1438, but during Alberti's second visit to the Este court in 1443 he advised the marquis on the commissioning of a bronze equestrian monument of his father, Niccolò III. Arising from this Alberti dedicated a treatise on the horse to Leonello and later claimed that his study of the principles of architecture was begun at the marquis' suggestion. Their association is also revealed in the *De Politia Litteraria* of the Milanese humanist Angelo Decembrio. Compiled in 1462 and dedicated to Pius II, Decembrio's work looks back at the life he had known at Ferrara around 1445. In recording discussions held at court, the work also reveals the impact of Alberti on Leonello's attitude to the arts. For example, while the marquis praises the achievements of Flemish tapestry weavers, he also criticises them in Albertian terms for indiscriminate use of colour and incoherent storytelling.[25]

Decembrio's retrospective picture of the marquis and his court may be flattering, but it is not false and it brings together much of the evidence for the connoisseurship of the arts which is a growing characteristic of the patronage of the period. Leonello was a collector of coins, gems, tapestries and antiquities. He held a competition for his portrait, Jacopo Bellini narrowly surpassing Pisanello. He was one of Pisanello's principal patrons and it was for the Este that the artist cast his first medals. In November 1447 the humanist Guarino Veronese advised the marquis on his plans to have the *studiolo* of his rural retreat at Belfiore decorated with representations of the muses from the hand of Agnolo da Siena.

It would, however, be a mistake to exaggerate the place of connoisseurship among the motives for the patronage of the arts. In the first place, the modern view of the collector accepts that there is also an 'art market' and that works of art can have considerable investment value. Possibly only in the case of the collections of *objets d'art* – easily moved, often in precious metals and often with a rarity or curiosity value as 'antiques' – was this calculation present. In 1471 Lorenzo de' Medici purchased items from the collection of Paul II. Of course the products of patronage, from chapels to illuminated manuscripts, did change hand; but the original patron had not had such an eventuality in mind, intending such works to remain in his own or his designated successor's possession. The members of the Florentine Brancacci family, when they paid for the construction and embellishment of a chapel in S. Maria del Carmine, did not imagine that it would become the meeting-place of a religious sorority following the disgrace and exile of Felice Brancacci in 1434.[26] Secondly, to place too much emphasis on the connoisseur and the private collector would be to create the false impression that the patronage and appreciation of the arts were the preserves of an elite, the rulers in Church and state and wealthy mercantile and noble families. In fact, the initiative for the commissioning of works of art was more widely distributed and it has been argued by Goldthwaite, among others, that the discussion of contracts and finished works of art in committee encouraged and educated the tastes of a relatively broad cross-section of the population.[27]

This was all the more marked in republican regimes where major projects for the glory of God or the state could be matters for wide discussion. A striking example of this survives in the minutes of a committee convened in Florence on 25 January 1504 to debate the location of Michelangelo's *David*, the participants revealing their awareness of aesthetic and political as well as of practical considerations.[28] Similar discussions could take place in the context of commissions of less prominence, if of equal immediacy for those concerned. On 11 June 1445 the Company of Mercy, a lay confraternity of Borgo San Sepolcro, drew up a detailed contract for a polyptych with Piero della Francesca. In 1525 the board of management of the confraternity of St Peter Martyr in Venice asked the government for permission not to accept the commission agreed to by a majority of the brothers, which the board felt would result in work of shoddy quality. Artistic and architectural projects could attract a wider public beyond the participating individuals and institutions. In Florence the competition held for the second set of baptistry doors in 1401 and the commissions given to Leonardo and Michelangelo to work in the hall of the Great Council in 1503 generated general interest. In 1505 the Florentine shopkeeper and chronicler Luca Landucci hawked round his own scheme for the improvement of the piazza of San Lorenzo.[29]

From such cases it becomes clear why Wackernagel insisted that art was central to the life of Renaissance Florence, but the same holds good elsewhere.[30] If the discussions which preceded acts of patronage tend to be better documented for the republics of Renaissance Italy, this is largely a result of the greater research carried out on their art patronage rather than a consequence of the greater freedom they enjoyed. It is of course true that lords, popes and monarchs had considerable initiative and influence, not only within court circles and over what might be called 'private' commissions but also in respect of larger and more 'public' projects carried out in their territories. From 1386 Giangaleazzo Visconti could intervene in discussions over the design of Milan Cathedral and the majority of the popes following Nicholas V concerned themselves with the rebuilding and reorientation of Rome outside the walls of their palaces. Princely patronage was, and still is, more conspicuous in the smaller cities. The determination of the Gonzaga to beautify Mantua 'to the honour of the Gonzaga family and the city' led to the destruction not only of unsightly houses round the Benedictine church of S. Andrea in 1470, but also of that church itself in favour of a new structure designed by Alberti.[31]

But in neither capital nor subject cities were princely patrons dictators of taste. Giangaleazzo's concern and intervention could not stop argument and jealousy among the builders involved in the cathedral project, and Gonzaga plans to rebuild S. Andrea struggled through in the face of the opposition of the Benedictine community. When, between 1492 and 1494 the Sforza began radically to alter the layout and appearance of the piazza at Vigevano the indignant residents, who were intended to be joint beneficiaries of the scheme, had to be calmed with tax exemptions.[32]

Otherwise it is probable that all over Italy discussions of the kind more familiarly documented for Florence or Venice accompanied the patronage of guilds, confraternities, religious institutions and autonomous communal authorities. The decoration of the oratory of S. Giovanni in Urbino by the Salimbeni brothers in 1416 was the product of collective patronage rather than the initiative of the Montefeltro dynasty. In 1477 a citizen committee in Florence's subject city of Pistoia argued over the commission for a funeral monument to honour their fellow-citizen, the Cardinal Niccolò Forteguerri. Lorenzo de' Medici became involved, not on his initiative but rather at the behest of one of the parties and as a ploy to endorse its choice. In Rome patronage was far from being the monopoly of popes and cardinals. In 1501 the guild of bakers commissioned Bramante and Antonio Sangallo the Younger to build S. Maria di Loreto; in 1516 the church of S. Eligio degli Orefici was built for the jewellers on the design of Raphael. This was even more true in Palermo, a royal capital but virtually deserted by the court, where patronage was in the hands of noble and bourgeois families, guilds and confraternities. The Chiaramonte were much more important as patrons of both secular and religious architecture in Palermo and Sicily than the crown.[33]

MAGNIFICENCE AND FAME

If it would be a mistake to see the patronage of the arts as the preserve of an elite, to concentrate too exclusively on the more esoteric tastes of that elite would be comparable to trying to understand the scholarship of Renaissance Italy in terms of the 'new' learning without reference to the 'old'. Patrons like Leonello and Isabella d'Este could be self-consciously striving after the new, especially in regard to the cult of antiquity, and the latter was clearly disappointed by Giovanni Bellini's extreme reluctance to work on a classical theme which would blend with the closet classicism of her *studiolo*. However, such endeavours belong – at least in general terms – to a much older tradition.

Magnificence had long been accepted as an attribute of the virtuous ruler and nobleman, although when magnificence spilled over into ostentation and vain display it could arouse criticism and trouble consciences. Writing in moralising mood in 1381, Coluccio Salutati underlined the superficial and transient splendour of the city of Florence. It is likely that Vasari was correct when he claimed that Cosimo de' Medici preferred Michelozzo over Brunelleschi when it came to designing a new palace because the former's design was less ostentatious, making the standing of the Medici in the district of S. Lorenzo less offensive to other families. Certainly Pius II recorded the resentment caused by Cosimo's lavish support of large-scale building projects. In a different political context the Florentine bookseller Vespasiano da Bisticci hinted at the doubts entertained by one of his heroes, Nicholas V, as to the righteousness of his building work in Rome. Obviously in these cases disquiet had been provoked by patronage on a grandiose and permanent scale, but the attacks in Florence after 1491 by Savonarola and his followers on 'vanities' show that the temptations of vainglory had proved widely irresistible.[34]

On the whole, however, the champions of a fitting magnificence carried the day; the older tradition, leaning on such authorities as Aquinas, received up-to-date support from Alberti and Filarete, who argued that buildings should be more than functional and should project the fame and virtue of their owner. The Neapolitan humanist Giovanni Pontano argued in his *De Magnificentia* (c. 1494) that magnificence was a duty for a prince. Expressed in modern terms, magnificence meant propaganda to project, enhance and enshrine the reputation whether of the state, the family, the guild, the religious community or the individual. In more contemporary terms it was closely related to the concern for fame which Burckhardt detected in the period; in his celebrated patent of 10 June 1468 Federigo da Montefeltro stressed his decision 'to make in our city of Urbino a beautiful residence worthy of the rank and fame of our ancestors and our own status'.[35]

Architecture was the clearest way of expressing such aspirations, and the palace was an obvious focus for the patron's attention. At the height of his power in the Papal States, Cardinal Giovanni Vitelleschi took over a group of buildings overlooking the principal entrance to his native town of Tarquinia to build his palace (1436–39) (see above, pp. 207–212). Towards the end of the century the communal council of Verona struggled to find the finance to build a new council hall to express its autonomy under Venetian rule. Architects could be employed on a still grander scale to satisfy such sentiments. Pienza was the name given by Pius II to his birthplace, the village of Corsignano near Siena, as it was rebuilt to his orders by Bernardo Rosellino between 1459 and 1464.

Of course, for full effect these buildings had to be decorated and furnished, and the comings and goings of the owner had to be attended with due ceremonial. The Ferrarese painter Cosimo Tura (c. 1430–95) is best remembered for the *Months of the Year* frescoes adorning the Este's Schifanoia palace in Ferrara, but as court painter from 1458 his duties were as much those of a decorator as those of an artist. The Este accounts reveal him to have been employed designing tapestries for chairbacks and ceremonial banners, as well as working on secular and religious commissions for the ruling house. A letter of 8 December 1490 reveals the impatience of Giangaleazzo Maria Sforza to have a ballroom in the *Castello Sforzesco* in Milan decorated with frescoes. At a more measured pace, throughout the period the Venetian government sought to have the interior of the ducal palace decorated with frescoes and paintings to proclaim the greatness and divine favour enjoyed by the republic; in a session of 21 September 1474 the Greater Council referred to its meeting-hall as 'among the foremost showpieces of our city'.[36]

In the expression of magnificence, patrons also turned to sculptors. From 1473 a preoccupation of Galeazzo Maria and Lodovico Sforza was the erection of an equestrian monument to Francesco, founder of the dynasty, as dukes of Milan. Doubtless having heard of this project, Leonardo da Vinci, in a letter to Lodovico of 1482, presented himself as able to execute it 'to the immortal glory and eternal honour of the prince your father of happy memory, and of the illustrious house of Sforza'. Leonardo laboured on the monument for around sixteen years, distracted by other work and daunted by the technical problem of fulfilling Lodovico's desire for a bronze statue four times larger than life. The clay model was on show in 1493, helping to adorn the wedding of Bona Sforza and the emperor Maximilian, but the model followed the fate of the dynasty and on the fall of the Sforza it was used for target practice, and nothing remains of the venture beyond the artist's notes and sketches.

A more manageable and extremely effective means of expressing a patron's reputation – and one that shared with the bronze equestrian statue an impeccable classical pedigree – was the medal. Popes from Pius II encouraged the practice of placing foundation medals in the buildings with which they were associated; Paul had medals by the Mantuan Cristoforo di Geremia buried in the structure of his palace of S. Marco. Other medals received a wider circulation. In 1506 the Milanese master Caradosso Foppa cast a medal for Julius II to commemorate the foundation of the new St Peter's which established the 'standard' portrait of the pope.[37]

The portrait was another art form which brought increasing work to sculptors and painters in the period. On the latter, the profile portrait as found on coins and medals was a powerful influence, and classical coins were probably one of the sources for Piero della Francesca's diptych portrait of Federigo da Montefeltro and his wife Battista Sforza (c. 1472–74).[38] A further influence came from the Netherlands in the form of the three-quarters portrait, which allowed the painter to convey more of the sitter's personality. It is possible that the Sforza court painter Zanetto Bugatto mastered this form after he had been sent to Flanders by Bianca Maria Visconti in 1463; certainly in 1468 her son Galeazzo Maria Sforza was so entranced by his portrait 'from the life' of his wife-to-be, Bona of Savoy, that he refused to send it on to his mother for inspection.[39] That painting does not survive, but a relatively early and very accomplished example of the three-quarters portrait which does is Leonardo's painting of Ginevra Benci, probably executed in connection with her marriage in 1474.

However, the growing interest in portraiture could cause embarrassment. Between 1474 and 1475 Lodovico Gonzaga corresponded with his ambassador at the Sforza court when told of the duke of Milan's pique at not being included among the portraits of famous contemporaries executed by Mantegna in the *Camera degli Sposi* of the Gonzaga palace in Mantua. The envoy was to mollify the duke with the opinion that portraiture was not Mantegna's *forte*, and to reassure him that the trial sketches had been burned.[40] This incident points to the fact that the pursuit of magnificence could stimulate other patrons to follow suit. On 28 July 1445 Filippo Maria Visconti was told that Alfonso I was 'making a sculptured, marble arch . . . worked in the antique manner, with sumptuous and marvellous architecture'. In this case Filippo Maria was not tempted to emulate the king of Naples, but the work in the 1460s of Antonio Rosellino on the tomb of Cardinal James of Portugal in the church of S. Miniato at Fiesole so impressed Antonio Piccolomini Duke of Amalfi that in 1470 he commissioned the sculptor to carve his wife's tomb in S. Maria Monteoliveto in Naples.[41] On 13 July 1494 Antonio Pollaiuolo – who had also been involved in work on the burial chapel for the cardinal of Portugal – wrote to the Roman noble Virginio Orsini suggesting that rather than confining himself to a bronze portrait bust, he should commission a bronze equestrian statue. It is likely that Pollaiuolo was trying to capitalise on the well-known achievements of Donatello and Verrocchio and the contemporary endeavours of Leonardo in Milan. The last were certainly in the mind of Ercole I d'Este in 1501 when he wrote to his ambassador asking him to get hold of one of Leonardo's models for the Sforza monument to assist in the construction of his own in Ferrara.

Lastly, by its very nature the cult of magnificence and fame could inflate the reputation of the patrons concerned, especially when they assumed the role of discerning experts. It is now accepted that the readiness of many aspiring patrons, from the citizens of Pistoia to the duke of Milan, to turn to Lorenzo de' Medici for advice has helped to exaggerate Lorenzo's own share of artistic patronage.

PATRONAGE AND PIETY

To insist too strongly on magnificence and the search for fame would be to create the misleading impression that the motives for the patronage of the arts and architecture can be clearly categorised. Not only is the source material not complete enough to encourage a pigeon-holing exercise, but where it does exist it tends to support the impression suggested by the works of art and architecture of the period themselves: that the motives of the patrons could be various, and that it would be unhistorical to place them in an order of priority. This point can be illustrated from architectural patronage. The castle Francesco Sforza rebuilt in Milan was certainly intended to project the authority of the ruling dynasty with its tall drum towers facing the city, set with carefully rusticated masonry to give a studied impression of strength, and carrying the Sforza coats of arms. At the same time it was a serious fortification, straddling the walls of Milan round what had been one of its principal gates. Finally it was a palace, with gardens, a courtyard and elaborately furnished apartments.

On a larger scale the work planned and initiated by Nicholas V on the Vatican, St Peter's, the Castel S. Angelo and the neighbouring districts of the *Borgo* and *Ponte* were in part to demonstrate the authority of the restored papacy, as recorded in the words attributed to the pope by his biographer Giannozzo Manetti:

if the authority of the Holy See were visibly displayed in majestic buildings, imperishable memorials and testimonials seemingly planted by the hand of God himself, belief would grow and strengthen from one generation to another, and all the world would accept and revere it.

Noble edifices combining taste and beauty with imposing proportions would contribute greatly to the exaltation of the 'throne of St Peter'. But other considerations must have been present: the need to defend the papacy, to provide accommodation and services for those attending the Curia, to restore the prosperity of Rome (see p. 109, 201 ff above).

Moving from a large to a small scale, the same point can be made from the commissioning of illuminated manuscripts, which could be regarded as prestige 'collector's items', valued in part for the artist's display of technical virtuosity. When the highly accomplished miniaturist Giovan Pietro Birago was working on the *Hours of Bona of Savoy* for the dowager duchess of Milan in the 1490s, some of the completed illuminations were stolen; Birago valued his lost work at 500 ducats, five times the value placed by Leonardo on his *Virgin of the Rocks*.[42] But at the same time the manuscript was an aid to personal devotion, and this serves to introduce a motive for the commissioning of works of art and architecture which was so prominent that it challenges the rather too secular – and even anachronistic – concept of the 'patronage of the arts'. Piety and religious observance meant that the creation of a reputation for magnificence through the employment of artists and architects was most often and most conspicuously set in a Christian context.

This can be illustrated from both individual and collective patronage in various forms and on various scales. Buildings of particular religious significance concerned the state, whether in princely or publican form. Giangaleazzo Visconti initiated the building of the Carthusian monastery, the Certosa of

Pavia, in 1396. The project suffered many interruptions but continued to receive the attention of both the Visconti and Sforza, doubtless encouraged by the fact that the first duke of Milan had indicated his enthusiasm for the strict Carthusian order by making its church his burial place. The same was true of smaller centres. The Viterbese chronicler Niccolò della Tuccia recorded how in 1458 the communal council, of which he was a member, had a *Madonna of Mercy* painted for its chapel, with the members of the government depicted from life, gathered under the Virgin's cloak.[43]

In Florence the maintenance and embellishment of the city's principal religious buildings devolved upon the greater guilds, and an element of inter-guild rivalry can be detected within the wider aim of expressing the city's faith and honouring its saints. From the first half of the fifteenth century perhaps the two most celebrated commissions were the two sets of bronze doors for the baptistry awarded by the Calimala, or cloth guild, to Lorenzo Ghiberti (1402–53) and the efforts of the Lana, or wool guild, to complete the structure of the cathedral with the raising of the great cupola to the design of Filippo Brunelleschi; but the competitiveness of the guilds can be seen more clearly in the sculptured decoration of the oratory known as Orsan-michele. Spurred on by the commune, the guilds of the city placed a series of commissions with artists of the calibre of Ghiberti and Donatello to fill the tabernacles allocated to them with appropriate sculptures. The element of prestige was underlined by the fact that the greater guilds were allowed to commission work in the expensive medium of bronze, while the others had to be content with marble.

Other sources of collective patronage demonstrating a concern for both prestige and piety were religious orders and lay confraternities. On 1 March 1445 the Benedictine monks of S. Pancrazio in Florence commissioned Neri de Bicci to execute frescoes in their cloister celebrating the Order's saints. In Venice from the later fifteenth century the number of *scuole* seek-ing canvases to decorate their meeting-halls resulted in large-scale commis-sions to painters like the Bellini and Carpaccio; the latter's cycle for the *scuola* of St Ursula (1490–98) are famous for the way the painter introduces portraits of members of the confraternity into the narrative scenes, the prom-inence given to members of the Loredan family reflecting their role in the *scuola* and its commission.

As this suggests, prestige and piety were also inextricably interwoven in the religious patronage of families and individuals. Larger civic churches could be identified as fashionable, leading to the employment of artists and craftsmen on side chapels or on the main body of the building. In some cases such devout attention was traditional. In Verona leading families had long favoured the Franciscan church of S. Fermo Maggiore and that of the Dominicans, S. Anastasia; in the former Pisanello painted a fresco of the *Annunciation* for the Brenzone family (*c.* 1425); in the latter he painted his enigmatic *St George and the Princess* in the Pellegrini chapel (*c.* 1440). In other cases special circumstances could encourage a wave of chapel endowment and the commissioning of works of art. The Roman church of S. Maria del

Popolo was granted to the Lombard congregation of the Augustinian canons by Sixtus IV, and radically rebuilt from 1472 to 1477. This inspired the intervention of a number of leading Roman families and churchmen. The much-sought-after Umbrian painter Pinturicchio was much employed in the building, for example on side chapels for cardinals Domenico della Rovere (c. 1489) and Lorenzo Maria Cybo (c. 1500), while for Pope Julius II he frescoed the ceiling of the choir (c. 1510). In 1473 Cardinal Rodrigo Borgia commissioned the Milanese architect and sculptor Andrea Bregno to create its high altar in the form of a triumphal arch.[44]

In some cases the wishes of the patron or his descendants led to the complete endowment of a chapel. After Filippo Strozzi had acquired a chapel to the right of the choir of S. Maria Novella in Florence in 1486, he lavished money on its lighting, its stained glass, the vestments of the officiating priests, and its decoration in fresco and sculpture. When he died in 1491 his will insisted that the work undertaken by the sculptor Benedetto da Maiano and the painter Filippino Lippi be completed. Strozzi had bought the chapel from the impoverished Boni family, but the embellishment of churches and the endowment of their chapels could provoke jealousy and dispute. When Piero de' Medici commissioned Michelozzo and Luca della Robbia to build and decorate the Tabernacle of the Crucifixion in S. Miniato in 1448 he had to acknowledge the church's traditional patrons, the Calimala guild, by allowing its emblem to occupy a more prominent position than his own. A quarrel with the Dominicans of S. Maria Novella persuaded the Florentine banker Francesco Sassetti to devote his energies to a chapel he had acquired in S. Trinità, which he chose as his own and his wife's burial place, and for which he commissioned an altarpiece and frescoes from Domenico Ghirlandaio (1483–86). The former, though dedicated to the life of St Francis, was flanked by portraits of the donor and his wife.[45]

As the Sassetti chapel recalls, the portrait makes its first prominent appearance in a religious context; hence its commemorative significance should not be ignored. Niccolò della Tuccia stressed that he was anxious to record his own and his contemporaries' portraits in the Viterbo *Madonna of Mercy* of 1458, 'not out of pride or vainglory, but only in case any of my successors wishes to see me, he can remember me better thus, and my soul may be commended to him'. In a more secularly minded world it is only too easy to scoff at such disclaimers and to overlook the piety that motivated other expressions of commemoration and religious dedication. The context could be essentially personal. Giangaleazzo Visconti commissioned a book of hours in 1388 to commemorate the birth of a male heir. Much more prominently Sigismondo Malatesta, to commemorate military victories in 1447, began to rebuild the church of S. Francesco in Rimini. Again the celebrity which has since surrounded certain works of art can obscure a more personal and private origin. In this category could be placed Jacopo della Quercia's tomb of Ilaria del Carretto, wife of the lord of Lucca (1405–13) or Raphael's *Deposition*, commissioned by Atalanta Baglioni to commemorate the murder of a son in 1507.[46]

Certainly in theory the idea survived that the arts were an aid to religious devotion and expression. For the Dominican friar Giovanni Dominici (*c.* 1356–1419), an illuminator of manuscripts as well as a reforming churchman, the arts retained their traditional value for Christianity – that of religious instruction. Another reformer, S. Antonino Pierozzi, archbishop of Florence from 1446 to 1459, criticised artists who misled or distracted congregations with false theology, 'apocryphal tales', and 'curiosities'; later Savonarola claimed that 'the pictures in the churches are the books of children and women'.[47] Even Alberti, for all the prevailingly secular tone of his *De Pictura* (1435), argued that painting could serve as an aid to worship, and when the religious art of the period is viewed 'in the round', its role was clearly far more varied and profound that the celebration of magnificence in a Christian context. The growing cult of the individual has to be set alongside other flourishing cults, themselves powerful sources of artistic inspiration, such as those attending the saints, the Virgin, the Rosary, the stations of the cross (see above, Chapter Seven, pp. 136–43). And if it is understandable why historical interest has tended to focus on major undertakings involving leading artists – such as the wall frescoes celebrating Christian orthodoxy, papal authority and the della Rovere family, commissioned by Sixtus IV in 1481 from a team of painters led by Perugino for his new chapel in the Vatican[48] – the larger number of artists and craftsmen producing woodcuts, terracottas and panel paintings for the insatiable market for devotional images deserves fuller study.

THE STATUS OF THE ARTIST

The patronage of the arts was far from being a new phenomenon, but there is evidence of a rising demand for the services of artists, architects and craftsmen in the period. This cannot be quantified; even if the record were complete, the arts do not normally lend themselves to that kind of analysis. But it is clear that the tastes of patrons developed and that they acquired new interests as collectors, connoisseurs and admirers of antiquity. They became more aware of the extent to which their reputations could be expressed through secular and religious commissions. They became more alive to the achievements of other patrons, whether public or private, individual or collective.

But behind the cumulative effect of fashion lay more powerful economic and social forces. It used to be believed that the Black Death and later attacks of the plague had a devastating and negative effect on the economy and society, both making only gradual and partial recoveries in the course of the fifteenth century. Now the view is one of massive dislocation, leading to a considerable redistribution of wealth from which the consequences were not so negative, and from which the economic recovery was quicker. More specifically, the funds made available and the profound anxieties aroused by the plague outbreaks were directed – at least in part – into projects which led to the employment of artists, craftsmen and architects. This can be seen clearly in the founding, or refounding, of hospitals and almshouses in the period. In Milan in 1456 Filarete began work on Francesco Sforza's Ospedale Maggiore; in Rome the hospital of S. Spirito was rebuilt and decorated with frescoes under Sixtus IV (1473–78). Moreover, the wealth circulated and the fears provoked by the plague deepened the commitment of the laity to confraternities, and through them to an intensification of collective patronage. In Palermo the level of gifts and bequests reaching confraternities made them leading patrons, commissioning altarpieces, banners for processions and painted necrologies to record the names and likenesses of past members. If the general piety of the period achieved little in the way of practical reform of the Church, it probably did contribute greatly to stimulating the economy, a point which can be illustrated from such sustained architectural programmes as those related to the cathedrals of Florence and Milan which were magnets for a wide range of arts, crafts and 'trades'.[49] The same economic point can be made in the secular field, for example in the context of the spate of palace-building which increasingly characterised both Florence and Rome in the course of the fifteenth century.

A further development which is both a symptom and a cause of the spiralling rate of patronage is the change in the reputation of the artist, if not his actual status. As has already been mentioned, one indication of this is the growing public interest and curiosity in the activities of artists and architects. In 1447 the physician and scholar Michele Savonarola claimed that when the opportunity presented itself crowds flocked to see the fresco of the *Paradiso* painted in the Greater Council Hall of the ducal palace of Venice by his fellow-Paduan, Guariento, between 1365 and 1368. Savonarola's pride in the achievement of a Paduan painter underlines a point already made: that men of letters began to pay increasing attention to the arts and architecture. The Florentine chronicler Filippo Villani was unusual in arguing that the painter was superior to the scholar because he depended on intellect and memory, while the scholar could fall back on the book-learning of others (1404).[50] More generally, men of letters became readier to praise and describe the work of contemporary or near-contemporary artists. They were also prepared to acknowledge the prestige accorded to works of art in antiquity and to turn a blind eye to the servile status of artists in ancient Rome. They provided artistic programmes, though not always with success. If Guarino of Verona's scheme of 1447 for Leonello d'Este's *studiolo* at Belfiore was accepted, Leonardo Bruni's suggested design for the third set of baptistry doors (*c.* 1425) was ignored by Ghiberti.[51] Lastly, inspired by the apparent example of ancient Greece, men of letters began to admit that the arts were worthy of study by patrons themselves; this argument was included by Castiglione in his *Courtier* (1508–28), but it had been mentioned earlier. In 1498 Francesco Negri, in a work dedicated to Doge Leonardo Loredan, advised that painting was a useful and uplifting exercise and that the Bellini were a fine example to the noble youth of Venice.[52]

However, as this case perhaps implies, the men of letters were serving only to encourage an attitude increasingly established among patrons. As discussed above, the esteem with which patrons, or would-be patrons, could hold the artist could be expressed more generally than in specific commissions; it could manifest itself in an interest in particular art forms and a fascination for the works of recognised masters. In the 1490s the marquis of Mantua was anxious to collect city views painted by the Bellini brothers, while his wife Isabella d'Este failed in 1498 to borrow from Cecilia Gallerani − the mistress of the duke of Milan − her portrait by Leonardo (now known as *The Lady with the Ermine*). Moreover, there is some evidence for close association and even friendship between patron and artist. Donatello received the active patronage and support of the Florentine Martelli family, while his association with the Medici was so close that he was buried near Cosimo in S. Lorenzo.

This particular relationship is confirmed not only by Medici commissions and acquisitions but by their correspondence, by contemporaries like Vespasiano da Bisticci and later by Vasari. Contemporary and later sources also suggest that Donatello was seen as a remarkable character, noted for his wit, his bohemian lifestyle and − perhaps − his interest in his workshop apprentices; and it is in this period that 'the artistic temperament' becomes more fully and sympathetically recorded. Here Vasari is a key source, and in the more detailed of his *Lives* he lays great stress on the personalities of his subjects as well as drawing together appropriately revealing anecdotes. Although many of his stories may be fictional or romanticised, that in itself is evidence for the growing acceptance of the artistic personality, and in many cases may also be understood to accentuate a facet of the artist's development. His story of Paolo Uccello's wife imploring her husband to leave his drawing board and come to bed, only to receive the reply, 'Oh what a delightful thing is this perspective!', underlined the fact that Uccello shared in the passion of leading Florentine artists for schemes of perspective. More sober and contemporary documentation can also express and recognise the artistic temperament; in a letter of 26 March 1436 Jacopo della Quercia told the officials of the building committee, or *Fabrica*, of S. Petronio in Bologna that he had temporarily abandoned work on the cathedral's central door because he was being pressurised, 'not to walk out upon my obligations, or depart from common reason, but to be free and not captive, because a captive man is neither heard nor understood.'[53]

Confidence in the status of the 'profession' can also be seen in the recognition artists could give each other; in a letter of 4 July 1428 to a Sienese patron, della Quercia praised two contemporary architects, Giovanni of Siena and Fioravante of Bologna, as accomplished men of ideas who did not demean themselves with manual labour. Later in the century Giovanni Santi, Raphael's father and himself a painter, praised the achievements of contemporary artists in his verse chronicle of the exploits of the duke of Urbino. Conversely, professional jealousy could often colour the relations between artists, as in the case of Sebastiano del Piombo and Raphael, both working for Cardinal Giulio de' Medici in Rome in 1518, while in the two examples of artistic 'generosity' just cited, it should be realised that della Quercia was himself very much 'in work' in 1428, while Santi was very much a minor artist.

The contemporary evidence also shows that artists could be confident – and occasionally aggressively so – about their own talents and status. In a letter of March 1507 to the commune of Siena, Pinturicchio staked out a claim for tax exemption by citing the recognition the ancient Romans accorded artists, and their acceptance of painting as an equal to the liberal arts and a rival to poetry.[54] Confidence and recognition can also be detected where artists signed their work. This was neither a new nor a universal practice. In the absence of an 'art market' it was probably not thought necessary, which makes the presence of an artist's signature in works intended to be admired all the more conspicuous. Sometimes this could be achieved by 'false modesty', as when Carpaccio placed his signature on a fragment of parchment painted on the lower right-hand corner of his *St Stephen with Six Companions*, executed for the Venetian *scuola* of St Stephen in 1511. In other cases the artist was bolder. The prominence of his name on the medals of Pisanello suggests that his patrons accepted the value of a signed work, and one that was intended to have some circulation.

Lastly, and most significantly, the confidence of artists and architects could be articulated in their own works of theory; many exist for the period, but three practitioner/authors signal a distinct advance. Cennino Cennini's *Craftsman's Handbook* of the 1390s tends to be described, rather dismissively, as the 'recipe book' of a medieval artist, but in fact it clearly expressed a craftsman's confidence in his own work and his pride in his professed descent from Giotto. Still more assertive are the *Commentaries* of Lorenzo Ghiberti which rehearsed the value placed on the arts in the ancient world, stressed the value of mathematics, optics and geometry for the artist, paid tribute to the achievements of his greater predecessors and – most originally – recorded the high points of his own career. Classical examples, academic disciplines and artistic theory were most forcefully expressed in the works of Alberti: the *De Pictura* (1435), *De Re Aedificatoria* (1452) and *De Statua* (c. 1450).

The first of these treatises was dedicated to the marquis of Mantua, and Alberti was later employed as an architectural consultant by the Gonzaga. That family were also the patrons of an artist whose relatively well-documented career embraces many of the points suggested above as evidence for the improved status and enhanced reputation of the artist in the period. Lodovico Gonzaga hired Andrea Mantegna as court painter in 1459. The rest of his career was largely spent in Gonzaga service, but the family did not prevent him from accepting commissions elsewhere, in Venice and Rome, or turn him into the kind of court painter who eagerly executed a miscellany of commissions. Though generously provided for, Mantegna was ready to complain bitterly to his patrons if he felt financially neglected. On the other hand, he does appear to have won the friendship and esteem of the ruling dynasty. A letter addressed to the marquis from Rome in 1489 is couched in terms of banter and familiarity; members of the family acted as godparents to his children. His artistic achievements were widely recognised, and distinguished visitors were shown the *Camera degli Sposi* frescoes he executed for the Gonzaga in the 1470s. Sometime after 1469 he acquired the title of count palatine from the emperor Frederick III. Giovanni Santi records how the duke of Urbino visited Mantua to inspect his work; in 1486 the duke of Ferrara came to view his progress on the *Triumphs of Caesar*, and when his *Madonna of Victory* was completed in 1496 it was carried in procession through Mantua. Leonardo da Vinci said in 1502 that Mantegna surpassed 'not only the artists of our own day but also those of antiquity'. This was a compliment which Mantegna would have appreciated. He associated with humanists and collected antiquities, while his art reveals him to have been a perceptive student of the antique; a description survives of a boating expedition taken by the painter in 1464 with fellow-enthusiasts to study the Roman remains and inscriptions on the shores of Lake Garda.[55]

However, Mantegna should not be regarded as typical. Few shared his talent or were able to command such sympathetic patronage, high salaries and personal security. A study of surviving contracts and correspondence reveals wide variations in career, calibre and circumstances. A contract of 10 June 1502 between the works committee of the Palazzo del Popolo of Florence and Andrea Sansovino could refer to him as a 'master and nobleman in sculpture', but then go on to impose stringent conditions on materials, working practices and price. Again, letters survive from artists indignantly demanding payment for work; but complaint could be couched in terms of a petition for redress or even help, depending on the status of the patron. Francesco Cossa could write to Borso d'Este on 25 March 1470 complaining about lack of payment, and stressing the claim that his growing reputation and continued study entitled him to be better treated than an artisan or apprentice, but the bluster subsided into supplication as Cossa asked for at least part payment.[56]

As this suggests, the economic circumstances of artists could vary considerably, and while a study of the assets of Lorenzo Ghiberti and his heirs reveals a comfortable affluence,[57] and while some celebrated talents like Raphael could command considerable sums, others, even when of proven ability and popularity, were not always so fortunate, as can be seen from cases where artists tendered or begged for work. On 28 July 1488 Alvise Vivarini petitioned the Venetian government to join the Bellini brothers working in the Greater Council Hall of the ducal palace, offering to work for nothing more than expenses until the quality of his work could be adjudged. His request was accepted, but this chance for work and celebrity did not save him from dying in debt to his principal patrons, the Morosini.[58]

Alvise had risen from, and then presided over, a busy workshop, but his later predicament − asking for work − supports evidence taken from the Peninsula as a whole suggesting that artists very rarely advanced beyond the economic and social conditions of the successful artisan. This is very much in contrast with the picture of the artist as hero, detectable in the period, encouraged by Vasari and fastened upon by art historians of the nineteenth and twentieth centuries. A basic reason why so few artists and architects dramatically advanced their social status is that most came from artisan backgrounds in the first place. There were exceptions. Alberti, although illegitimate, came from the Florentine patriciate and Baldassare d'Este (d. 1504) was an illegitimate son of the ruling house of Ferrara, but even as exceptions these cases do not seriously modify the rule; architects tended to be distinguished from other artists because of their acquaintance with the disciplines of mathematics and geometry, because their supervisory or co-ordinating role separated them from the men with the trowels, saws and chisels and because the monumental architecture of ancient Rome was its most obvious legacy and one supported on a literary level by Vitruvius' *De Architectura* – the Roman theorist of the first century B.C. receiving growing attention in the period, his work being printed in Rome in 1486. This explains the tone of a letter of 29 April 1491 from the government of Lucca to the commune of Siena thanking it for the privilege of sharing in the genius of the Sienese architect Francesco di Giorgio.[59]

But even within such criteria Alberti was exceptional, not having risen from the ranks of sculptors, craftsmen or builders as was more generally the case. Indeed, he had more of the status of a consultant than a practising architect, and while his works of theory appealed to a few discerning patrons – like Nicholas V and the Gonzaga – and a few artists – like Leonardo da Vinci – the majority of his 'colleagues' approached the 'profession' in a much more empirical and *ad hoc* fashion; that included Brunelleschi, whom Alberti addressed by name in his *De Pictura*.[60] Baldassare d'Este's family connections earned him employment at court, partly as a portrait painter, but they did not absolve him from exacting contracts and lower fees, as when he was commissioned in 1472 to paint a fresco cycle for the chapel of Simone Ruffino in Ferrara. The contract specified the principal colours and materials to be used, the general subject matter, the inclusions of portraits, the supervisory role of the patron and the provision of assessors.[61]

In practical economic and social terms, therefore, the vast majority of artists and even architects never emerged beyond the status of highly paid artisans or craftsmen, and their working lives were shaped by the workshop – often the family workshop. For painters, sculptors and craftsmen in most of the larger cities the guild was also present in their working lives. Many of these conditions applied to Mantegna. Born around 1430, he was the son of a carpenter. Between 1441 and 1446 he registered with the guild of painters in Padua as an apprentice in the large workshop of Francesco Squarcione (1397–1468), whose adopted son he became, taking the name 'Andrea Squarcione'. He left that workshop with some bitterness in 1448, and became involved in a number of partnerships commissioned to fresco the chapel of the Ovetari family in the Paduan church of the Eremitani. In 1453 he became associated with one of the largest and most productive of Venice's family workshops by marrying Jacopo Bellini's daughter. If his subsequent career, based largely in Mantua, distanced him from the world of the guild and the workshop, he did not leave it completely. He trained his own sons as artists and despite the commissions and recognition bestowed on him during his working life, towards the end of his career (1506) he was heavily in debt and forced to contemplate selling Isabella d'Este one of his most treasured pieces of Roman sculpture.

However, if dramatic social mobility was rarely a feature of the lives of artists and architects it would be anachronistic to see them as oppressed and inhibited by the 'medieval' restrictions of contract, *bottega* (workshop) and guild. Contracts, however detailed, did not always prove binding and defaulting artists appear to have been rarely taken to court. The demanding terms of a contract entered into by Donatello on 14 July 1428 for an external pulpit for Prato Cathedral were ignored by the sculptor, but so anxious was the commune of Prato to obtain his services that it drew up a fresh contract in 1434.[62] For artists and craftsmen with a large 'turnover', like the painters of *cassone* panels, a workshop was essential, and for masters the *bottega* was a reservoir not only of models but of assistance and expertise to various levels of accomplishment valuable in such labour-intensive processes as working in fresco. Despite the popular myth, Michelangelo probably did not work alone in the Sistine Chapel.

For the aspiring artist there was no other way of acquiring a training, as was recognised on 18 December 1489 when Brescia accepted the petition of its citizen Vincenzo Foppa to become the commune's official artist, impressed not only by his reputation as a painter and architect but also by his willingness to 'teach and instruct the young'.[63] If the *bottega* could produce bitterness, as between Squarcione and Mantegna, it could also create a more positive and harmonious tradition. Jacopo Bellini was so indebted to his master Gentile da Fabriano that he named his eldest son after him; it was to Gentile Bellini that Jacopo passed his massive portfolio of drawings, and Gentile remained as the unchallenged head of the 'family firm' despite the fact that his younger brother Giovanni became recognised as the more accomplished artist. It is also likely that the *bottega* prepared men to work in partnership. Of course some did prefer to work alone, as Domenico Veneziano indicated when asking Piero de' Medici for work on 1 April 1483. But for others partnerships could prove congenial and productive, as has been shown recently in the case of Donatello and Michelozzo.[64]

Of all aspects of the status of the artist, the various guilds to which they belonged as full or associate members are among the least examined, perhaps because it has been assumed that guild membership was inhibiting. Certainly the guilds tried to be protectionist, shielding their members from foreign competition – although in the cosmopolitan city of Genoa a guild was created for foreign painters. Like other trade and craft guilds, they tried to establish working practices and to protect the spiritual well-being of their members. Otherwise there is little evidence – at present – to suggest that guilds were anything more than occasionally irksome to their members or to outsiders. Indeed, they could provide both a stimulus and employment. Around 1413 the Florentine sculptor Nanni di Banco executed a commission for the masters of the guild of workers in stone and wood, to which he himself belonged. The work celebrated the 'Four Crowned Martyrs', sculptors persecuted by

Diocletian. The commission, the subject matter, the location of the finished sculptures in the prestigious shrine of Orsanmichele and the remarkable, innovative quality of di Banco's work does not suggest that guild membership was necessarily an incubus.

Moreover, when an artist enjoyed the employment of a powerful patron he could probably ignore guild requirements. In 1483 Giovanni Bellini was allowed the privilege of exemption from guild duties because of his work in the hall of the Greater Council in Venice, and while Albrecht Dürer complained in 1506 about the summonses and fees he had to face as a foreigner in Venice, they did not stop him from working in the city. While it is true that for the few artists of the first rank the guild became increasingly an anachronism, for the majority it remained a feature of their working lives. In fact the evidence suggests that in cities like Padua, Siena and Rome the fifteenth century saw an increase in the number of guilds embracing artists and craftsmen, as well as the extensive revision of guild statutes. Seen in the context of the period and from the viewpoint of the majority of artists and craftsmen, this was probably a further indication of an increase in demand and a related improvement in their status.[65]

MUSIC[66]

The music of Renaissance Italy is neither as familiar nor as accessible as its art and architecture; though increasing in number, performances and recordings still remain relatively rare. This is to be regretted. The subject is an illuminating one, and its importance has long been recognised by more specialised scholars – not least because it challenges the accuracy of the concept of 'revival' to characterise the whole culture of the age. Indeed, in recent years the volume of research has markedly increased and has resulted in the editing of texts, the reconstruction of musical instruments and performance practices and the study of individual musicians. For example, the exploration of the Sforza archives has revealed that the association of Josquin des Prez with the dynasty and the city of Milan was much longer than used to be thought. He was a singer at the cathedral from 1459, fourteen years before his more direct association with the Sforza; moreover, his recognition and remuneration by the dynasty were much more generous than was once believed.[67]

However, as with the study of Renaissance art, modern musical research also points to lacunae in the evidence. Little of the music of the Venetian confraternities, even that of the wealthier *scuole*, has survived.[68] The same can be said for the music which accompanied theatrical performances and pageants, and for that which was performed in a more private setting. An attribute of Italian singers and musicians was the ability to improvise accompaniments to their own or others' verses. Such spontaneous music-making has left little record beyond the high reputation of a few poet-performers like Serafino d'Aquila (1466–1500), whose skills were secured by Cardinal Ascanio Sforza before impressing audiences in other north Italian courts.

However, awareness of such lacunae serves to underline the presence and importance of music in society. More positively, this can be seen from the role frequently assigned to artists to enhance musical performances. This could result in remarkable commissions, as in the case of the singing galleries, or *cantoria*, decorated with marble reliefs, commissioned for the cathedral of Florence from Donatello (1438) and Luca della Robbia (1439). More commonly, the skills of woodcarvers and *intarsia* workers were employed on the choir stalls of principal churches; in the early fifteenth century, Mariano Taccola worked on the choir stalls of Siena Cathedral. Organ screens were another conspicuous area where the artist could be employed to enhance the performance of music; in 1469 Cosimo Tura painted the screens for the organ of Ferrara Cathedral. Less publicly, manuscript painters could be employed to illuminate the songbooks used in religious services; on 10 February 1478 Taddeo Crivelli received such a commission from the works committee of the cathedral of S. Petronio in Bologna. Lastly, music could have a prominent place in works of art, whether in an obvious if secondary position, as with Carpaccio's lute-playing angels attending the Madonna, or in a subtler, more central role, as in the allegorical paintings commissioned by Isabella d'Este for her *grotta* and *studiolo* in Mantua.

Still more positive and direct evidence for the importance of music in Renaissance Italy is provided by the multifarious activity of musicians of various degrees of ability and professionalism. As elsewhere in Europe, towns like Siena and Lucca had their bands of trumpeters and pipe-players, while in 1483 the Venetian Council of Ten became alarmed at the popularity and behaviour of 'glee clubs' in the city. By way of marked contrast, when the house of Savoy set out to reform the ducal chapel of Sainte Chapelle at Chambéry in the 1460s its concern was directed not only at the clergy and the state of the building and its decoration, but also towards its choir and organ. For the theatrical pageantry accompanying the marriage of Giangaleazzo Sforza and Isabella of Aragon in 1489, Lodovico Sforza employed Josquin des Prez for the music while Leonardo da Vinci designed the floats and sets.

Further evidence for the importance of music to the society of Renaissance Italy is its appreciation of the skills of foreign musicians from Germany, Spain and England, but above all from northern France and Flanders; whereas the northern influence on Italian pictorial art is receiving a somewhat belated recognition, the key importance of the north for Italian music has long been recognised, as has the fact that it is only with the sixteenth century that the tide of influence begins to run strongly in the other direction.[69] Indeed, the fact that the influence of antiquity, whether real or imagined, was only marginal while that of contemporary northern music was so great as to amount to dominance means that the history of music presents a contrast to the history of art and challenges any attempt to characterise the cultural life of the Peninsula too narrowly, in terms of a 'Renaissance' of classical antiquity.

The taste and demand for foreign musical talent can be seen in various ways. Leading musicians, whether composers, theorists or performers, were wooed and employed on shorter or more permanent bases. From at least 1476 the Fleming Iohannes Tinctoris was in the service of Ferrante I where he not only composed, but taught the royal children and wrote twelve musical treatises, some of which were dedicated to his royal patrons. In 1493, Ferrante I tried in vain to tempt the Fleming Alexander Agricola into his service with the offer of the remarkably high salary of 300 ducats a year.[70] Ercole d'Este was advised by one of his agents that to secure Josquin des Prez, from Hainault, would be to elevate his chapel choir above all others, and the duke of Ferrara, one of the most discerning music patrons of the period, was doubtless delighted to employ him as *maestro di capella* from 1503 to 1504.

In other cases, if patrons failed to secure the personal services of a composer, they were keen to acquire copies of his compositions for local performance. Thus a large collection of English music was put together at the court of Leonello d'Este, and the interest shown in the works of Dufay (from Cambrai) at Ferrara and elsewhere bore no close relationship to the composer's actual working presence.[71] Around 1450 he wrote to Piero and Giovanni de' Medici from Geneva, sending them some of his latest compositions and telling them of other new pieces. But foreign influences can be detected more generally. Dufay's first period of service in the papal choir (1428 to 1433) illustrates not only his growing reputation as a composer and performer but also the fact that throughout the fifteenth century singers for the papal choir were recruited from Cambrai, as well as from elsewhere in the north. This was not unusual. Alfonso I recruited choristers in Spain, while in 1487 Tinctoris travelled in northern Europe hiring singers for Ferrante I. Lastly, many instrument-makers came from France and Germany; Germans built the organ for Milan Cathedral.[72]

Possibly the value placed on non-Italian musicians has been exaggerated by historians; the appearance of Flemish names in Italian archives or the use of French in motets dedicated to the Malatesta of Pesaro or the doges of Venice naturally stand out. Possibly the Italian contribution has been underestimated, in part as a consequence of the expertise of Italian performers as improvisers, at least in the secular context. And the fashion for foreign – especially for northern – musicians may have been to a certain extent self-perpetuating as the talent scouts sent out by Italian patrons returned to familiar recruiting grounds; in 1467, for example, the Medici were impressed by the singers Dufay sent them from Cambrai.

More positively, the Italian contribution could be illustrated in several ways, from the career of the celebrated blind Florentine organist and composer Francesco Landini (1335–97) to that of the Lombard composer, collector, organist, theorist and choirmaster Franceschino Gaffurio (1451–1522); from Leonello d'Este's virtuoso lutanist Pietrobono da Ferrara to Ottaviano Petrucci (1466–1539), who established himself in Venice around 1500 as the first large-scale music publisher. On the other hand, the impression remains that

Italy's greatest contribution to the history of music, certainly before 1500, lay in its enthusiastic and ambitious patronage of foreign musicians, and the prevalent influence of northern music cannot be denied. Of all leading centres of patronage, only the court of Mantua under the guidance of Isabella d'Este after 1490 was dominated by Italians. This was possibly in part due to the fact that the rulers of Mantua came to an ambitious patronage of music relatively late in the day. It might also have been a consequence of Isabella's own preference for secular music-making in more intimate surroundings; certainly the two key figures of her court, Bartolomeo Tromboncino and Marchetto Cara, were both Italian specialists in a secular form of music called, loosely, the *frottola* which was direct and accessible and drew on a more native tradition of improvisation and the use of popular melodies.[73]

More generally, however, it appears to have been the northerners' mastery of polyphony, especially effective on ceremonial and religious occasions, that drew the attention of Italian patrons. Polyphonic music was technically more demanding, and required a greater range of trained voices. Its encouragement at the papal, Savoyard, Sforza, Este and Aragonese courts helps to disprove the theory that princely patronage tended to be more conservative or restrictive than that found in the Italian republics. As Lewis Lockwood has emphasised, Ercole d'Este's patronage of music was not noted simply for its scale – bringing together one of the largest choirs in Europe, of between thirty and forty singers – but also for the duke's own interest and discernment. Not that music was unappreciated in the republics; in 1403 the Venetian government recruited singers, 'since it reflects on the fame and honour of our dominion if our church of S. Marco has good singers'. But it was only towards the end of the fifteenth century that the musical resources of the ducal chapel in Venice, the baptistry and cathedral of Florence and the cathedral of S. Petronio in Bologna began to approach the resources of the above-mentioned courts in a conscious effort to master the prestigious and growing polyphonic repertoire.

In part, the initiative achieved by princely patrons was due to a greater ability to concentrate resources on the building-up of choirs, and it is significant that in Florence the concern of the Medici lay more or less openly behind improvements in the city's public music-making.[74] It was also due to the personal interests and tastes of the patrons; connoisseurship has been offered as one of the explanations for the patronage of the fine arts, but in the case of music the enthusiasm and knowledgeability of a small number of influential patrons stands out more sharply. This can be traced in the statements of the patrons themselves and in the comments of contemporaries. Lodovico Duke of Savoy (1440–65) loved to hear 'numerous and sumptuous singers'. On 29 January 1473, Galeazzo Maria Sforza wrote to the pope: 'Since we have for a long time taken delight in music and song, more so than in any other entertainment, we have taken measures to engage singers to establish a chapel.' The musical interests of Giovanni de' Medici, later Leo X, were widely acknowledged – sometimes with approval, as in Paolo Cortese's *De Cardinalatu* of 1510; sometimes critically, as when a Venetian ambassador reported complaints in 1513 that the pope 'values nothing except to sound the lute'.[75]

The interest of patrons can also be seen in the way musicians could be regarded as a source of companionship, consolation and delight. When Francesco Gonzaga languished in a Venetian prison in 1509 his wife sent him Marchetto Cara from Mantua; musicians encouraged his successor Federico II to take the waters at Caldiero and helped to cheer the marquis and his companions after the ordeal.[76] In 1520 the doge of Venice sent a virtuoso fluatist to entertain Leo X, who was duly impressed by this 'kinsman of the muses'. Moreover, a number of princely patrons had had a musical education which left them not only with a taste for music, but with some personal expertise. Music and dance formed part of the curriculum of Vittorino da Feltre's influential school established at the Gonzaga court in 1423. In 1476 Tinctoris dedicated one of his treatises to a star pupil, Beatrice of Aragon, daughter of Ferrante I and wife of Matthias Corvinus of Hungary. Isabella d'Este, brought up in one of the most musically aware courts in Italy, was able to play a number of string and keyboard instruments, her own personal musical device was worked into the ceiling tiles and *intarsia* wall panels of her private apartments and she owned collections of French *chansons* and a treatise by Gaffurio. When, in his *Book of the Courtier*, Castiglione, himself both an appreciative listener and a competent performer, argued that his courtier should demonstrate more than a passing acquaintance with music he was addressing a sympathetic audience.[77]

In such courtly circles musicians had a role as entertainers, as soloists, singers, accompanists to song and dance. Their role as entertainers could also be required in a more public context, for example in pageants and spectacles, in theatrical productions and in the carnival festivities so encouraged by Lorenzo de' Medici, for whom the German composer Heinrich Isaac wrote direct and accessible secular pieces as well as more elaborate and solemn Masses. On occasions of greater solemnity musicians would be commissioned to mark matters of moment for dynasty, state and Church. One of the earliest northern composers of distinction to work in Italy, Giovanni Cicogna from Liège, composed a motet to honour the election of Michele Steno as doge of Venice in 1400, in terms which presented the office of doge in a much more influential light than is generally recognised by constitutional historians. Dufay's earliest compositions for Italian patrons were for the Malatesta of Pesaro; in 1423 he composed a *ballata* to celebrate the marriage of Carlo with Vittoria Colonna, niece of Martin V. Later he composed a *ballata* praising the virtues of Niccolò III d'Este (1430s) and motets for the election of Eugenius IV (1431), the coronation of Sigismund (1433), the completion of the dome of Florence Cathedral (1436) and the installation of Donatello's high altar in Sant'Antonio in Padua (1450).

Dufay was clearly one of the most sought-after musicians of the first half of the fifteenth century, and in 1467 Piero de' Medici described him as 'the greatest ornament of our age'. His career should be seen in the context of the competitiveness which could characterise the relations between the more ambitious patrons as they sought to recruit and retain chapel choirs and leading musicians. Galeazzo Maria Sforza enticed the singer and *maestro di capella* Antonio Guinati from the service of the duke of Savoy. On the fall of the Sforza in 1499 many of their musicians were snapped up by the Este. In 1502 an Este agent was arrested in Savoy trying to lure singers to Ferrara, but in 1510 the political difficulties of the Este themselves allowed the Gonzaga to recruit singers from Ferrara to help establish a cathedral choir in Mantua.

Altogether, the evidence might suggest that musicians did enjoy a high status, possibly higher than that achieved by leading artists and architects, a hypothesis supported by the fact that from the late fifteenth century an increasing number of leading artists (Leonardo, Giorgione, Titian) enjoyed a reputation as musicians, while the converse did not apply. Musicians clearly benefited from the fact that music was a traditional university discipline. As theorists like Tinctoris were anxious to underline, its high standing had been endorsed by ancient and early Christian authorities and further enhanced by the achievements of such near contemporaries as Dunstable and Dufay. Moreover, as has been mentioned, the ability to sing, to play a string or keyboard instrument and to dance was regarded as desirable for the courtier and the prince, which helps to account for the informed enthusiasm of some patrons. Threats to the status of music came from some religious reformers, like Savonarola, who denounced polyphony as a distraction from the worship of God and whose influence led to the temporary disbandment of the leading choirs of Florence. Leonardo, for all his interest in the theory and practice of music, argued that painting was a superior art as its images were not fleeting, and some humanists claimed that the poet and the word came before the musician and the setting. In general, however, the status enjoyed by music went unchallenged, and this position was bound to have an effect on the standing of at least the leading musicians.

The more ambitious patrons, like Galeazzo Maria and Lodovico Sforza, Ercole d'Este and Ferrante I, recognised the need to reward their principal musicians well, and to do so sought papal permission to allocate them benefices in their dominions. When Gaspard van Werbecke from Oudenarde temporarily left Sforza service, where he had been relatively well paid, Lodovico tried to entice him back from Rome with the offer of benefices, 'to whatever value should appear convenient'. Perhaps even more than with artists, it is difficult to assess precisely the economic position of musicians, to take account of their earnings in the form of benefices (in the case of clergy), gifts, rents from property, fees from pupils, payments in kind, as well as from regular salaries. However, it certainly seems true that leading musicians could command high salaries; Josquin's 200 ducats a year while at Ferrara, itself a high sum, presumably came on top of other revenues from his northern benefices, while the lay musician Marchetto Cara, with a salary from the Gonzaga of over 150 ducats a year, was approaching Mantegna's 180 ducats a year.

But, as with painters, sculptors and architects, men of the calibre and success of a Dufay or a Josquin were exceptions. Musicians at the the other end of the spectrum were the more numerous. The choristers at S. Petronio in Bologna, belonging to one of the largest cathedral choirs of the sixteenth century, approached the economic position of skilled artisans, and their choirmaster's salary was between a quarter and a third of that received by a university professor. Apprentice choristers at Florence received a musical training in lieu of payment. Many musicians, especially the instrumentalists who made up town bands and who were drafted in to make up the numbers on special occasions, were part-time; the same is true for the singers and instrumentalists who provided the music for the services and processions organised by the wealthier confraternities, the *Scuole Grandi*, in Venice. Moreover, not all musicians shared the same status, solo singers and players of string and keyboard instruments generally standing higher than wind players. While Vespasiano da Bisticci emphasised Federigo da Montefeltro's love of music he stressed his preference for 'delicate to loud instruments, caring little for trombones and the like'.

Finally, musicians, like other artists, were susceptible to changes in political and economic circumstances; indeed, choir members were particularly vulnerable, dependent as they were on a collectivity. On the murder of Galeazzo Maria Sforza in 1476 a number of his singers were dismissed, and Alfonso d'Este's war with the papacy in 1510 meant the dispersal of his chapel choir. Moreover, the tastes of patrons could vary; Borso d'Este did not continue Leonello's interest in music. If Dufay and Josquin enjoyed an international reputation, other musicians can be found soliciting employment. In 1466 and 1469 Jachetto di Marvilla tried in vain to enter the service of Lorenzo de' Medici as a choirmaster and talent scout. And running through Tinctoris's dedications to Ferrante I is the anxiety that the interest and the liberality of the prince be sustained.

NOTES AND REFERENCES

1. F. Ames-Lewis and J. Wright, *Drawing in the Italian Renaissance Workshop* (London, 1983).
2. B. Cole, *The Renaissance Artist at Work* (Bloomington and London, 1983).
3. Throughout I have made extensive use of two valuable collections of contemporary material: D. S. Chambers, *Patrons and Artists in the Italian Renaissance* (London, 1970) and C. E. Gilbert, *Italian Art 1400–1500* (Englewood Cliffs, 1980).
4. M. Baxandall, *Painting and Experience in Fifteenth Century Italy* (Oxford, 1972).
5. E. R. Driscoll, 'Alfonso of Aragon as a patron of art', *Essays in Memory of K. Lehmann*, ed. L. F. Sandler (New York, 1964); G. L. Hersey, *Alfonso II and the Artistic Renewal of Naples* (New Haven and London, 1969), and *The Aragonese Arch at Naples* (New Haven and London, 1973).
6. D. Galis, 'Concealed wisdom, Renaissance hieroglyphs and Lorenzo Lotto's Bergamo *Intarsie*', *Art B.*, vol. lxii, no. 3 (1980).

7. J. Hook, *Siena* (London, 1980), pp. 98–100.

8. C. H. Clough, 'Federigo da Montefeltro's patronage of the arts', in *The Duchy of Urbino in the Renaissance* (London, 1981), ch. viii.

9. J. Anderson, 'The "Casa Longobarda" in Asolo', *B.M.*, vol. cxvi, no. 855 (1974).

10. M. Evans, 'Northern artists in Italy during the Renaissance', *Bulletin of the Society for Renaissance Studies*, vol. iii, no. ii (1985).

11. L. Castelfranchi Vegas, *International Gothic Art in Italy* (London, 1968), pp. 38–9.

12. G. Maluzzani, 'Observations on the Sforza triptych in the Brussels Museum', *B.M.*, vol. cxiii, no. 818 (1971).

13. G. Bresc-Bautier, *Artistes, patriciens et confrères. Production et consommation de l'œuvre d'art à Palerme et en Sicile occidentale* (Rome, 1979).

14. A. Rizzi, *Mostra della Scultura Lignea in Friuli* (Udine, 1983).

15. We are indebted to Annabelle Pelta for advice on this point.

16. B. Rackham, *Italian Maiolica* (London, 1952); G. Cora, *Storia della Maiolica di Firenze e del Contado*, 2 vols (Florence, 1973); J. Pope-Hennessy, *Luca della Robbia* (Oxford, 1980).

17. A. Chastel in *The Encyclopedia of World Art*, vol. viii (New York–Toronto–London, 1963), coll. 129–33; M. J. Thornton, '*Tarsie: Designs and designers*', *J.W.C.I.* vol. xxxvi (1973).

18. R. Trexler, 'The Magi enter Florence. The Ubriachi of Florence and Venice', *Studies in Med. and Ren. Hist.*, n.s., vol. i (1978); G. A. dell'Acqua, *Il Trittico di Pavia* (Milan, 1982).

19. T. Verdon, *The Art of Guido Mazzoni* (New York and London, 1978).

20. J. M. Fletcher, 'Patronage in Venice', in *The Genius of Venice*, ed. J. Martineau and C. Hope (London, 1983).

21. M. Baxandall, 'Bartholomeus Facius on painting', *J.W.C.I.*, vol. xxvii (1964).

22. C. H. Clough, 'Francis I and the Courtiers of Castiglione's *Courtier*', in *The Duchy of Urbino in the Renaissance*, ch. xvi, p. 32.

23. A. Radcliffe and C. Avery, 'The Chellini Madonna', *B.M.*, vol. cxvii, no. 879 (1976).

24. J. Beck, 'The historical "Taccola" and emperor Sigismund in Siena', *Art B.*, vol. xl (1968).

25. M. Baxandall, 'A dialogue on art from the court of Leonello d'Este', *J.W.C.I.*, vol. xxvi (1963).

26. A. Molho, 'The Brancacci chapel', *J.W.C.I.*, vol. xl (1977).

27. R. A. Goldthwaite, *The Building of Renaissance Florence* (Baltimore and London, 1980).

28. S. Levine, 'The location of Michelangelo's *David*', *Art. B.*, vol. lvi (1974).

29. L. Landucci, *A Florentine Diary*, trans. A. de Rosen Jervis (London, 1927), p. 217.

30. M. Wackernagel, *The World of the Florentine Renaissance Artist* (Princeton, 1981).

31. D. S. Chambers, 'Sant'Andrea at Mantua and Gonzaga patronage', *J.W.C.I.*, vol. xl (1977).

32. A. Colombo, 'La piazza ducale in Vigevano', *L'Arte*, vol. v (1902).

33. G. Spatrisano, *Lo Steri di Palermo e l'Architettura Siciliana del Trecento* (Palermo, 1972).

34. Hersey, *Alfonso II*, pp. 22–3; A. D. Frazer Jenkins, 'Cosimo de' Medici's patronage of architecture and the theory of Magnificence', *J.W.C.I.*, vol. xxxiii

(1970); S. Lang, 'Sforzinda, Filarete and Filelfo', *J.W.C.I.*, vol. xxxv (1972); M. King, 'The moral philosophy of Giovanni Caldiera', *Ren. Q.*, vol. xxviii (1975). pp. 547, 551–2; Goldthwaite, op. cit., pp. 83–4.

35. Chambers, *Patrons*, pp. 164–6.
36. Chambers, op. cit., p. 79.
37. R. Weiss, 'The medals of Julius II', *J.W.C.I.*, vol. xxviii (1965), pp. 163–182; G. Hill and G. Pollard, *Medals of the Renaissance* (London, 1978), p. 65.
38. Clough, 'Federigo da Montefeltro's patronage'.
39. Gilbert, op. cit., pp. 121–2.
40. Gilbert, op. cit., pp. 130–31.
41. F. Hartt, G. Corti and C. Kennedy, *The Chapel of the Cardinal of Portugal* (Philadelphia, 1964).
42. M. Evans, 'Italian manuscript illumination', in T. Kren (ed.), *Renaissance Painting in Manuscripts* (New York, 1983), pp. 113–22.
43. Gilbert, op. cit., pp. 211–13.
44. R. Cannatà *et al.*, 'Umanesimo e Primo Rinascimento in Santa Maria del Popolo', in *Il Quattrocento a Roma e nel Lazio* (Rome, 1981).
45. Wackernagel, op. cit., p. 212 and *passim*; E. Borsook and G. Corti, 'Documents for Filippo Strozzi's chapel in Sta Maria Novella', *B.M.*, vol. cxiii, no. 822 (1970); E. Borsook and J. Offerhaus, *Francesco Sassetti and Ghirlandaio at Sta Trinità* (Doornspijk, 1981).
46. J. Harthan, *Books of Hours* (Milan, 1977), pp. 76–7; M. Jacobson, 'A Sforza miniature', *B.M.*, vol. cxvi, no. 851 (1974); A. Luchs, 'A note on Raphael's Perugian patrons', *B.M.*, vol. cxxv, no. 958 (1983).
47. Gilbert, op. cit., ch. 5.
48. L. D. Ettlinger, *The Sistine Chapel before Michelangelo* (Oxford, 1965).
49. Goldthwaite, op. cit., *passim*.
50. J. Larner, 'The artist and the intellectuals in fourteenth century Italy', *History*, vol. liv (1969).
51. Chambers, op. cit., pp. 47–48; M. Baxandall, *Giotto and the Orators* (Oxford, 1971).
52. J. Fletcher, 'Marcantonio Michiel: his friends and collectors', *B.M.*, vol. cxxiii, no. 941 (1981).
53. Chambers, op. cit., pp. 7–8.
54. Ibid., pp. 197–8.
55. M. Bellonci and N. Garaviglia, *Mantegna* (Milan, 1967).
56. Chambers, op. cit., pp. 162–4.
57. T. Krautheimer-Hess, 'More Ghibertiana', *Art B.*, vol. xlvi (1964).
58. Chambers, op. cit., pp. 80–81; J. Fletcher, review of J. Steer, *Alvise Vivarini* (Cambridge, 1982), in *B.M.*, vol. cxxv. no. 959 (1983), pp. 99–100.
59. Chambers, op. cit., pp. 76–7.
60. J. S. Ackerman, 'Architectural practice in the Italian Renaissance', *Journal of the Soc. of Architectural Historians*, vol. xiii (1954).
61. Chambers, op. cit., pp. 169–71; Matthieson Fine Art Ltd, *From Borso to Cesare d'Este* (London, 1984), pp. 64–6.
62. Chambers, op. cit., pp. 63–5.
63. Gilbert, op. cit., pp. 41–2.
64. H. McNeil Caplow, 'Sculptors' partnerships in Michelozzo's Florence', *Studies in the Renaissance*, vol. xxi (1974).
65. E. Battisti in *The Encyclopedia of World Art*, vol. viii, coll. 141–50; D. Rosand,

Painting in Cinquecento Venice (New Haven and London, 1982). ch. 1; Pope-Hennessy, op. cit., pp. 55–6, 247–8.

66. This section has benefited greatly from the advice of Alison Smith, and *The New Grove Dictionary of Music and Musicians* (London, 1980) was a valuable reference work.

67. E. Lowinsky and B. Blackburn (eds), *Josquin des Prez – Proceedings of the International Josquin Festival Conference* (London, 1976).

68. J. E. Glixon, 'Music at the Venetian *Scuole Grandi*', in *Music in Medieval and Early Modern Europe*, ed. I. Fenlon (Cambridge, 1981).

69. L. Lockwood, 'Strategies of music patronage in the fifteenth century: the capella of Ercole I d'Este', in Fenlon, op. cit. We have not had the chance to consult Lockwood's *Music in Renaissance Ferrara* (Oxford, 1984). An older general study of Este music patronage is L. F. Valdrighi, 'Cappelle, concerti e musiche di casa d'Este', *Atti e Mem. delle R. Deputazioni di Storia Patria per le Provincie Modenesi e Parmensi*, ser. iii, vol. ii (1884).

70. A. Atlas, 'Alexander Agricola and Ferrante I of Naples', *Journal of the American Musicological Soc.*, vol. xxx (1977).

71. On Dufay, A. W. Atlas (ed.), *Papers Read at the Dufay Quincentenary Conference* (New York, 1976); D. Fallows, *Dufay* (London, 1982).

72. On Sforza patronage, E. Motta, 'Musici alla Corte degli Sforza', *A.S.L.*, ser. ii, vol. xiv (1887); F. Malaguzzi Valeri, *La Corte di Ludovico il Moro*, vol. iv (Milan, 1923).

73. On Mantua, W. F. Prizer, 'Marchetto Cara at Mantua', *Musica Disciplina*, vol. xxxii (1978); I. Fenlon, *Music and Patronage in Sixteenth Century Mantua*, (Cambridge, 1981). vol. i; idem., 'The Gonzaga and Music', in D. S. Chambers and J. Martineau eds, *The Splendours of the Gonzaga* (London, 1982).

74. F. d'Accone, 'The singers of San Giovanni in Florence', *J. of the American Musicological Soc.*, vol. xiv (1961).

75. A. Pirro, 'Leo X and Music', *Musical Quarterly*, vol. xxi (1935).

76. D. S. Chambers, 'Federico Gonzaga ai Bagni di Caldiero', *Civiltà Mantovana*, n.s., vol. iv (1984).

77. W. H. Kemp, 'Music in "Il Libro del Cortegiano"', in *Essays in Honour of P. O. Kristeller*, ed. C. H. Clough (Manchester, 1976).

Appendix
The papal succession
1370–1534

Gregory XI (Pierre Roger)	1370–78
Urban VI (Bartolomeo Prignani)	1378–89
Boniface IX (Pietro Tomacelli)	1389–1404
Innocent VII (Cosimo Migliorati)	1404–06
Gregory XII (Angelo Correr)	1406–09
Alexander V (Pietro Filargi)	1409–10
John XXIII (Baldassare Cossa)	1410–15
Martin V (Otto Colonna)	1417–31
Eugenius IV (Gabriele Condulmer)	1431–47
Nicholas V (Tommaso Parentucelli)	1447–55
Calixtus III (Alfonso Borgia)	1455–58
Pius II (Enea Silvio Piccolomini)	1458–64
Paul II (Pietro Barbo)	1464–71
Sixtus IV (Francesco della Rovere)	1471–84
Innocent VIII (Giovanni Battista Cibo)	1484–92
Alexander VI (Rodrigo Borgia)	1492–1503
Pius III (Francesco Todeschini–Piccolomini)	1503
Julius II (Giuliano della Rovere)	1503–13
Leo X (Giovanni de' Medici)	1513–22
Hadrian VI (Adrian Florensz)	1522–23
Clement VII (Giulio de' Medici)	1523–34

Genealogical tables

Table 1 **The kingdom of Naples: Anjou–Durazzo**

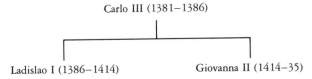

Carlo III (1381–1386)

Ladislao I (1386–1414)   Giovanna II (1414–35)

Table 2 **The kingdom of Naples: Aragon–Trastamara**

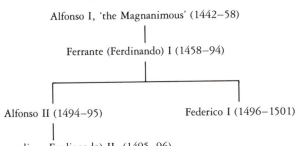

Alfonso I, 'the Magnanimous' (1442–58)

Ferrante (Ferdinando) I (1458–94)

Alfonso II (1494–95)   Federico I (1496–1501)

Ferrante (Ferrandino, Ferdinando) II, (1495–96)

Table 3 **The kingdom of Naples: Anjou–Provence, and the French claim to Naples**

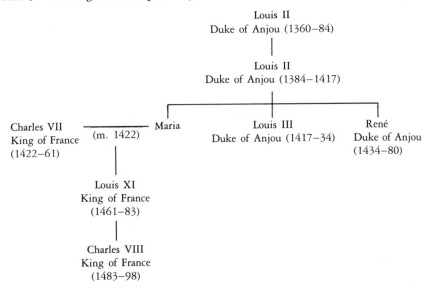

Louis II
Duke of Anjou (1360–84)

Louis II
Duke of Anjou (1384–1417)

Charles VII ——— Maria   Louis III   René
King of France (m. 1422)   Duke of Anjou (1417–34)   Duke of Anjou
(1422–61)   (1434–80)

Louis XI
King of France
(1461–83)

Charles VIII
King of France
(1483–98)

Table 4 **The Kingdom of Sicily: The house of Barcelona**

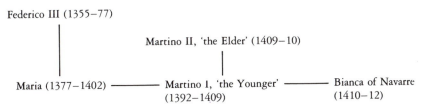

Federico III (1355–77)

Martino II, 'the Elder' (1409–10)

Maria (1377–1402) ——— Martino I, 'the Younger' ——— Bianca of Navarre
(1392–1409)   (1410–12)

347

Table 5 **The house of Trastamara**

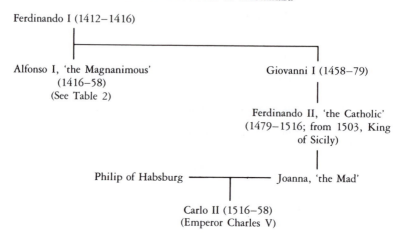

Ferdinando I (1412–1416)

Alfonso I, 'the Magnanimous'
(1416–58)
(See Table 2)

Giovanni I (1458–79)

Ferdinando II, 'the Catholic'
(1479–1516; from 1503, King
of Sicily)

Philip of Habsburg —————— Joanna, 'the Mad'

Carlo II (1516–58)
(Emperor Charles V)

Table 6 **The house of Savoy**

Amedeo VII
(1383–91)

Amedeo VIII (first duke)
(1391–1451)

Amedeo
(d. 1431)

Lodovico (second duke)
(1451–65)

Amedeo IX (third duke)
(1465–72)

Filippo *senza Terra* (seventh duke)
(1496–97)

Filiberto I (fourth duke)
(1472–82)

Carlo I (fifth duke)
(1482–90)

Carlo Giovanni Amedeo (sixth duke)
(1490–96)

Filiberto II (eighth duke)
(1497–1503)

Carlo II (ninth duke)
(1503–53)

Table 7 **The Visconti and the Sforza**

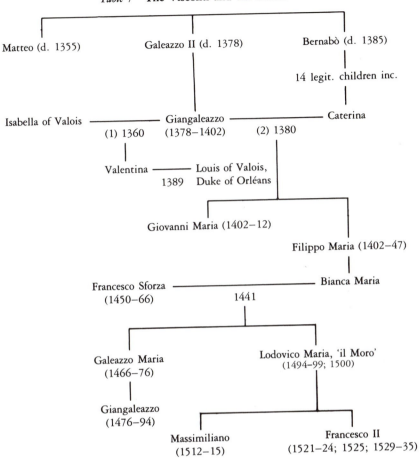

Table 8 **The French claim to Milan**

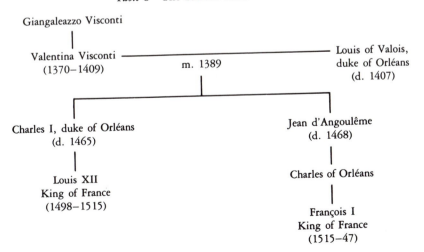

Table 9 **The leading Medici** (italicised dates indicate periods of leadership)

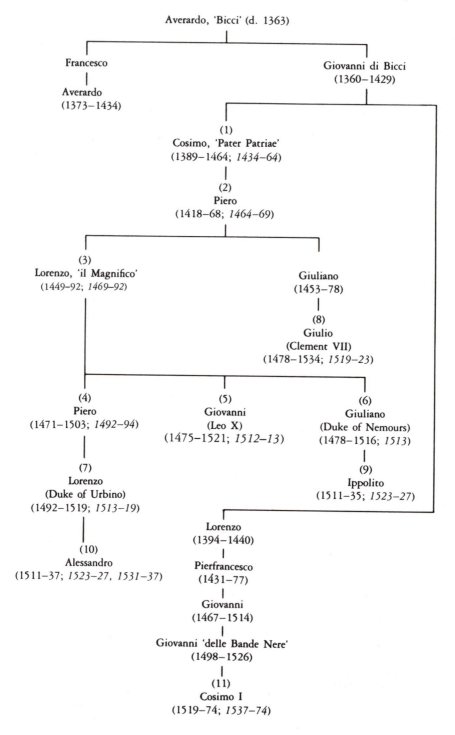

Averardo, 'Bicci' (d. 1363)

Francesco

Averardo
(1373–1434)

Giovanni di Bicci
(1360–1429)

(1)
Cosimo, 'Pater Patriae'
(1389–1464; *1434–64*)

(2)
Piero
(1418–68; *1464–69*)

(3)
Lorenzo, 'il Magnifico'
(1449–92; *1469–92*)

Giuliano
(1453–78)

(8)
Giulio
(Clement VII)
(1478–1534; *1519–23*)

(4)
Piero
(1471–1503; *1492–94*)

(5)
Giovanni
(Leo X)
(1475–1521; *1512–13*)

(6)
Giuliano
(Duke of Nemours)
(1478–1516; *1513*)

(7)
Lorenzo
(Duke of Urbino)
(1492–1519; *1513–19*)

(9)
Ippolito
(1511–35; *1523–27*)

(10)
Alessandro
(1511–37; *1523–27, 1531–37*)

Lorenzo
(1394–1440)

Pierfrancesco
(1431–77)

Giovanni
(1467–1514)

Giovanni 'delle Bande Nere'
(1498–1526)

(11)
Cosimo I
(1519–74; *1537–74*)

Maps

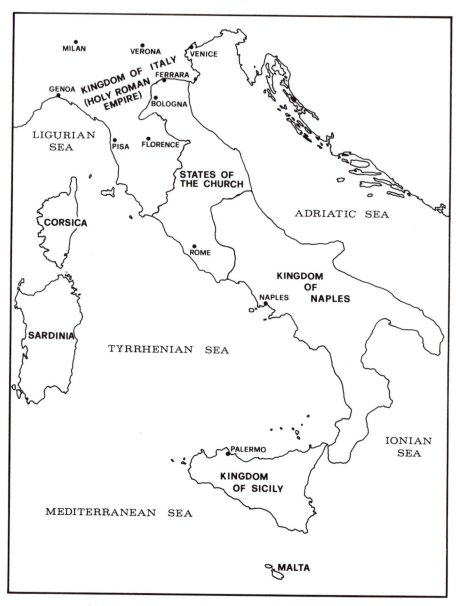

Map 1.   Renaissance Italy: the main political divisions

Map 2.   The Aragonese territories

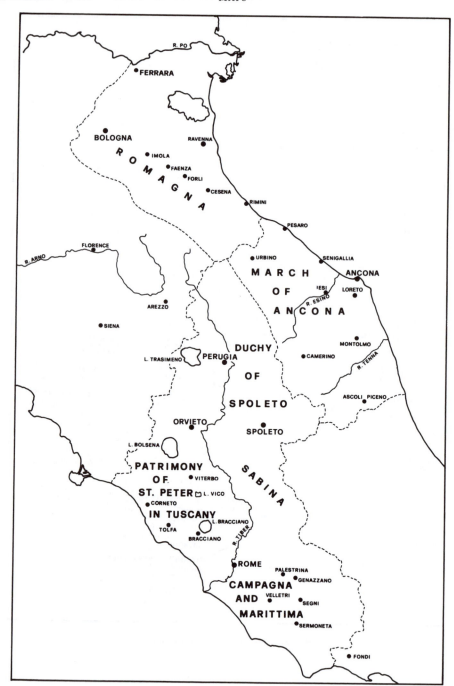

Map 3.   The States of the Church

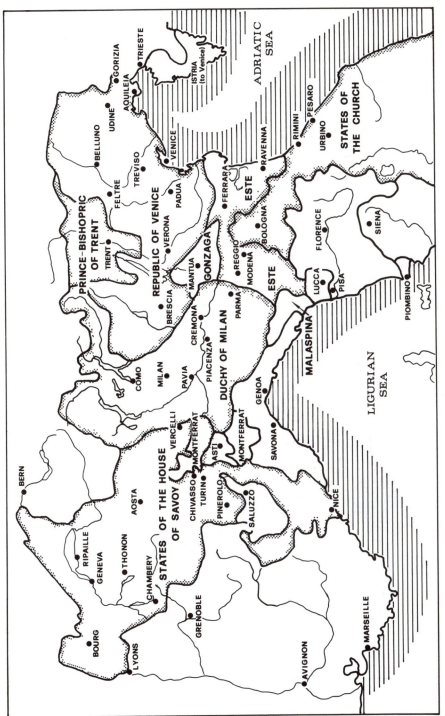

Map 4. Northern Italy in the mid-fifteenth century

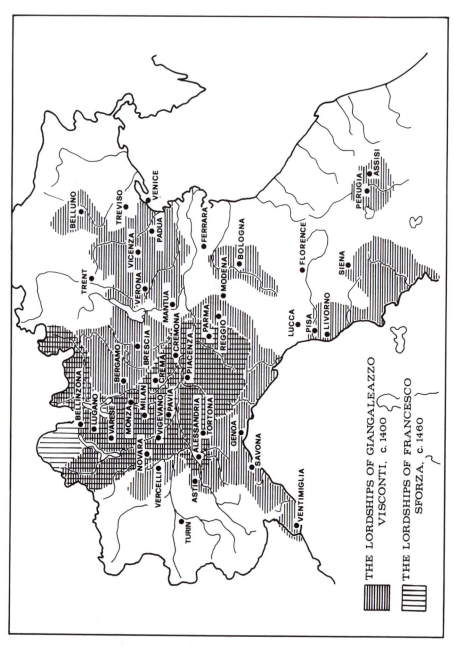

Map 5. The Visconti and Sforza duchies

THE LORDSHIPS OF GIANGALEAZZO
VISCONTI, c. 1400

THE LORDSHIPS OF FRANCESCO
SFORZA, c. 1460

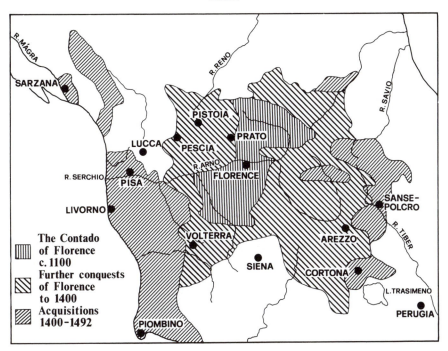

Map 6.   The expansion of Florence

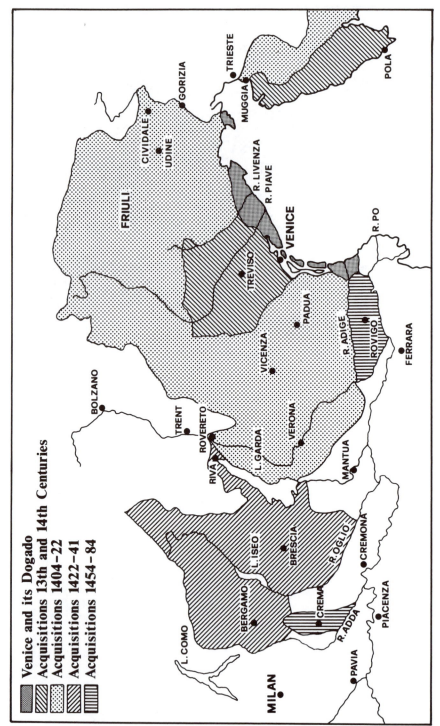

Venice and its Dogado
Acquisitions 13th and 14th Centuries
Acquisitions 1404–22
Acquisitions 1422–41
Acquisitions 1454–84

TRIESTE

POLA

MUGGIA

GORIZIA

CIVIDALE

UDINE

R. LIVENZA

R. PIAVE

FRIULI

VENICE

R. PO

TREVISO

PADUA

R. ADIGE

ROVIGO

FERRARA

VICENZA

BOLZANO

R. ADIGE

TRENT

ROVERETO

VERONA

MANTUA

L. GARDA

RIVA

L. SEO

BRESCIA

R. OGLIO

CREMONA

BERGAMO

CREMA

PIACENZA

R. ADDA

L. COMO

PAVIA

MILAN

Map 7. The expansion of Venice

Index